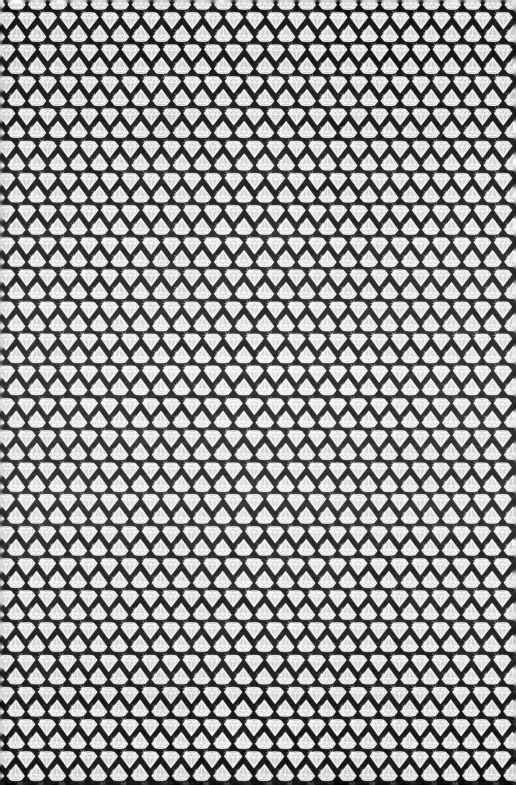

JoJo's BIZARRE ADVENTURE

HIROHIKO ARAKI

PART 4 ★ DIAMOND IS UNBREAKABLE

7

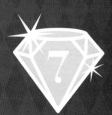

JoJo's
BIZARRE ADVENTURE

PART 4 ★ DIAMOND IS UNBREAKABLE

CONTENTS

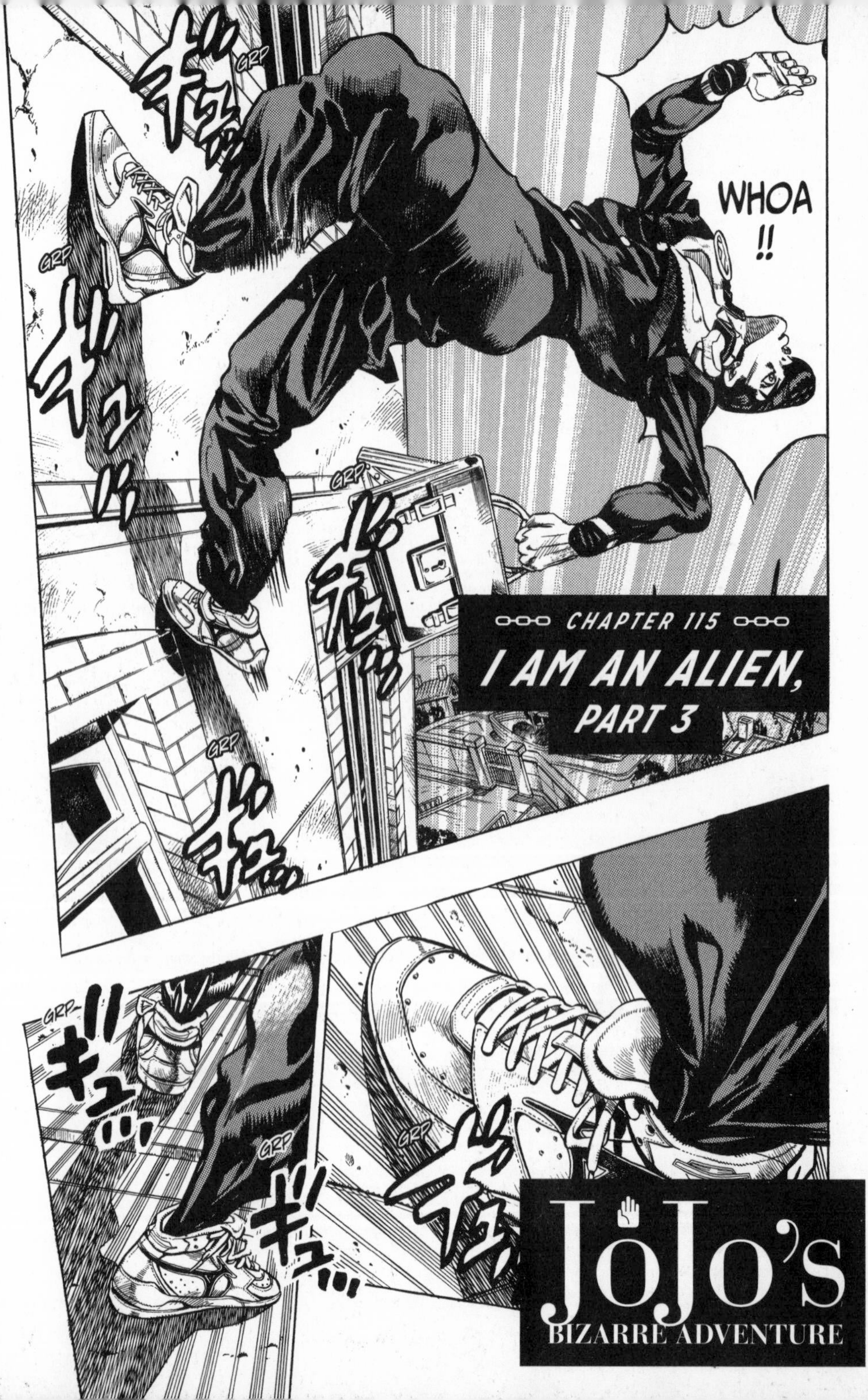
WHOA !!
GRP
GRP
GRP
GRP
CHAPTER 115
I AM AN ALIEN, PART 3
GRP
GRP
GRP
JoJo's
BIZARRE ADVENTURE

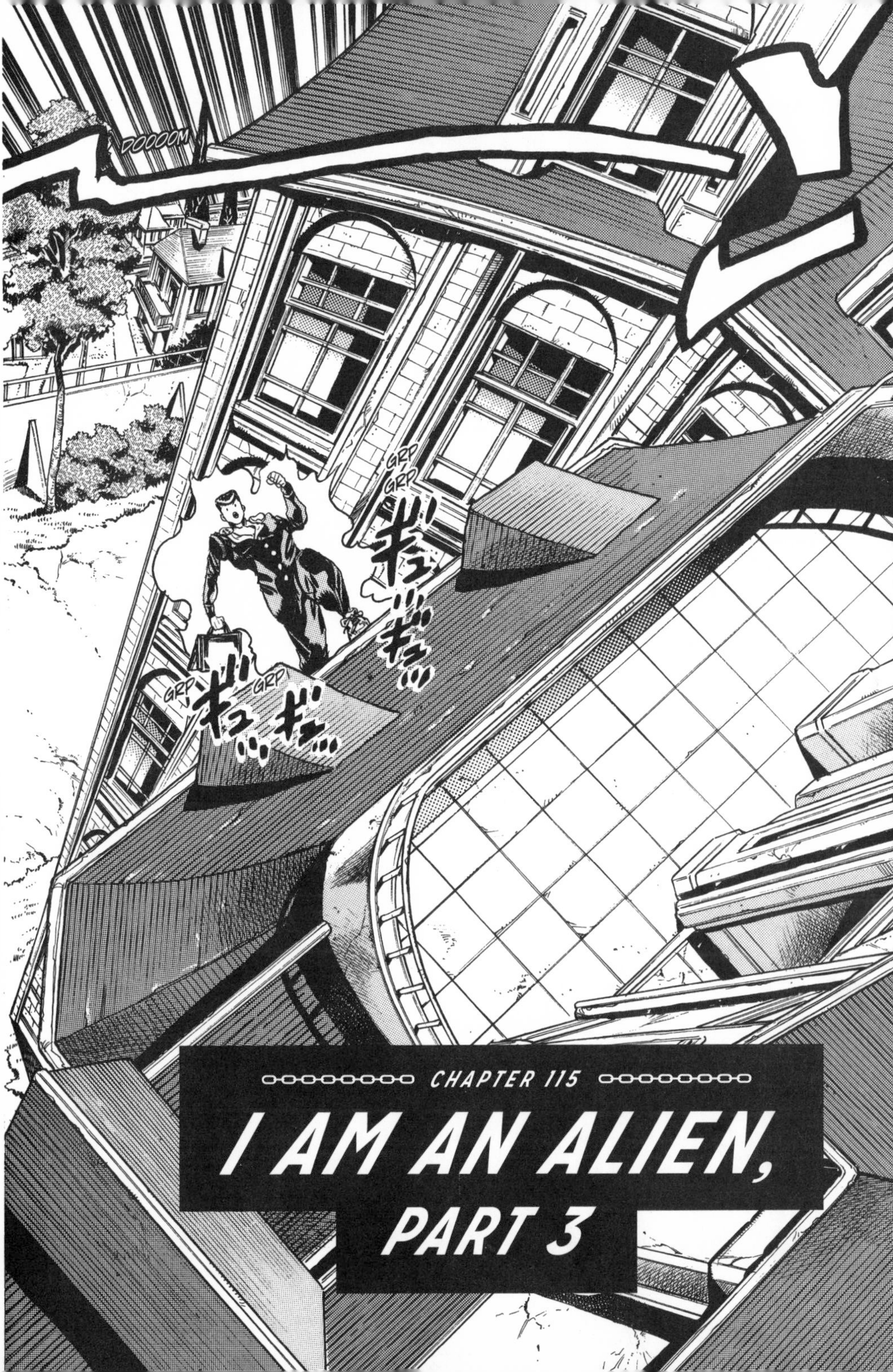
DOOOOM
GRP GRP
ギュ ギュ
GRP GRP
ギュ ギュ
CHAPTER 115
I AM AN ALIEN, PART 3

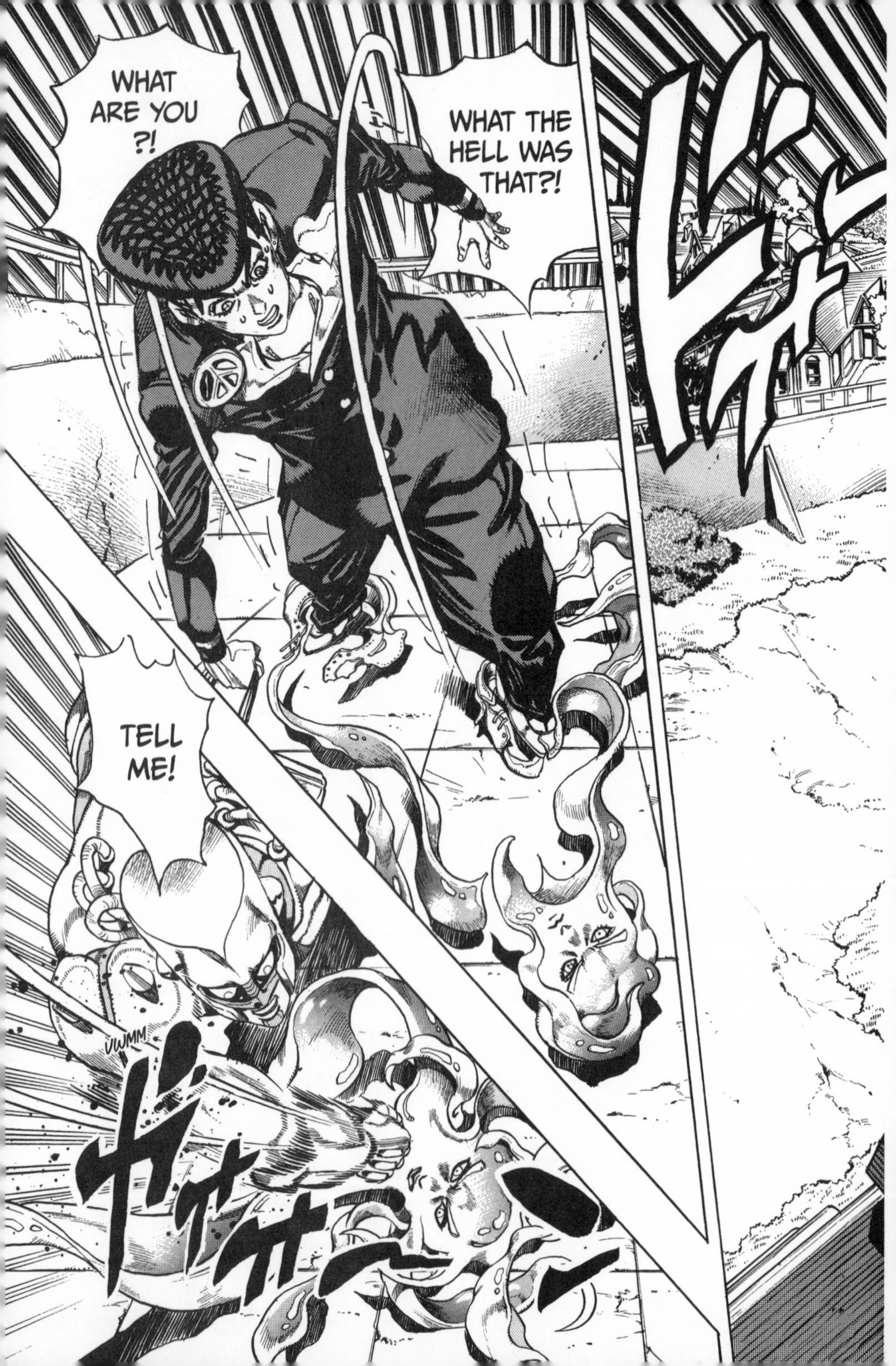
WHAT THE HELL WAS THAT?!
WHAT ARE YOU ?!
TELL ME!
VWMM

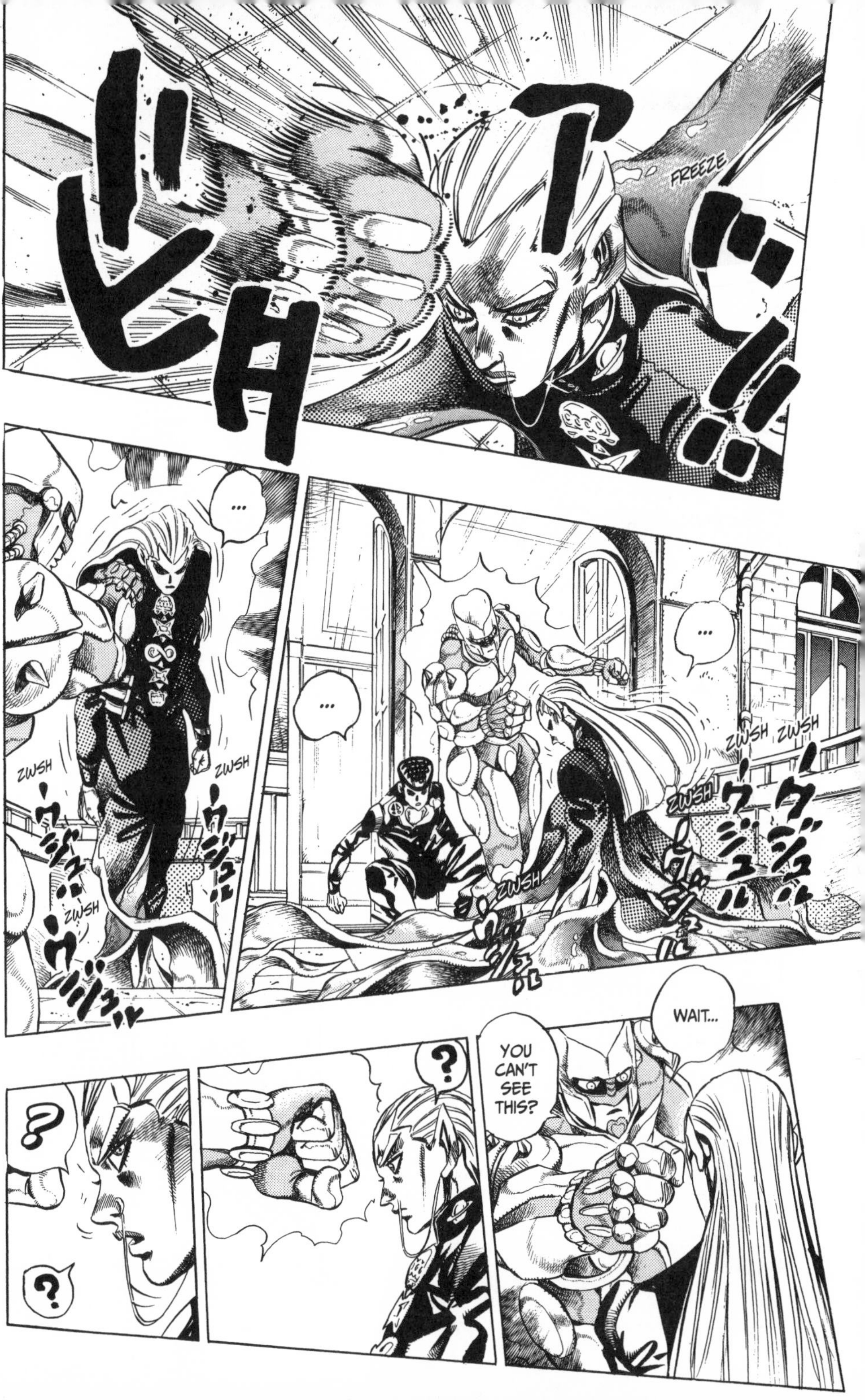
FREEZE
...
...
ZWSH
ZWSH
ZWSH
ZWSH
...
ZWSH
ZWSH
ZWSH
WAIT...
YOU CAN'T SEE THIS?
?
?
?

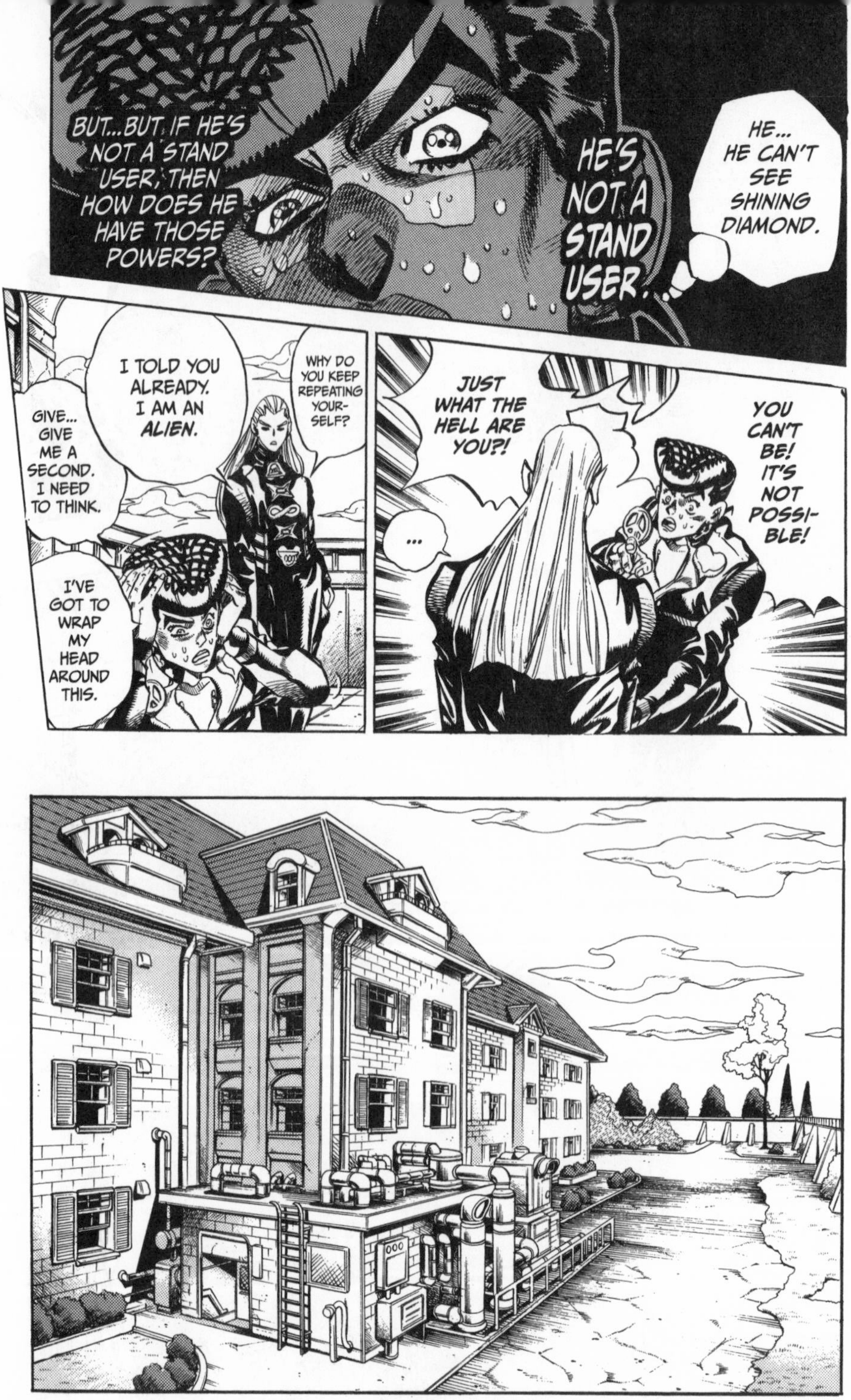
HE... HE CAN'T SEE SHINING DIAMOND.
HE'S NOT A STAND USER...
BUT...BUT IF HE'S NOT A STAND USER, THEN HOW DOES HE HAVE THOSE POWERS?
YOU CAN'T BE! IT'S NOT POSSI-BLE!
JUST WHAT THE HELL ARE YOU?!
...
WHY DO YOU KEEP REPEATING YOUR-SELF?
I TOLD YOU ALREADY. I AM AN ALIEN.
GIVE... GIVE ME A SECOND. I NEED TO THINK.
I'VE GOT TO WRAP MY HEAD AROUND THIS.

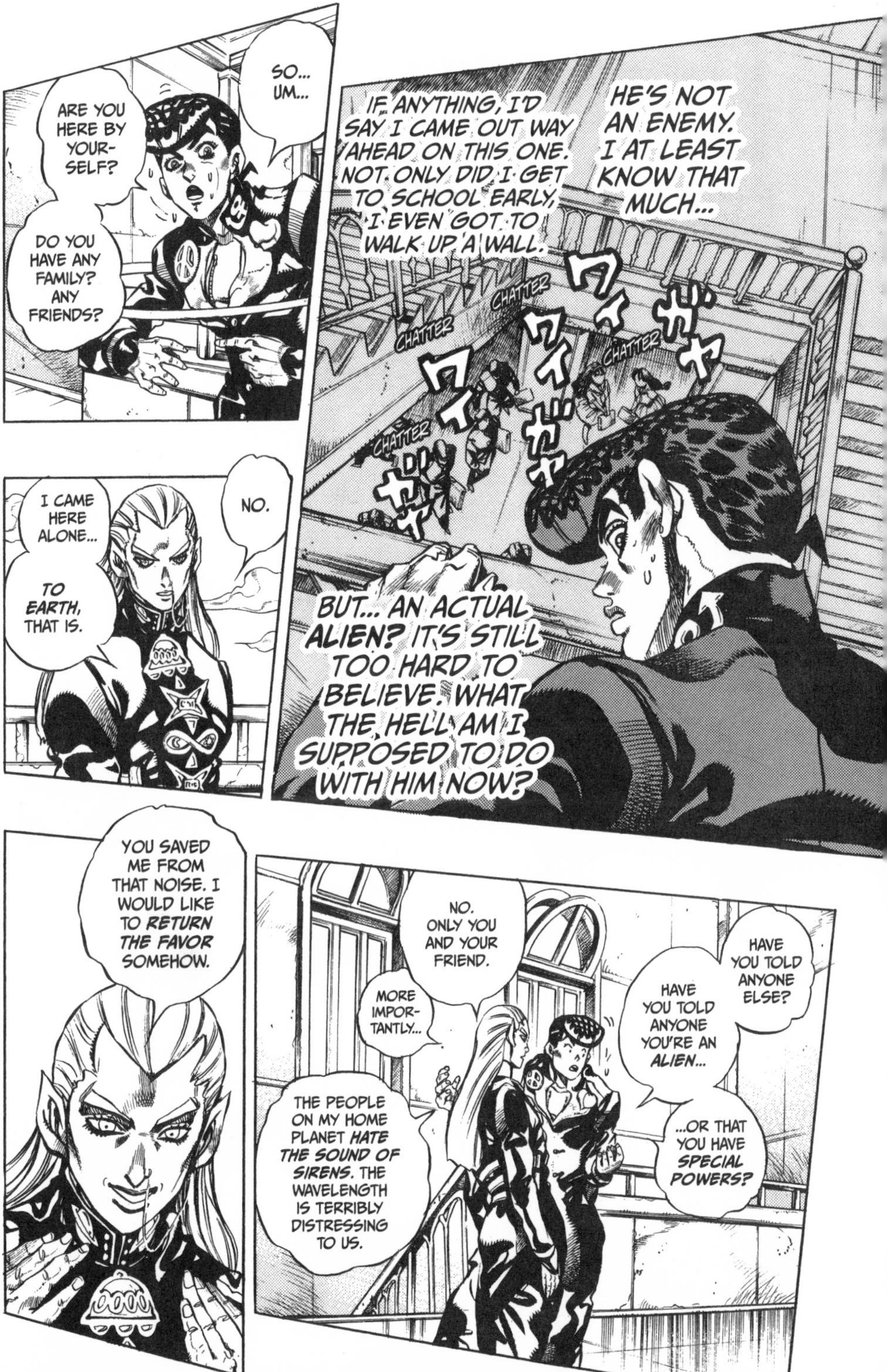
HE'S NOT AN ENEMY. I AT LEAST KNOW THAT MUCH...
IF ANYTHING, I'D SAY I CAME OUT WAY AHEAD ON THIS ONE. NOT ONLY DID I GET TO SCHOOL EARLY, I EVEN GOT TO WALK UP A WALL.
ガヤガヤ
ワイワイ
CHATTER
CHATTER
CHATTER
CHATTER
BUT... AN ACTUAL ALIEN? IT'S STILL TOO HARD TO BELIEVE. WHAT THE HELL AM I SUPPOSED TO DO WITH HIM NOW?
SO... UM...
ARE YOU HERE BY YOUR-SELF?
DO YOU HAVE ANY FAMILY? ANY FRIENDS?
NO.
I CAME HERE ALONE...
TO EARTH, THAT IS.
HAVE YOU TOLD ANYONE ELSE?
HAVE YOU TOLD ANYONE YOU'RE AN ALIEN...
...OR THAT YOU HAVE SPECIAL POWERS?
NO. ONLY YOU AND YOUR FRIEND.
MORE IMPOR-TANTLY...
THE PEOPLE ON MY HOME PLANET HATE THE SOUND OF SIRENS. THE WAVELENGTH IS TERRIBLY DISTRESSING TO US.
YOU SAVED ME FROM THAT NOISE. I WOULD LIKE TO RETURN THE FAVOR SOMEHOW.

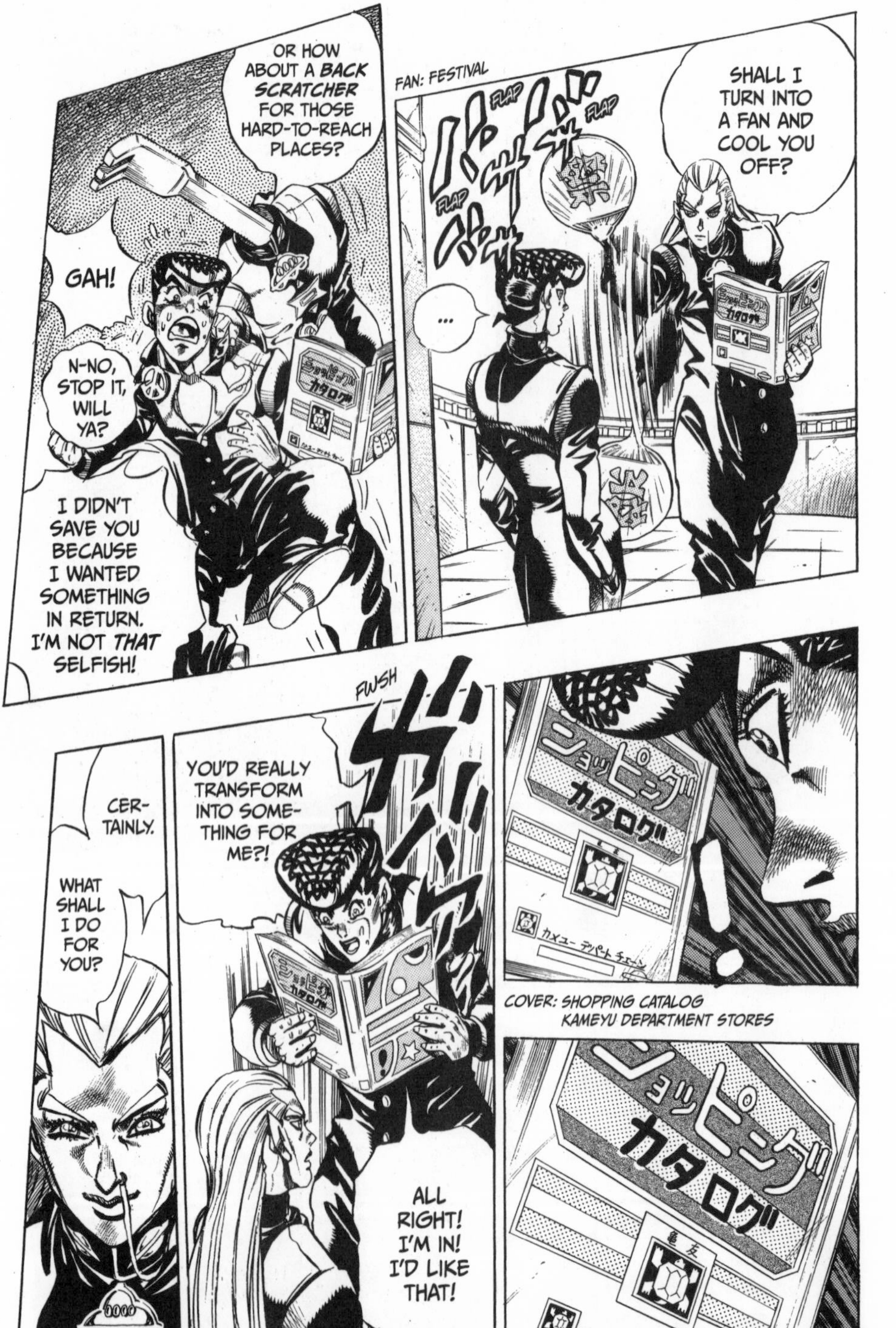
FAN: FESTIVAL
SHALL I TURN INTO A FAN AND COOL YOU OFF?
FLAP
FLAP
FLAP
...
OR HOW ABOUT A *BACK SCRATCHER* FOR THOSE HARD-TO-REACH PLACES?
GAH!
N-NO, STOP IT, WILL YA?
I DIDN'T SAVE YOU BECAUSE I WANTED SOMETHING IN RETURN. I'M NOT *THAT* SELFISH!
COVER: SHOPPING CATALOG
KAMEYU DEPARTMENT STORES
FWSH
YOU'D REALLY TRANSFORM INTO SOME-THING FOR ME?!
ALL RIGHT! I'M IN! I'D LIKE THAT!
CER-TAINLY.
WHAT SHALL I DO FOR YOU?

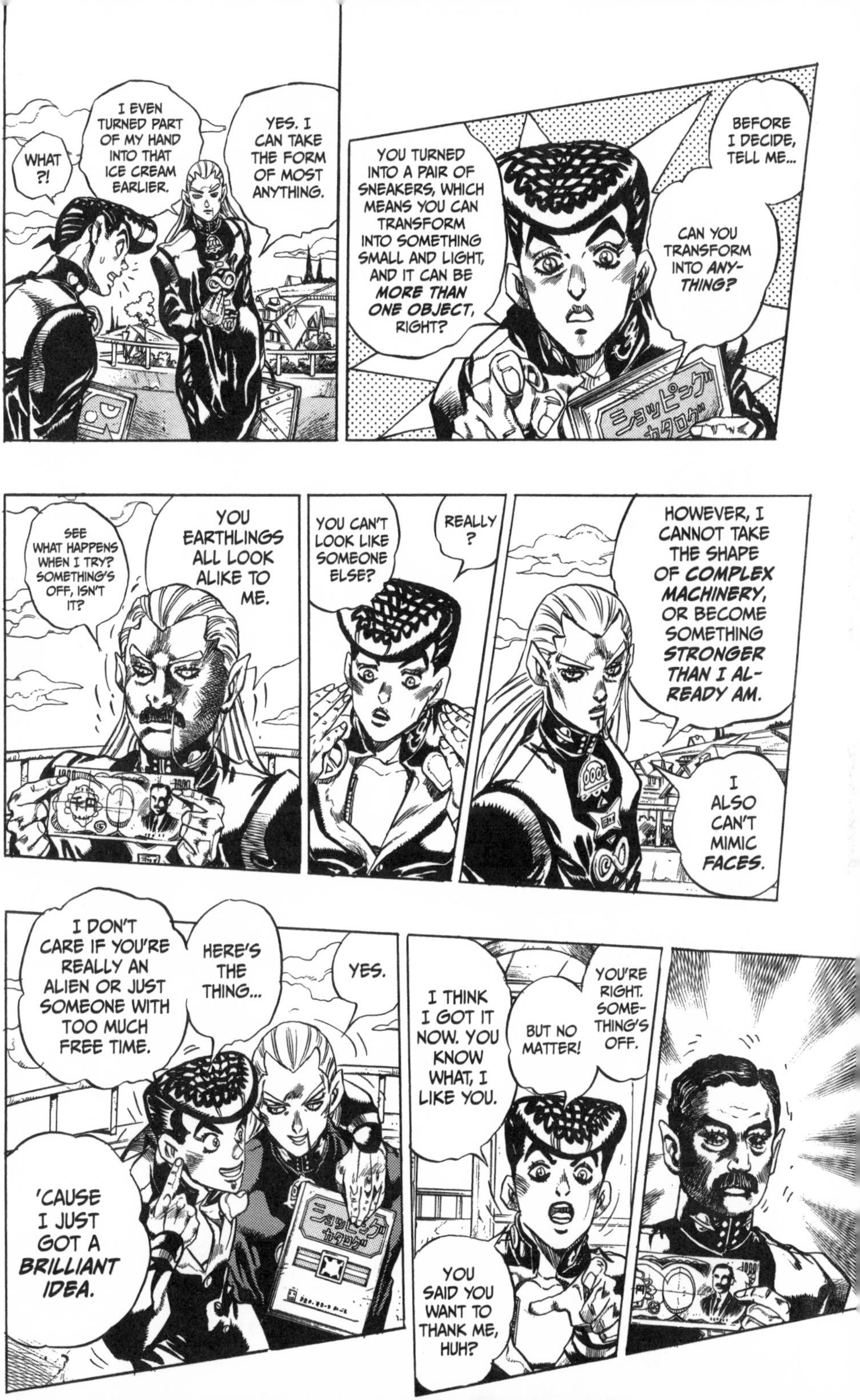
BEFORE I DECIDE, TELL ME...
CAN YOU TRANSFORM INTO *ANYTHING?*
YOU TURNED INTO A PAIR OF SNEAKERS, WHICH MEANS YOU CAN TRANSFORM INTO SOMETHING SMALL AND LIGHT, AND IT CAN BE ***MORE THAN ONE OBJECT***, RIGHT?
ショッピングカタログ
YES. I CAN TAKE THE FORM OF MOST ANYTHING.
I EVEN TURNED PART OF MY HAND INTO THAT ICE CREAM EARLIER.
WHAT ?!
HOWEVER, I CANNOT TAKE THE SHAPE OF ***COMPLEX MACHINERY***, OR BECOME SOMETHING ***STRONGER THAN I ALREADY AM***.
I ALSO CAN'T MIMIC ***FACES***.
REALLY ?
YOU CAN'T LOOK LIKE SOMEONE ELSE?
YOU EARTHLINGS ALL LOOK ALIKE TO ME.
SEE WHAT HAPPENS WHEN I TRY? SOMETHING'S OFF, ISN'T IT?
YOU'RE RIGHT. SOMETHING'S OFF.
BUT NO MATTER!
I THINK I GOT IT NOW. YOU KNOW WHAT, I LIKE YOU.
YOU SAID YOU WANT TO THANK ME, HUH?
YES.
HERE'S THE THING...
I DON'T CARE IF YOU'RE REALLY AN ALIEN OR JUST SOMEONE WITH TOO MUCH FREE TIME.
'CAUSE I JUST GOT A ***BRILLIANT IDEA.***

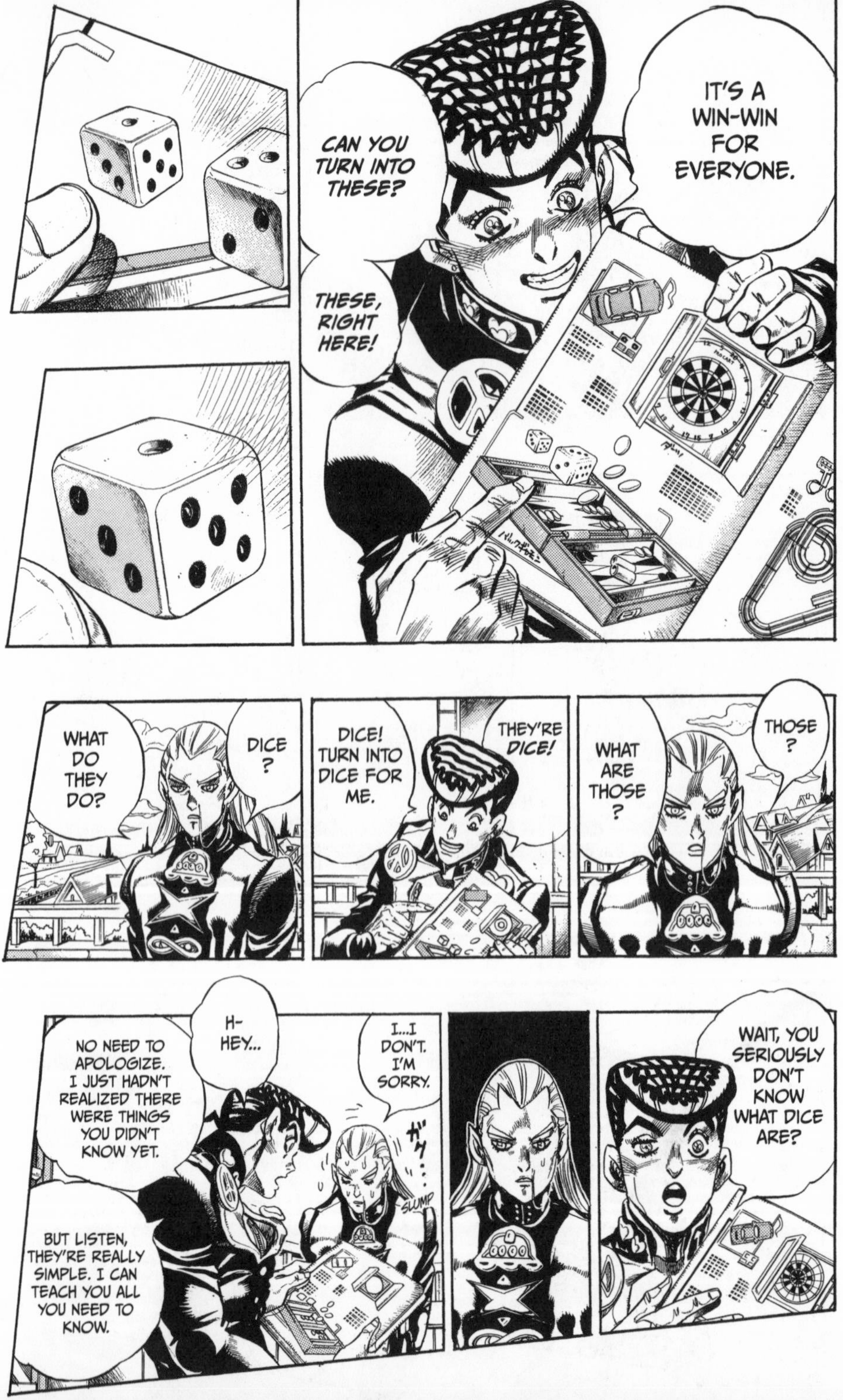
IT'S A WIN-WIN FOR EVERYONE.
CAN YOU TURN INTO THESE?
THESE, RIGHT HERE!
THOSE?
WHAT ARE THOSE?
THEY'RE DICE!
DICE! TURN INTO DICE FOR ME.
DICE?
WHAT DO THEY DO?
WAIT, YOU SERIOUSLY DON'T KNOW WHAT DICE ARE?
I...I DON'T. I'M SORRY.
SLUMP
H-HEY...
NO NEED TO APOLOGIZE. I JUST HADN'T REALIZED THERE WERE THINGS YOU DIDN'T KNOW YET.
BUT LISTEN, THEY'RE REALLY SIMPLE. I CAN TEACH YOU ALL YOU NEED TO KNOW.

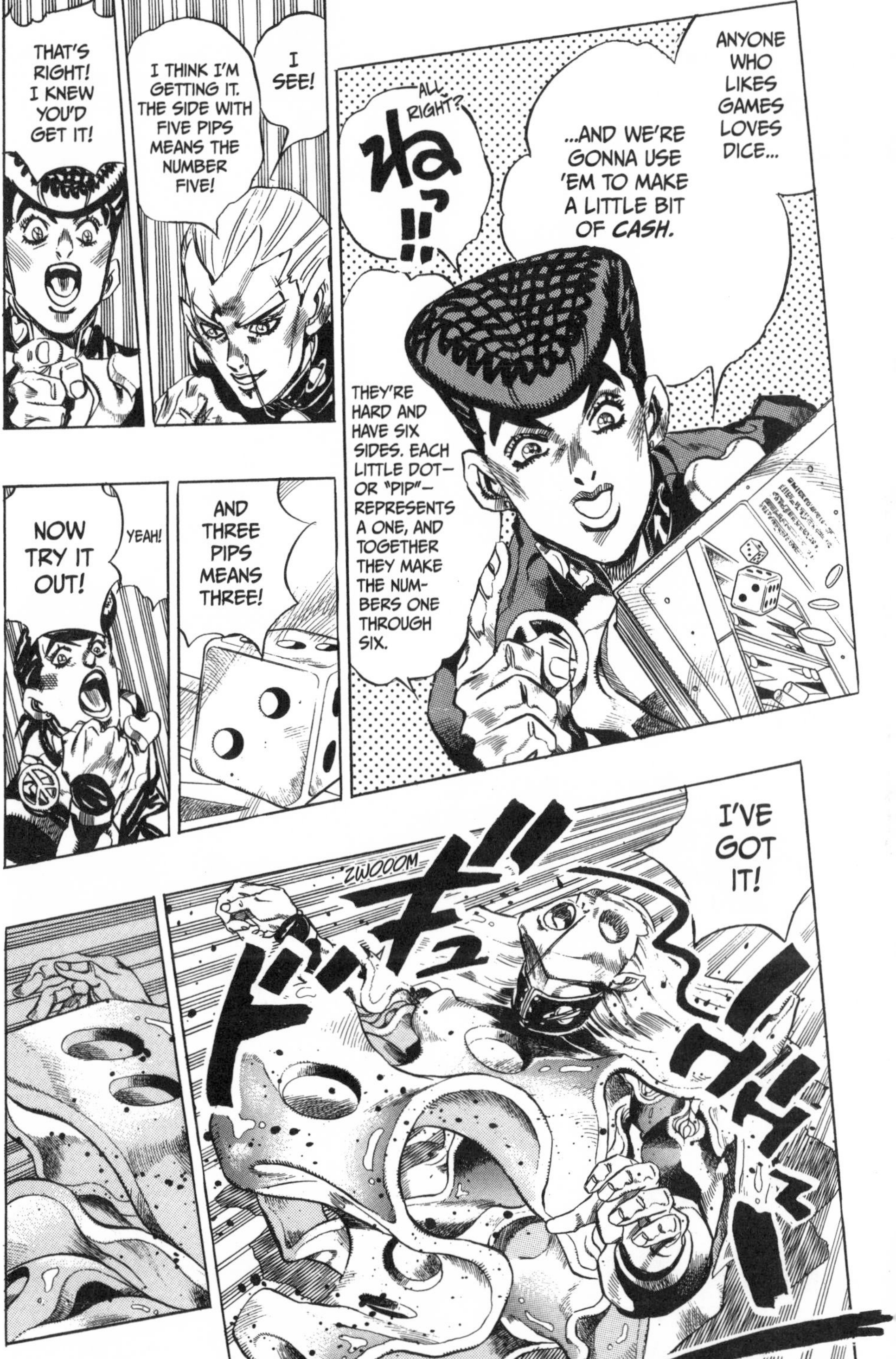

ANYONE WHO LIKES GAMES LOVES DICE...
...AND WE'RE GONNA USE 'EM TO MAKE A LITTLE BIT OF CASH.
ねっ!!
ALL RIGHT?
THEY'RE HARD AND HAVE SIX SIDES. EACH LITTLE DOT—OR "PIP"—REPRESENTS A ONE, AND TOGETHER THEY MAKE THE NUMBERS ONE THROUGH SIX.
I SEE!
I THINK I'M GETTING IT. THE SIDE WITH FIVE PIPS MEANS THE NUMBER FIVE!
THAT'S RIGHT! I KNEW YOU'D GET IT!
AND THREE PIPS MEANS THREE!
YEAH!
NOW TRY IT OUT!
I'VE GOT IT!
ZWOOOM

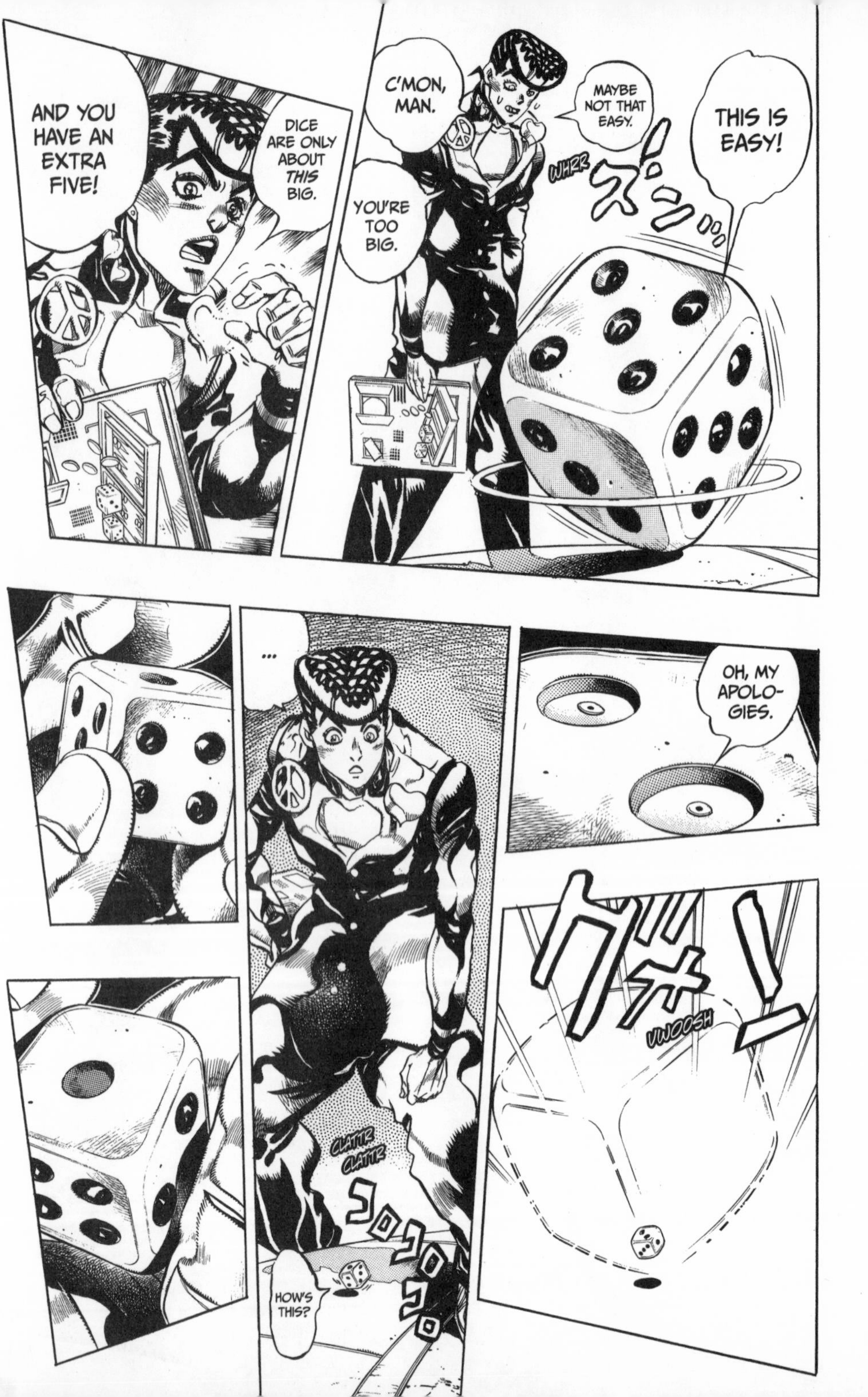
THIS IS EASY!
MAYBE NOT THAT EASY.
WHRR
C'MON, MAN.
YOU'RE TOO BIG.
DICE ARE ONLY ABOUT *THIS* BIG.
AND YOU HAVE AN EXTRA FIVE!
OH, MY APOLOGIES.
VWOOSH
...
CLATTR CLATTR
HOW'S THIS?

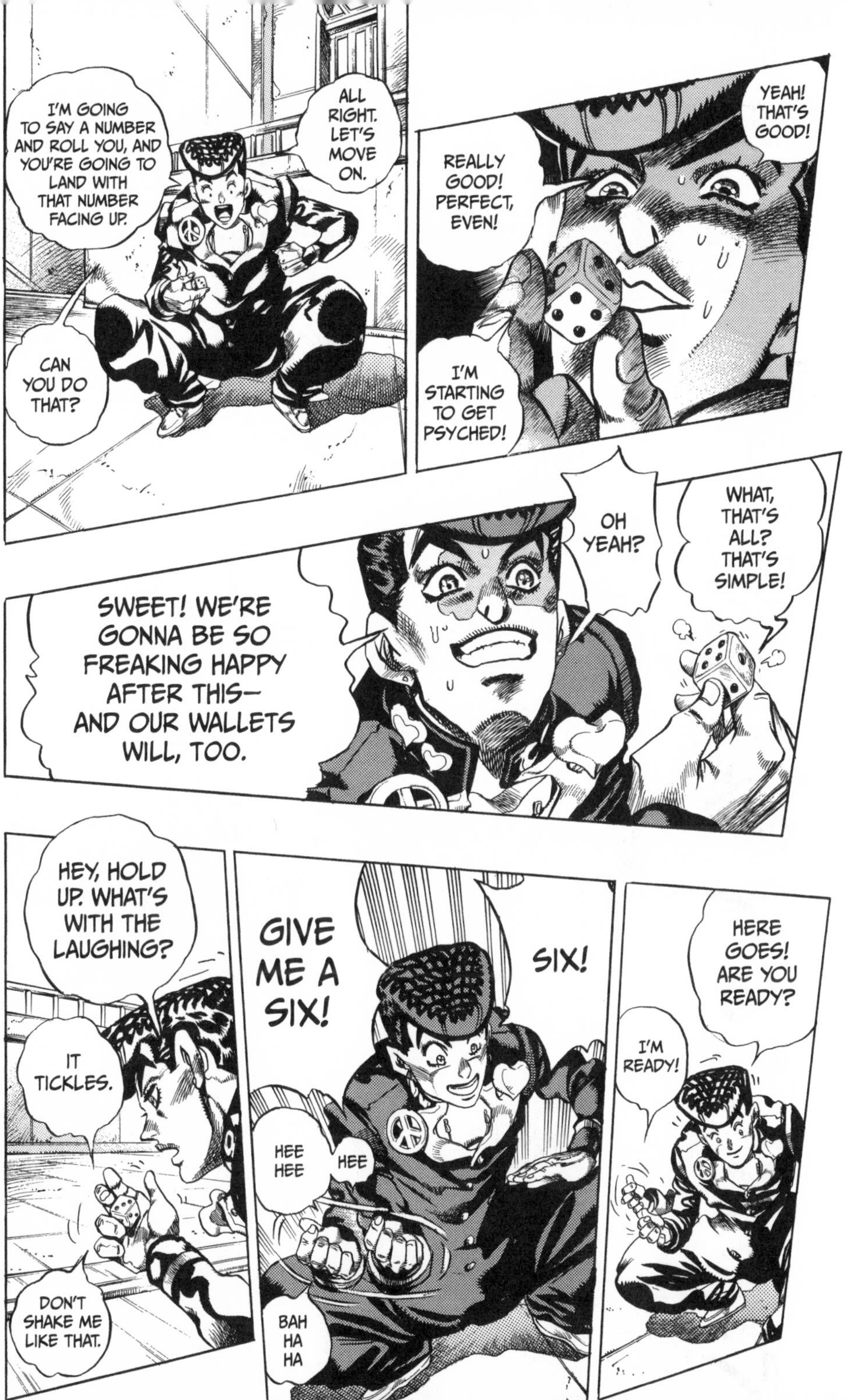
YEAH! THAT'S GOOD!
REALLY GOOD! PERFECT, EVEN!
I'M STARTING TO GET PSYCHED!
ALL RIGHT. LET'S MOVE ON.
I'M GOING TO SAY A NUMBER AND ROLL YOU, AND YOU'RE GOING TO LAND WITH THAT NUMBER FACING UP.
CAN YOU DO THAT?
WHAT, THAT'S ALL? THAT'S SIMPLE!
OH YEAH?
SWEET! WE'RE GONNA BE SO FREAKING HAPPY AFTER THIS— AND OUR WALLETS WILL, TOO.
HERE GOES! ARE YOU READY?
I'M READY!
SIX!
GIVE ME A SIX!
HEE
HEE HEE
BAH HA HA
HEY, HOLD UP. WHAT'S WITH THE LAUGHING?
IT TICKLES.
DON'T SHAKE ME LIKE THAT.

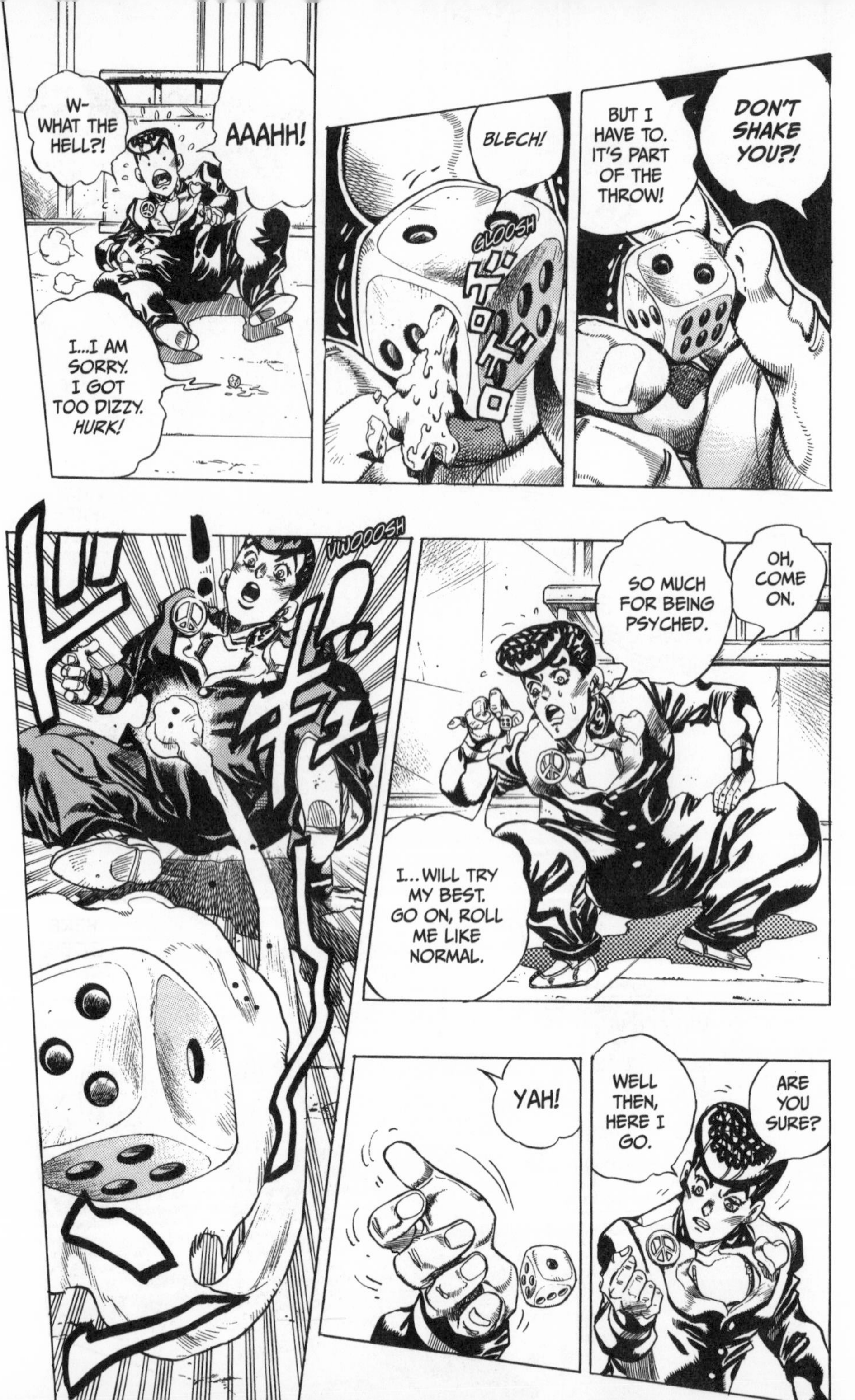
DON'T SHAKE YOU?!
BUT I HAVE TO. IT'S PART OF THE THROW!
BLECH!
GLOOSH
AAAHH!
W- WHAT THE HELL?!
I...I AM SORRY. I GOT TOO DIZZY. HURK!
OH, COME ON.
SO MUCH FOR BEING PSYCHED.
I...WILL TRY MY BEST. GO ON, ROLL ME LIKE NORMAL.
ARE YOU SURE?
WELL THEN, HERE I GO.
YAH!
UWOOOSH

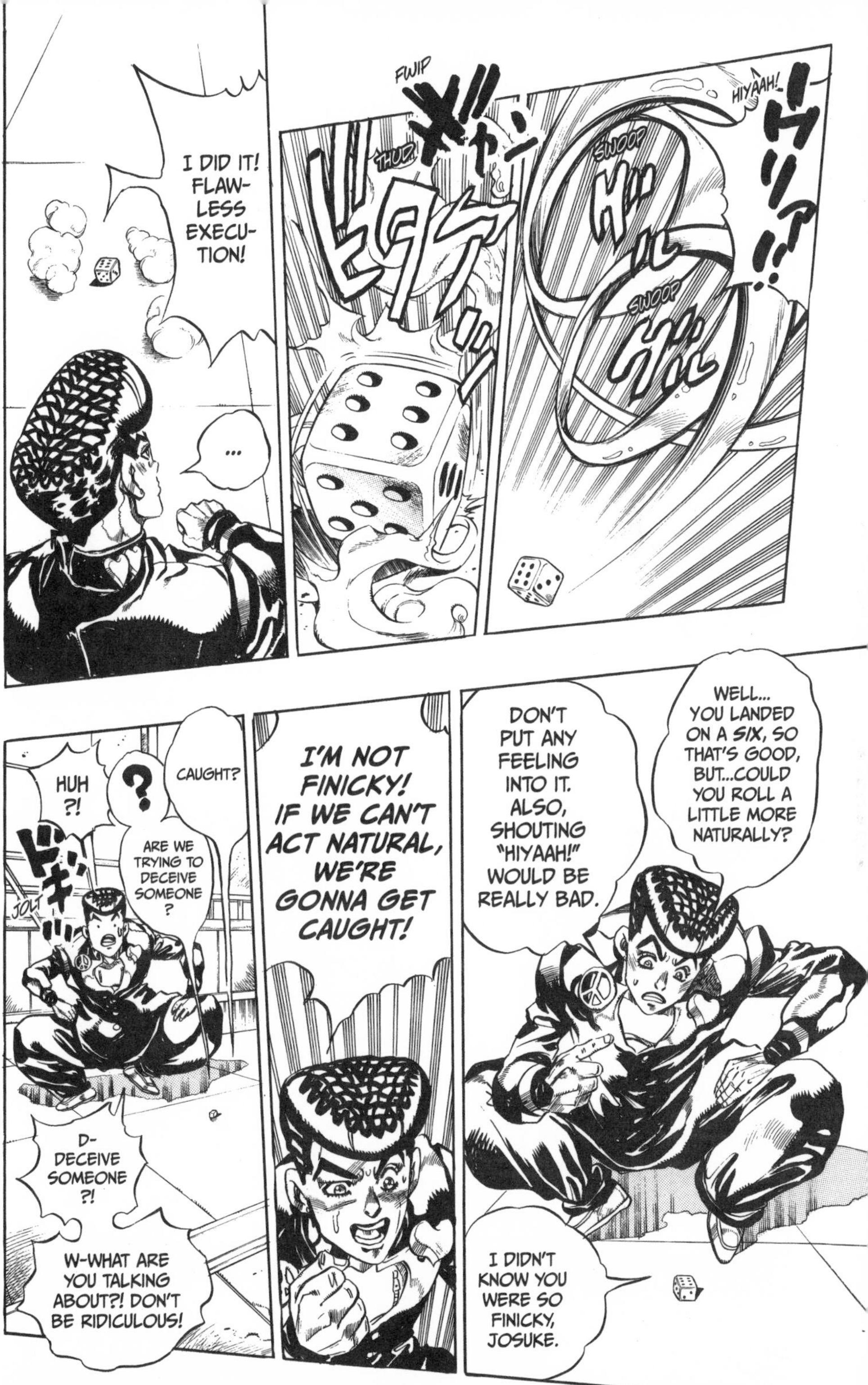
HIYAAH!
SWOOP
SWOOP
FWIP
THUD
I DID IT! FLAW-LESS EXECU-TION!
...
WELL... YOU LANDED ON A SIX, SO THAT'S GOOD, BUT...COULD YOU ROLL A LITTLE MORE NATURALLY?
DON'T PUT ANY FEELING INTO IT. ALSO, SHOUTING "HIYAAH!" WOULD BE REALLY BAD.
I DIDN'T KNOW YOU WERE SO FINICKY, JOSUKE.
I'M NOT FINICKY! IF WE CAN'T ACT NATURAL, WE'RE GONNA GET CAUGHT!
CAUGHT?
ARE WE TRYING TO DECEIVE SOMEONE?
HUH?!
JOLT
D-DECEIVE SOMEONE?!
W-WHAT ARE YOU TALKING ABOUT?! DON'T BE RIDICULOUS!

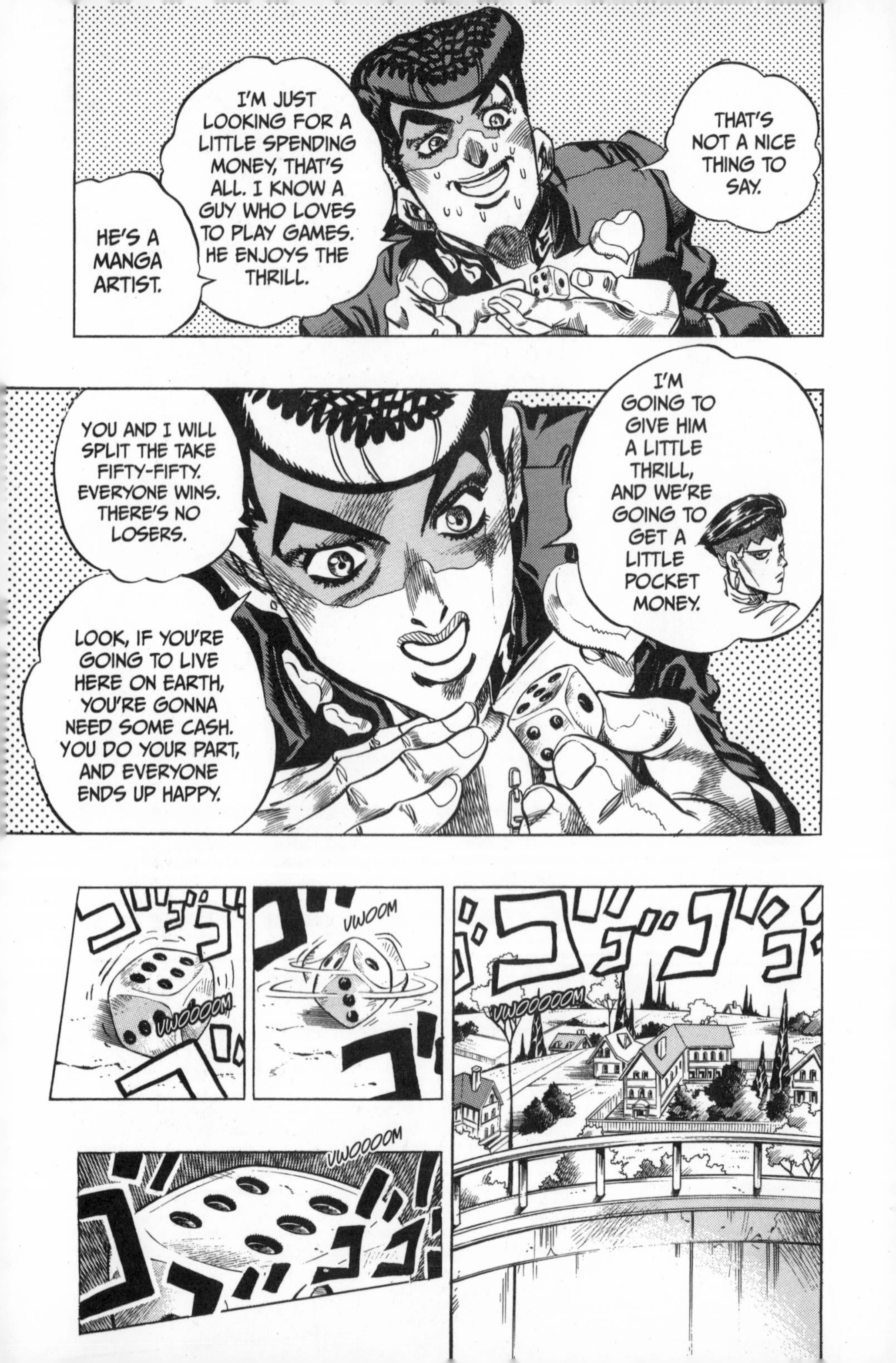
THAT'S NOT A NICE THING TO SAY.
I'M JUST LOOKING FOR A LITTLE SPENDING MONEY, THAT'S ALL. I KNOW A GUY WHO LOVES TO PLAY GAMES. HE ENJOYS THE THRILL.
HE'S A MANGA ARTIST.
I'M GOING TO GIVE HIM A LITTLE THRILL, AND WE'RE GOING TO GET A LITTLE POCKET MONEY.
YOU AND I WILL SPLIT THE TAKE FIFTY-FIFTY. EVERYONE WINS. THERE'S NO LOSERS.
LOOK, IF YOU'RE GOING TO LIVE HERE ON EARTH, YOU'RE GONNA NEED SOME CASH. YOU DO YOUR PART, AND EVERYONE ENDS UP HAPPY.
VWOOOOOOM
VWOOM
VWOOOOOM
VWOOOOOM

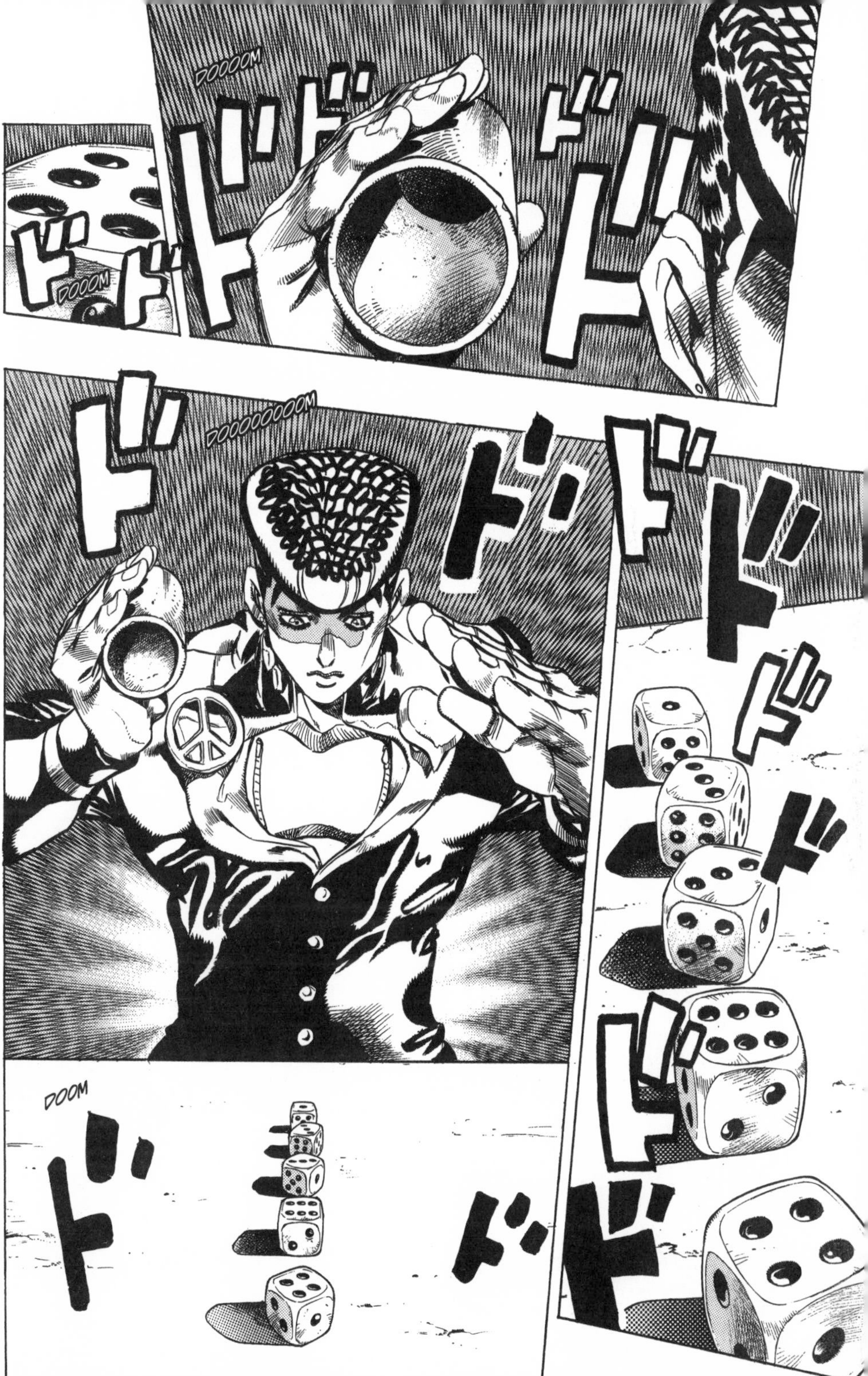
DOOOOM
DOOOM
DOOOOOOOOM
DOOM

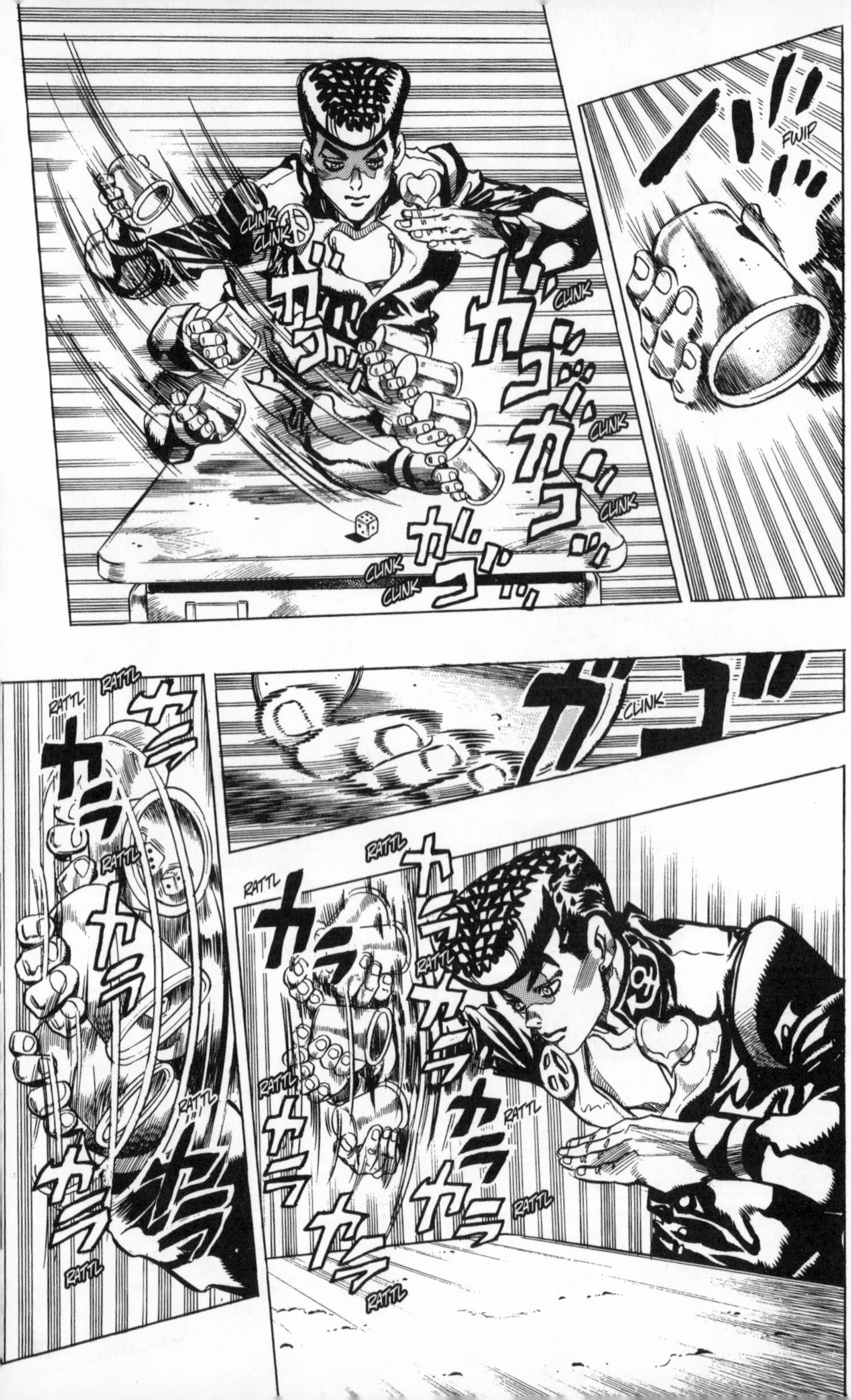
バ
FWIP
ガゴ
CLINK
CLINK
CLINK
ガゴ
CLINK
CLINK
ガゴ
CLINK
CLINK
ガゴ
CLINK
ガゴ
CLINK
カラ
RATTL
カラ
RATTL
カラ
RATTL
カラ
RATTL
カラ
RATTL
カラ
RATTL
カラ
RATTL
カラ
RATTL
カラ
RATTL
カラ
RATTL
カラ
RATTL
カラ
RATTL

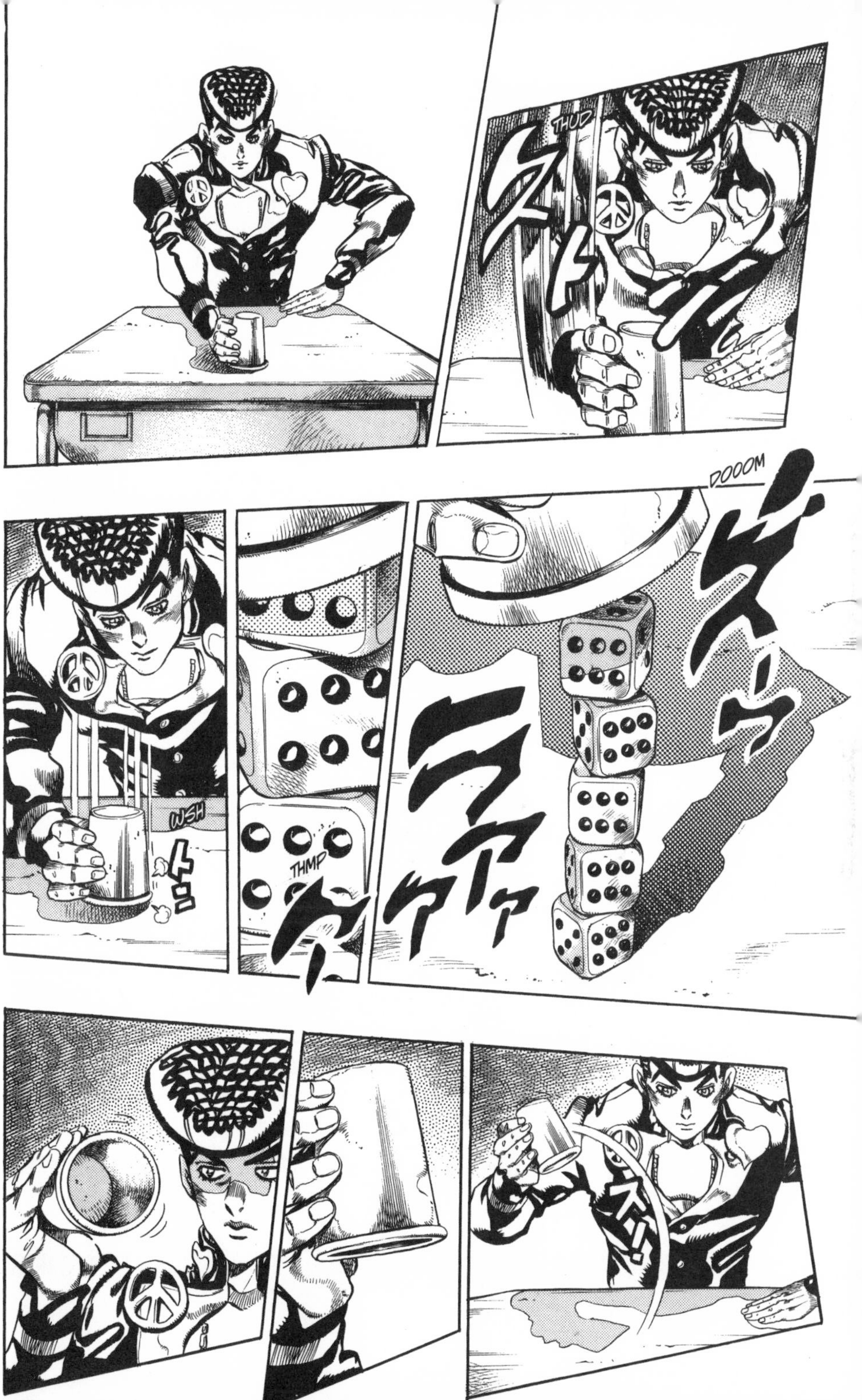
THUD
DOOOM
THMP
WSH

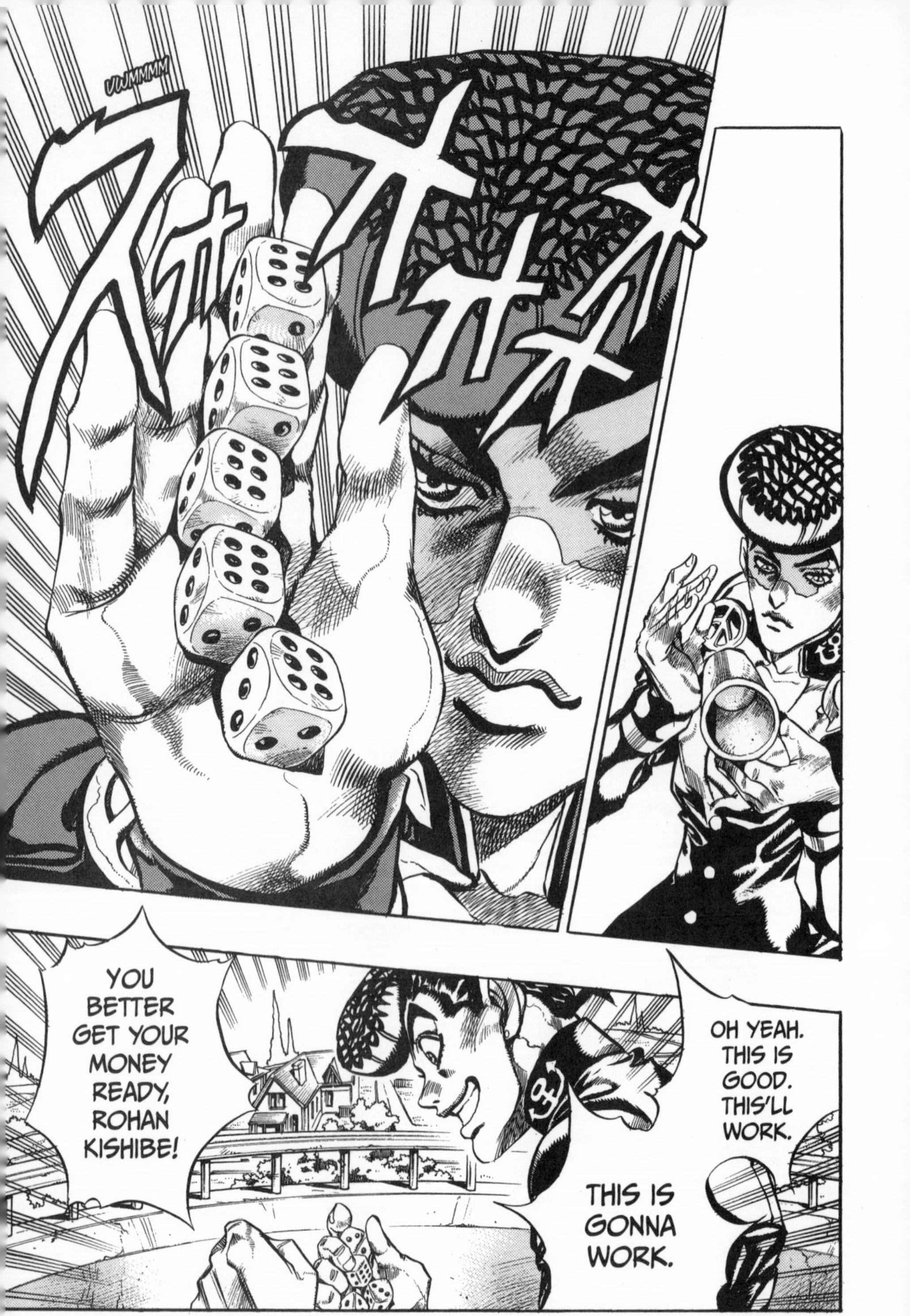
UWMMMM
OH YEAH. THIS IS GOOD. THIS'LL WORK.
THIS IS GONNA WORK.
YOU BETTER GET YOUR MONEY READY, ROHAN KISHIBE!

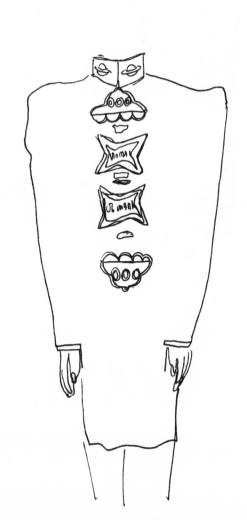

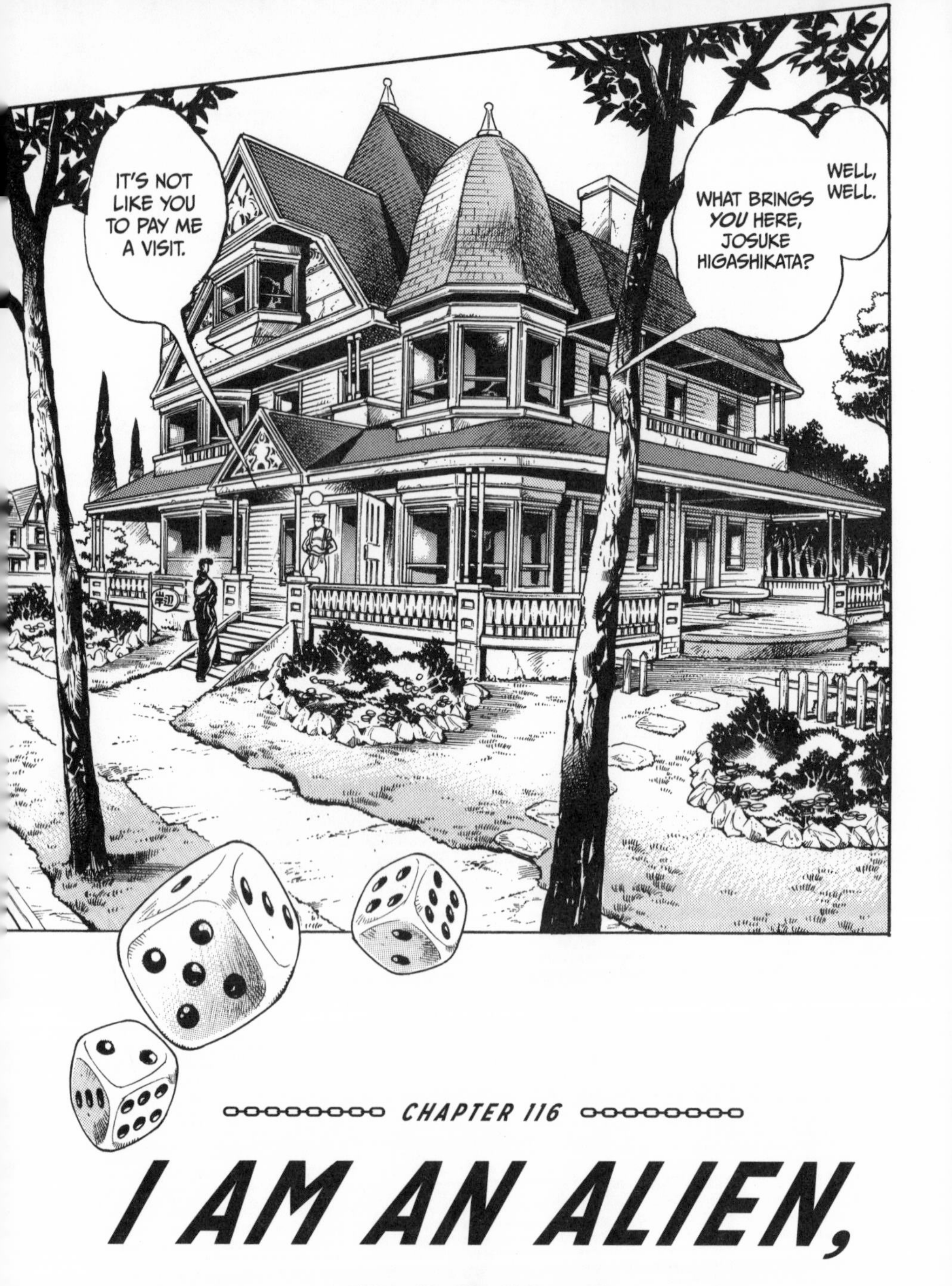
WELL, WELL.
WHAT BRINGS *YOU* HERE, JOSUKE HIGASHIKATA?
IT'S NOT LIKE YOU TO PAY ME A VISIT.

CHAPTER 116

I AM AN ALIEN, PART 4

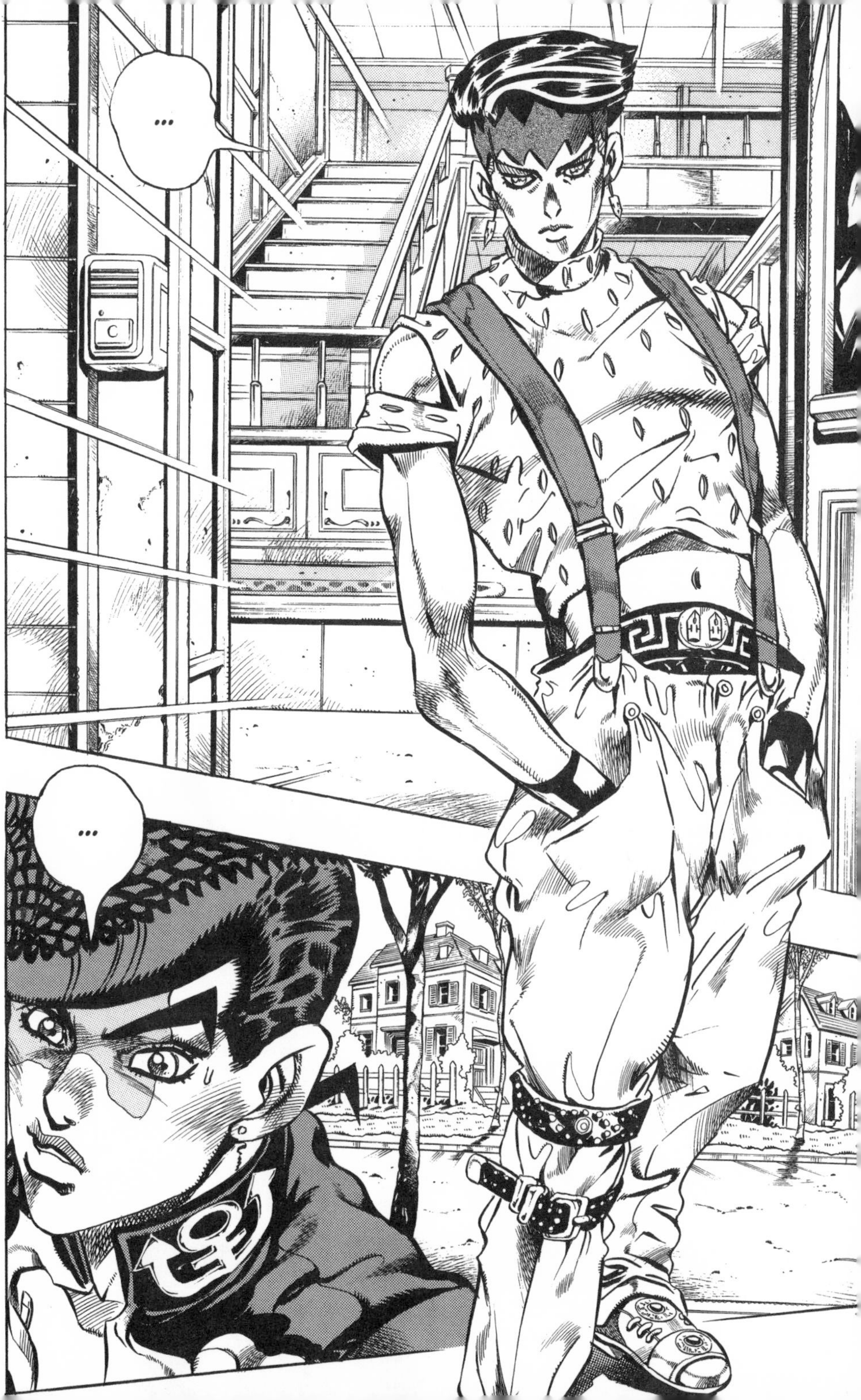
...
...

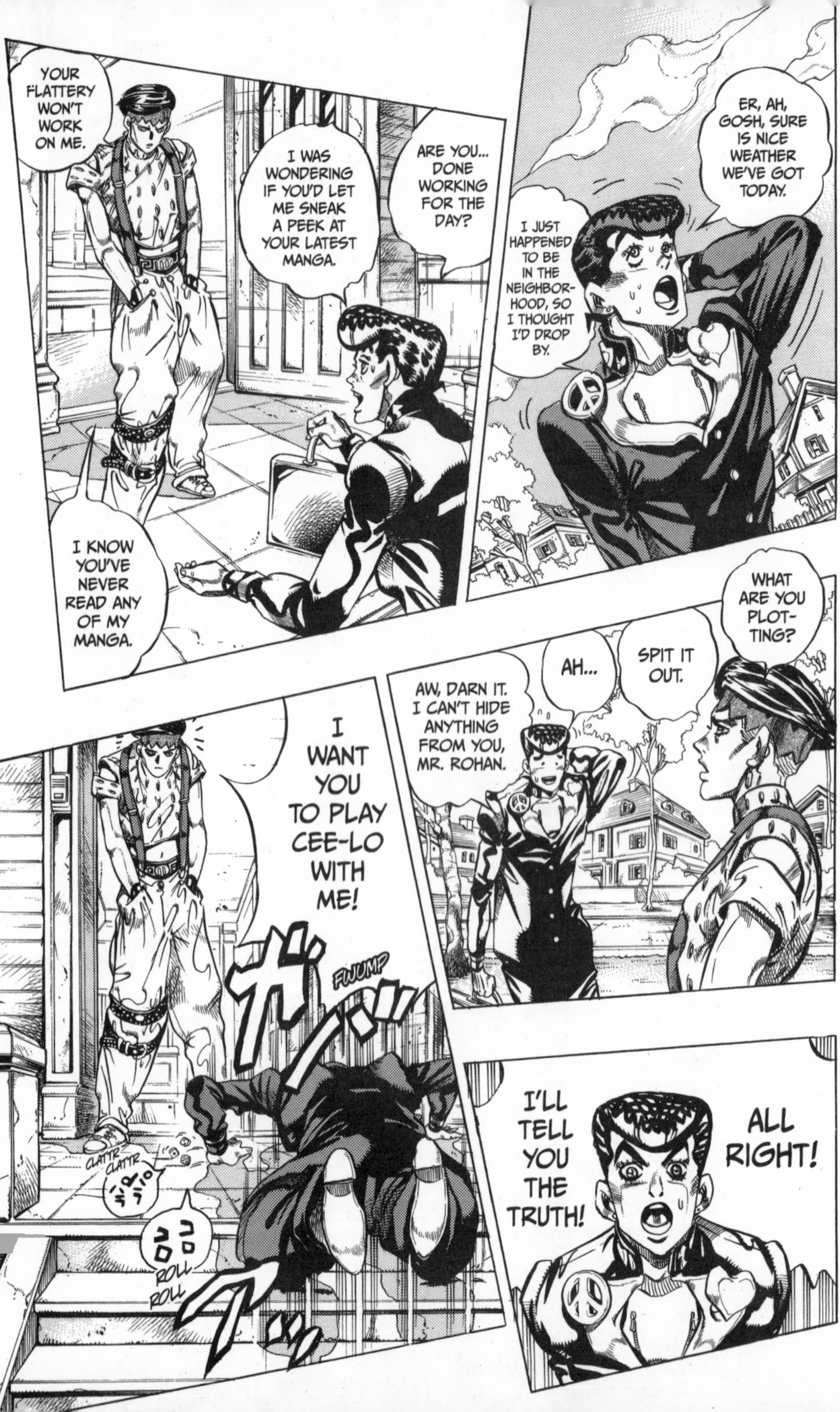
ER, AH, GOSH, SURE IS NICE WEATHER WE'VE GOT TODAY.
I JUST HAPPENED TO BE IN THE NEIGHBORHOOD, SO I THOUGHT I'D DROP BY.
ARE YOU... DONE WORKING FOR THE DAY?
I WAS WONDERING IF YOU'D LET ME SNEAK A PEEK AT YOUR LATEST MANGA.
YOUR FLATTERY WON'T WORK ON ME.
I KNOW YOU'VE NEVER READ ANY OF MY MANGA.
WHAT ARE YOU PLOTTING?
SPIT IT OUT.
AH...
AW, DARN IT. I CAN'T HIDE ANYTHING FROM YOU, MR. ROHAN.
ALL RIGHT!
I'LL TELL YOU THE TRUTH!
I WANT YOU TO PLAY CEE-LO WITH ME!
FWUMP
CLATTR CLATTR
ROLL ROLL

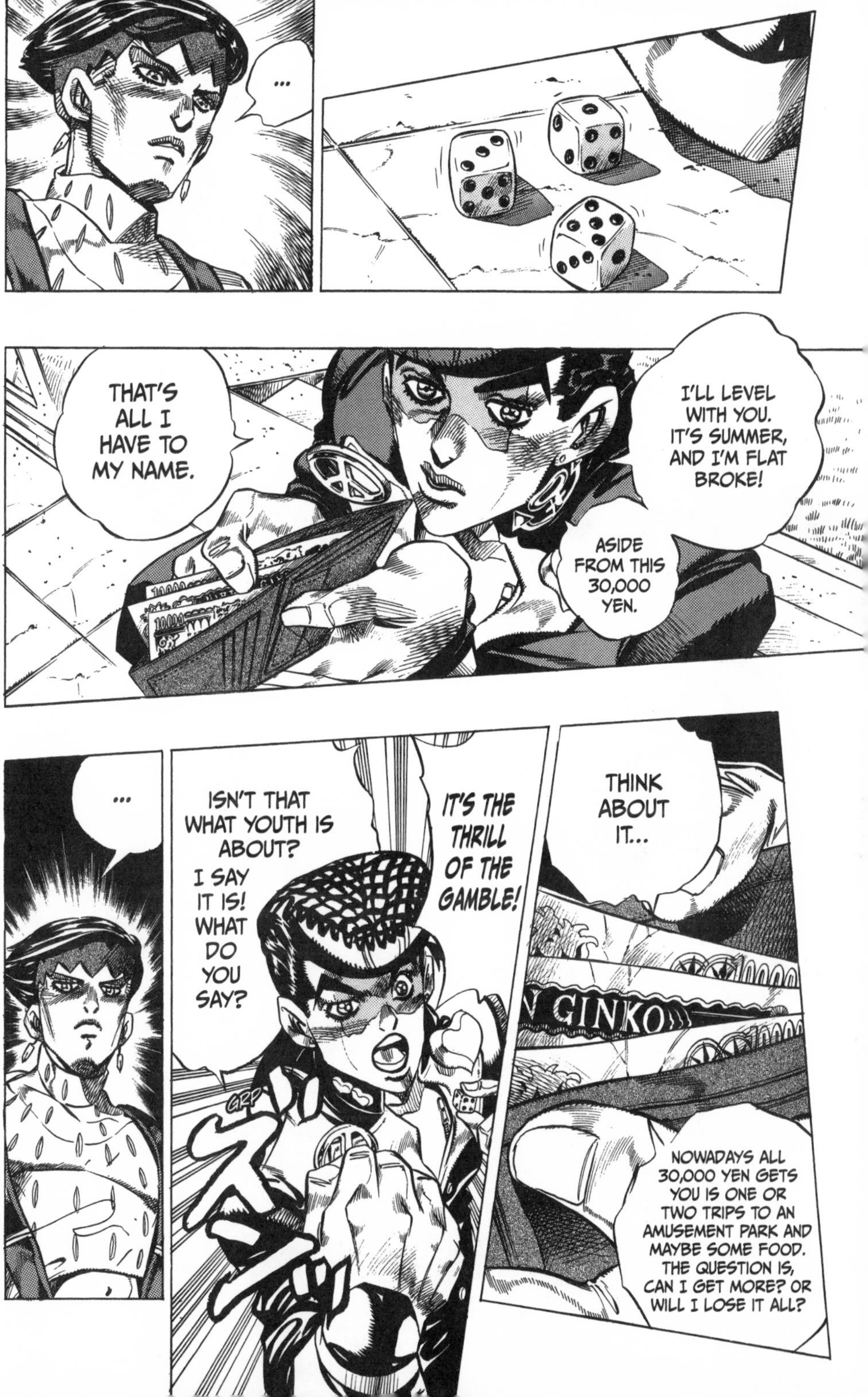
...
I'LL LEVEL WITH YOU. IT'S SUMMER, AND I'M FLAT BROKE!
ASIDE FROM THIS 30,000 YEN.
THAT'S ALL I HAVE TO MY NAME.
THINK ABOUT IT...
NOWADAYS ALL 30,000 YEN GETS YOU IS ONE OR TWO TRIPS TO AN AMUSEMENT PARK AND MAYBE SOME FOOD. THE QUESTION IS, CAN I GET MORE? OR WILL I LOSE IT ALL?
IT'S THE THRILL OF THE GAMBLE!
ISN'T THAT WHAT YOUTH IS ABOUT?
I SAY IT IS! WHAT DO YOU SAY?
GRP
...

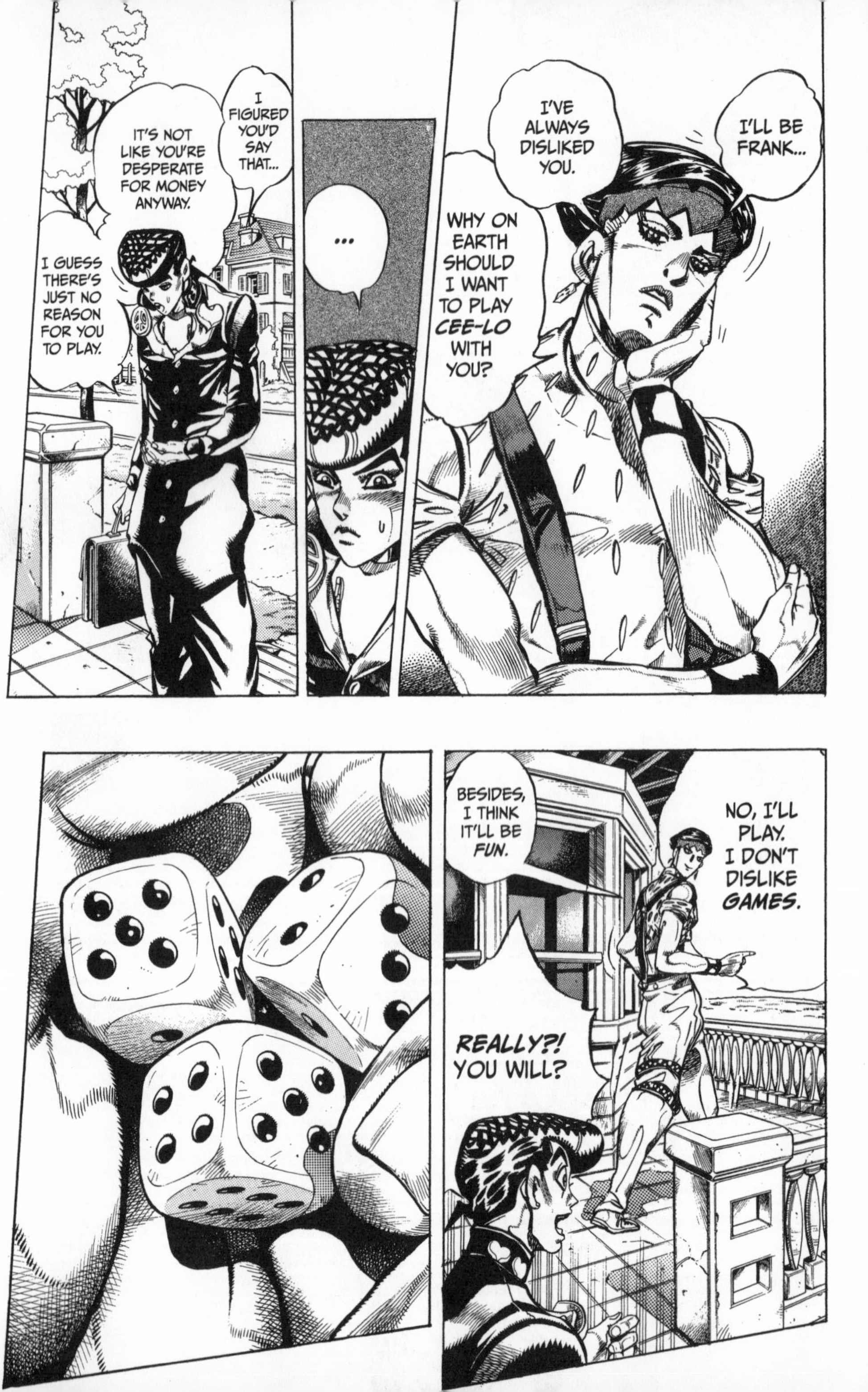
I'LL BE FRANK...
I'VE ALWAYS DISLIKED YOU.
WHY ON EARTH SHOULD I WANT TO PLAY *CEE-LO* WITH YOU?
...
I FIGURED YOU'D SAY THAT...
IT'S NOT LIKE YOU'RE DESPERATE FOR MONEY ANYWAY.
I GUESS THERE'S JUST NO REASON FOR YOU TO PLAY.
NO, I'LL PLAY. I DON'T DISLIKE ***GAMES***.
BESIDES, I THINK IT'LL BE ***FUN***.
REALLY?! YOU WILL?

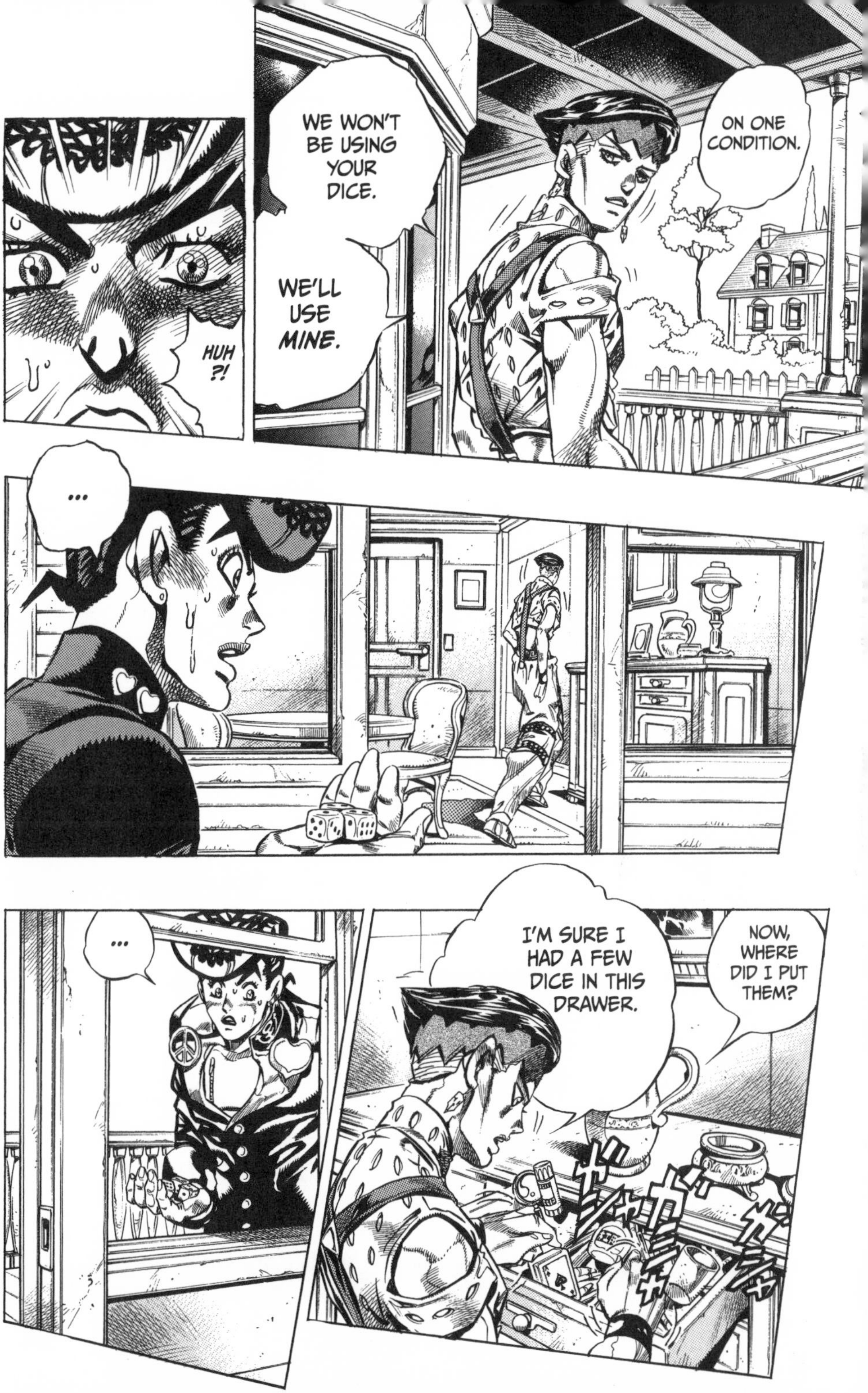
ON ONE CONDITION.
WE WON'T BE USING YOUR DICE.
WE'LL USE *MINE*.
HUH ?!
...
NOW, WHERE DID I PUT THEM?
I'M SURE I HAD A FEW DICE IN THIS DRAWER.
...

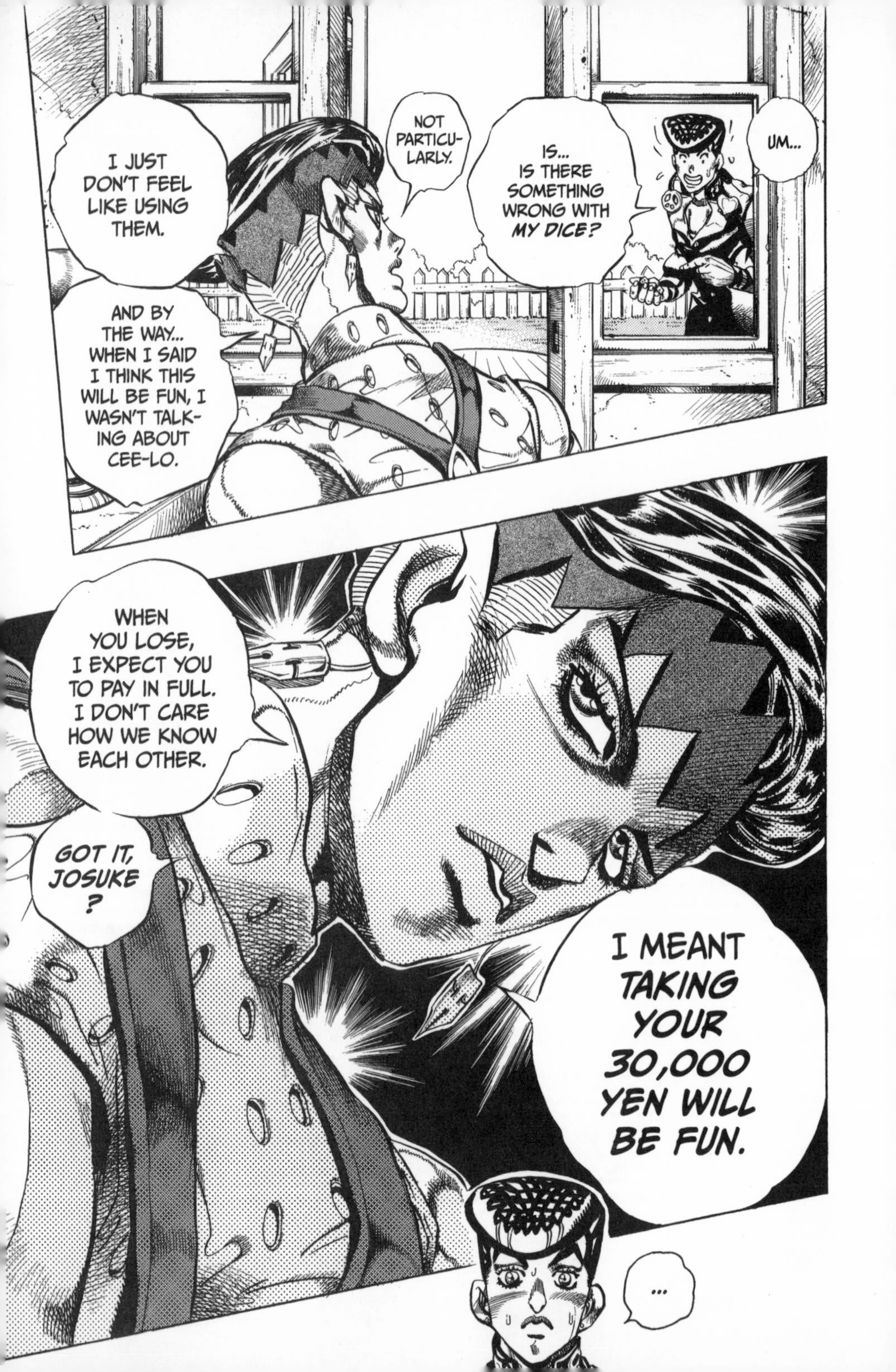
UM...
IS... IS THERE SOMETHING WRONG WITH *MY DICE?*
NOT PARTICULARLY.
I JUST DON'T FEEL LIKE USING THEM.
AND BY THE WAY... WHEN I SAID I THINK THIS WILL BE FUN, I WASN'T TALKING ABOUT CEE-LO.
I MEANT *TAKING YOUR 30,000 YEN WILL BE FUN.*
WHEN YOU LOSE, I EXPECT YOU TO PAY IN FULL. I DON'T CARE HOW WE KNOW EACH OTHER.
GOT IT, JOSUKE?
...

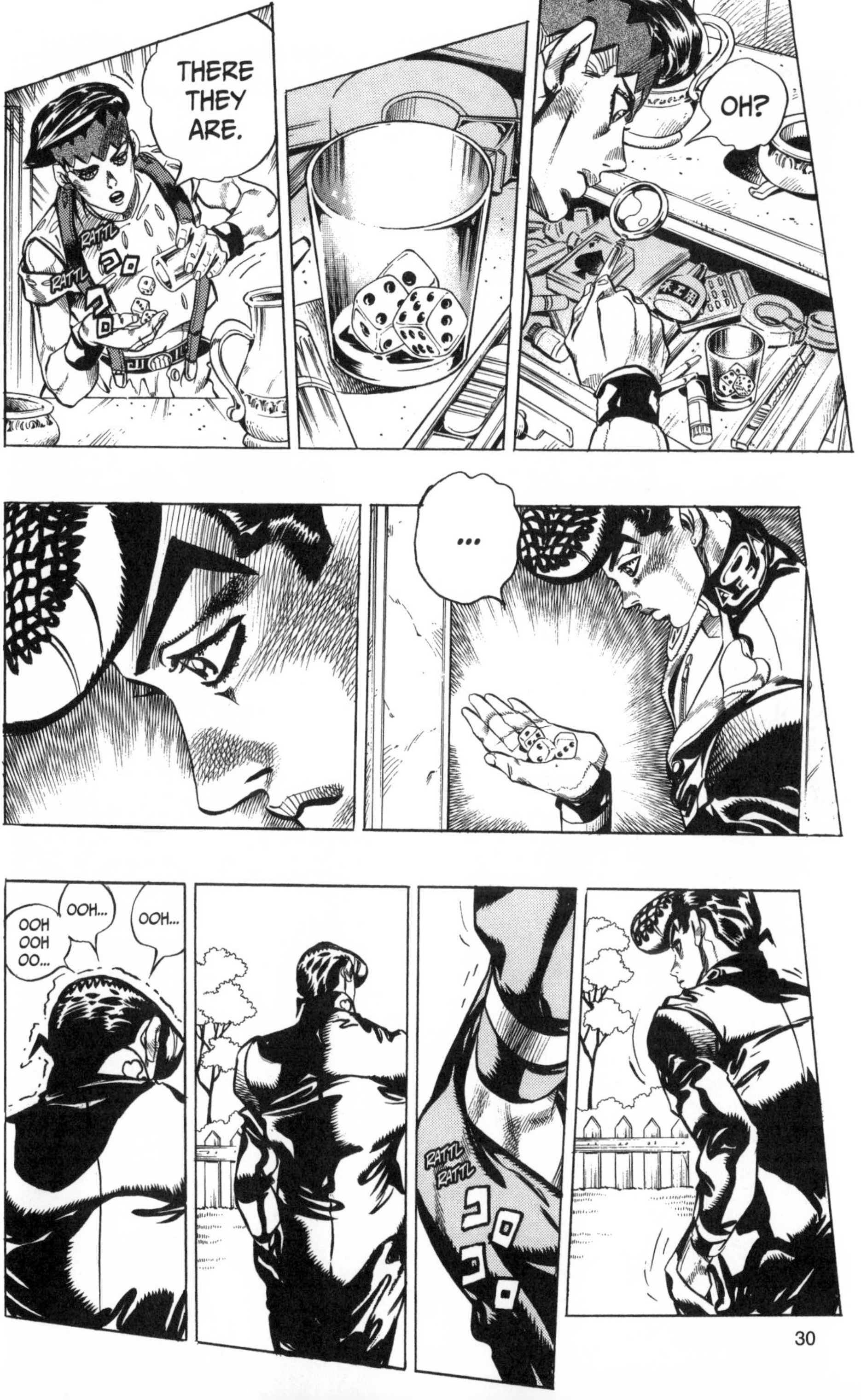
OH?
THERE THEY ARE.
RATTL
RATTL
...
RATTL
RATTL
OOH...
OOH...
OOH OOH OO...

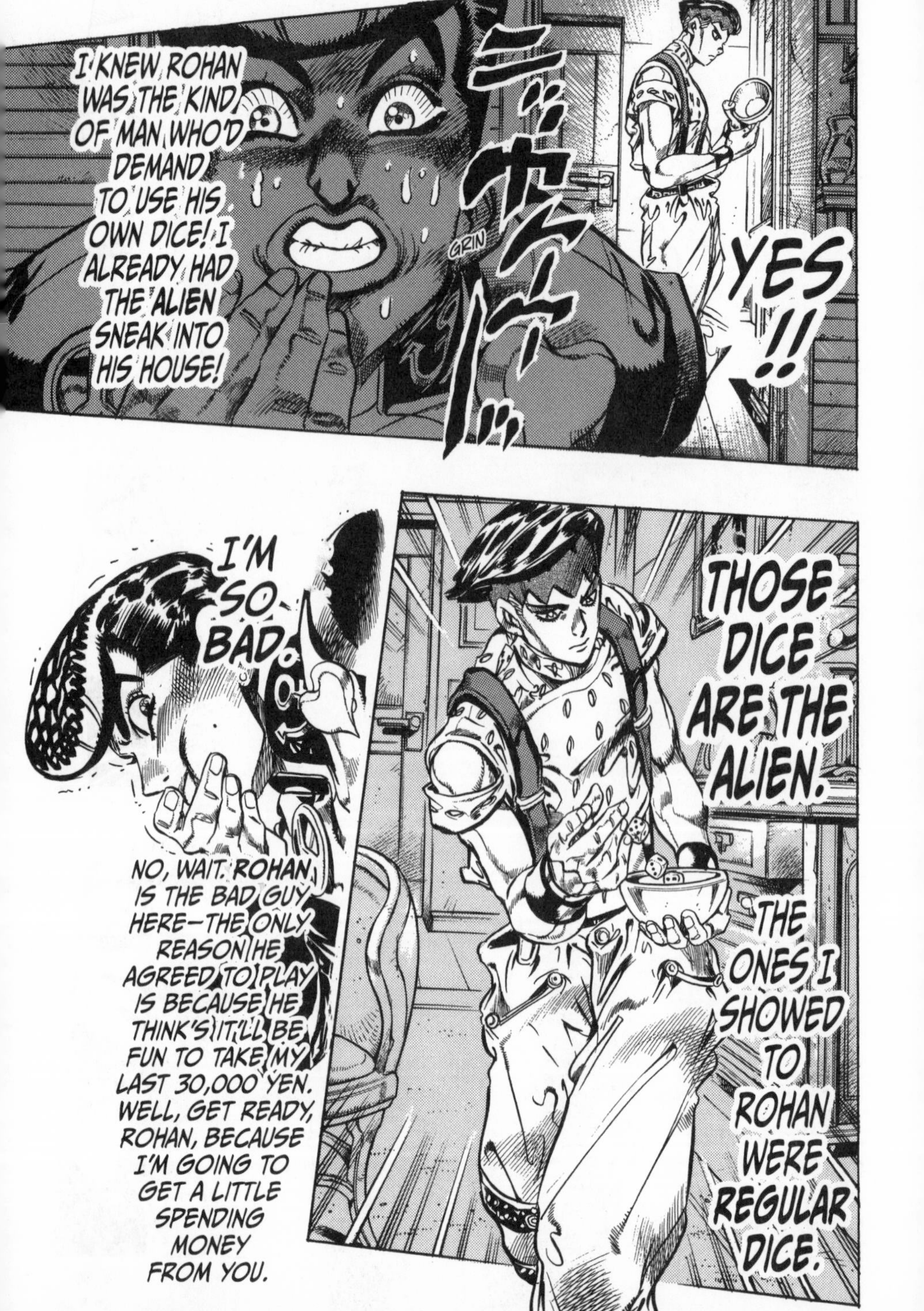
YES!!
GRIN
I KNEW ROHAN WAS THE KIND OF MAN WHO'D DEMAND TO USE HIS OWN DICE! I ALREADY HAD THE ALIEN SNEAK INTO HIS HOUSE!
THOSE DICE ARE THE ALIEN.
THE ONES I SHOWED TO ROHAN WERE REGULAR DICE.
I'M SO BAD.
NO, WAIT. ROHAN IS THE BAD GUY HERE—THE ONLY REASON HE AGREED TO PLAY IS BECAUSE HE THINK'S IT'LL BE FUN TO TAKE MY LAST 30,000 YEN. WELL, GET READY, ROHAN, BECAUSE I'M GOING TO GET A LITTLE SPENDING MONEY FROM YOU.

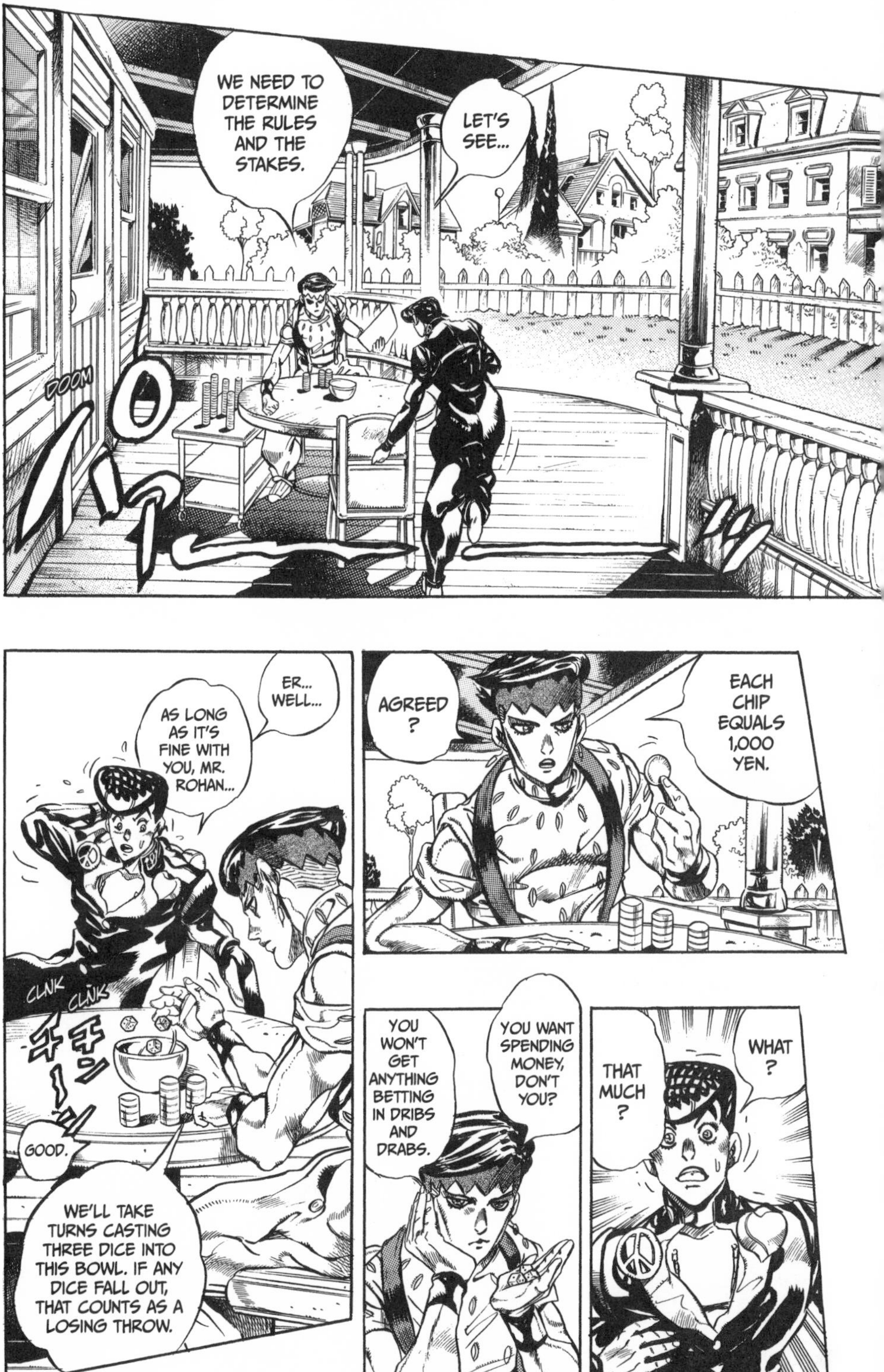
LET'S SEE...
WE NEED TO DETERMINE THE RULES AND THE STAKES.
DOOM
EACH CHIP EQUALS 1,000 YEN.
AGREED?
WHAT?
THAT MUCH?
YOU WANT SPENDING MONEY, DON'T YOU?
YOU WON'T GET ANYTHING BETTING IN DRIBS AND DRABS.
ER... WELL...
AS LONG AS IT'S FINE WITH YOU, MR. ROHAN...
CLNK CLNK
GOOD.
WE'LL TAKE TURNS CASTING THREE DICE INTO THIS BOWL. IF ANY DICE FALL OUT, THAT COUNTS AS A LOSING THROW.

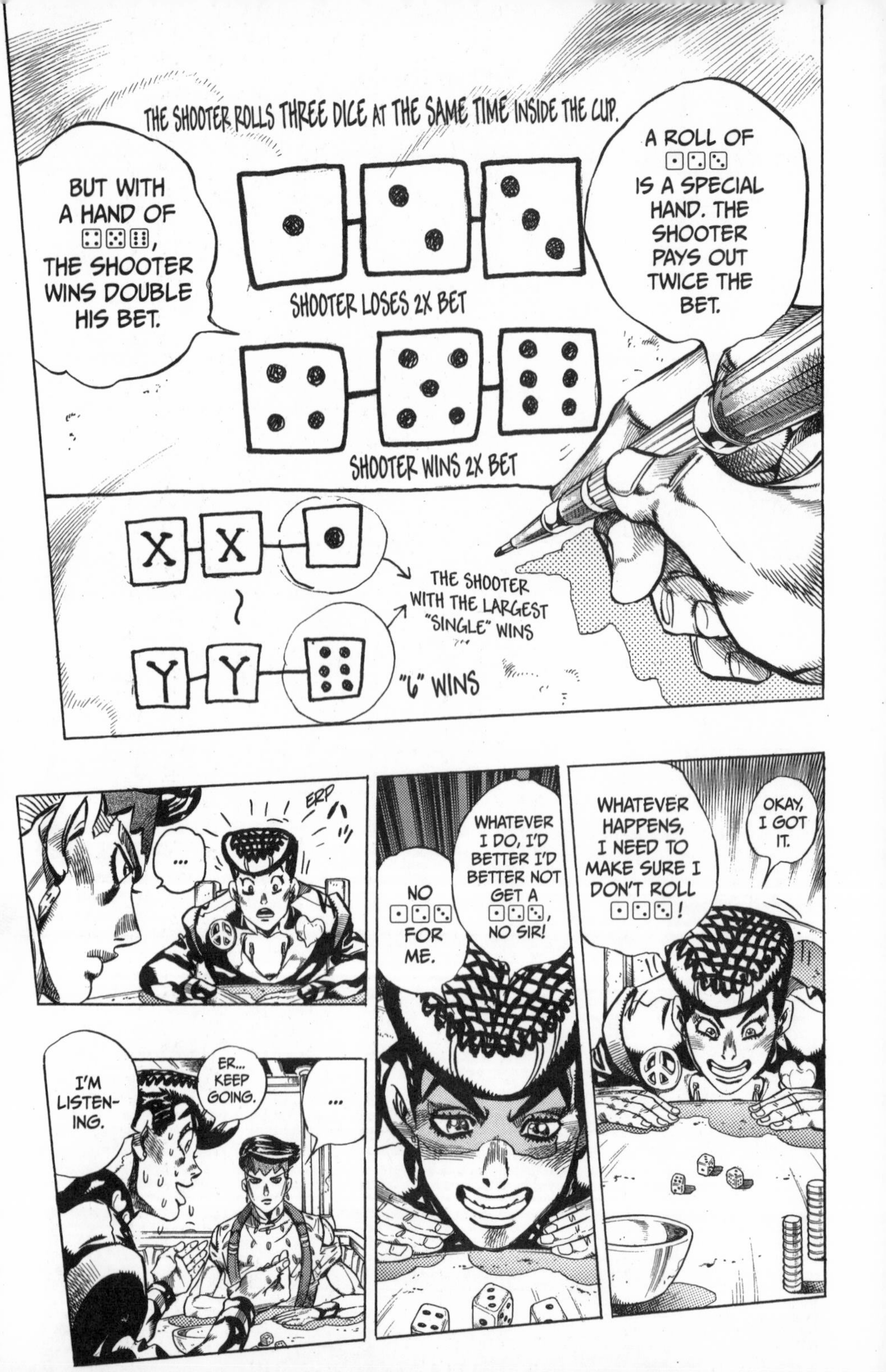
THE SHOOTER ROLLS THREE DICE AT THE SAME TIME INSIDE THE CUP.
A ROLL OF ⚀⚁⚂ IS A SPECIAL HAND. THE SHOOTER PAYS OUT TWICE THE BET.
BUT WITH A HAND OF ⚃⚄⚅, THE SHOOTER WINS DOUBLE HIS BET.
SHOOTER LOSES 2X BET
SHOOTER WINS 2X BET
X X ⚀
Y Y ⚅
THE SHOOTER WITH THE LARGEST "SINGLE" WINS
"6" WINS
OKAY, I GOT IT.
WHATEVER HAPPENS, I NEED TO MAKE SURE I DON'T ROLL ⚀⚁⚂!
WHATEVER I DO, I'D BETTER I'D BETTER NOT GET A ⚀⚁⚂, NO SIR!
NO ⚀⚁⚂ FOR ME.
ERP
...
...
ER... KEEP GOING.
I'M LISTENING.

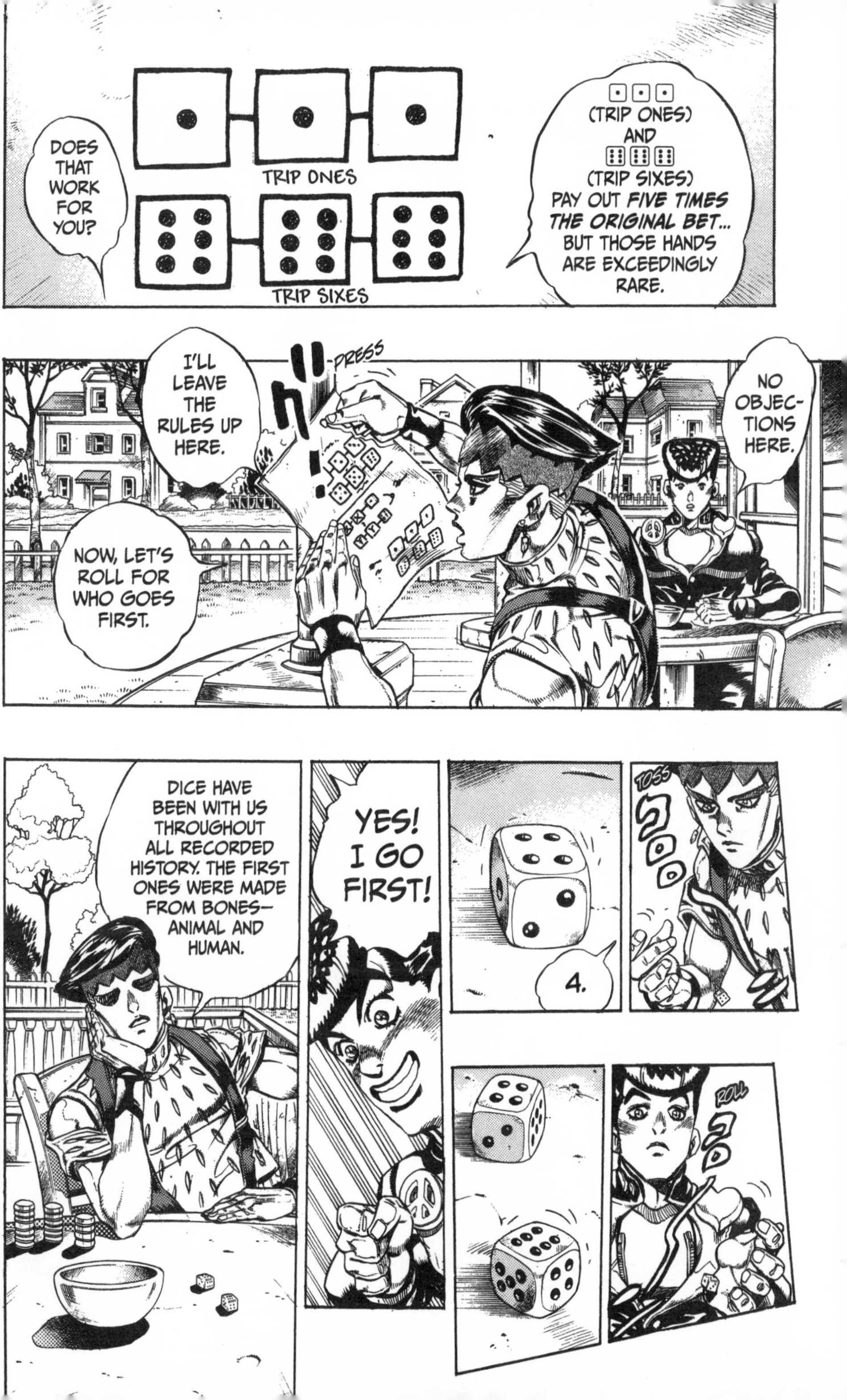
(TRIP ONES) AND (TRIP SIXES) PAY OUT *FIVE TIMES THE ORIGINAL BET*... BUT THOSE HANDS ARE EXCEEDINGLY RARE.
TRIP ONES
TRIP SIXES
DOES THAT WORK FOR YOU?
NO OBJECTIONS HERE.
-PRESS
I'LL LEAVE THE RULES UP HERE.
NOW, LET'S ROLL FOR WHO GOES FIRST.
TOSS
4.
ROLL
YES! I GO FIRST!
DICE HAVE BEEN WITH US THROUGHOUT ALL RECORDED HISTORY. THE FIRST ONES WERE MADE FROM BONES— ANIMAL AND HUMAN.

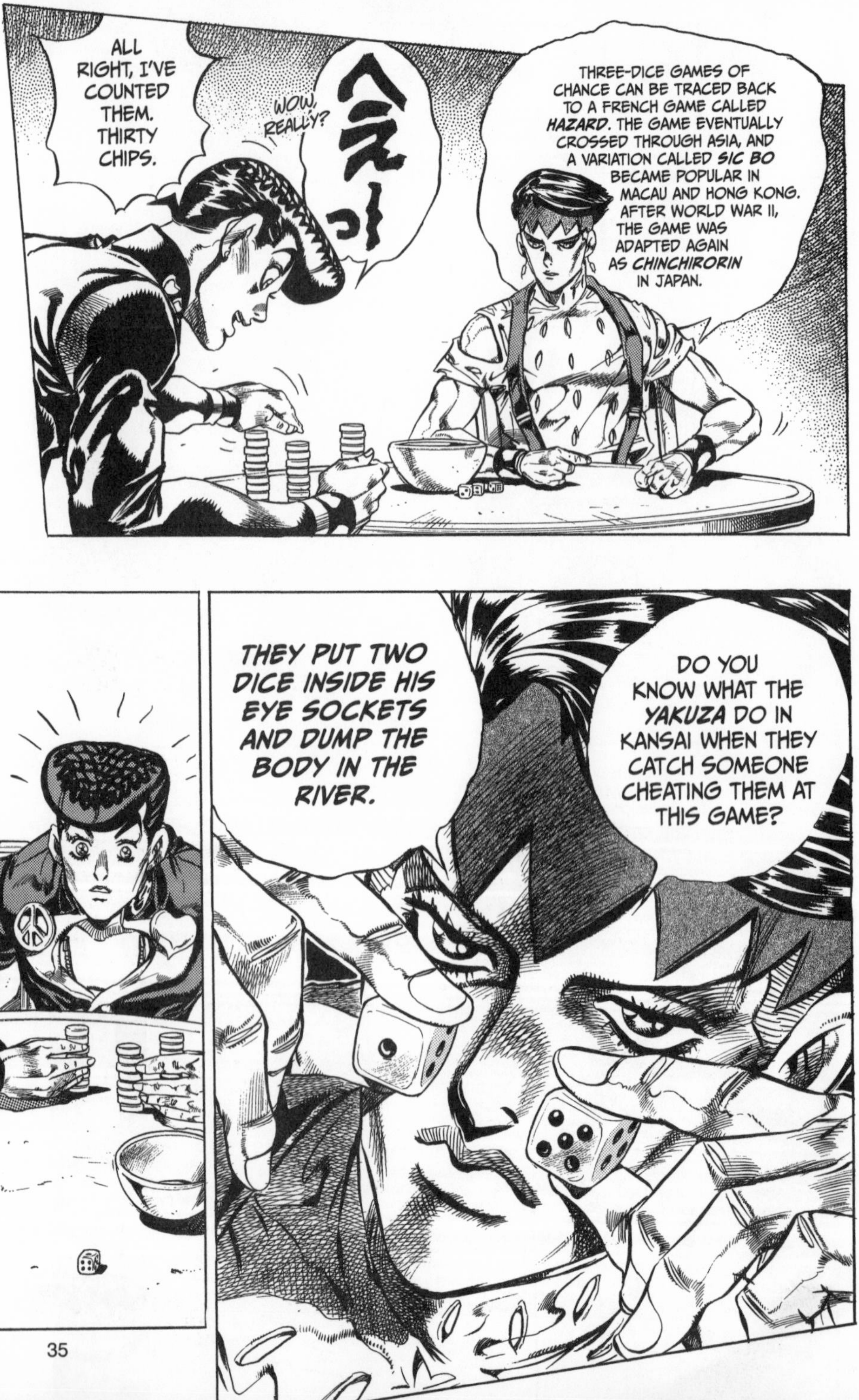
THREE-DICE GAMES OF CHANCE CAN BE TRACED BACK TO A FRENCH GAME CALLED *HAZARD*. THE GAME EVENTUALLY CROSSED THROUGH ASIA, AND A VARIATION CALLED *SIC BO* BECAME POPULAR IN MACAU AND HONG KONG. AFTER WORLD WAR II, THE GAME WAS ADAPTED AGAIN AS *CHINCHIRORIN* IN JAPAN.
へえーっ
WOW, REALLY?
ALL RIGHT, I'VE COUNTED THEM. THIRTY CHIPS.
DO YOU KNOW WHAT THE *YAKUZA* DO IN KANSAI WHEN THEY CATCH SOMEONE CHEATING THEM AT THIS GAME?
THEY PUT TWO DICE INSIDE HIS EYE SOCKETS AND DUMP THE BODY IN THE RIVER.

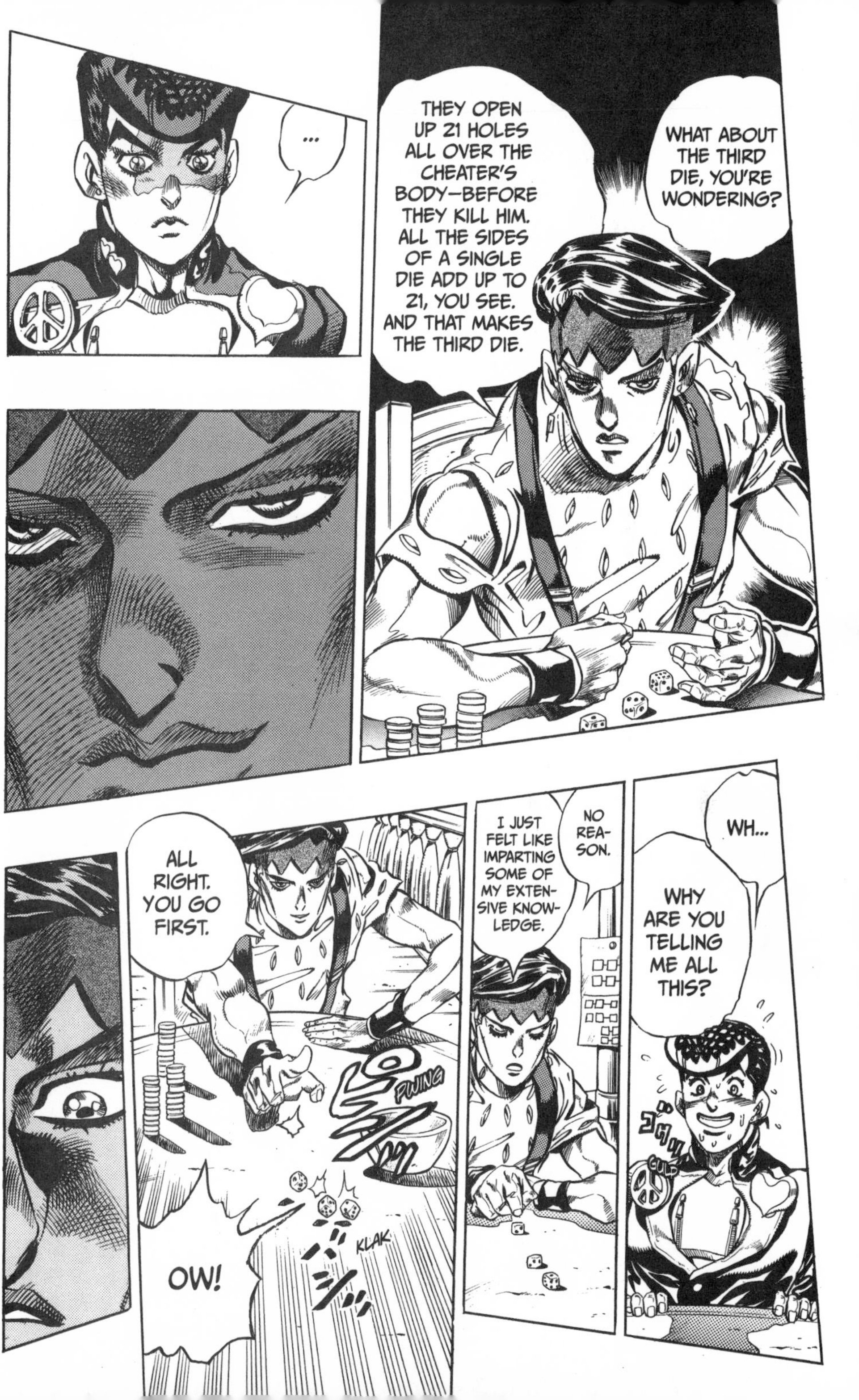

WHAT ABOUT THE THIRD DIE, YOU'RE WONDERING?
THEY OPEN UP 21 HOLES ALL OVER THE CHEATER'S BODY—BEFORE THEY KILL HIM. ALL THE SIDES OF A SINGLE DIE ADD UP TO 21, YOU SEE. AND THAT MAKES THE THIRD DIE.
...
WH...
WHY ARE YOU TELLING ME ALL THIS?
GULP
NO REA-SON.
I JUST FELT LIKE IMPARTING SOME OF MY EXTEN-SIVE KNOW-LEDGE.
ALL RIGHT. YOU GO FIRST.
PWING
KLAK
OW!

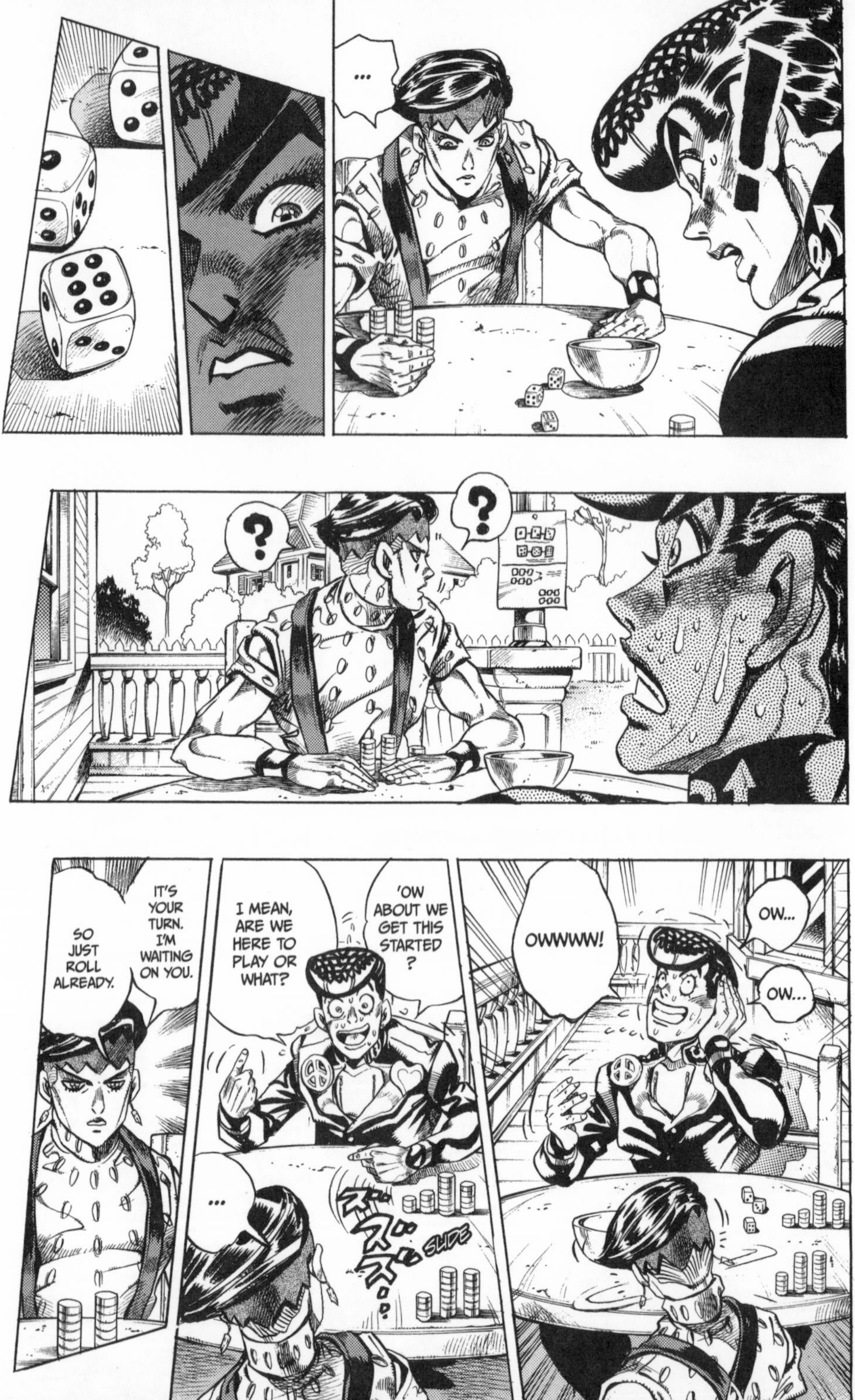
...
?
?
OW...
OWWWW!
OW...
'OW ABOUT WE GET THIS STARTED?
I MEAN, ARE WE HERE TO PLAY OR WHAT?
...
SLIDE
IT'S YOUR TURN. I'M WAITING ON YOU.
SO JUST ROLL ALREADY.

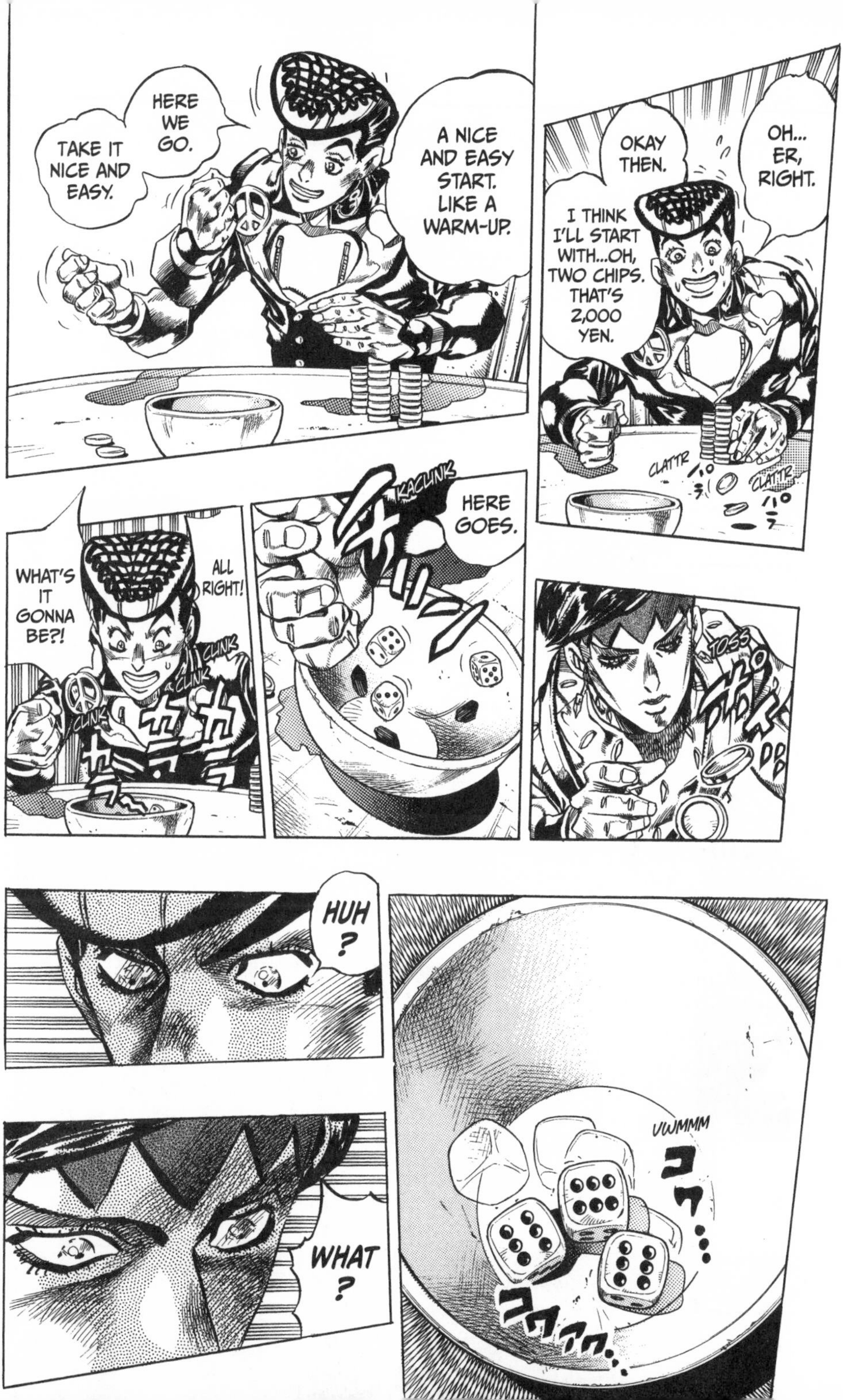
OH... ER, RIGHT.
OKAY THEN.
I THINK I'LL START WITH...OH, TWO CHIPS. THAT'S 2,000 YEN.
CLATTR
CLATTR
A NICE AND EASY START. LIKE A WARM-UP.
HERE WE GO.
TAKE IT NICE AND EASY.
TOSS
DDD
KACUNK
HERE GOES.
ALL RIGHT!
CLUNK
CLUNK
CLUNK
WHAT'S IT GONNA BE?!
UWMMM
HUH?
WHAT?

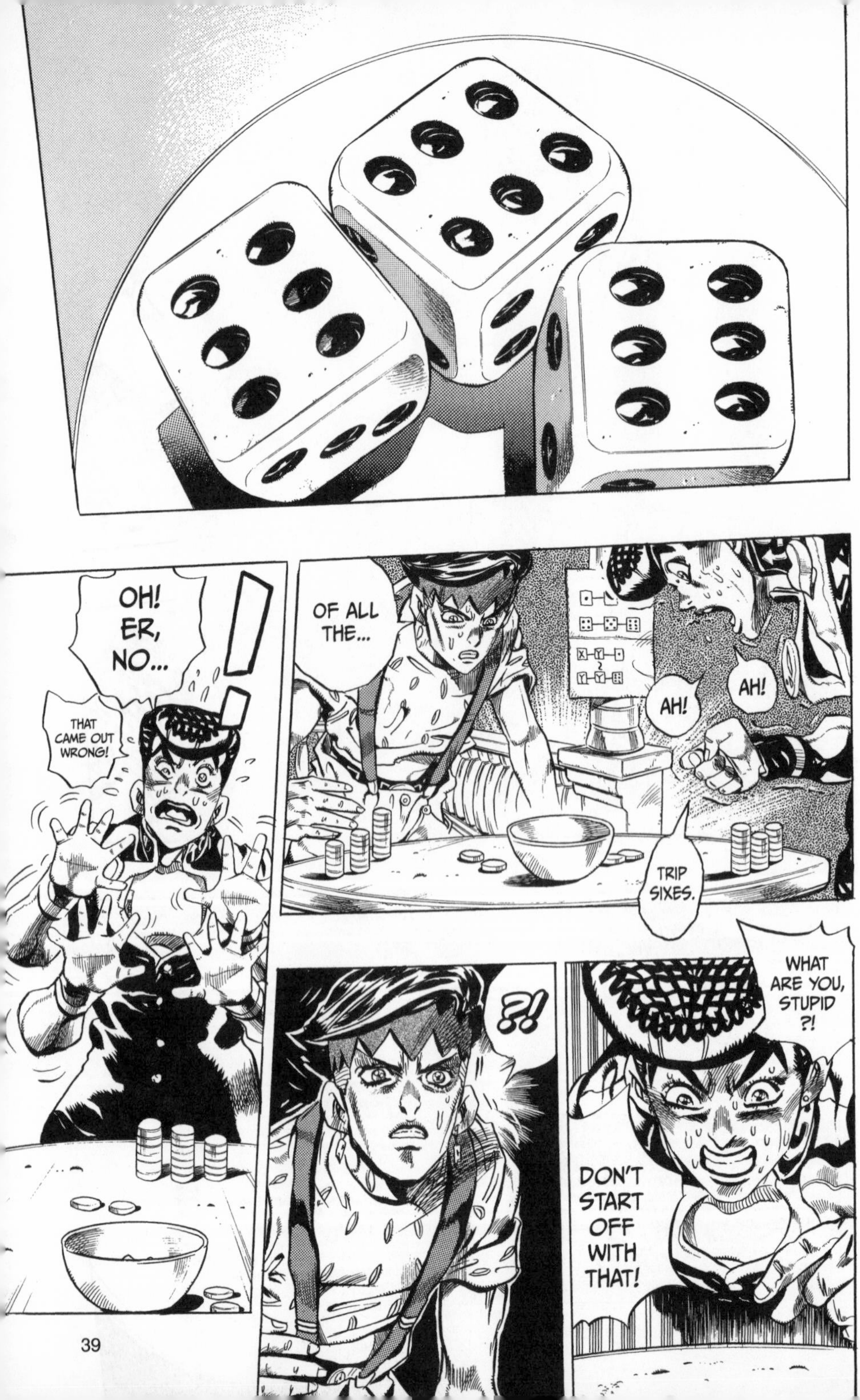
AH!
AH!
OF ALL THE...
TRIP SIXES.
WHAT ARE YOU, STUPID ?!
DON'T START OFF WITH THAT!
?!
OH! ER, NO...
THAT CAME OUT WRONG!

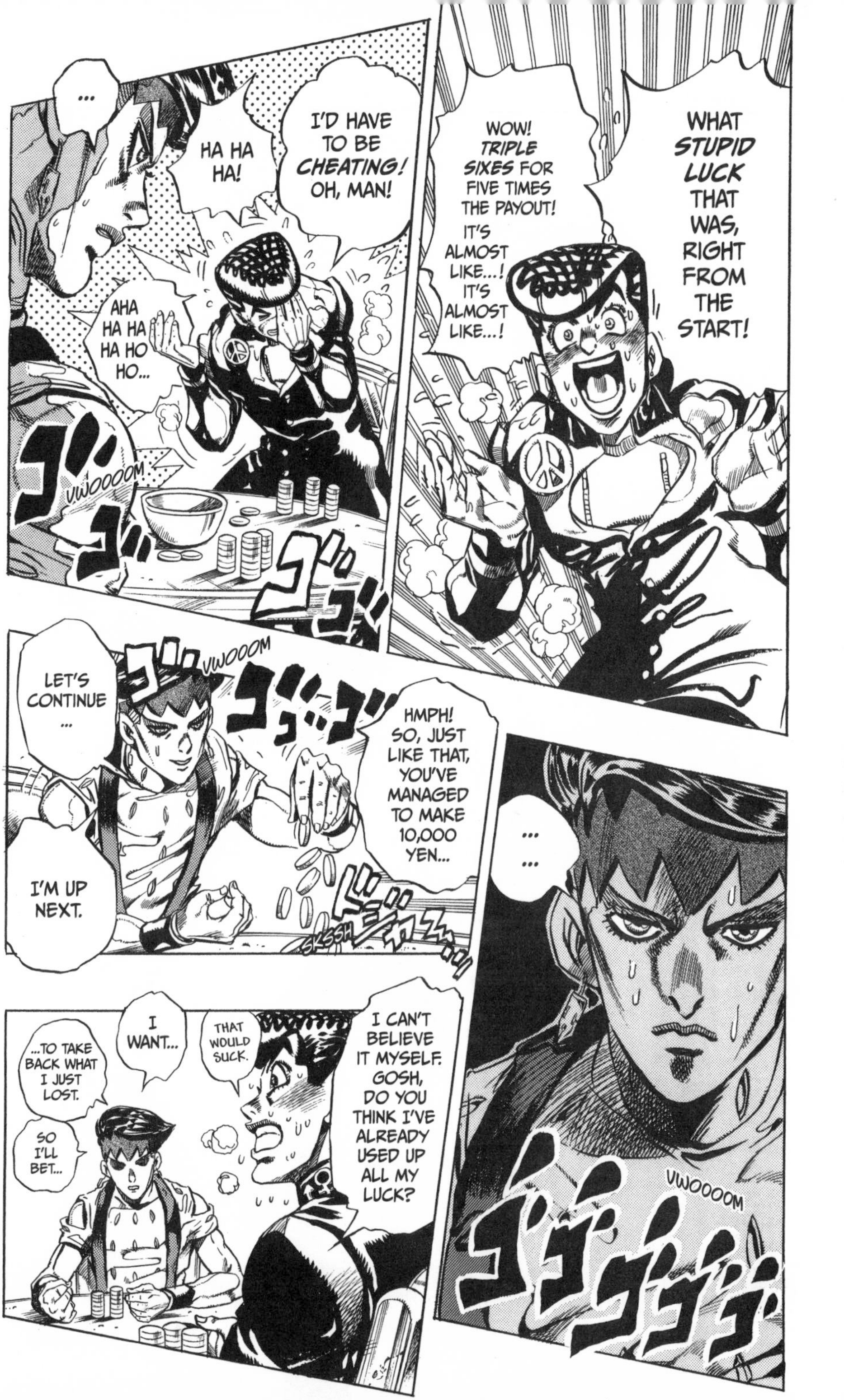
WHAT STUPID LUCK THAT WAS, RIGHT FROM THE START!
WOW! TRIPLE SIXES FOR FIVE TIMES THE PAYOUT!
IT'S ALMOST LIKE...! IT'S ALMOST LIKE...!
I'D HAVE TO BE CHEATING! OH, MAN!
HA HA HA!
...
AHA HA HA HA HO HO...
VWOOOOM
...
...
VWOOOOM
HMPH! SO, JUST LIKE THAT, YOU'VE MANAGED TO MAKE 10,000 YEN...
VWOOOM
LET'S CONTINUE ...
I'M UP NEXT.
SKSSH
I CAN'T BELIEVE IT MYSELF. GOSH, DO YOU THINK I'VE ALREADY USED UP ALL MY LUCK?
THAT WOULD SUCK.
I WANT...
...TO TAKE BACK WHAT I JUST LOST.
SO I'LL BET...

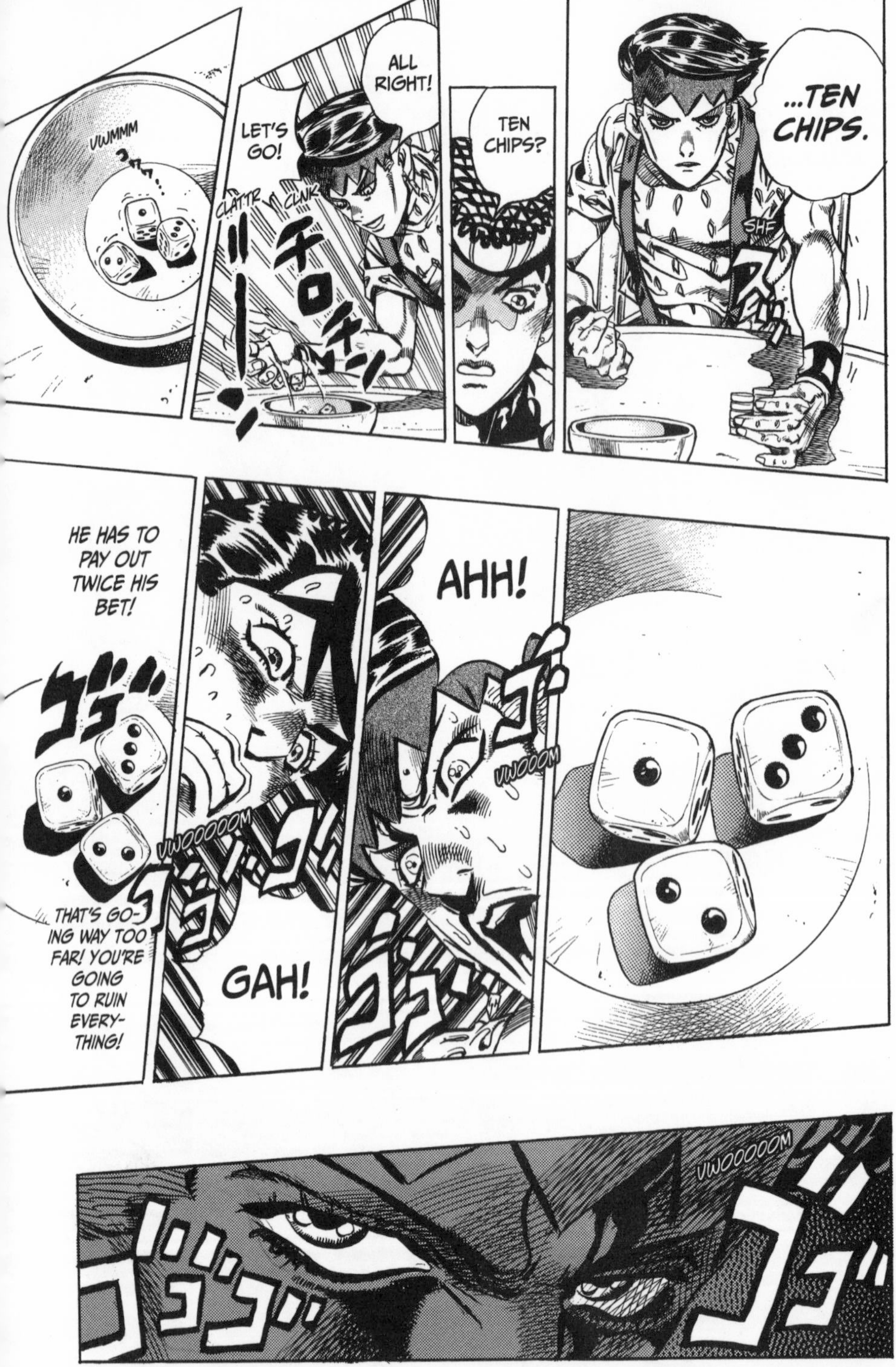
...TEN CHIPS.
SHF
TEN CHIPS?
ALL RIGHT!
LET'S GO!
CLNK
CLATTR
VWMMM
AHH!
VWOOOM
GAH!
HE HAS TO PAY OUT TWICE HIS BET!
VWOOOOOM
THAT'S GO-ING WAY TOO FAR! YOU'RE GOING TO RUIN EVERY-THING!
VWOOOOOM

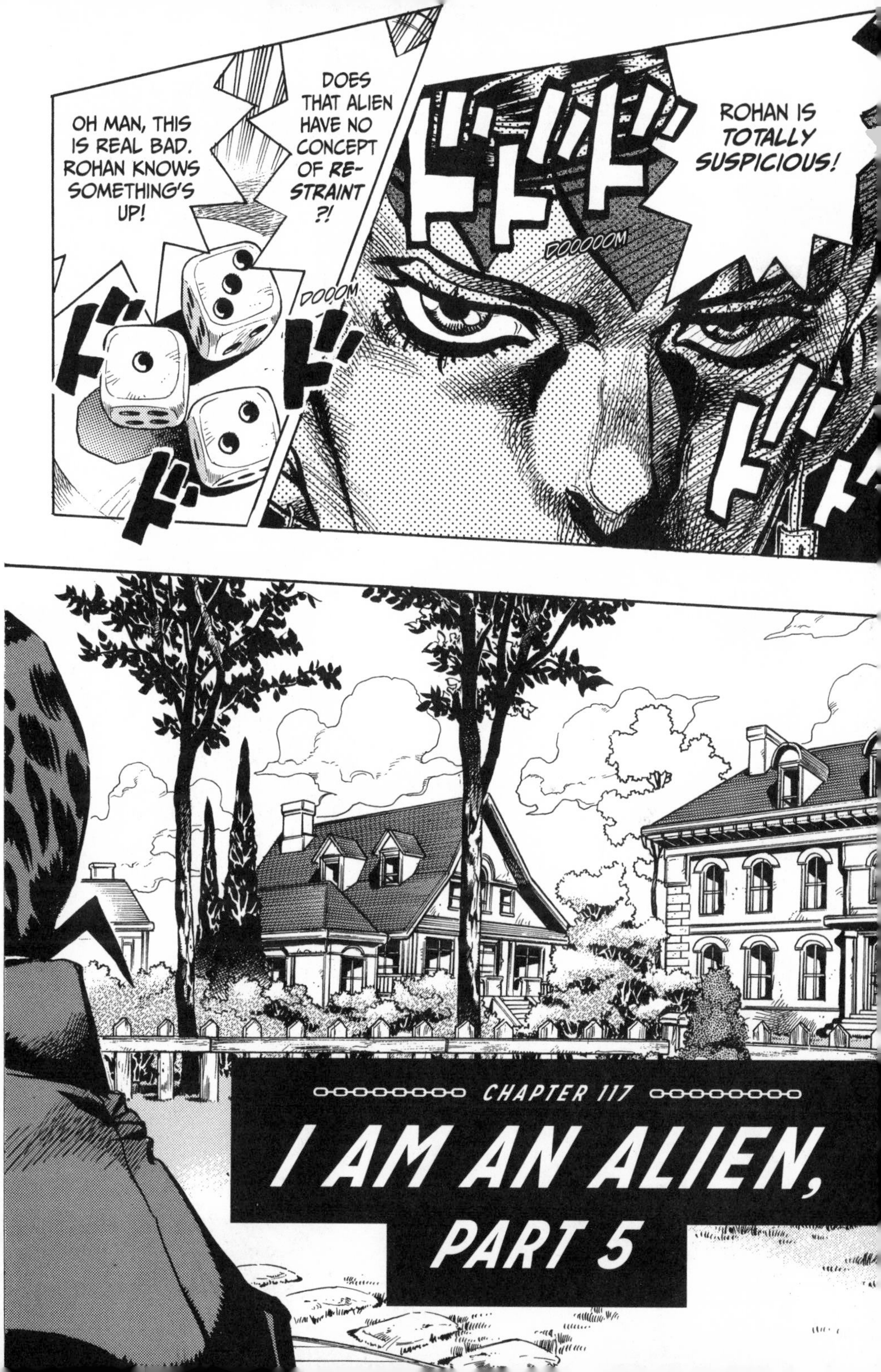
ROHAN IS TOTALLY SUSPICIOUS!
DOOOOOM
DOES THAT ALIEN HAVE NO CONCEPT OF RE-STRAINT ?!
OH MAN, THIS IS REAL BAD. ROHAN KNOWS SOMETHING'S UP!
DOOOM
CHAPTER 117
I AM AN ALIEN, PART 5

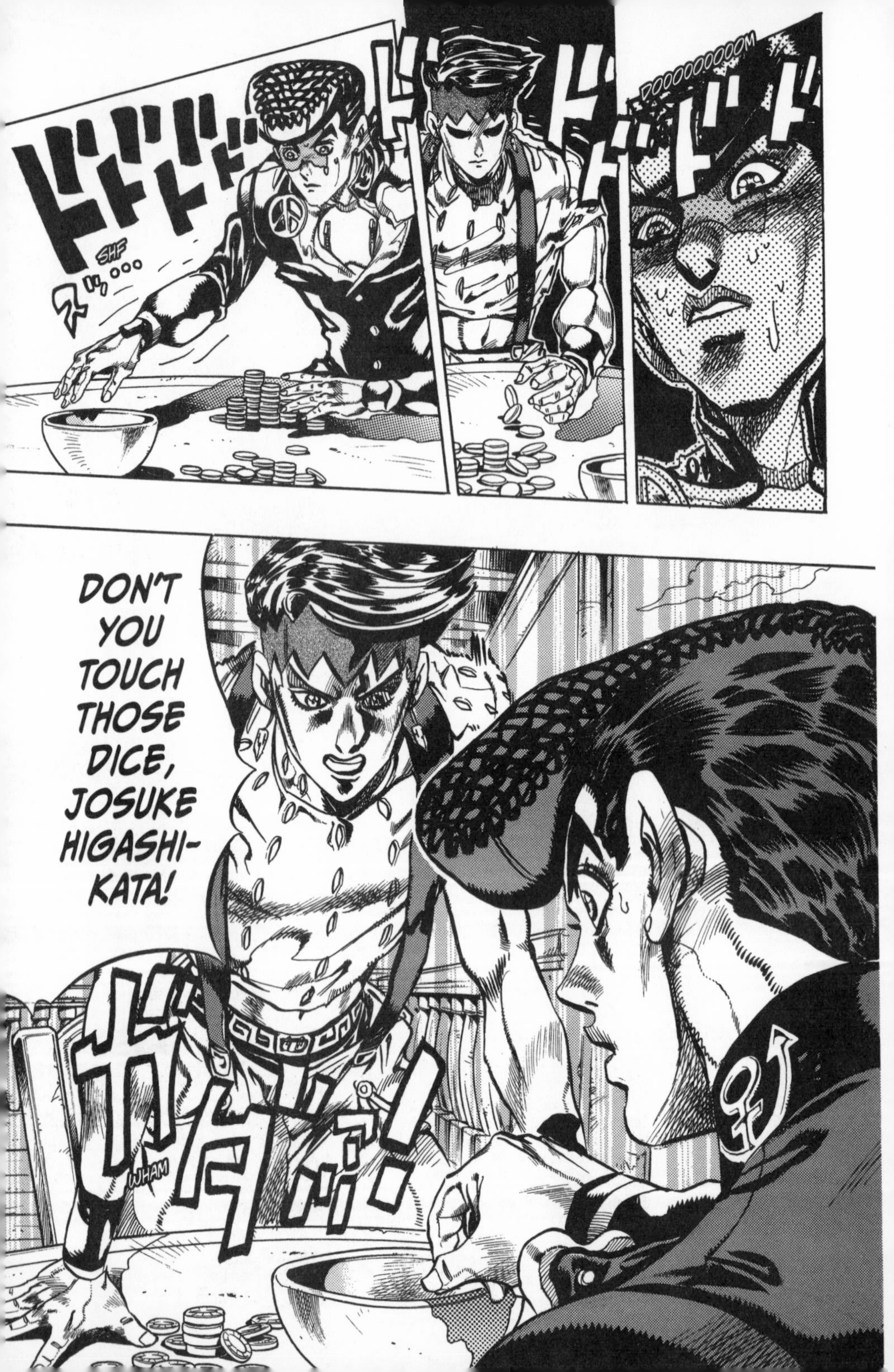
DOOOOOOOOOOM
SHF
DON'T YOU TOUCH THOSE DICE, JOSUKE HIGASHIKATA!
WHAM

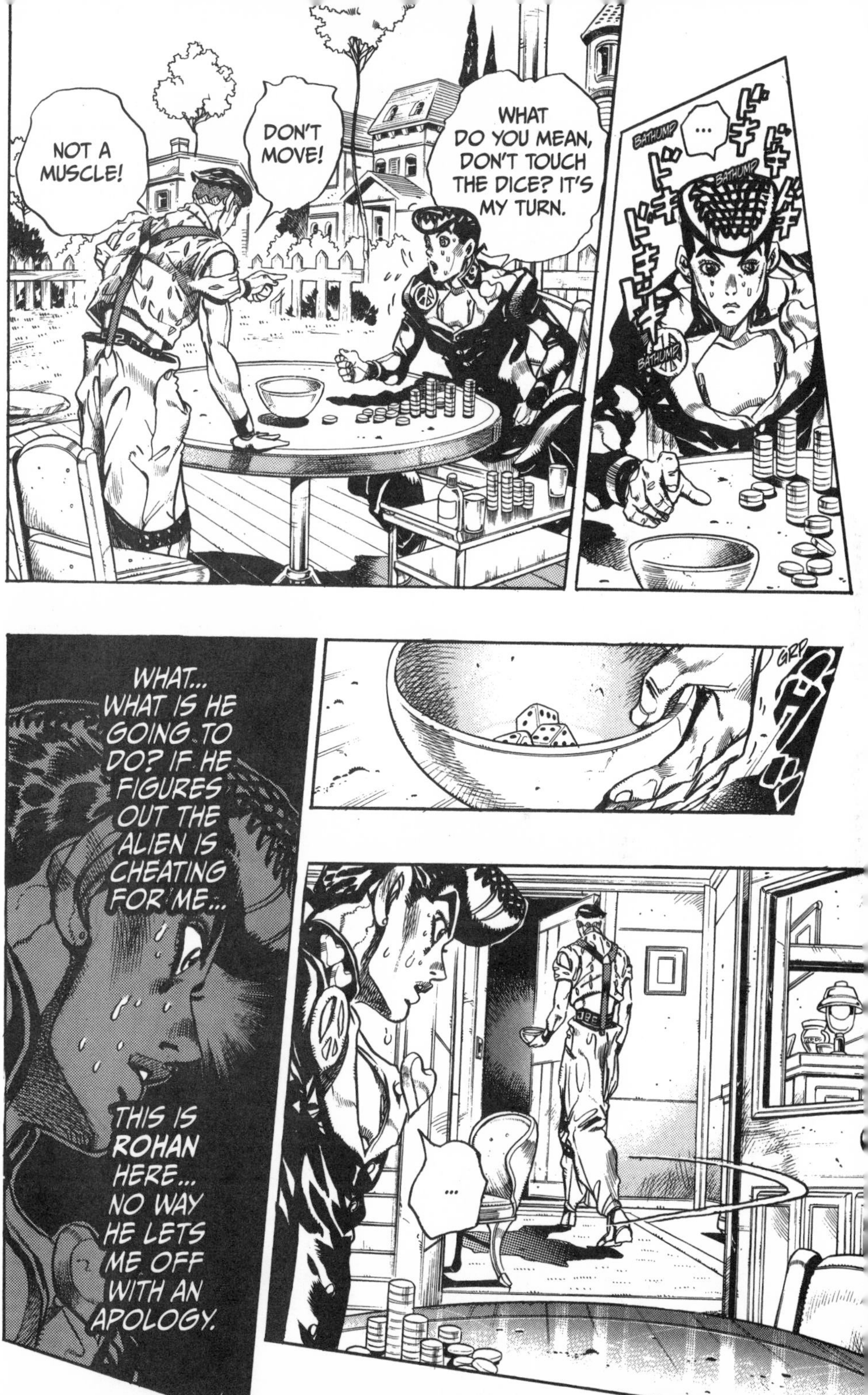
BATHUMP
...
BATHUMP
BATHUMP
WHAT DO YOU MEAN, DON'T TOUCH THE DICE? IT'S MY TURN.
DON'T MOVE!
NOT A MUSCLE!
GRP
...
WHAT... WHAT IS HE GOING TO DO? IF HE FIGURES OUT THE ALIEN IS CHEATING FOR ME...
THIS IS ROHAN HERE... NO WAY HE LETS ME OFF WITH AN APOLOGY.

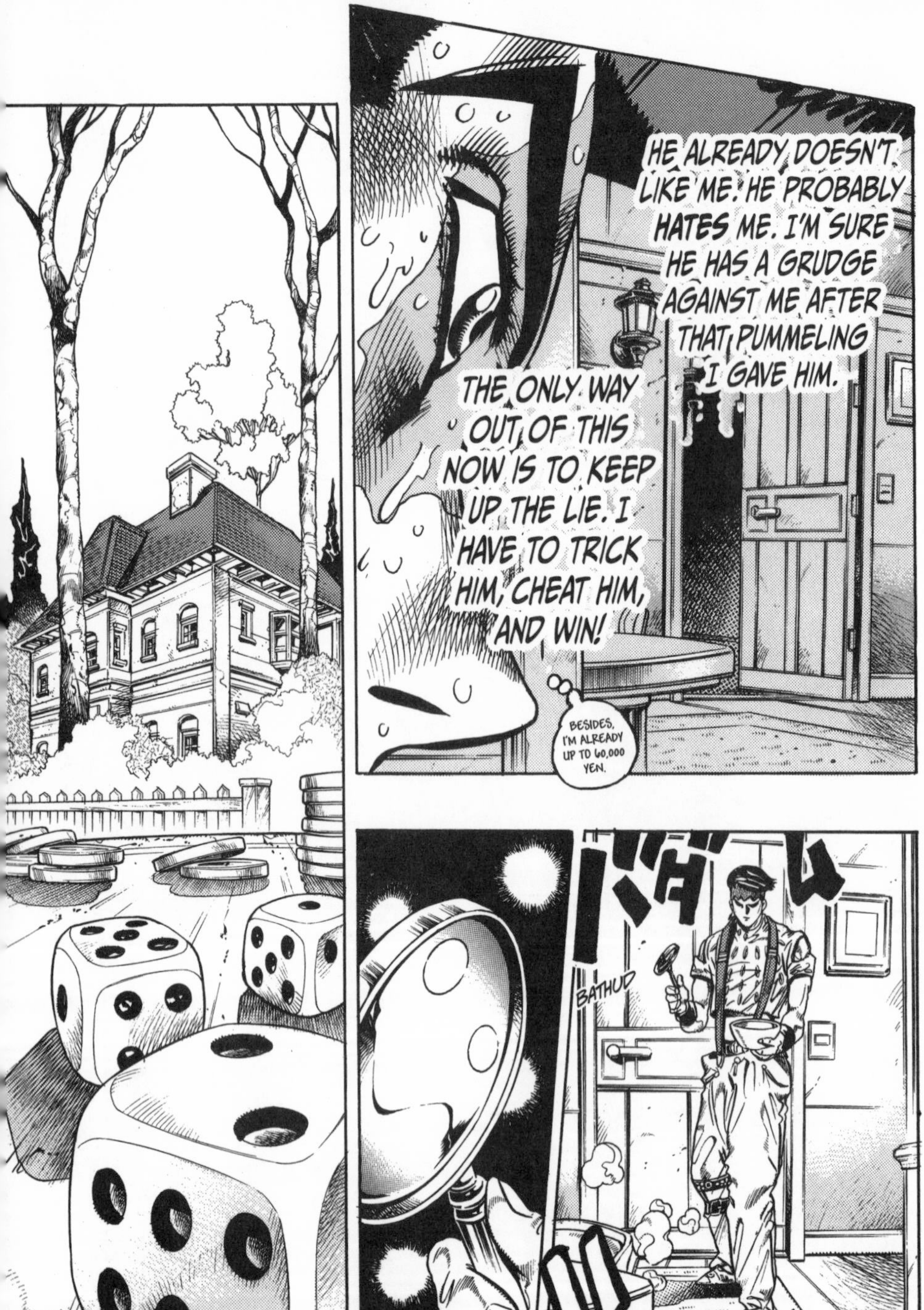
HE ALREADY DOESN'T LIKE ME. HE PROBABLY HATES ME. I'M SURE HE HAS A GRUDGE AGAINST ME AFTER THAT PUMMELING I GAVE HIM.
THE ONLY WAY OUT OF THIS NOW IS TO KEEP UP THE LIE. I HAVE TO TRICK HIM, CHEAT HIM, AND WIN!
BESIDES, I'M ALREADY UP TO 60,000 YEN.
BATHUD

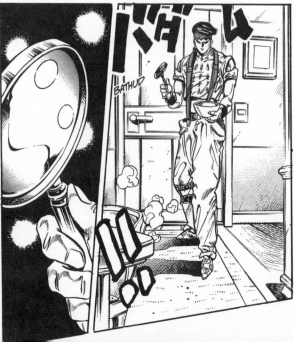

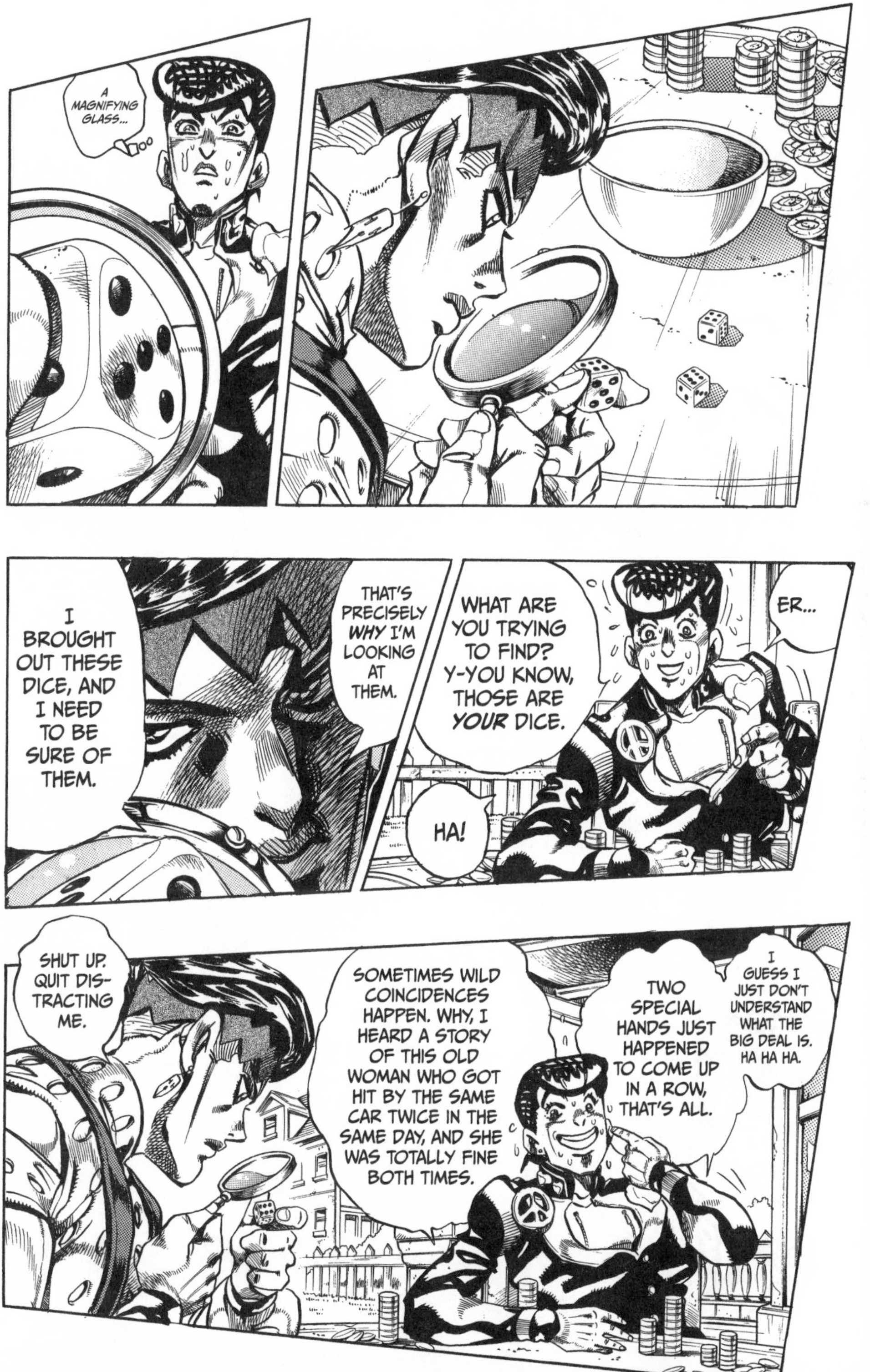
A MAGNIFYING GLASS...
ER...
WHAT ARE YOU TRYING TO FIND? Y-YOU KNOW, THOSE ARE *YOUR* DICE.
HA!
THAT'S PRECISELY *WHY* I'M LOOKING AT THEM.
I BROUGHT OUT THESE DICE, AND I NEED TO BE SURE OF THEM.
I GUESS I JUST DON'T UNDERSTAND WHAT THE BIG DEAL IS. HA HA HA.
TWO SPECIAL HANDS JUST HAPPENED TO COME UP IN A ROW, THAT'S ALL.
SOMETIMES WILD COINCIDENCES HAPPEN. WHY, I HEARD A STORY OF THIS OLD WOMAN WHO GOT HIT BY THE SAME CAR TWICE IN THE SAME DAY, AND SHE WAS TOTALLY FINE BOTH TIMES.
SHUT UP. QUIT DIS-TRACTING ME.

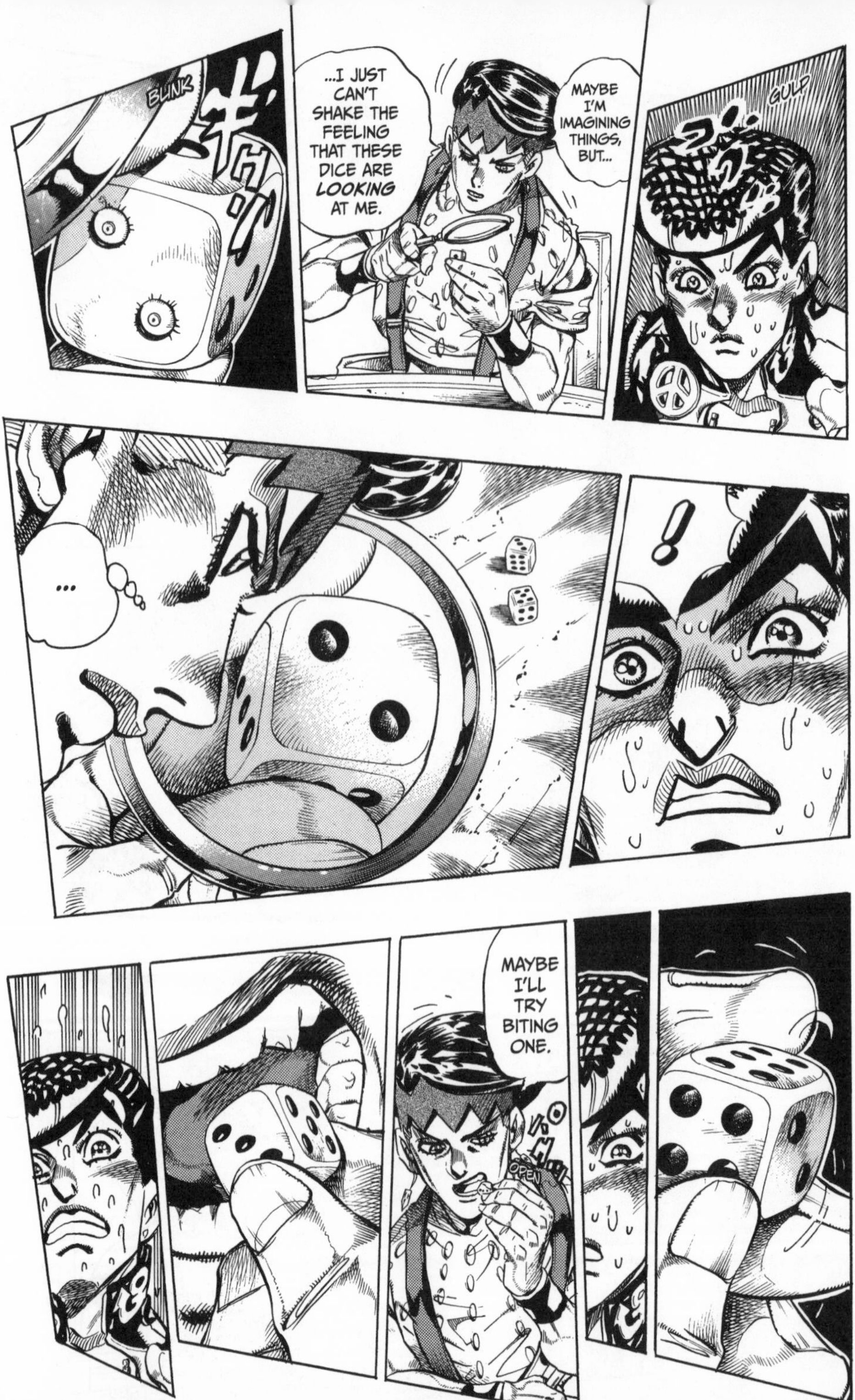
GULP
MAYBE I'M IMAGINING THINGS, BUT...
...I JUST CAN'T SHAKE THE FEELING THAT THESE DICE ARE *LOOKING* AT ME.
BLINK
!
...
MAYBE I'LL TRY BITING ONE.
OPEN

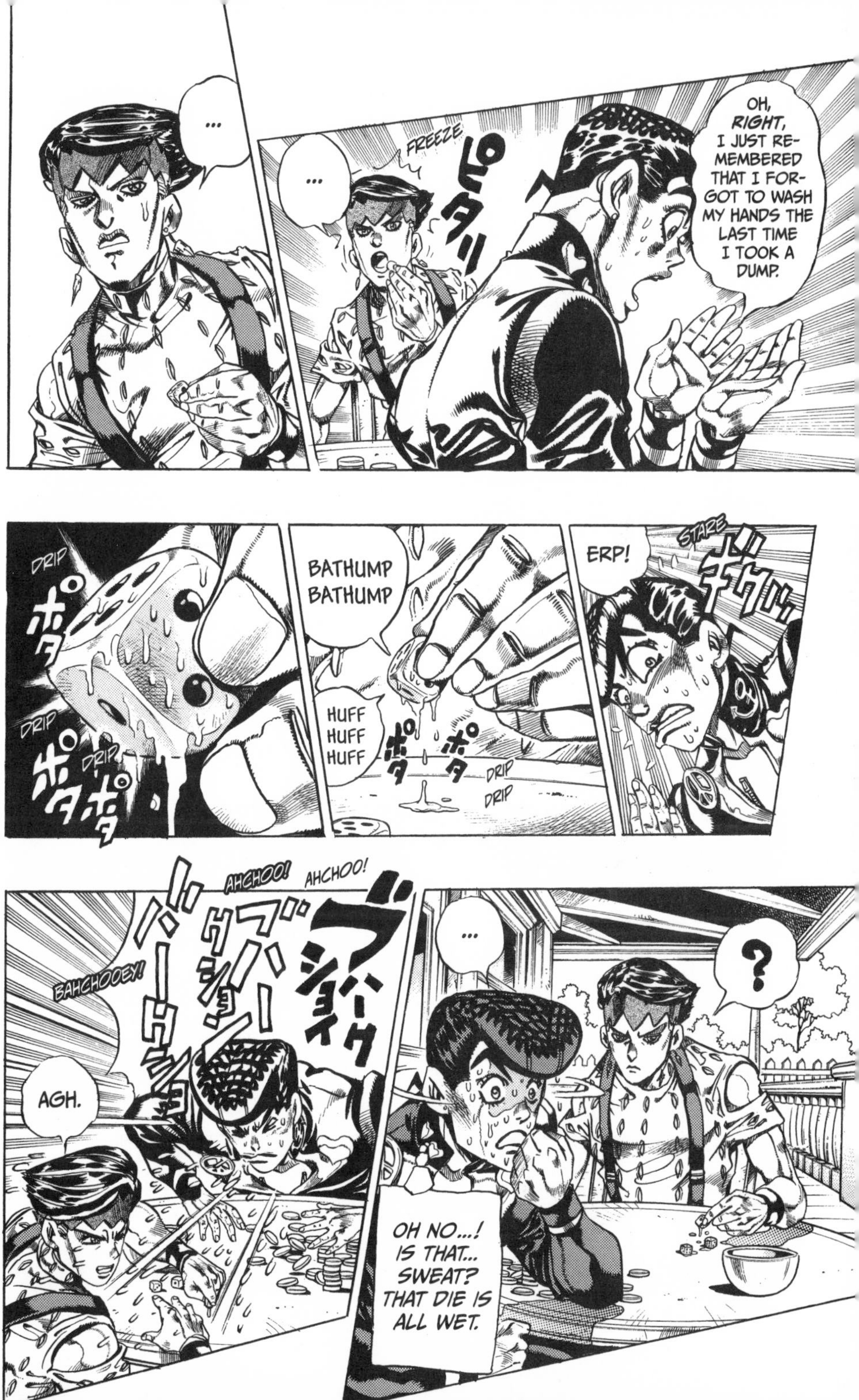
OH, RIGHT, I JUST REMEMBERED THAT I FORGOT TO WASH MY HANDS THE LAST TIME I TOOK A DUMP.
FREEZE
...
...
STARE
ERP!
BATHUMP BATHUMP
HUFF HUFF HUFF
DRIP
DRIP
DRIP
DRIP
DRIP
?
...
OH NO...! IS THAT... SWEAT? THAT DIE IS ALL WET.
AHCHOO!
AHCHOO!
BAHCHOOEY!
AGH.

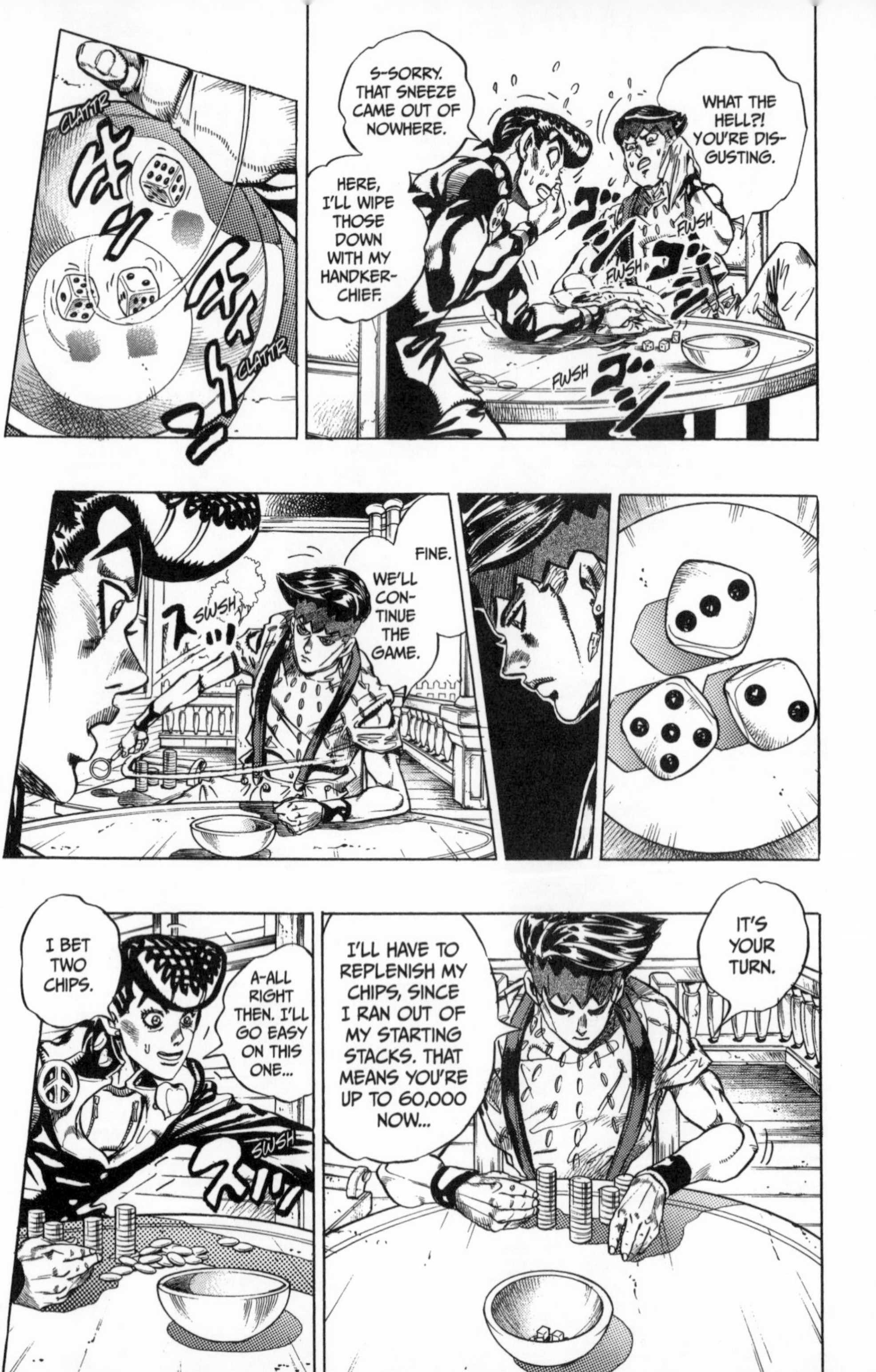
WHAT THE HELL?! YOU'RE DISGUSTING.
S-SORRY. THAT SNEEZE CAME OUT OF NOWHERE.
HERE, I'LL WIPE THOSE DOWN WITH MY HANDKERCHIEF.
FWSH
FWSH
FWSH
CLATTR
CLATTR
FINE. WE'LL CONTINUE THE GAME.
SWSH
IT'S YOUR TURN.
I'LL HAVE TO REPLENISH MY CHIPS, SINCE I RAN OUT OF MY STARTING STACKS. THAT MEANS YOU'RE UP TO 60,000 NOW...
A-ALL RIGHT THEN. I'LL GO EASY ON THIS ONE...
I BET TWO CHIPS.
SWSH

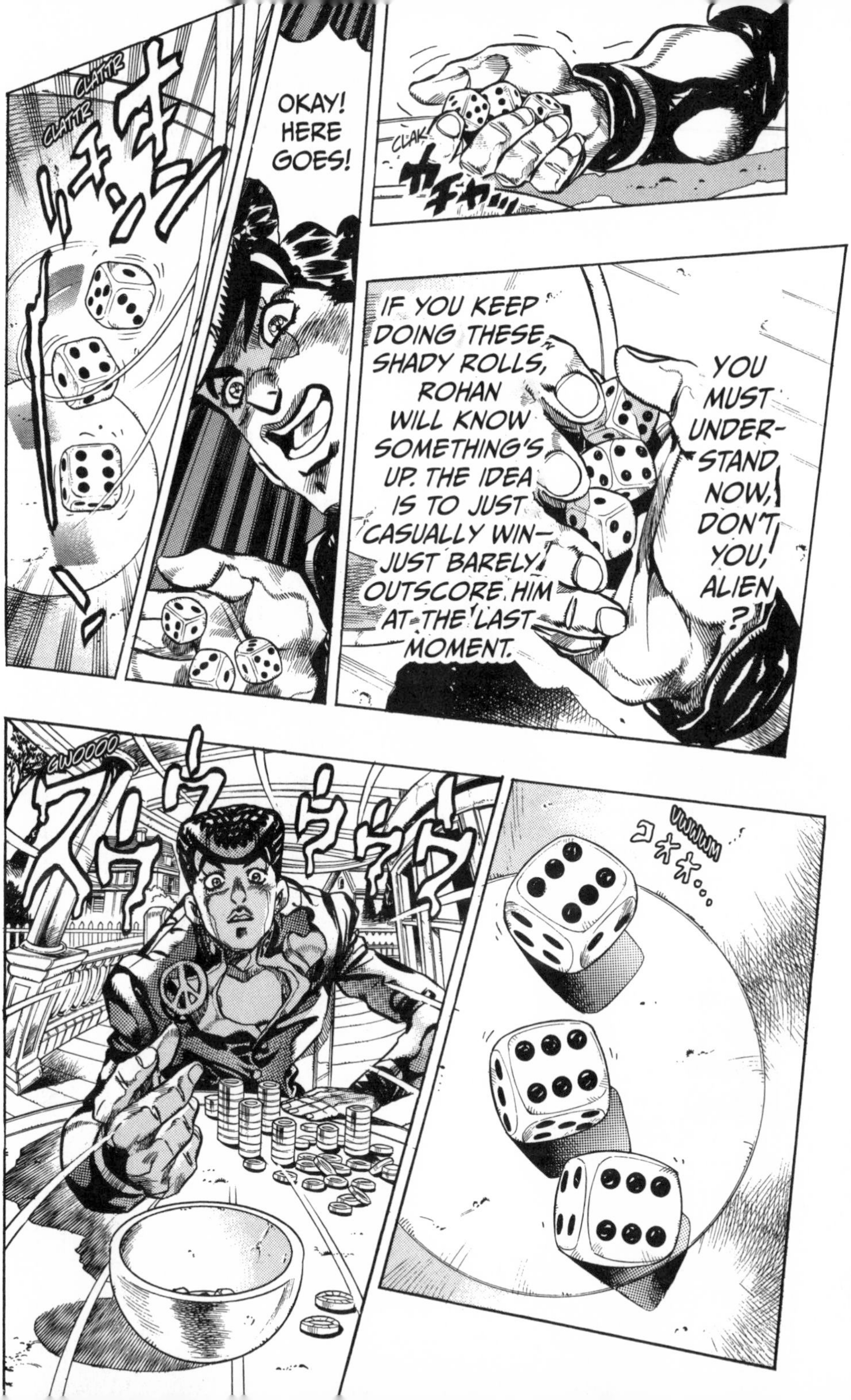
CLAK
IF YOU KEEP DOING THESE SHADY ROLLS, ROHAN WILL KNOW SOMETHING'S UP. THE IDEA IS TO JUST CASUALLY WIN-- JUST BARELY OUTSCORE HIM AT THE LAST MOMENT.
YOU MUST UNDER-STAND NOW, DON'T YOU, ALIEN?
OKAY! HERE GOES!
CLATTR CLATTR
VWNNM
GWOOOO

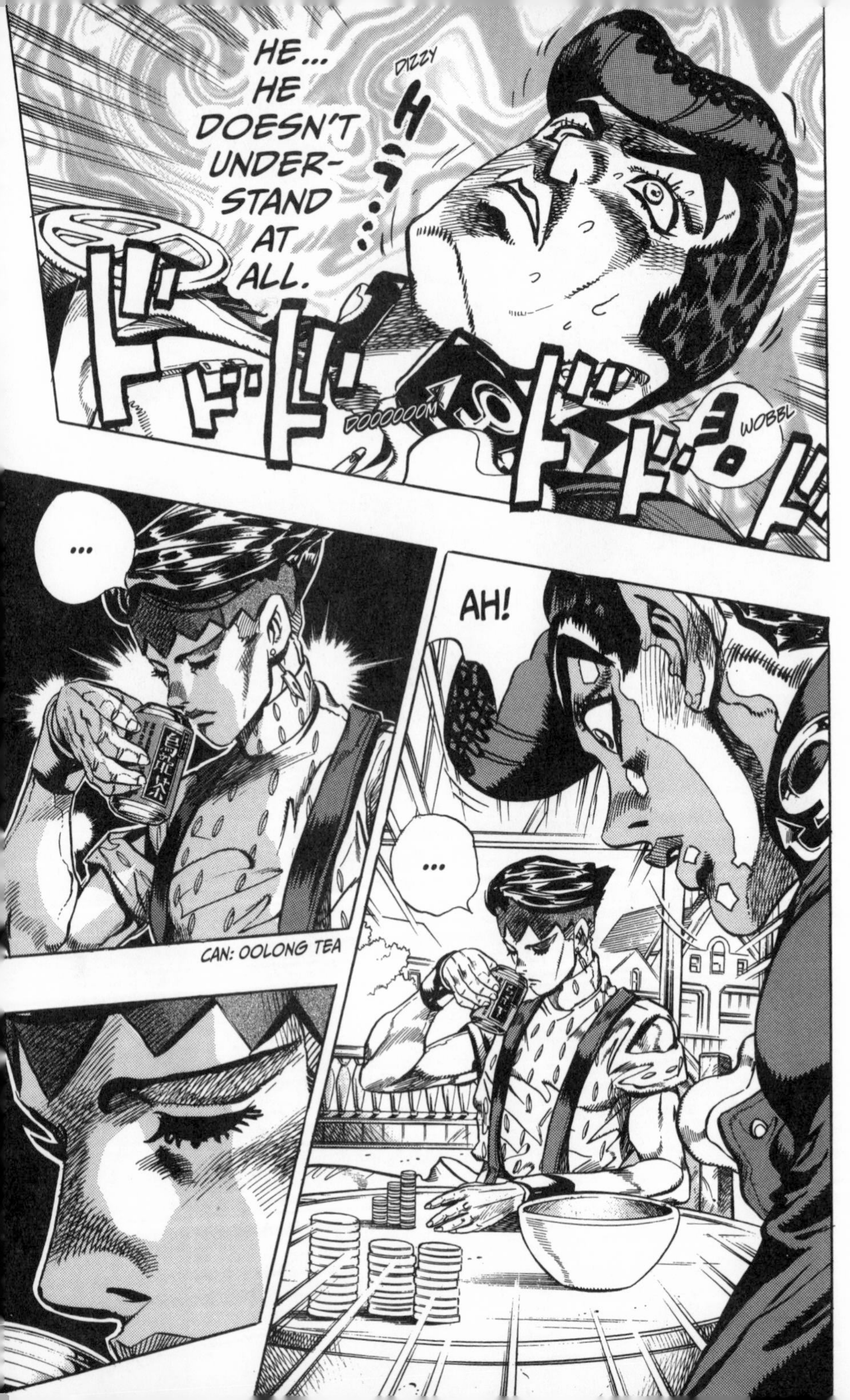
HE... HE DOESN'T UNDER-STAND AT ALL.
DIZZY
DOOOOOOOM
WOBBL
AH!
...
...
CAN: OOLONG TEA

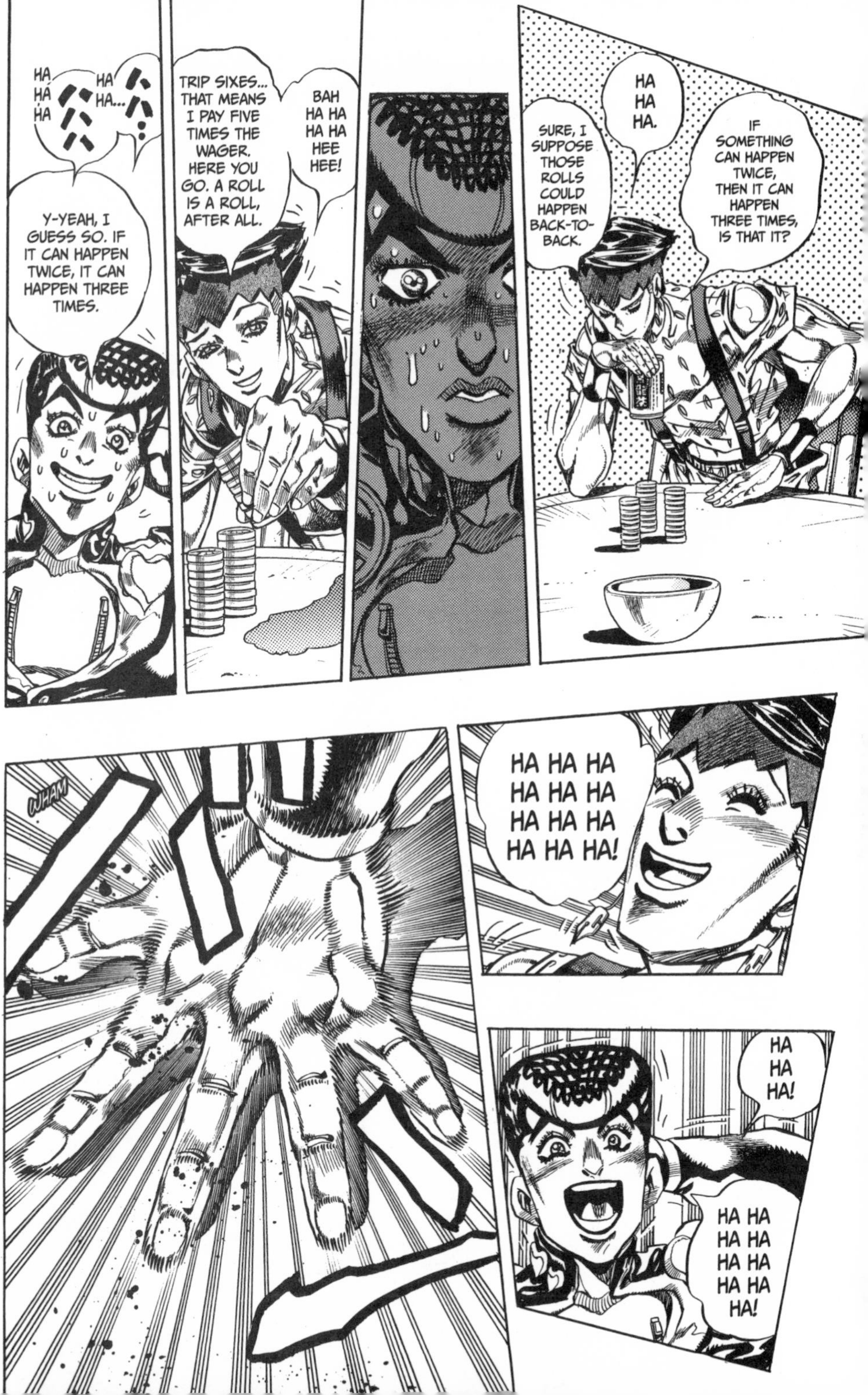

IF SOMETHING CAN HAPPEN TWICE, THEN IT CAN HAPPEN THREE TIMES, IS THAT IT?
HA HA HA.
SURE, I SUPPOSE THOSE ROLLS COULD HAPPEN BACK-TO-BACK.
BAH HA HA HA HA HEE HEE!
TRIP SIXES... THAT MEANS I PAY FIVE TIMES THE WAGER. HERE YOU GO. A ROLL IS A ROLL, AFTER ALL.
HA HA...
HA HA HA
Y-YEAH, I GUESS SO. IF IT CAN HAPPEN TWICE, IT CAN HAPPEN THREE TIMES.
HA HA HA HA HA HA HA HA HA HA HA HA!
HA HA HA!
HA HA HA HA HA HA HA HA HA!
WHAM

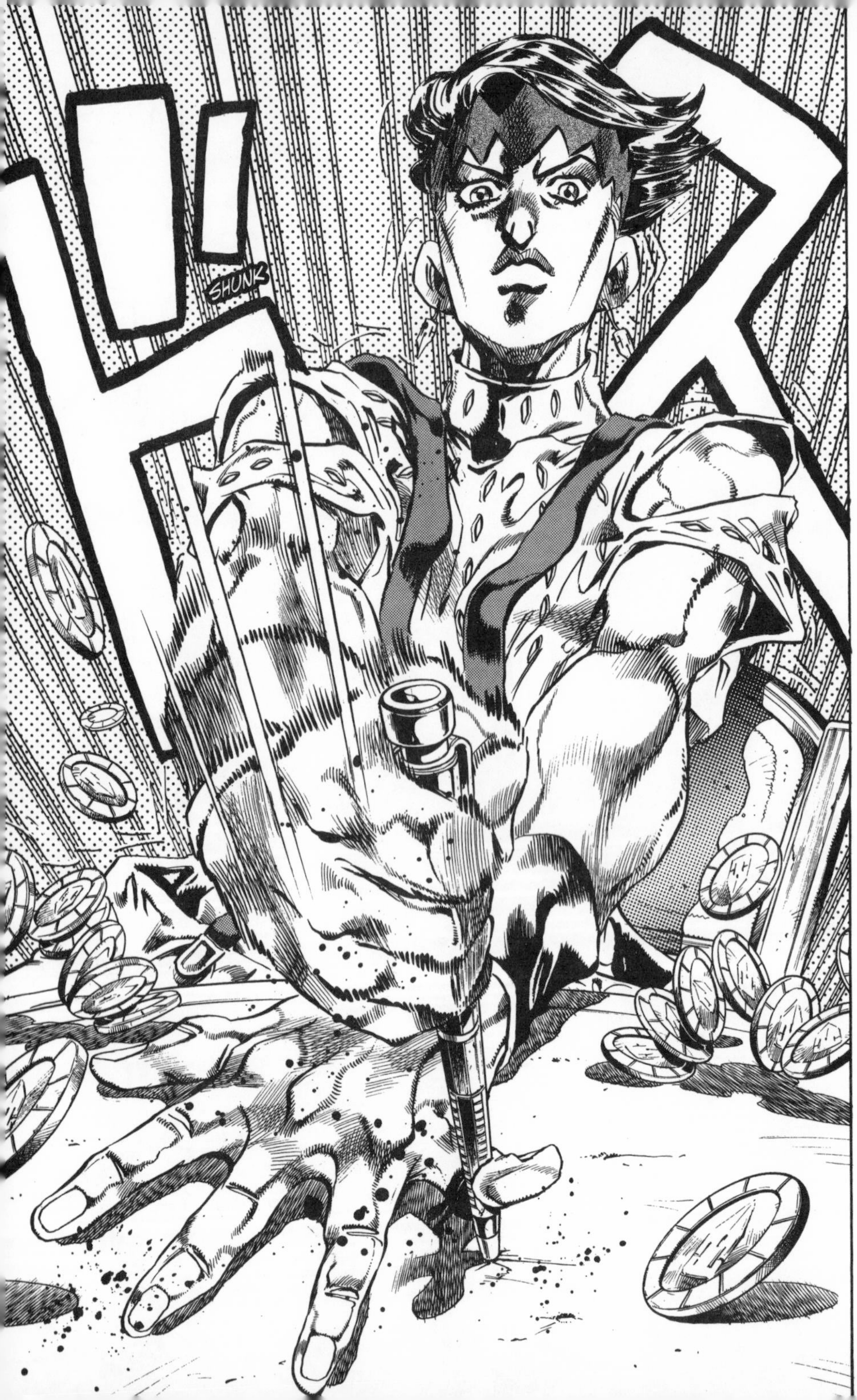
SHUNK

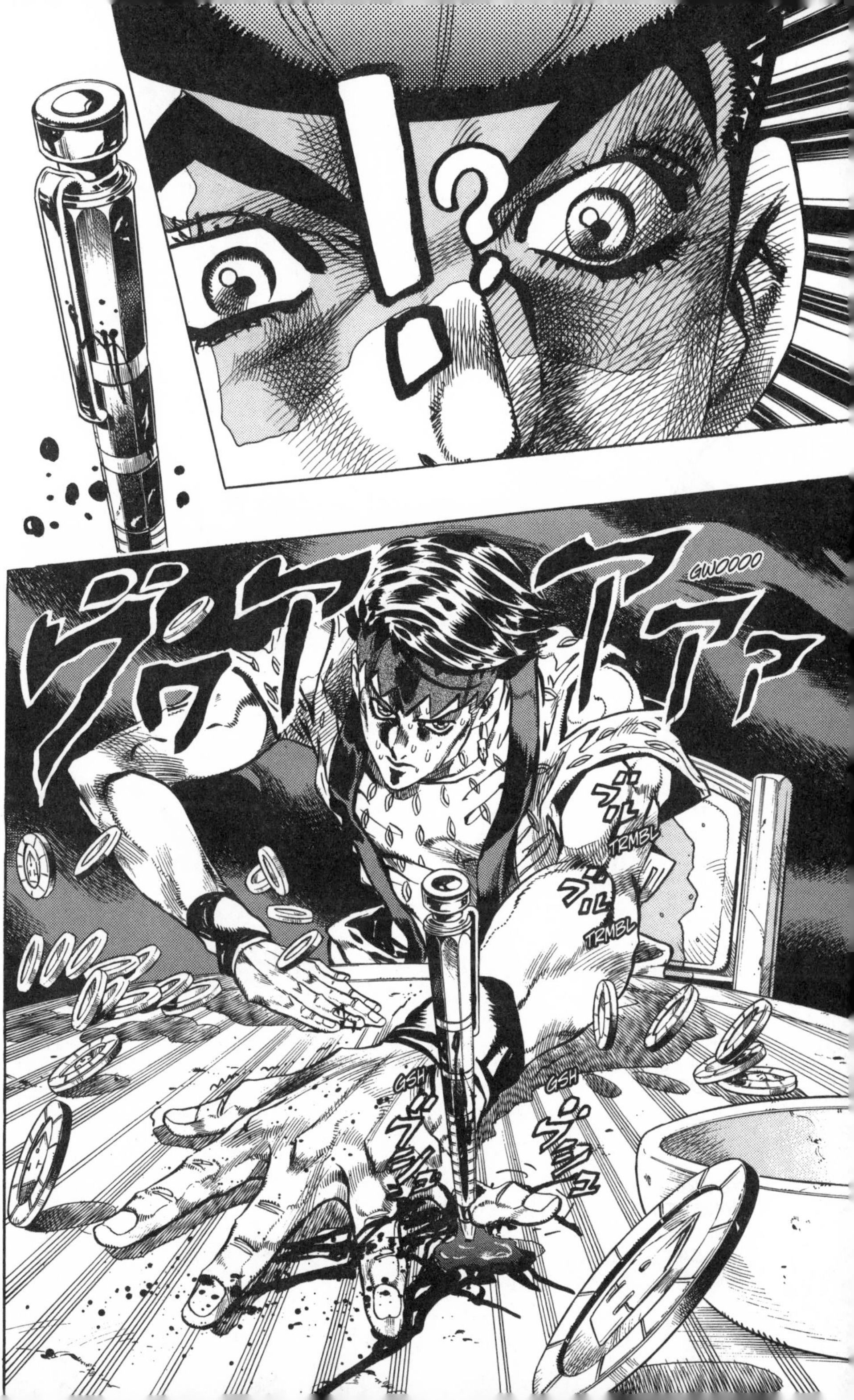
!?
ヴウアアァ
GWOOOO
ブル
TRMBL
ブル
TRMBL
GSH
GSH

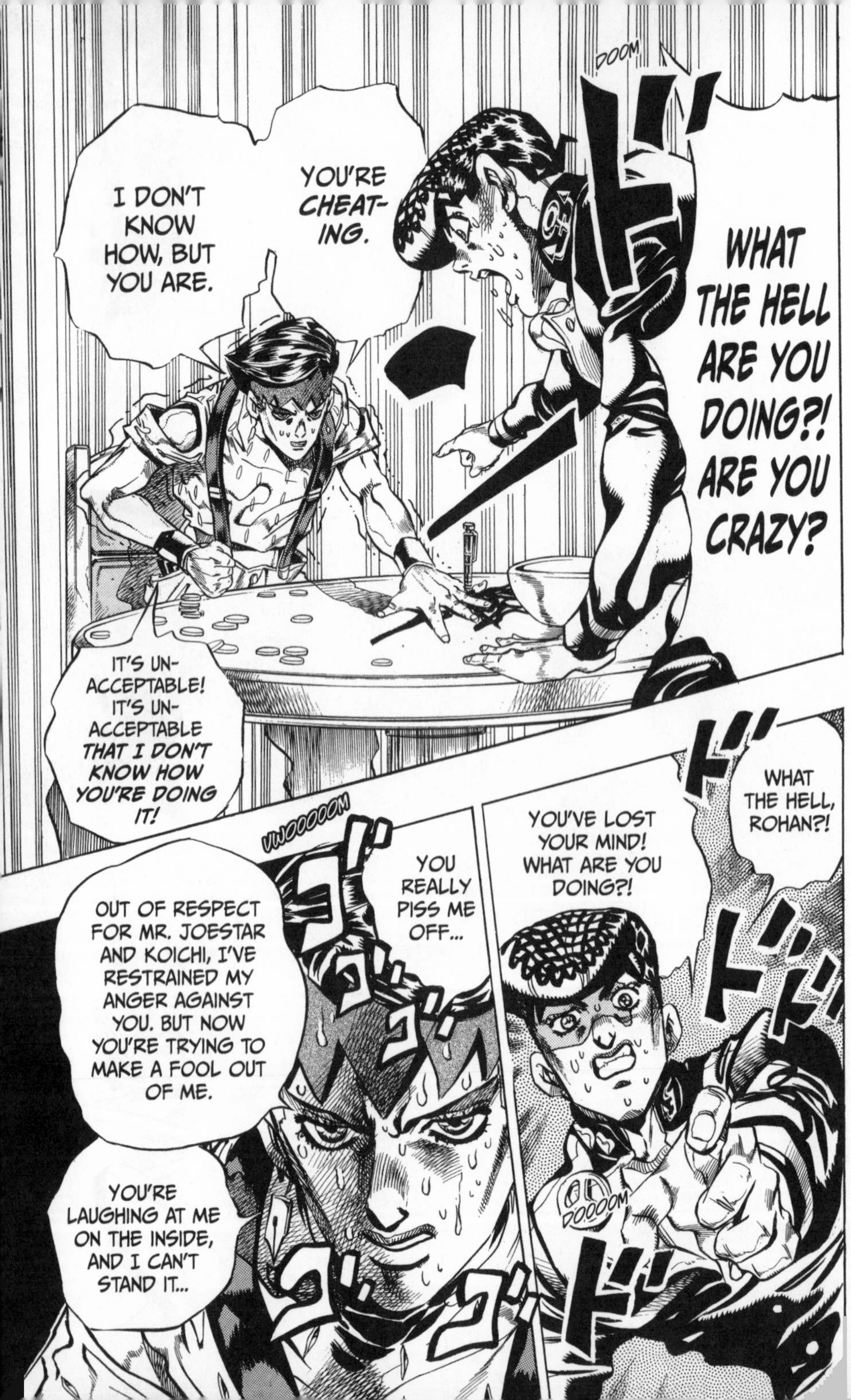
DOOM
WHAT THE HELL ARE YOU DOING?! ARE YOU CRAZY?
YOU'RE CHEAT-ING.
I DON'T KNOW HOW, BUT YOU ARE.
IT'S UN-ACCEPTABLE! IT'S UN-ACCEPTABLE THAT I DON'T KNOW HOW YOU'RE DOING IT!
WHAT THE HELL, ROHAN?!
YOU'VE LOST YOUR MIND! WHAT ARE YOU DOING?!
DOOOOM
UWOOOOOM
YOU REALLY PISS ME OFF...
OUT OF RESPECT FOR MR. JOESTAR AND KOICHI, I'VE RESTRAINED MY ANGER AGAINST YOU. BUT NOW YOU'RE TRYING TO MAKE A FOOL OUT OF ME.
YOU'RE LAUGHING AT ME ON THE INSIDE, AND I CAN'T STAND IT...

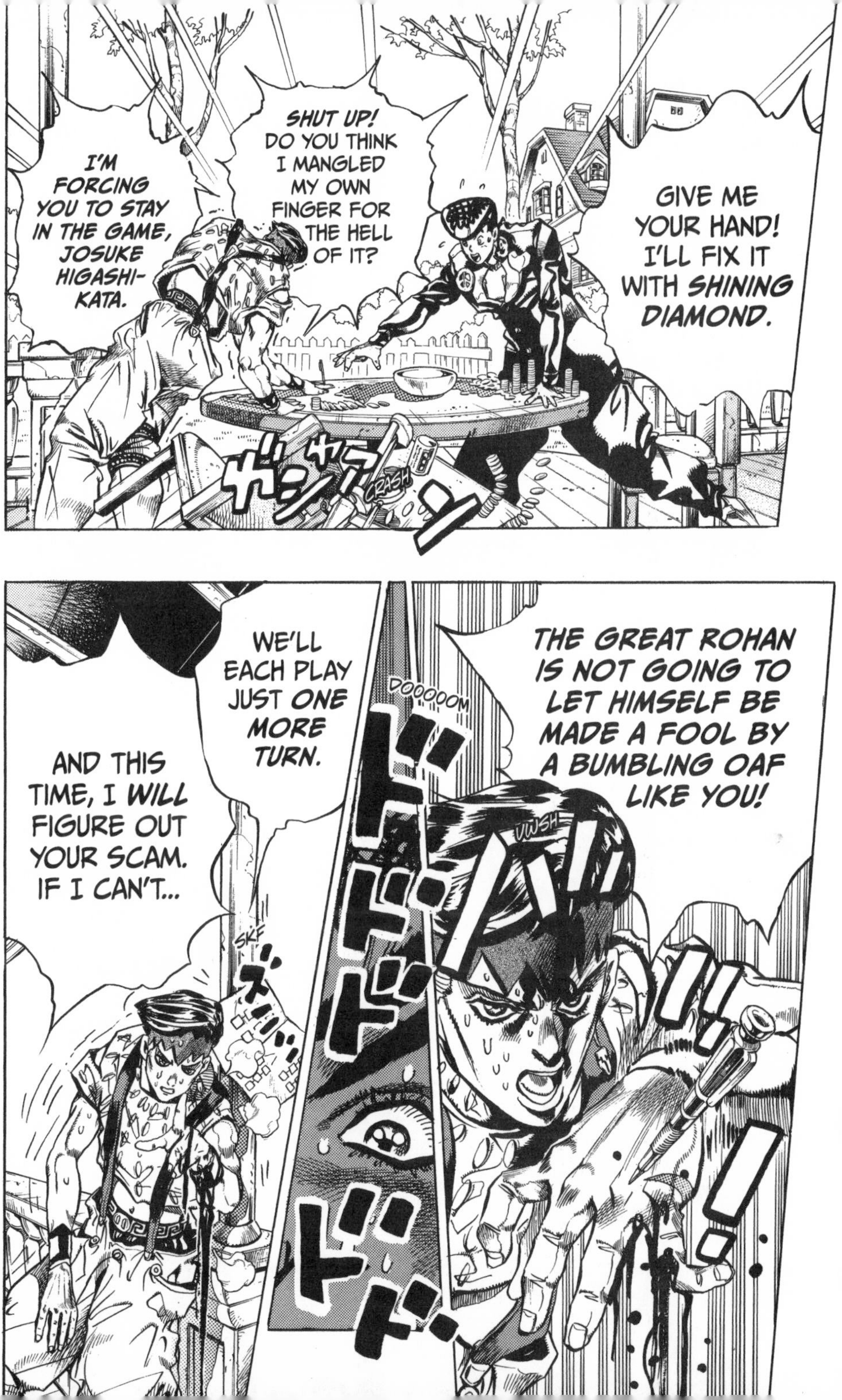
GIVE ME YOUR HAND! I'LL FIX IT WITH *SHINING DIAMOND.*
SHUT UP! DO YOU THINK I MANGLED MY OWN FINGER FOR THE HELL OF IT?
I'M FORCING YOU TO STAY IN THE GAME, JOSUKE HIGASHI-KATA.
CRASH
THE GREAT ROHAN IS NOT GOING TO LET HIMSELF BE MADE A FOOL BY A BUMBLING OAF LIKE YOU!
DOOOOOM
VWSH
WE'LL EACH PLAY JUST *ONE MORE* TURN.
AND THIS TIME, I *WILL* FIGURE OUT YOUR SCAM. IF I CAN'T...
SKF

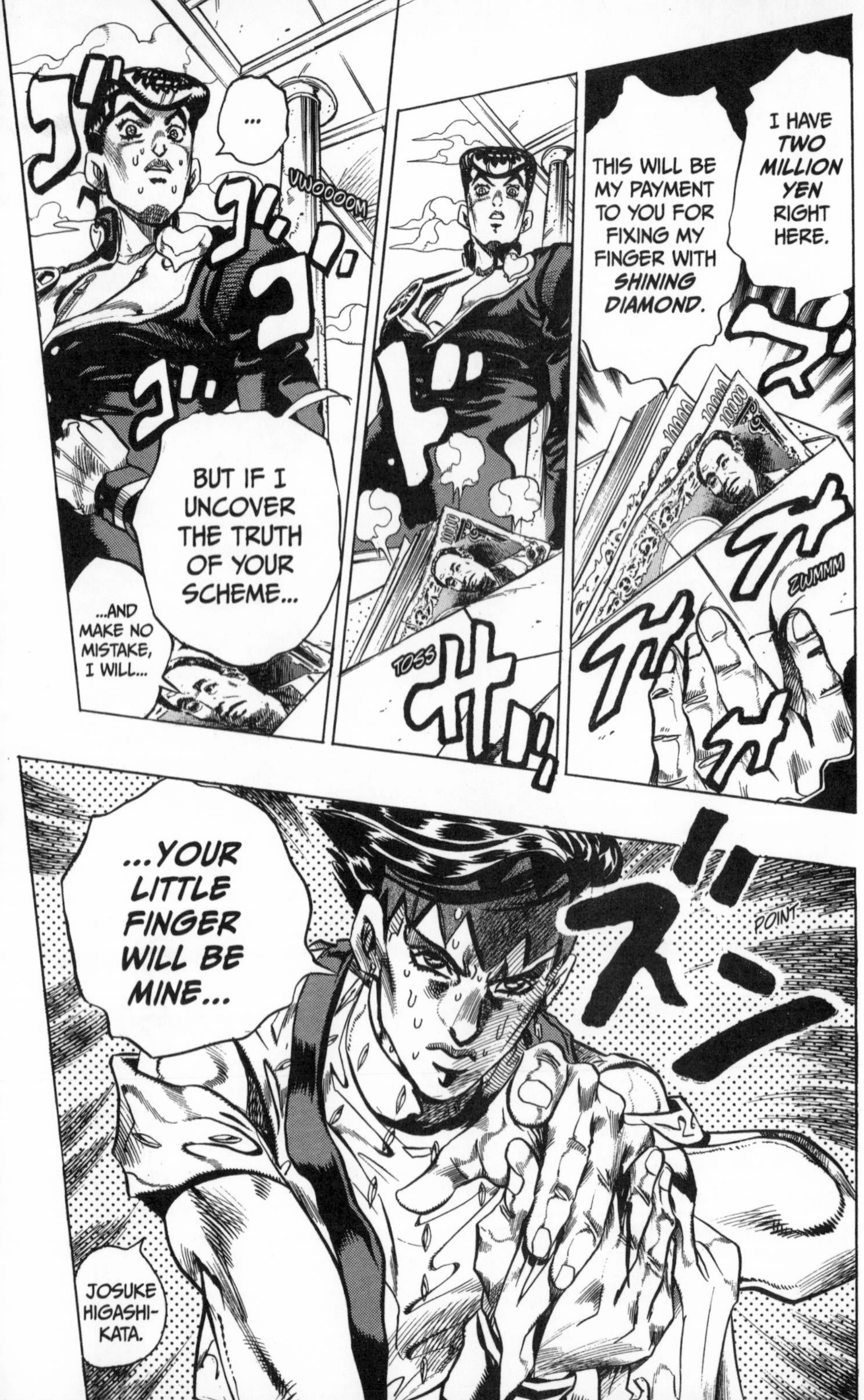
I HAVE TWO MILLION YEN RIGHT HERE.
THIS WILL BE MY PAYMENT TO YOU FOR FIXING MY FINGER WITH SHINING DIAMOND.
ZWMMM
TOSS
...
VWOOOOM
BUT IF I UNCOVER THE TRUTH OF YOUR SCHEME...
...AND MAKE NO MISTAKE, I WILL...
...YOUR LITTLE FINGER WILL BE MINE...
POINT
JOSUKE HIGASHI-KATA.

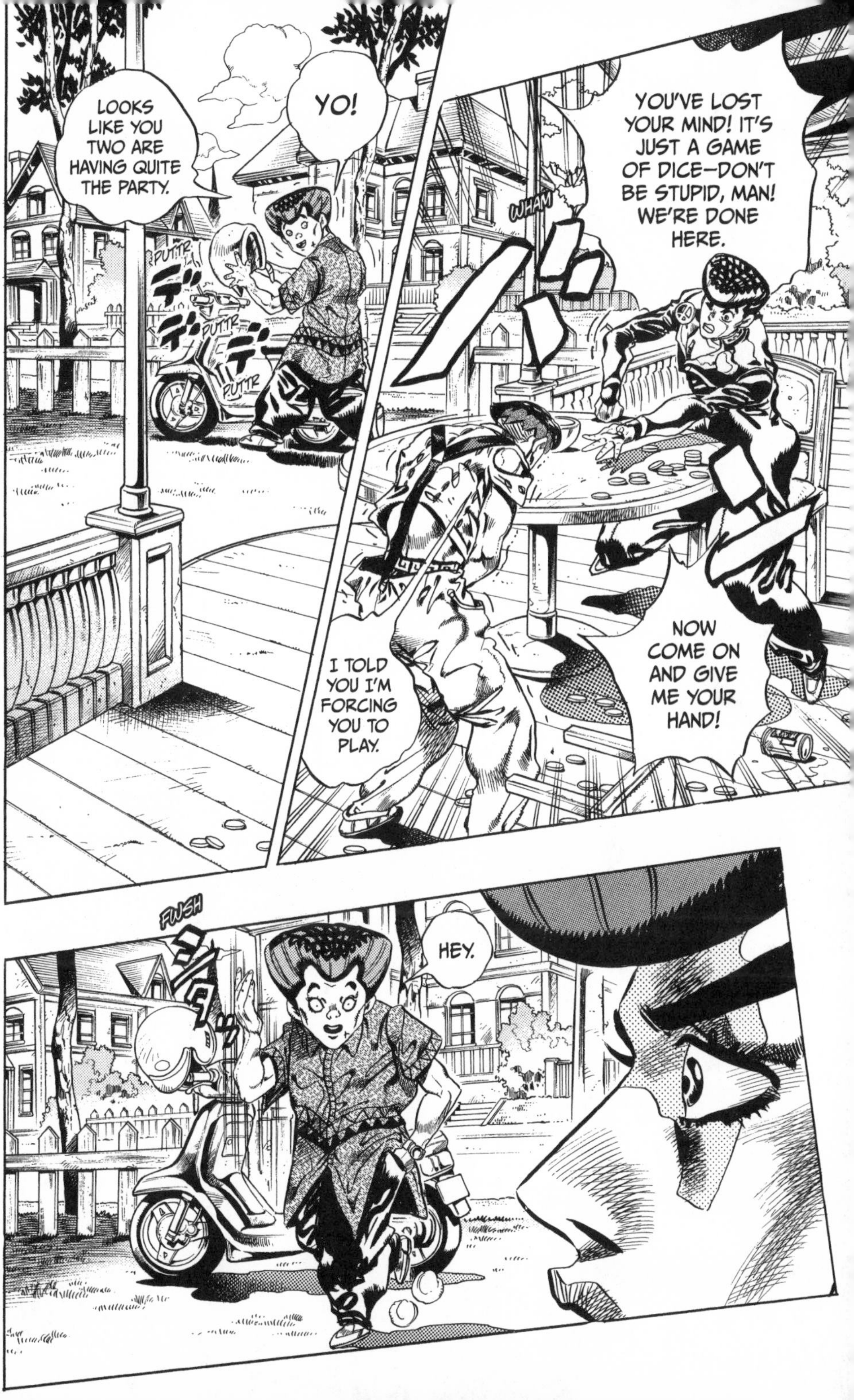
YOU'VE LOST YOUR MIND! IT'S JUST A GAME OF DICE—DON'T BE STUPID, MAN! WE'RE DONE HERE.
WHAM
NOW COME ON AND GIVE ME YOUR HAND!
I TOLD YOU I'M FORCING YOU TO PLAY.
YO!
LOOKS LIKE YOU TWO ARE HAVING QUITE THE PARTY.
PUTTR PUTTR PUTTR
HEY.
FWSH

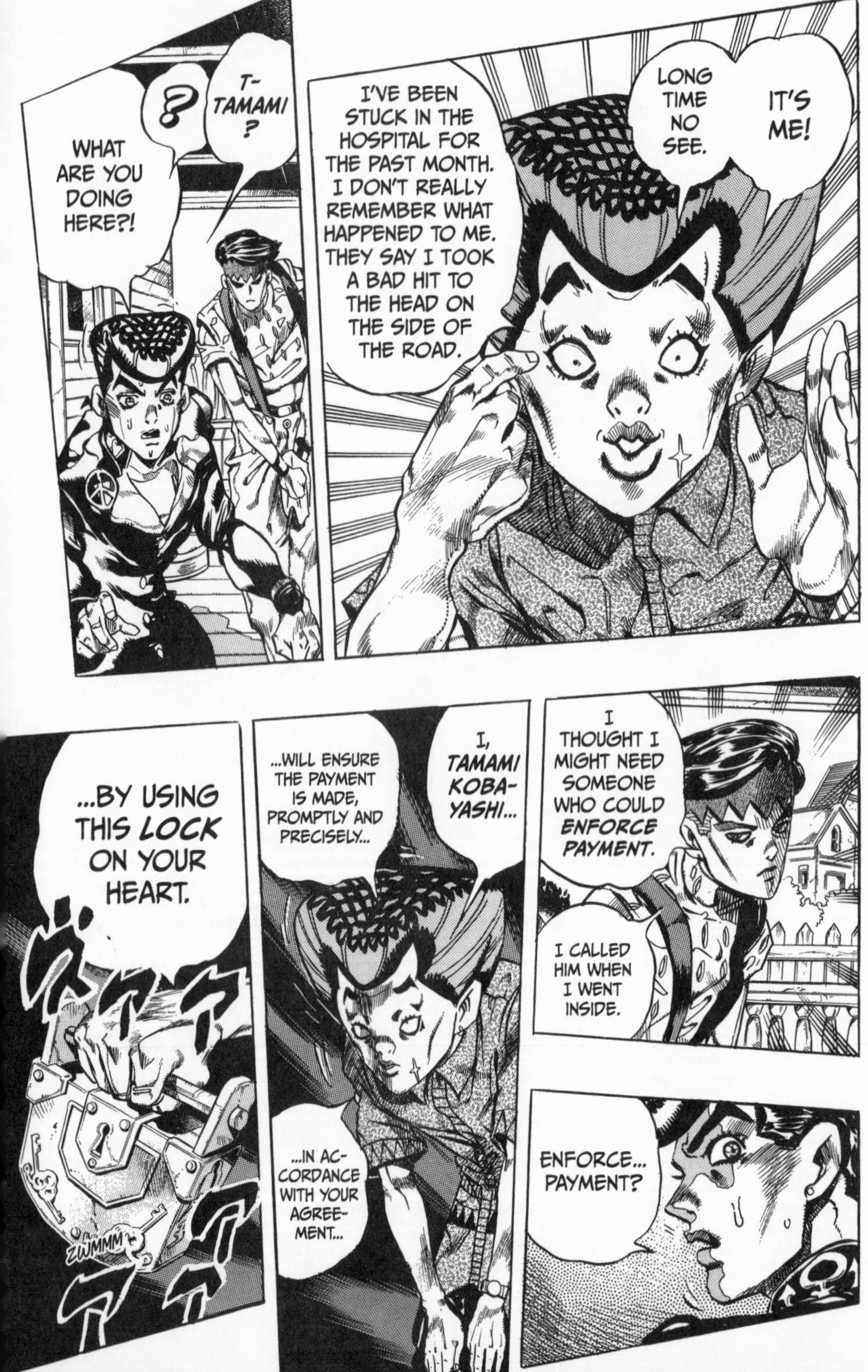
IT'S ME!
LONG TIME NO SEE.
I'VE BEEN STUCK IN THE HOSPITAL FOR THE PAST MONTH. I DON'T REALLY REMEMBER WHAT HAPPENED TO ME. THEY SAY I TOOK A BAD HIT TO THE HEAD ON THE SIDE OF THE ROAD.
T-TAMAMI?
?
WHAT ARE YOU DOING HERE?!
I THOUGHT I MIGHT NEED SOMEONE WHO COULD ENFORCE PAYMENT.
I CALLED HIM WHEN I WENT INSIDE.
ENFORCE... PAYMENT?
I, TAMAMI KOBAYASHI...
...WILL ENSURE THE PAYMENT IS MADE, PROMPTLY AND PRECISELY...
...IN ACCORDANCE WITH YOUR AGREEMENT...
...BY USING THIS LOCK ON YOUR HEART.
ZWMMM

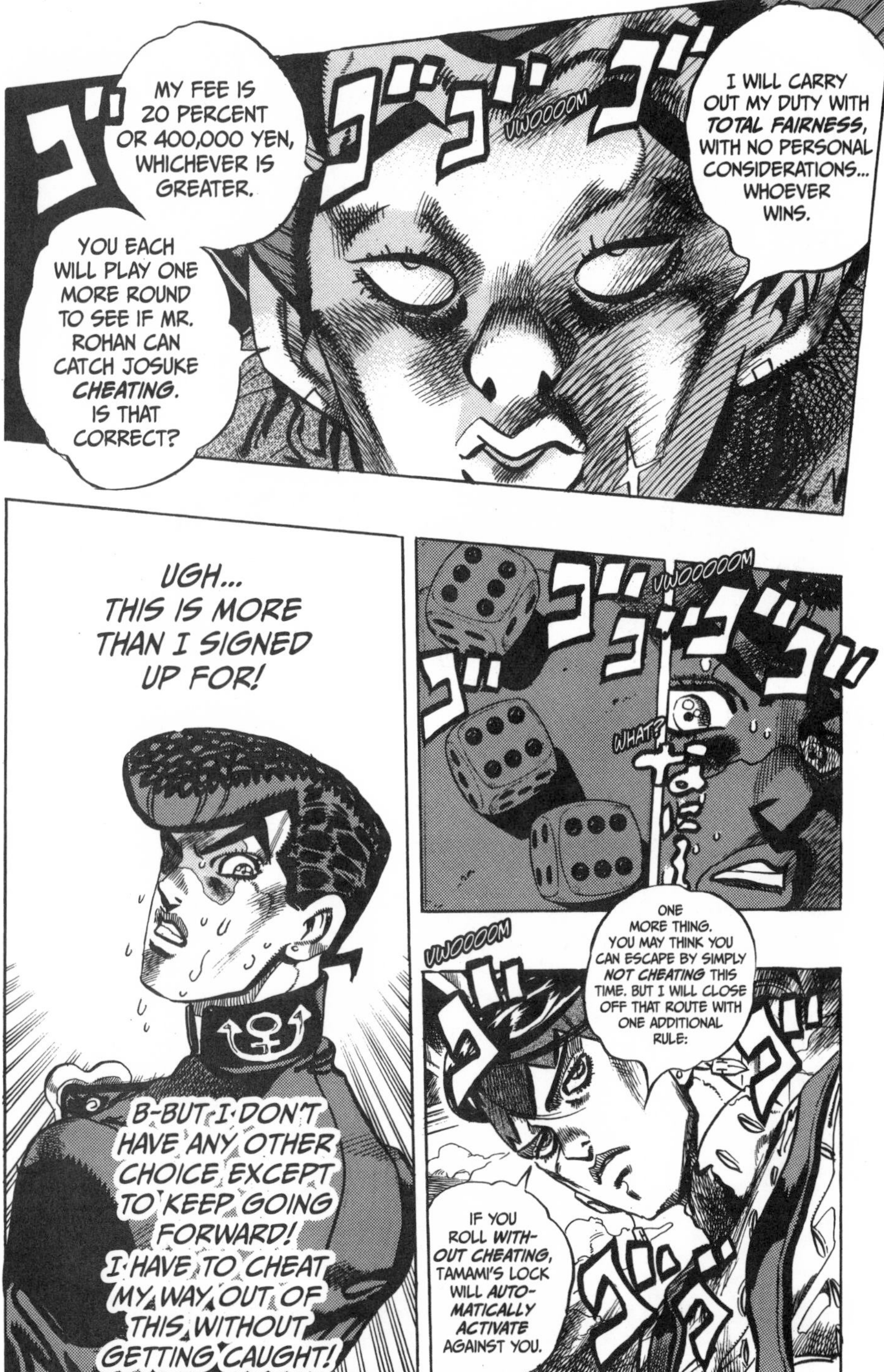
I WILL CARRY OUT MY DUTY WITH TOTAL FAIRNESS, WITH NO PERSONAL CONSIDERATIONS... WHOEVER WINS.
VWOOOOM
MY FEE IS 20 PERCENT OR 400,000 YEN, WHICHEVER IS GREATER.
YOU EACH WILL PLAY ONE MORE ROUND TO SEE IF MR. ROHAN CAN CATCH JOSUKE CHEATING. IS THAT CORRECT?
VWOOOOOM
WHAT?
VWOOOOM
ONE MORE THING. YOU MAY THINK YOU CAN ESCAPE BY SIMPLY NOT CHEATING THIS TIME. BUT I WILL CLOSE OFF THAT ROUTE WITH ONE ADDITIONAL RULE:
IF YOU ROLL WITHOUT CHEATING, TAMAMI'S LOCK WILL AUTOMATICALLY ACTIVATE AGAINST YOU.
UGH... THIS IS MORE THAN I SIGNED UP FOR!
B-BUT I DON'T HAVE ANY OTHER CHOICE EXCEPT TO KEEP GOING FORWARD! I HAVE TO CHEAT MY WAY OUT OF THIS WITHOUT GETTING CAUGHT!

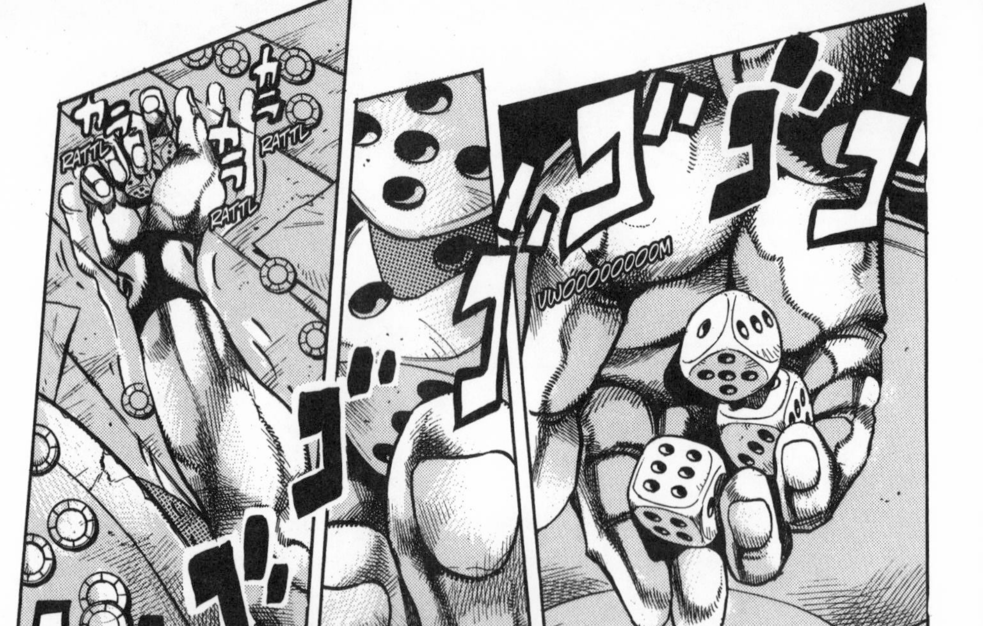
VWOOOOOOOOOM
RATTL
RATTL
RATTL

CHAPTER 118

I AM AN ALIEN, PART 6

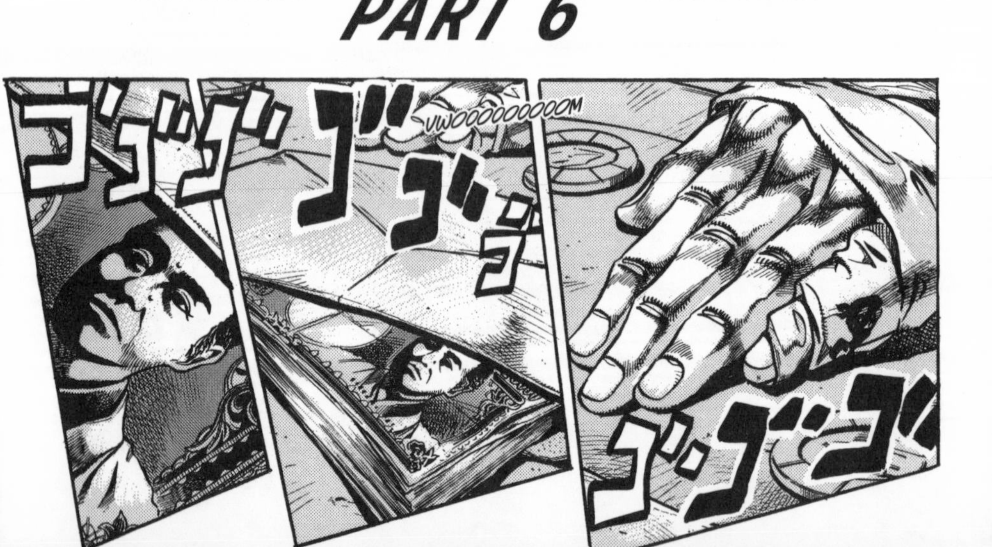
VWOOOOOOOOOOOM

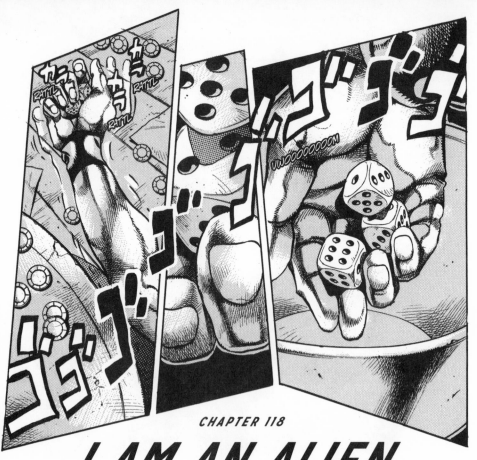

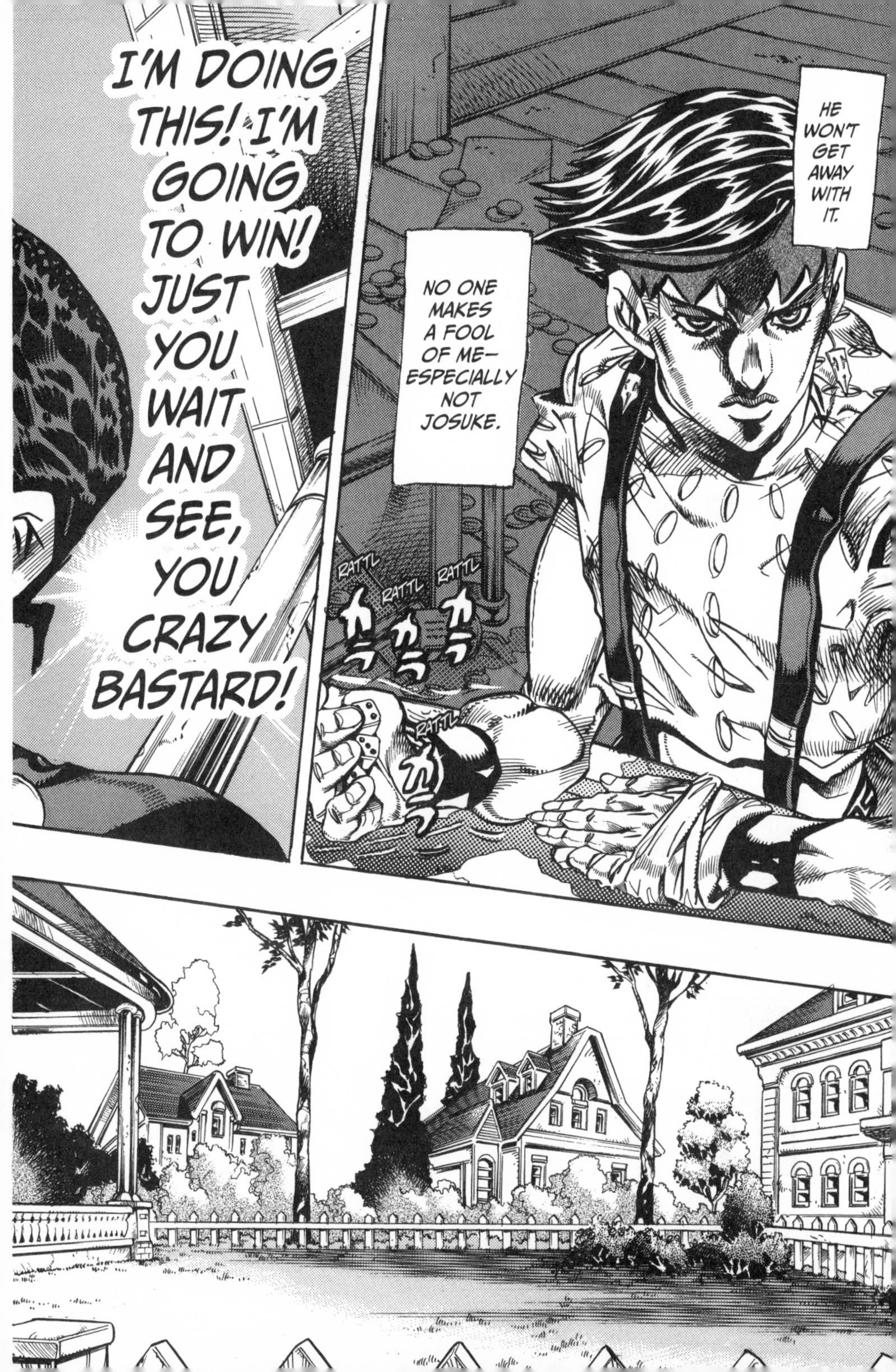
HE WON'T GET AWAY WITH IT.
NO ONE MAKES A FOOL OF ME—ESPECIALLY NOT JOSUKE.
RATTL
カラ
RATTL
カラ
RATTL
カラ
RATTL
カラ
I'M DOING THIS! I'M GOING TO WIN! JUST YOU WAIT AND SEE, YOU CRAZY BASTARD!

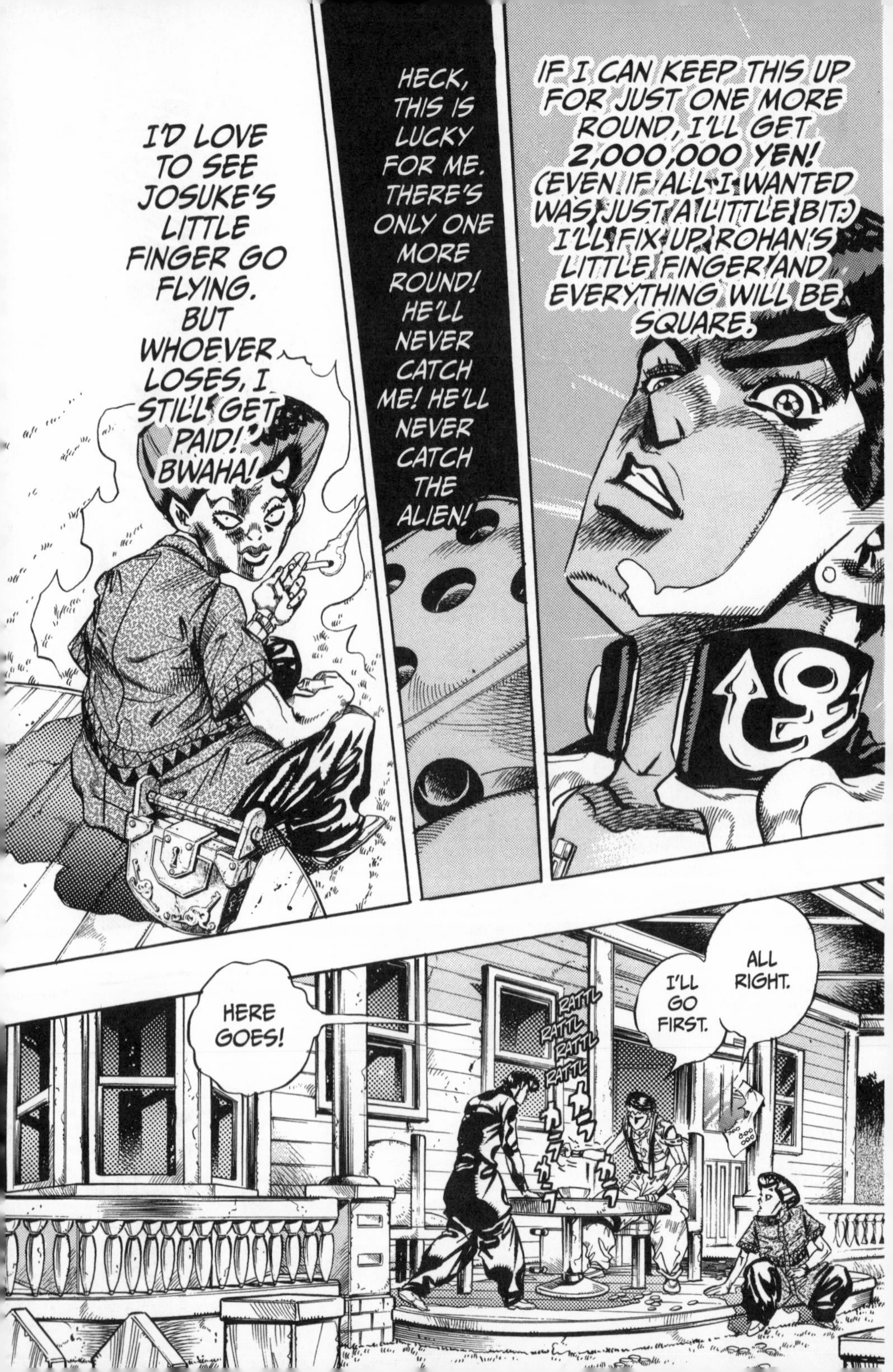
IF I CAN KEEP THIS UP FOR JUST ONE MORE ROUND, I'LL GET **2,000,000 YEN!** (EVEN IF ALL I WANTED WAS JUST A LITTLE BIT.) I'LL FIX UP ROHAN'S LITTLE FINGER AND EVERYTHING WILL BE SQUARE.
HECK, THIS IS LUCKY FOR ME. THERE'S ONLY ONE MORE ROUND! HE'LL NEVER CATCH ME! HE'LL NEVER CATCH THE ALIEN!
I'D LOVE TO SEE JOSUKE'S LITTLE FINGER GO FLYING. BUT WHOEVER LOSES, I STILL GET PAID! BWAHA!
ALL RIGHT. I'LL GO FIRST.
RATTL RATTL RATTL RATTL
HERE GOES!

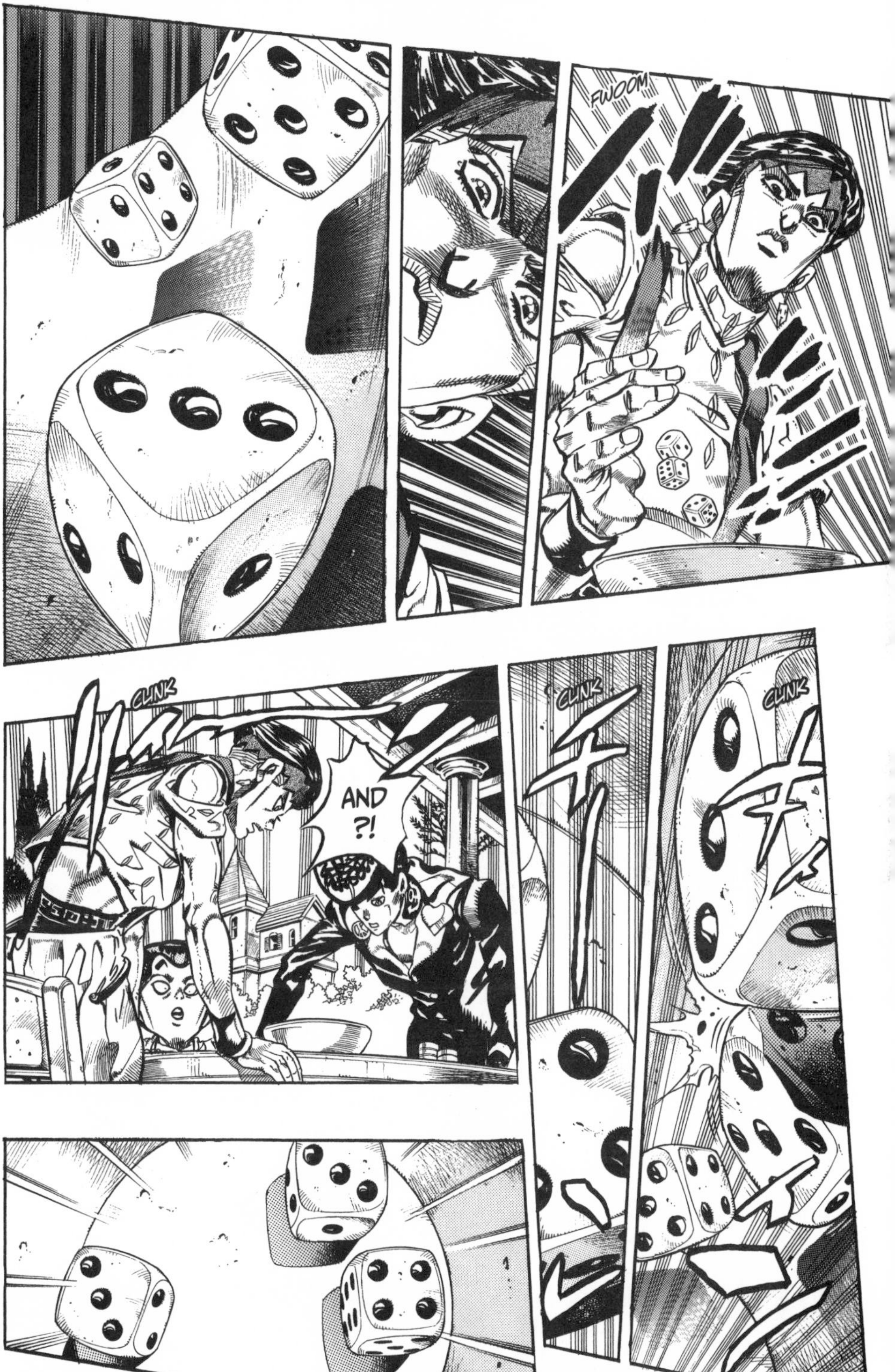
FWOOM
CLINK
CLINK
CLINK
AND ?!

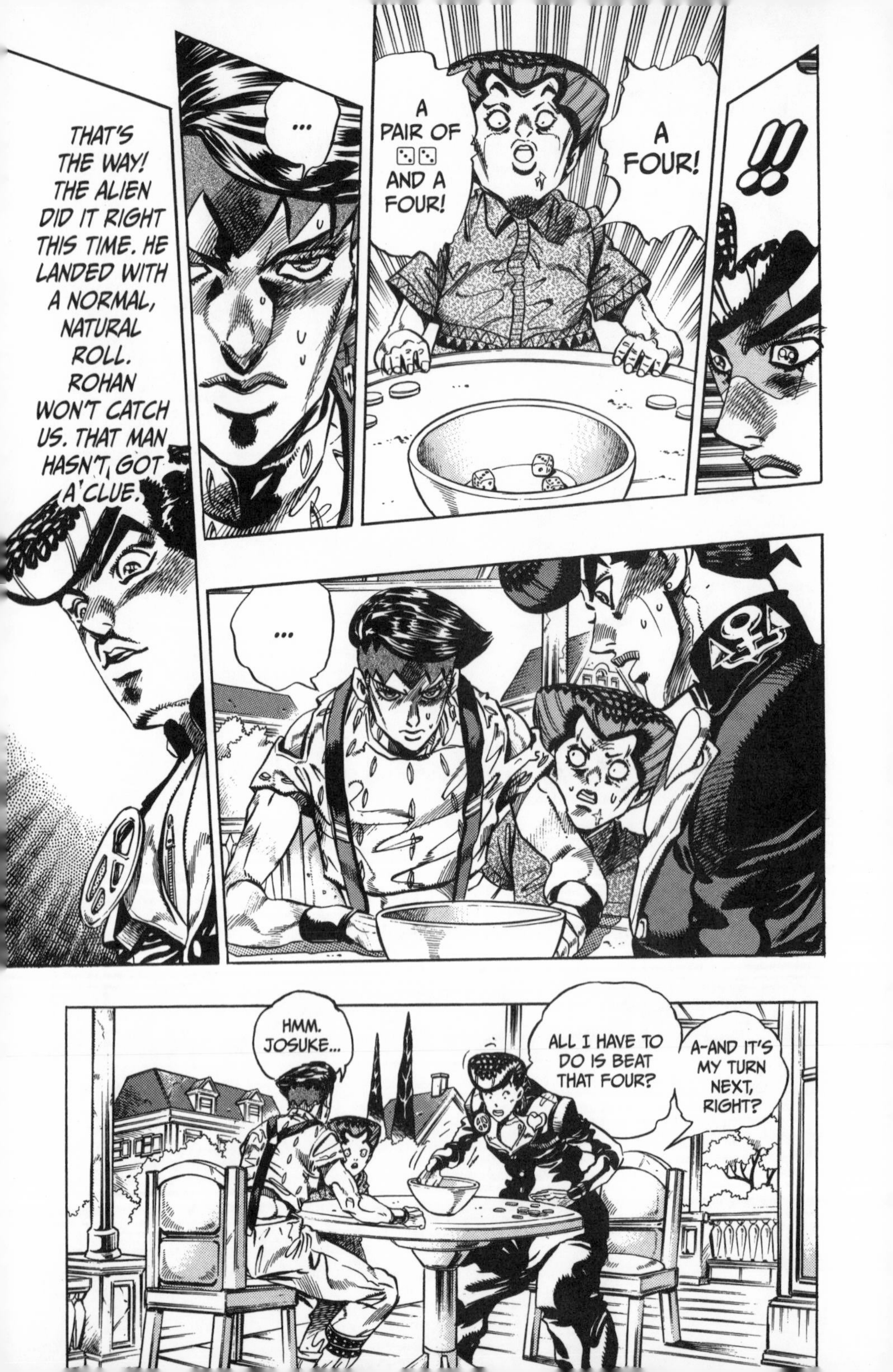
!!
A PAIR OF ⚂⚂ AND A FOUR!
A FOUR!
...
THAT'S THE WAY! THE ALIEN DID IT RIGHT THIS TIME. HE LANDED WITH A NORMAL, NATURAL ROLL. ROHAN WON'T CATCH US. THAT MAN HASN'T GOT A CLUE.
...
A-AND IT'S MY TURN NEXT, RIGHT?
ALL I HAVE TO DO IS BEAT THAT FOUR?
HMM. JOSUKE...

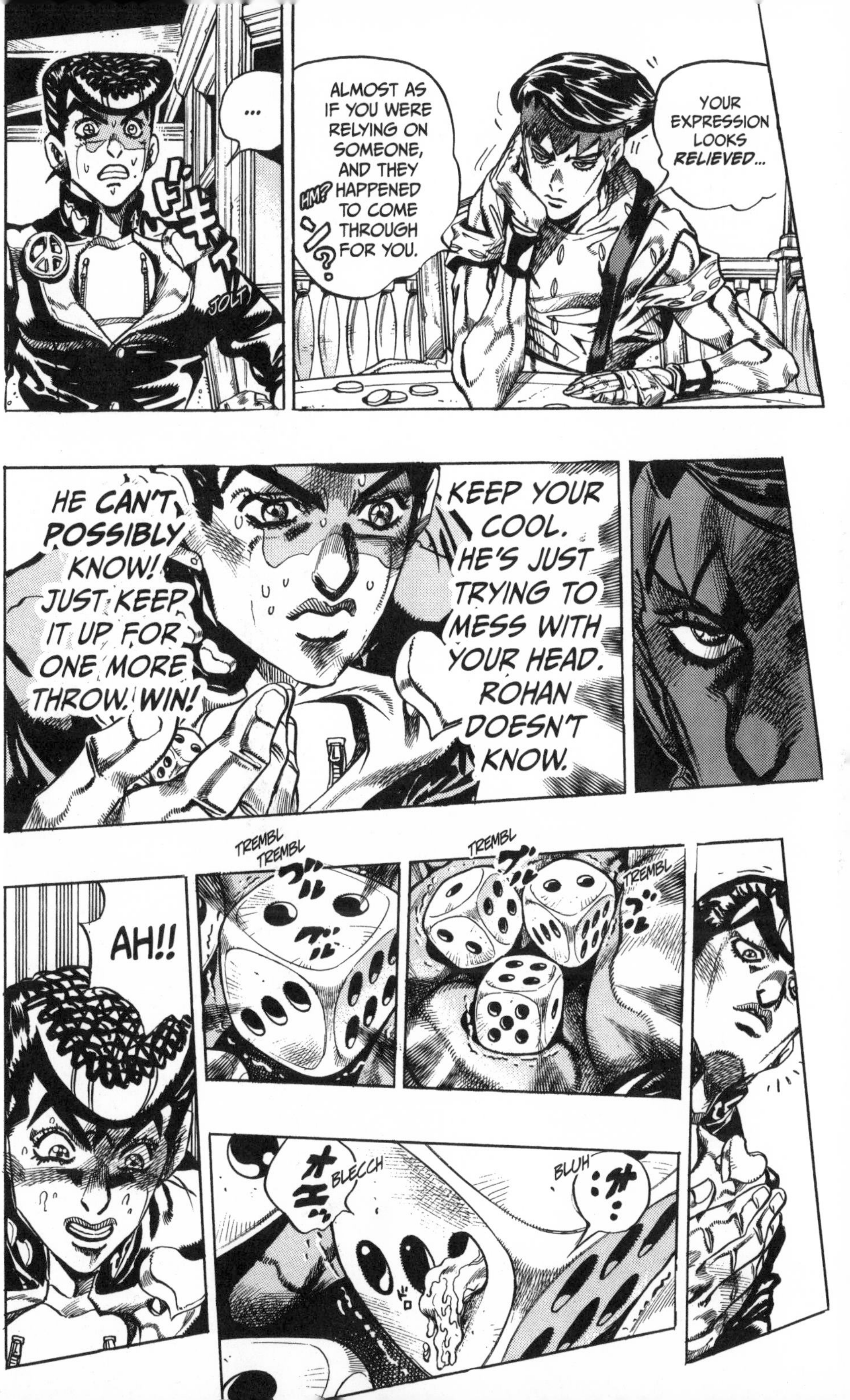
YOUR EXPRESSION LOOKS RELIEVED...
ALMOST AS IF YOU WERE RELYING ON SOMEONE, AND THEY HAPPENED TO COME THROUGH FOR YOU.
HM?
...
JOLT
KEEP YOUR COOL. HE'S JUST TRYING TO MESS WITH YOUR HEAD. ROHAN DOESN'T KNOW.
HE CAN'T POSSIBLY KNOW! JUST KEEP IT UP FOR ONE MORE THROW. WIN!
TREMBL
TREMBL
TREMBL TREMBL
BLUH
BLECCH
AH!!

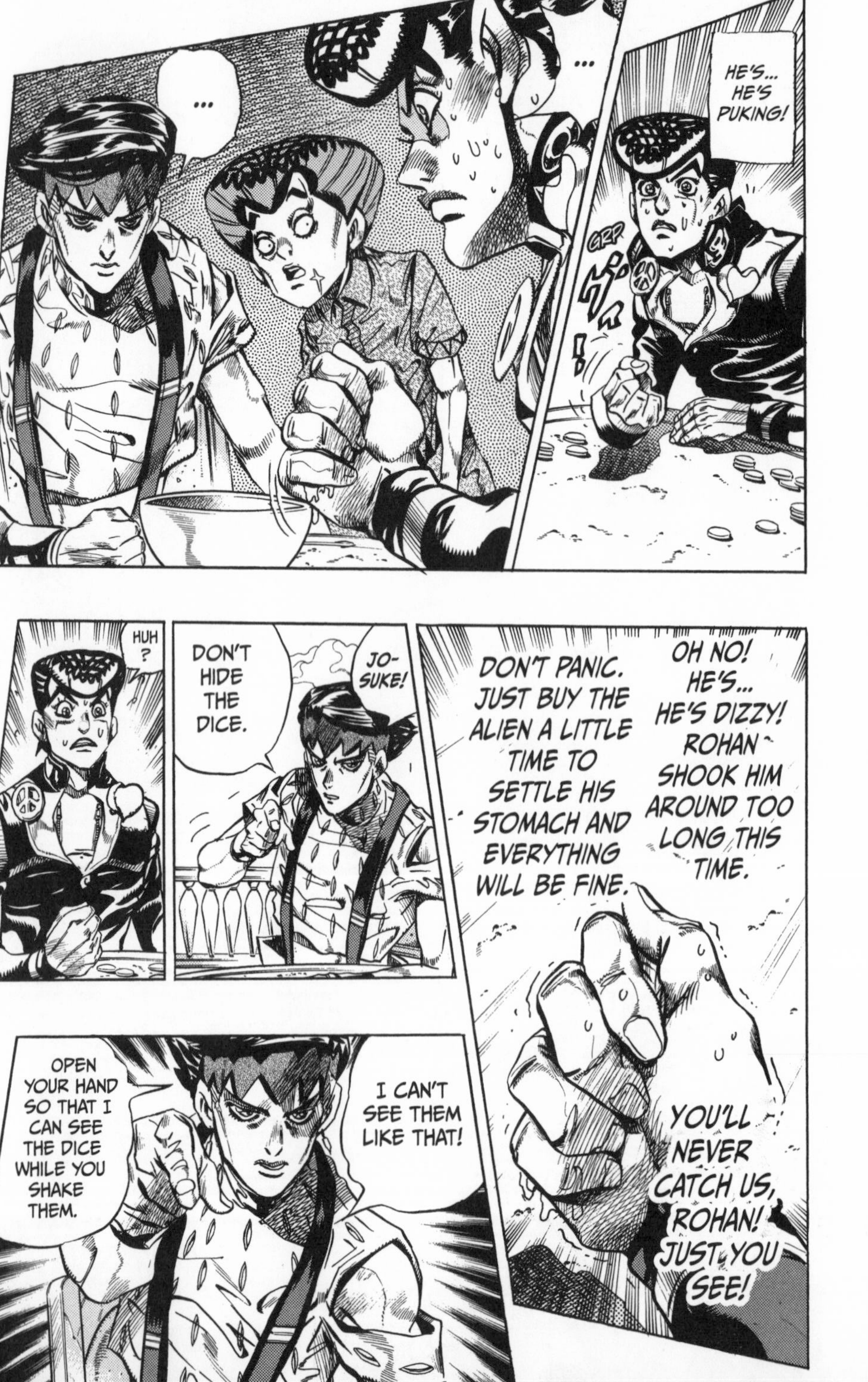
HE'S... HE'S PUKING!
GRP
...
...
OH NO! HE'S... HE'S DIZZY! ROHAN SHOOK HIM AROUND TOO LONG THIS TIME.
DON'T PANIC. JUST BUY THE ALIEN A LITTLE TIME TO SETTLE HIS STOMACH AND EVERYTHING WILL BE FINE.
YOU'LL NEVER CATCH US, ROHAN! JUST YOU SEE!
JO-SUKE!
DON'T HIDE THE DICE.
HUH ?
I CAN'T SEE THEM LIKE THAT!
OPEN YOUR HAND SO THAT I CAN SEE THE DICE WHILE YOU SHAKE THEM.

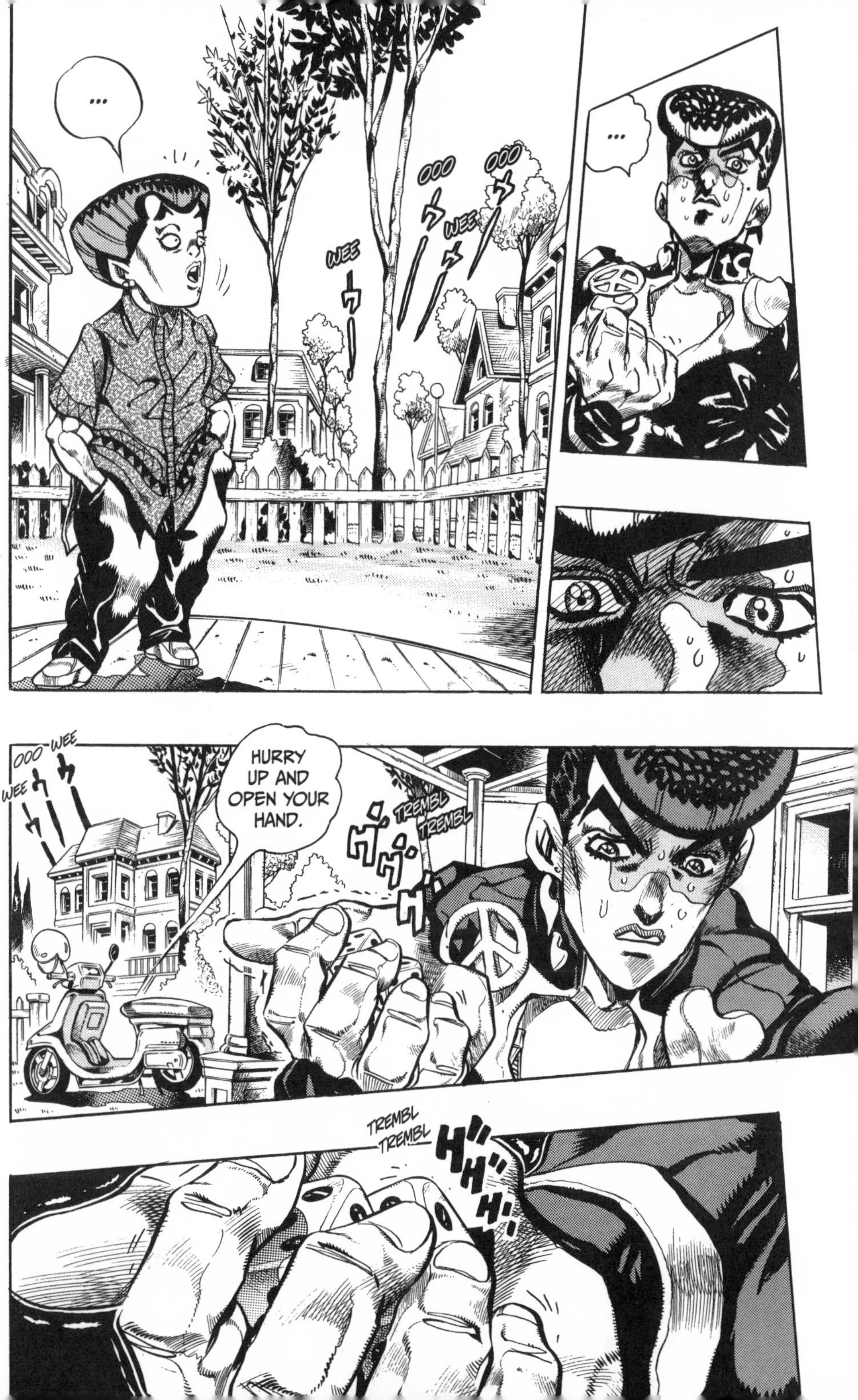
...
...
OOO
WEE
OOO
WEE
WEE
HURRY UP AND OPEN YOUR HAND.
TREMBL TREMBL
OOO WEE
WEE
TREMBL TREMBL

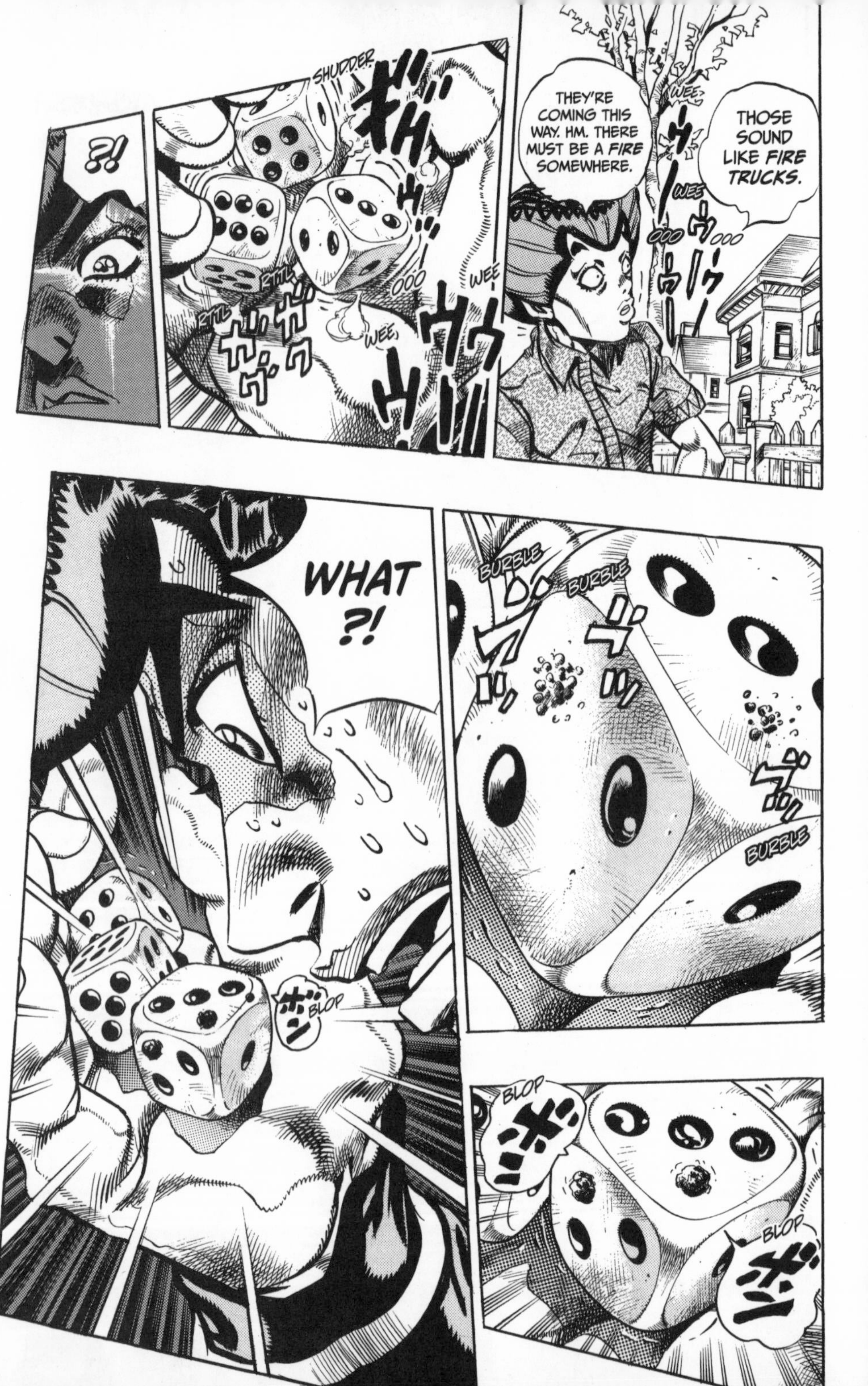
THOSE SOUND LIKE FIRE TRUCKS.
WEE
WEE
OOO
OOO
THEY'RE COMING THIS WAY. HM. THERE MUST BE A FIRE SOMEWHERE.
SHUDDER
WEE
OOO
WEE
RTTL
RTTL
?!
BURBLE
BURBLE
BURBLE
BLOP
BLOP
WHAT ?!
BLOP

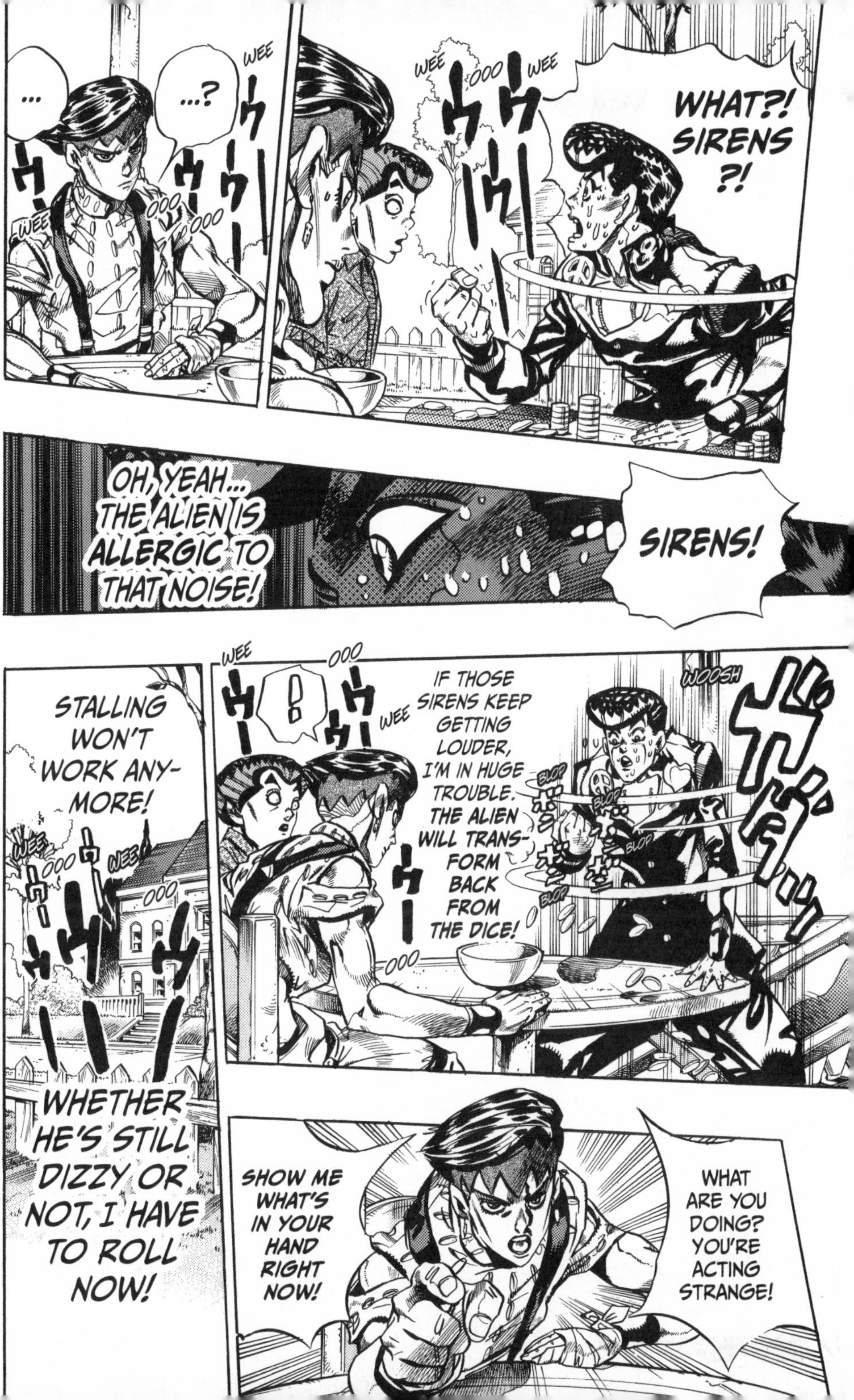
WEE
OOO
WEE
WHAT?! SIRENS ?!
WEE
...?
...
WEE
OOO
OOO
SIRENS!
OH, YEAH... THE ALIEN IS ALLERGIC TO THAT NOISE!
WOOSH
BLOP
BLOP
BLOP
BLOP
IF THOSE SIRENS KEEP GETTING LOUDER, I'M IN HUGE TROUBLE. THE ALIEN WILL TRANS-FORM BACK FROM THE DICE!
OOO
WEE
!
WEE
OOO
WHAT ARE YOU DOING? YOU'RE ACTING STRANGE!
SHOW ME WHAT'S IN YOUR HAND RIGHT NOW!
STALLING WON'T WORK ANY-MORE!
WEE
OOO
WEE
OOO
WHETHER HE'S STILL DIZZY OR NOT, I HAVE TO ROLL NOW!

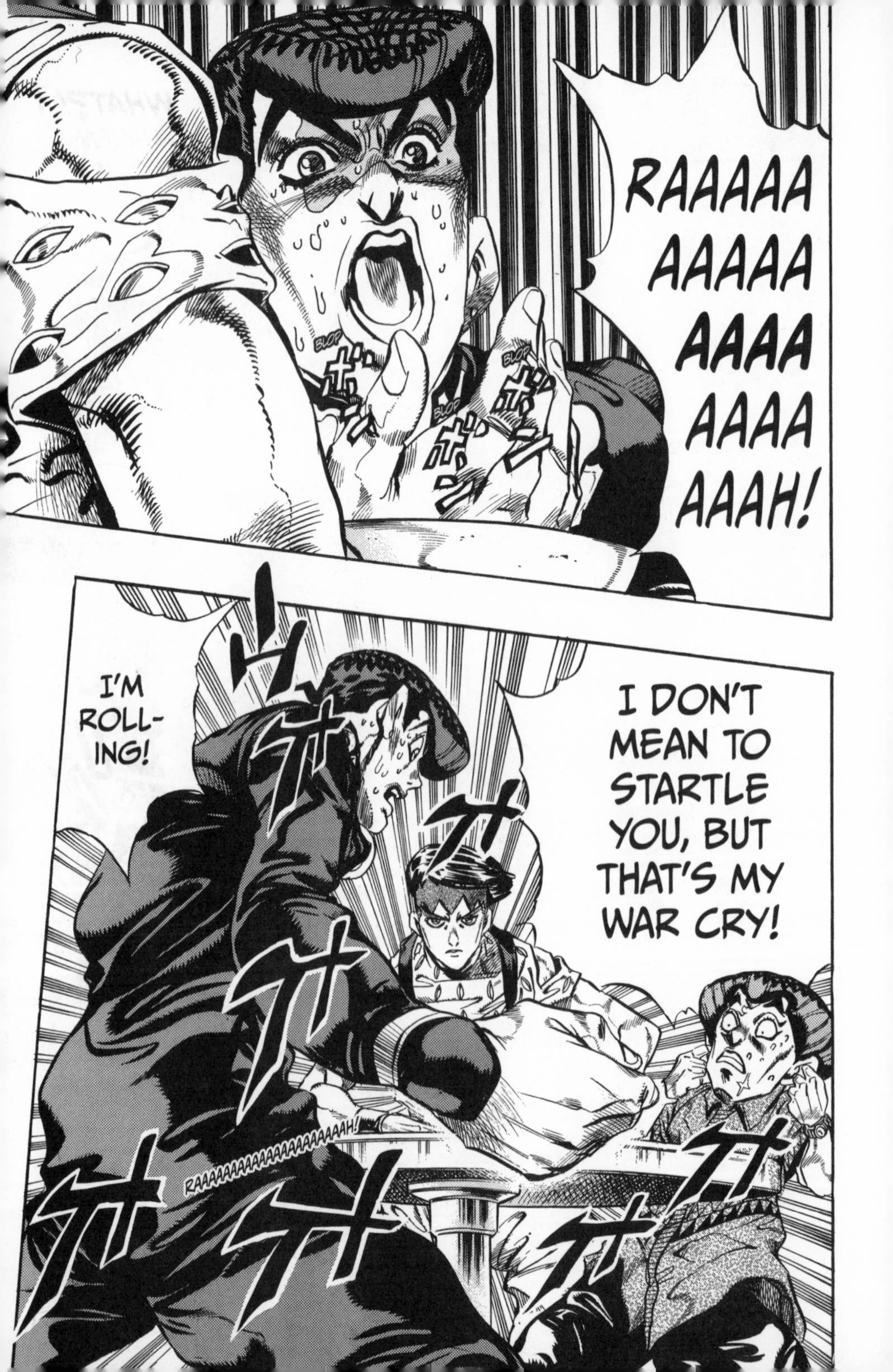
RAAAAA
AAAAA
AAAA
AAAA
AAAH!
BLOP
BLOP
BLOP
I DON'T MEAN TO STARTLE YOU, BUT THAT'S MY WAR CRY!
I'M ROLL-ING!
RAAAAAAAAAAAAAAAAAAAAAAH!

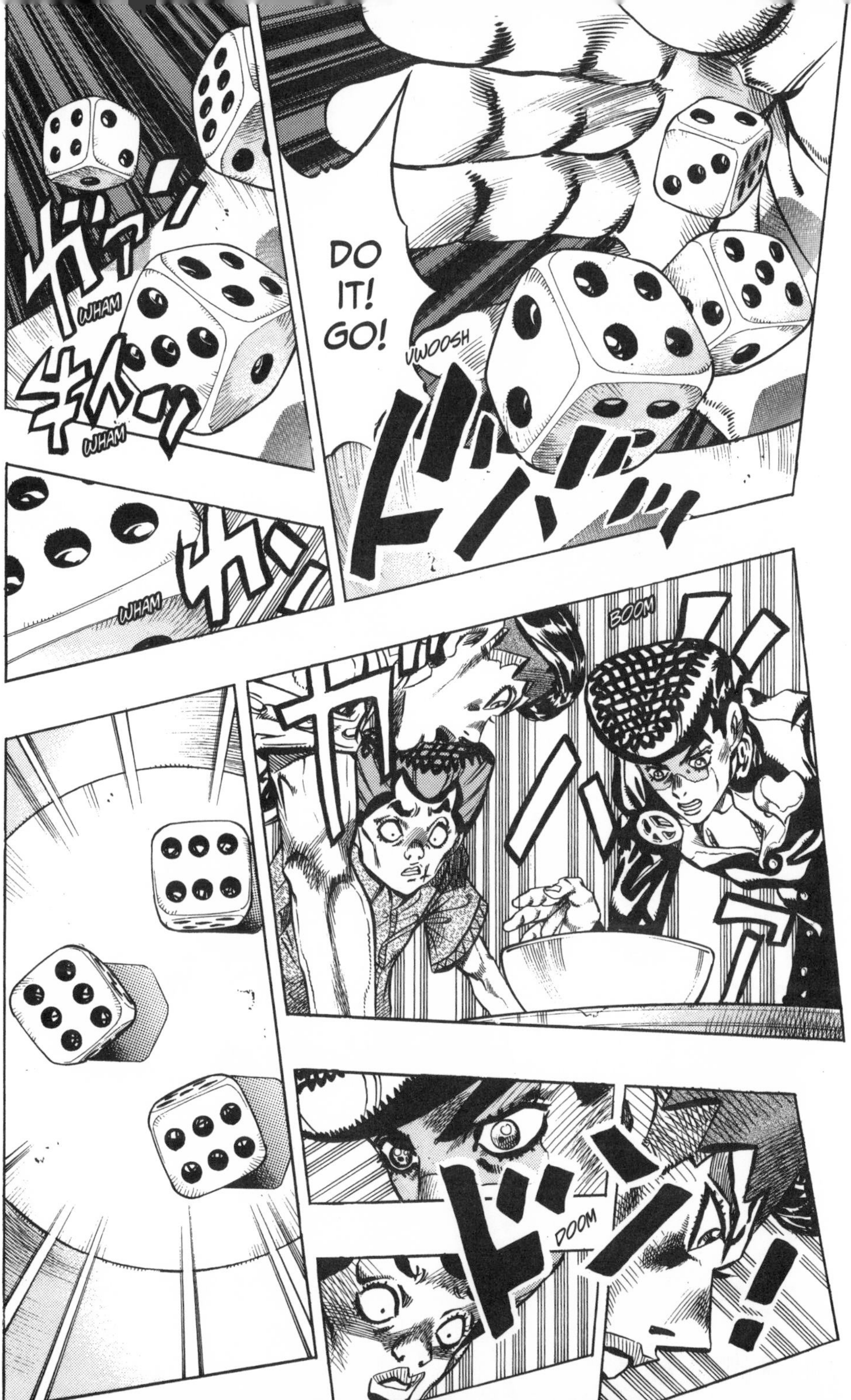
DO IT! GO!
VWOOSH
WHAM
WHAM
WHAM
BOOM
DOOM

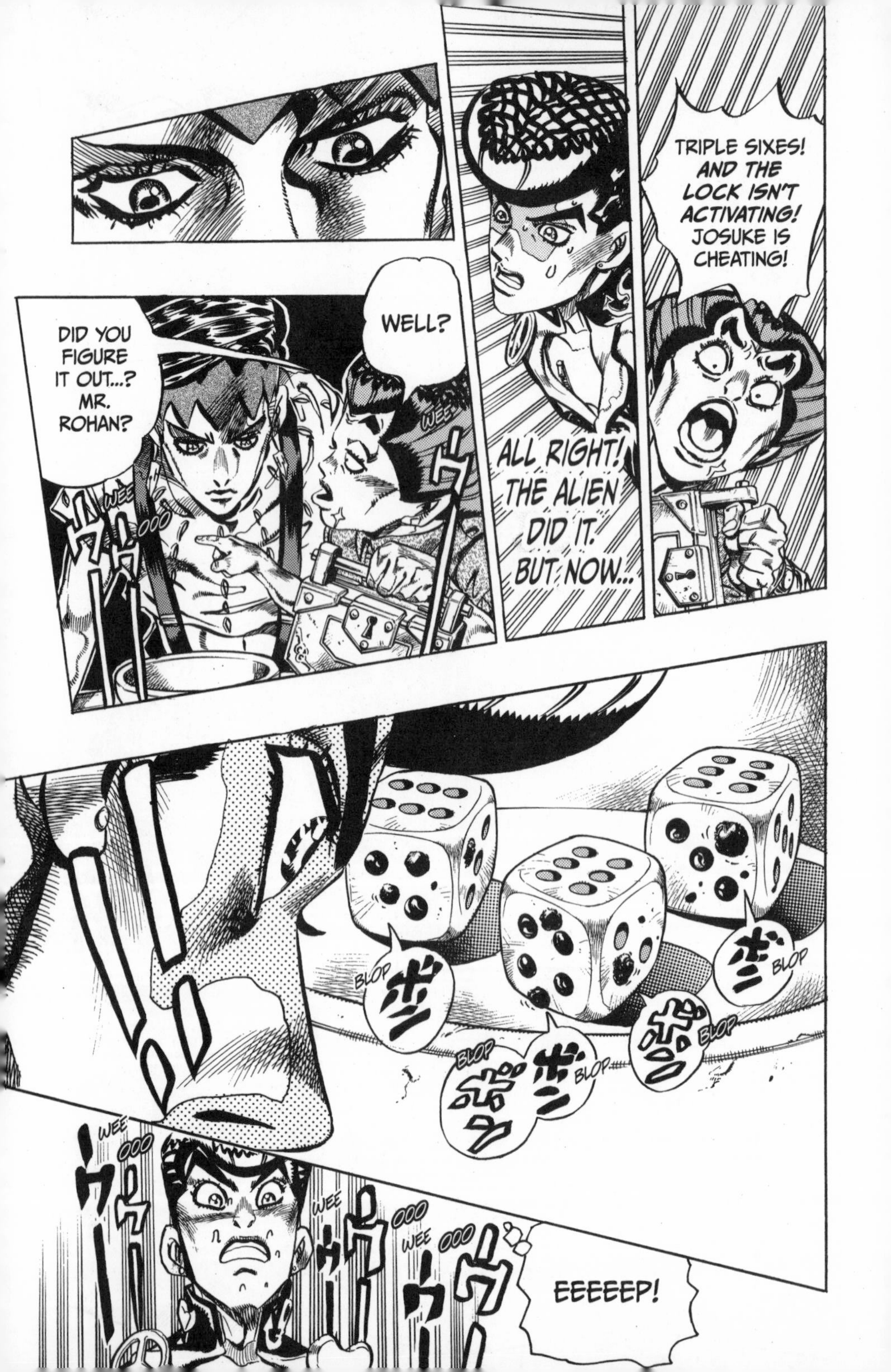
TRIPLE SIXES! AND THE LOCK ISN'T ACTIVATING! JOSUKE IS CHEATING!
ALL RIGHT! THE ALIEN DID IT. BUT NOW...
WELL?
DID YOU FIGURE IT OUT...? MR. ROHAN?
WEE
WEE OOO
BLOP
BLOP
BLOP
BLOP
BLOP
WEE OOO
WEE OOO
WEE OOO
EEEEEP!

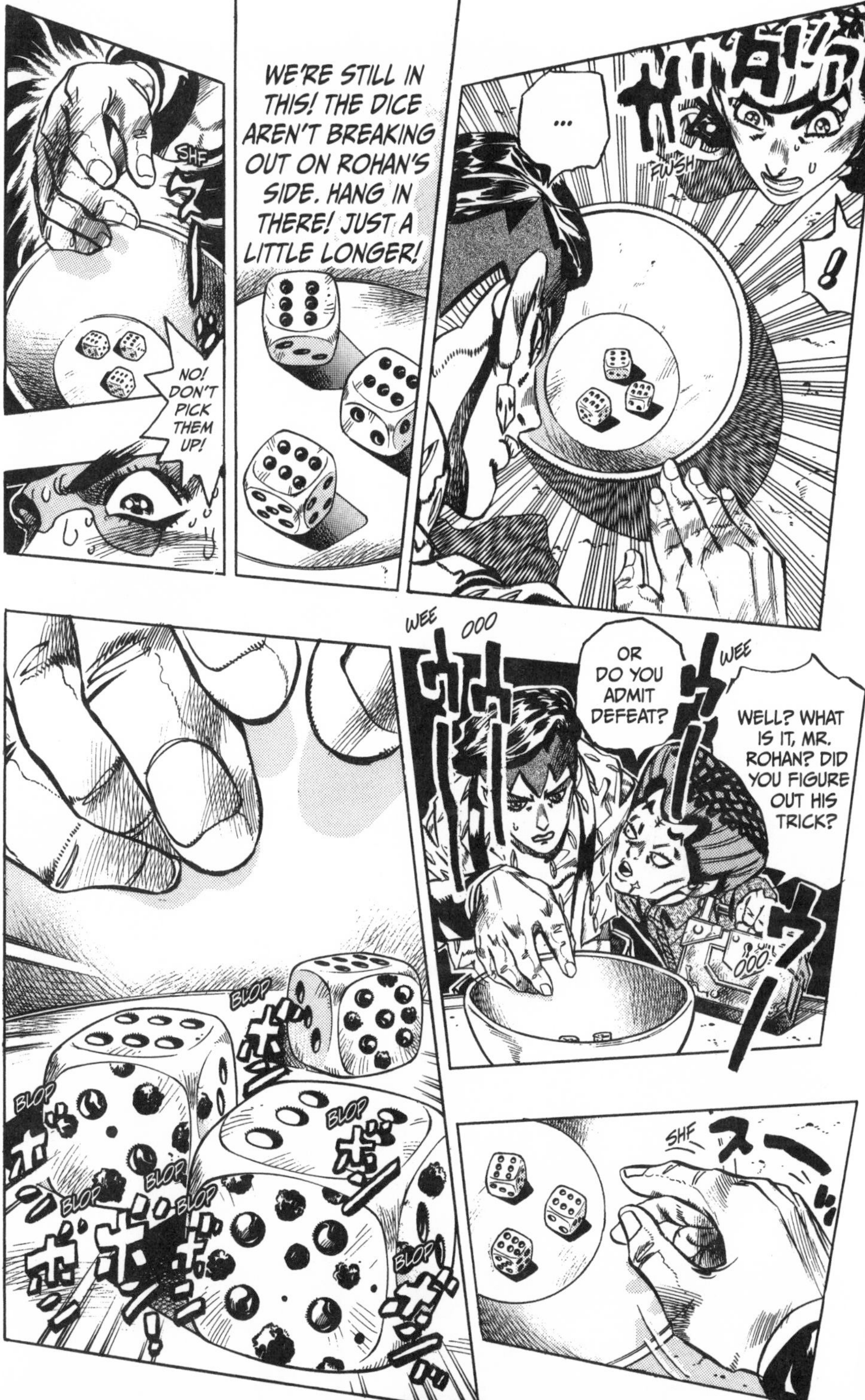
...
FWSH
!
WE'RE STILL IN THIS! THE DICE AREN'T BREAKING OUT ON ROHAN'S SIDE. HANG IN THERE! JUST A LITTLE LONGER!
SHF
NO! DON'T PICK THEM UP!
WEE
OOO
WELL? WHAT IS IT, MR. ROHAN? DID YOU FIGURE OUT HIS TRICK?
OR DO YOU ADMIT DEFEAT?
WEE
OOO
SHF
BLOP
BLOP
BLOP
BLOP
BLOP
BLOP

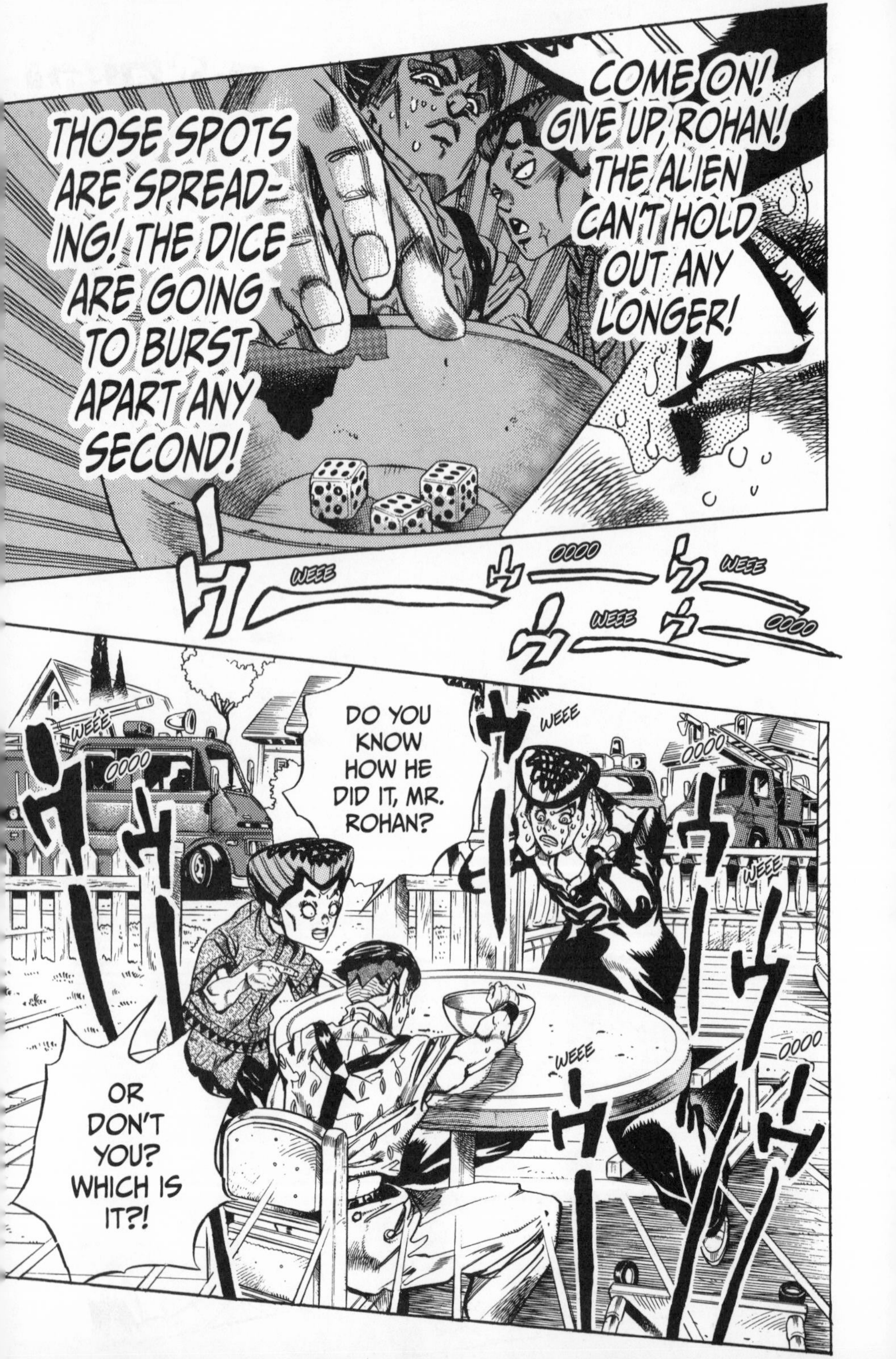
COME ON! GIVE UP, ROHAN! THE ALIEN CAN'T HOLD OUT ANY LONGER!
THOSE SPOTS ARE SPREAD-ING! THE DICE ARE GOING TO BURST APART ANY SECOND!
WEEE
OOOO
WEEE
WEEE
OOOO
WEEE
OOOO
DO YOU KNOW HOW HE DID IT, MR. ROHAN?
WEEE
OOOO
WEEE
OOOO
WEEE
OR DON'T YOU? WHICH IS IT?!

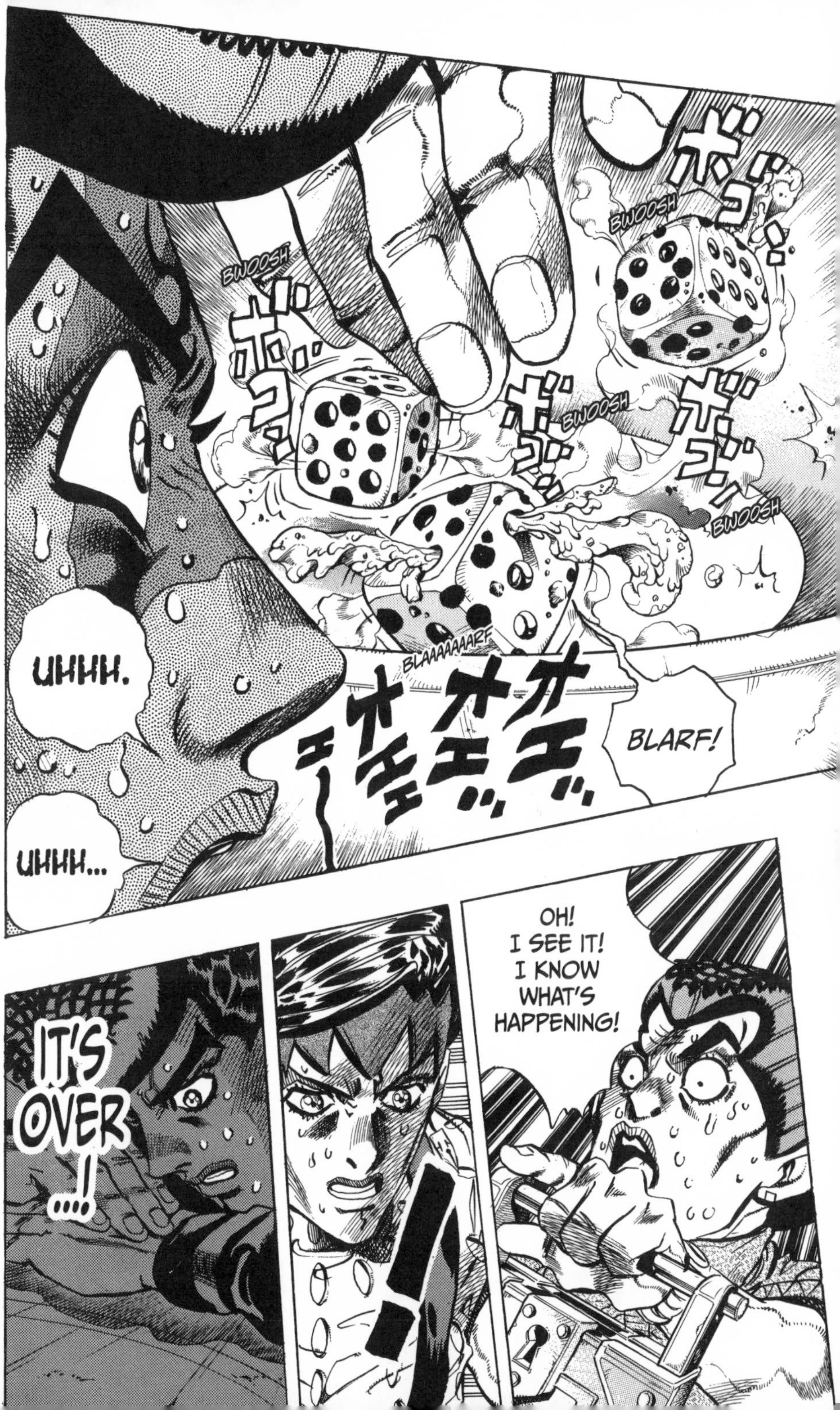
BWOOSH
BWOOSH
BWOOSH
BWOOSH
BLAAAAAAARF
BLARF!
UHHH.
UHHH...
OH! I SEE IT! I KNOW WHAT'S HAPPENING!
IT'S OVER ...!

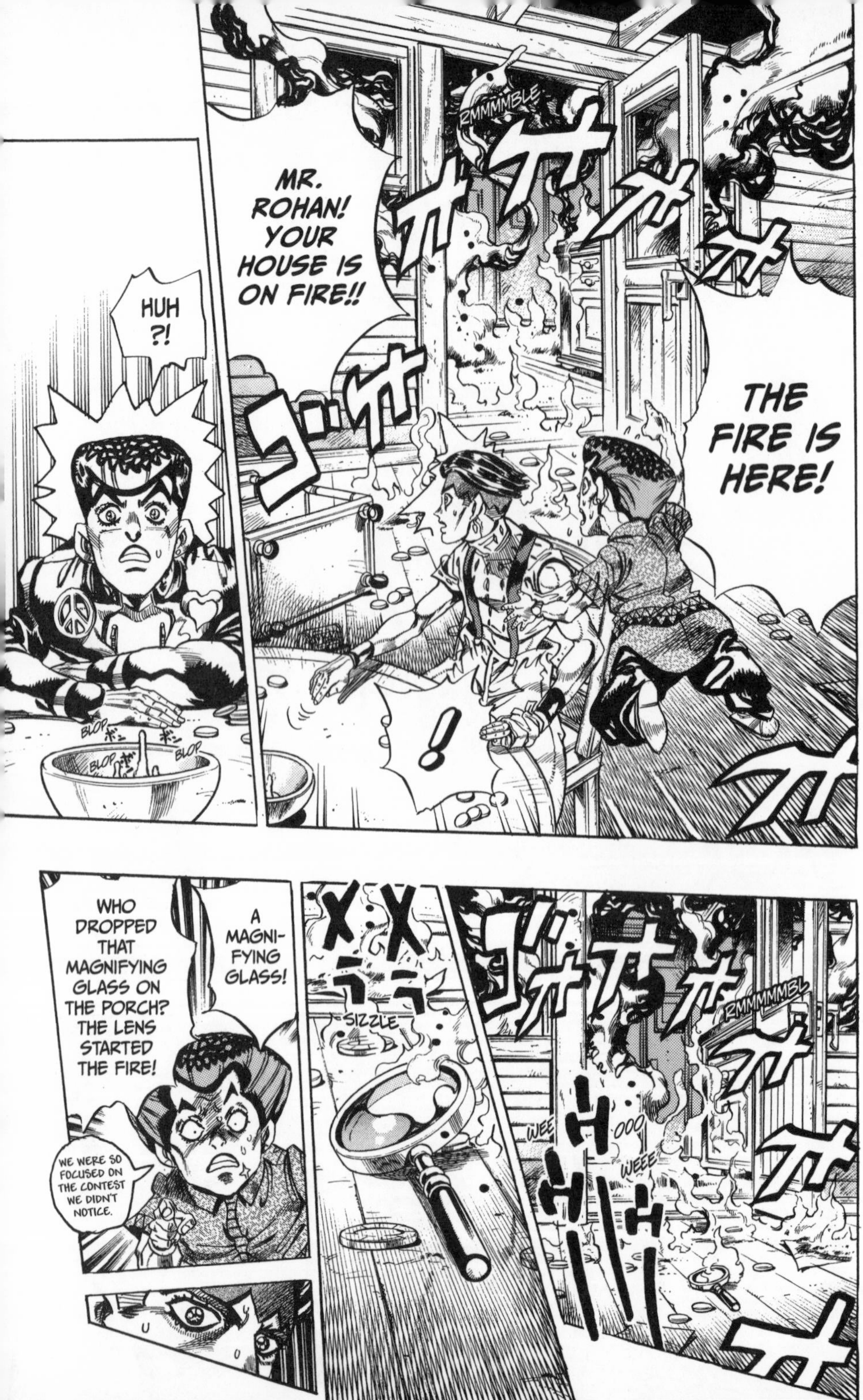
RMMMMBLE
MR. ROHAN! YOUR HOUSE IS ON FIRE!!
THE FIRE IS HERE!
!
HUH ?!
BLOP
BLOP
BLOP
RMMMMMBL
WEEE
OOO
WEEE
SIZZLE
A MAGNI-FYING GLASS!
WHO DROPPED THAT MAGNIFYING GLASS ON THE PORCH? THE LENS STARTED THE FIRE!
WE WERE SO FOCUSED ON THE CONTEST WE DIDN'T NOTICE.

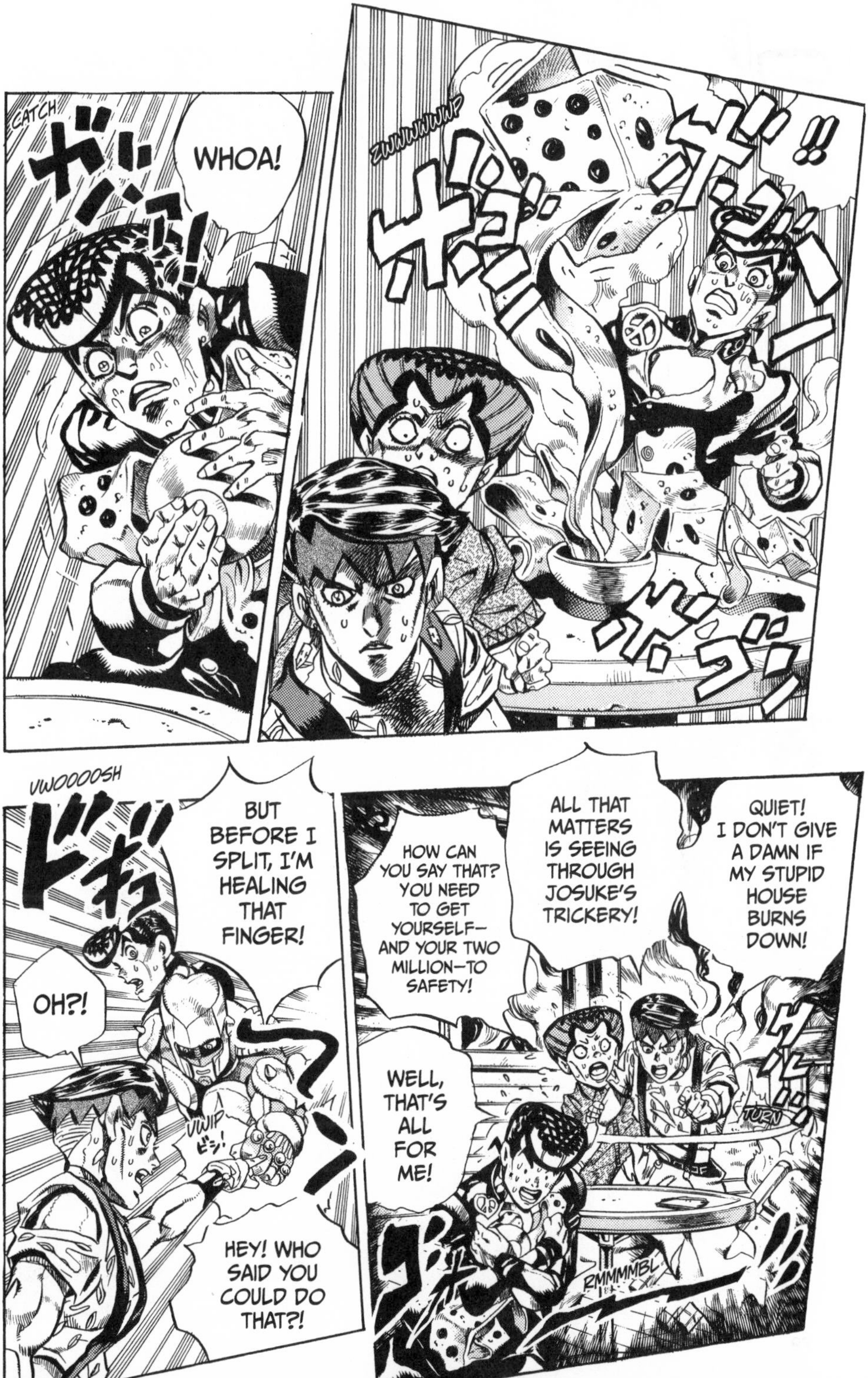
ZWWWWWWWP
CATCH
WHOA!
QUIET! I DON'T GIVE A DAMN IF MY STUPID HOUSE BURNS DOWN!
ALL THAT MATTERS IS SEEING THROUGH JOSUKE'S TRICKERY!
HOW CAN YOU SAY THAT? YOU NEED TO GET YOURSELF—AND YOUR TWO MILLION—TO SAFETY!
TURN
WELL, THAT'S ALL FOR ME!
RMMMMBL
BUT BEFORE I SPLIT, I'M HEALING THAT FINGER!
VWOOOOSH
OH?!
VWIP
HEY! WHO SAID YOU COULD DO THAT?!

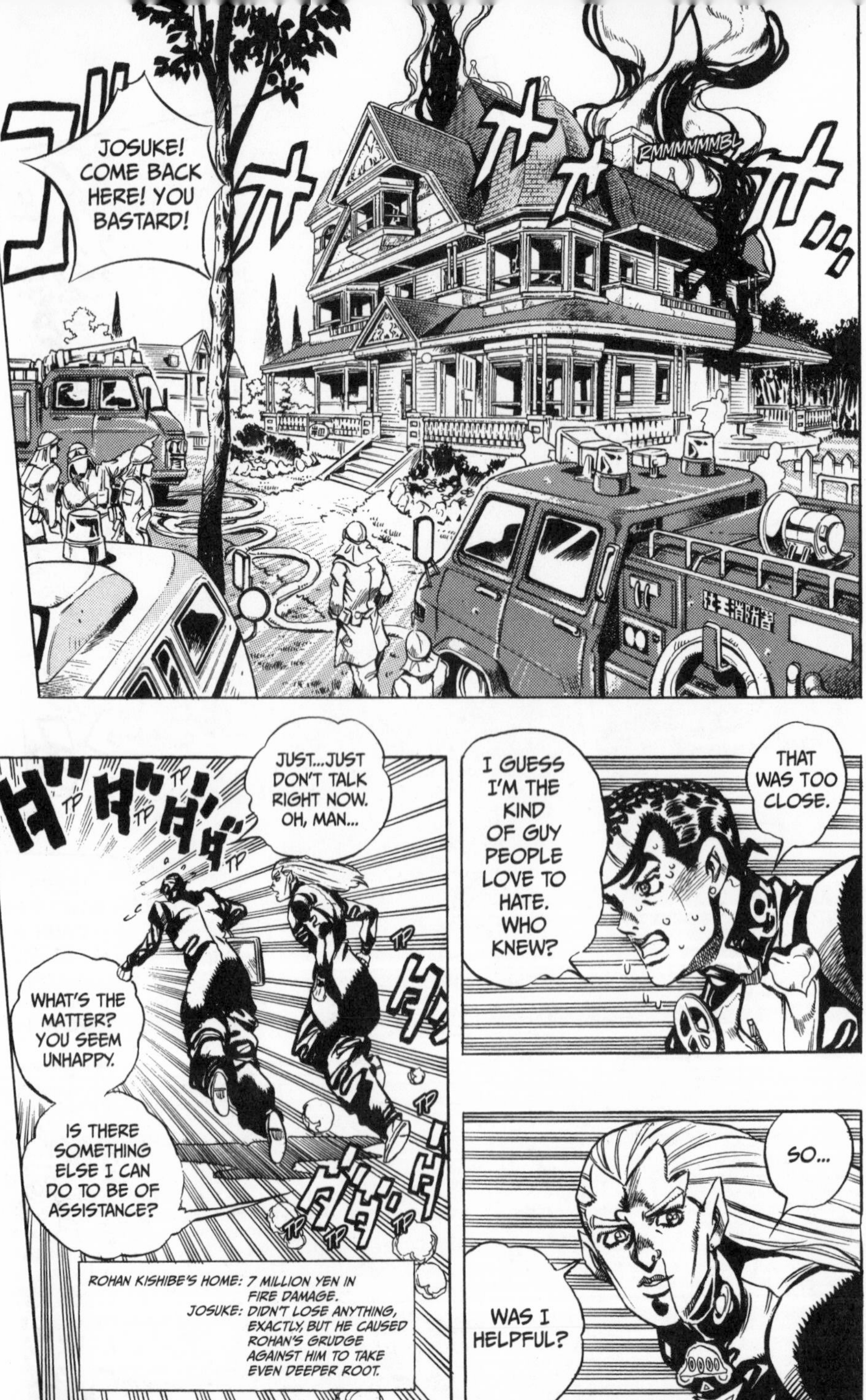
RMMMMMMBL
JOSUKE! COME BACK HERE! YOU BASTARD!
THAT WAS TOO CLOSE.
I GUESS I'M THE KIND OF GUY PEOPLE LOVE TO HATE. WHO KNEW?
SO...
WAS I HELPFUL?
JUST...JUST DON'T TALK RIGHT NOW. OH, MAN...
WHAT'S THE MATTER? YOU SEEM UNHAPPY.
IS THERE SOMETHING ELSE I CAN DO TO BE OF ASSISTANCE?
ROHAN KISHIBE'S HOME: 7 MILLION YEN IN FIRE DAMAGE.
JOSUKE: DIDN'T LOSE ANYTHING, EXACTLY, BUT HE CAUSED ROHAN'S GRUDGE AGAINST HIM TO TAKE EVEN DEEPER ROOT.

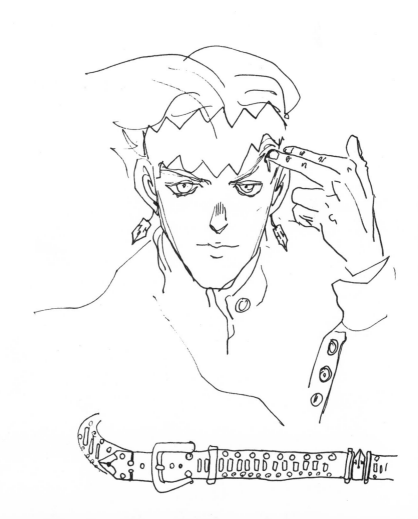

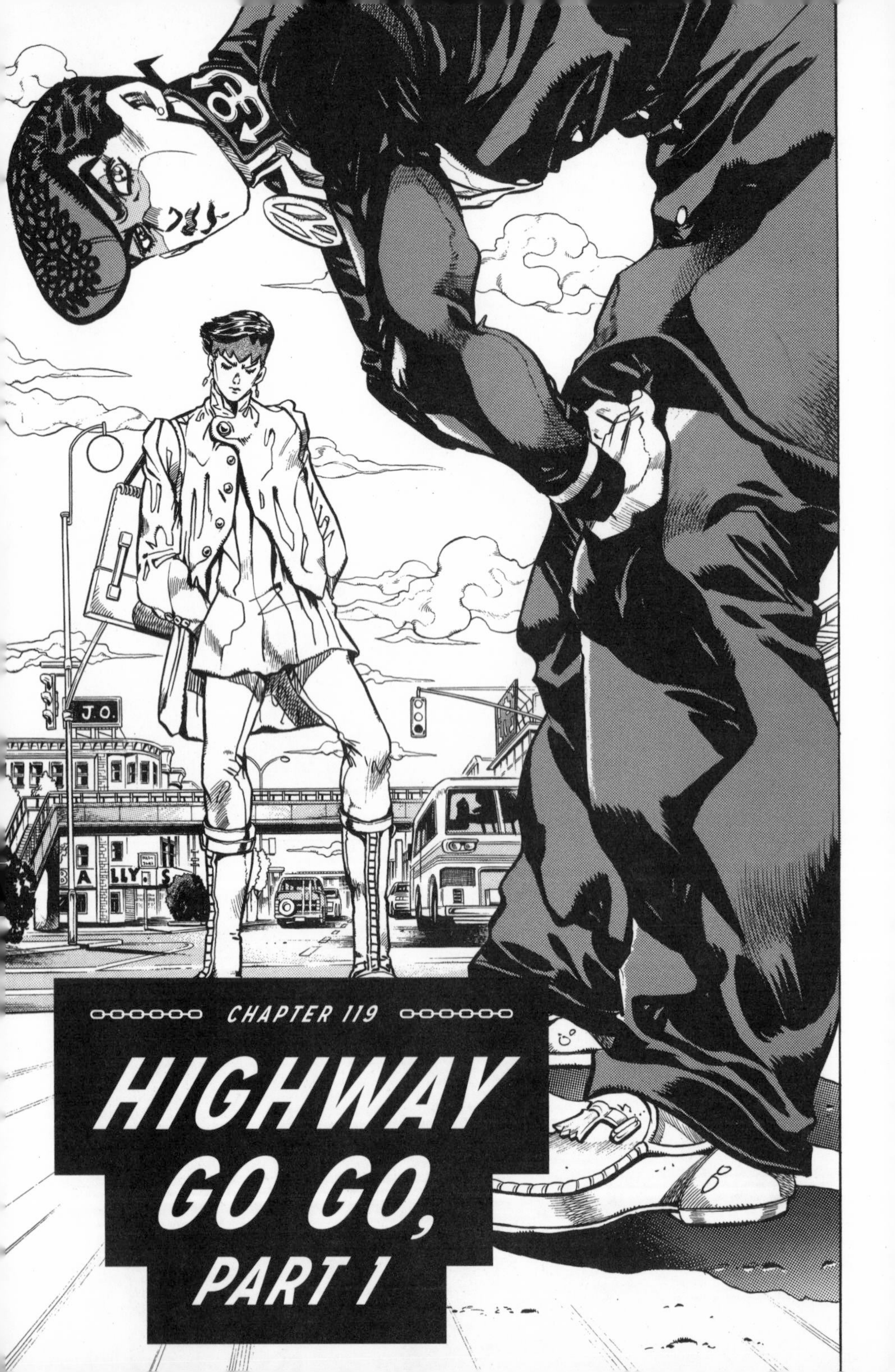
J.O.
CHAPTER 119
HIGHWAY GO GO, PART 1

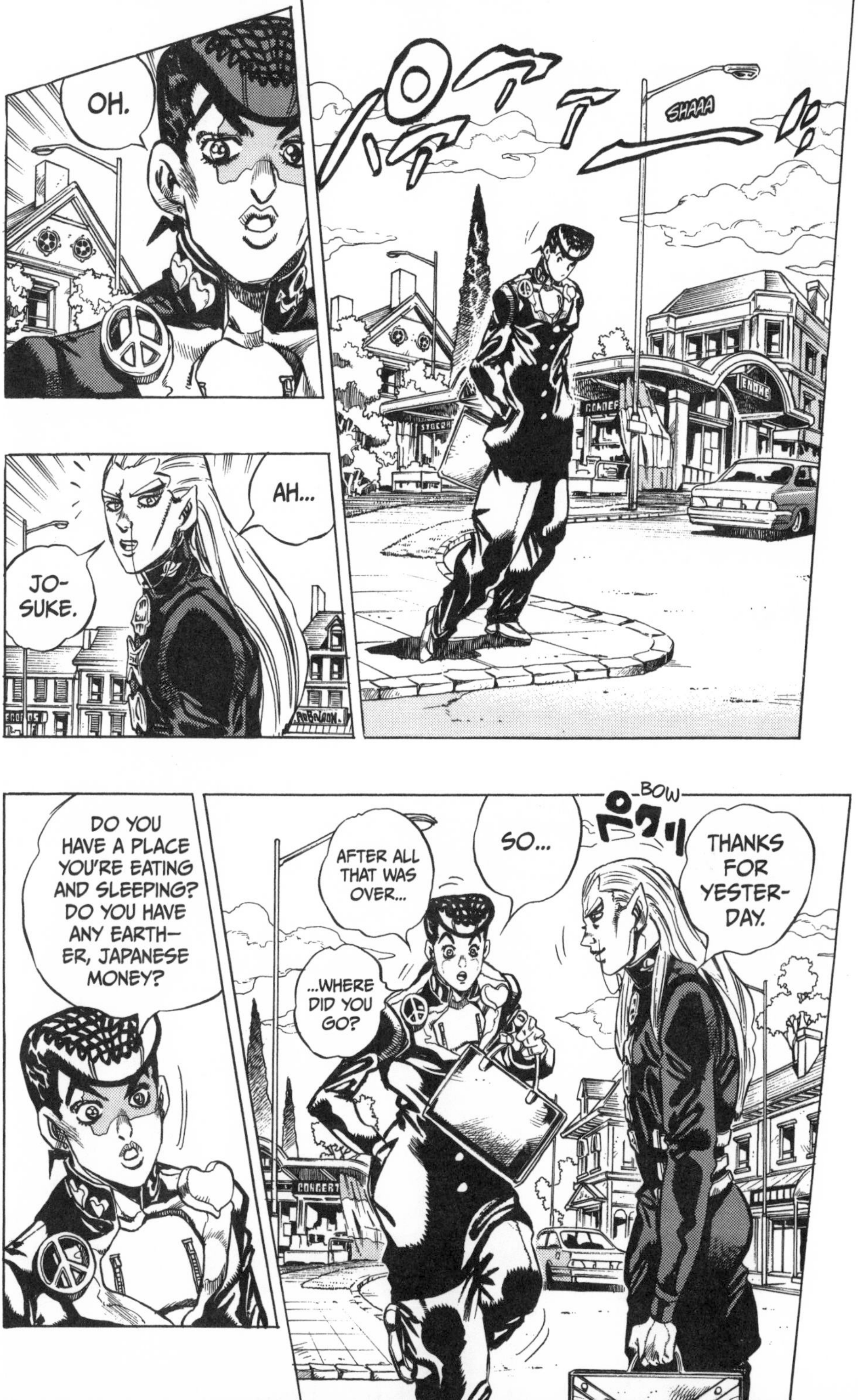
SHAAA
OH.
AH...
JO-SUKE.
BOW
THANKS FOR YESTER-DAY.
SO...
AFTER ALL THAT WAS OVER...
...WHERE DID YOU GO?
DO YOU HAVE A PLACE YOU'RE EATING AND SLEEPING? DO YOU HAVE ANY EARTH— ER, JAPANESE MONEY?

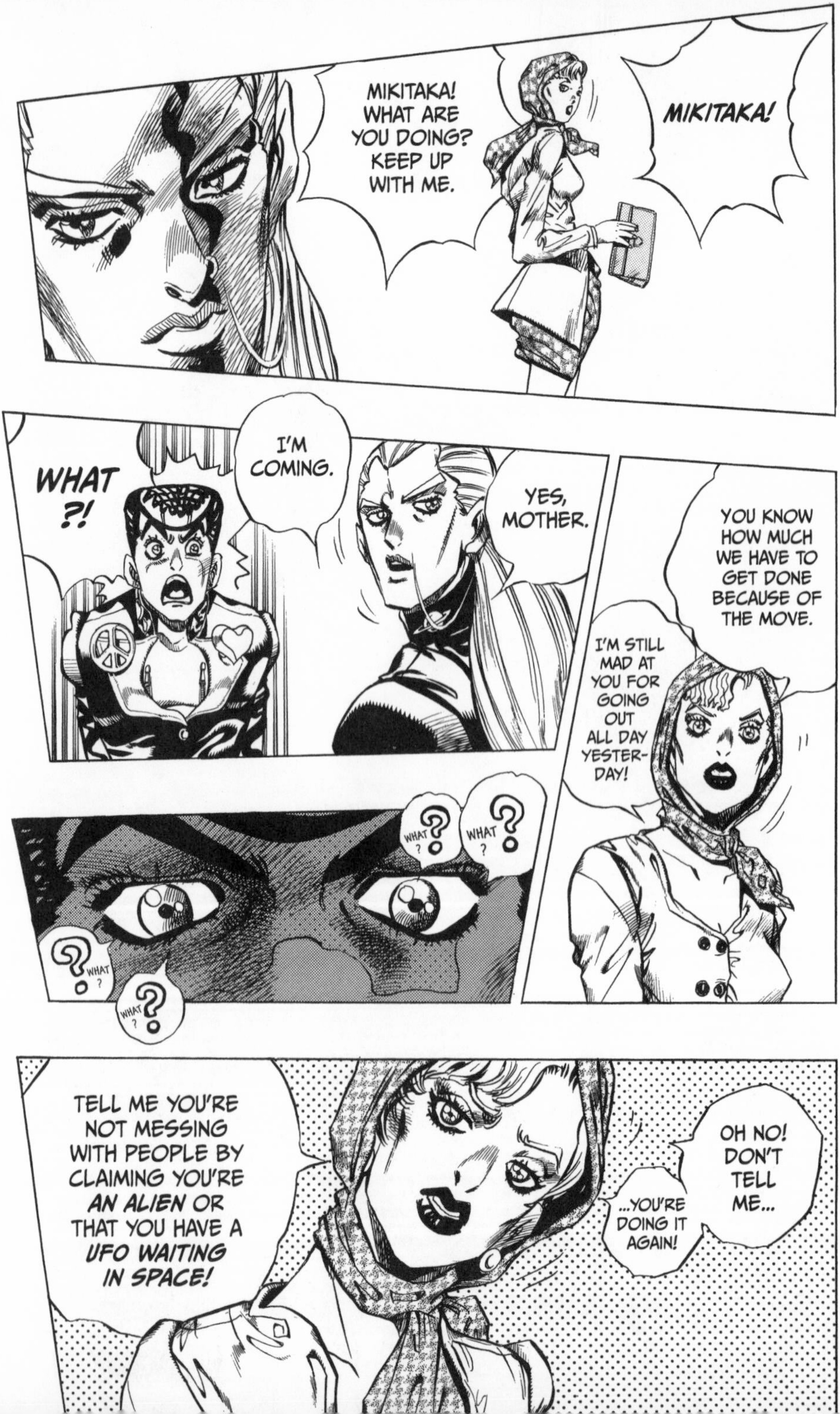

MIKITAKA!
MIKITAKA! WHAT ARE YOU DOING? KEEP UP WITH ME.
YOU KNOW HOW MUCH WE HAVE TO GET DONE BECAUSE OF THE MOVE.
I'M STILL MAD AT YOU FOR GOING OUT ALL DAY YESTER-DAY!
YES, MOTHER.
I'M COMING.
WHAT ?!
WHAT ?
WHAT ?
WHAT ?
WHAT ?
OH NO! DON'T TELL ME...
...YOU'RE DOING IT AGAIN!
TELL ME YOU'RE NOT MESSING WITH PEOPLE BY CLAIMING YOU'RE AN ALIEN OR THAT YOU HAVE A UFO WAITING IN SPACE!

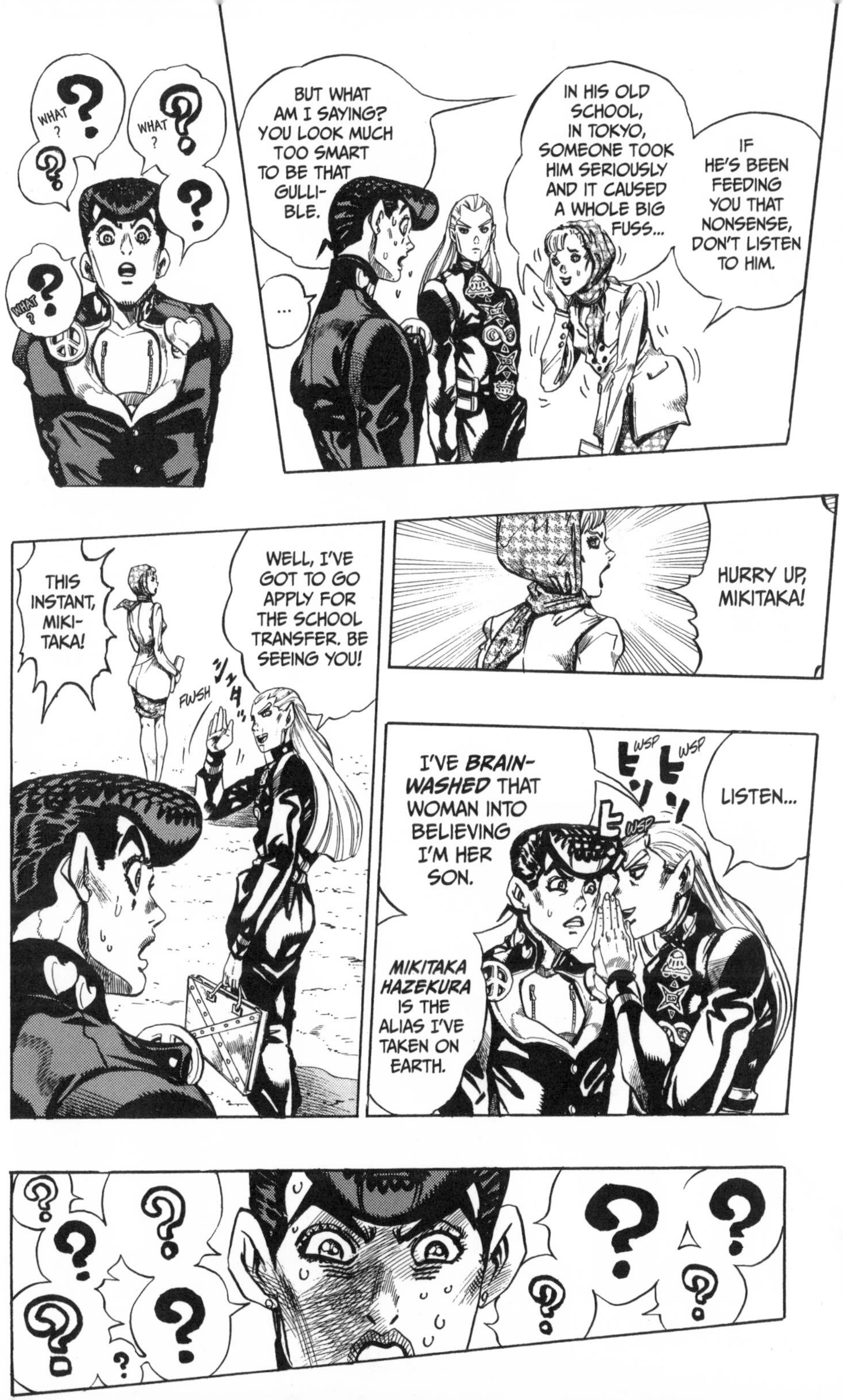
IF HE'S BEEN FEEDING YOU THAT NONSENSE, DON'T LISTEN TO HIM.
IN HIS OLD SCHOOL, IN TOKYO, SOMEONE TOOK HIM SERIOUSLY AND IT CAUSED A WHOLE BIG FUSS...
BUT WHAT AM I SAYING? YOU LOOK MUCH TOO SMART TO BE THAT GULLI-BLE.
...
WHAT ?
WHAT ?
WHAT ?
HURRY UP, MIKITAKA!
LISTEN...
WSP
WSP
WSP
I'VE ***BRAIN-WASHED*** THAT WOMAN INTO BELIEVING I'M HER SON.
MIKITAKA HAZEKURA IS THE ALIAS I'VE TAKEN ON EARTH.
WELL, I'VE GOT TO GO APPLY FOR THE SCHOOL TRANSFER. BE SEEING YOU!
FWSH
THIS INSTANT, MIKI-TAKA!

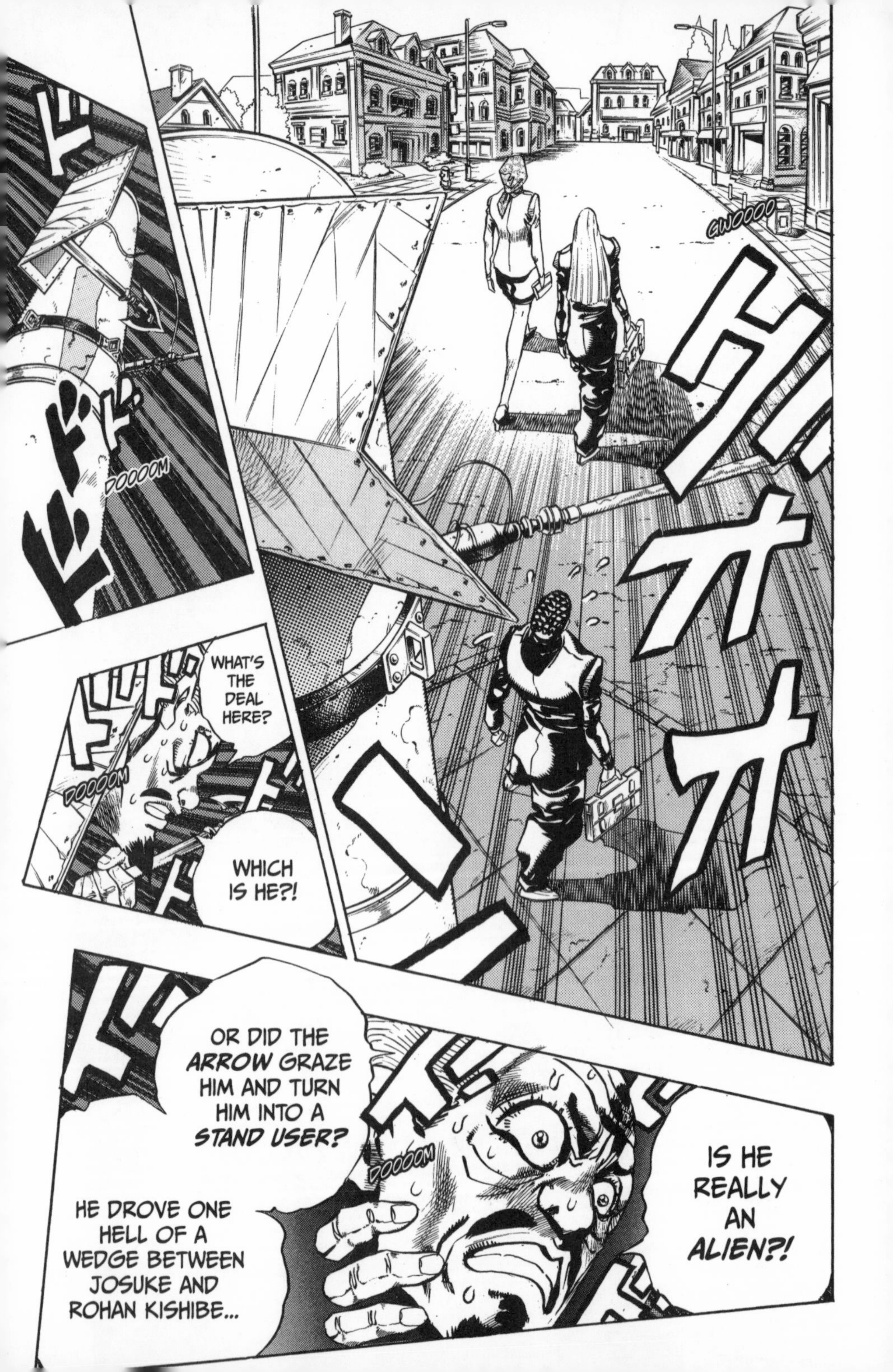
GWOOOO
DOOOOM
WHAT'S THE DEAL HERE?
DOOOOM
WHICH IS HE?!
IS HE REALLY AN *ALIEN*?!
DOOOOM
OR DID THE *ARROW* GRAZE HIM AND TURN HIM INTO A *STAND USER?*
HE DROVE ONE HELL OF A WEDGE BETWEEN JOSUKE AND ROHAN KISHIBE...

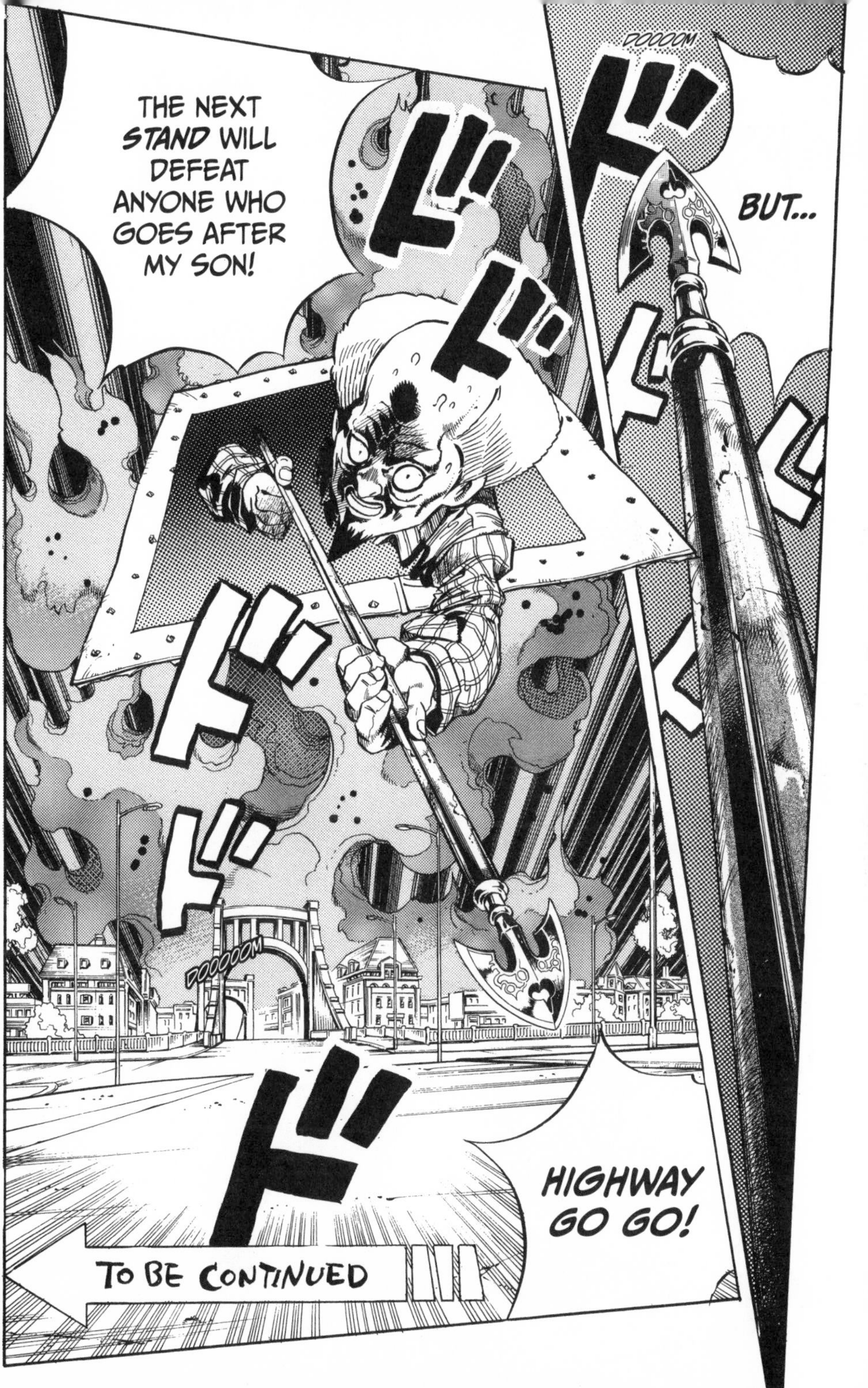
DOOOOM
BUT...
THE NEXT STAND WILL DEFEAT ANYONE WHO GOES AFTER MY SON!
DOOOOOM
HIGHWAY GO GO!
TO BE CONTINUED

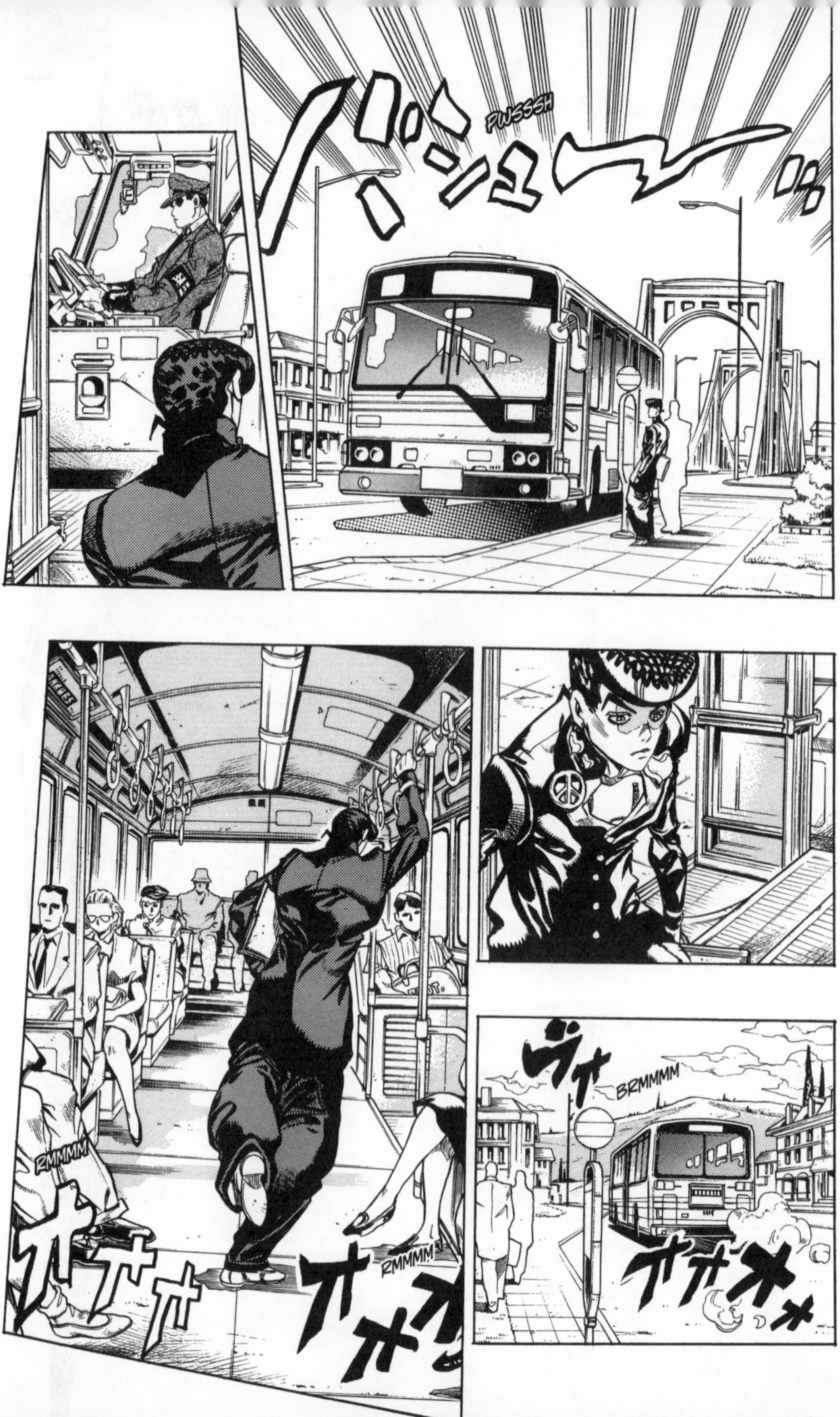
PWSSSH
BRMMMM
RMMMM
RMMMM

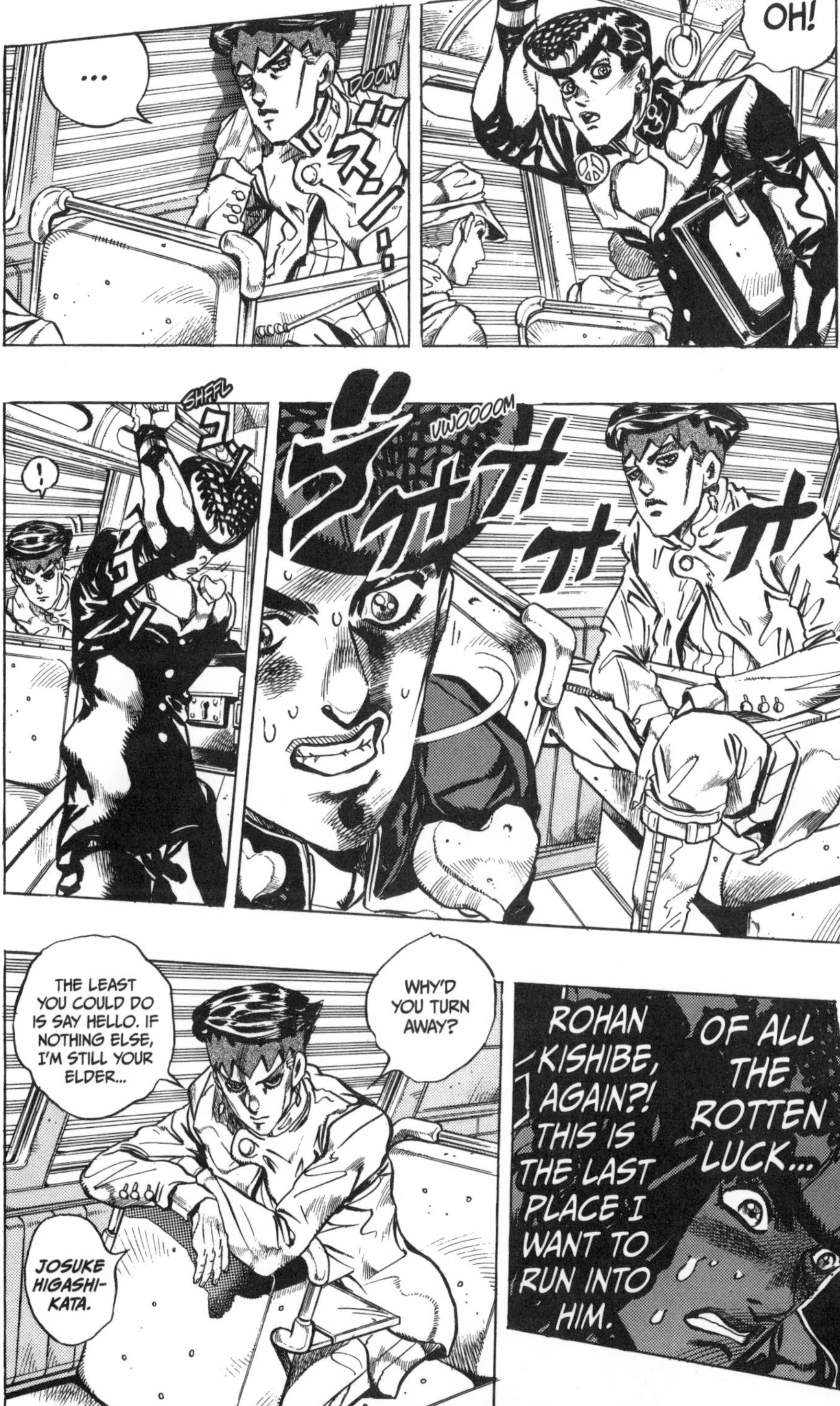
OH!
...
DOOM
VWOOOOM
SHFFL
!
OF ALL THE ROTTEN LUCK...
ROHAN KISHIBE, AGAIN?! THIS IS THE LAST PLACE I WANT TO RUN INTO HIM.
WHY'D YOU TURN AWAY?
THE LEAST YOU COULD DO IS SAY HELLO. IF NOTHING ELSE, I'M STILL YOUR ELDER...
JOSUKE HIGASHI-KATA.

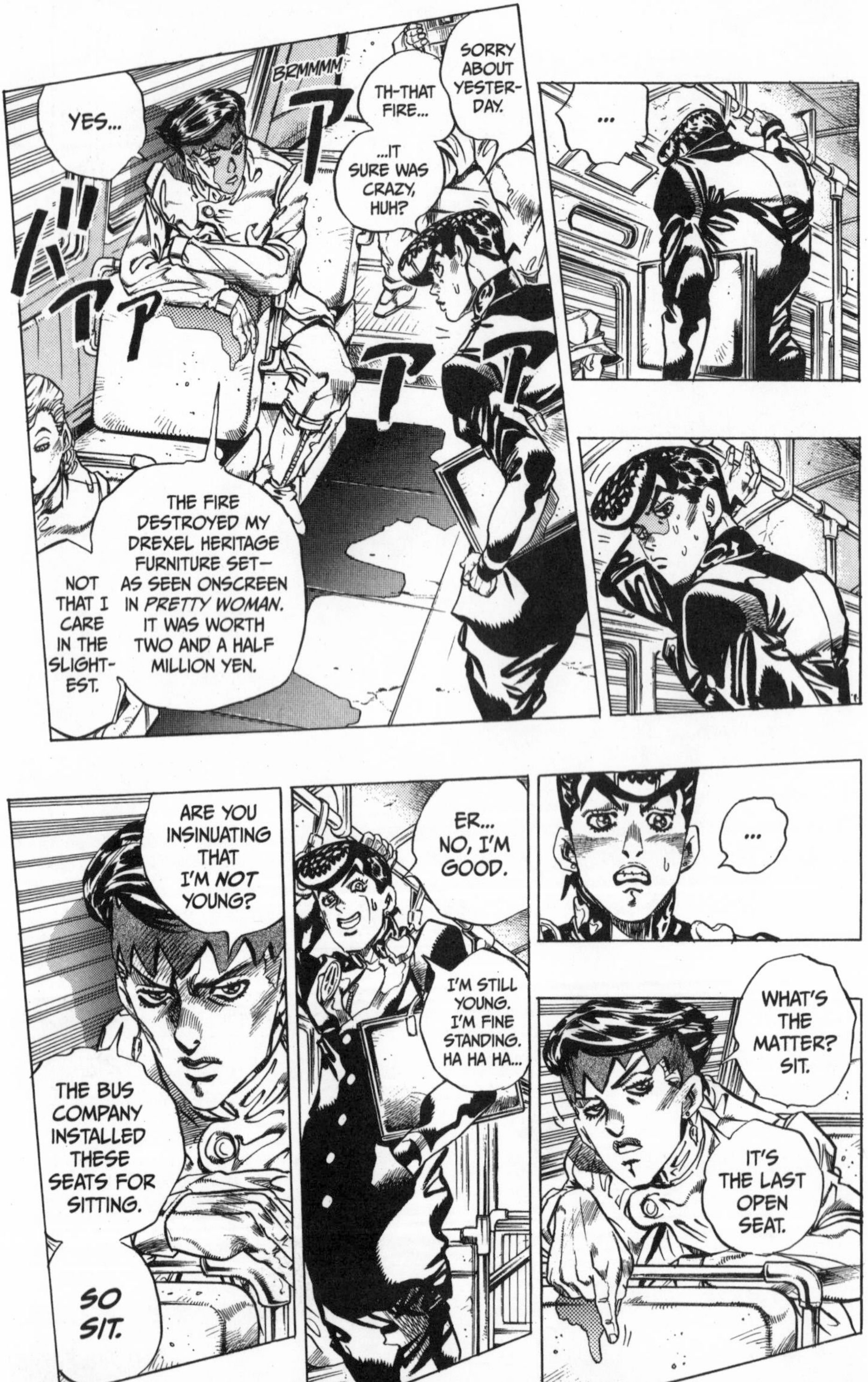
...
SORRY ABOUT YESTER-DAY.
TH-THAT FIRE...
...IT SURE WAS CRAZY, HUH?
BRMMMM
YES...
THE FIRE DESTROYED MY DREXEL HERITAGE FURNITURE SET—AS SEEN ONSCREEN IN *PRETTY WOMAN*. IT WAS WORTH TWO AND A HALF MILLION YEN.
NOT THAT I CARE IN THE SLIGHT-EST.
...
WHAT'S THE MATTER? SIT.
IT'S THE LAST OPEN SEAT.
ER... NO, I'M GOOD.
I'M STILL YOUNG. I'M FINE STANDING. HA HA HA...
ARE YOU INSINUATING THAT I'M *NOT* YOUNG?
THE BUS COMPANY INSTALLED THESE SEATS FOR SITTING.
SO SIT.

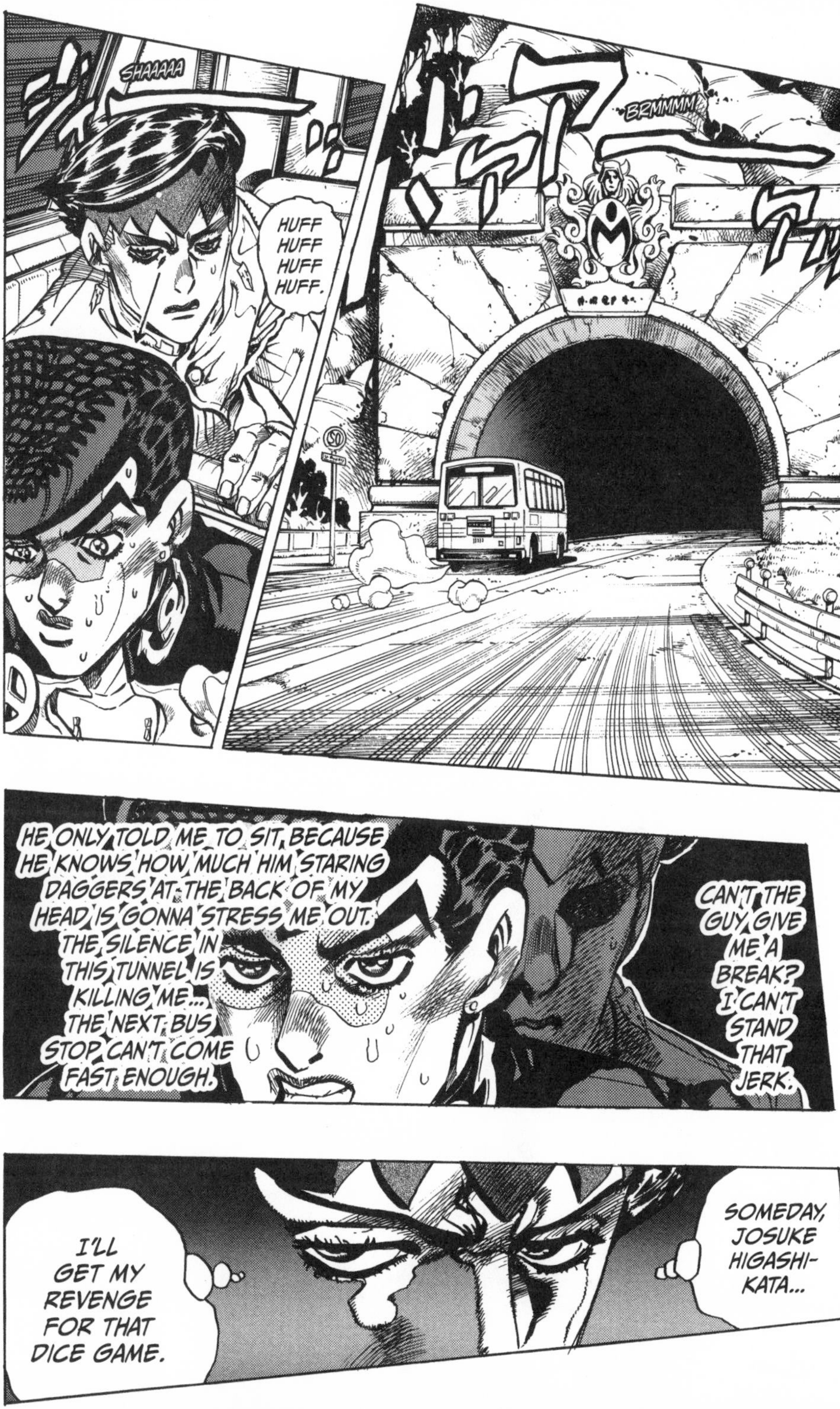
BRMMMM
SHAAAAA
HUFF HUFF HUFF HUFF.
CAN'T THE GUY GIVE ME A BREAK? I CAN'T STAND THAT JERK.
HE ONLY TOLD ME TO SIT BECAUSE HE KNOWS HOW MUCH HIM STARING DAGGERS AT THE BACK OF MY HEAD IS GONNA STRESS ME OUT.
THE SILENCE IN THIS TUNNEL IS KILLING ME... THE NEXT BUS STOP CAN'T COME FAST ENOUGH.
SOMEDAY, JOSUKE HIGASHI-KATA...
I'LL GET MY REVENGE FOR THAT DICE GAME.

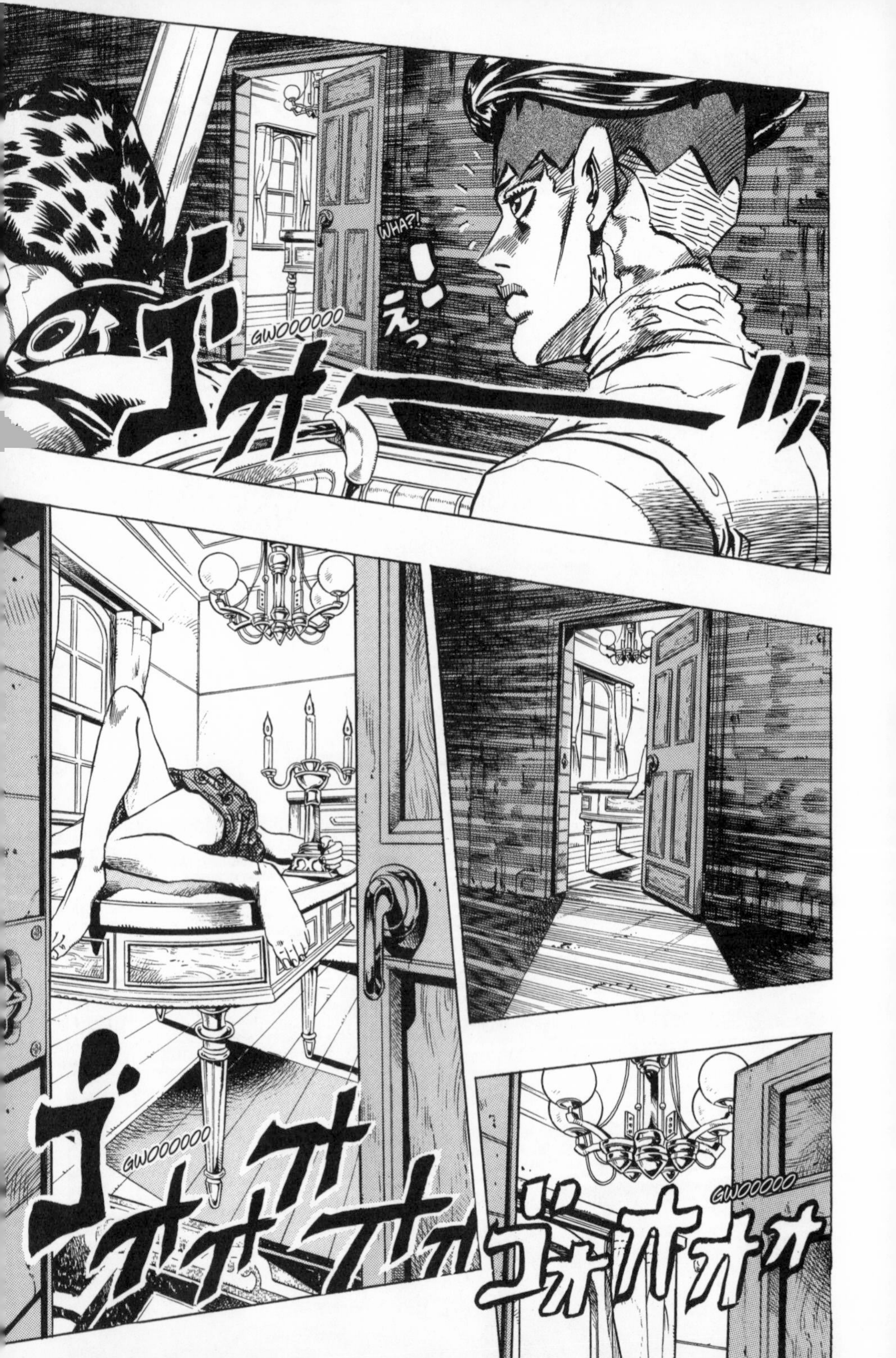
WHA?!
えっ
GWOOOOOO
ゴオオーーーッ
GWOOOOO
ゴォオオオオ
GWOOOOOO
ゴオオオオオ

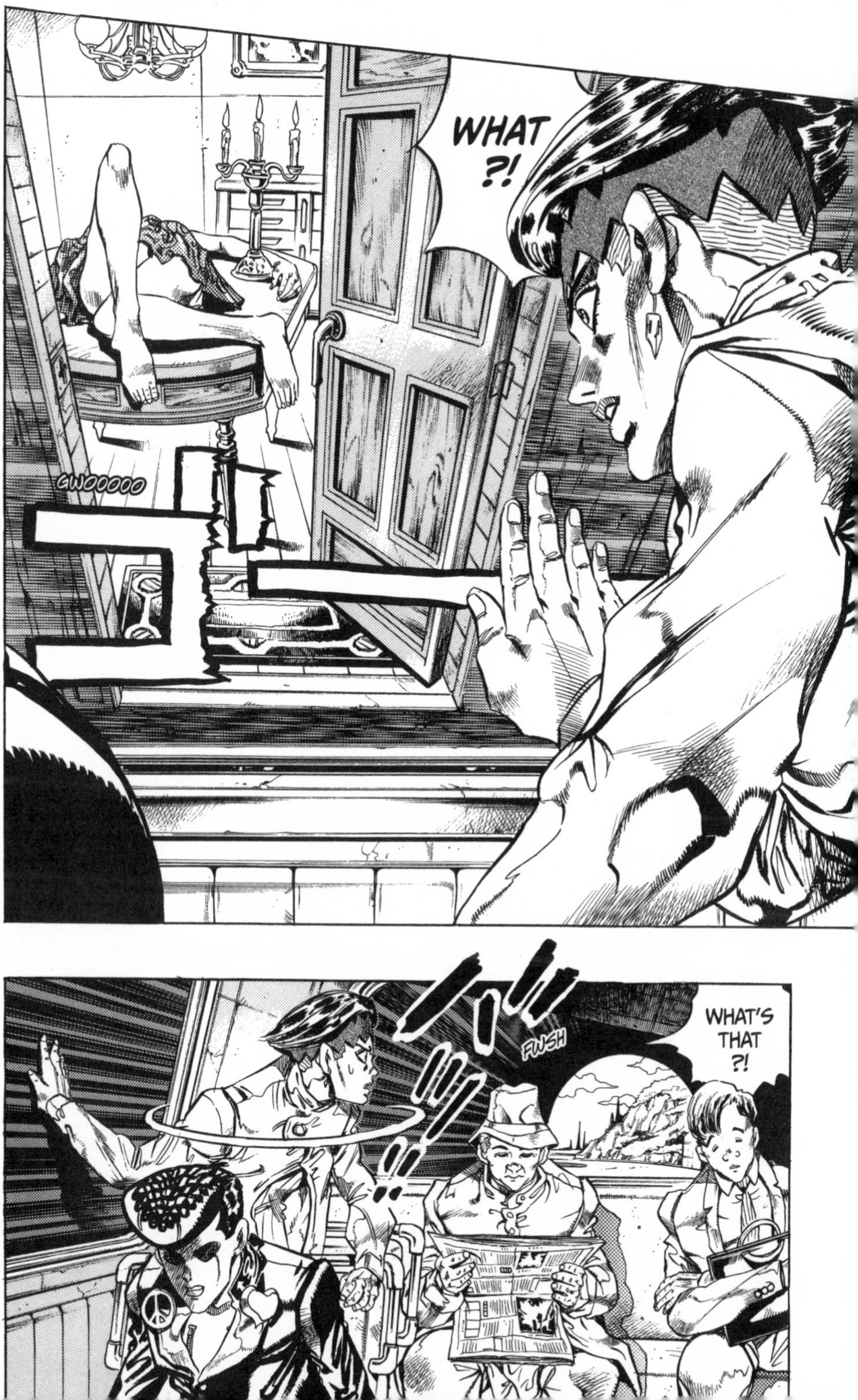
WHAT ?!
GWOOOOO
WHAT'S THAT ?!
FWSH

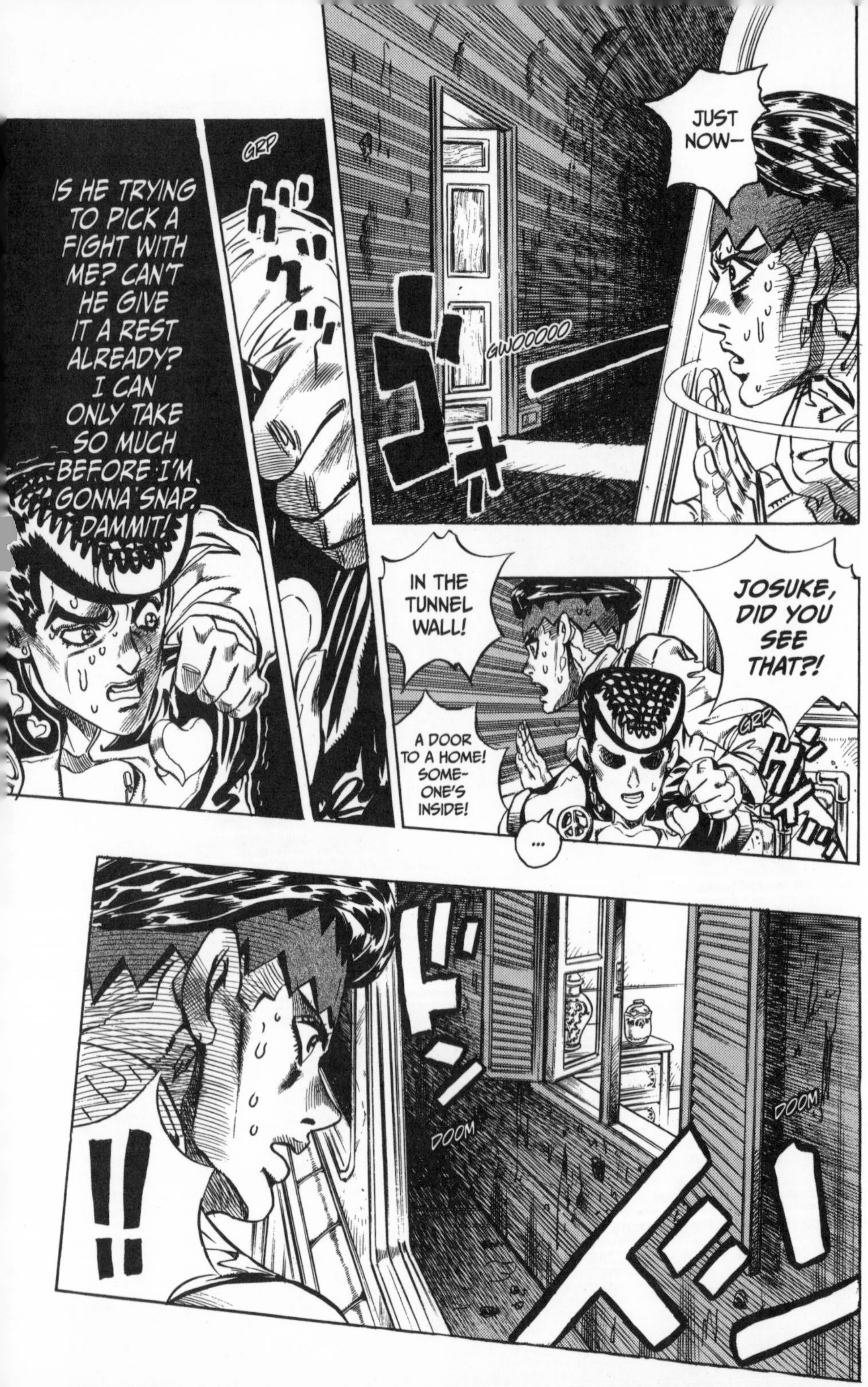

JUST NOW—
GWOOOOO
JOSUKE, DID YOU SEE THAT?!
IN THE TUNNEL WALL!
A DOOR TO A HOME! SOME-ONE'S INSIDE!
GRP
...
GRP
IS HE TRYING TO PICK A FIGHT WITH ME? CAN'T HE GIVE IT A REST ALREADY? I CAN ONLY TAKE SO MUCH BEFORE I'M GONNA SNAP, DAMMIT!
DOOM
DOOM
!!

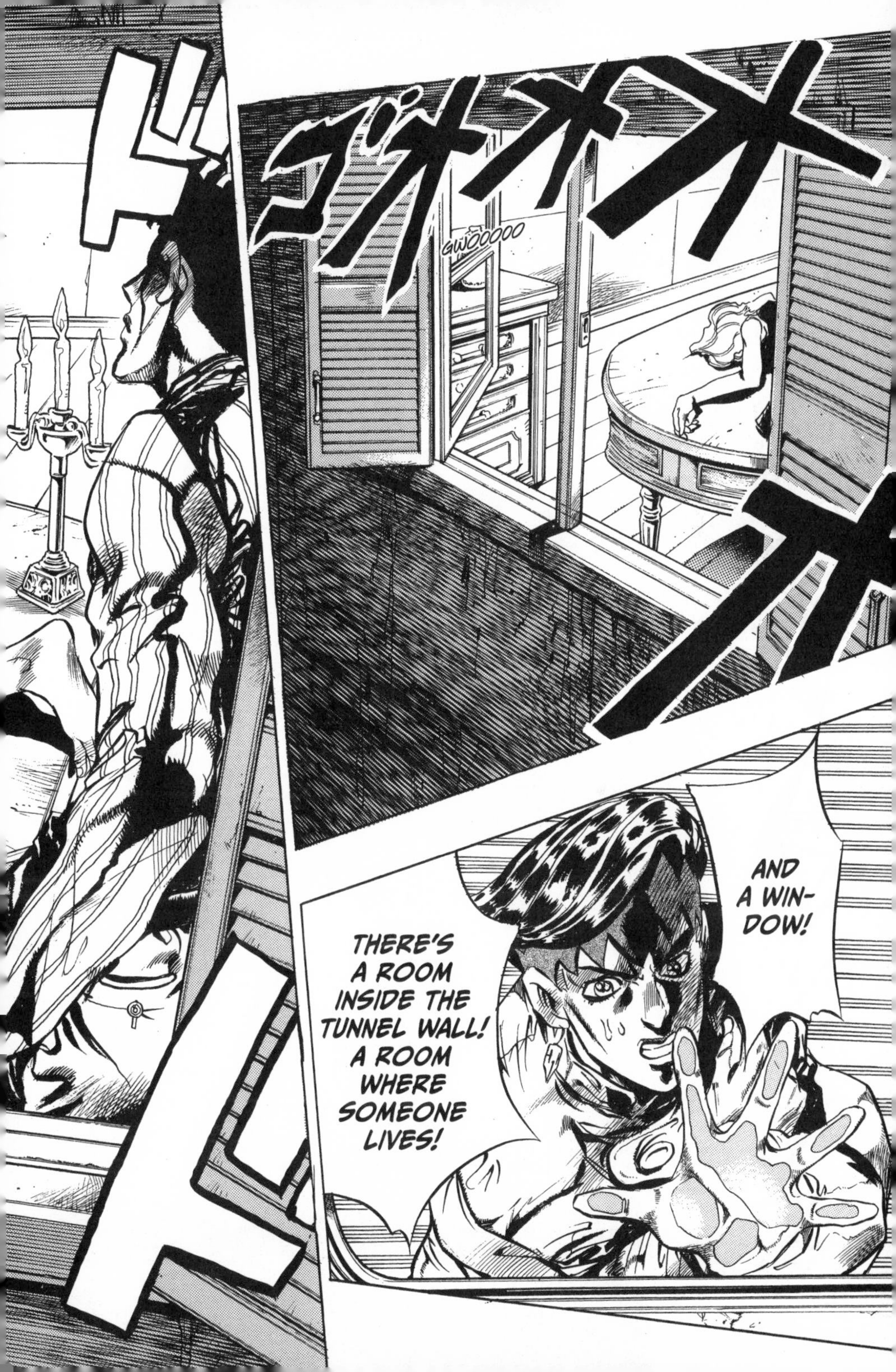
ゴオオオオ
GWOOOOO
THERE'S A ROOM INSIDE THE TUNNEL WALL! A ROOM WHERE SOMEONE LIVES!
AND A WIN-DOW!
ドド

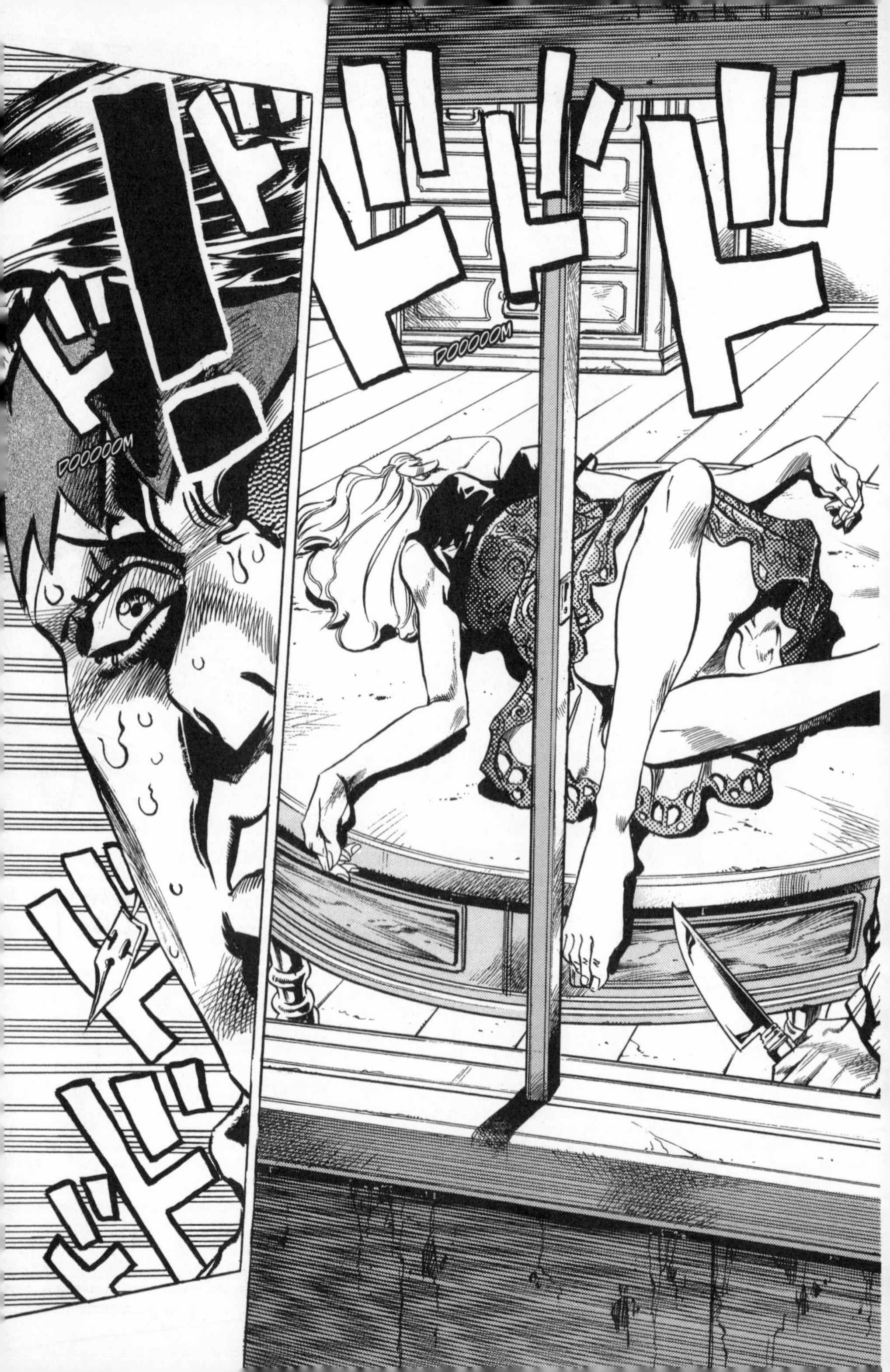
DOOOOOM
DOOOOOM

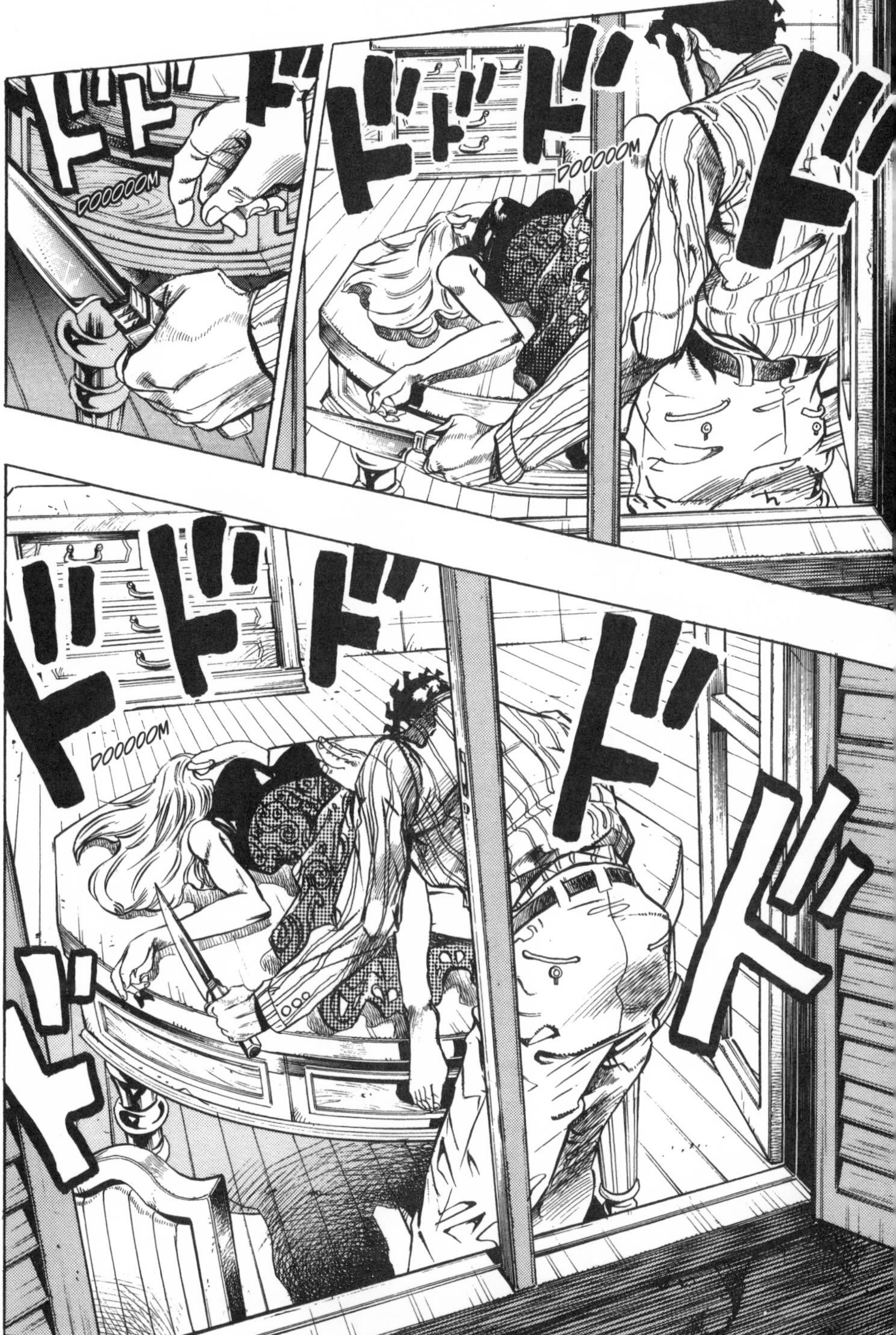
ドド
ドドドド
DOOOOOM
ドドドド
DOOOOOM
ドドド
ドドドド
DOOOOOM
ドド

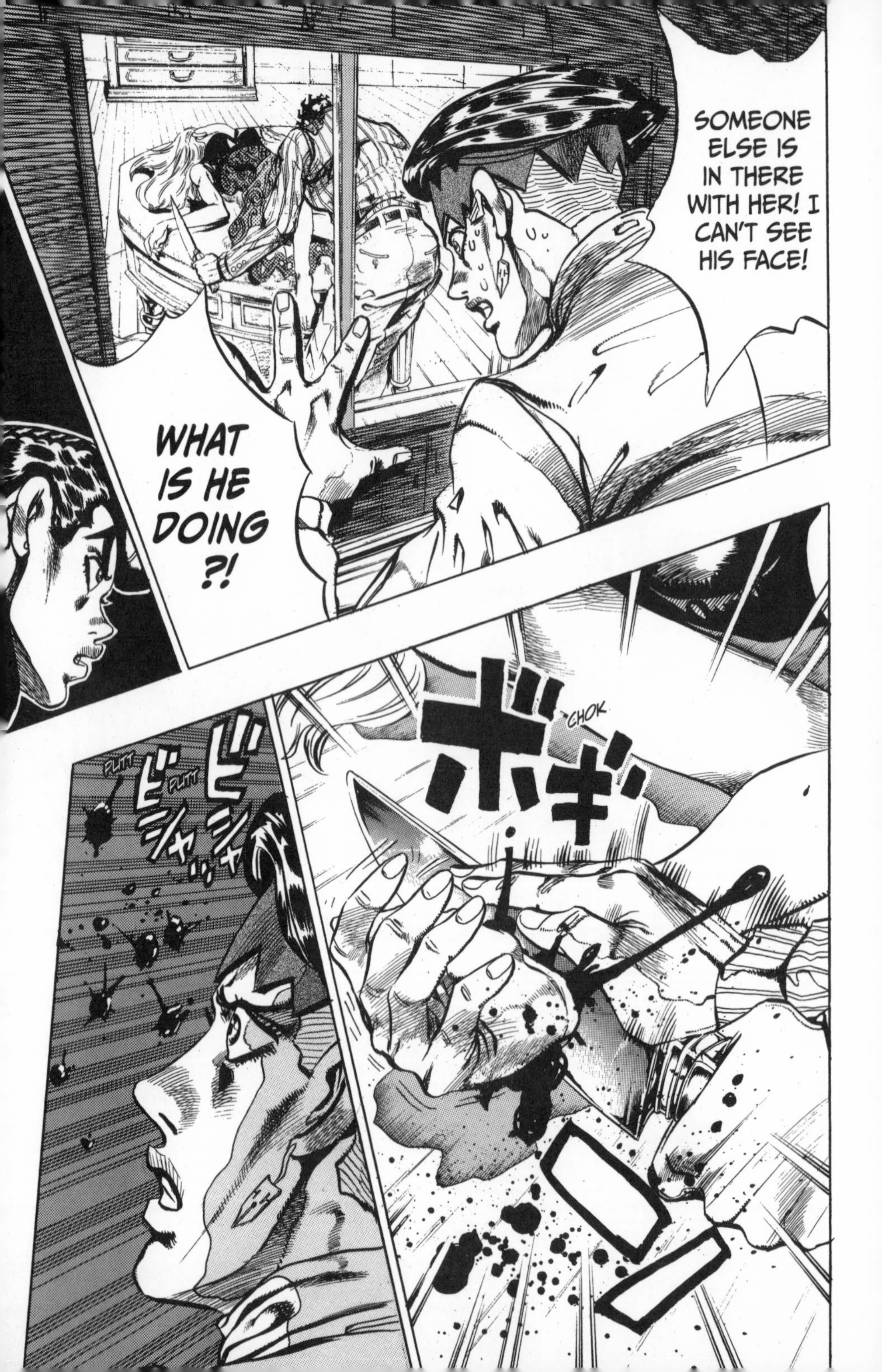
SOMEONE ELSE IS IN THERE WITH HER! I CAN'T SEE HIS FACE!
WHAT IS HE DOING ?!
ボギ
CHOK
ビシャッ ビシャ
PLITT PLITT

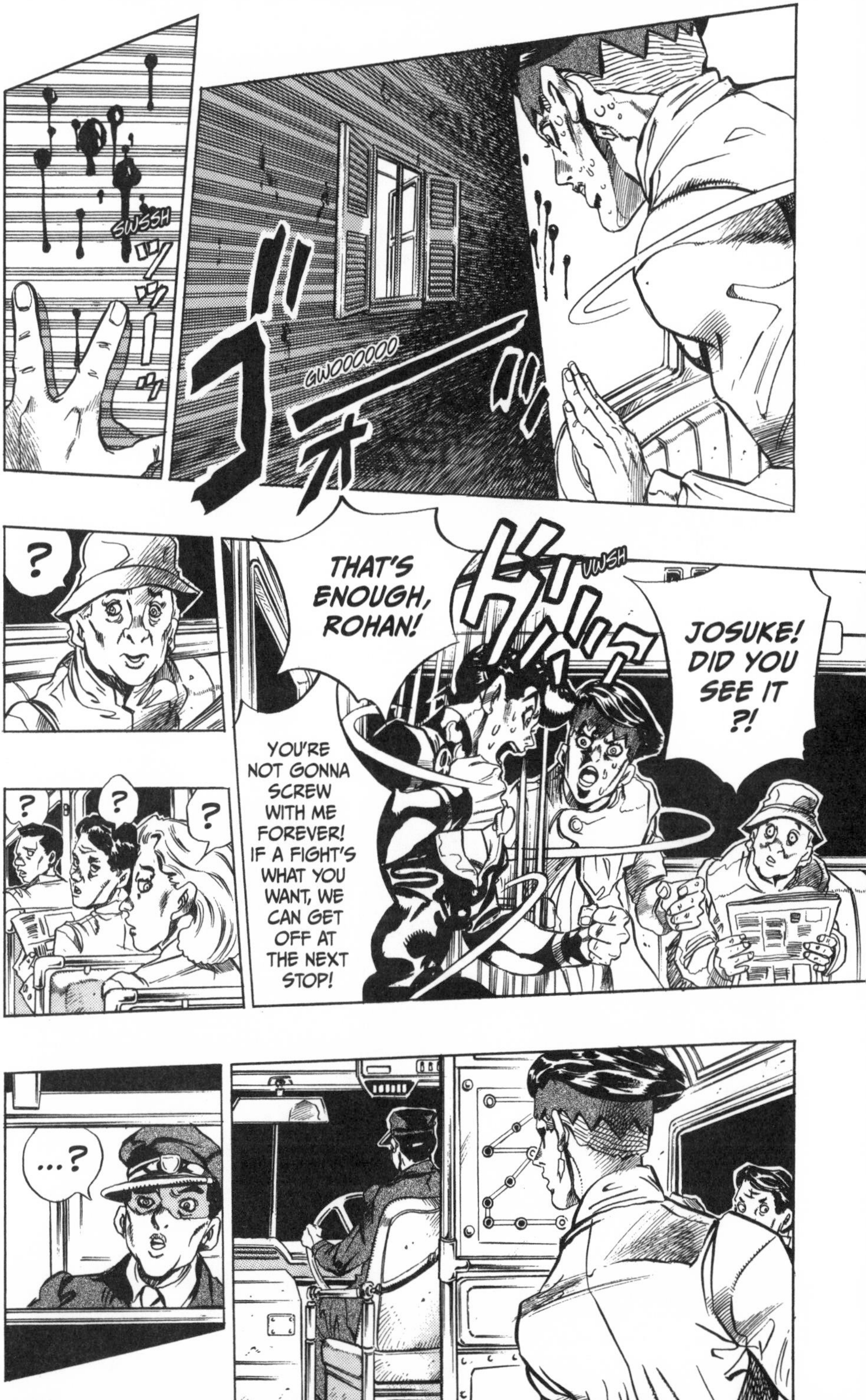
GWOOOOO
SWSSH
JOSUKE! DID YOU SEE IT ?!
THAT'S ENOUGH, ROHAN!
UWSH
YOU'RE NOT GONNA SCREW WITH ME FOREVER! IF A FIGHT'S WHAT YOU WANT, WE CAN GET OFF AT THE NEXT STOP!
?
?
?
?
...?

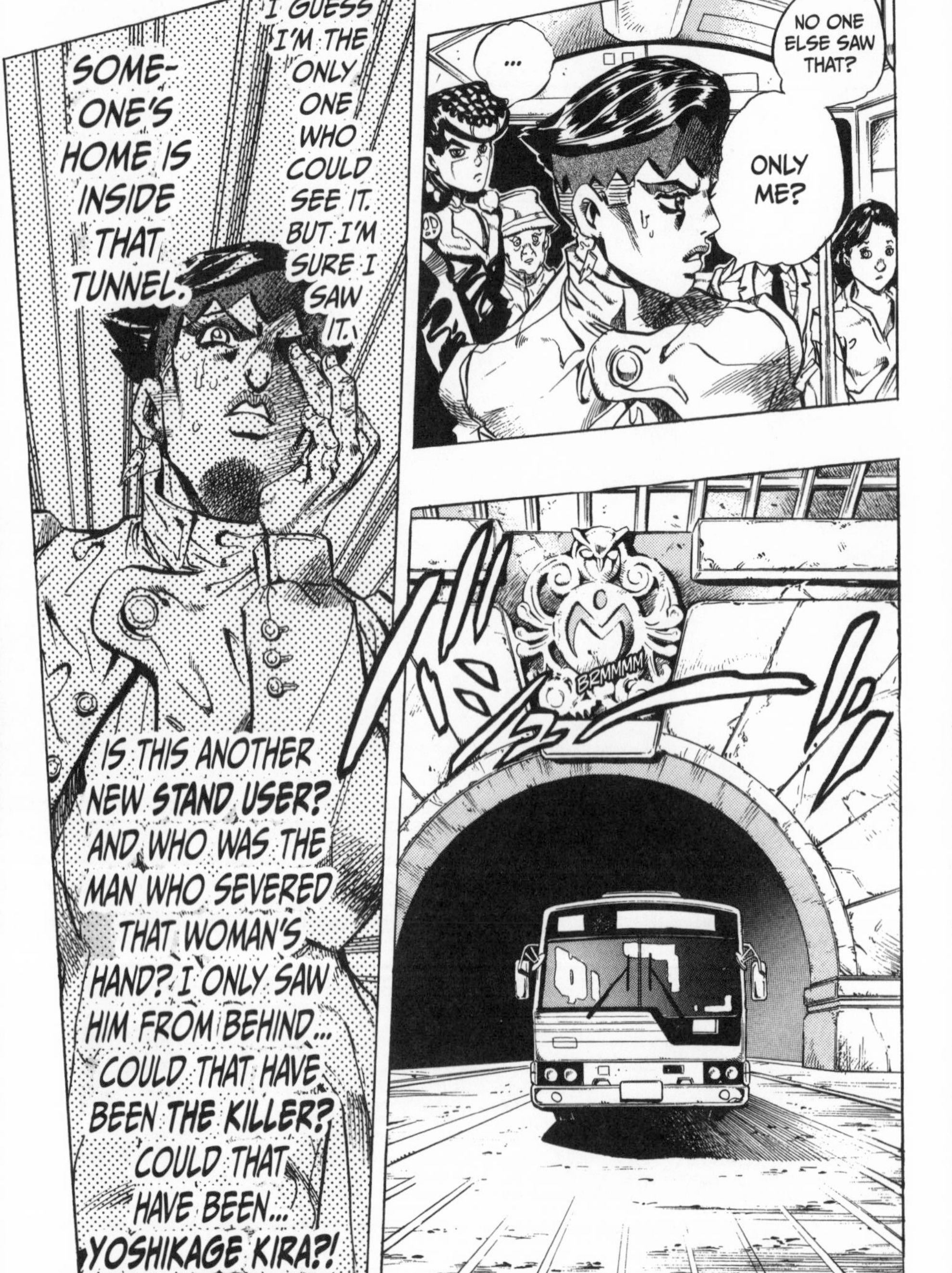

NO ONE ELSE SAW THAT?
...
ONLY ME?
BRMMMM
I GUESS I'M THE ONLY ONE WHO COULD SEE IT. BUT I'M SURE I SAW IT.
SOME-ONE'S HOME IS INSIDE THAT TUNNEL.
IS THIS ANOTHER NEW STAND USER? AND WHO WAS THE MAN WHO SEVERED THAT WOMAN'S HAND? I ONLY SAW HIM FROM BEHIND... COULD THAT HAVE BEEN THE KILLER? COULD THAT HAVE BEEN... YOSHIKAGE KIRA?!

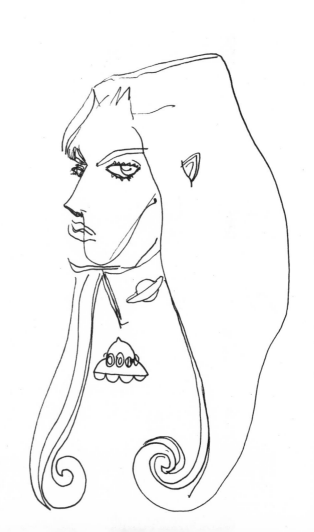

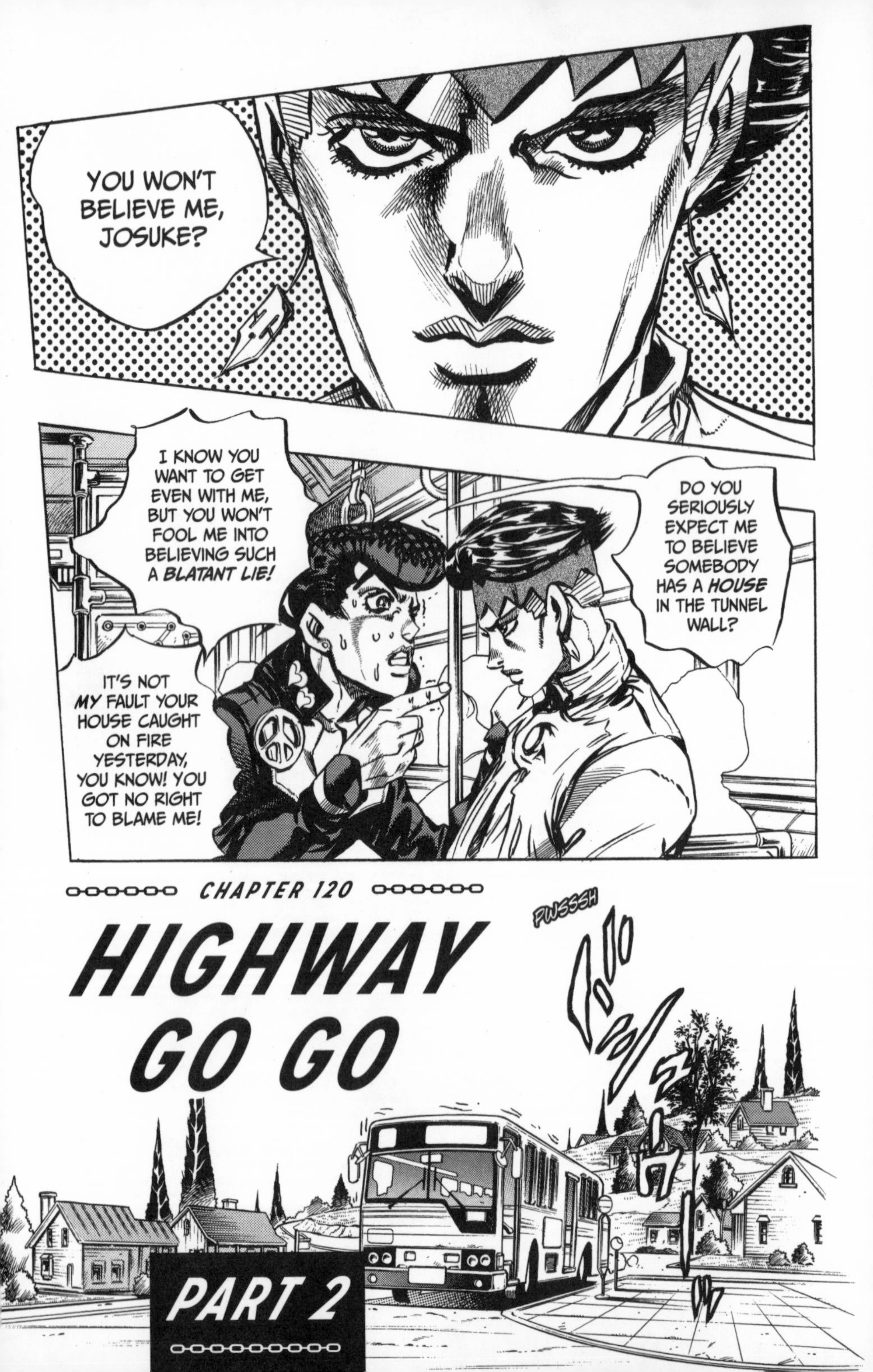
YOU WON'T BELIEVE ME, JOSUKE?
DO YOU SERIOUSLY EXPECT ME TO BELIEVE SOMEBODY HAS A *HOUSE* IN THE TUNNEL WALL?
I KNOW YOU WANT TO GET EVEN WITH ME, BUT YOU WON'T FOOL ME INTO BELIEVING SUCH A *BLATANT LIE!*
IT'S NOT *MY* FAULT YOUR HOUSE CAUGHT ON FIRE YESTERDAY, YOU KNOW! YOU GOT NO RIGHT TO BLAME ME!
CHAPTER 120
HIGHWAY GO GO
PART 2
PWSSSH

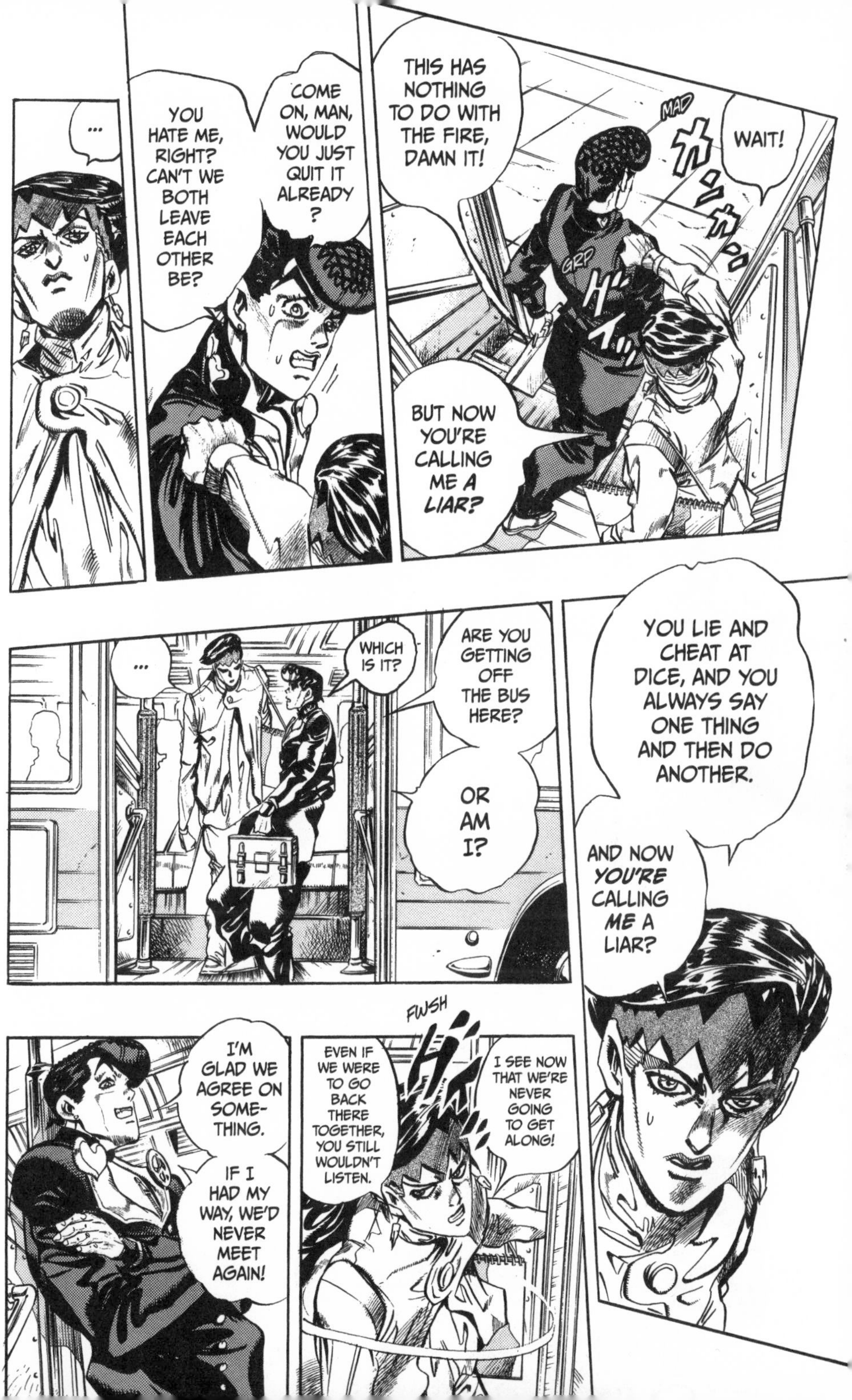
MAD
WAIT!
THIS HAS NOTHING TO DO WITH THE FIRE, DAMN IT!
GRP
BUT NOW YOU'RE CALLING ME A *LIAR?*
COME ON, MAN, WOULD YOU JUST QUIT IT ALREADY?
YOU HATE ME, RIGHT? CAN'T WE BOTH LEAVE EACH OTHER BE?
...
YOU LIE AND CHEAT AT DICE, AND YOU ALWAYS SAY ONE THING AND THEN DO ANOTHER.
AND NOW *YOU'RE* CALLING *ME* A LIAR?
ARE YOU GETTING OFF THE BUS HERE?
OR AM I?
WHICH IS IT?
...
I SEE NOW THAT WE'RE NEVER GOING TO GET ALONG!
FWSH
EVEN IF WE WERE TO GO BACK THERE TOGETHER, YOU STILL WOULDN'T LISTEN.
I'M GLAD WE AGREE ON SOME-THING.
IF I HAD MY WAY, WE'D NEVER MEET AGAIN!

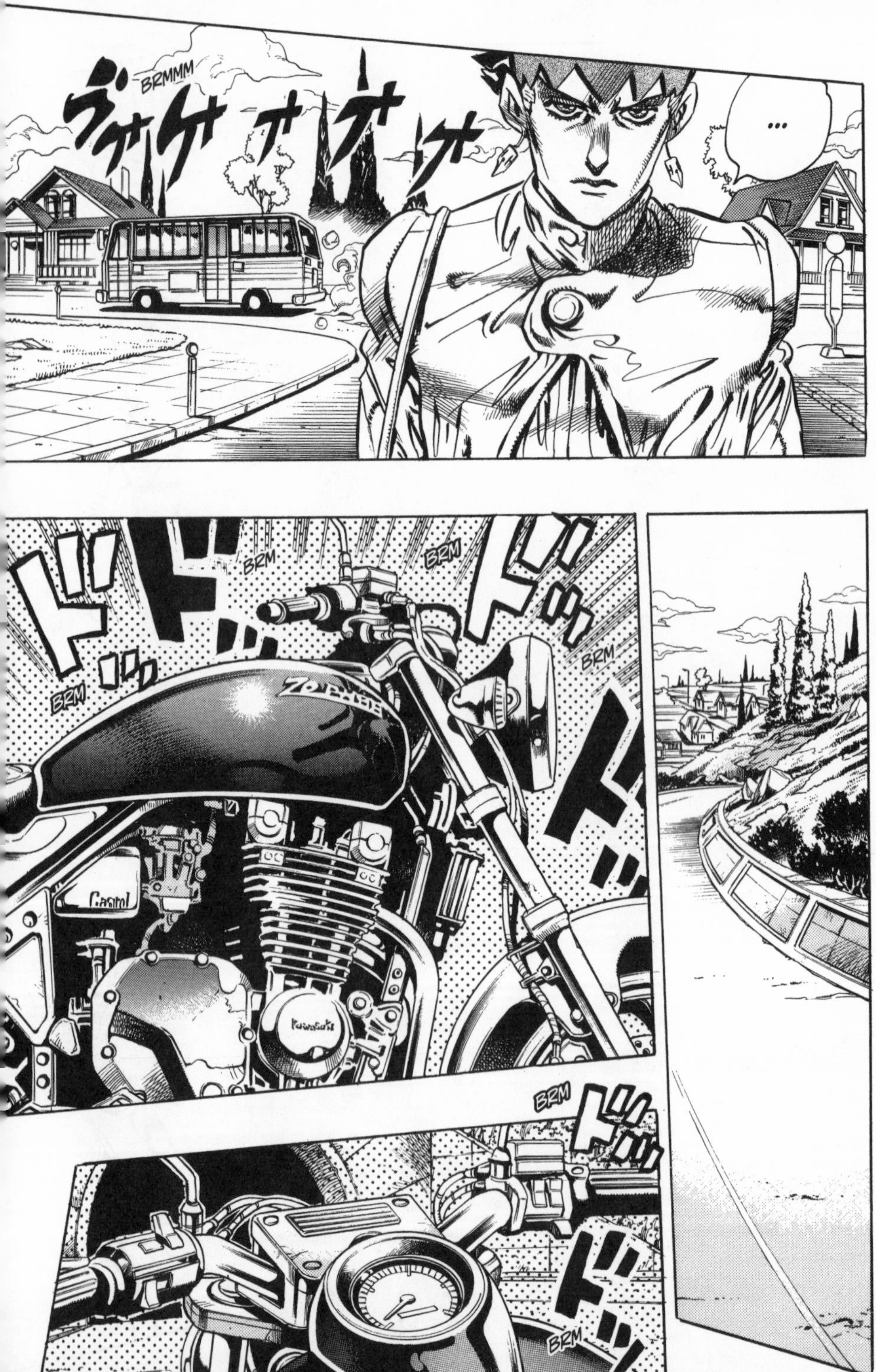

BRMMM
...
BRM
BRM
BRM
BRM
BRM
BRM

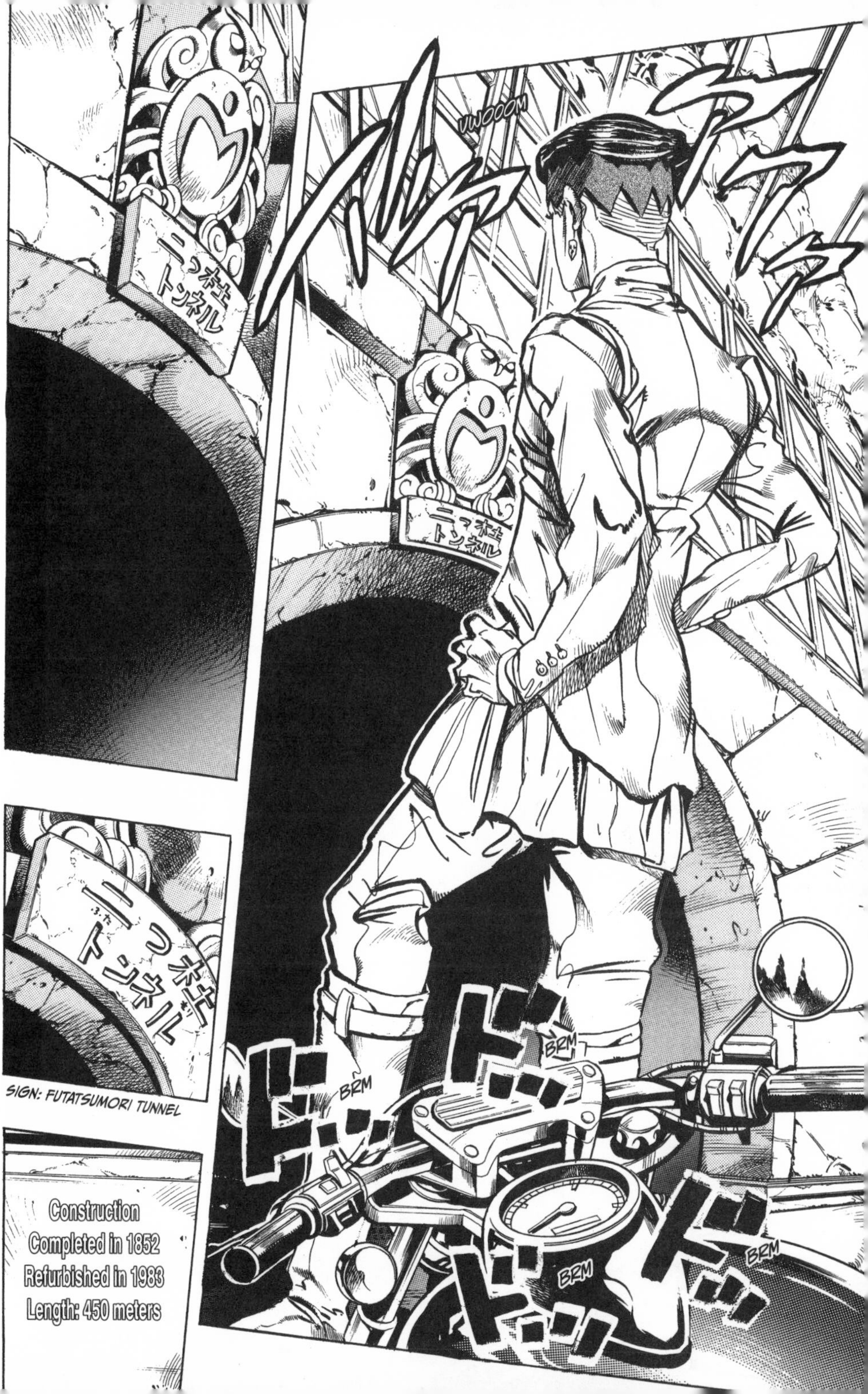
UWOOOM
BRM
BRM
BRM
BRM
SIGN: FUTATSUMORI TUNNEL
Construction
Completed in 1852
Refurbished in 1983
Length: 450 meters

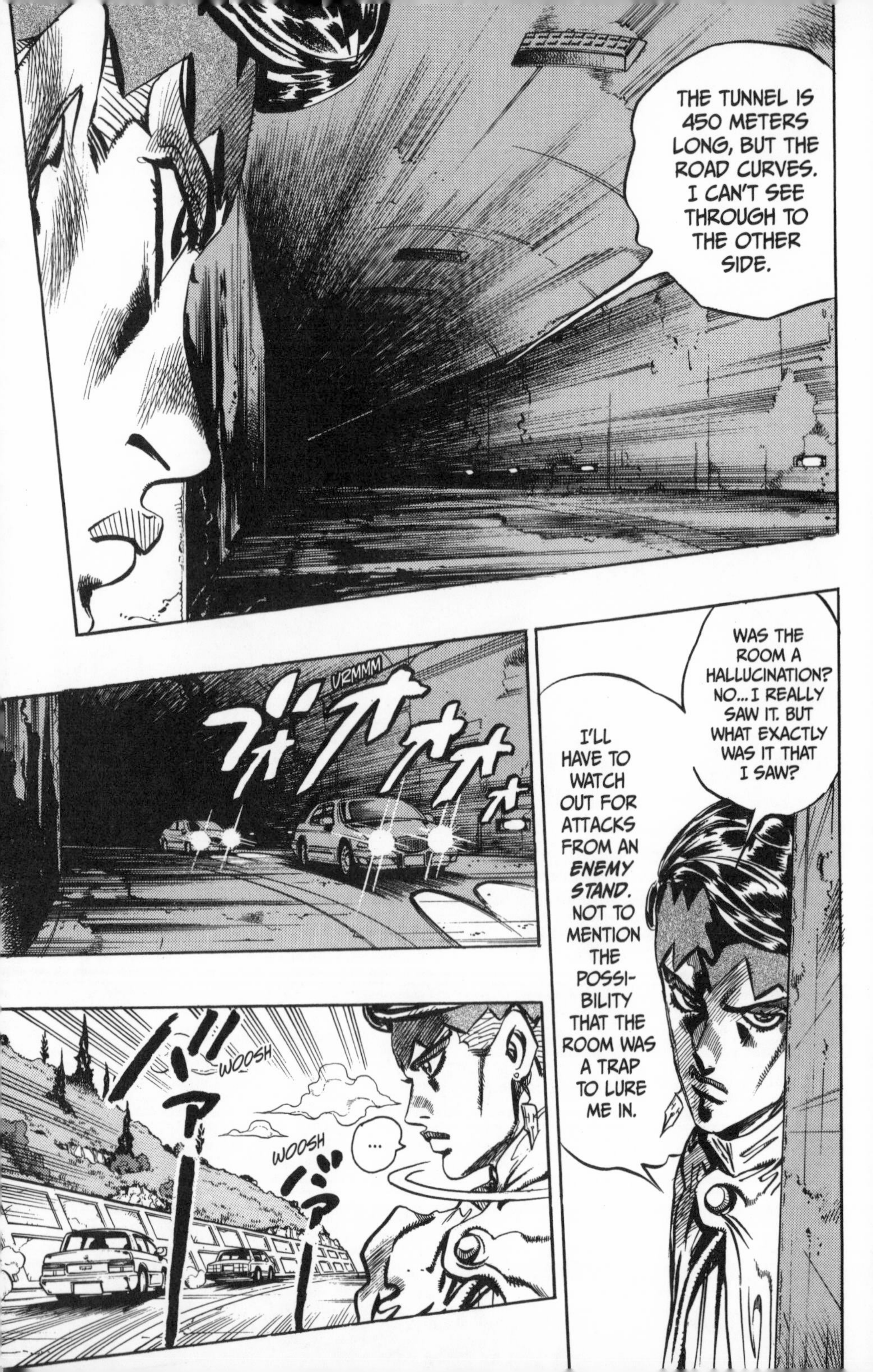
THE TUNNEL IS 450 METERS LONG, BUT THE ROAD CURVES. I CAN'T SEE THROUGH TO THE OTHER SIDE.
WAS THE ROOM A HALLUCINATION? NO...I REALLY SAW IT. BUT WHAT EXACTLY WAS IT THAT I SAW?
I'LL HAVE TO WATCH OUT FOR ATTACKS FROM AN *ENEMY STAND*. NOT TO MENTION THE POSSIBILITY THAT THE ROOM WAS A TRAP TO LURE ME IN.
URMMM
WOOSH
WOOSH
...

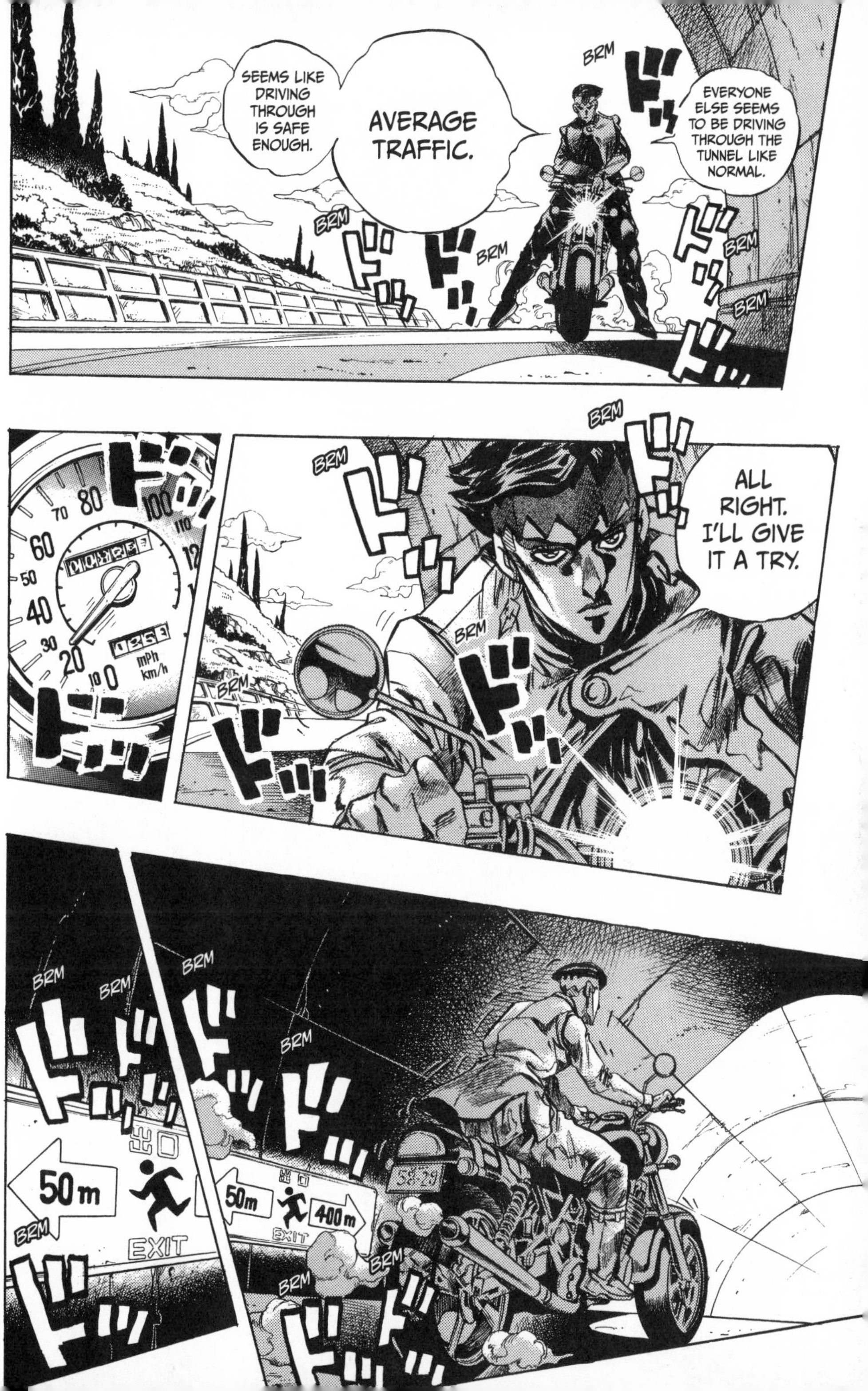
EVERYONE ELSE SEEMS TO BE DRIVING THROUGH THE TUNNEL LIKE NORMAL.
AVERAGE TRAFFIC.
SEEMS LIKE DRIVING THROUGH IS SAFE ENOUGH.
ALL RIGHT. I'LL GIVE IT A TRY.
mph
km/h
出口
50m
400m
EXIT
50m
EXIT

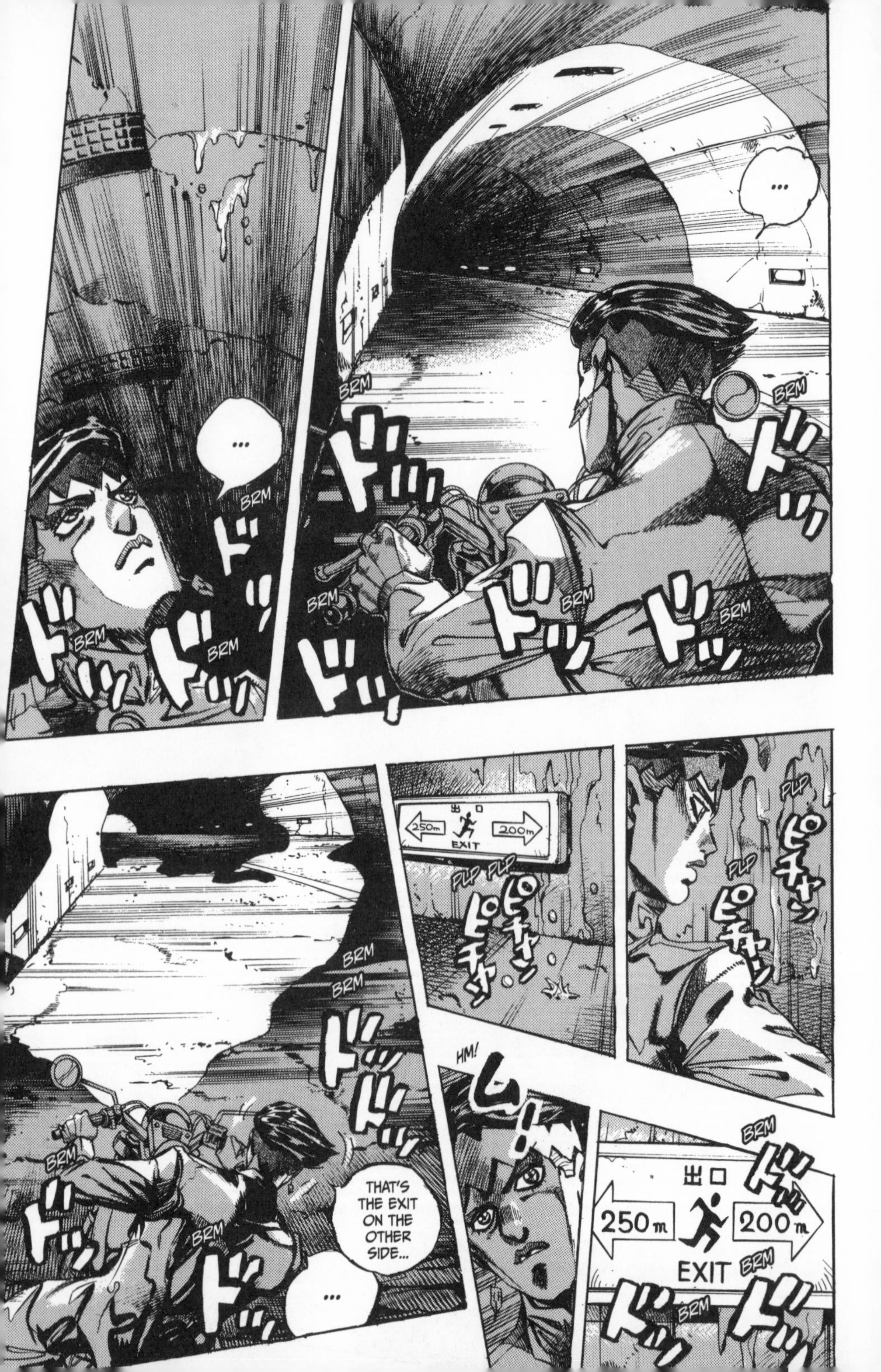
...
BRM
BRM
BRM
BRM
BRM
...
BRM
BRM
BRM
PLP
PLP
出口
250m
200m
EXIT
PLP PLP
BRM
出口
250m
200m
EXIT
BRM
BRM
HM!
BRM
BRM
BRM
THAT'S THE EXIT ON THE OTHER SIDE...
BRM
...

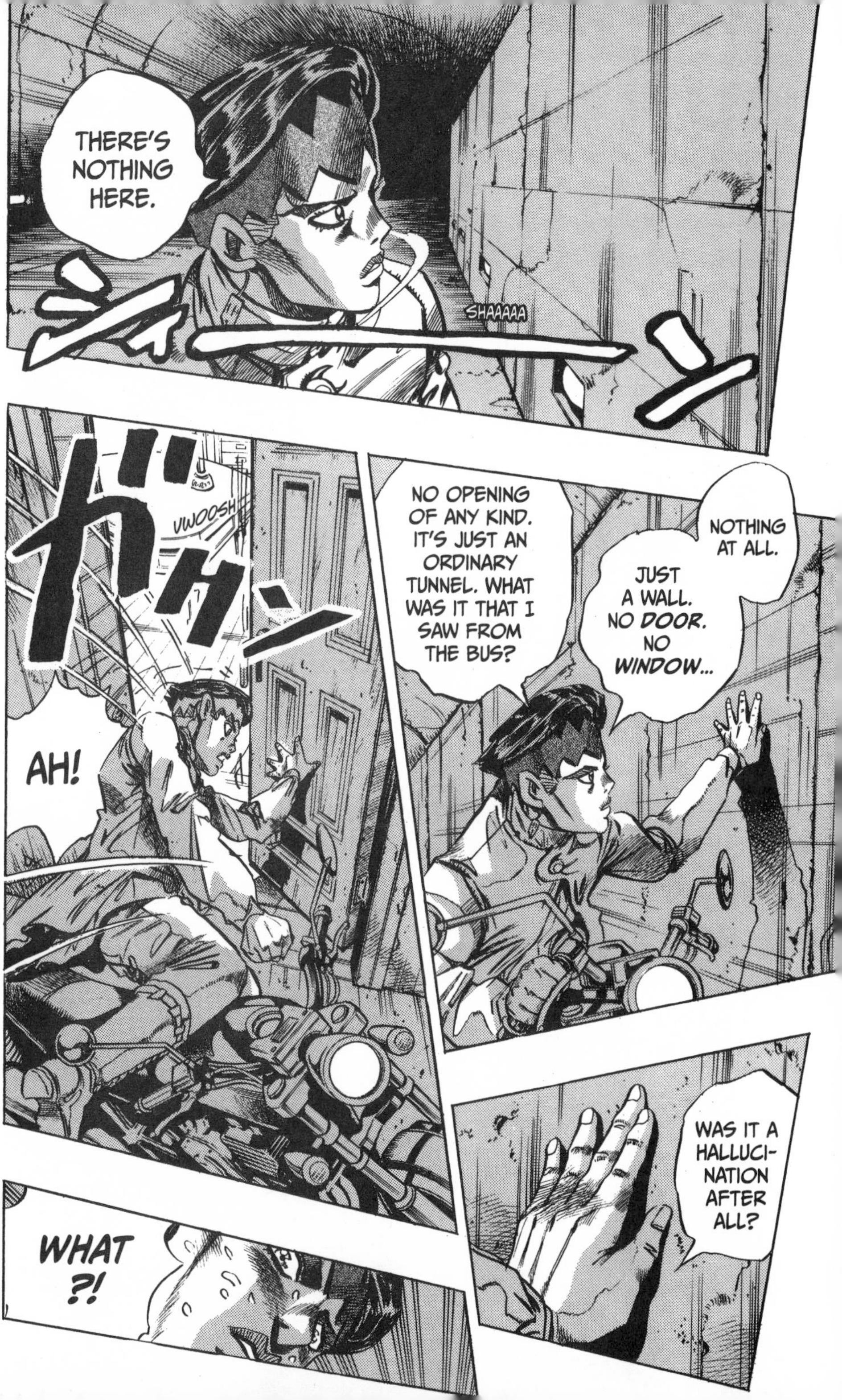
THERE'S NOTHING HERE.
SHAAAAA
NOTHING AT ALL.
JUST A WALL. NO DOOR. NO WINDOW...
NO OPENING OF ANY KIND. IT'S JUST AN ORDINARY TUNNEL. WHAT WAS IT THAT I SAW FROM THE BUS?
WAS IT A HALLUCINATION AFTER ALL?
ガッ
VWOOSH
AH!
WHAT ?!

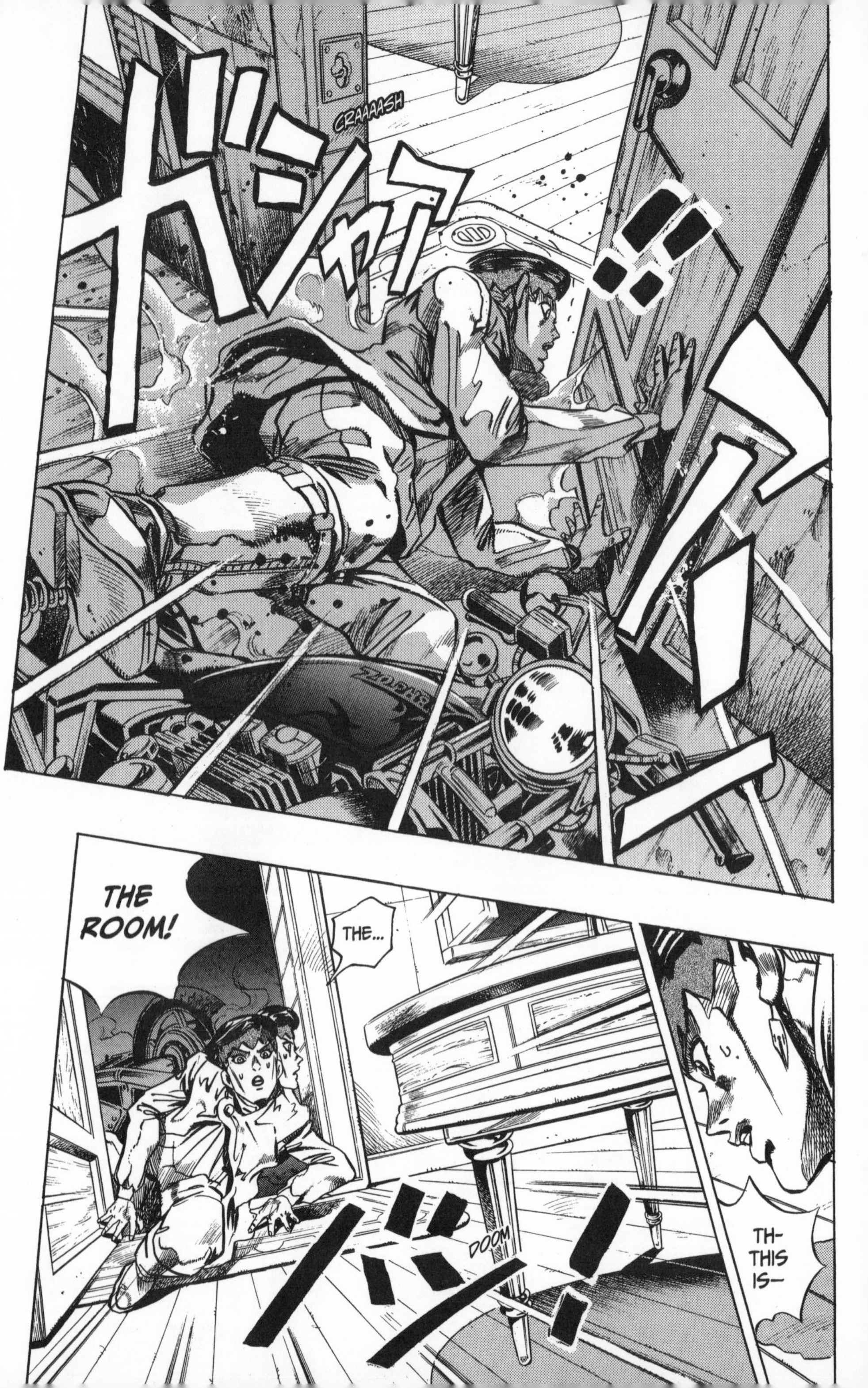
CRAAAASH
THE...
THE ROOM!
TH-
THIS
IS—
DOOM

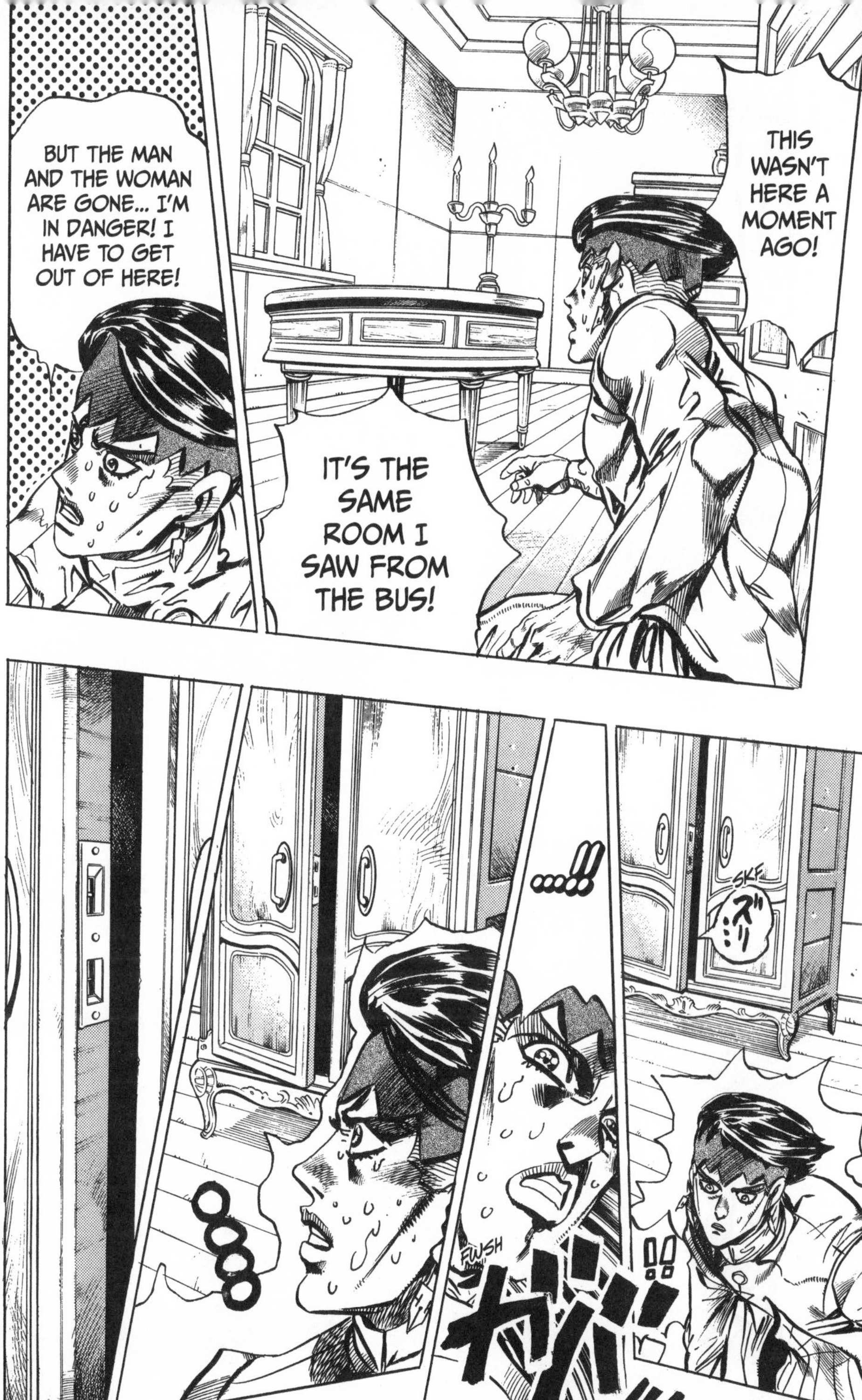
THIS WASN'T HERE A MOMENT AGO!
IT'S THE SAME ROOM I SAW FROM THE BUS!
BUT THE MAN AND THE WOMAN ARE GONE... I'M IN DANGER! I HAVE TO GET OUT OF HERE!
SKF
!!
FWSH
...!!

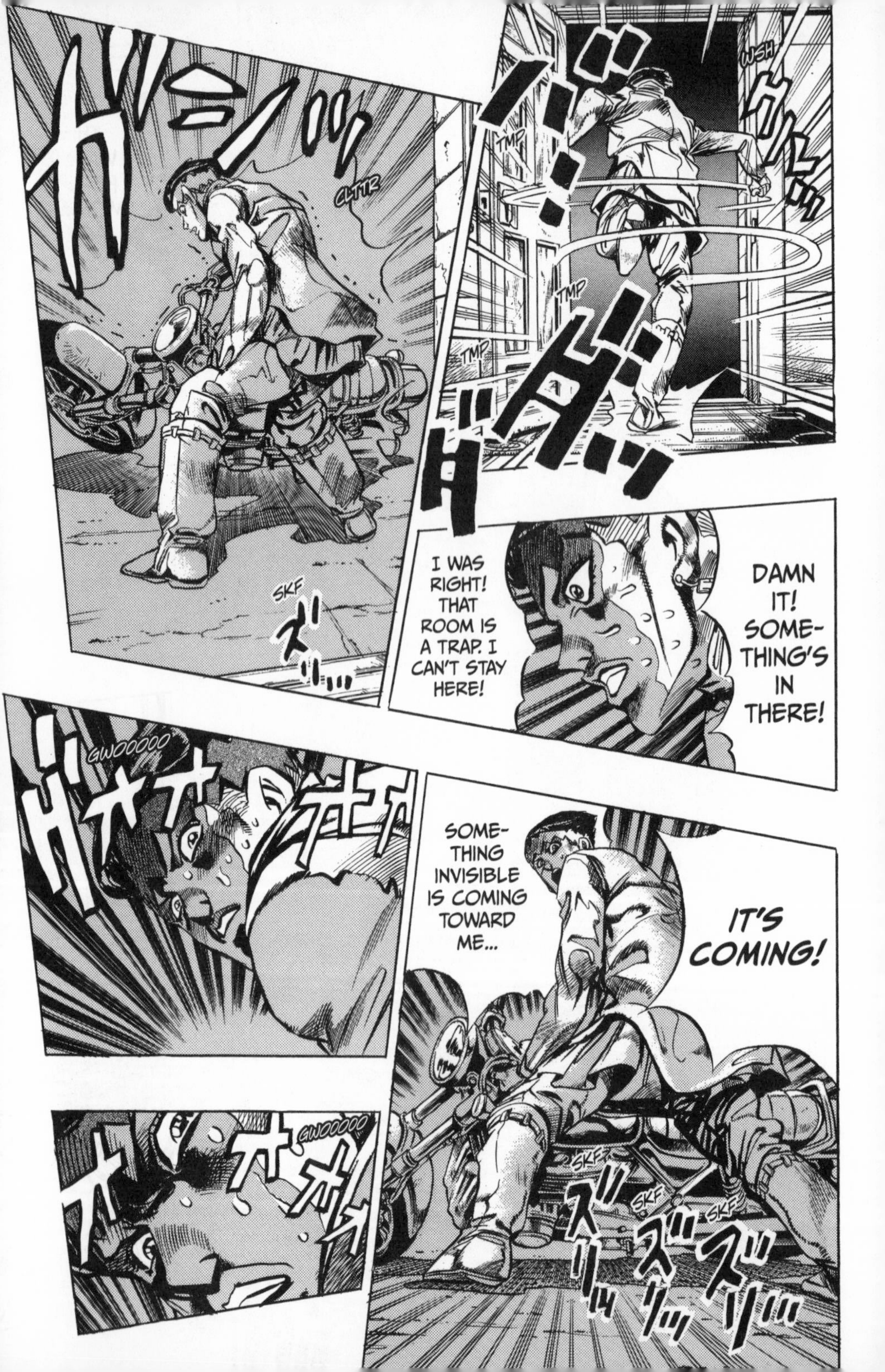
WSH
TMP
TMP
TMP
DAMN IT! SOME-THING'S IN THERE!
I WAS RIGHT! THAT ROOM IS A TRAP. I CAN'T STAY HERE!
CLTTR
SKF
IT'S COMING!
SOME-THING INVISIBLE IS COMING TOWARD ME...
SKF
SKF
SKF
GWOOOOO
GWOOOOO

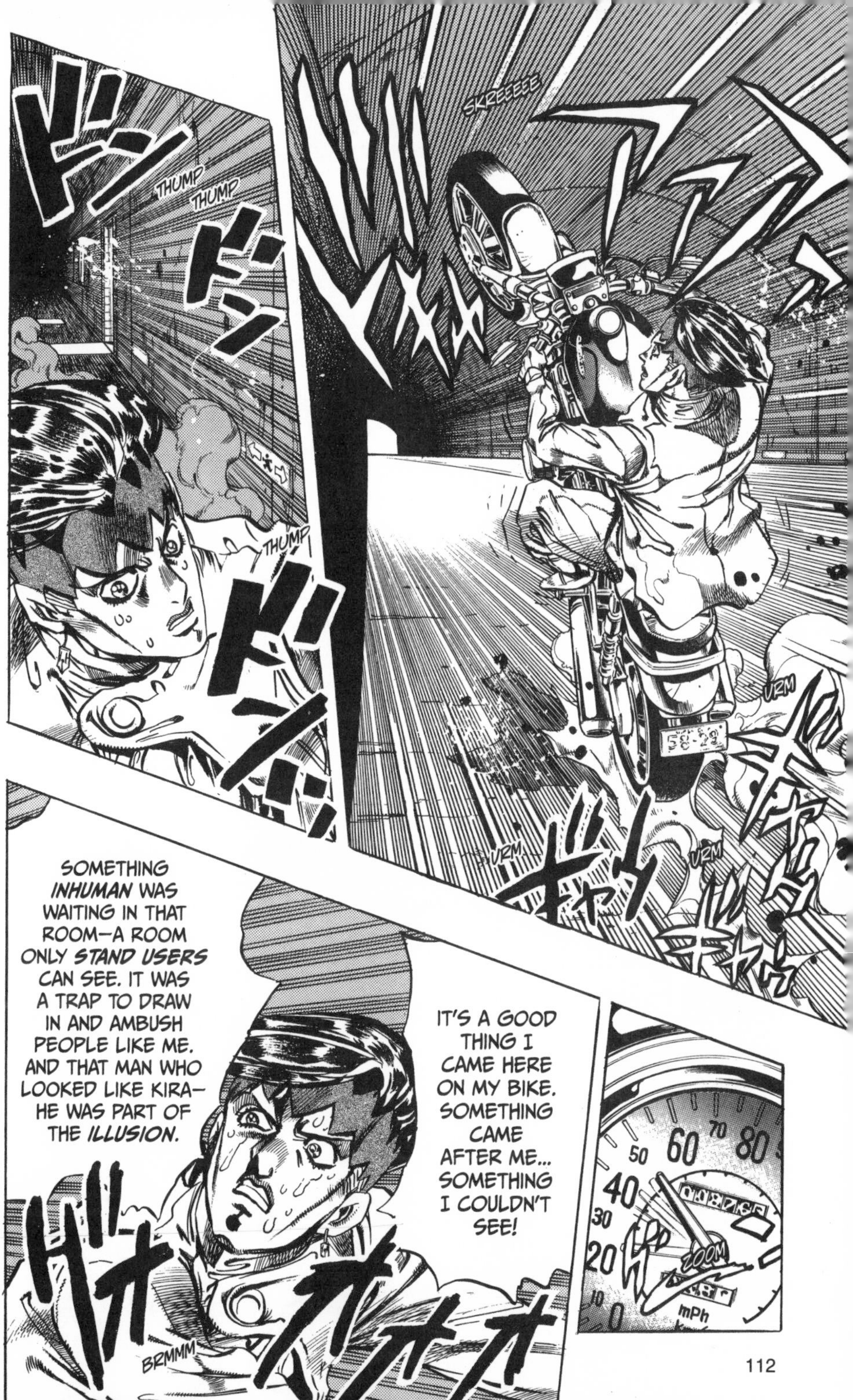
SKREEEEE
URM
URM
URM
THUMP
THUMP
THUMP
IT'S A GOOD THING I CAME HERE ON MY BIKE. SOMETHING CAME AFTER ME... SOMETHING I COULDN'T SEE!
SOMETHING *INHUMAN* WAS WAITING IN THAT ROOM—A ROOM ONLY **STAND USERS** CAN SEE. IT WAS A TRAP TO DRAW IN AND AMBUSH PEOPLE LIKE ME. AND THAT MAN WHO LOOKED LIKE KIRA—HE WAS PART OF THE *ILLUSION*.
BRMMM
ZOOM
mPh

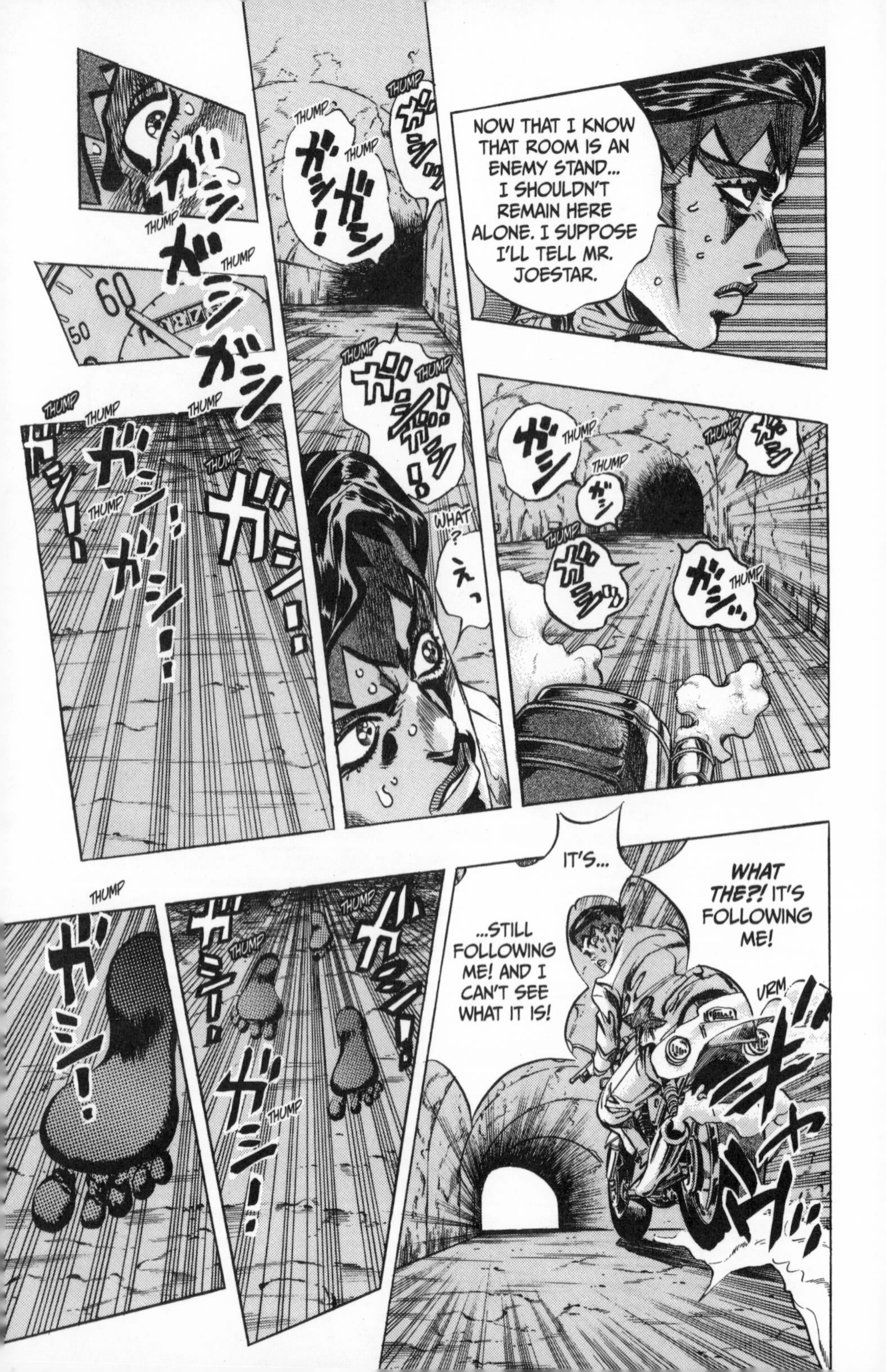
NOW THAT I KNOW THAT ROOM IS AN ENEMY STAND... I SHOULDN'T REMAIN HERE ALONE. I SUPPOSE I'LL TELL MR. JOESTAR.
THUMP
THUMP
THUMP
THUMP
THUMP
THUMP
60
50
THUMP
THUMP
THUMP
THUMP
THUMP
THUMP
THUMP
THUMP
THUMP
THUMP
THUMP
WHAT?
えっ
IT'S...
WHAT THE?! IT'S FOLLOWING ME!
...STILL FOLLOWING ME! AND I CAN'T SEE WHAT IT IS!
URM
THUMP
THUMP
THUMP
THUMP

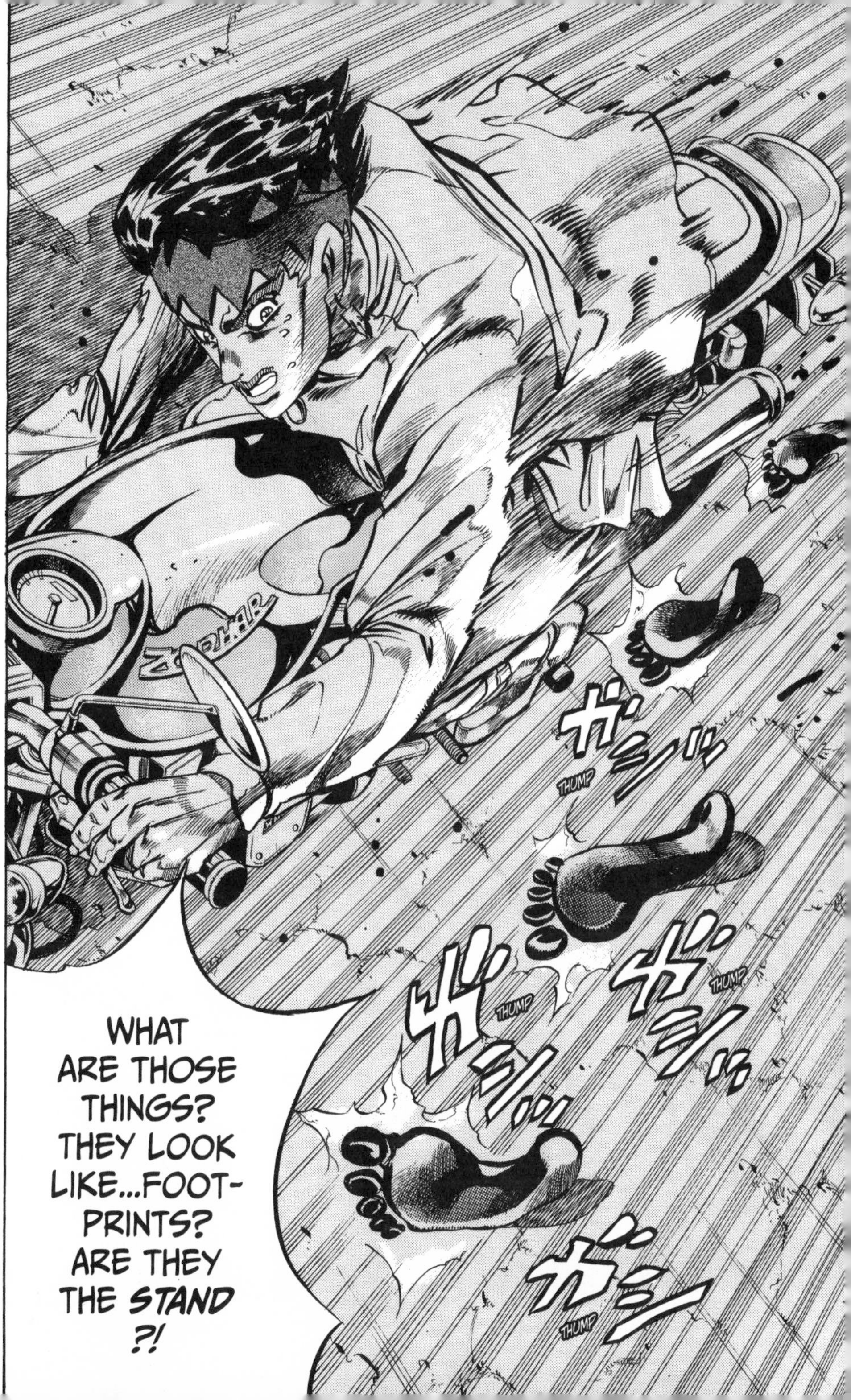
THUMP
THUMP
THUMP
WHAT ARE THOSE THINGS? THEY LOOK LIKE...FOOT-PRINTS? ARE THEY THE STAND ?!
THUMP

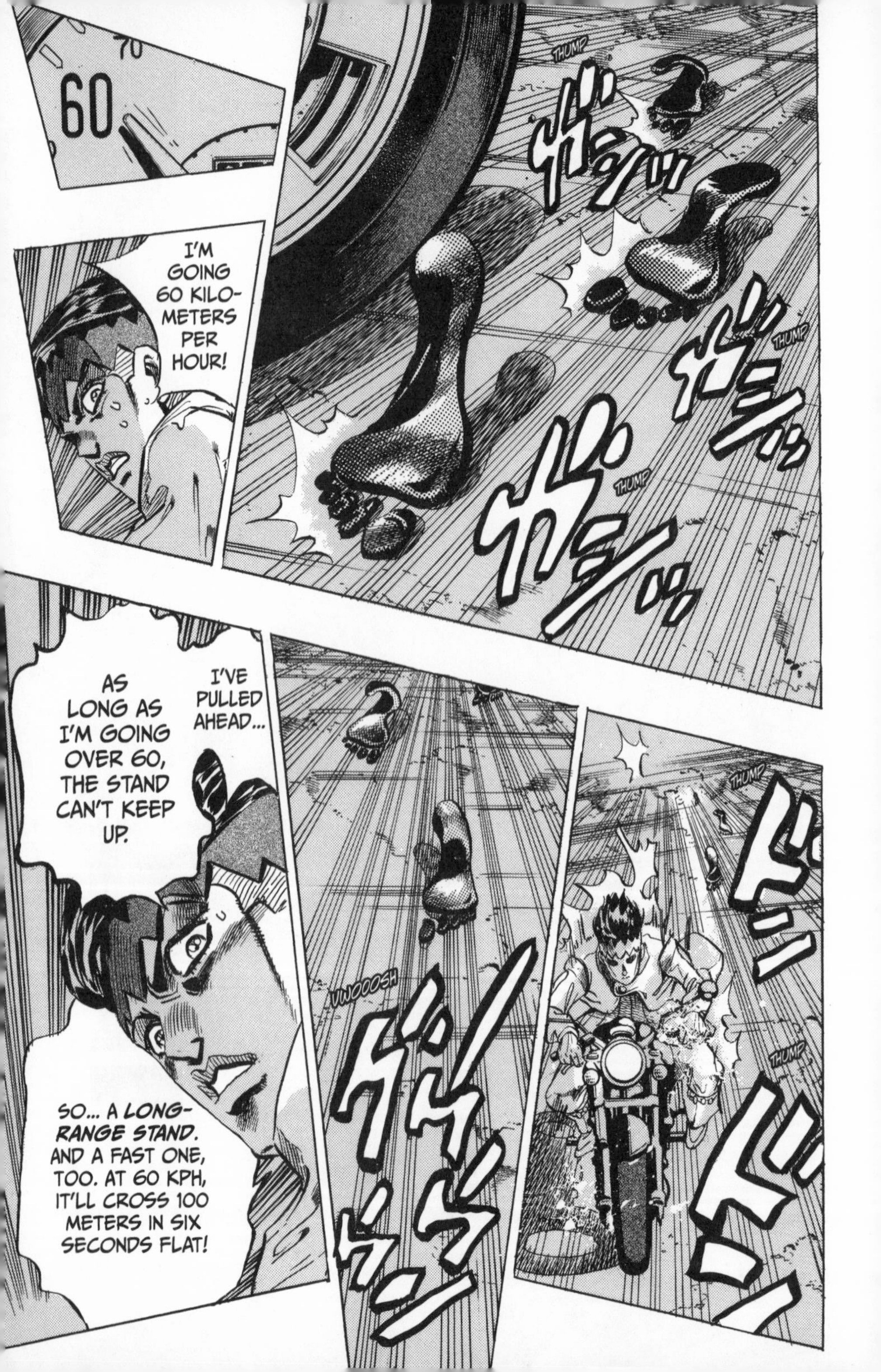
THUMP
THUMP
THUMP
70
60
I'M GOING 60 KILO-METERS PER HOUR!
THUMP
THUMP
UWOOOSH
I'VE PULLED AHEAD...
AS LONG AS I'M GOING OVER 60, THE STAND CAN'T KEEP UP.
SO... A ***LONG-RANGE STAND.*** AND A FAST ONE, TOO. AT 60 KPH, IT'LL CROSS 100 METERS IN SIX SECONDS FLAT!

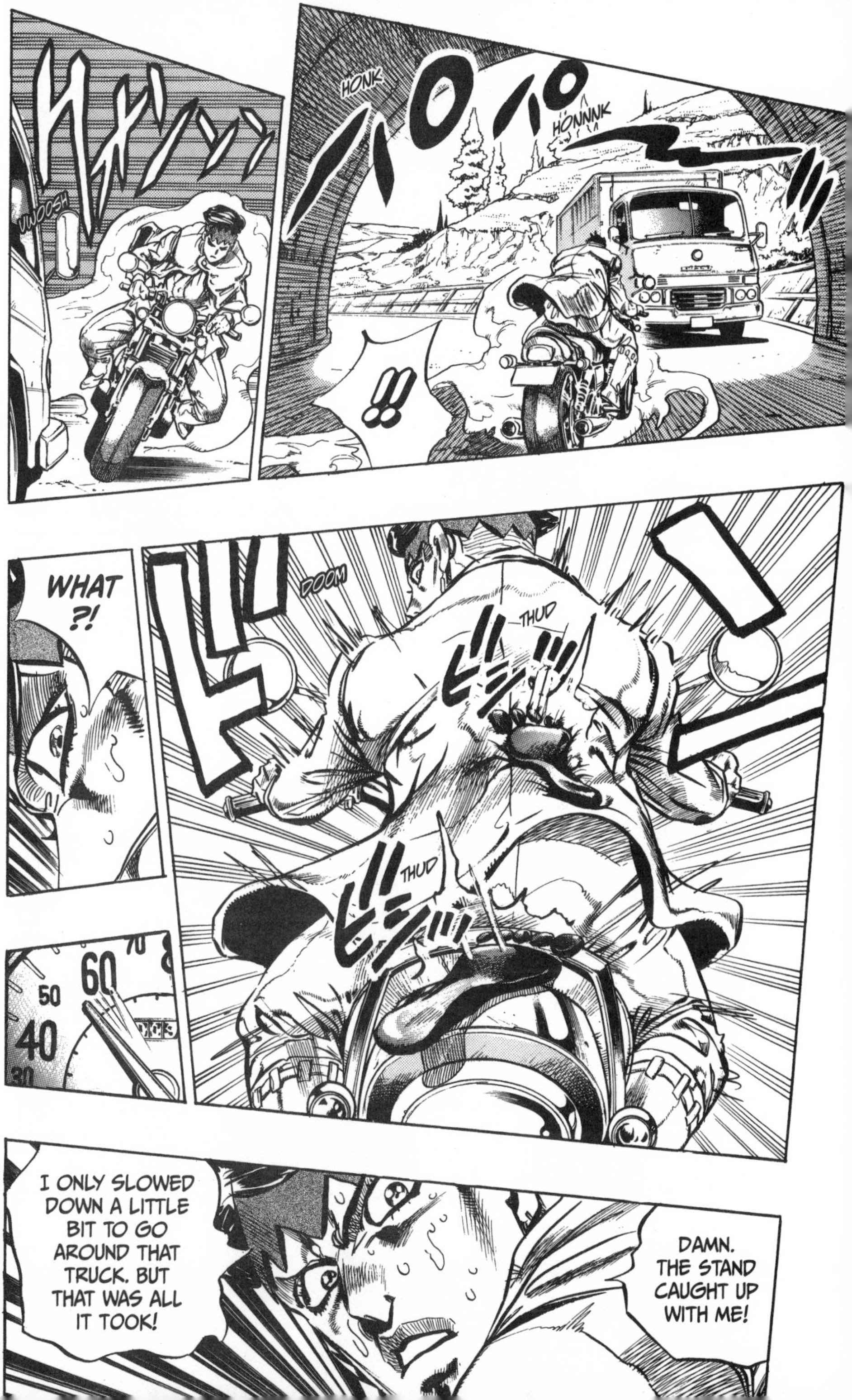
HONK
HONNNK
!!
WOOSH
DOOM
THUD
THUD
WHAT ?!
DAMN. THE STAND CAUGHT UP WITH ME!
I ONLY SLOWED DOWN A LITTLE BIT TO GO AROUND THAT TRUCK. BUT THAT WAS ALL IT TOOK!

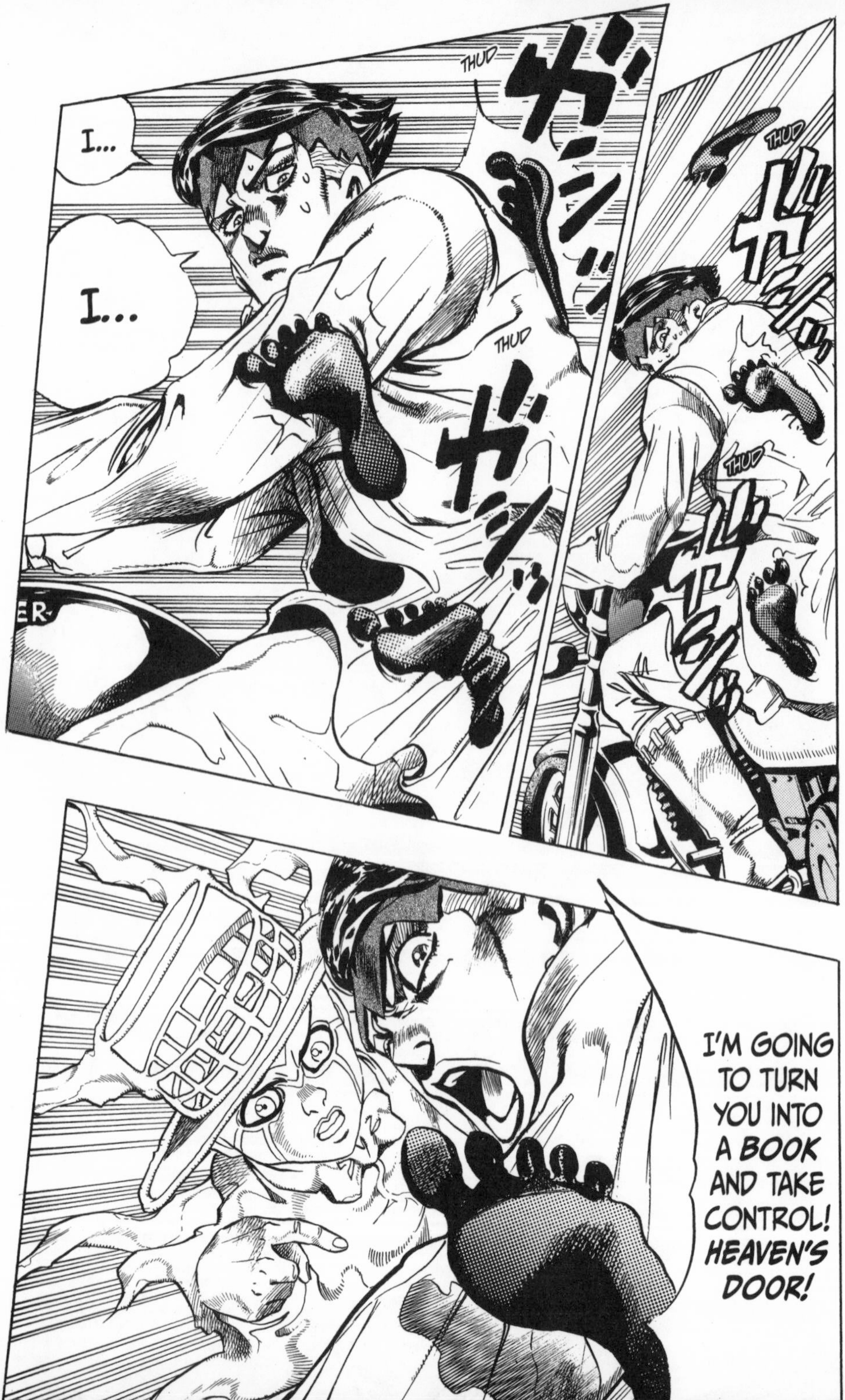
THUD
THUD
THUD
I...
I...
THUD
I'M GOING TO TURN YOU INTO A *BOOK* AND TAKE CONTROL! ***HEAVEN'S DOOR!***

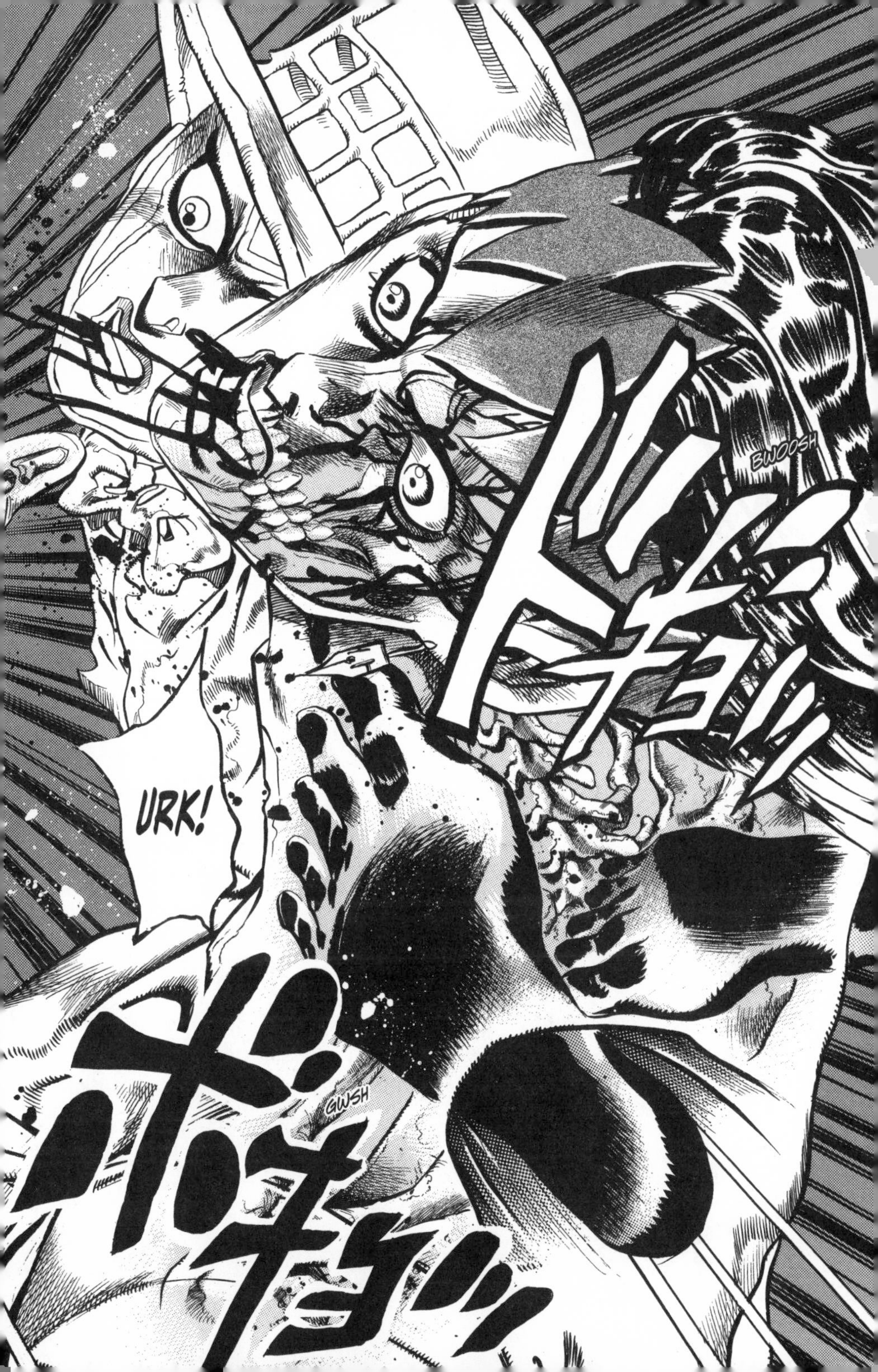
BWOOSH
URK!
GWSH

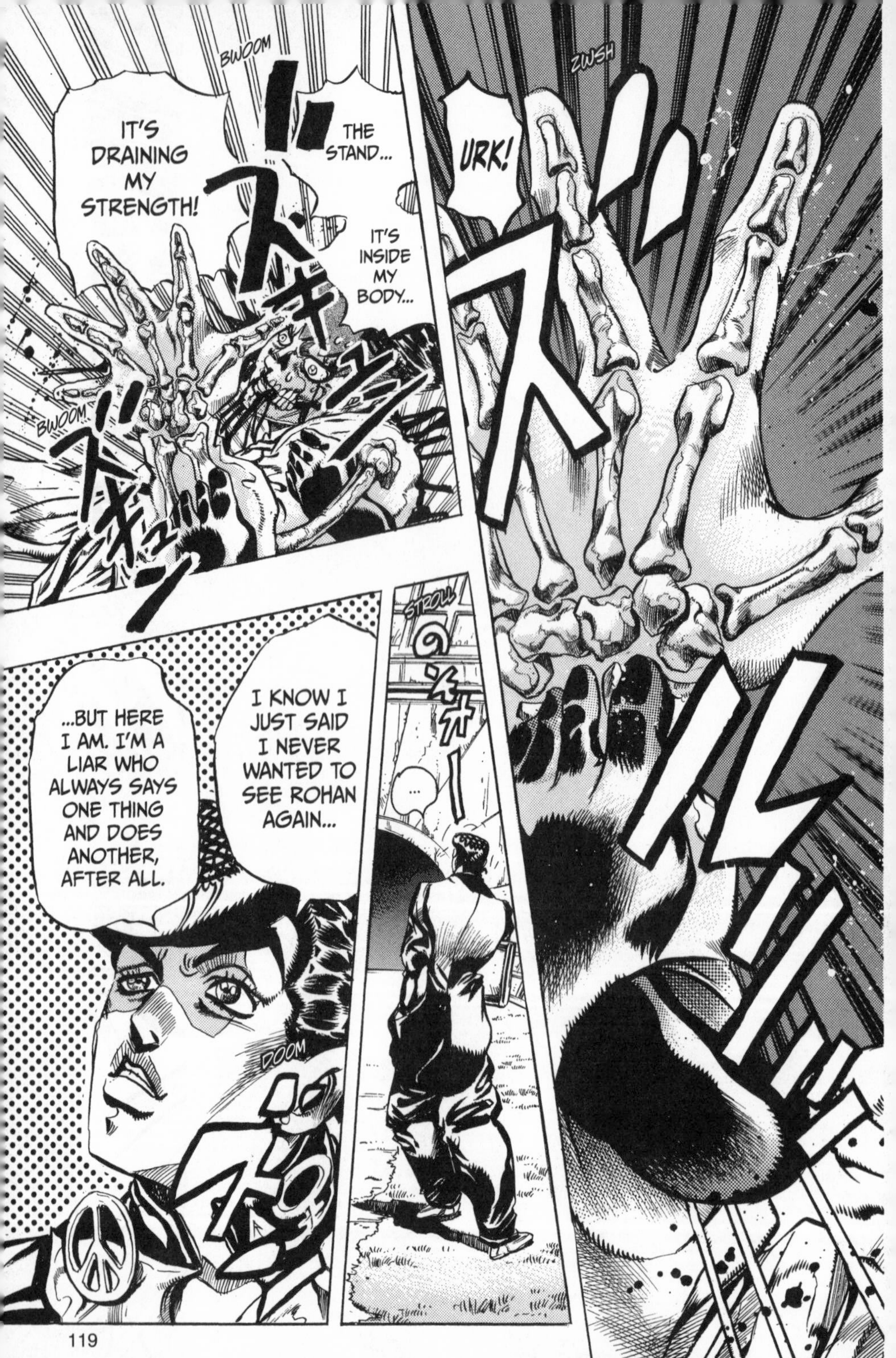
ZWSH
URK!
BWOOM
THE STAND...
IT'S INSIDE MY BODY...
IT'S DRAINING MY STRENGTH!
BWOOM
STROLL
...
I KNOW I JUST SAID I NEVER WANTED TO SEE ROHAN AGAIN...
...BUT HERE I AM. I'M A LIAR WHO ALWAYS SAYS ONE THING AND DOES ANOTHER, AFTER ALL.
DOOM

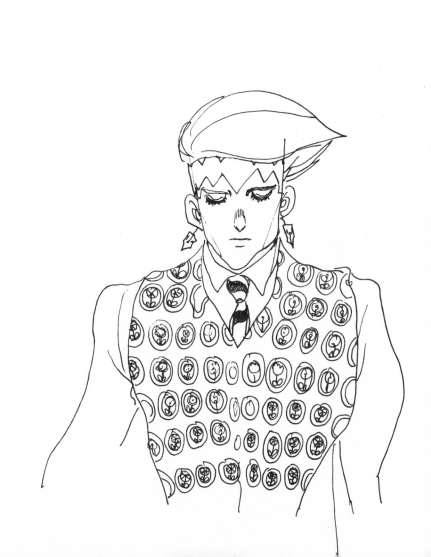

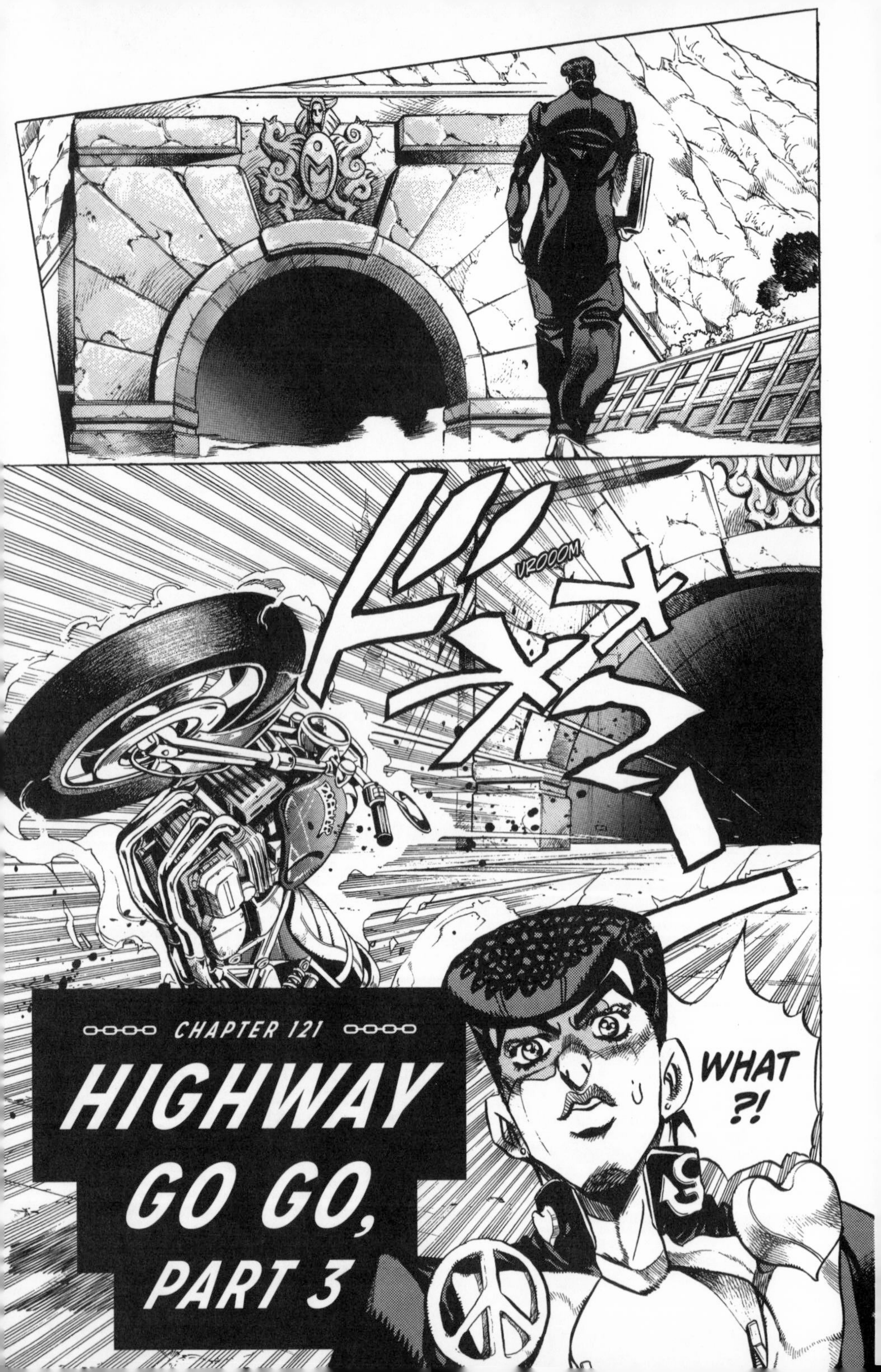
VROOOM
CHAPTER 121
HIGHWAY GO GO, PART 3
WHAT ?!

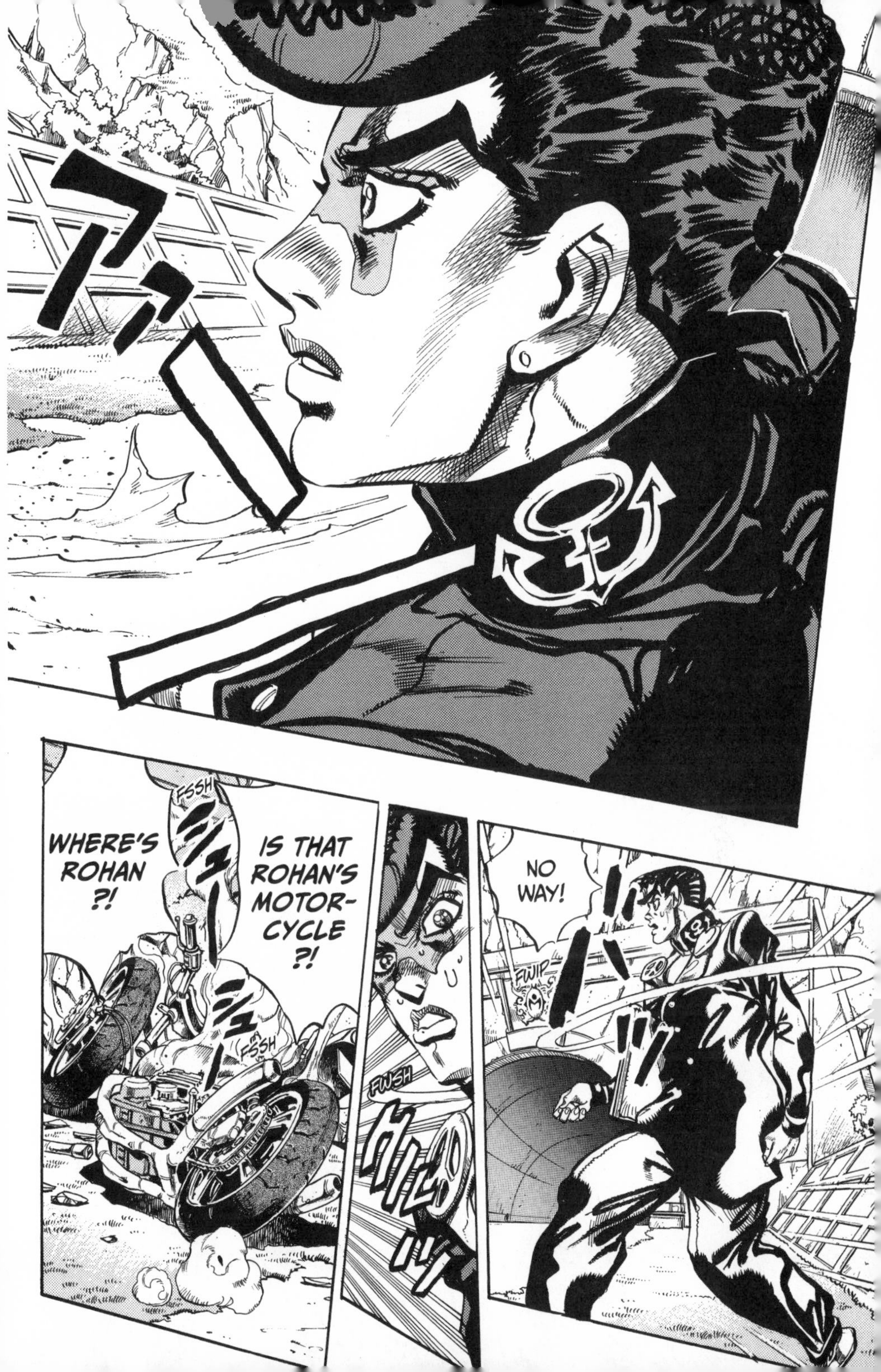
NO WAY!
FWIP
FWSH
FSSH
IS THAT ROHAN'S MOTORCYCLE ?!
WHERE'S ROHAN ?!
FSSH

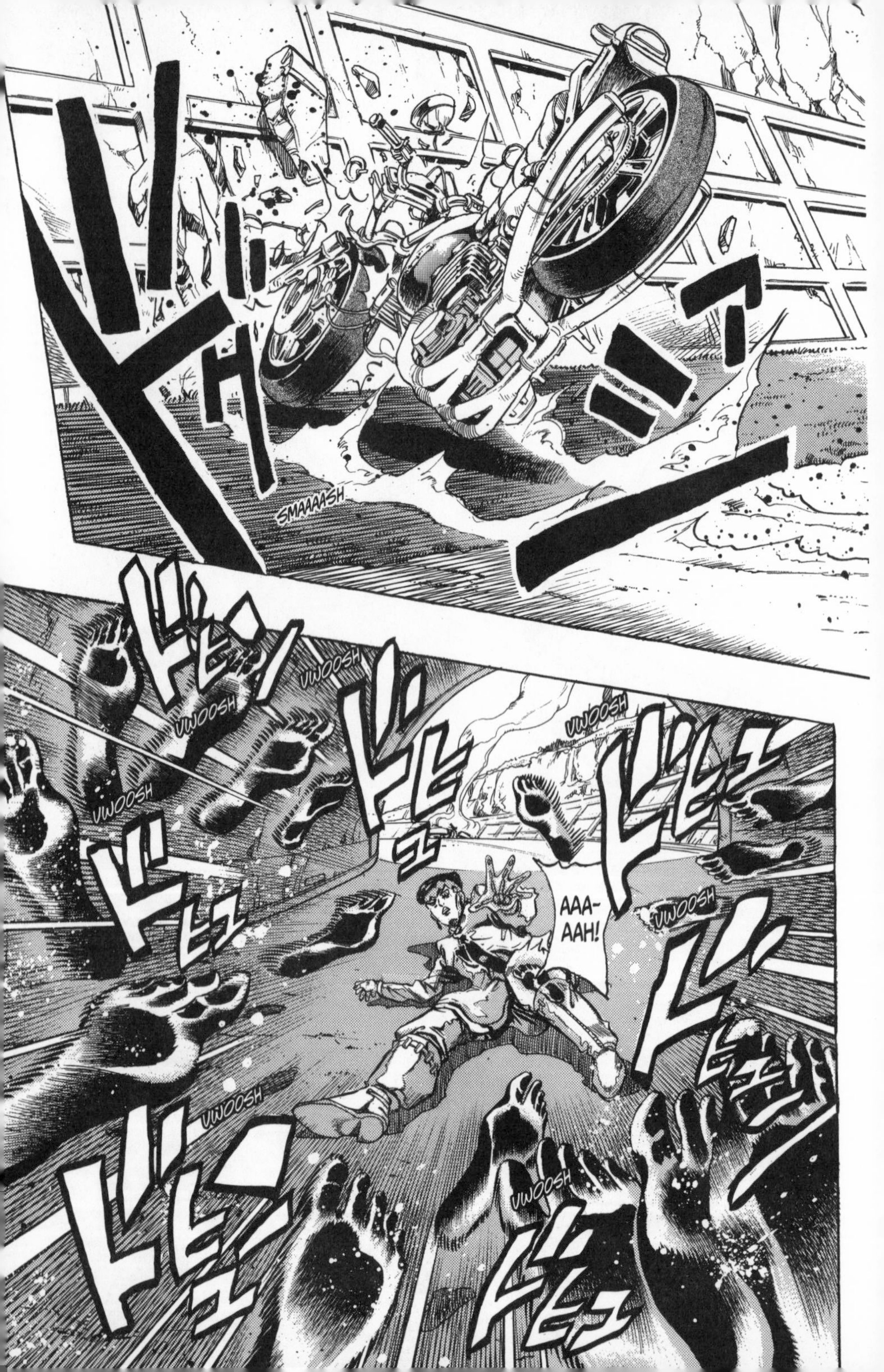
SMAAAASH
VWOOSH
VWOOSH
VWOOSH
VWOOSH
AAA-AAH!
VWOOSH
VWOOSH
VWOOSH

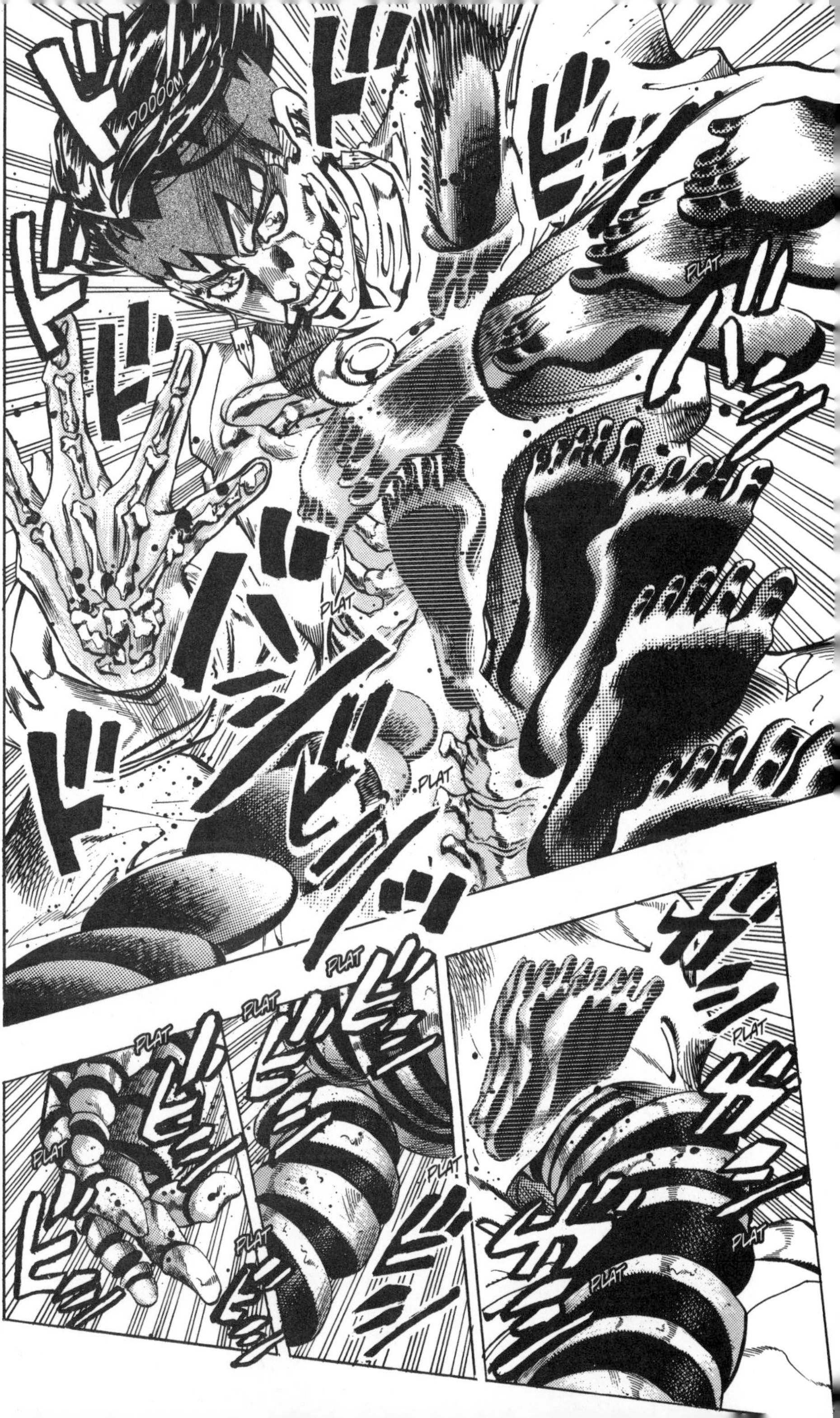
DOOOOM
PLAT
PLAT
PLAT
PLAT
PLAT
PLAT
PLAT
PLAT
PLAT
PLAT
PLAT

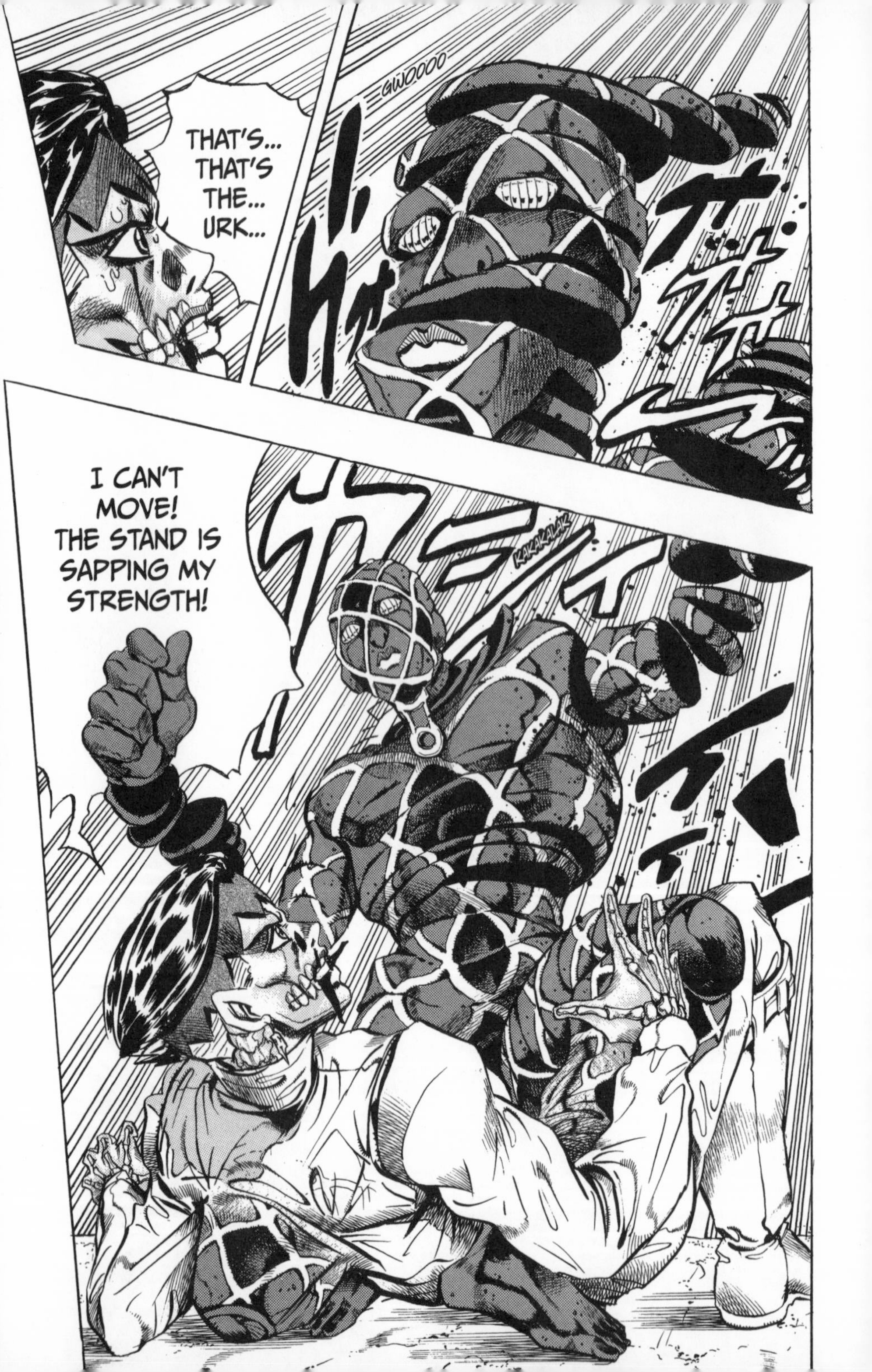
GWOOOO
THAT'S... THAT'S THE... URK...
KAKAKALAK
I CAN'T MOVE! THE STAND IS SAPPING MY STRENGTH!

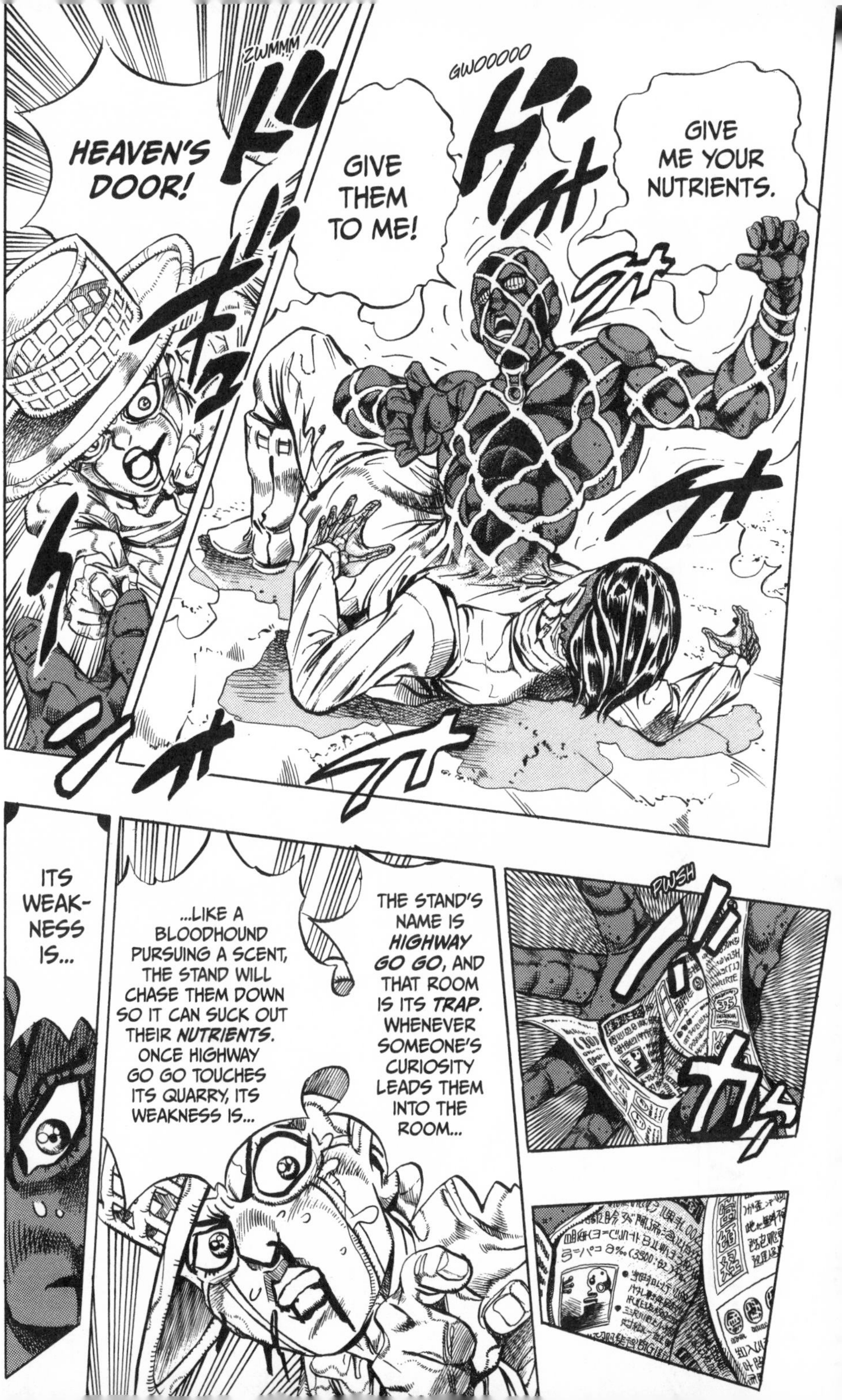
GIVE ME YOUR NUTRIENTS.
GWOOOOO
GIVE THEM TO ME!
ZWUMMM
HEAVEN'S DOOR!
PWSH
THE STAND'S NAME IS *HIGHWAY GO GO*, AND THAT ROOM IS ITS *TRAP*. WHENEVER SOMEONE'S CURIOSITY LEADS THEM INTO THE ROOM...
...LIKE A BLOODHOUND PURSUING A SCENT, THE STAND WILL CHASE THEM DOWN SO IT CAN SUCK OUT THEIR *NUTRIENTS*. ONCE HIGHWAY GO GO TOUCHES ITS QUARRY, ITS WEAKNESS IS...
ITS WEAK-NESS IS...

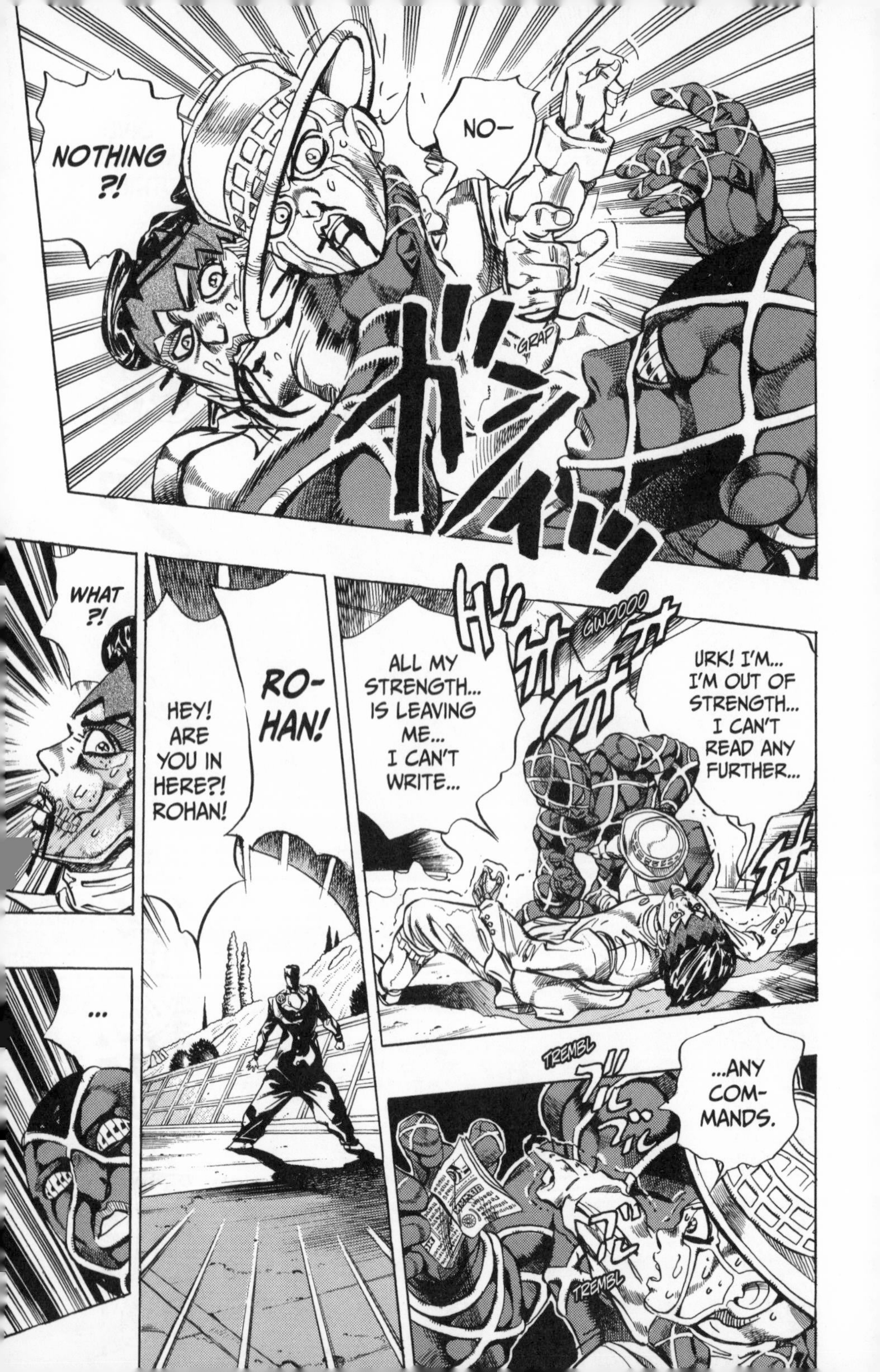
NO–
NOTHING ?!
GRAP
GWOOOO
URK! I'M... I'M OUT OF STRENGTH... I CAN'T READ ANY FURTHER...
ALL MY STRENGTH... IS LEAVING ME... I CAN'T WRITE...
TREMBL
...ANY COM-MANDS.
TREMBL
RO-HAN!
HEY! ARE YOU IN HERE?! ROHAN!
WHAT ?!
...

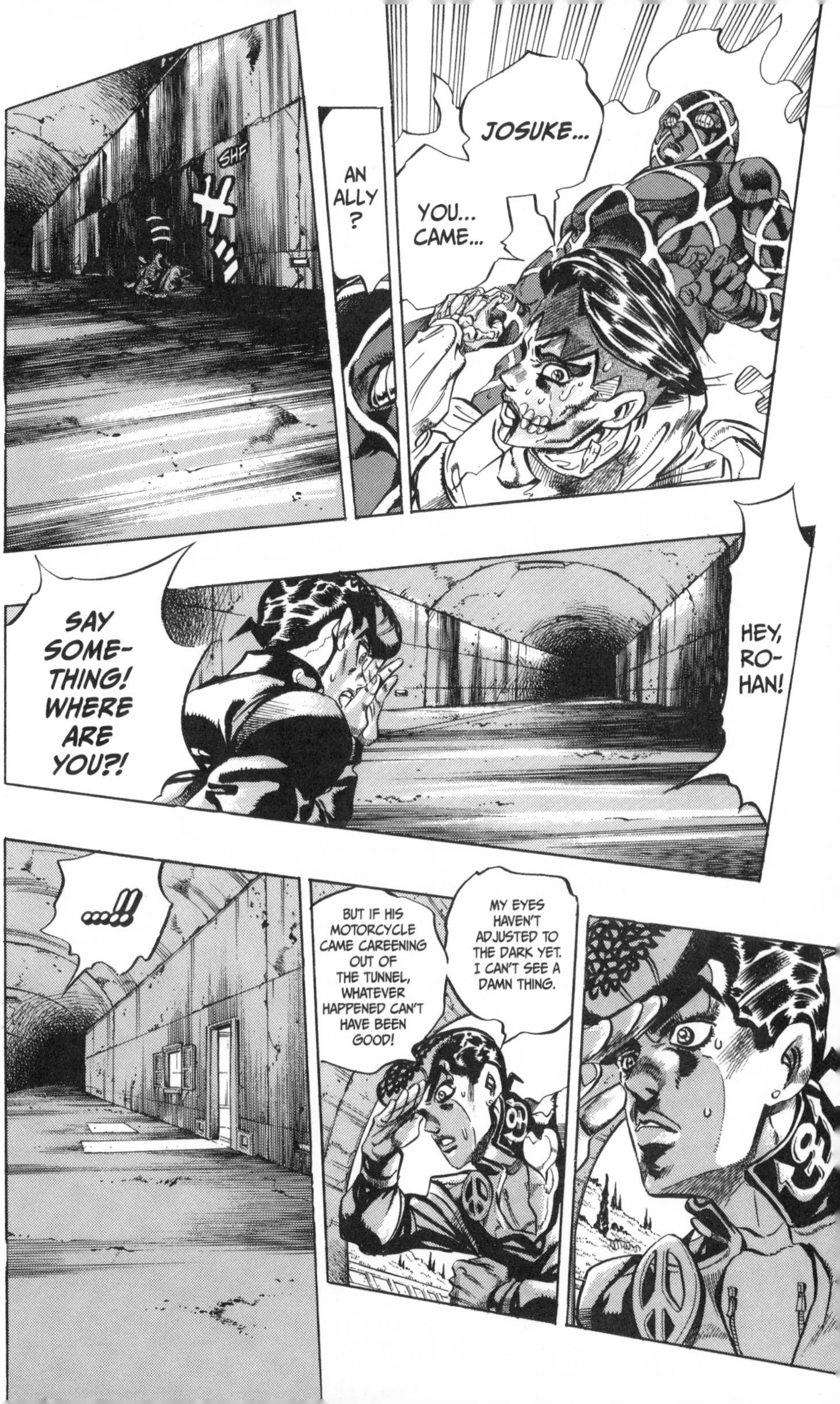
JOSUKE...
YOU... CAME...
AN ALLY ?
SHF
HEY, RO-HAN!
SAY SOME-THING! WHERE ARE YOU?!
MY EYES HAVEN'T ADJUSTED TO THE DARK YET. I CAN'T SEE A DAMN THING.
BUT IF HIS MOTORCYCLE CAME CAREENING OUT OF THE TUNNEL, WHATEVER HAPPENED CAN'T HAVE BEEN GOOD!
...!!

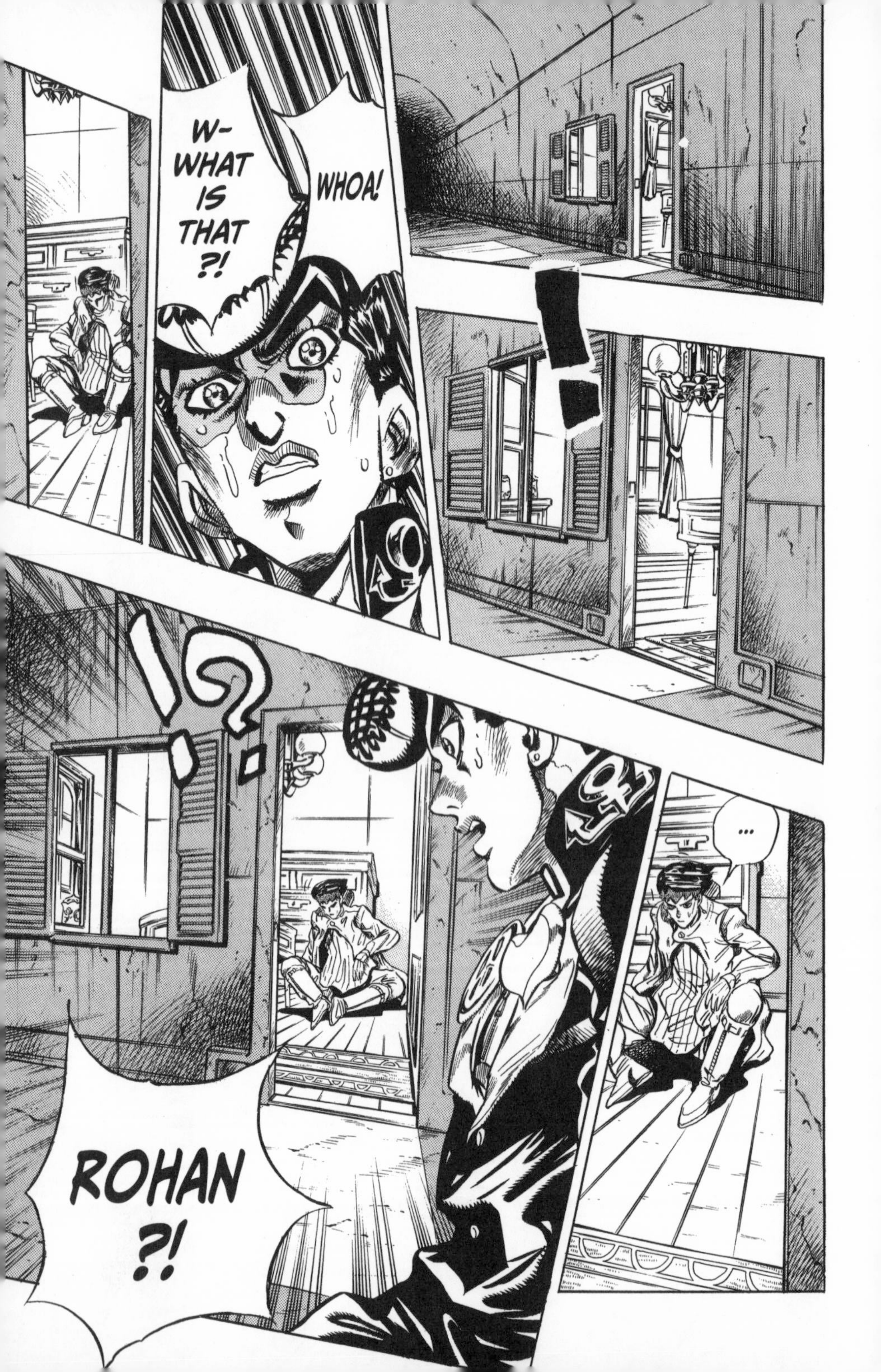
WHOA!
W-WHAT IS THAT?!
...
ROHAN?!

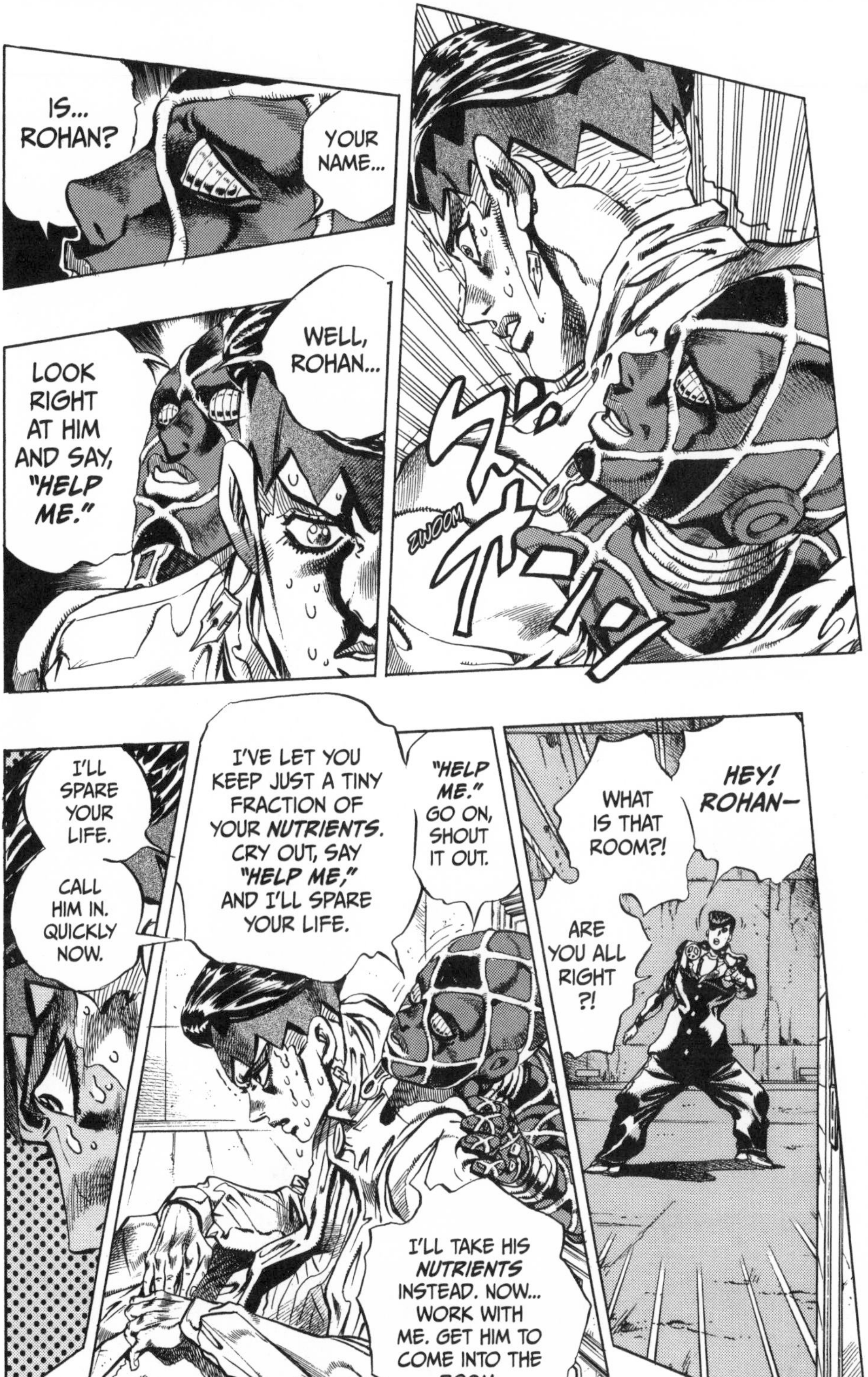
ZWOOM
YOUR NAME...
IS... ROHAN?
WELL, ROHAN...
LOOK RIGHT AT HIM AND SAY, *"HELP ME."*
HEY! ROHAN—
WHAT IS THAT ROOM?!
ARE YOU ALL RIGHT ?!
"HELP ME." GO ON, SHOUT IT OUT.
I'VE LET YOU KEEP JUST A TINY FRACTION OF YOUR *NUTRIENTS*. CRY OUT, SAY *"HELP ME,"* AND I'LL SPARE YOUR LIFE.
I'LL SPARE YOUR LIFE.
CALL HIM IN. QUICKLY NOW.
I'LL TAKE HIS *NUTRIENTS* INSTEAD. NOW... WORK WITH ME. GET HIM TO COME INTO THE ROOM.

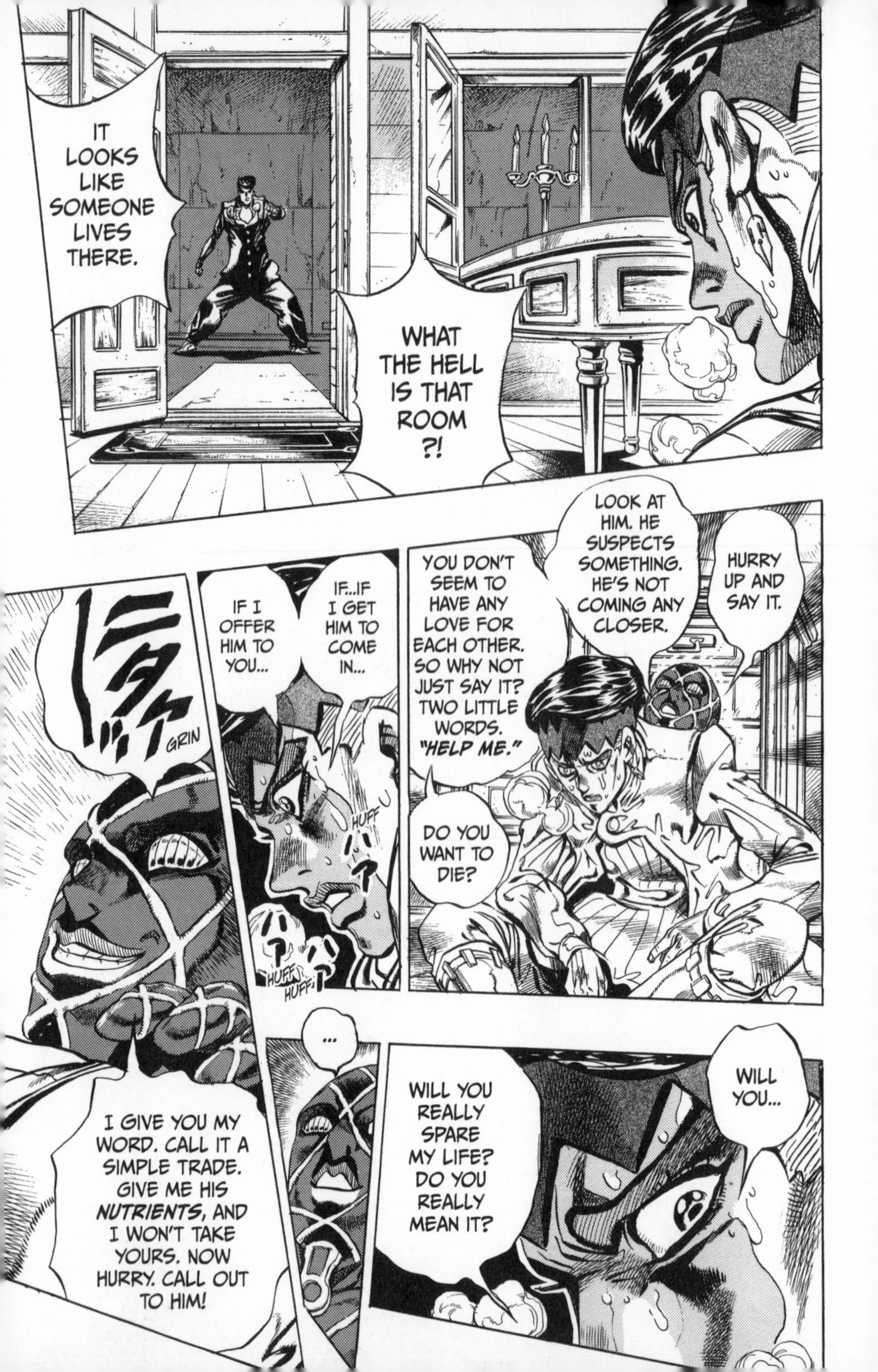
WHAT THE HELL IS THAT ROOM ?!
IT LOOKS LIKE SOMEONE LIVES THERE.
HURRY UP AND SAY IT.
LOOK AT HIM. HE SUSPECTS SOMETHING. HE'S NOT COMING ANY CLOSER.
YOU DON'T SEEM TO HAVE ANY LOVE FOR EACH OTHER. SO WHY NOT JUST SAY IT? TWO LITTLE WORDS. ***"HELP ME."***
DO YOU WANT TO DIE?
IF...IF I GET HIM TO COME IN...
IF I OFFER HIM TO YOU...
HUFF
HUFF HUFF
WILL YOU...
WILL YOU REALLY SPARE MY LIFE? DO YOU REALLY MEAN IT?
...
ニタァ
GRIN
I GIVE YOU MY WORD. CALL IT A SIMPLE TRADE. GIVE ME HIS ***NUTRIENTS***, AND I WON'T TAKE YOURS. NOW HURRY. CALL OUT TO HIM!

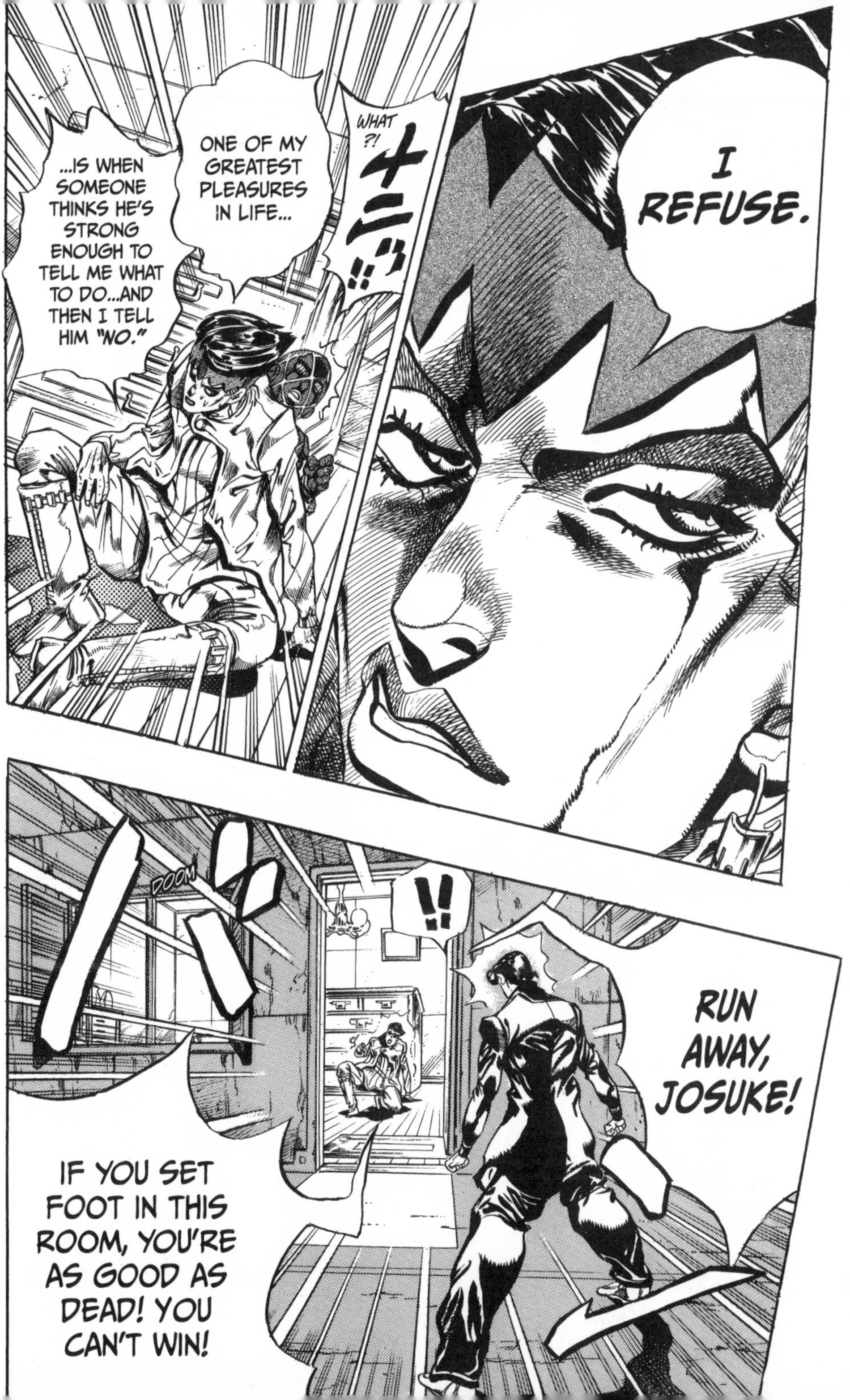
I REFUSE.
WHAT ?!
ONE OF MY GREATEST PLEASURES IN LIFE...
...IS WHEN SOMEONE THINKS HE'S STRONG ENOUGH TO TELL ME WHAT TO DO...AND THEN I TELL HIM "NO."
!!
RUN AWAY, JOSUKE!
DOOM
IF YOU SET FOOT IN THIS ROOM, YOU'RE AS GOOD AS DEAD! YOU CAN'T WIN!

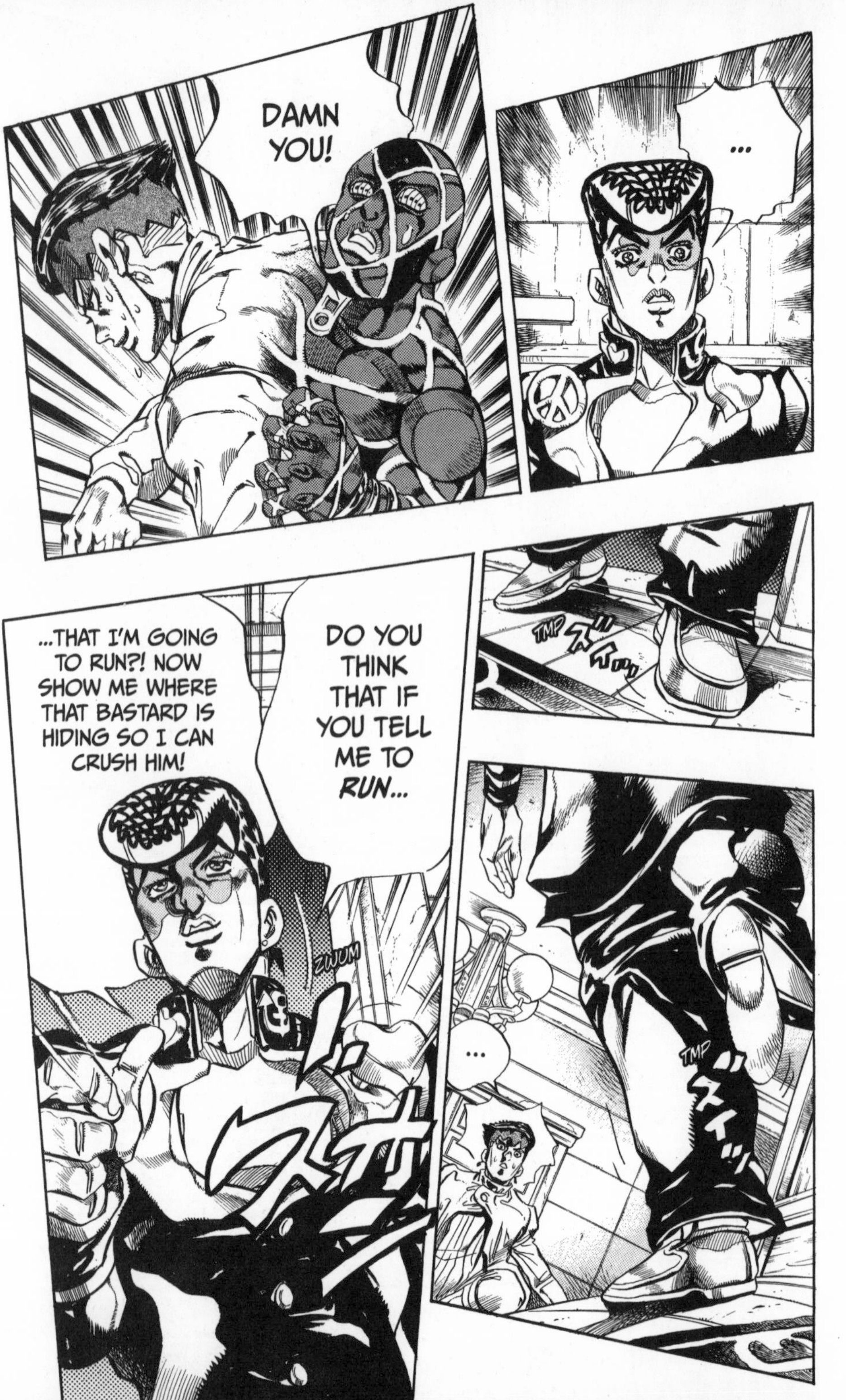
...
DAMN YOU!
TMP
...
TMP
DO YOU THINK THAT IF YOU TELL ME TO *RUN*...
...THAT I'M GOING TO RUN?! NOW SHOW ME WHERE THAT BASTARD IS HIDING SO I CAN CRUSH HIM!
ZWUM

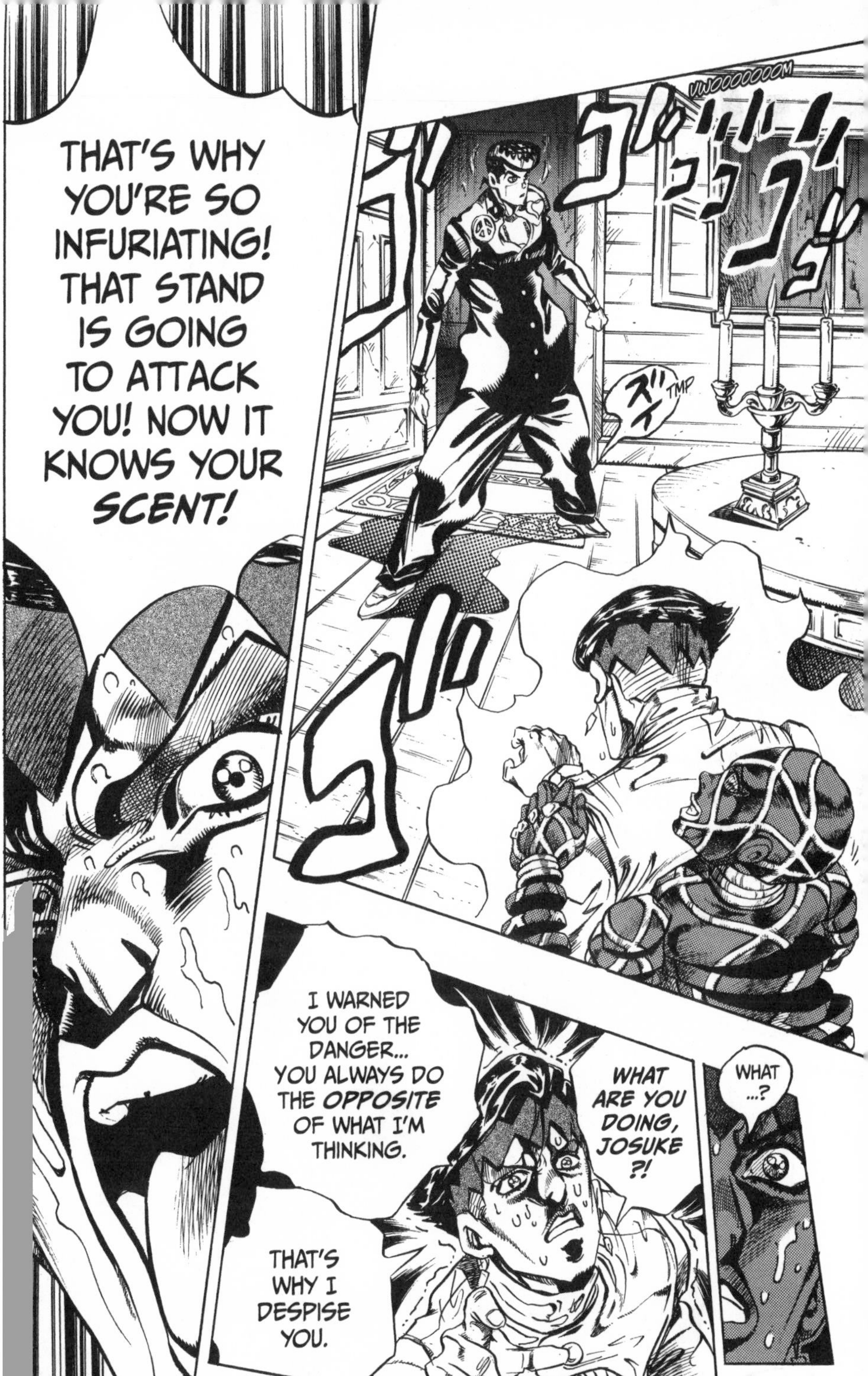
VWOOOOOOOM
ズイ TMP
WHAT ...?
WHAT ARE YOU DOING, JOSUKE?!
I WARNED YOU OF THE DANGER... YOU ALWAYS DO THE *OPPOSITE* OF WHAT I'M THINKING.
THAT'S WHY I DESPISE YOU.
THAT'S WHY YOU'RE SO INFURIATING! THAT STAND IS GOING TO ATTACK YOU! NOW IT KNOWS YOUR *SCENT!*

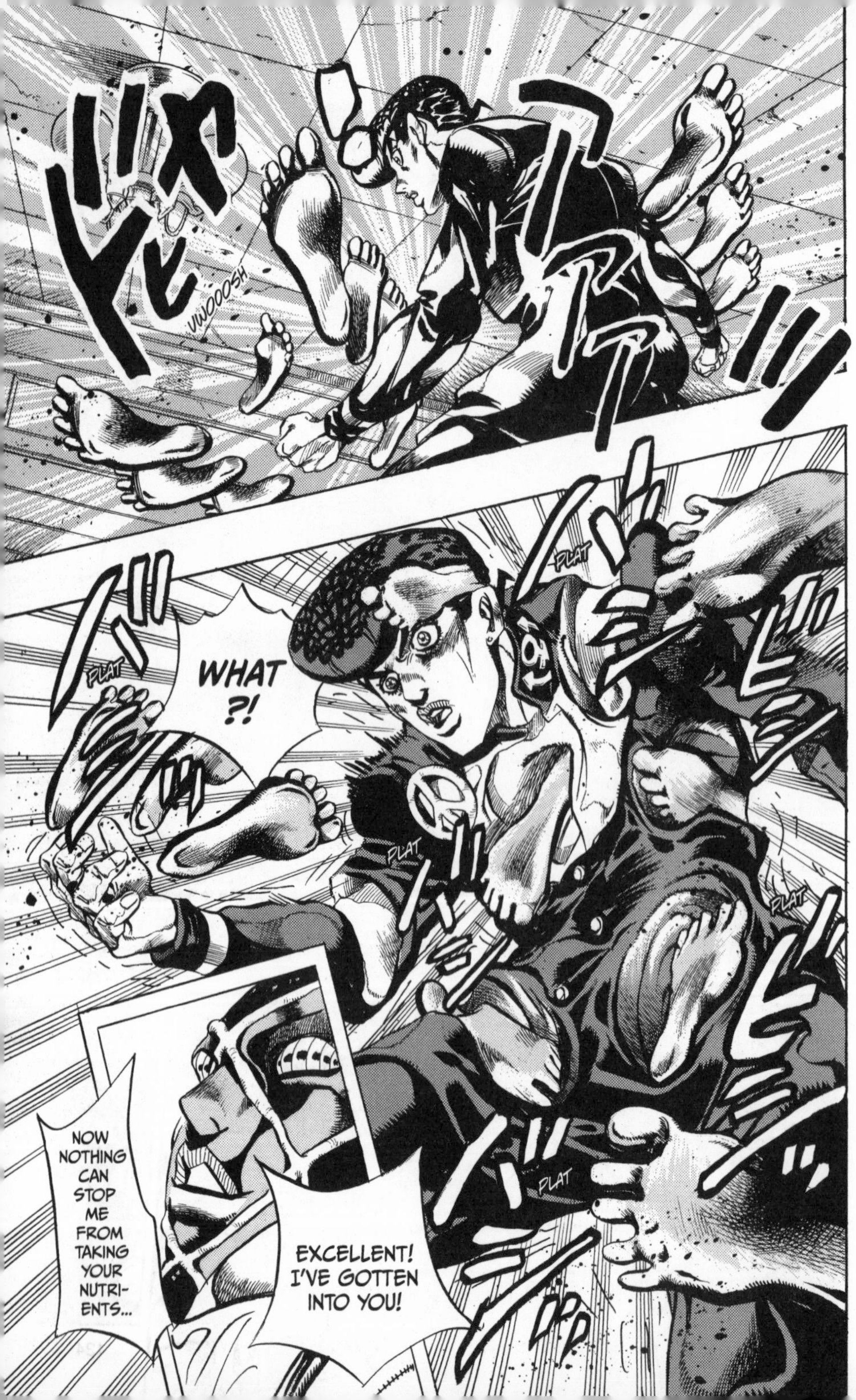

VWOOOSH
PLAT
WHAT ?!
PLAT
PLAT
PLAT
PLAT
EXCELLENT! I'VE GOTTEN INTO YOU!
NOW NOTHING CAN STOP ME FROM TAKING YOUR NUTRI-ENTS...

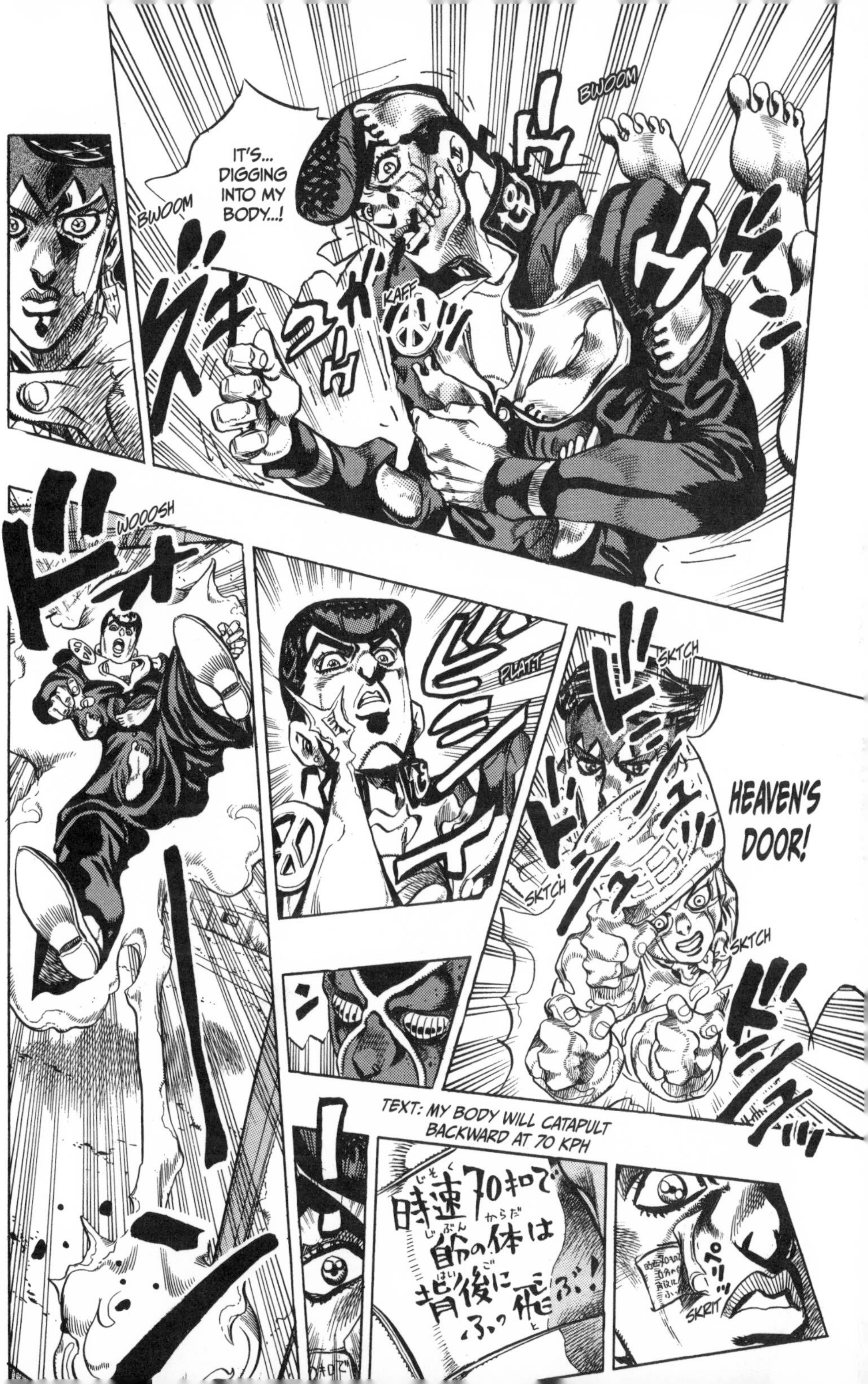
BWOOM
IT'S... DIGGING INTO MY BODY...!
BWOOM
KAFF
SKTCH
HEAVEN'S DOOR!
SKTCH
SKTCH
PLATT
WOOOSH
TEXT: MY BODY WILL CATAPULT BACKWARD AT 70 KPH
時速70キロで節の体は背後にふっ飛ぶ!
SKRIT

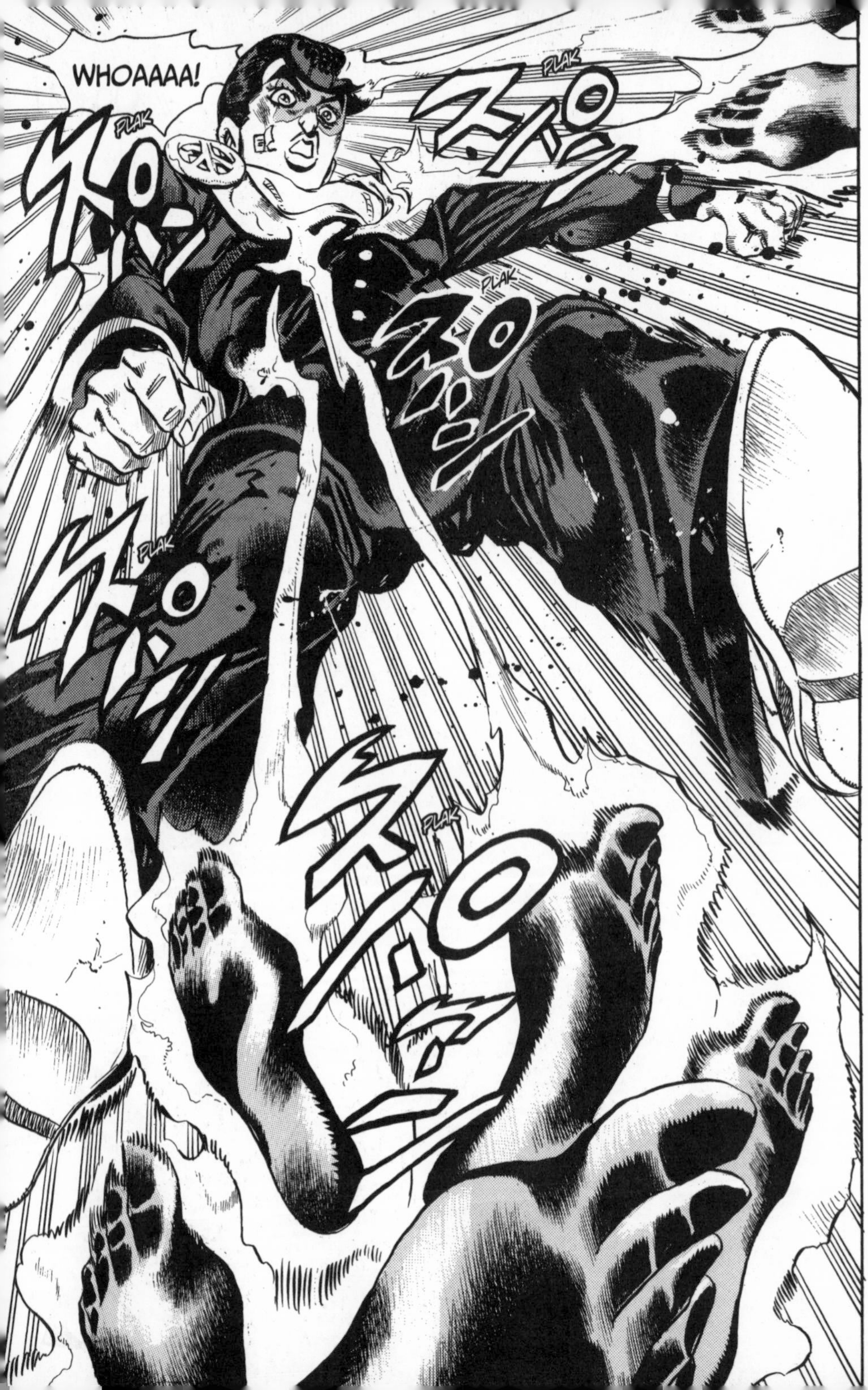
WHOAAAA!
PLAK
PLAK
PLAK
PLAK
PLAK

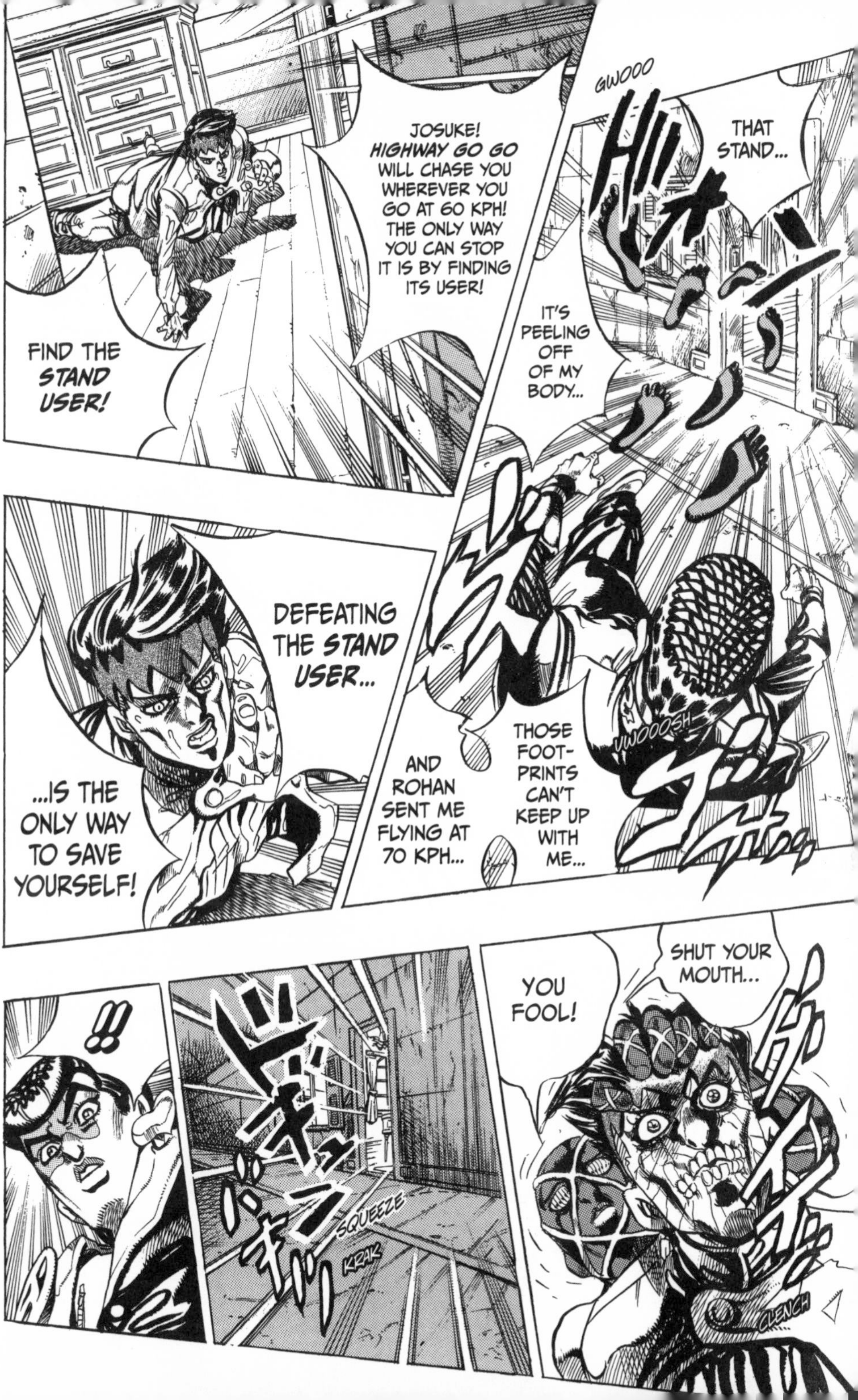
GWOOO
THAT STAND...
IT'S PEELING OFF OF MY BODY...
THOSE FOOT-PRINTS CAN'T KEEP UP WITH ME...
AND ROHAN SENT ME FLYING AT 70 KPH...
UWOOOSH
JOSUKE! HIGHWAY GO GO WILL CHASE YOU WHEREVER YOU GO AT 60 KPH! THE ONLY WAY YOU CAN STOP IT IS BY FINDING ITS USER!
FIND THE STAND USER!
DEFEATING THE STAND USER...
...IS THE ONLY WAY TO SAVE YOURSELF!
SHUT YOUR MOUTH...
YOU FOOL!
CLENCH
SQUEEZE
KRAK
!!

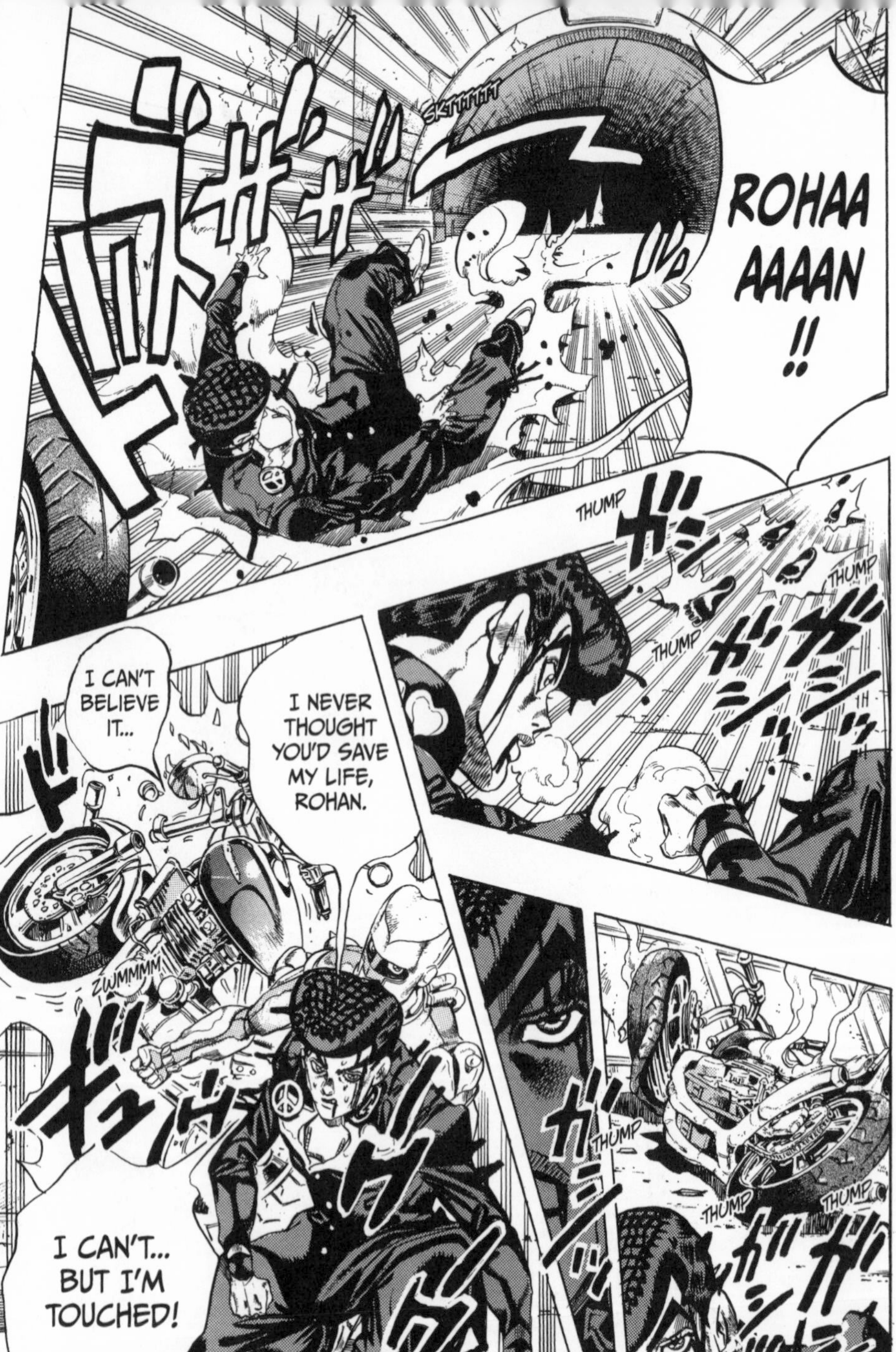
SKTTTTTT
ROHAA AAAAN !!
THUMP
THUMP
THUMP
THUMP
THUMP
THUMP
ZWMMMM
I CAN'T BELIEVE IT...
I NEVER THOUGHT YOU'D SAVE MY LIFE, ROHAN.
I CAN'T... BUT I'M TOUCHED!

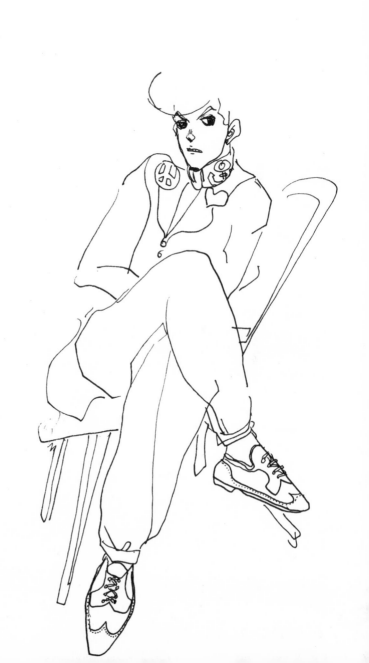

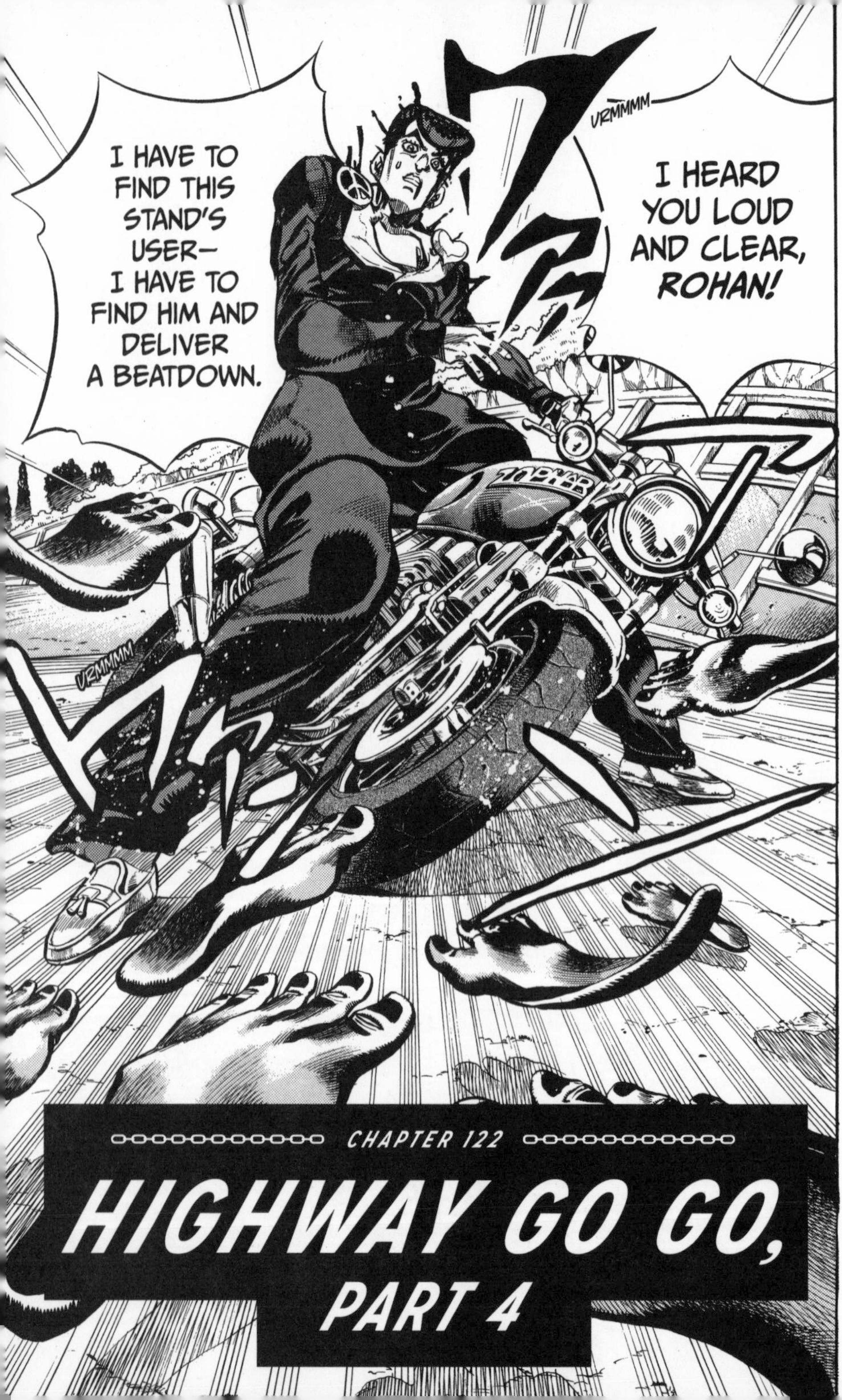
VRMMMM
I HEARD YOU LOUD AND CLEAR, ROHAN!
I HAVE TO FIND THIS STAND'S USER— I HAVE TO FIND HIM AND DELIVER A BEATDOWN.
VRMMMM
CHAPTER 122
HIGHWAY GO GO, PART 4

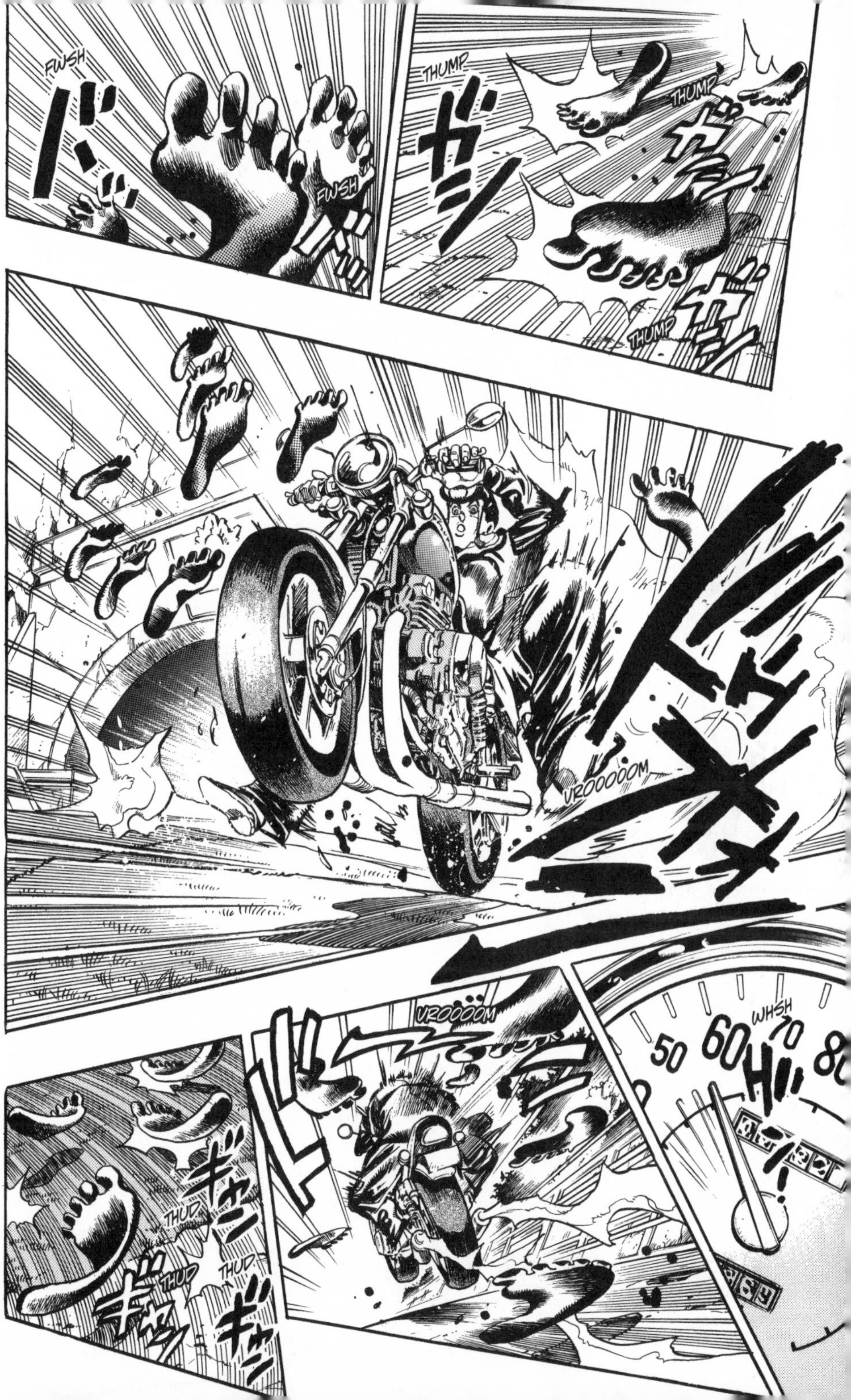
THUMP
THUMP
THUMP
FWSH
FWSH
VROOOOOM
WHSH
VROOOOM
THUD
THUD
THUD

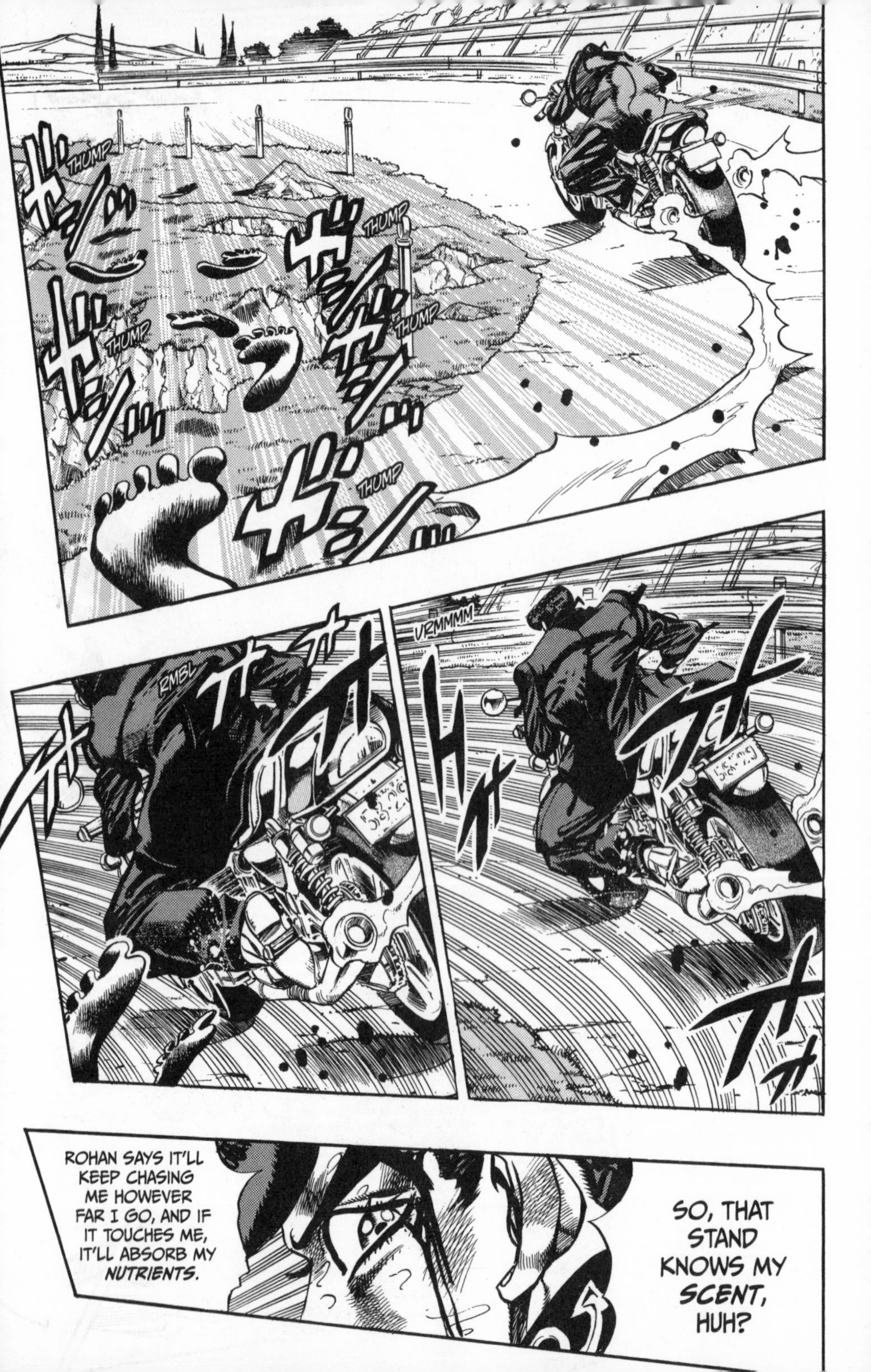
THUMP
THUMP
THUMP
THUMP
THUMP
URMMMM
RMBL
SO, THAT STAND KNOWS MY *SCENT*, HUH?
ROHAN SAYS IT'LL KEEP CHASING ME HOWEVER FAR I GO, AND IF IT TOUCHES ME, IT'LL ABSORB MY *NUTRIENTS*.

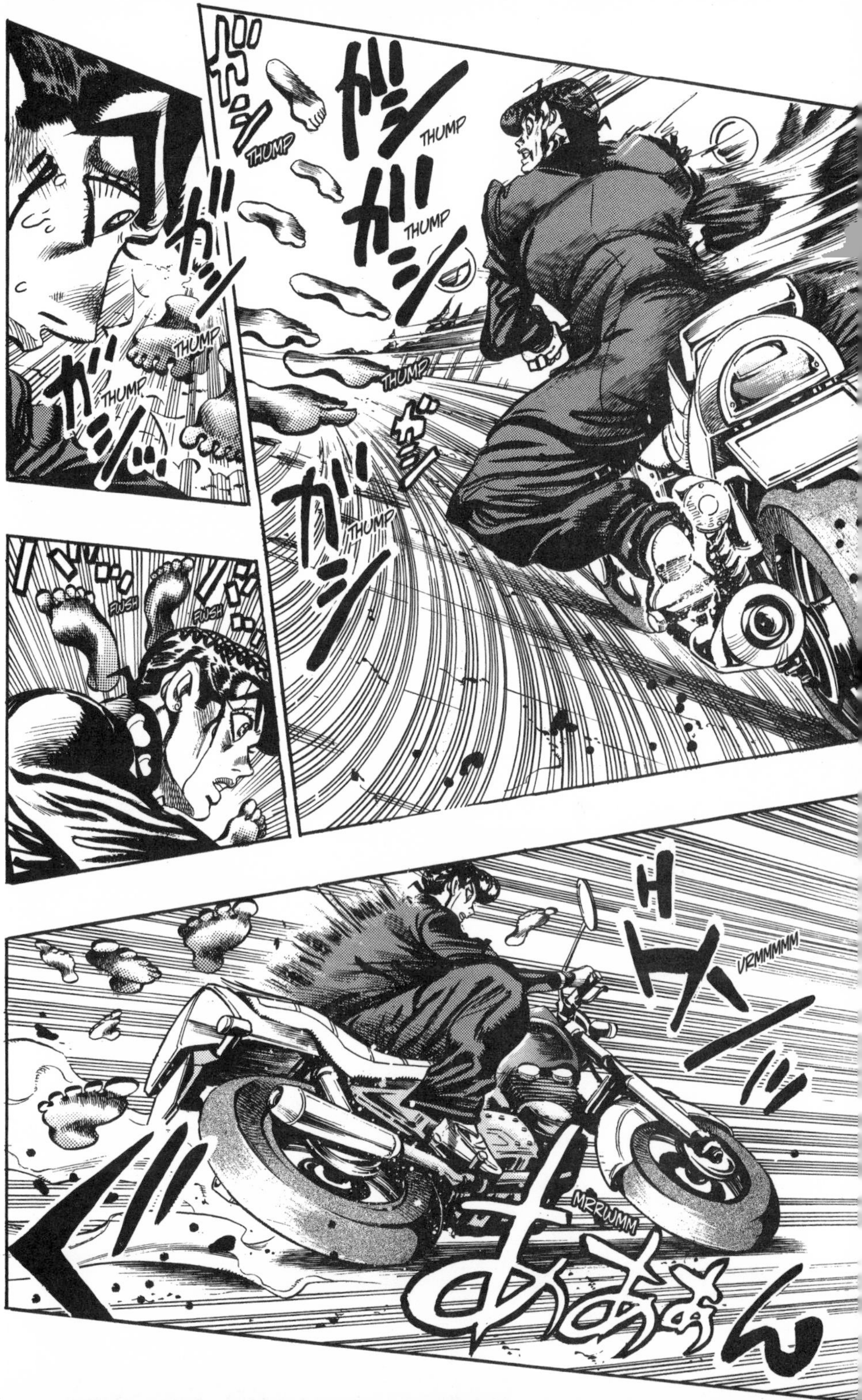
THUMP
THUMP
THUMP
THUMP
THUMP
THUMP
THUMP
THUMP
FWSH
FWSH
URMMMMM
MRRWMM

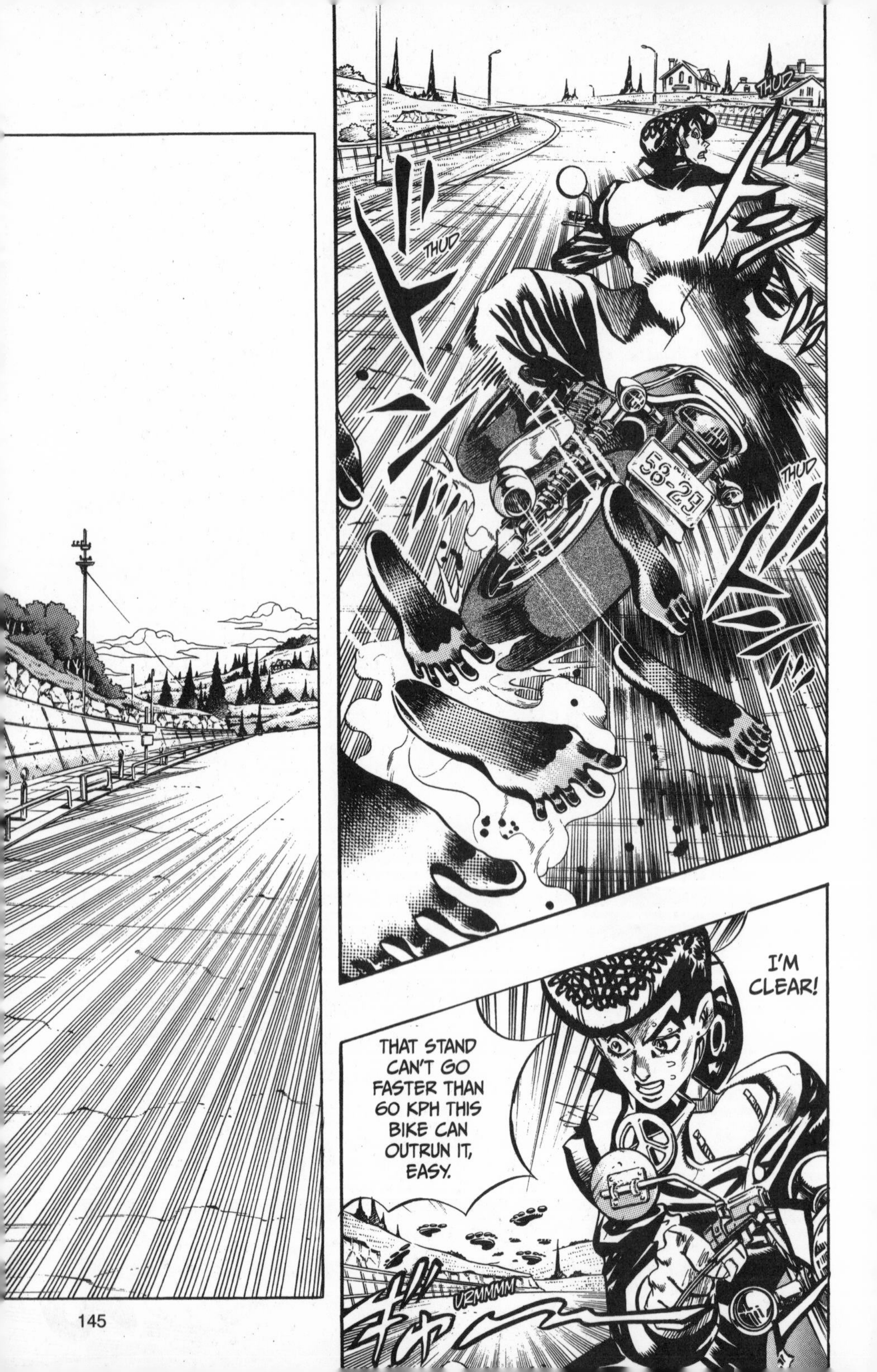
THUD
THUD
THUD
I'M CLEAR!
THAT STAND CAN'T GO FASTER THAN 60 KPH THIS BIKE CAN OUTRUN IT, EASY.
URMMMM

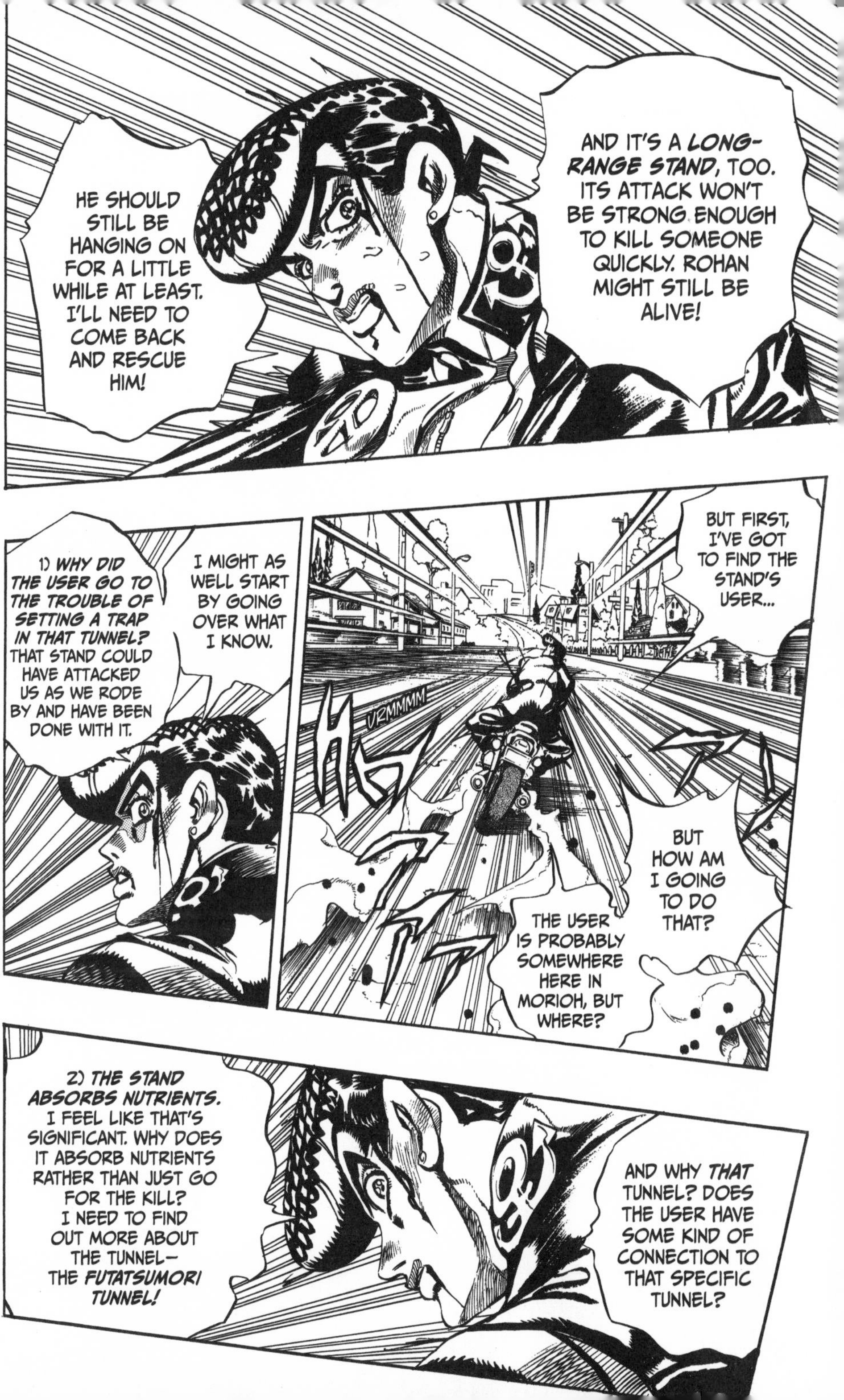
AND IT'S A *LONG-RANGE STAND*, TOO. ITS ATTACK WON'T BE STRONG ENOUGH TO KILL SOMEONE QUICKLY. ROHAN MIGHT STILL BE ALIVE!
HE SHOULD STILL BE HANGING ON FOR A LITTLE WHILE AT LEAST. I'LL NEED TO COME BACK AND RESCUE HIM!
BUT FIRST, I'VE GOT TO FIND THE STAND'S USER...
BUT HOW AM I GOING TO DO THAT?
THE USER IS PROBABLY SOMEWHERE HERE IN MORIOH, BUT WHERE?
VRMMMM
I MIGHT AS WELL START BY GOING OVER WHAT I KNOW.
1) *WHY DID THE USER GO TO THE TROUBLE OF SETTING A TRAP IN THAT TUNNEL?* THAT STAND COULD HAVE ATTACKED US AS WE RODE BY AND HAVE BEEN DONE WITH IT.
2) *THE STAND ABSORBS NUTRIENTS.* I FEEL LIKE THAT'S SIGNIFICANT. WHY DOES IT ABSORB NUTRIENTS RATHER THAN JUST GO FOR THE KILL? I NEED TO FIND OUT MORE ABOUT THE TUNNEL— THE *FUTATSUMORI TUNNEL!*
AND WHY *THAT* TUNNEL? DOES THE USER HAVE SOME KIND OF CONNECTION TO THAT SPECIFIC TUNNEL?

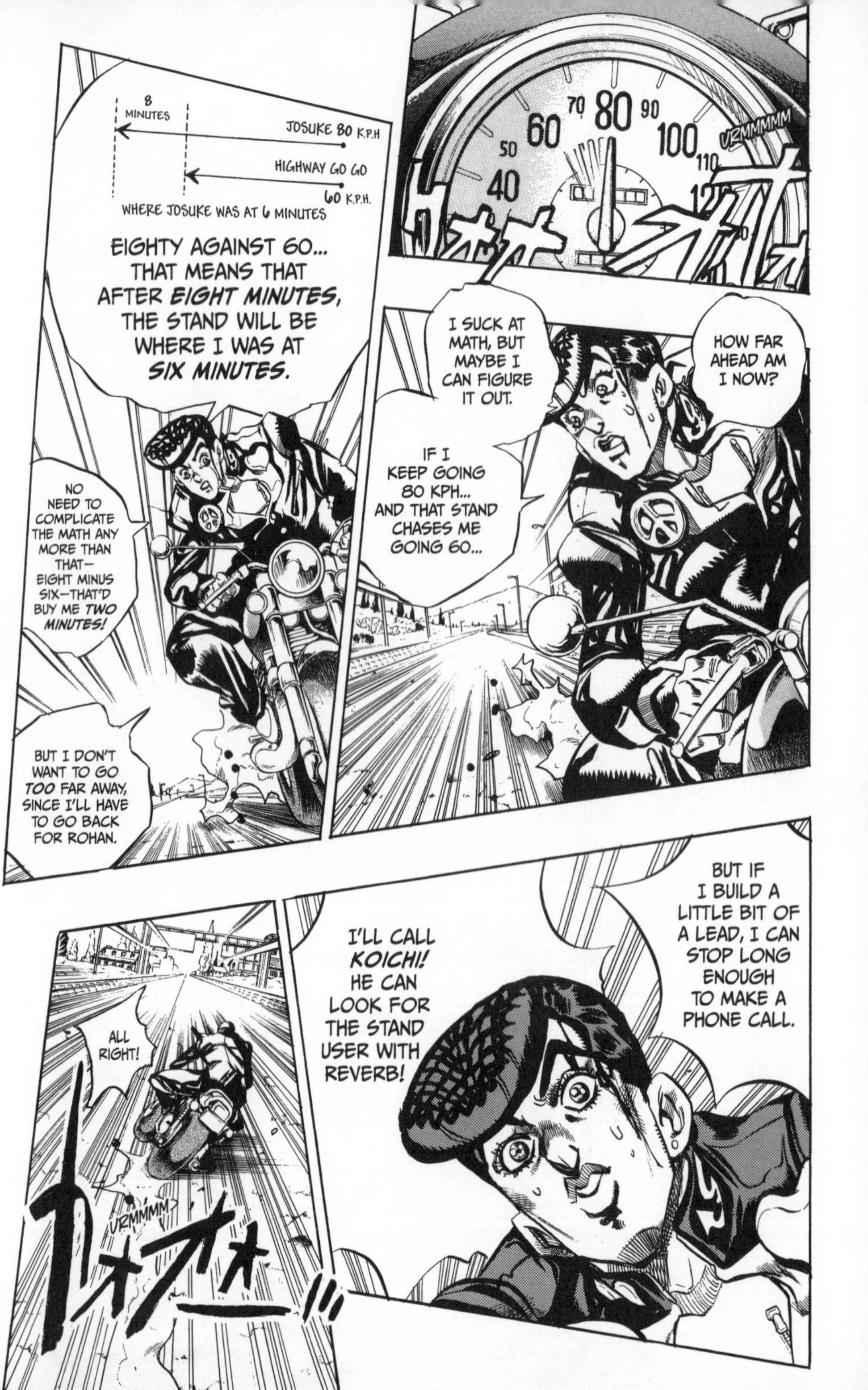
URMMMMM
HOW FAR AHEAD AM I NOW?
I SUCK AT MATH, BUT MAYBE I CAN FIGURE IT OUT.
IF I KEEP GOING 80 KPH... AND THAT STAND CHASES ME GOING 60...
8 MINUTES
JOSUKE 80 K.P.H
HIGHWAY GO GO 60 K.P.H.
WHERE JOSUKE WAS AT 6 MINUTES
EIGHTY AGAINST 60... THAT MEANS THAT AFTER *EIGHT MINUTES*, THE STAND WILL BE WHERE I WAS AT *SIX MINUTES*.
NO NEED TO COMPLICATE THE MATH ANY MORE THAN THAT— EIGHT MINUS SIX—THAT'D BUY ME *TWO MINUTES!*
BUT I DON'T WANT TO GO *TOO* FAR AWAY, SINCE I'LL HAVE TO GO BACK FOR ROHAN.
BUT IF I BUILD A LITTLE BIT OF A LEAD, I CAN STOP LONG ENOUGH TO MAKE A PHONE CALL.
I'LL CALL *KOICHI!* HE CAN LOOK FOR THE STAND USER WITH REVERB!
ALL RIGHT!
URMMMMM

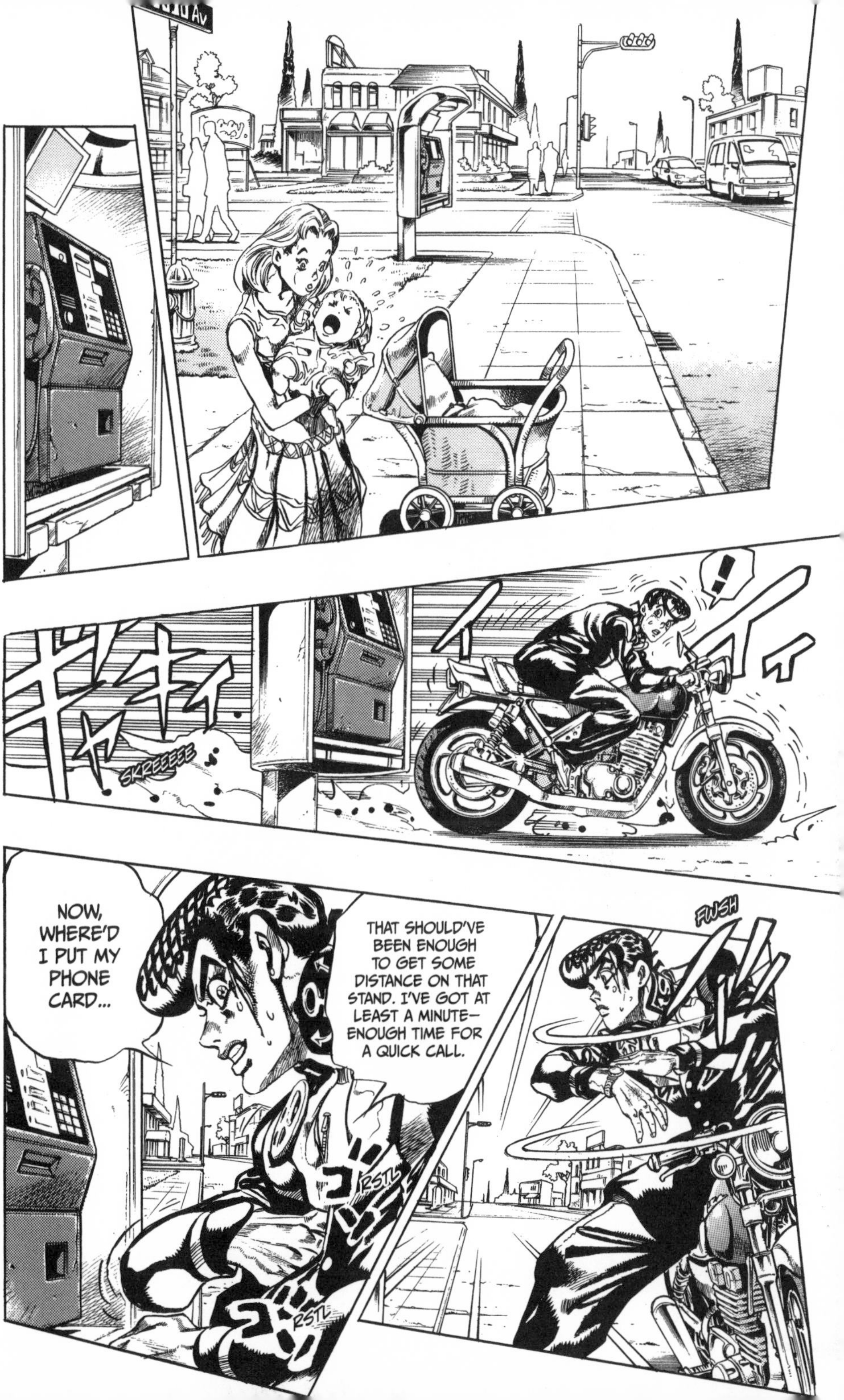

!
SKREEEEEE
FWSH
THAT SHOULD'VE BEEN ENOUGH TO GET SOME DISTANCE ON THAT STAND. I'VE GOT AT LEAST A MINUTE— ENOUGH TIME FOR A QUICK CALL.
NOW, WHERE'D I PUT MY PHONE CARD...
RSTL
RSTL

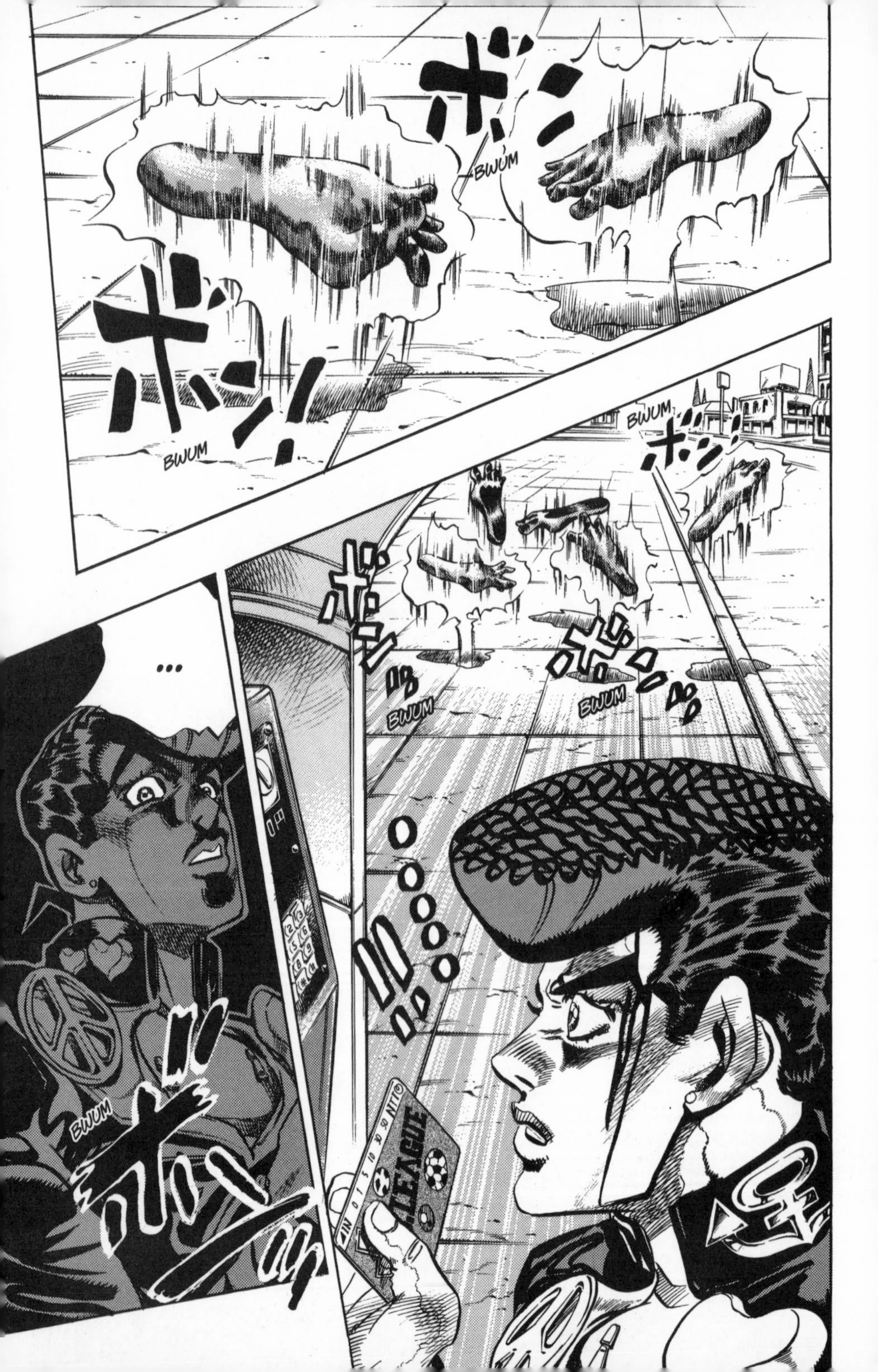

ボン
BWUM
ボン！
BWUM
ボン
BWUM
ボン
BWUM
ボン
BWUM
ボン
BWUM
…
BWUM

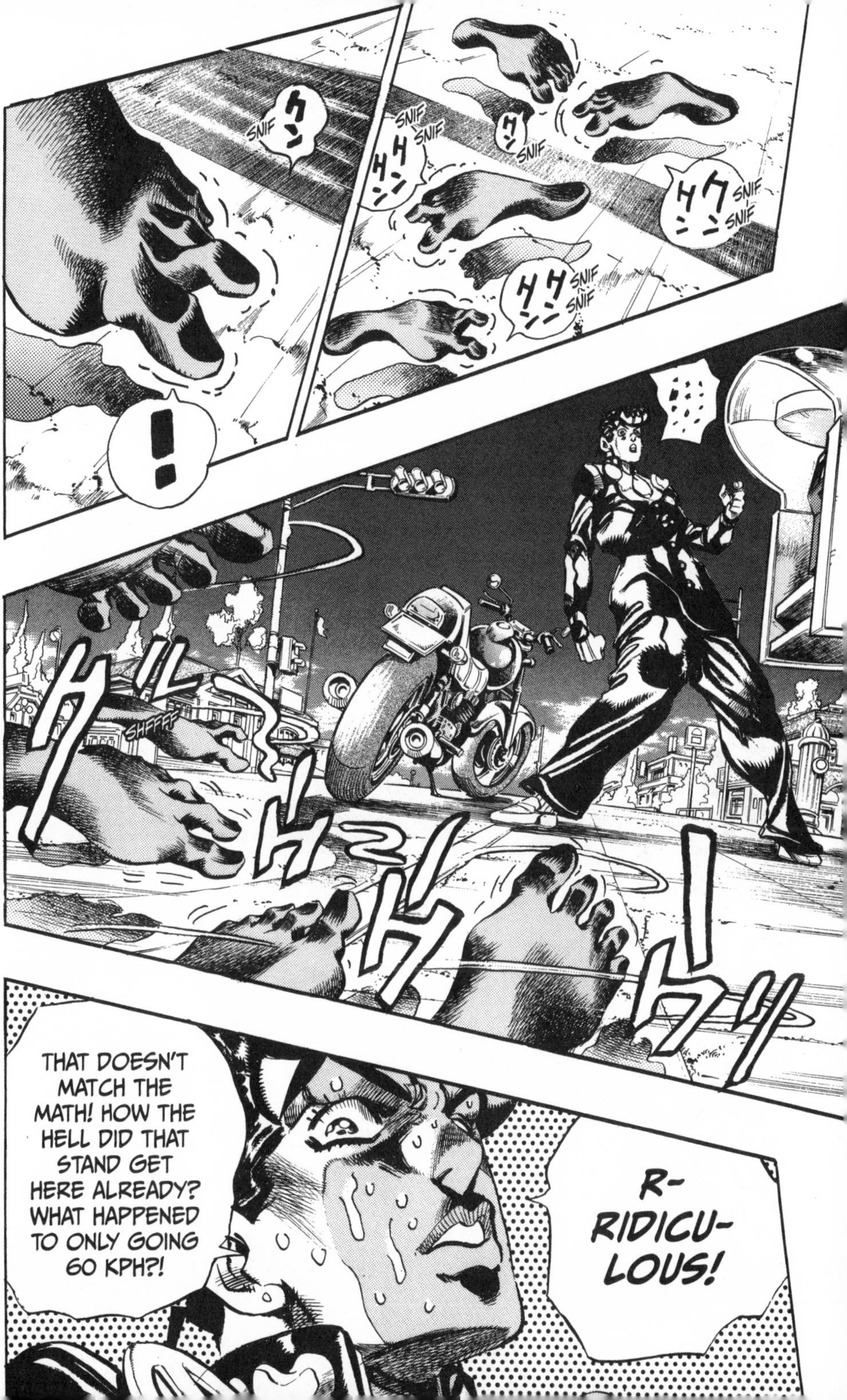
SNIF SNIF
SNIF
SNIF SNIF
SNIF SNIF
SNIF
!
SHFFFF
R-RIDICU-LOUS!
THAT DOESN'T MATCH THE MATH! HOW THE HELL DID THAT STAND GET HERE ALREADY? WHAT HAPPENED TO ONLY GOING 60 KPH?!

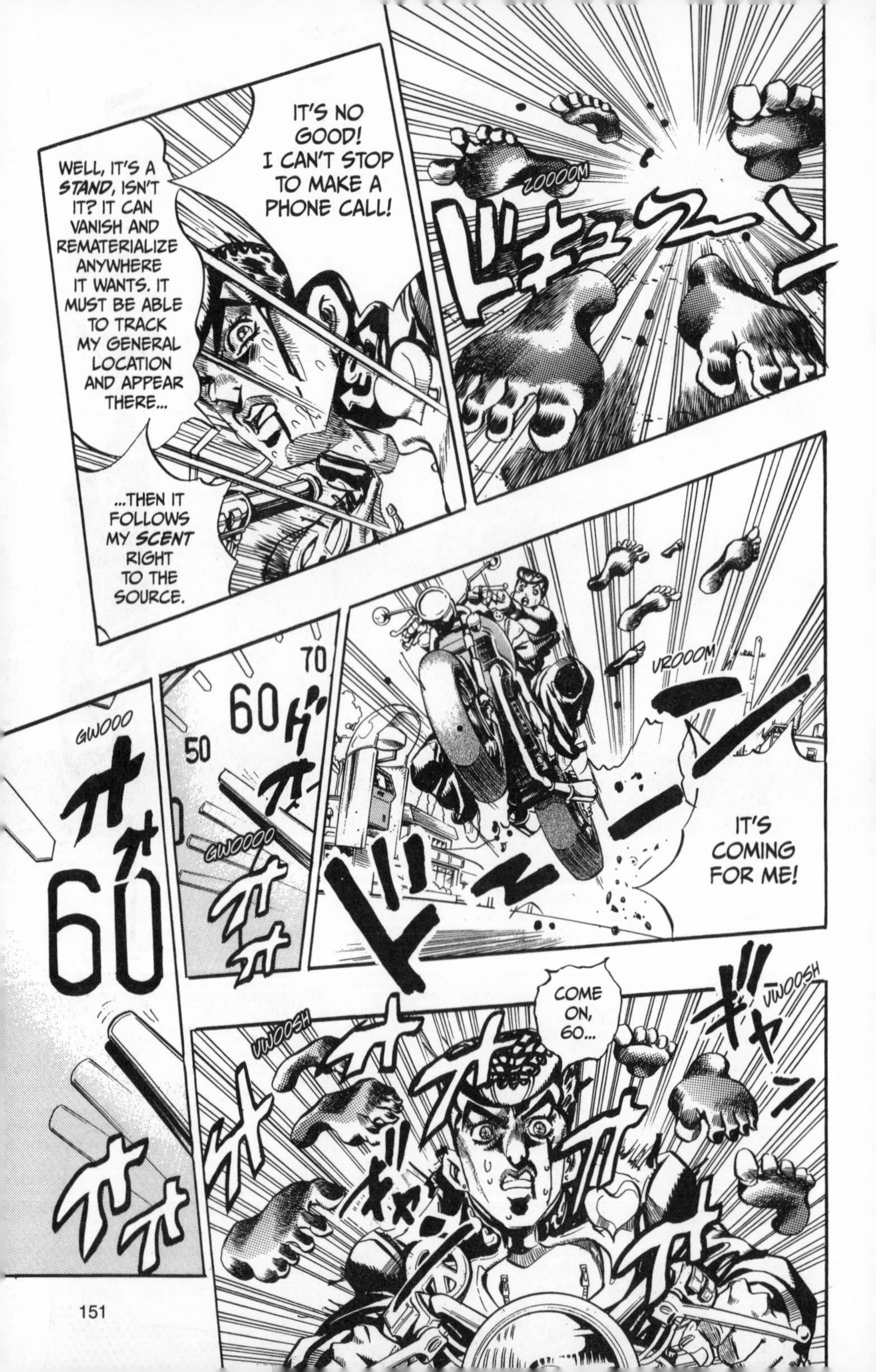
ZOOOOM
IT'S NO GOOD! I CAN'T STOP TO MAKE A PHONE CALL!
WELL, IT'S A *STAND*, ISN'T IT? IT CAN VANISH AND REMATERIALIZE ANYWHERE IT WANTS. IT MUST BE ABLE TO TRACK MY GENERAL LOCATION AND APPEAR THERE...
...THEN IT FOLLOWS MY *SCENT* RIGHT TO THE SOURCE.
VROOOM
IT'S COMING FOR ME!
70
60
50
GWOOOO
GWOOO
60
VWOOSH
COME ON, 60...
VWOOSH

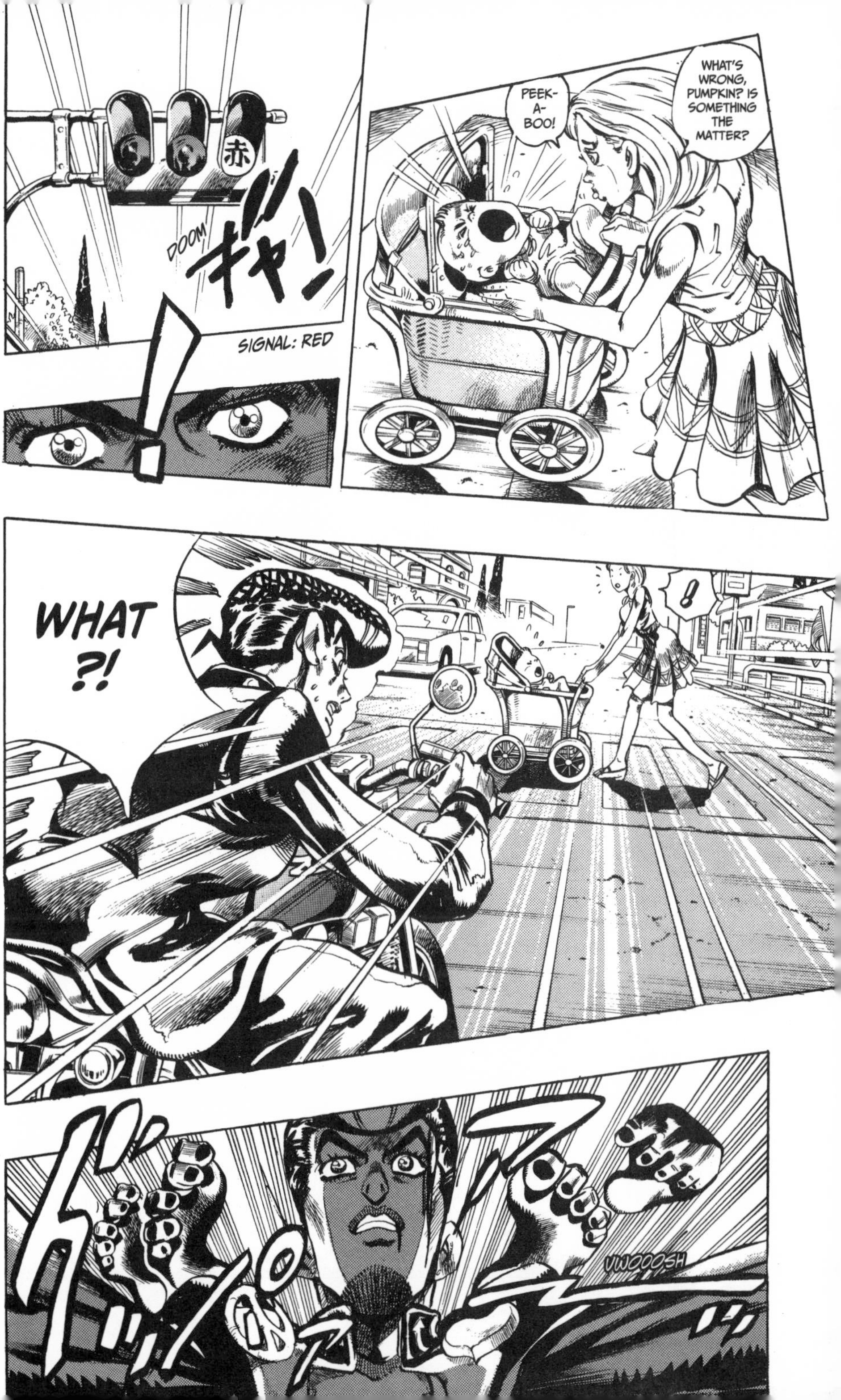
WHAT'S WRONG, PUMPKIN? IS SOMETHING THE MATTER?
PEEK-A-BOO!
赤
DOOM
SIGNAL: RED
WHAT ?!
VWOOOSH

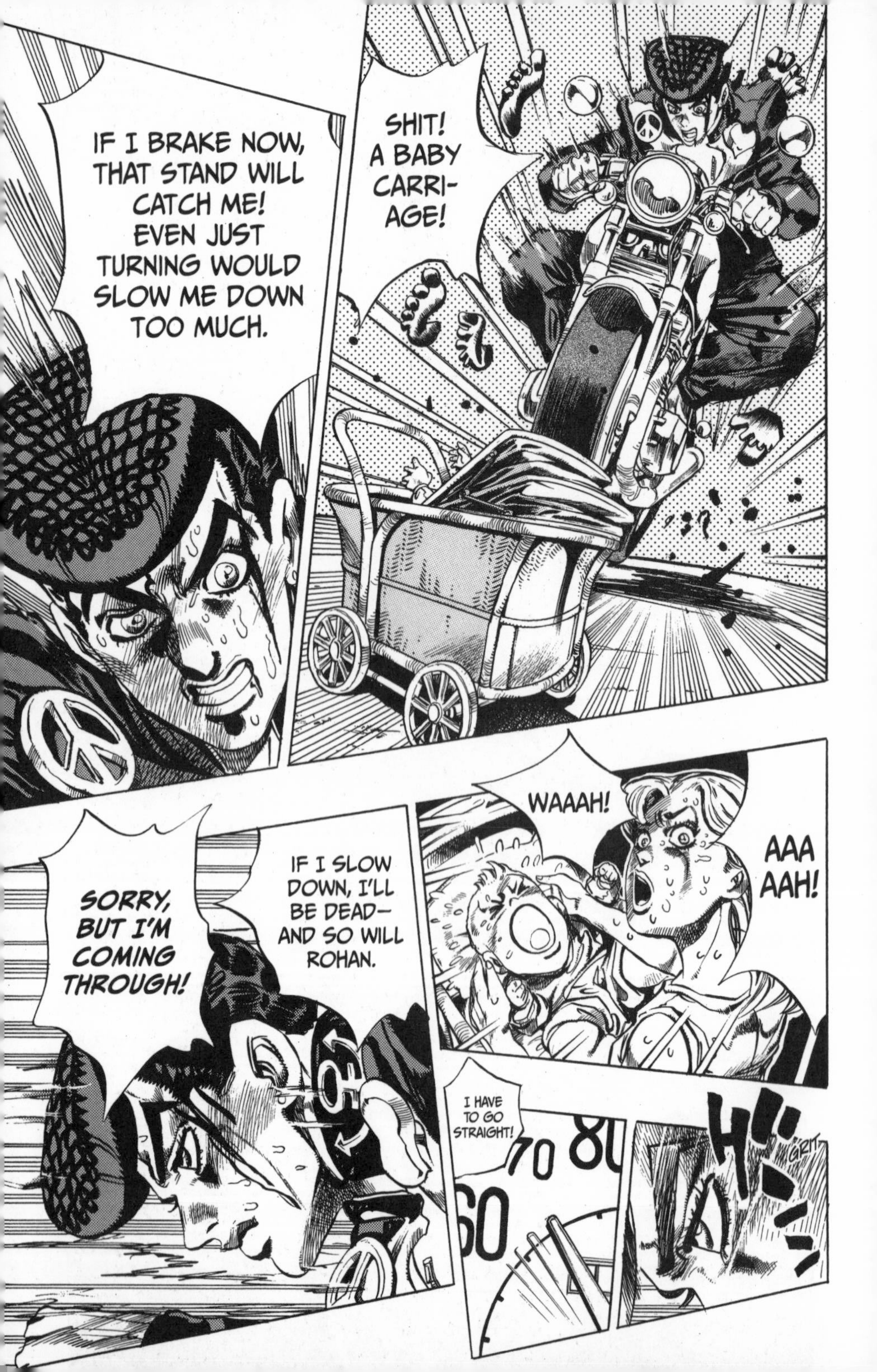
SHIT! A BABY CARRIAGE!
IF I BRAKE NOW, THAT STAND WILL CATCH ME! EVEN JUST TURNING WOULD SLOW ME DOWN TOO MUCH.
WAAAH!
AAA AAH!
GRIT
I HAVE TO GO STRAIGHT!
70 80
60
IF I SLOW DOWN, I'LL BE DEAD— AND SO WILL ROHAN.
SORRY, BUT I'M COMING THROUGH!

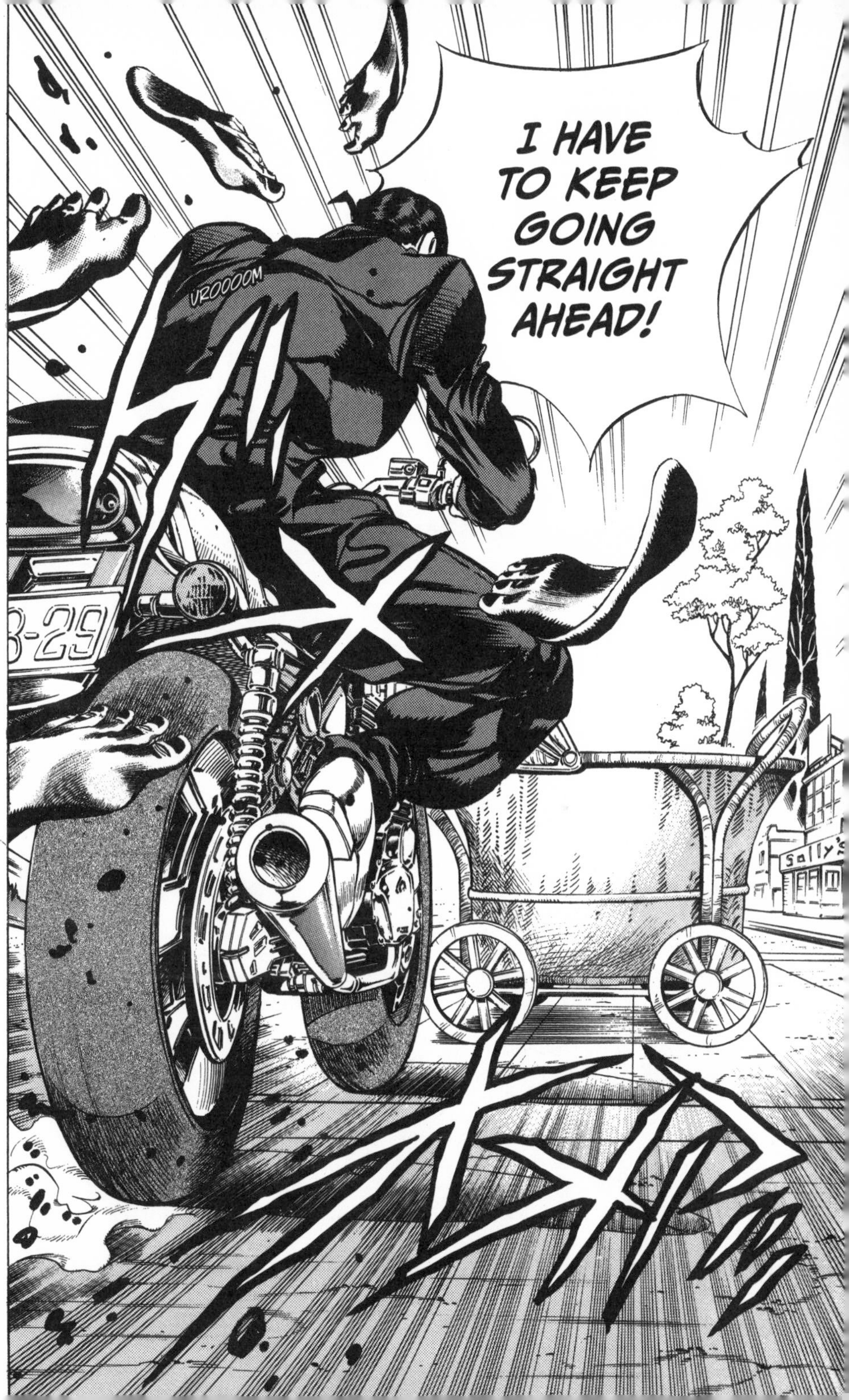
I HAVE TO KEEP GOING STRAIGHT AHEAD!
VROOOOM
Sally

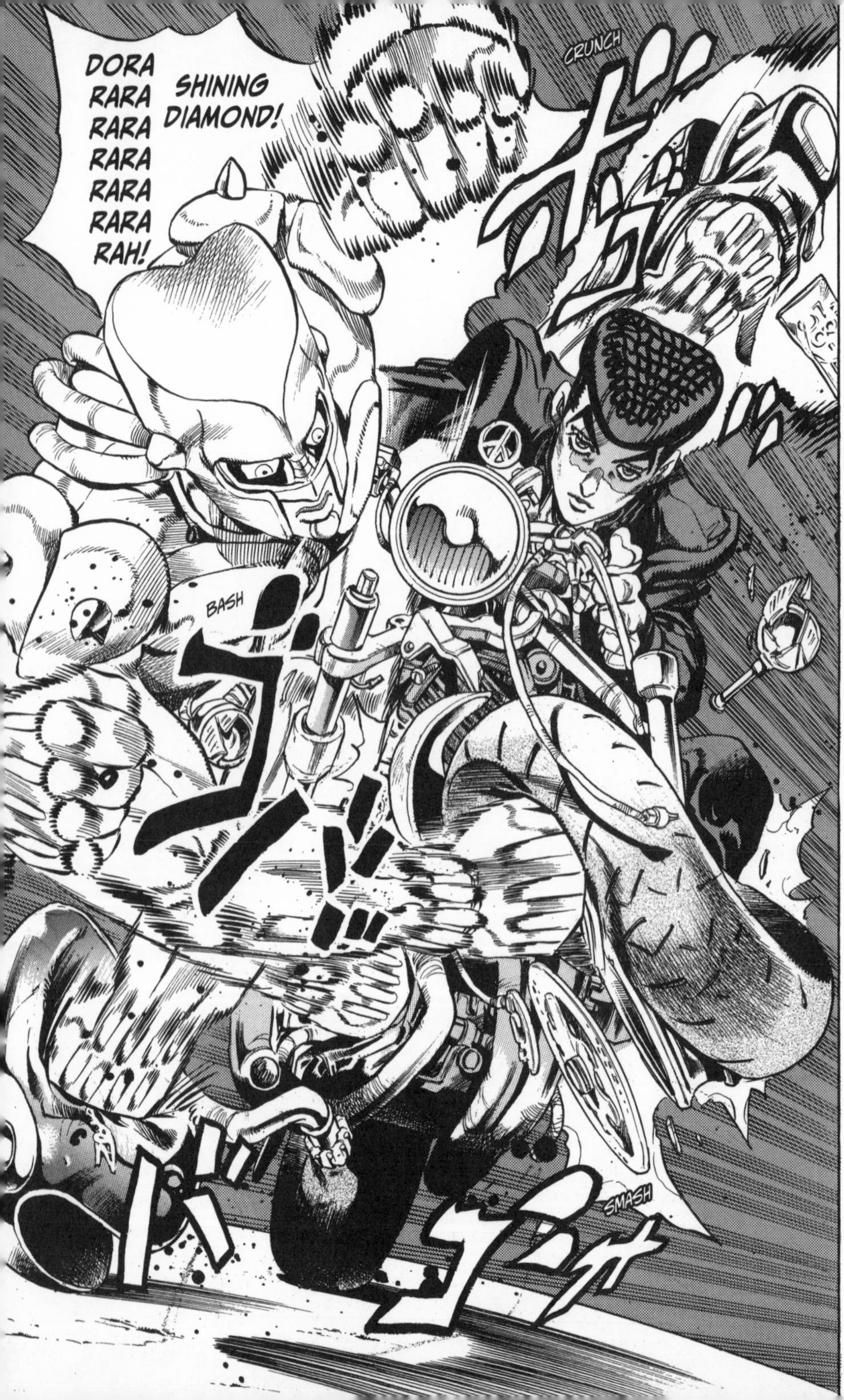
CRUNCH
SHINING DIAMOND!
DORA RARA RARA RARA RARA RARA RAH!
BASH
SMASH

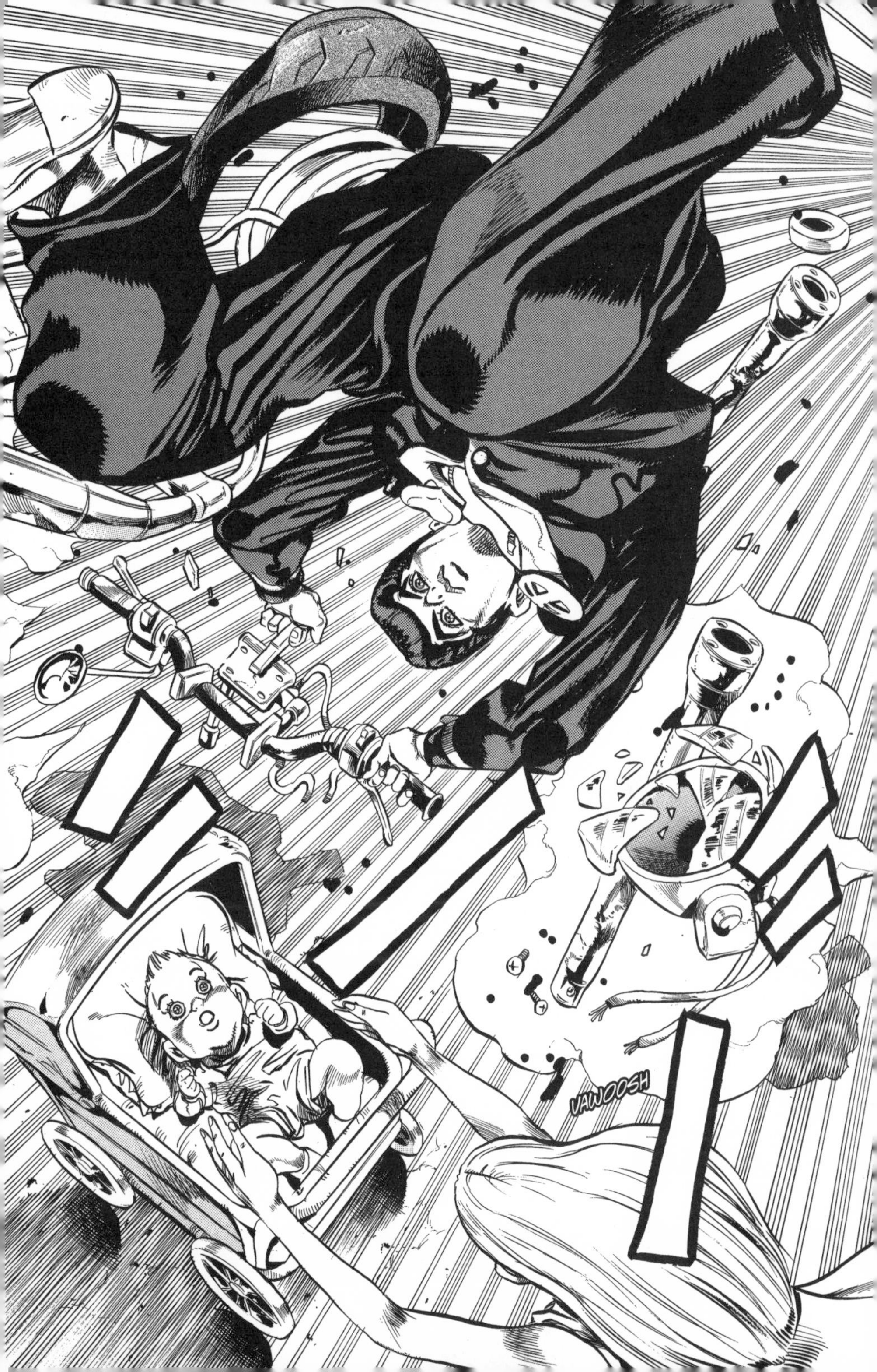
VAWOOSH

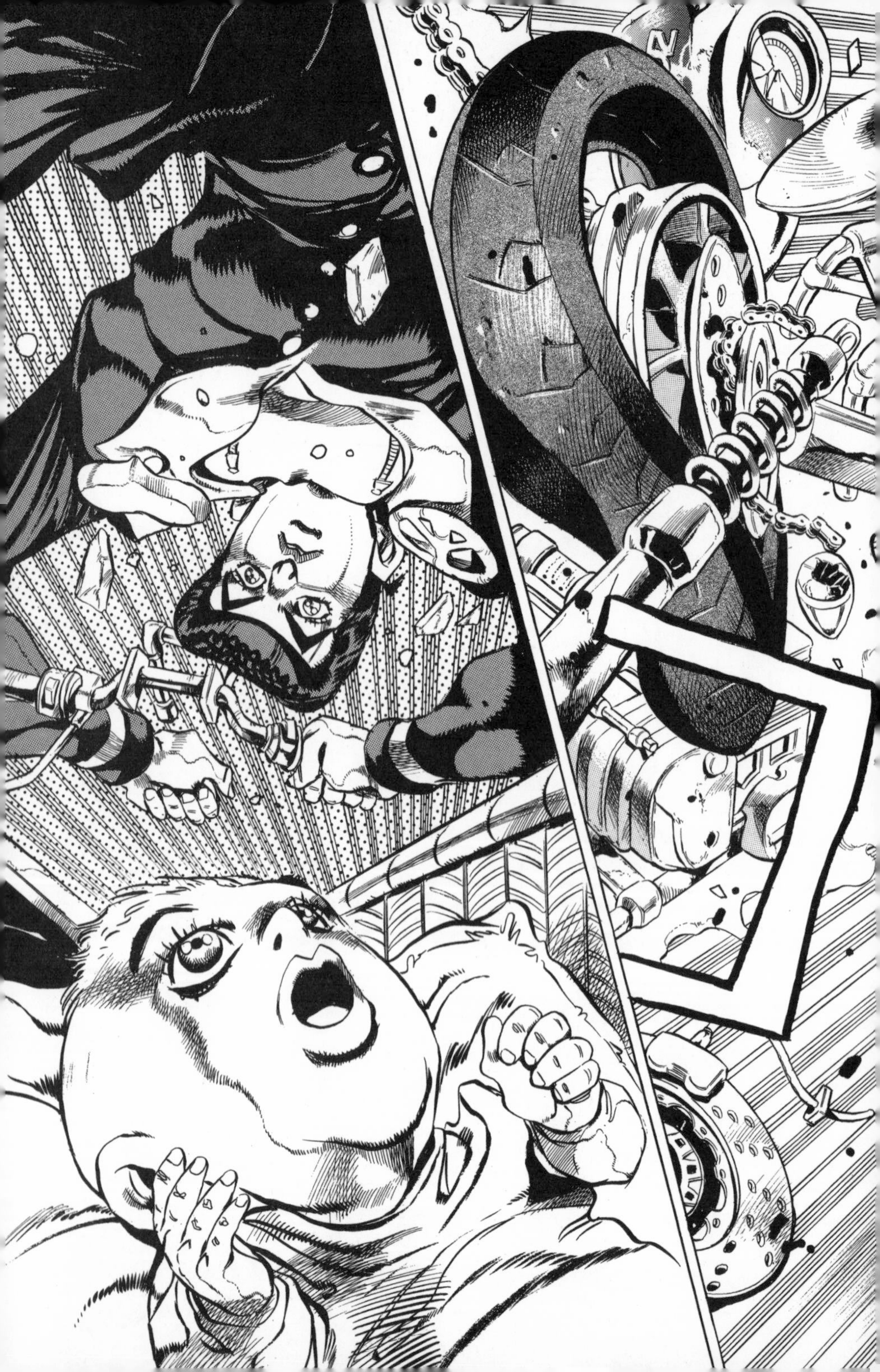

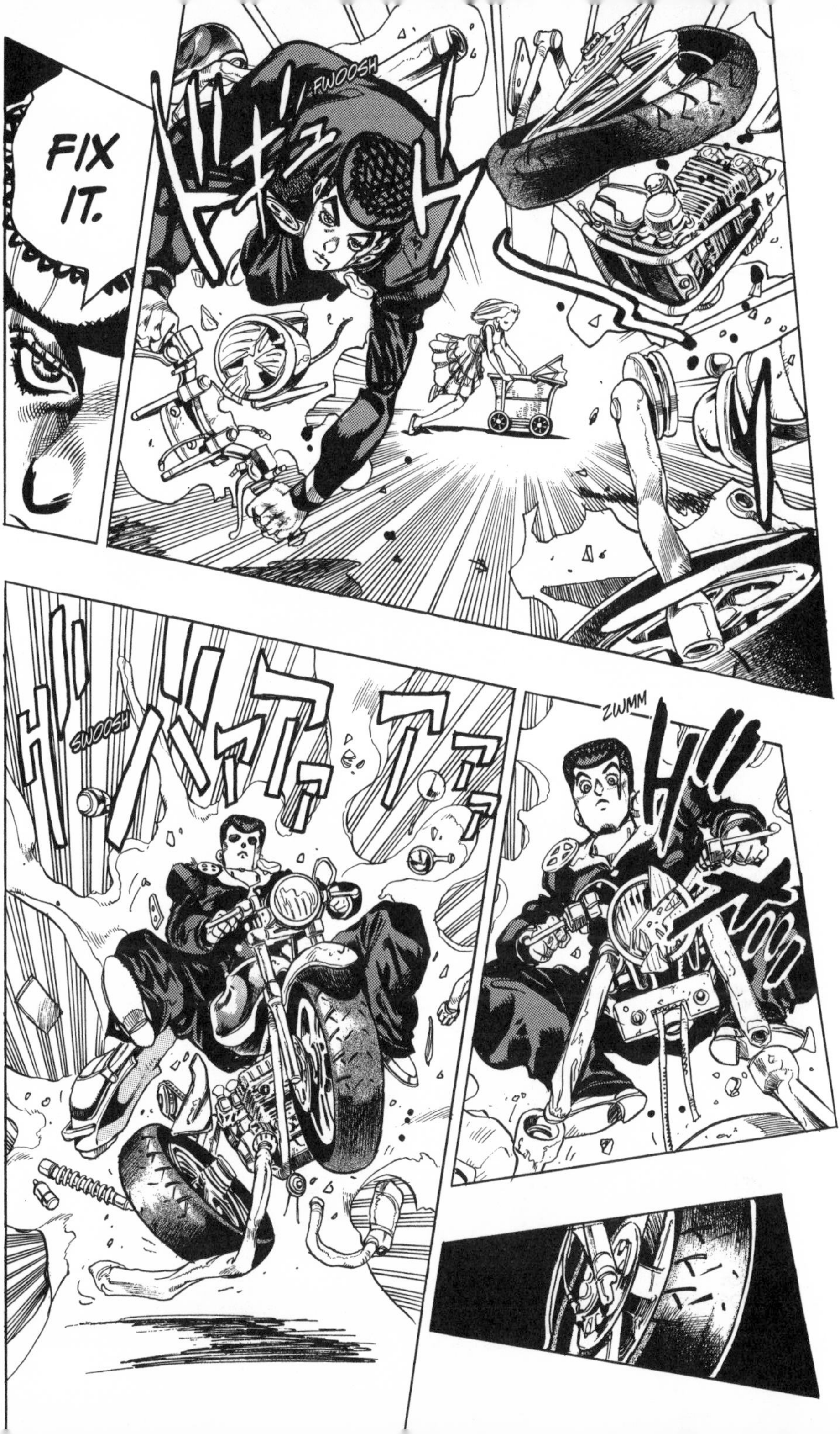
FWOOSH
FIX IT.
ZWMM
SWOOSH

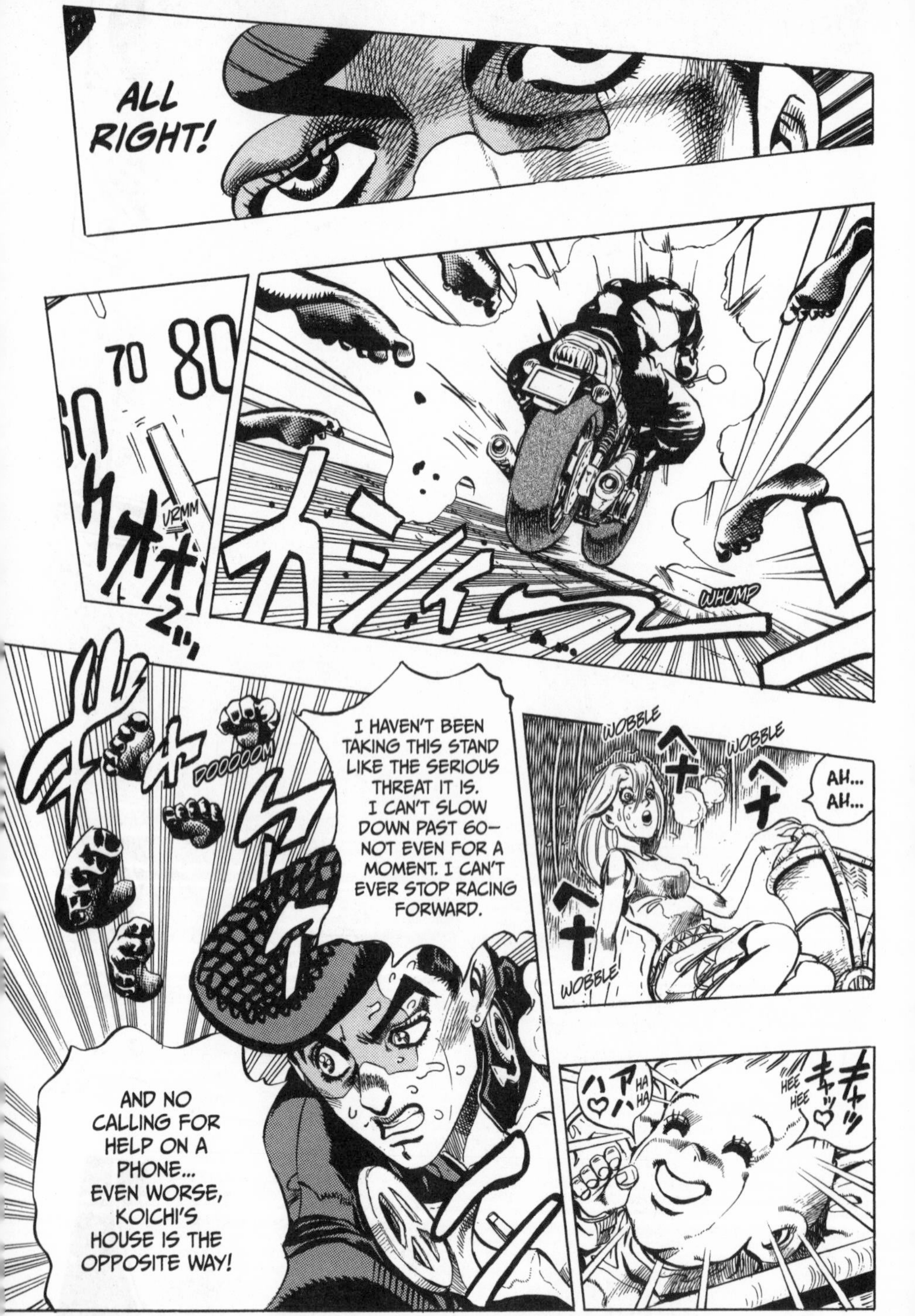

ALL RIGHT!
WHUMP
60
70
80
URMM
WOBBLE
WOBBLE
WOBBLE
AH... AH...
HEE HEE
HA HA
DOOOOOM
I HAVEN'T BEEN TAKING THIS STAND LIKE THE SERIOUS THREAT IT IS. I CAN'T SLOW DOWN PAST 60— NOT EVEN FOR A MOMENT. I CAN'T EVER STOP RACING FORWARD.
AND NO CALLING FOR HELP ON A PHONE... EVEN WORSE, KOICHI'S HOUSE IS THE OPPOSITE WAY!

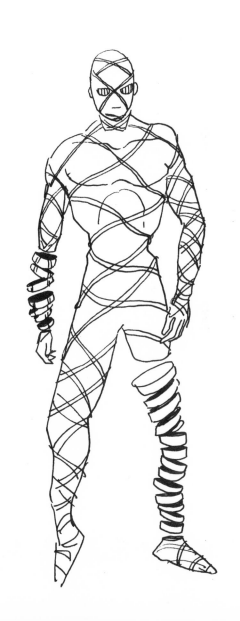

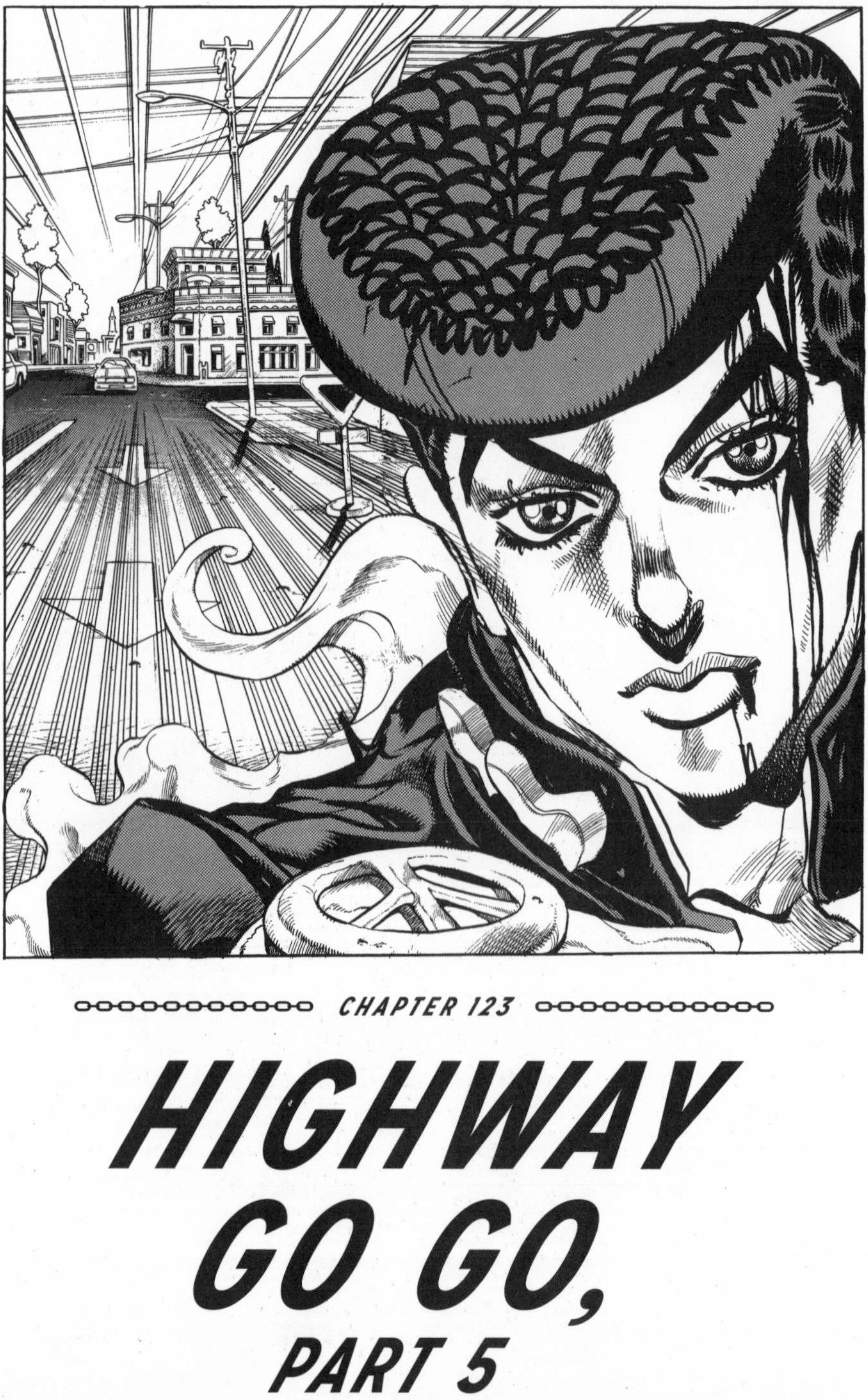

CHAPTER 123

HIGHWAY GO GO, PART 5

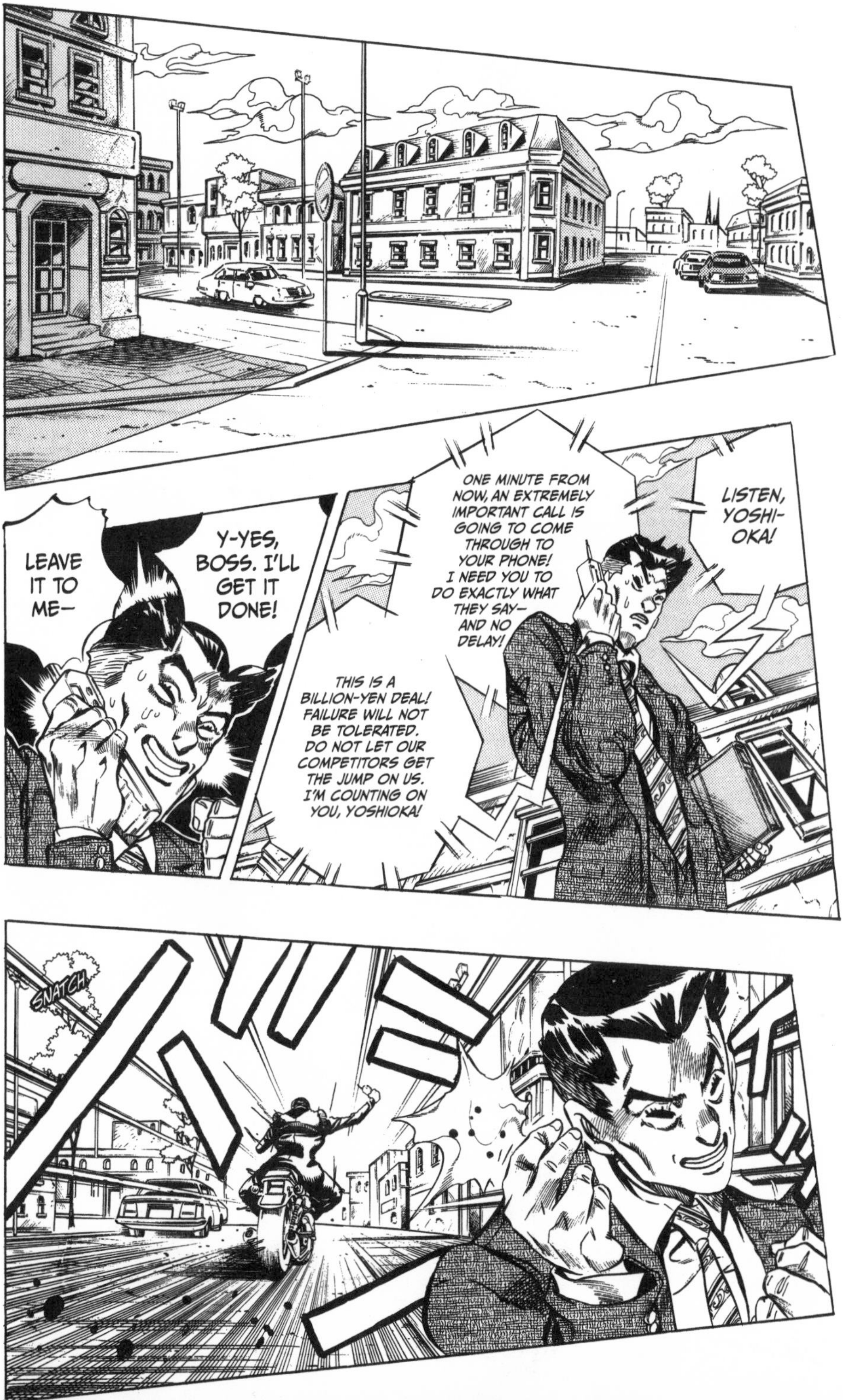
LISTEN, YOSHIOKA!
ONE MINUTE FROM NOW, AN EXTREMELY IMPORTANT CALL IS GOING TO COME THROUGH TO YOUR PHONE! I NEED YOU TO DO EXACTLY WHAT THEY SAY— AND NO DELAY!
THIS IS A BILLION-YEN DEAL! FAILURE WILL NOT BE TOLERATED. DO NOT LET OUR COMPETITORS GET THE JUMP ON US. I'M COUNTING ON YOU, YOSHIOKA!
Y-YES, BOSS. I'LL GET IT DONE!
LEAVE IT TO ME—
SNATCH

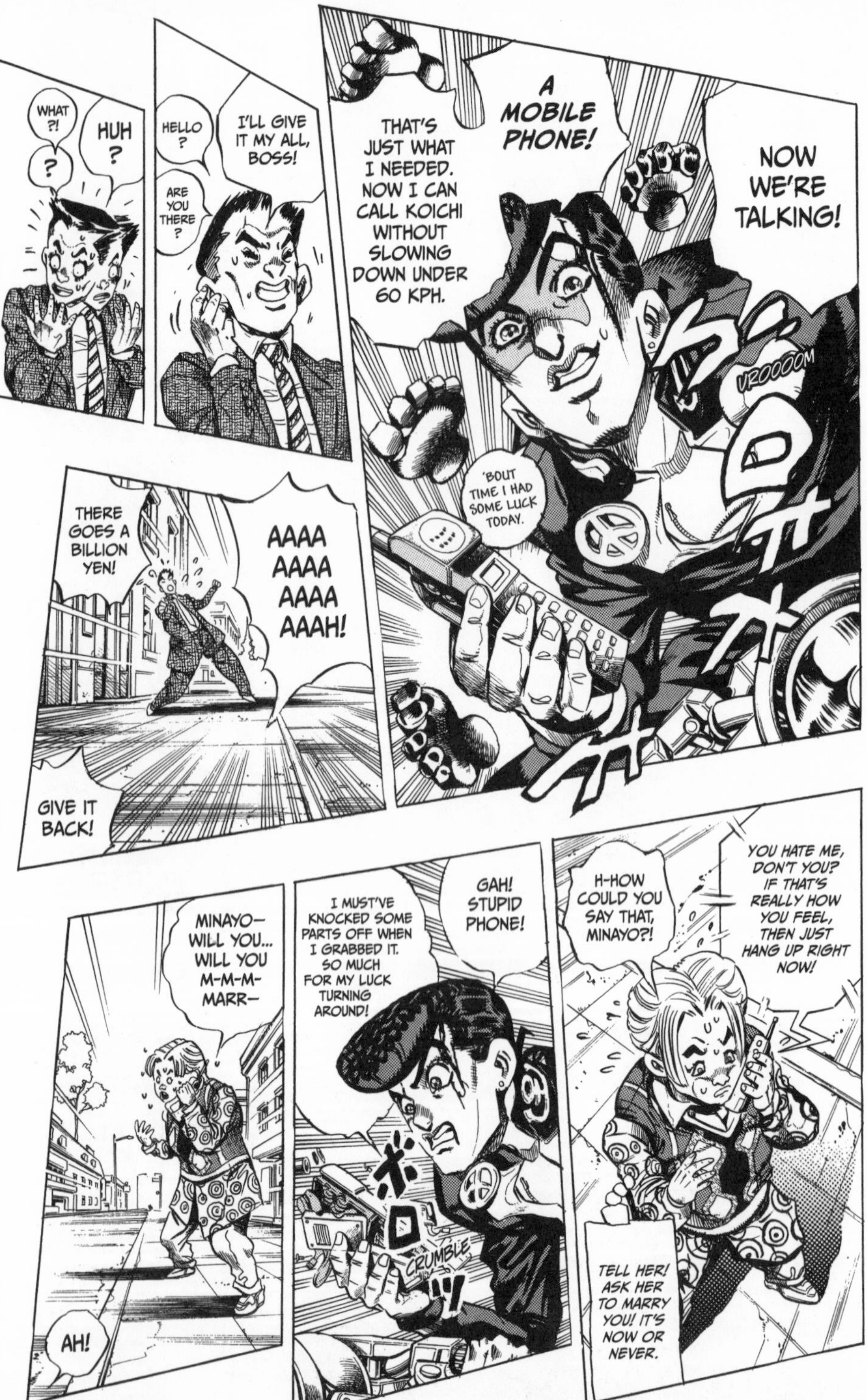
NOW WE'RE TALKING!
A MOBILE PHONE!
THAT'S JUST WHAT I NEEDED. NOW I CAN CALL KOICHI WITHOUT SLOWING DOWN UNDER 60 KPH.
VROOOOOM
'BOUT TIME I HAD SOME LUCK TODAY.
I'LL GIVE IT MY ALL, BOSS!
HELLO?
ARE YOU THERE?
HUH?
WHAT?!
?
AAAA AAAA AAAA AAAH!
THERE GOES A BILLION YEN!
GIVE IT BACK!
YOU HATE ME, DON'T YOU? IF THAT'S REALLY HOW YOU FEEL, THEN JUST HANG UP RIGHT NOW!
H-HOW COULD YOU SAY THAT, MINAYO?!
TELL HER! ASK HER TO MARRY YOU! IT'S NOW OR NEVER.
GAH! STUPID PHONE!
I MUST'VE KNOCKED SOME PARTS OFF WHEN I GRABBED IT. SO MUCH FOR MY LUCK TURNING AROUND!
CRUMBLE
MINAYO— WILL YOU... WILL YOU M-M-M-MARR—
AH!

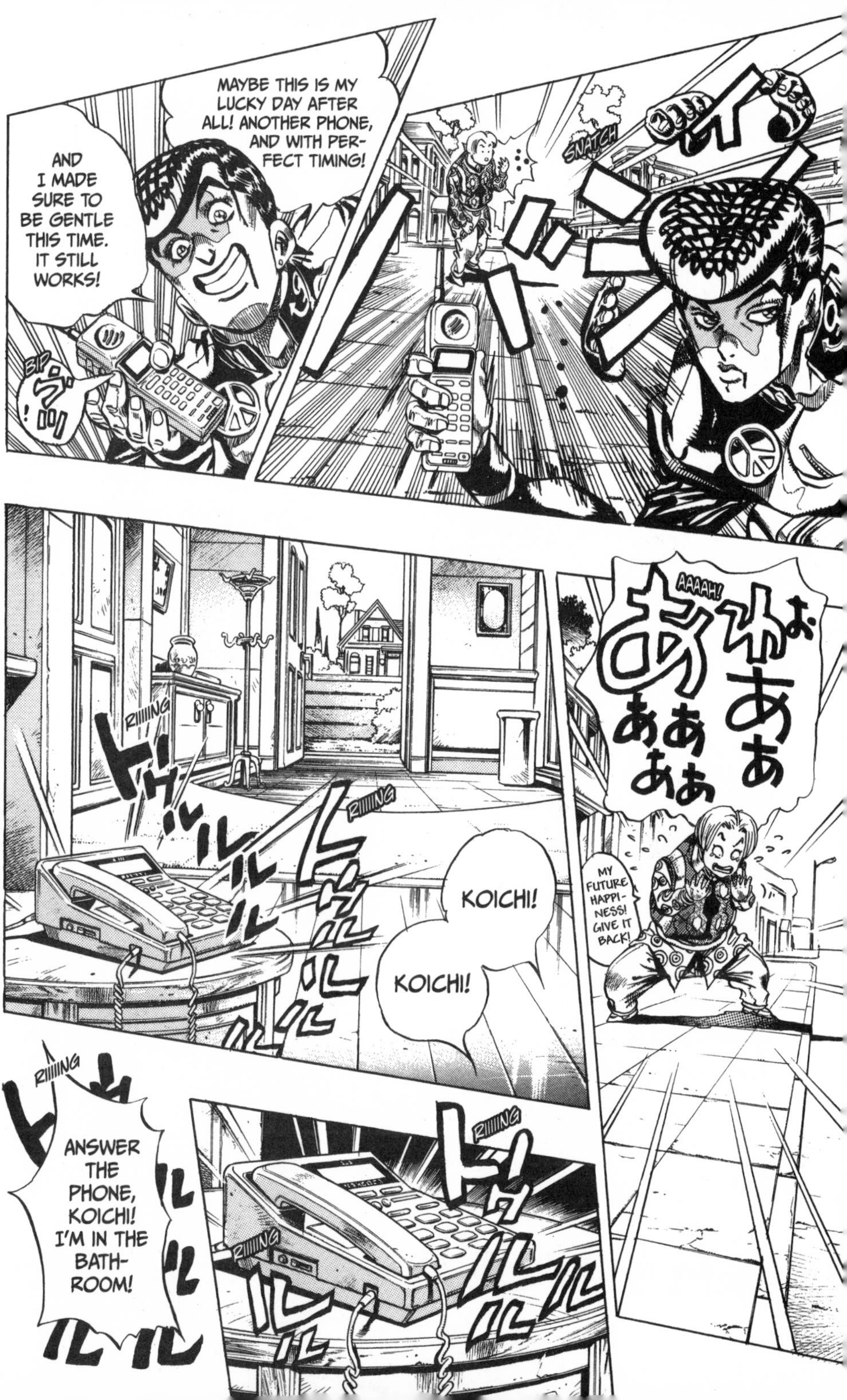
SNATCH
MAYBE THIS IS MY LUCKY DAY AFTER ALL! ANOTHER PHONE, AND WITH PERFECT TIMING!
AND I MADE SURE TO BE GENTLE THIS TIME. IT STILL WORKS!
BIP
AAAAH!
MY FUTURE HAPPINESS! GIVE IT BACK!
RIIIING
RIIIING
KOICHI!
KOICHI!
RIIIING
RIIIING
RIIIING
ANSWER THE PHONE, KOICHI! I'M IN THE BATHROOM!

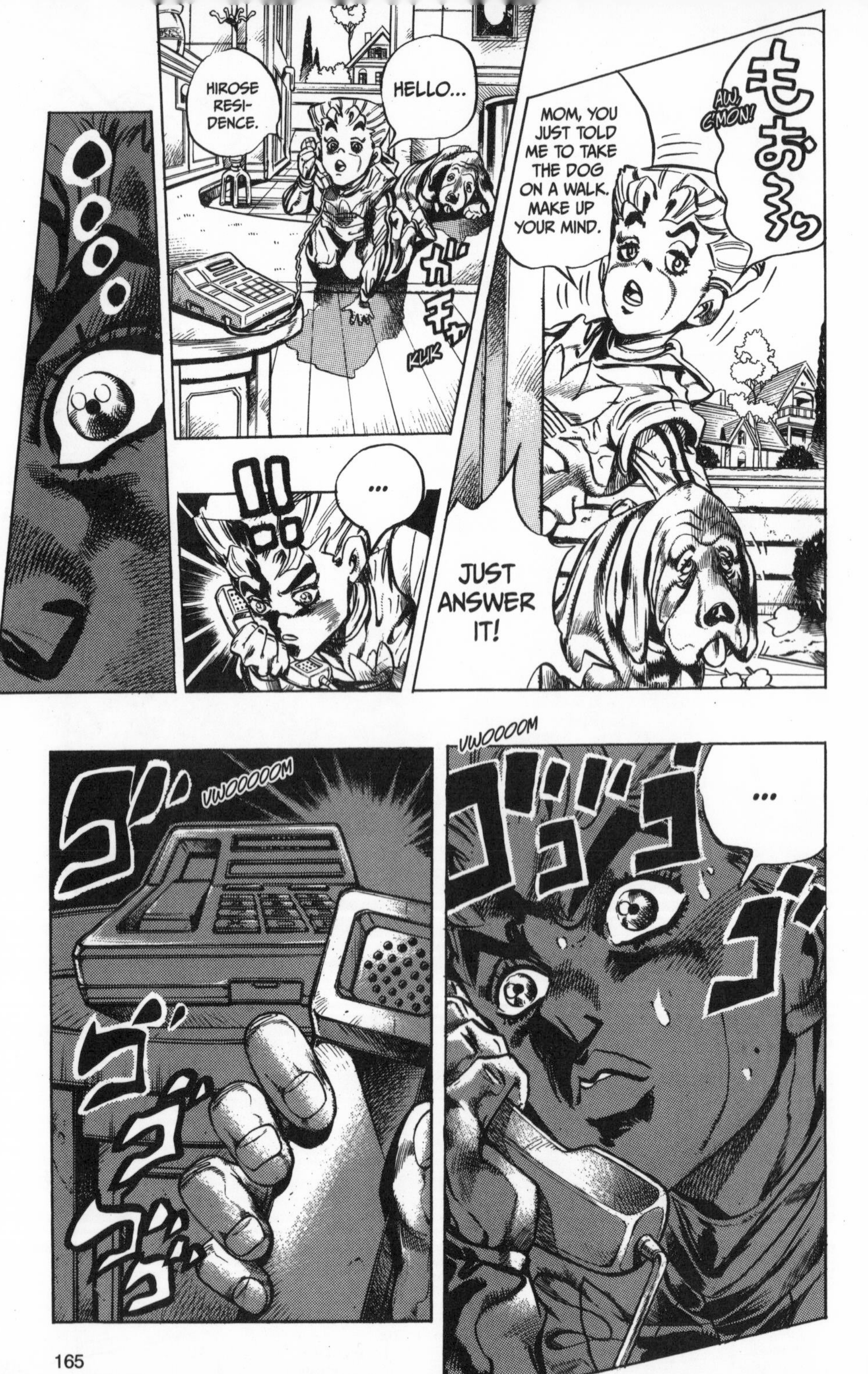
AW, C'MON!
MOM, YOU JUST TOLD ME TO TAKE THE DOG ON A WALK. MAKE UP YOUR MIND.
JUST ANSWER IT!
HELLO...
HIROSE RESI-DENCE.
ガチャ
KLIK
...
VWOOOOM
...
VWOOOOOM

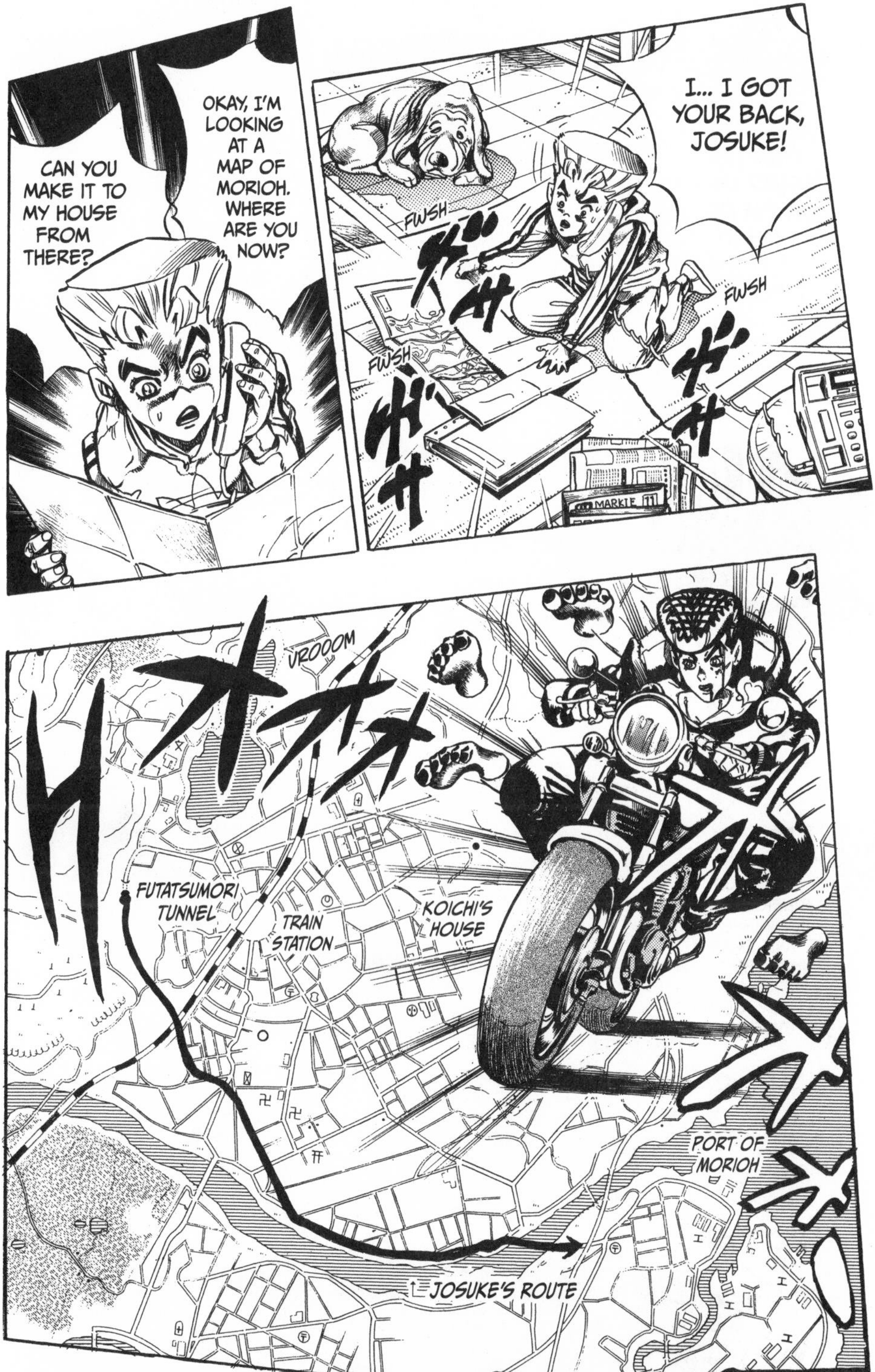
I... I GOT YOUR BACK, JOSUKE!
FWSH
FWSH
FWSH
MARKIE
OKAY, I'M LOOKING AT A MAP OF MORIOH. WHERE ARE YOU NOW?
CAN YOU MAKE IT TO MY HOUSE FROM THERE?
VROOOM
FUTATSUMORI TUNNEL
TRAIN STATION
KOICHI'S HOUSE
PORT OF MORIOH
JOSUKE'S ROUTE

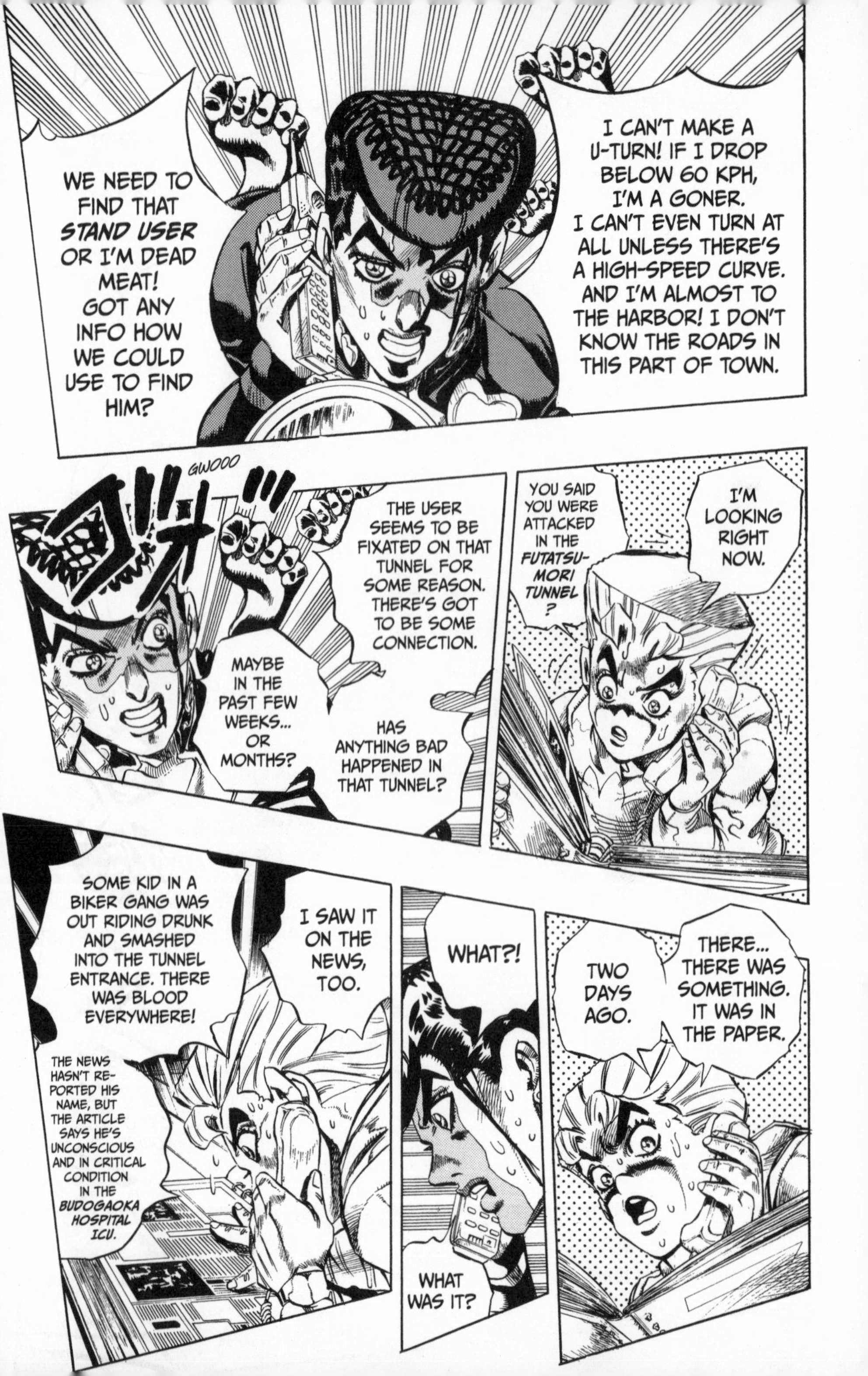
I CAN'T MAKE A U-TURN! IF I DROP BELOW 60 KPH, I'M A GONER. I CAN'T EVEN TURN AT ALL UNLESS THERE'S A HIGH-SPEED CURVE. AND I'M ALMOST TO THE HARBOR! I DON'T KNOW THE ROADS IN THIS PART OF TOWN.
WE NEED TO FIND THAT *STAND USER* OR I'M DEAD MEAT! GOT ANY INFO HOW WE COULD USE TO FIND HIM?
I'M LOOKING RIGHT NOW.
YOU SAID YOU WERE ATTACKED IN THE *FUTATSU-MORI TUNNEL*?
GWOOO
THE USER SEEMS TO BE FIXATED ON THAT TUNNEL FOR SOME REASON. THERE'S GOT TO BE SOME CONNECTION.
HAS ANYTHING BAD HAPPENED IN THAT TUNNEL?
MAYBE IN THE PAST FEW WEEKS... OR MONTHS?
THERE... THERE WAS SOMETHING. IT WAS IN THE PAPER.
TWO DAYS AGO.
WHAT?!
WHAT WAS IT?
I SAW IT ON THE NEWS, TOO.
SOME KID IN A BIKER GANG WAS OUT RIDING DRUNK AND SMASHED INTO THE TUNNEL ENTRANCE. THERE WAS BLOOD EVERYWHERE!
THE NEWS HASN'T REPORTED HIS NAME, BUT THE ARTICLE SAYS HE'S UNCONSCIOUS AND IN CRITICAL CONDITION IN THE *BUDOGAOKA HOSPITAL ICU*.

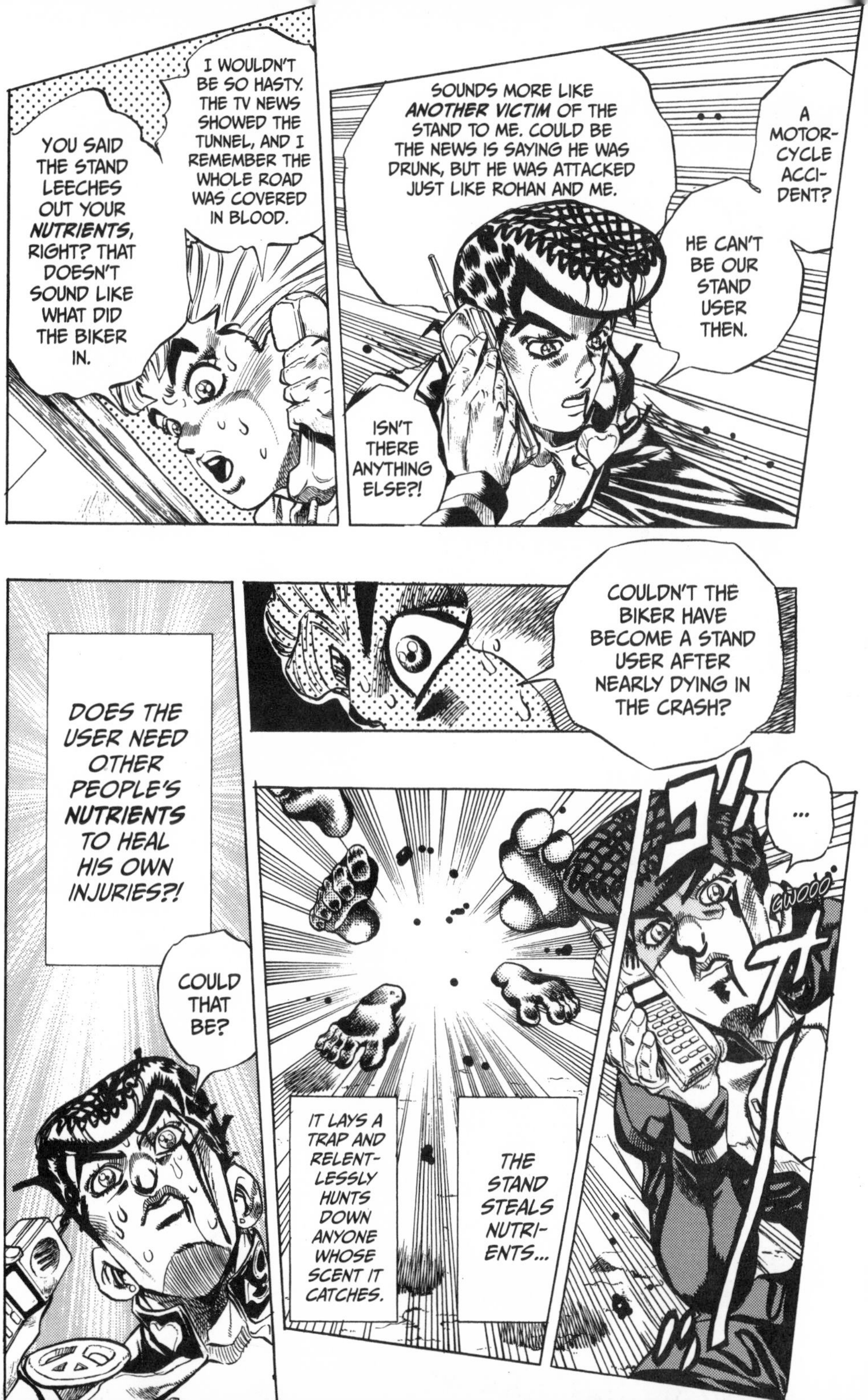
A MOTOR-CYCLE ACCI-DENT?
HE CAN'T BE OUR STAND USER THEN.
SOUNDS MORE LIKE ANOTHER VICTIM OF THE STAND TO ME. COULD BE THE NEWS IS SAYING HE WAS DRUNK, BUT HE WAS ATTACKED JUST LIKE ROHAN AND ME.
ISN'T THERE ANYTHING ELSE?!
I WOULDN'T BE SO HASTY. THE TV NEWS SHOWED THE TUNNEL, AND I REMEMBER THE WHOLE ROAD WAS COVERED IN BLOOD.
YOU SAID THE STAND LEECHES OUT YOUR NUTRIENTS, RIGHT? THAT DOESN'T SOUND LIKE WHAT DID THE BIKER IN.
COULDN'T THE BIKER HAVE BECOME A STAND USER AFTER NEARLY DYING IN THE CRASH?
...
GWOOO
THE STAND STEALS NUTRI-ENTS...
IT LAYS A TRAP AND RELENT-LESSLY HUNTS DOWN ANYONE WHOSE SCENT IT CATCHES.
DOES THE USER NEED OTHER PEOPLE'S NUTRIENTS TO HEAL HIS OWN INJURIES?!
COULD THAT BE?

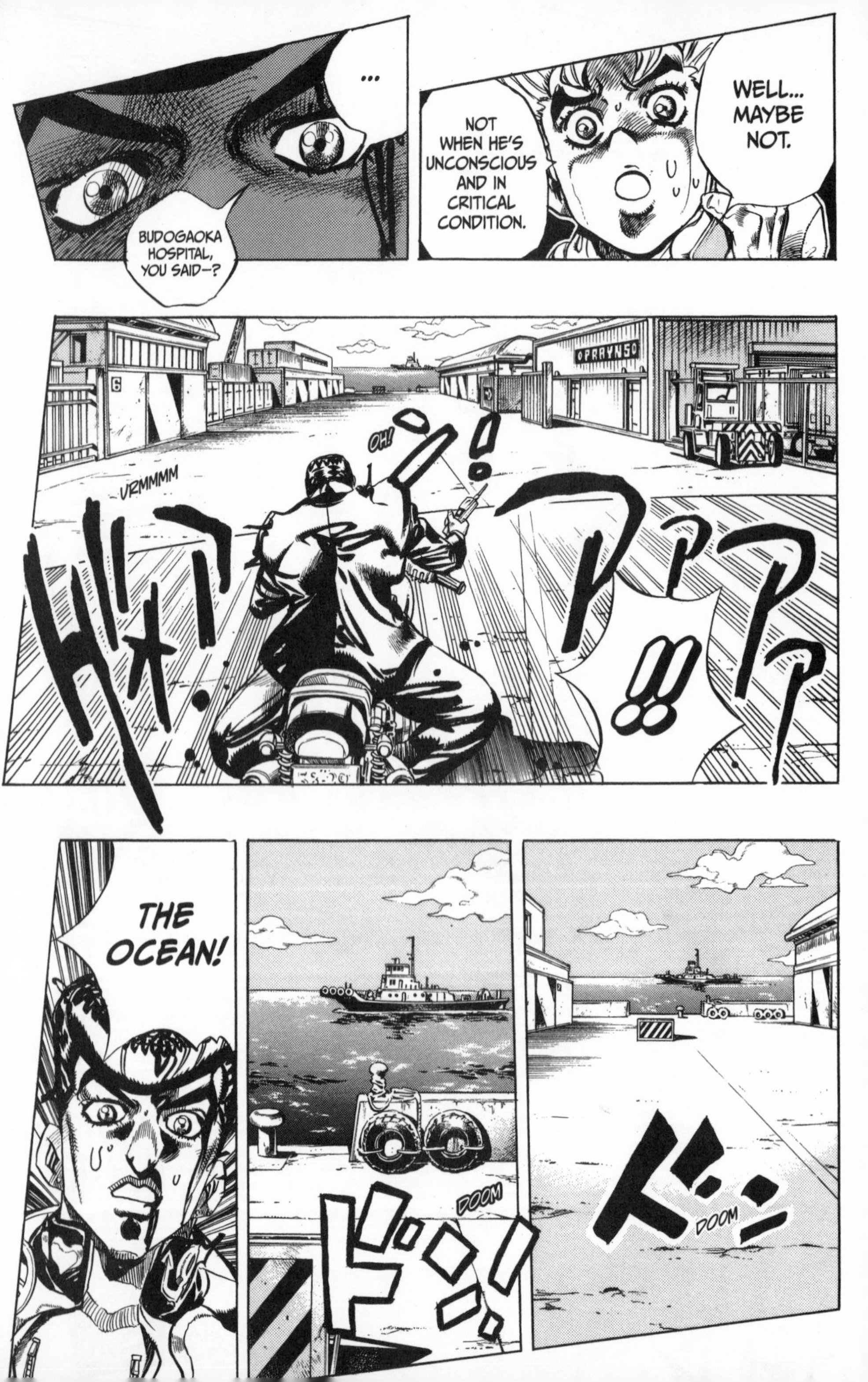
WELL... MAYBE NOT.
NOT WHEN HE'S UNCONSCIOUS AND IN CRITICAL CONDITION.
...
BUDOGAOKA HOSPITAL, YOU SAID—?
OH!
URMMMM
DOOM
DOOM
THE OCEAN!

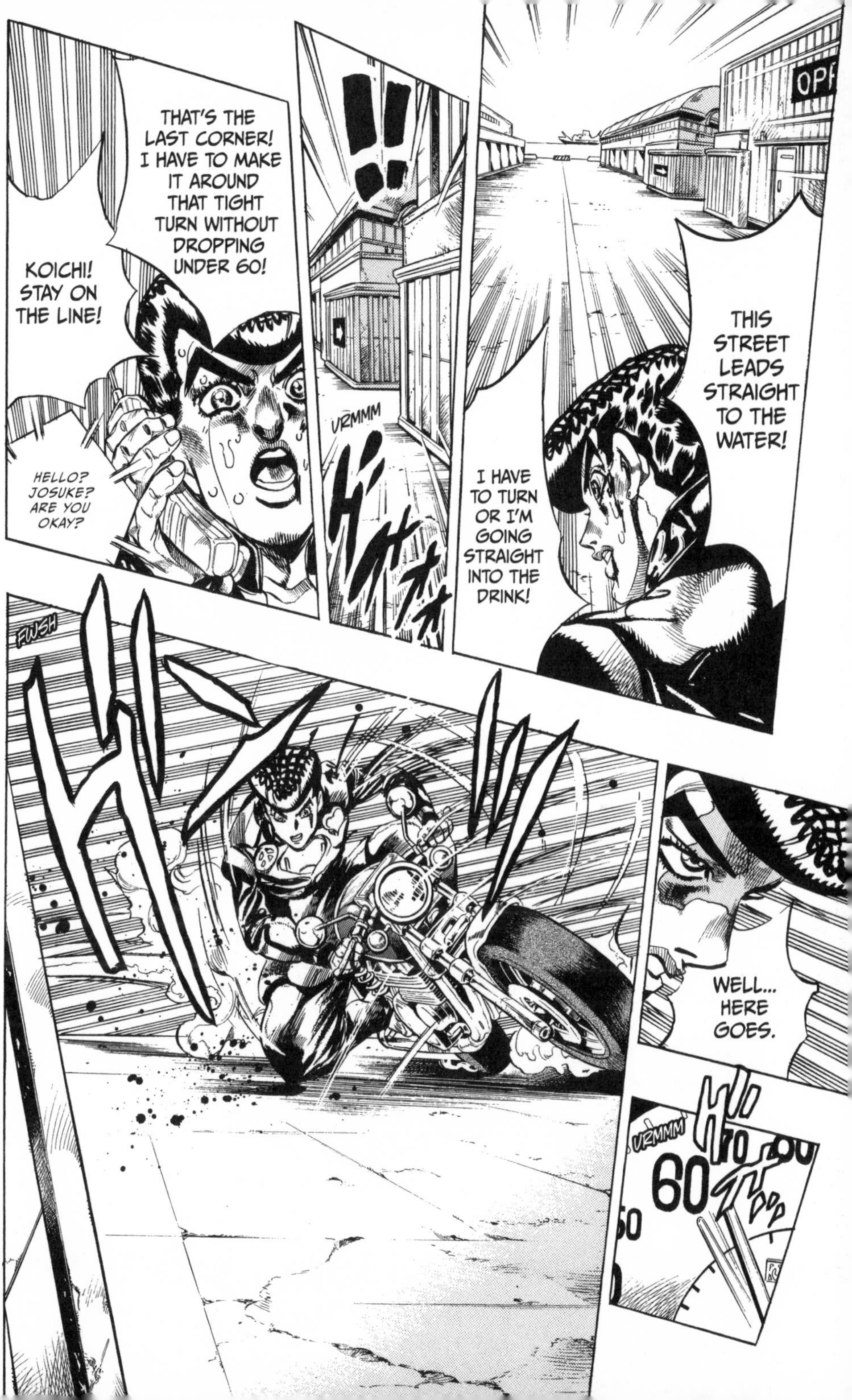

THIS STREET LEADS STRAIGHT TO THE WATER!
I HAVE TO TURN OR I'M GOING STRAIGHT INTO THE DRINK!
!!
URMMM
THAT'S THE LAST CORNER! I HAVE TO MAKE IT AROUND THAT TIGHT TURN WITHOUT DROPPING UNDER 60!
KOICHI! STAY ON THE LINE!
HELLO? JOSUKE? ARE YOU OKAY?
WELL... HERE GOES.
URMMM
60
FWSH

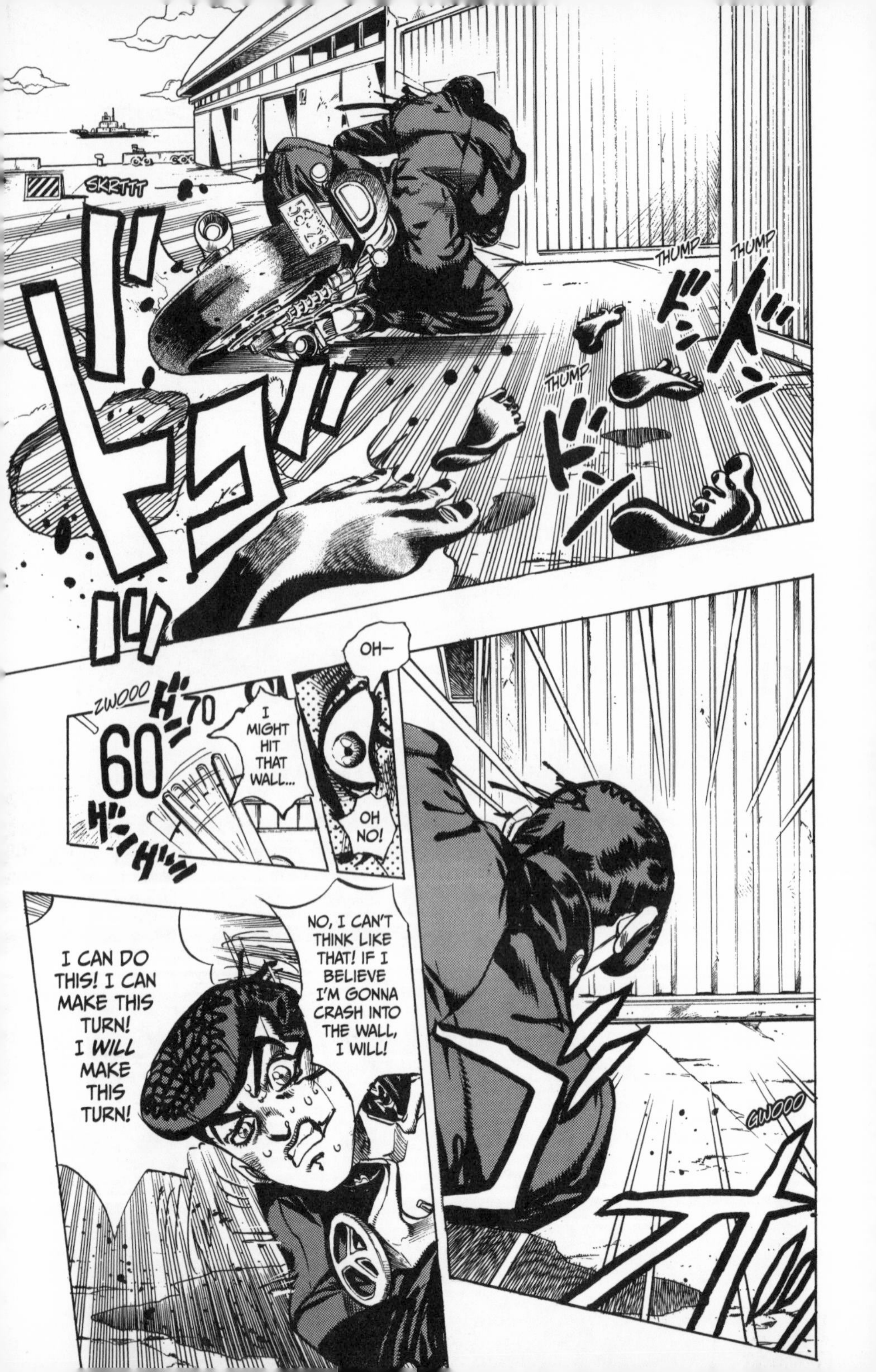
THUMP
THUMP
SKRTTT
THUMP
OH—
OH NO!
ZWOOO
70
60
I MIGHT HIT THAT WALL...
GWOOO
NO, I CAN'T THINK LIKE THAT! IF I BELIEVE I'M GONNA CRASH INTO THE WALL, I WILL!
I CAN DO THIS! I CAN MAKE THIS TURN! I *WILL* MAKE THIS TURN!

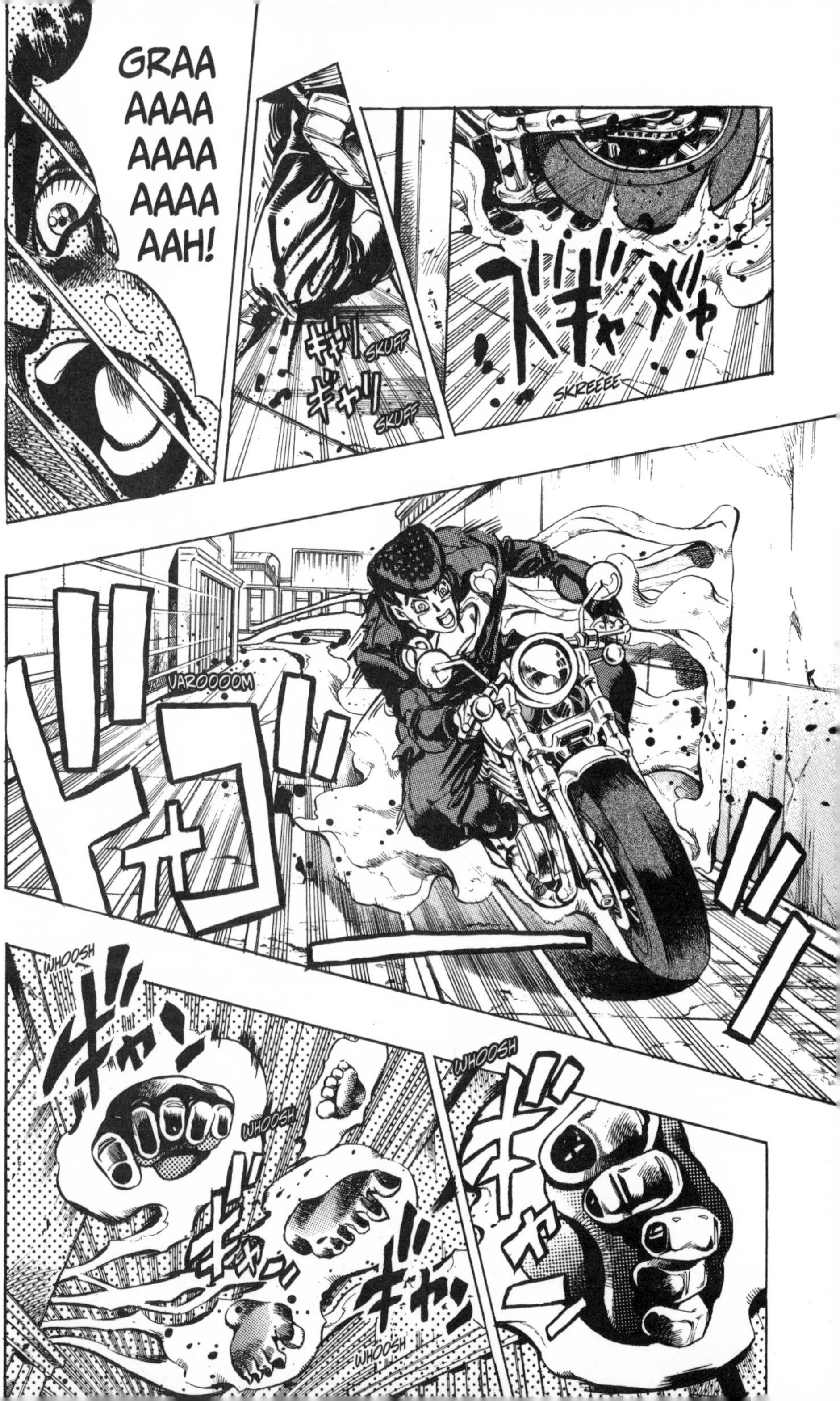
SKREEEE
ギャリ
SKUFF
ギャリ
SKUFF
GRAA
AAAA
AAAA
AAAA
AAH!
VAROOOOM
WHOOSH
WHOOSH
ギャン
WHOOSH
WHOOSH
ギャン

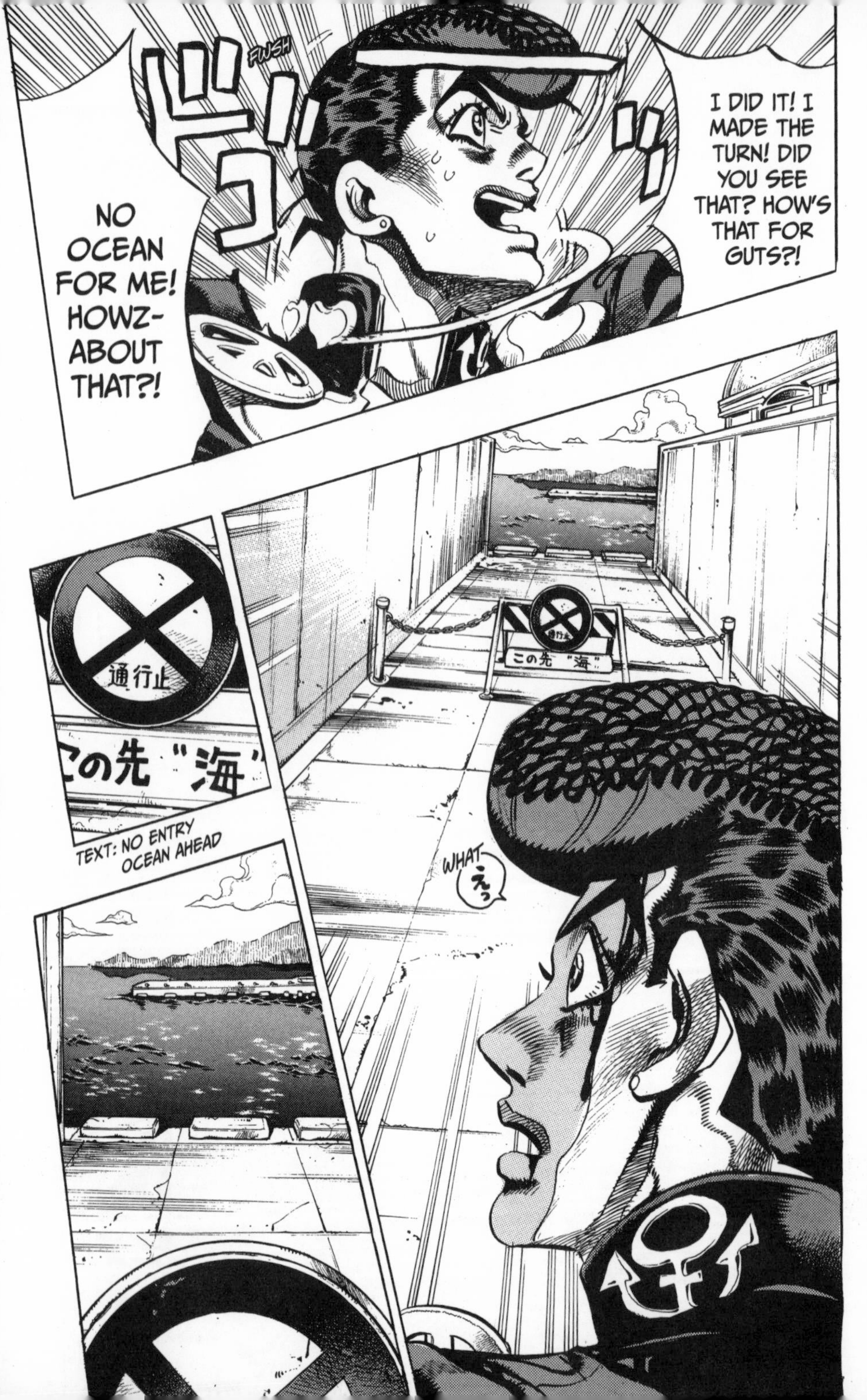
FWSH
I DID IT! I MADE THE TURN! DID YOU SEE THAT? HOW'S THAT FOR GUTS?!
NO OCEAN FOR ME! HOWZ-ABOUT THAT?!
通行止
この先"海"
通行止
この先"海"
TEXT: NO ENTRY OCEAN AHEAD
WHAT えっ

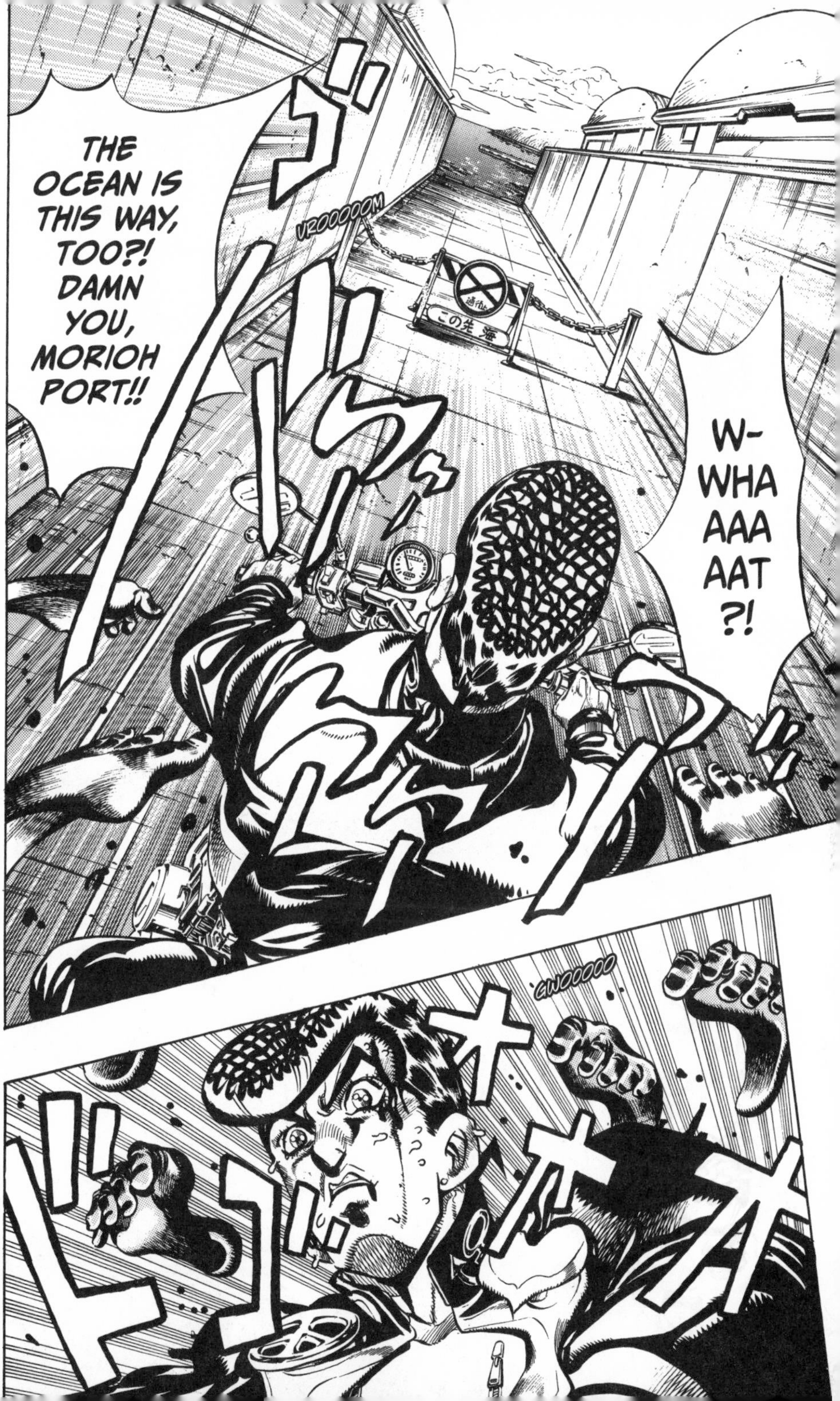

W-WHAAAAAAT?!
THE OCEAN IS THIS WAY, TOO?! DAMN YOU, MORIOH PORT!!
VROOOOOOM
通行止
この先 海
GWOOOOO

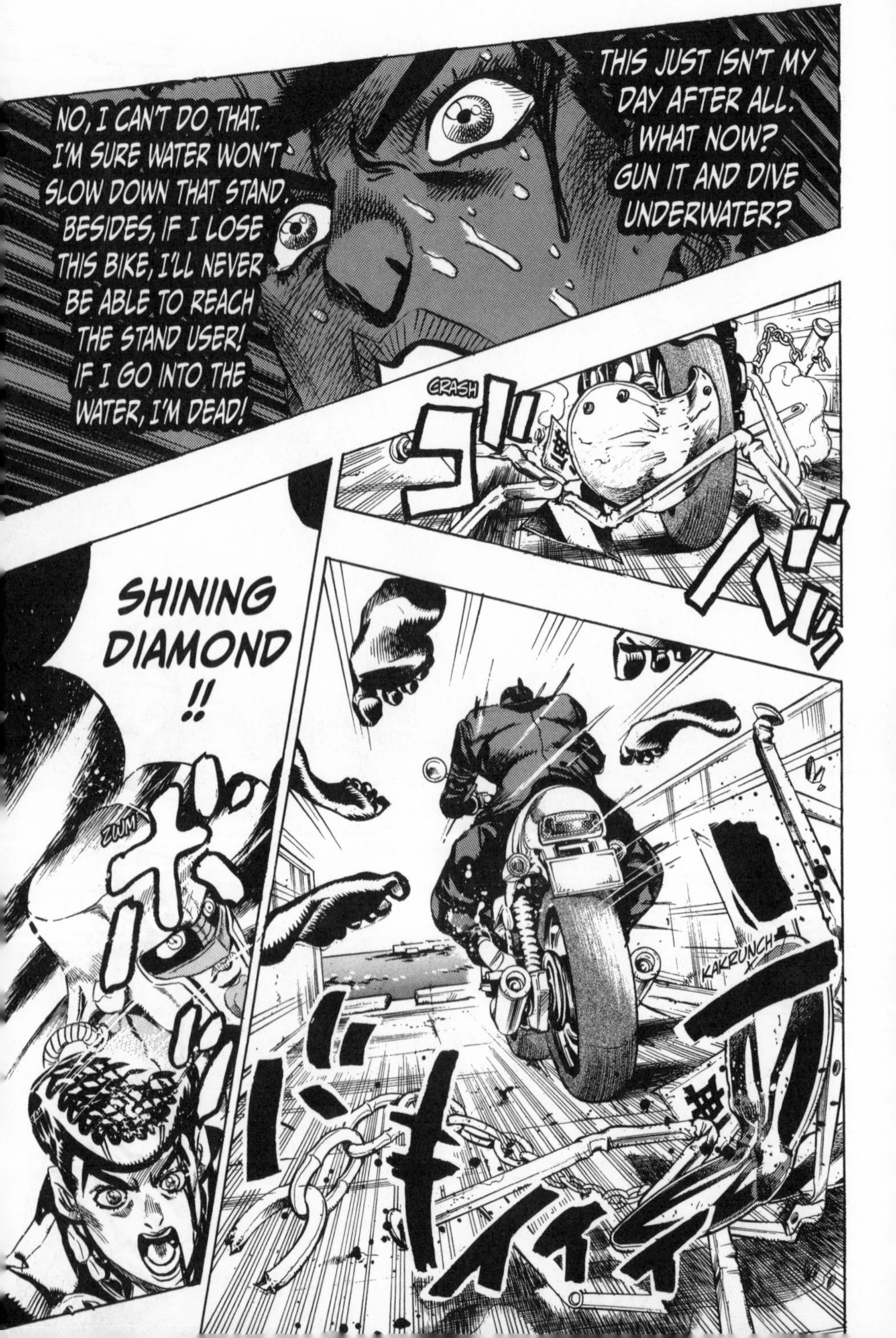
THIS JUST ISN'T MY DAY AFTER ALL. WHAT NOW? GUN IT AND DIVE UNDERWATER?
NO, I CAN'T DO THAT. I'M SURE WATER WON'T SLOW DOWN THAT STAND. BESIDES, IF I LOSE THIS BIKE, I'LL NEVER BE ABLE TO REACH THE STAND USER! IF I GO INTO THE WATER, I'M DEAD!
CRASH
KAKRUNCH
SHINING DIAMOND !!
ZWM

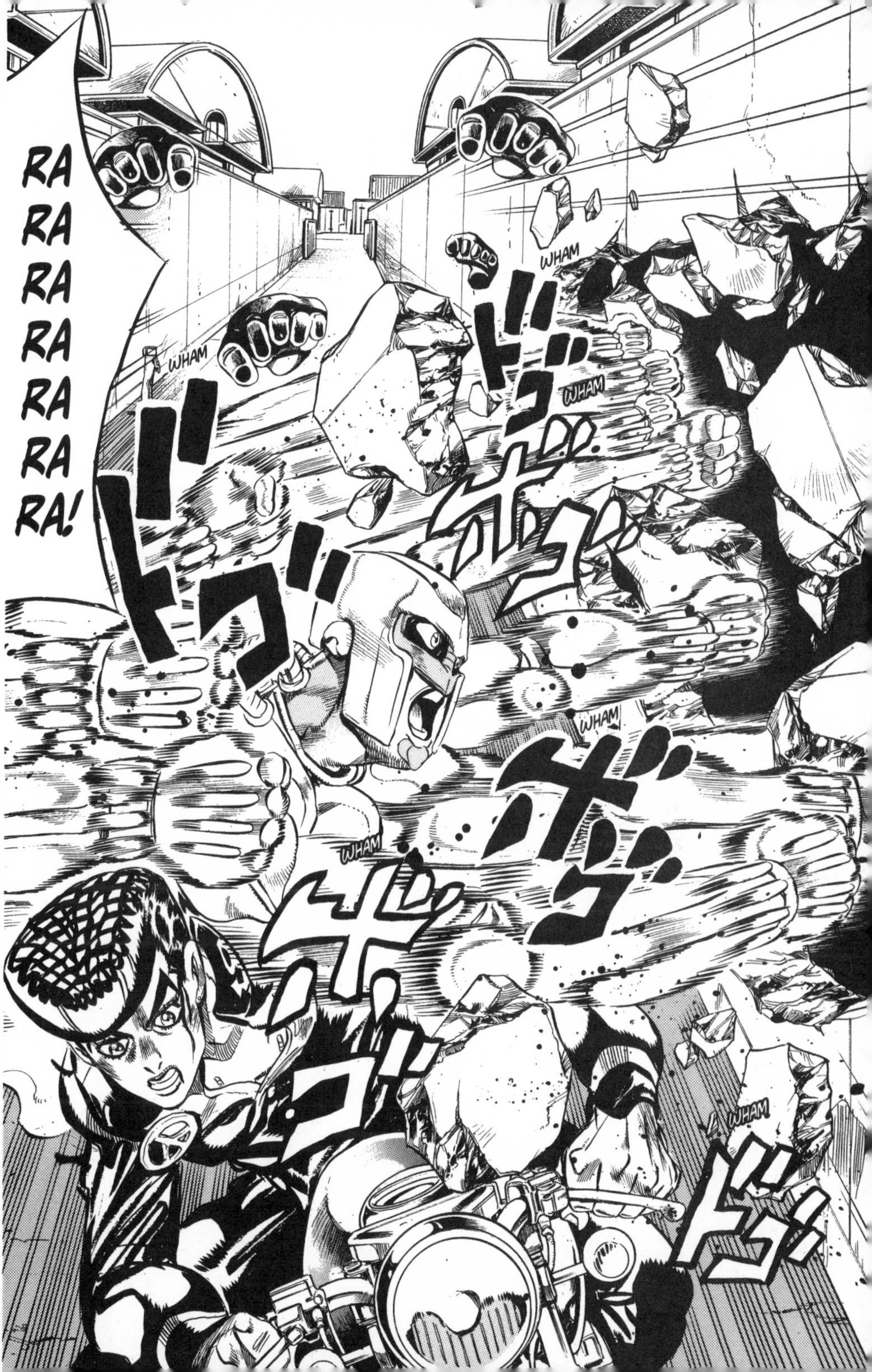
RA RA RA RA RA RA RA RA!
WHAM
WHAM
WHAM
WHAM
WHAM
WHAM

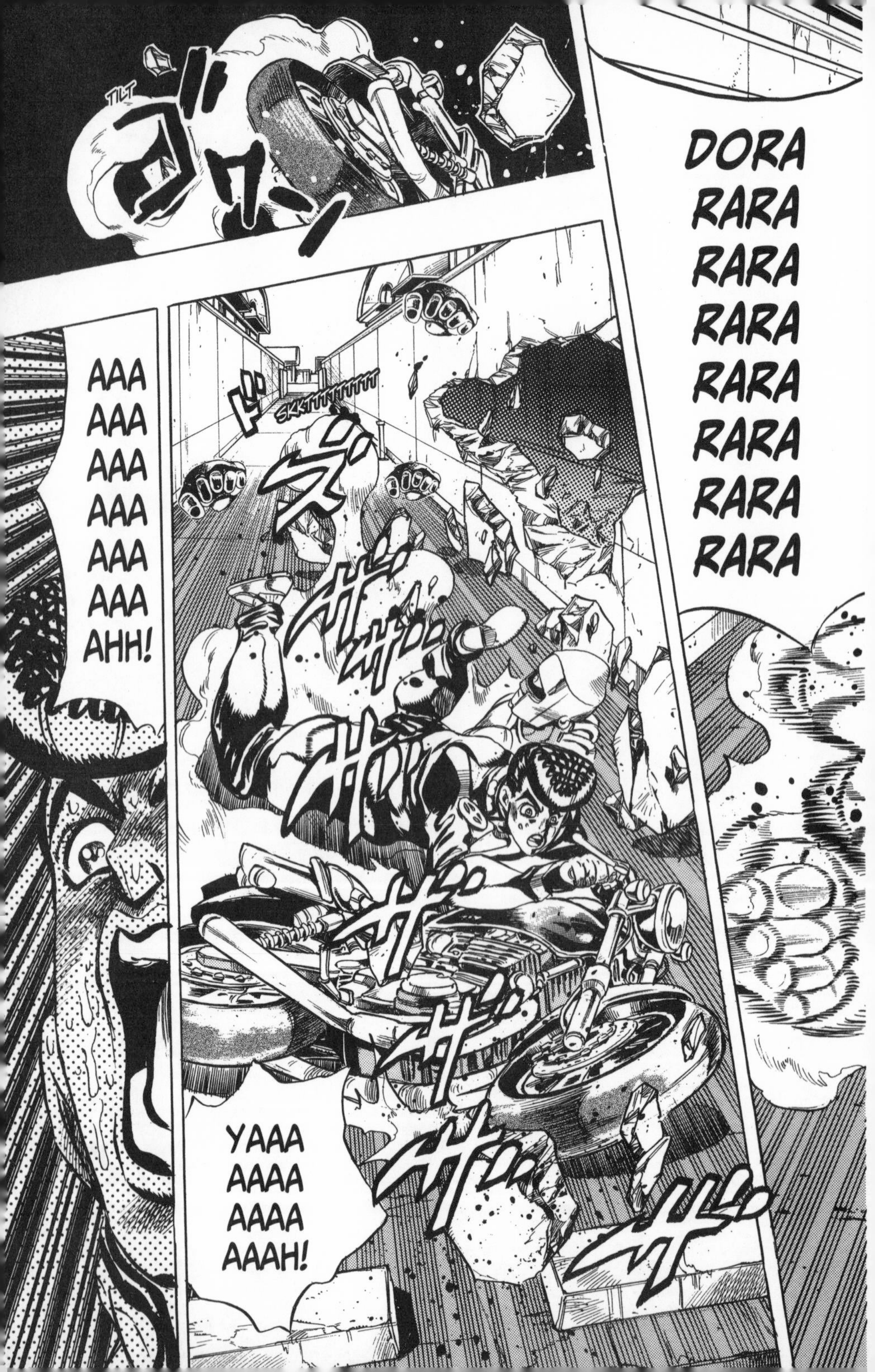
DORA RARA RARA RARA RARA RARA RARA RARA
TILT
SKKTTTTTTTTTT
YAAA AAAA AAAA AAAH!
AAA AAA AAA AAA AAA AAA AHH!

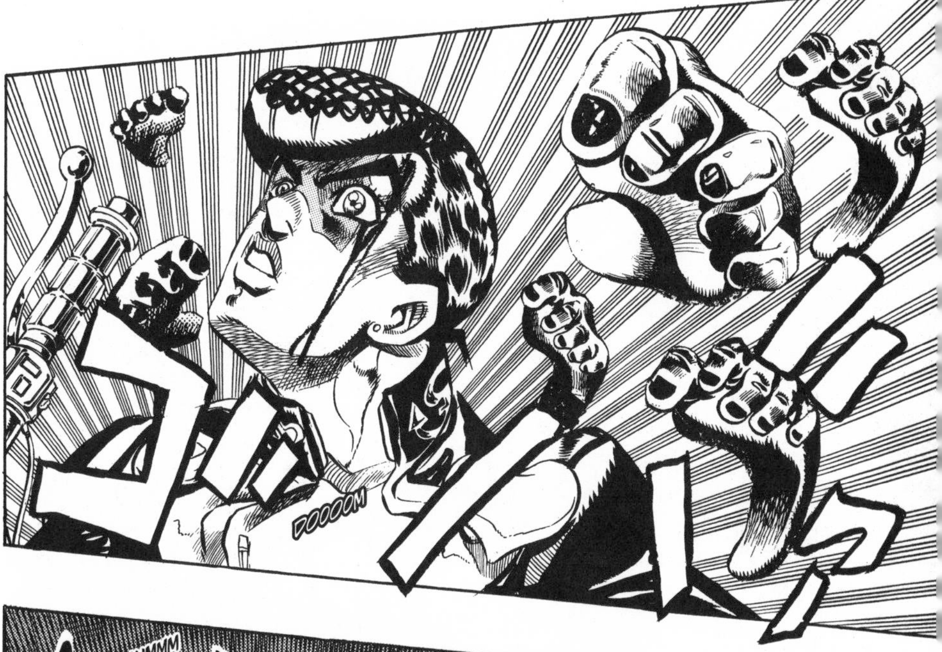
DOOOOM

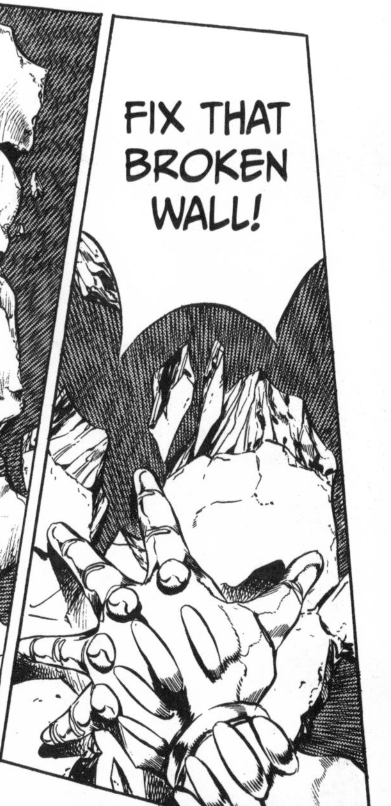
FIX THAT
BROKEN
WALL!

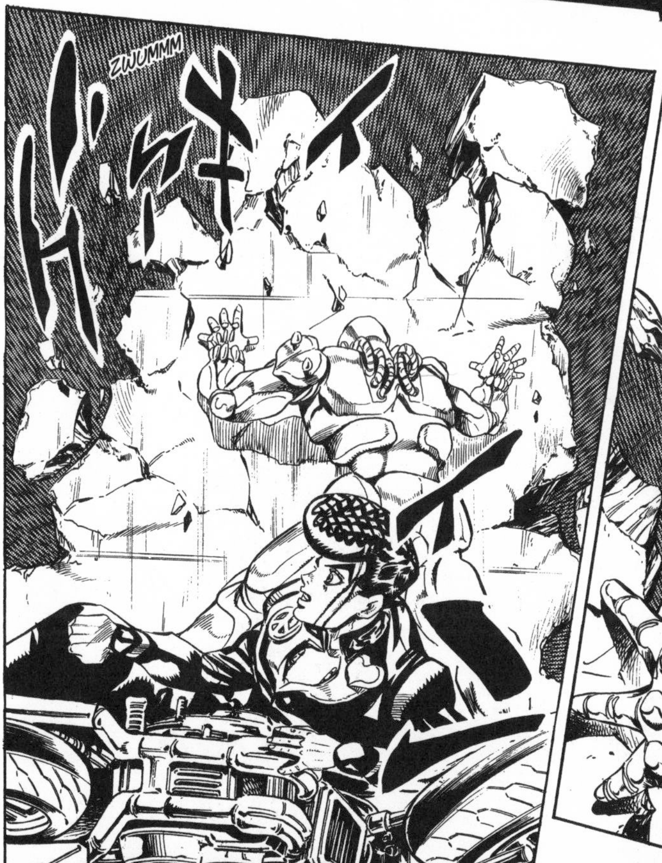
ZWUMMM

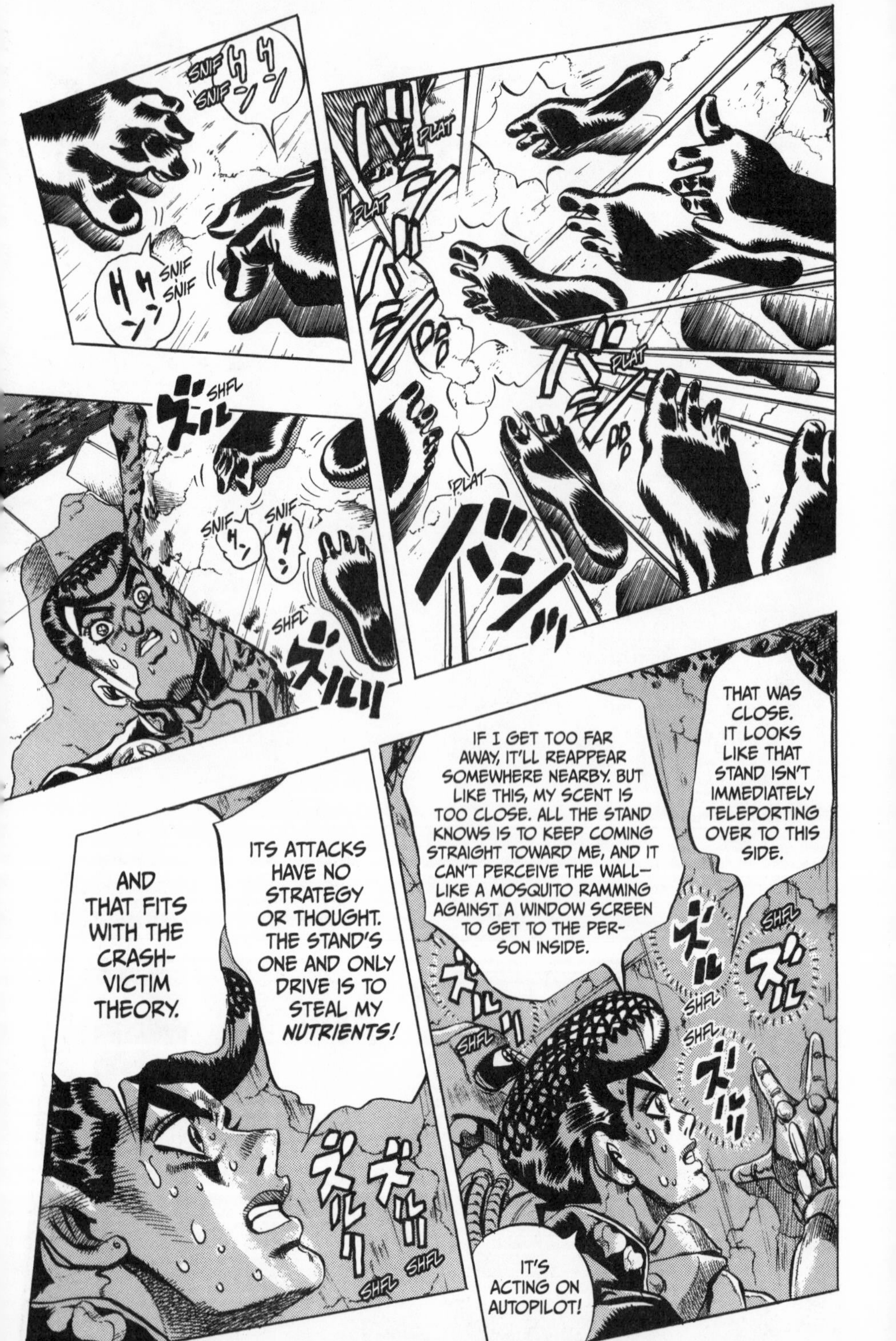
PLAT
PLAT
PLAT
PLAT
SNIF SNIF
SNIF SNIF
SHFL
SNIF
SNIF
SHFL
THAT WAS CLOSE. IT LOOKS LIKE THAT STAND ISN'T IMMEDIATELY TELEPORTING OVER TO THIS SIDE.
IF I GET TOO FAR AWAY, IT'LL REAPPEAR SOMEWHERE NEARBY. BUT LIKE THIS, MY SCENT IS TOO CLOSE. ALL THE STAND KNOWS IS TO KEEP COMING STRAIGHT TOWARD ME, AND IT CAN'T PERCEIVE THE WALL— LIKE A MOSQUITO RAMMING AGAINST A WINDOW SCREEN TO GET TO THE PER-SON INSIDE.
SHFL
SHFL
SHFL
SHFL
IT'S ACTING ON AUTOPILOT!
ITS ATTACKS HAVE NO STRATEGY OR THOUGHT. THE STAND'S ONE AND ONLY DRIVE IS TO STEAL MY *NUTRIENTS*!
AND THAT FITS WITH THE CRASH-VICTIM THEORY.
SHFL
SHFL

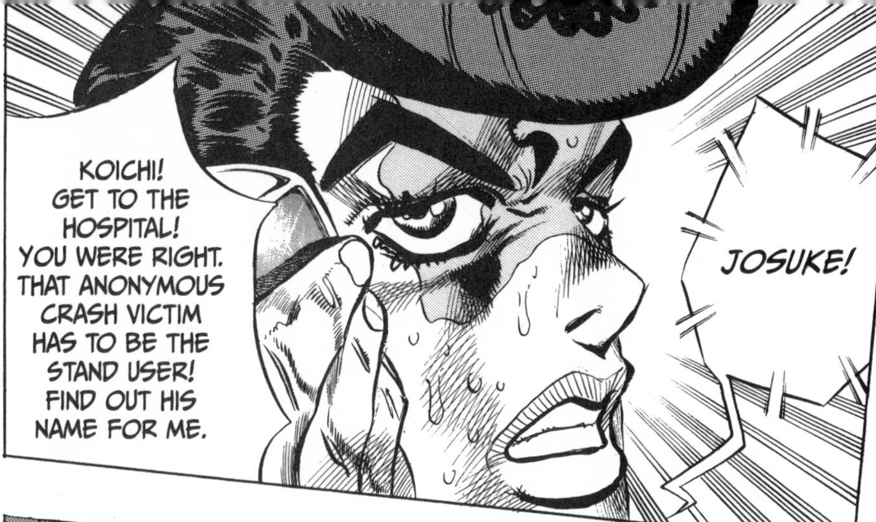
JOSUKE!
KOICHI! GET TO THE HOSPITAL! YOU WERE RIGHT. THAT ANONYMOUS CRASH VICTIM HAS TO BE THE STAND USER! FIND OUT HIS NAME FOR ME.

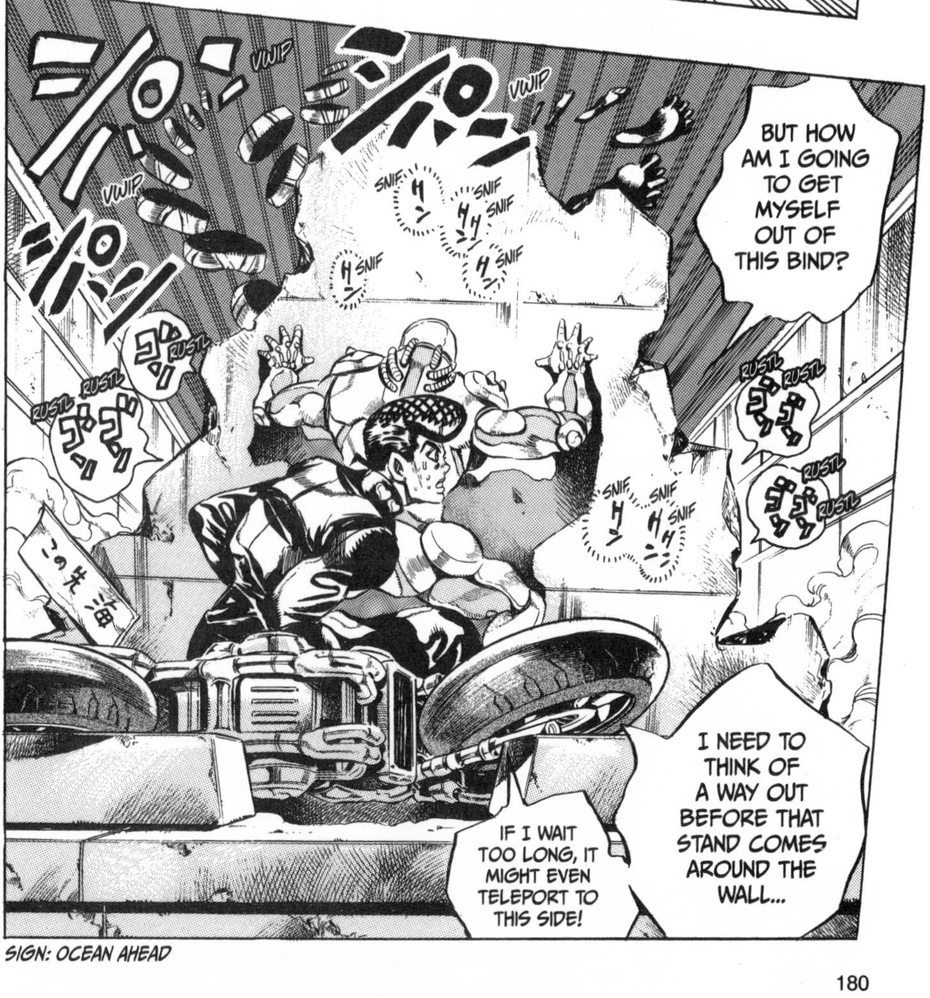
BUT HOW AM I GOING TO GET MYSELF OUT OF THIS BIND?
VWIP
VWIP
VWIP
SNIF SNIF SNIF SNIF
RUSTL RUSTL
RUSTL RUSTL
RUSTL RUSTL RUSTL
SNIF SNIF SNIF
I NEED TO THINK OF A WAY OUT BEFORE THAT STAND COMES AROUND THE WALL...
IF I WAIT TOO LONG, IT MIGHT EVEN TELEPORT TO THIS SIDE!

SIGN: OCEAN AHEAD

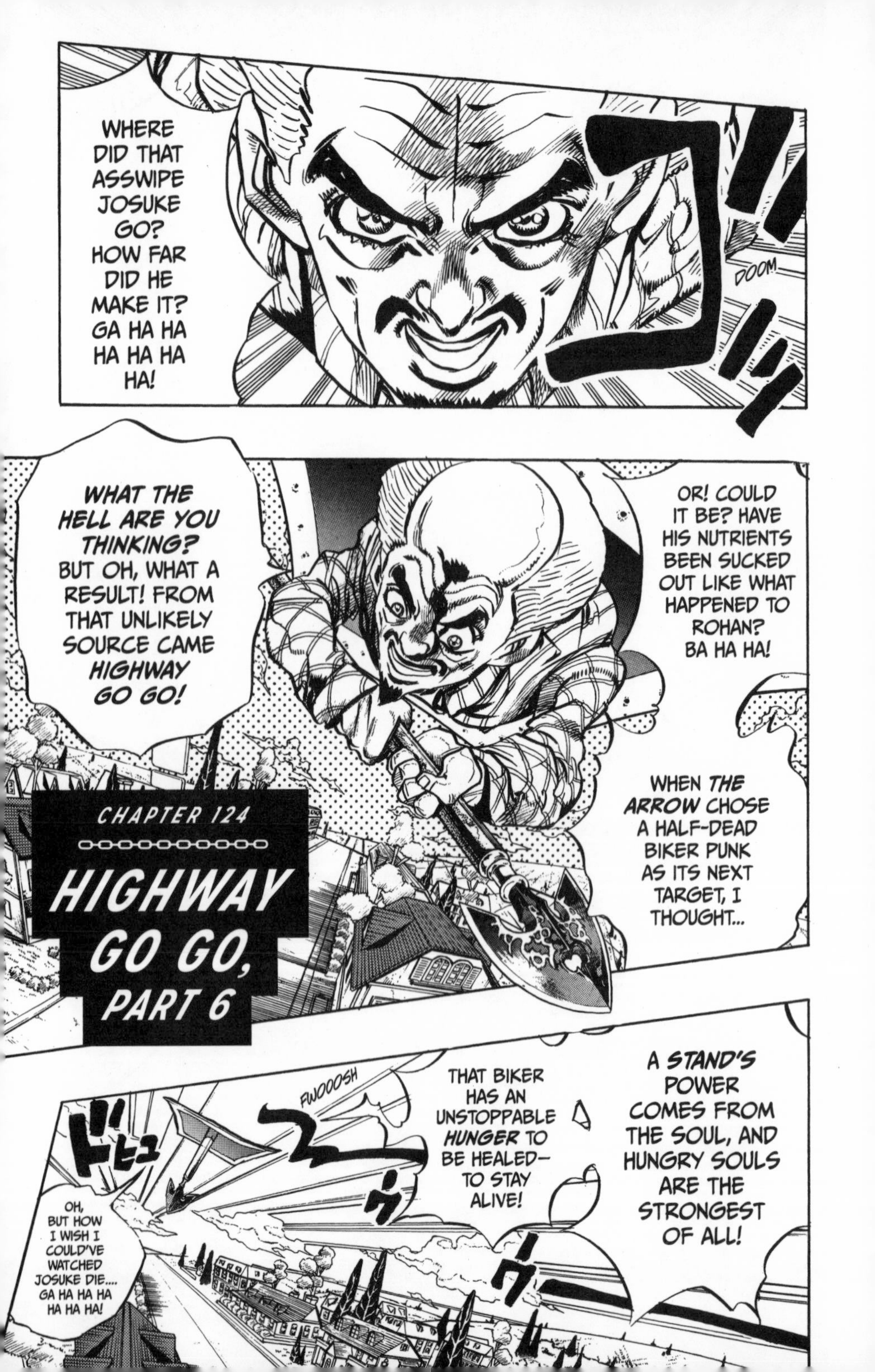
WHERE DID THAT ASSWIPE JOSUKE GO? HOW FAR DID HE MAKE IT? GA HA HA HA HA HA HA!
DOOM
OR! COULD IT BE? HAVE HIS NUTRIENTS BEEN SUCKED OUT LIKE WHAT HAPPENED TO ROHAN? BA HA HA!
WHEN THE ARROW CHOSE A HALF-DEAD BIKER PUNK AS ITS NEXT TARGET, I THOUGHT...
WHAT THE HELL ARE YOU THINKING? BUT OH, WHAT A RESULT! FROM THAT UNLIKELY SOURCE CAME HIGHWAY GO GO!
CHAPTER 124
HIGHWAY GO GO, PART 6
A STAND'S POWER COMES FROM THE SOUL, AND HUNGRY SOULS ARE THE STRONGEST OF ALL!
THAT BIKER HAS AN UNSTOPPABLE HUNGER TO BE HEALED— TO STAY ALIVE!
FWOOOSH
OH, BUT HOW I WISH I COULD'VE WATCHED JOSUKE DIE.... GA HA HA HA HA HA HA!

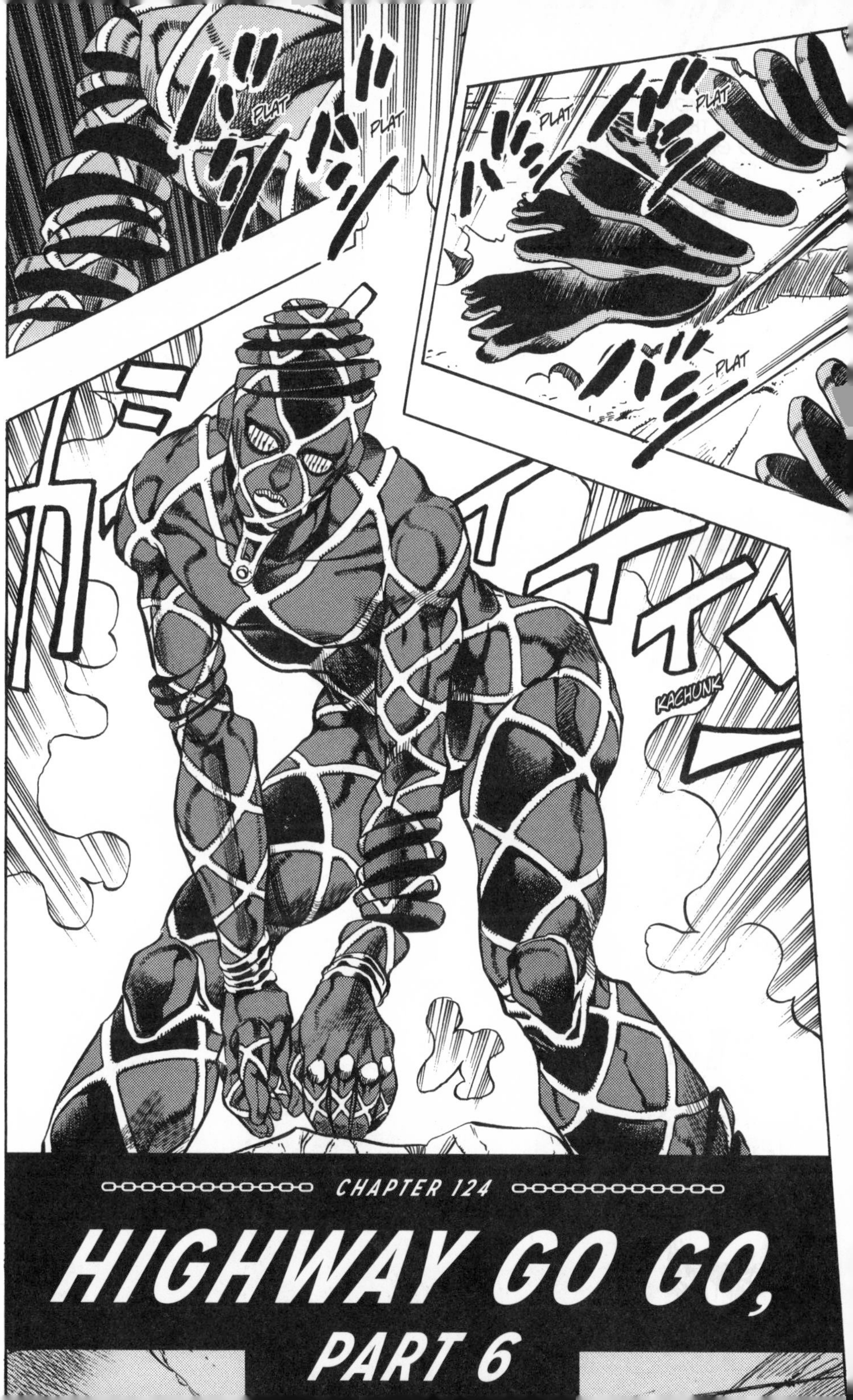
PLAT
PLAT
PLAT
PLAT
PLAT
KACHUNK

CHAPTER 124

HIGHWAY GO GO, PART 6

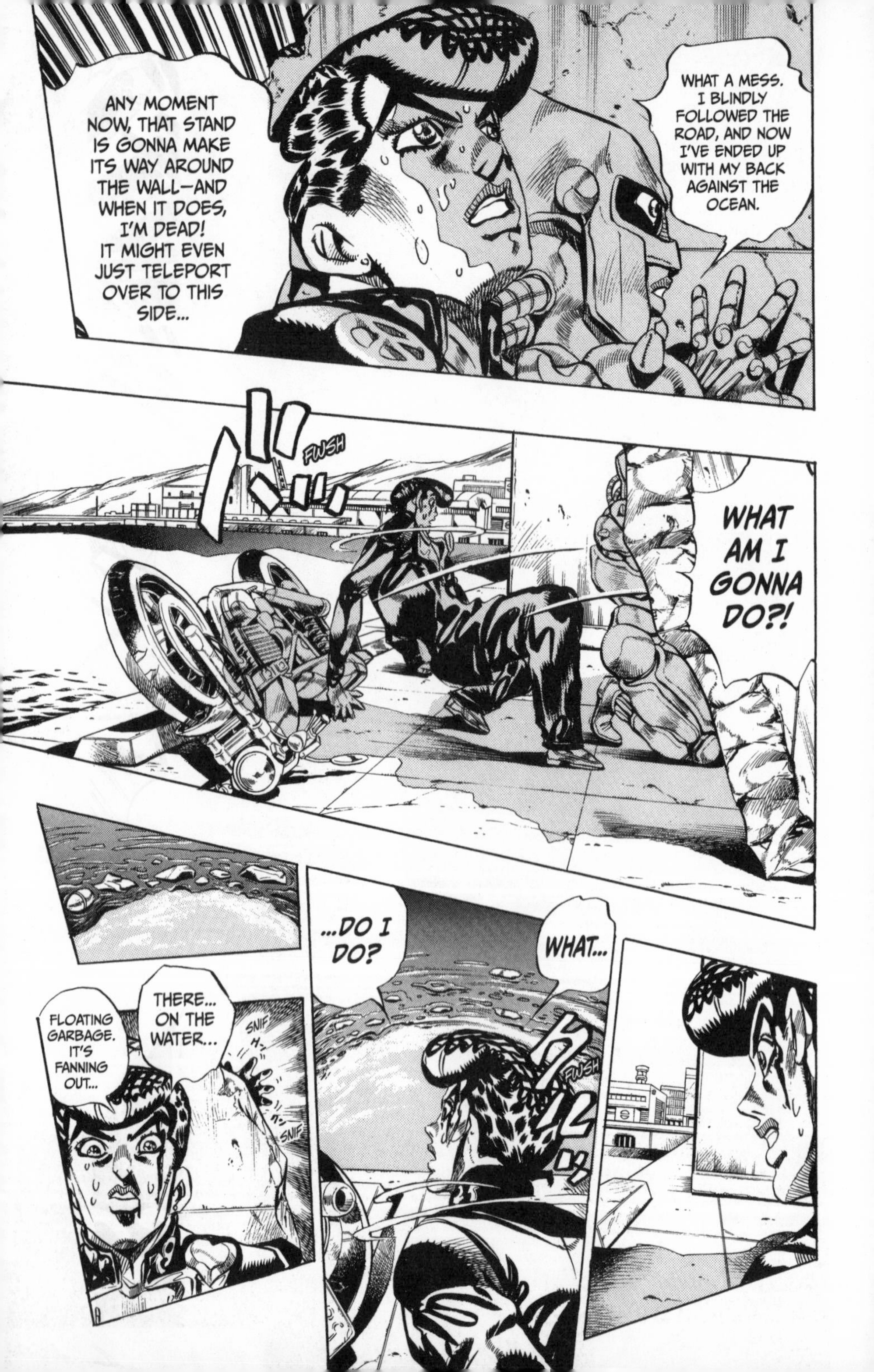
WHAT A MESS. I BLINDLY FOLLOWED THE ROAD, AND NOW I'VE ENDED UP WITH MY BACK AGAINST THE OCEAN.
ANY MOMENT NOW, THAT STAND IS GONNA MAKE ITS WAY AROUND THE WALL—AND WHEN IT DOES, I'M DEAD! IT MIGHT EVEN JUST TELEPORT OVER TO THIS SIDE...
FWSH
WHAT AM I GONNA DO?!
WHAT...
...DO I DO?
FWSH
THERE... ON THE WATER...
SNIF
SNIF
FLOATING GARBAGE. IT'S FANNING OUT...

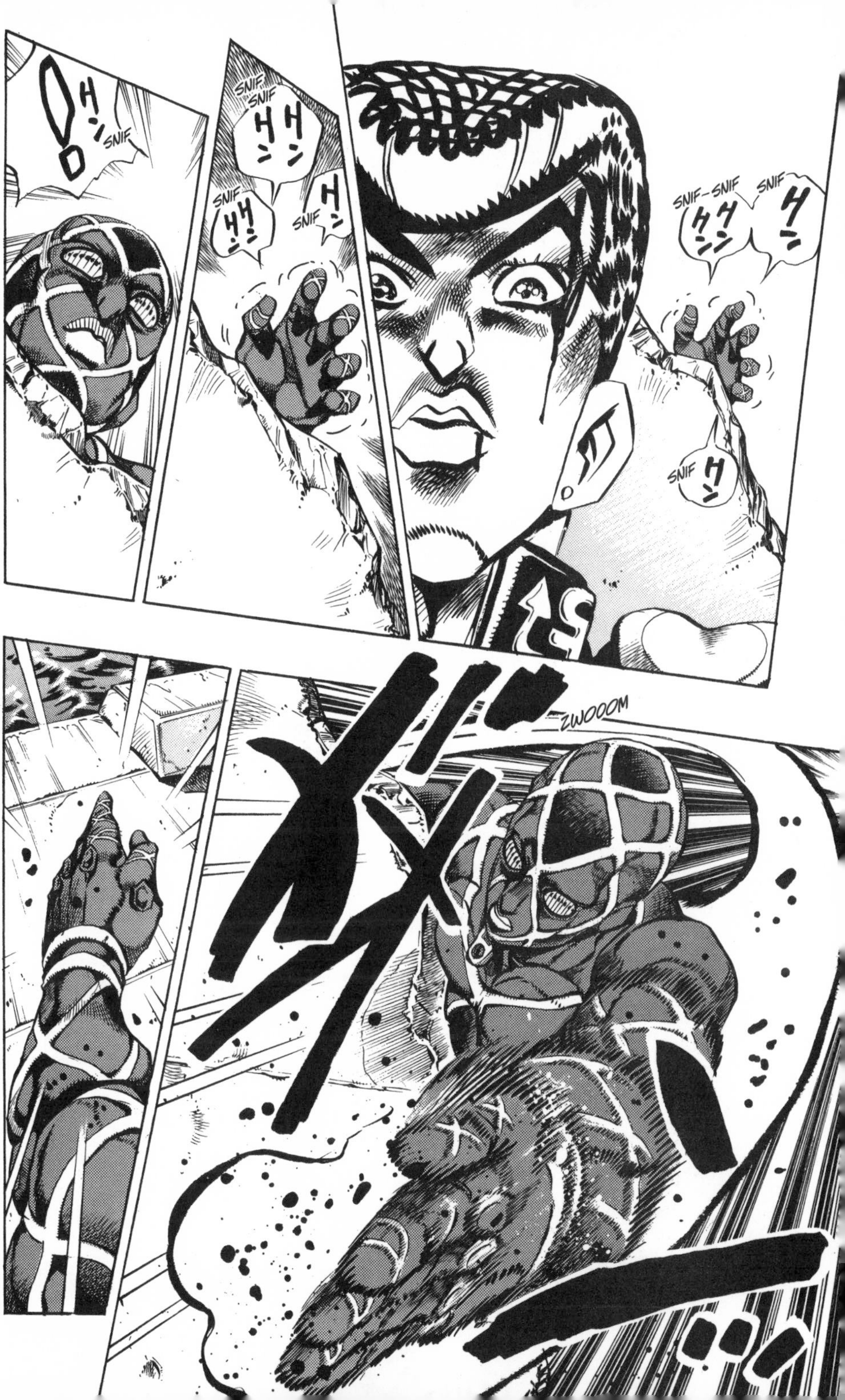
SNIF-SNIF
SNIF
SNIF
SNIF
SNIF
HH
SNIF
HH
SNIF
H
H
SNIF
ZWOOOM

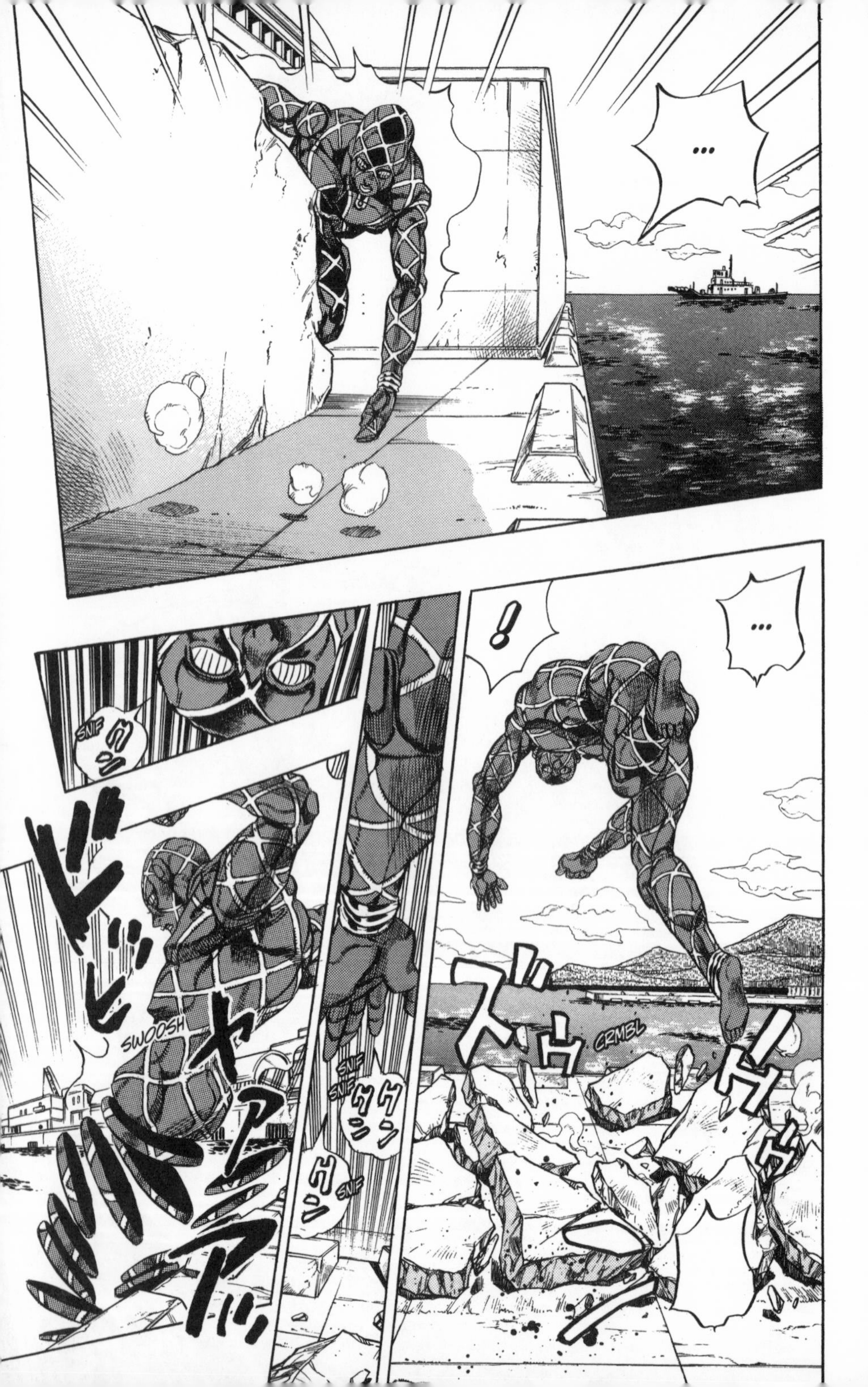
...
!
...
CRMBL
SNIF SNIF
SNIF
SNIF
SWOOSH

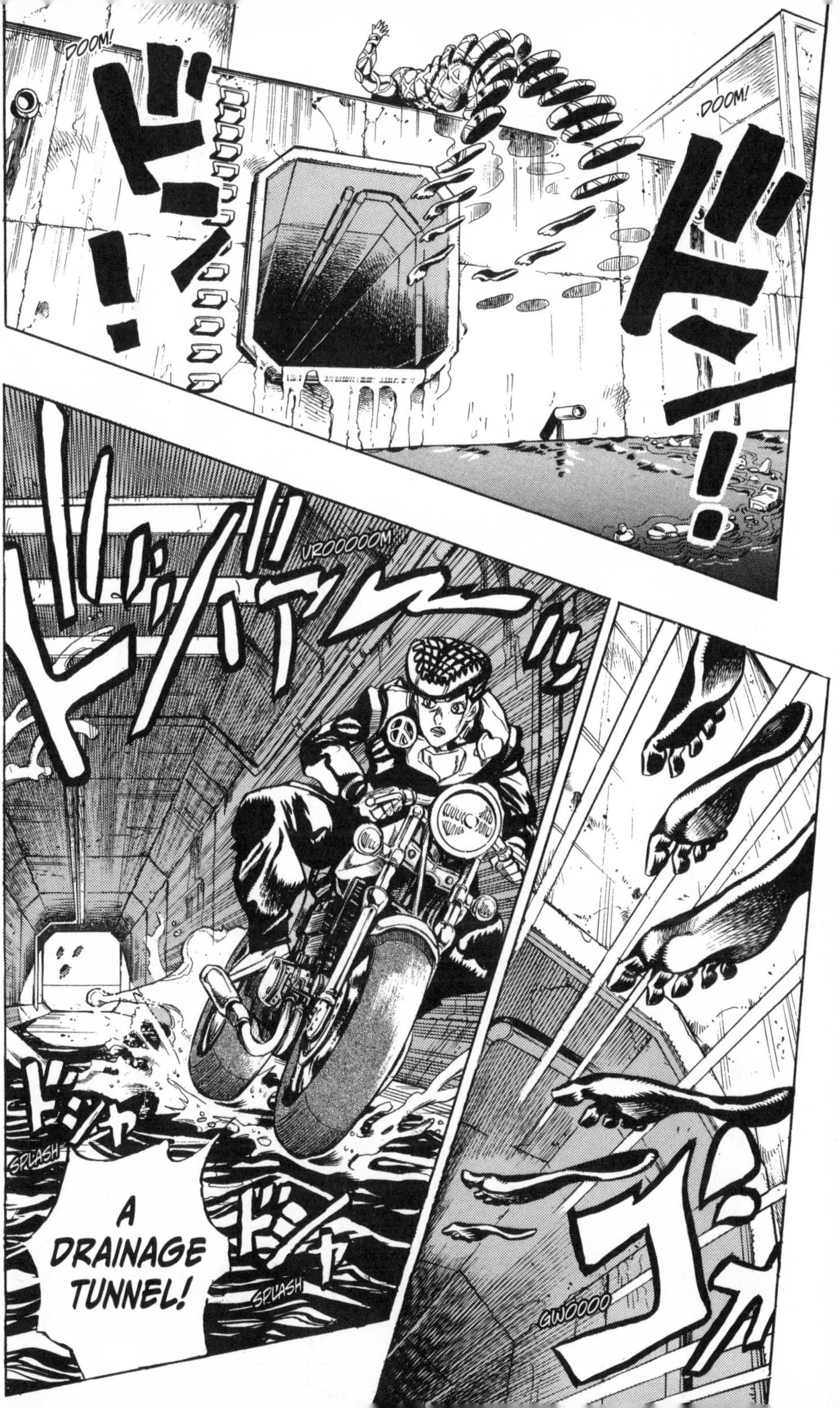
DOOM!
DOOM!
GWOOOO
VROOOOOM
SPLASH
A DRAINAGE TUNNEL!
SPLASH

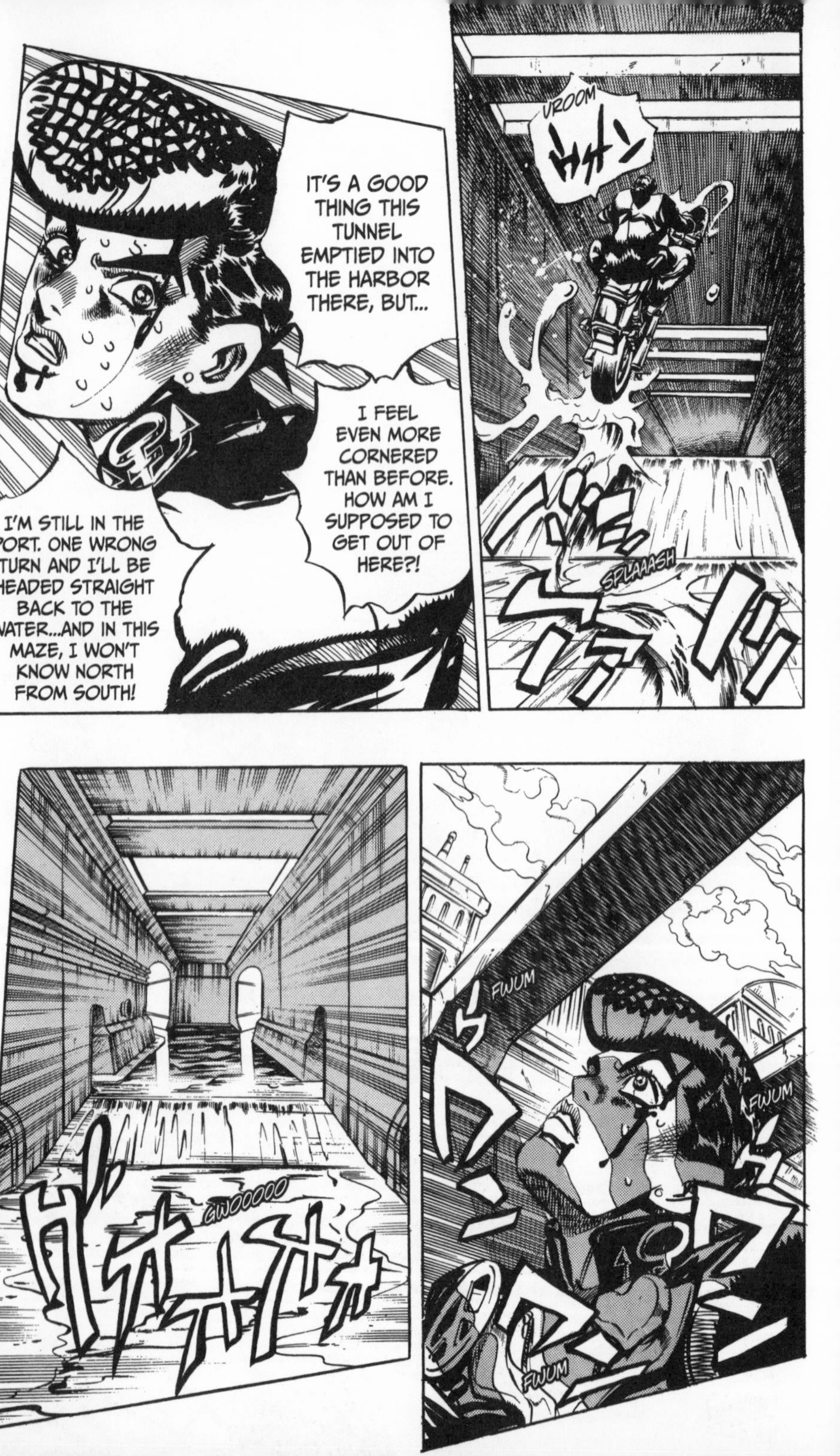
VROOM
SPLAAASH
IT'S A GOOD THING THIS TUNNEL EMPTIED INTO THE HARBOR THERE, BUT...
I FEEL EVEN MORE CORNERED THAN BEFORE. HOW AM I SUPPOSED TO GET OUT OF HERE?!
I'M STILL IN THE PORT. ONE WRONG TURN AND I'LL BE HEADED STRAIGHT BACK TO THE WATER...AND IN THIS MAZE, I WON'T KNOW NORTH FROM SOUTH!
FWUM
FWUM
FWUM
GWOOOOO

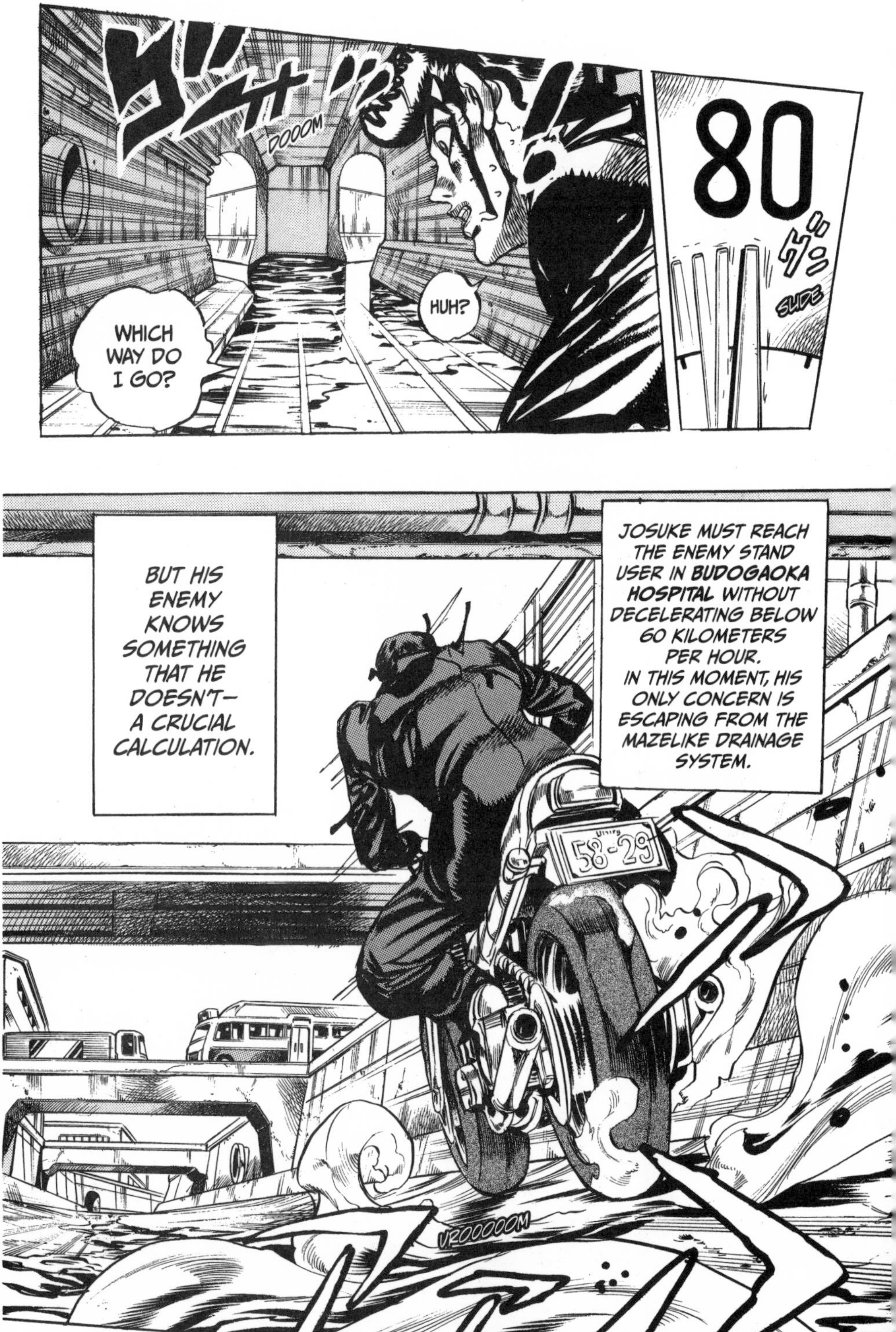
80
SLIDE
DOOOM
HUH?
WHICH WAY DO I GO?
JOSUKE MUST REACH THE ENEMY STAND USER IN **BUDOGAOKA HOSPITAL** WITHOUT DECELERATING BELOW 60 KILOMETERS PER HOUR. IN THIS MOMENT, HIS ONLY CONCERN IS ESCAPING FROM THE MAZELIKE DRAINAGE SYSTEM.
BUT HIS ENEMY KNOWS SOMETHING THAT HE DOESN'T— A CRUCIAL CALCULATION.
VROOOOOM

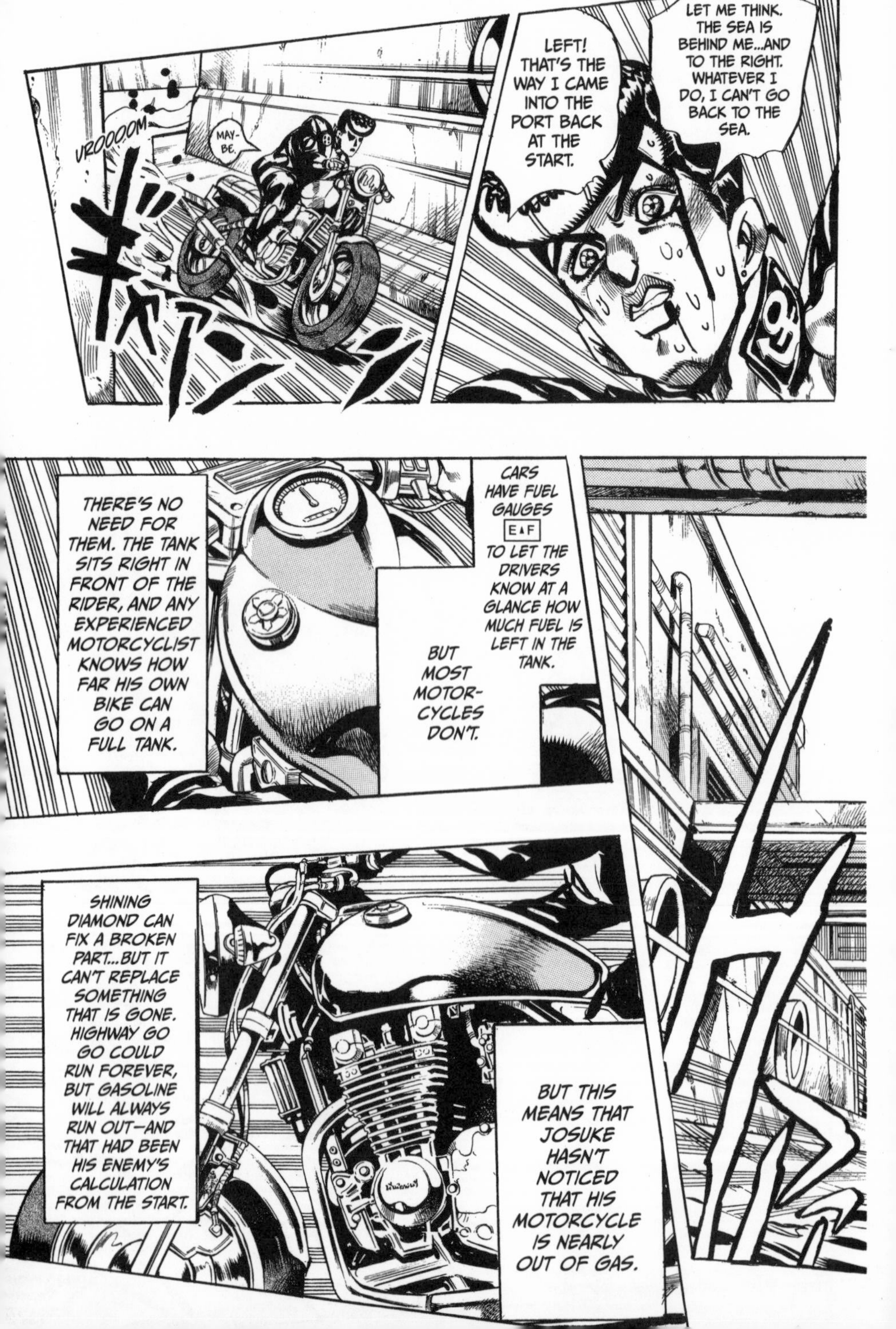
LET ME THINK. THE SEA IS BEHIND ME...AND TO THE RIGHT. WHATEVER I DO, I CAN'T GO BACK TO THE SEA.
LEFT! THAT'S THE WAY I CAME INTO THE PORT BACK AT THE START.
MAY-BE.
UROOOOM
CARS HAVE FUEL GAUGES
E F
TO LET THE DRIVERS KNOW AT A GLANCE HOW MUCH FUEL IS LEFT IN THE TANK.
BUT MOST MOTOR-CYCLES DON'T.
THERE'S NO NEED FOR THEM. THE TANK SITS RIGHT IN FRONT OF THE RIDER, AND ANY EXPERIENCED MOTORCYCLIST KNOWS HOW FAR HIS OWN BIKE CAN GO ON A FULL TANK.
BUT THIS MEANS THAT JOSUKE HASN'T NOTICED THAT HIS MOTORCYCLE IS NEARLY OUT OF GAS.
SHINING DIAMOND CAN FIX A BROKEN PART...BUT IT CAN'T REPLACE SOMETHING THAT IS GONE. HIGHWAY GO GO COULD RUN FOREVER, BUT GASOLINE WILL ALWAYS RUN OUT—AND THAT HAD BEEN HIS ENEMY'S CALCULATION FROM THE START.

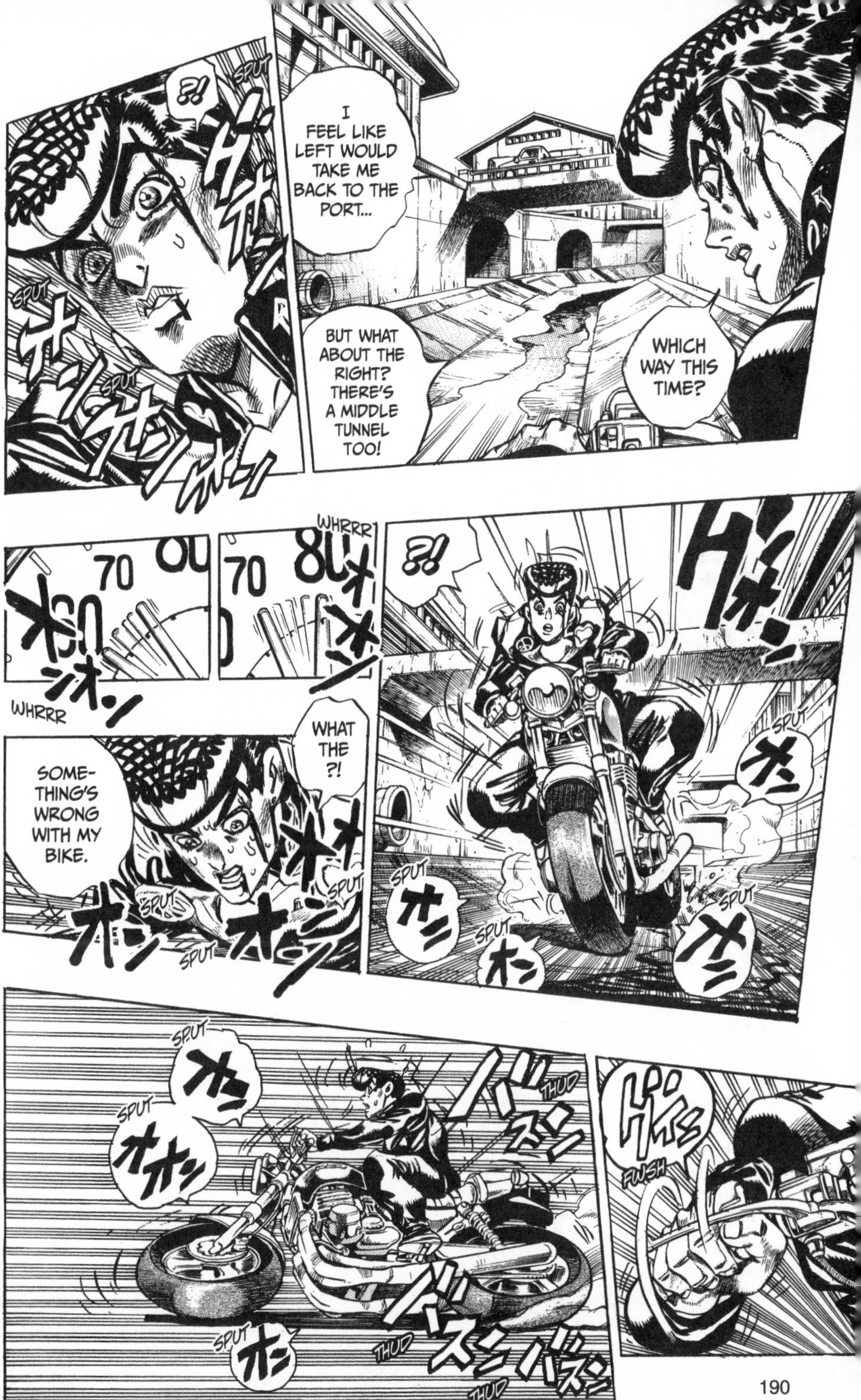
WHICH WAY THIS TIME?
I FEEL LIKE LEFT WOULD TAKE ME BACK TO THE PORT...
BUT WHAT ABOUT THE RIGHT? THERE'S A MIDDLE TUNNEL TOO!
?!
SPUT
SPUT
SPUT
?!
SPUT
SPUT
SPUT
SPUT
WHRRR
70
70
WHRRR
WHAT THE ?!
SOME-THING'S WRONG WITH MY BIKE.
SPUT
SPUT
SPUT
FWSH
THUD
SPUT
SPUT
SPUT
THUD
THUD

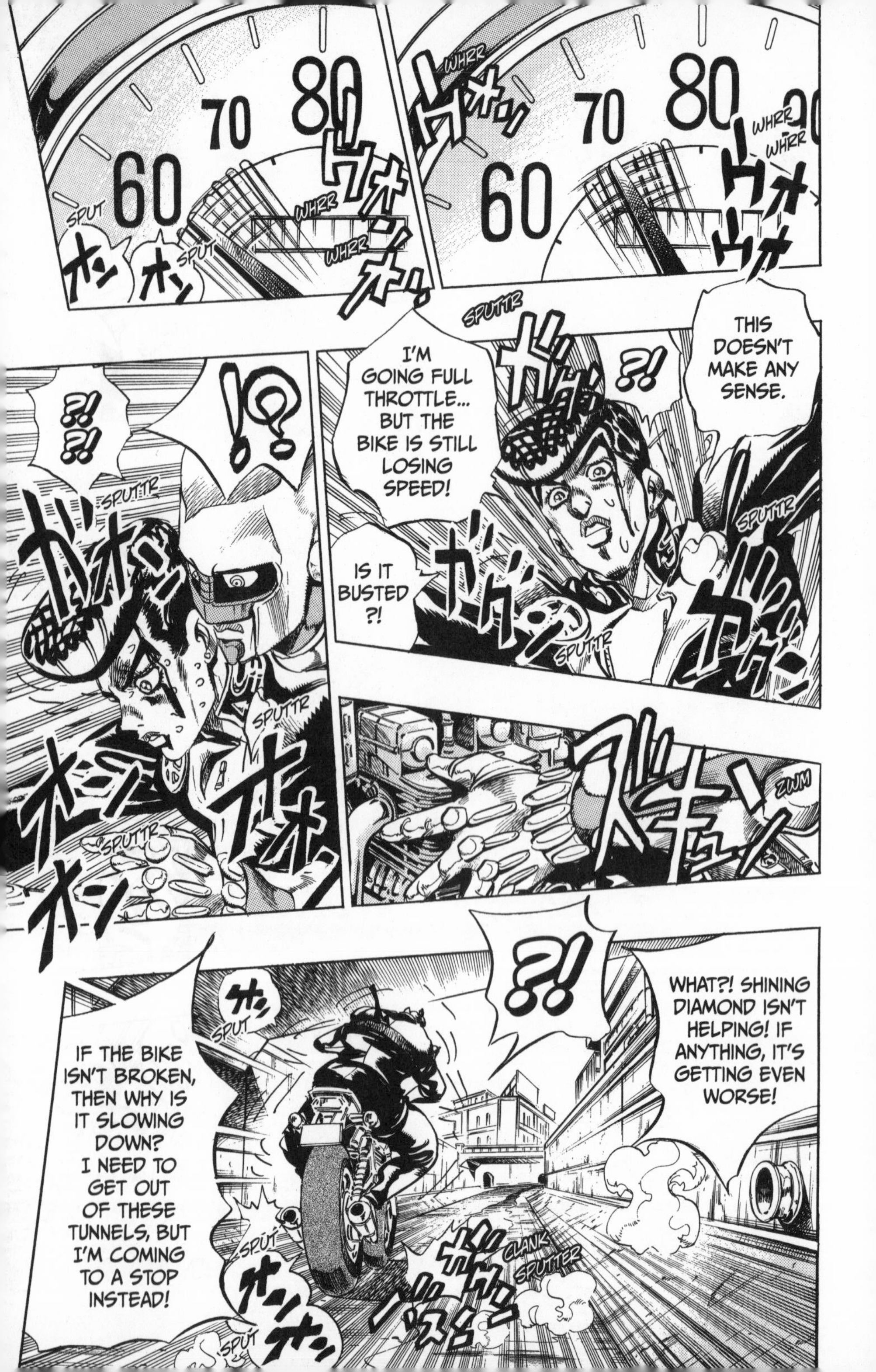
WHRR
80
70
60
WHRR
WHRR
WHRR
80
70
60
SPUT
SPUT
WHRR
WHRR
THIS DOESN'T MAKE ANY SENSE.
?!
SPUTTR
I'M GOING FULL THROTTLE... BUT THE BIKE IS STILL LOSING SPEED!
IS IT BUSTED?!
SPUTTR
SPUTTR
ZWUM
?! ?!
!?
SPUTTR
SPUTTR
SPUTTR
WHAT?! SHINING DIAMOND ISN'T HELPING! IF ANYTHING, IT'S GETTING EVEN WORSE!
?!
SPUT
IF THE BIKE ISN'T BROKEN, THEN WHY IS IT SLOWING DOWN? I NEED TO GET OUT OF THESE TUNNELS, BUT I'M COMING TO A STOP INSTEAD!
CLANK
SPUTTER
SPUT
SPUT

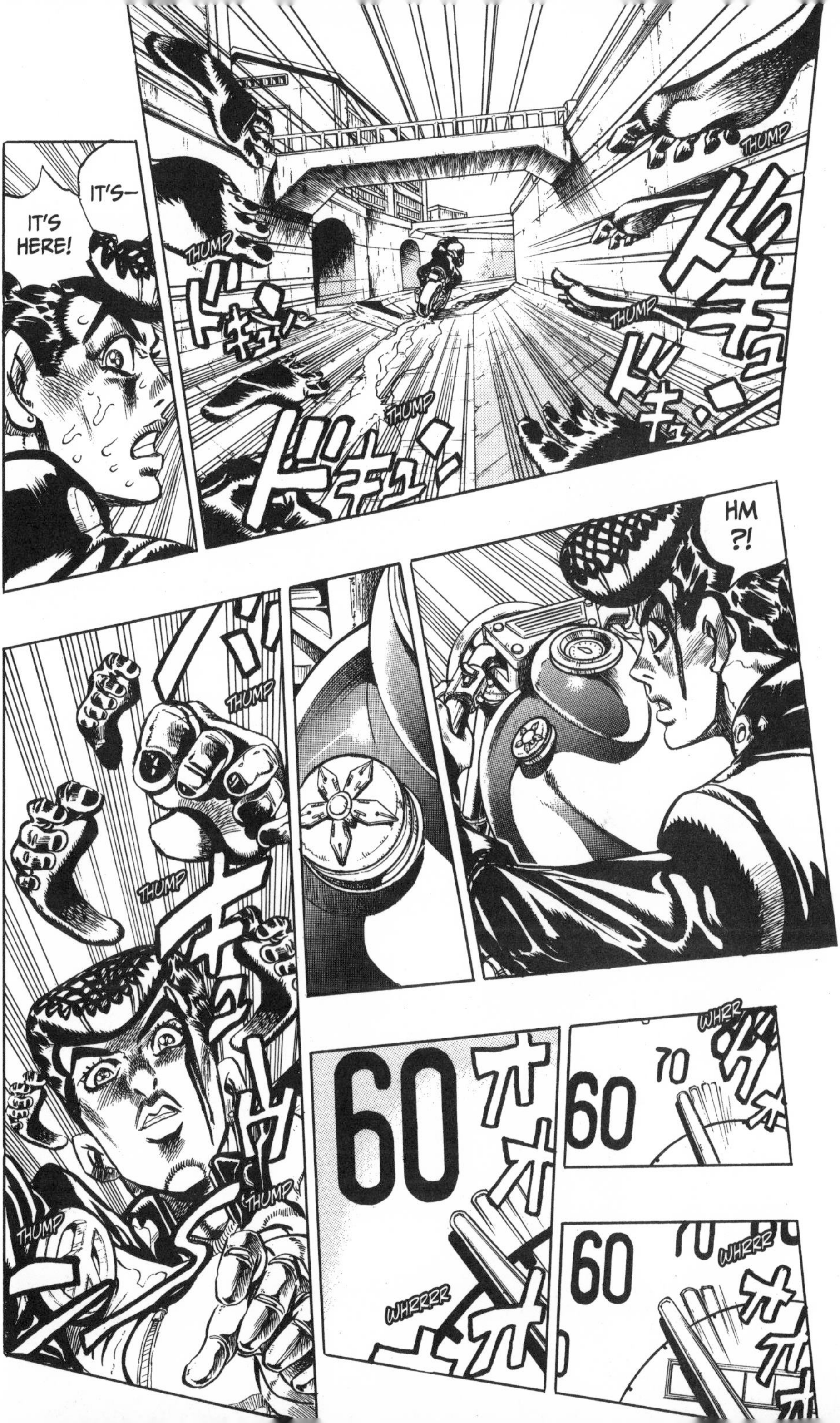
THUMP
THUMP
THUMP
THUMP
IT'S—
IT'S HERE!
HM ?!
WHRR
60
70
WHRRR
60
WHRRRR
60
THUMP
THUMP
THUMP
THUMP

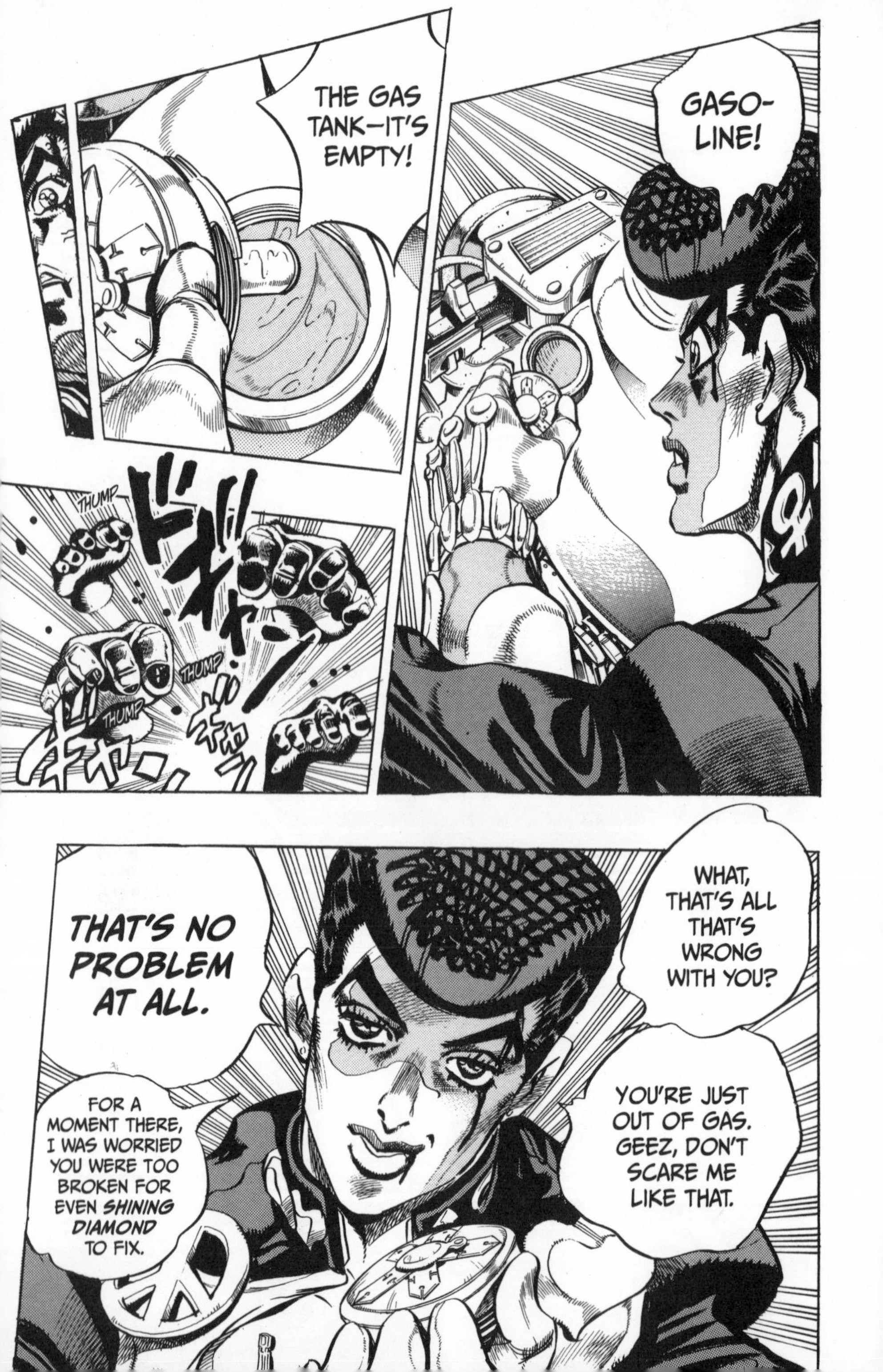
GASO-LINE!
THE GAS TANK—IT'S EMPTY!
THUMP
THUMP
THUMP
WHAT, THAT'S ALL THAT'S WRONG WITH YOU?
THAT'S NO PROBLEM AT ALL.
YOU'RE JUST OUT OF GAS. GEEZ, DON'T SCARE ME LIKE THAT.
FOR A MOMENT THERE, I WAS WORRIED YOU WERE TOO BROKEN FOR EVEN SHINING DIAMOND TO FIX.

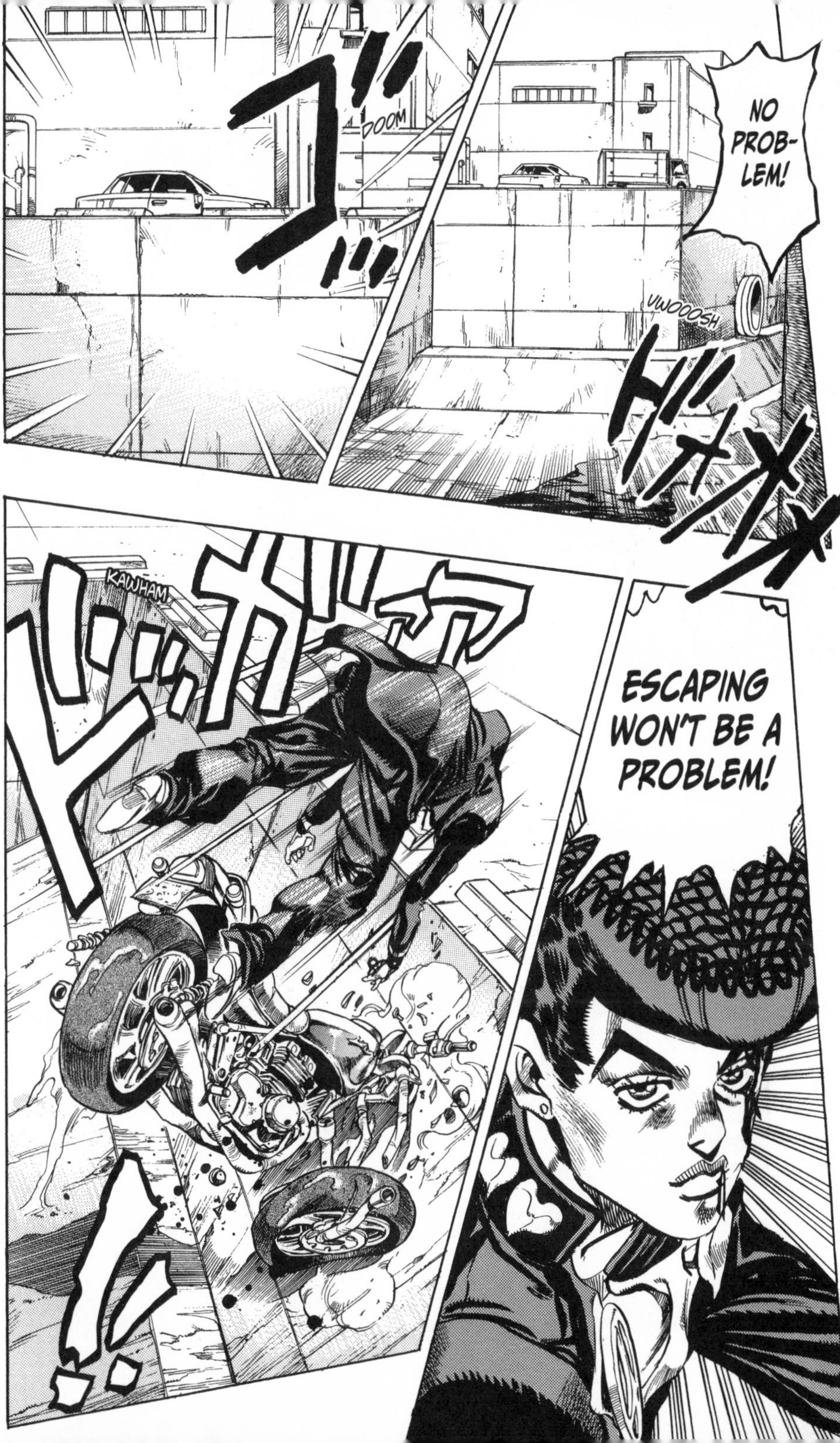
NO PROB-
LEM!
VWOOOSH
DOOM
ESCAPING WON'T BE A PROBLEM!
KAWHAM

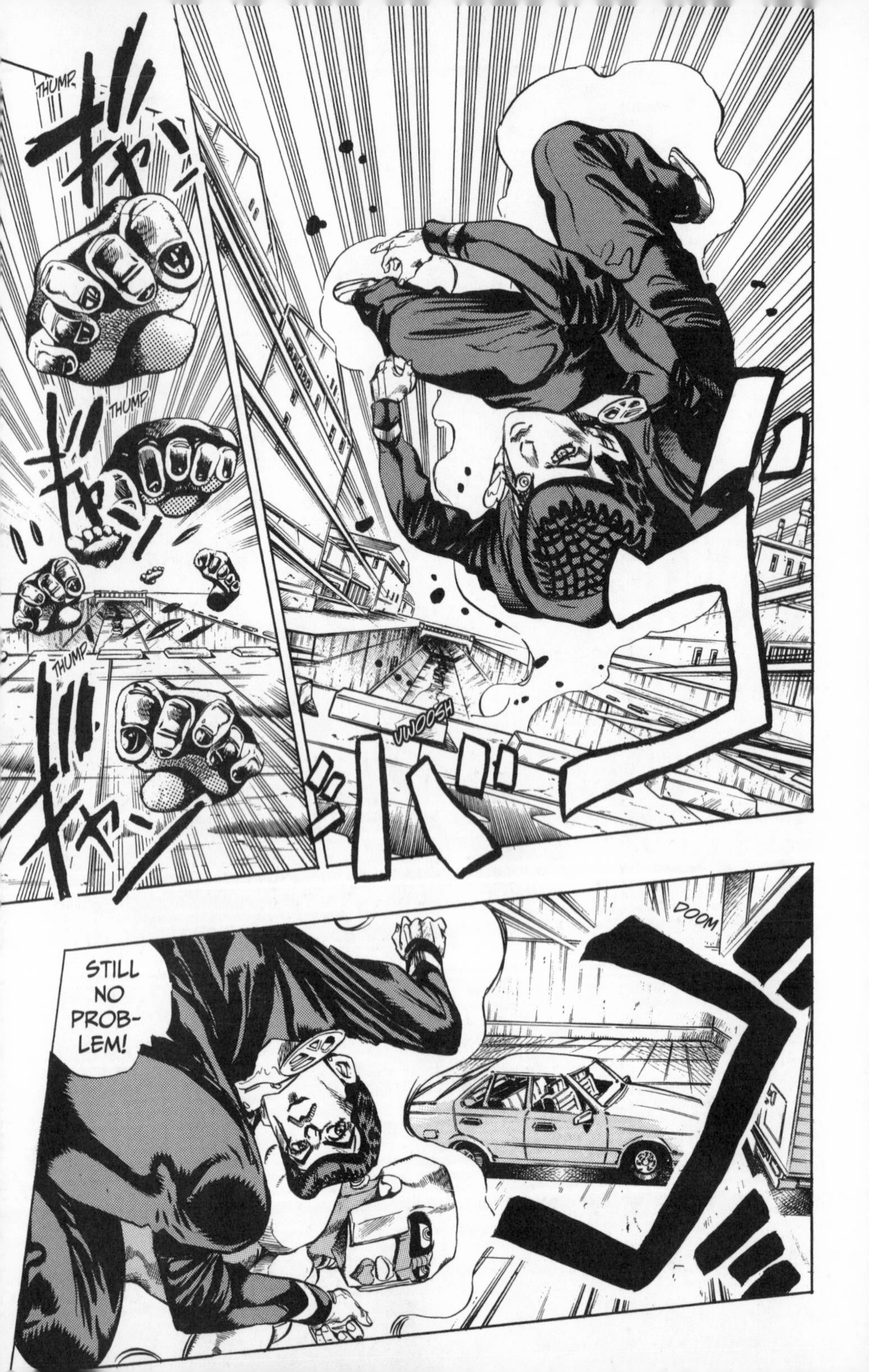
WOOSH
THUMP
THUMP
THUMP
DOOM
STILL NO PROB-LEM!

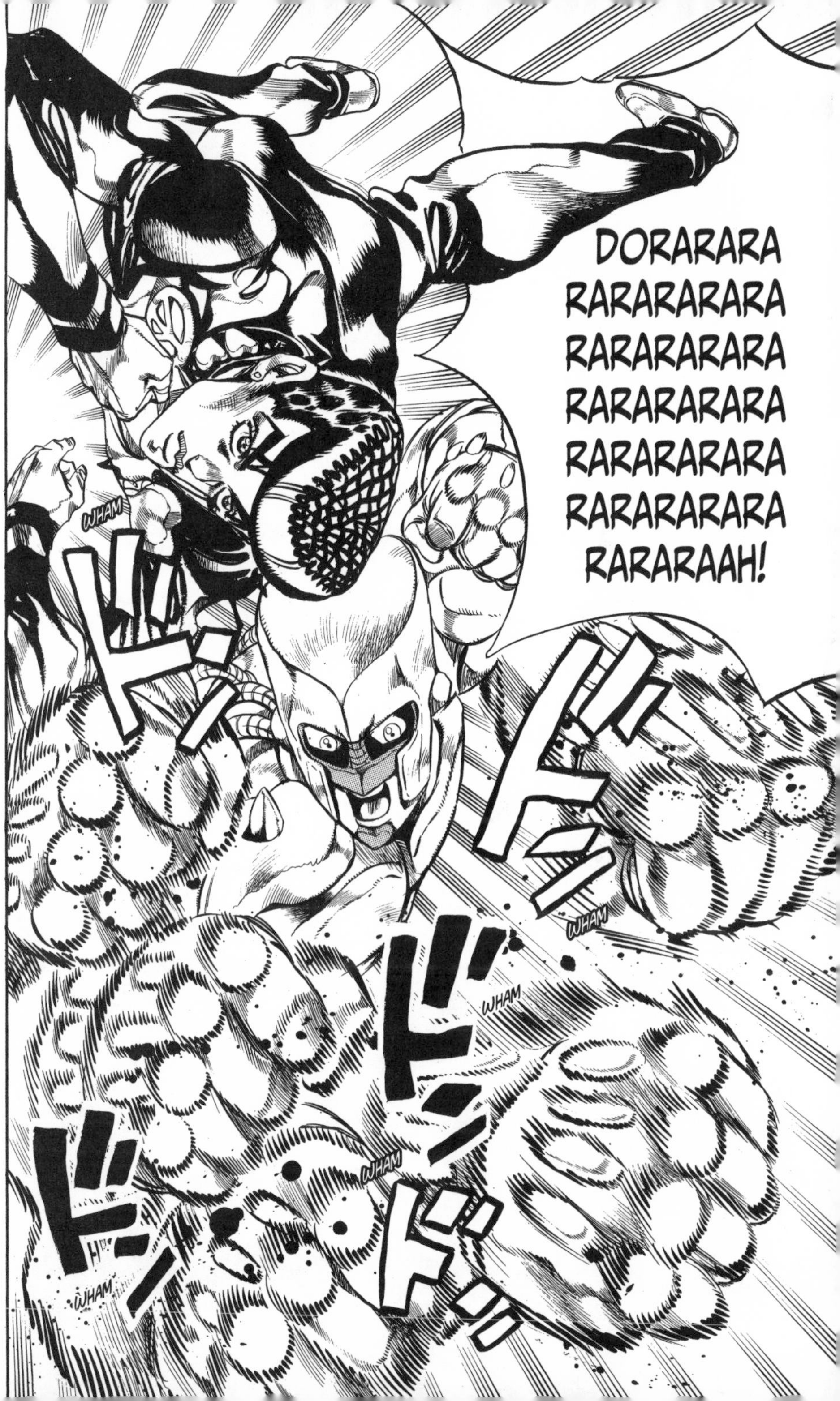
DORARARA RARARARARA RARARARARA RARARARARA RARARARARA RARARARARA RARARAAH!
WHAM
WHAM
WHAM
WHAM
WHAM

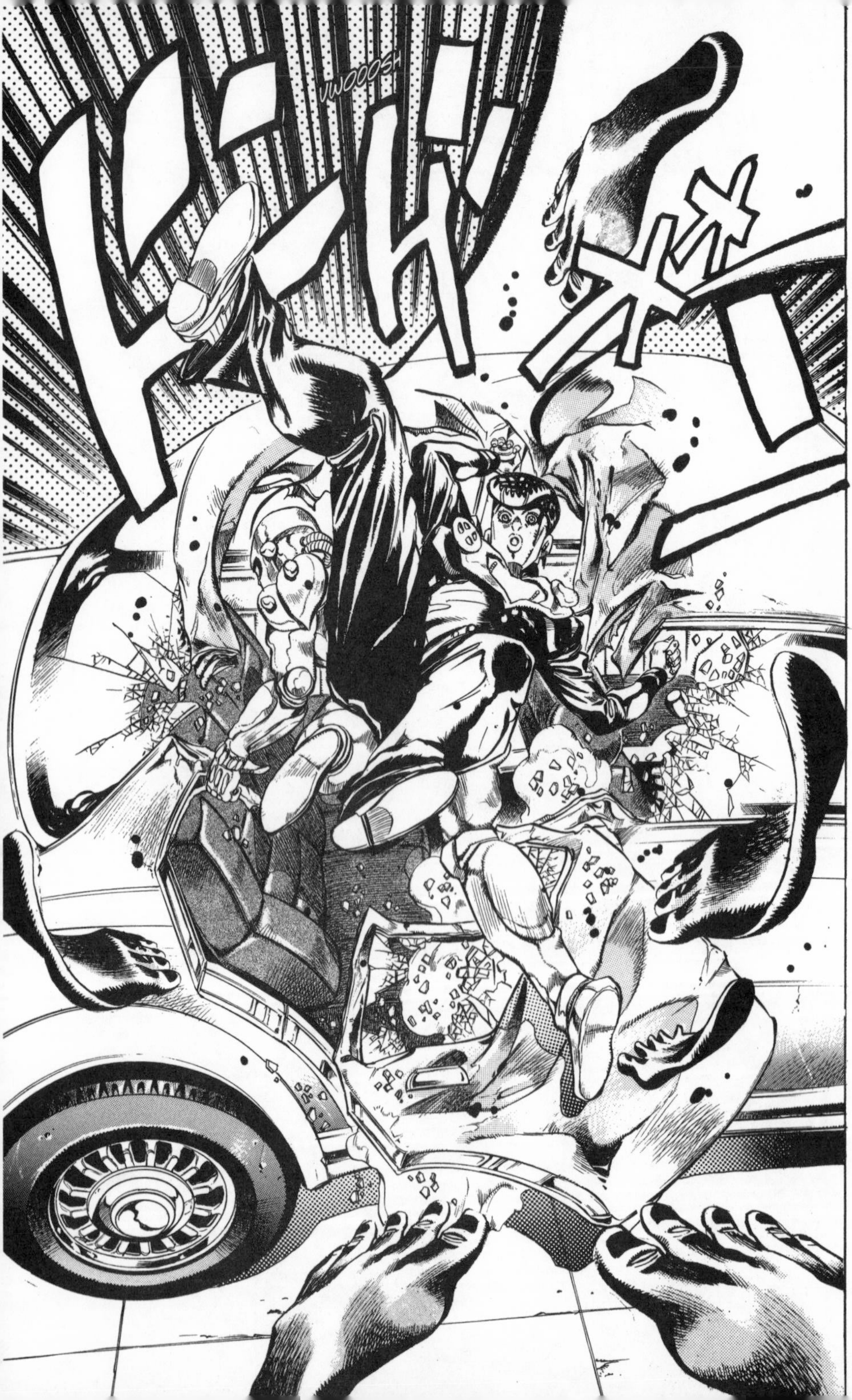
VWOOOSH

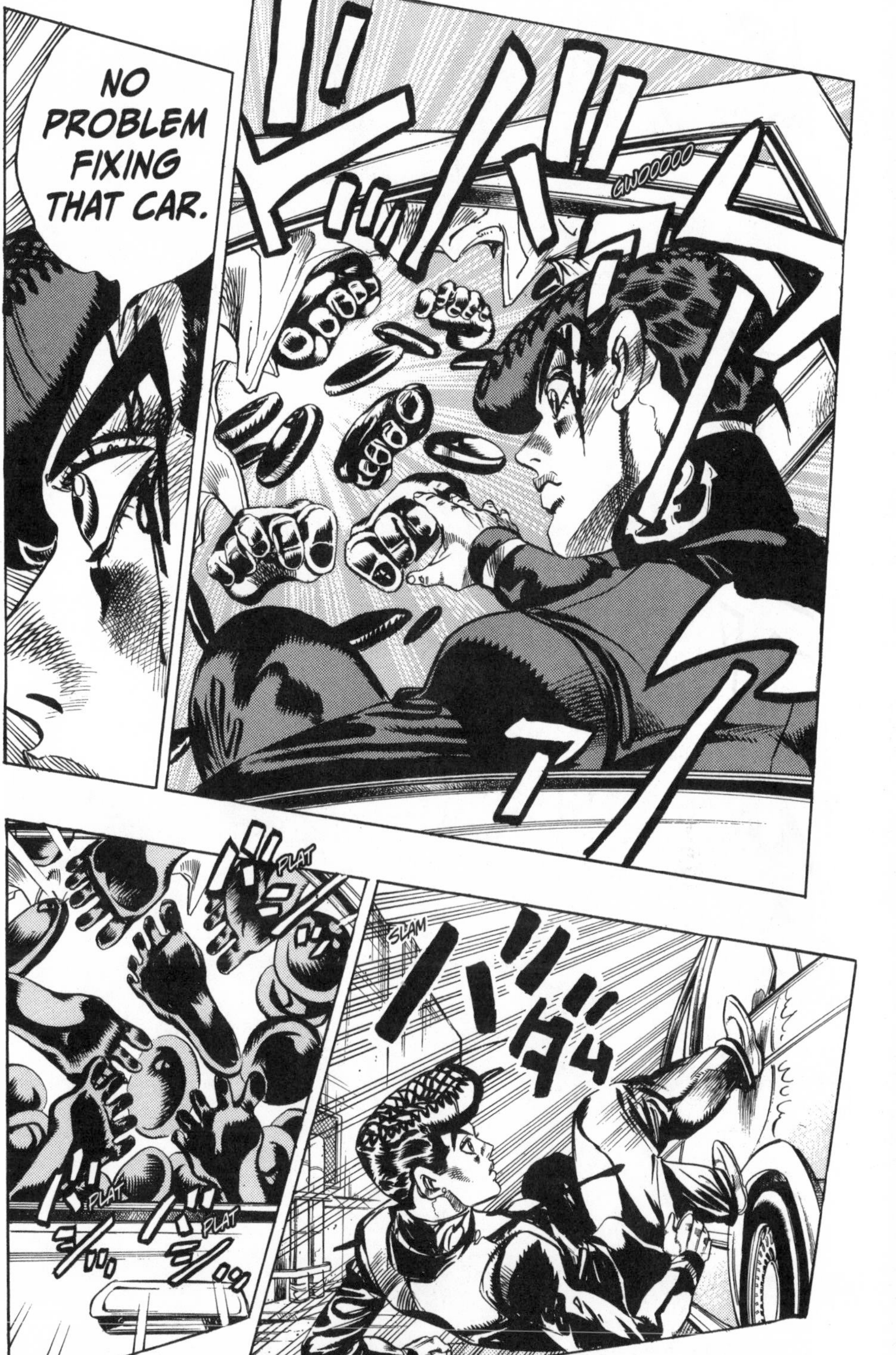
GWOOOOO
NO PROBLEM FIXING THAT CAR.
SLAM
PLAT
PLAT
PLAT

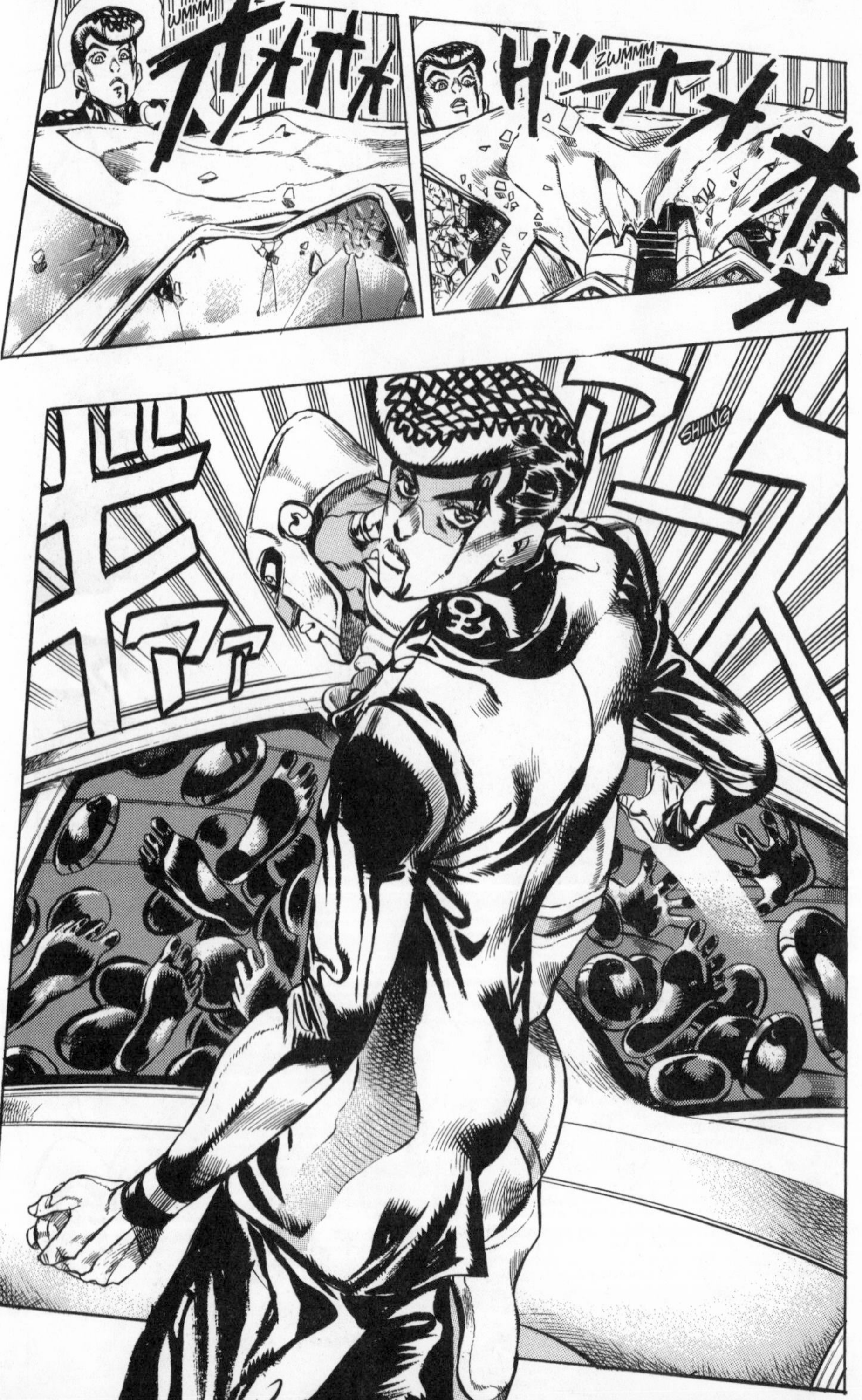
ZWMMM
WMMM
SHIIING

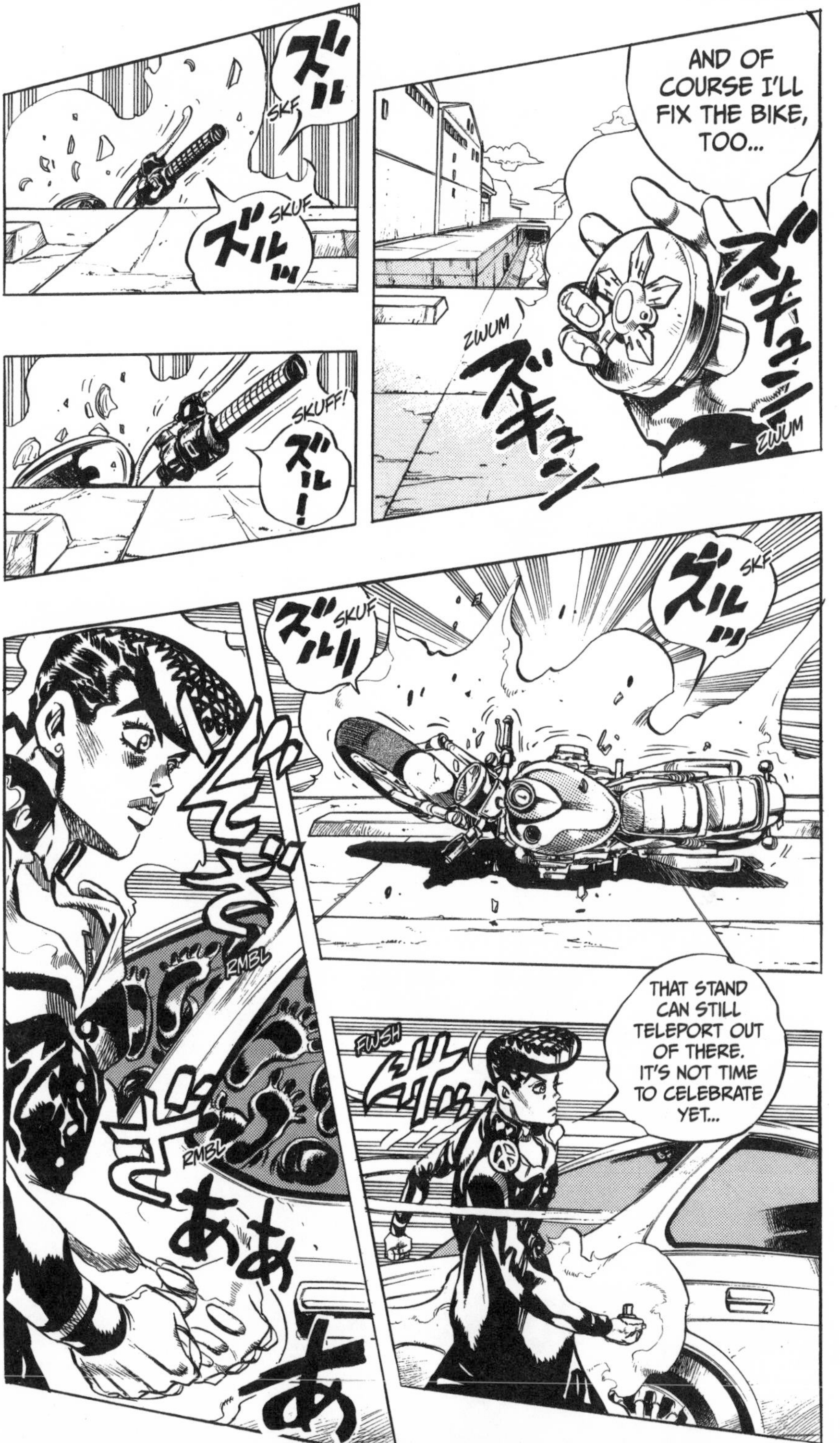
AND OF COURSE I'LL FIX THE BIKE, TOO...
ズギュン
ZWUUM
ズギュン
ZWUUM
ズル
SKF
ズル
SKUF
ズルー!
SKUFF!
ズル
SKF
ズル
SKUF
THAT STAND CAN STILL TELEPORT OUT OF THERE. IT'S NOT TIME TO CELEBRATE YET...
FWSH
RMBL
RMBL

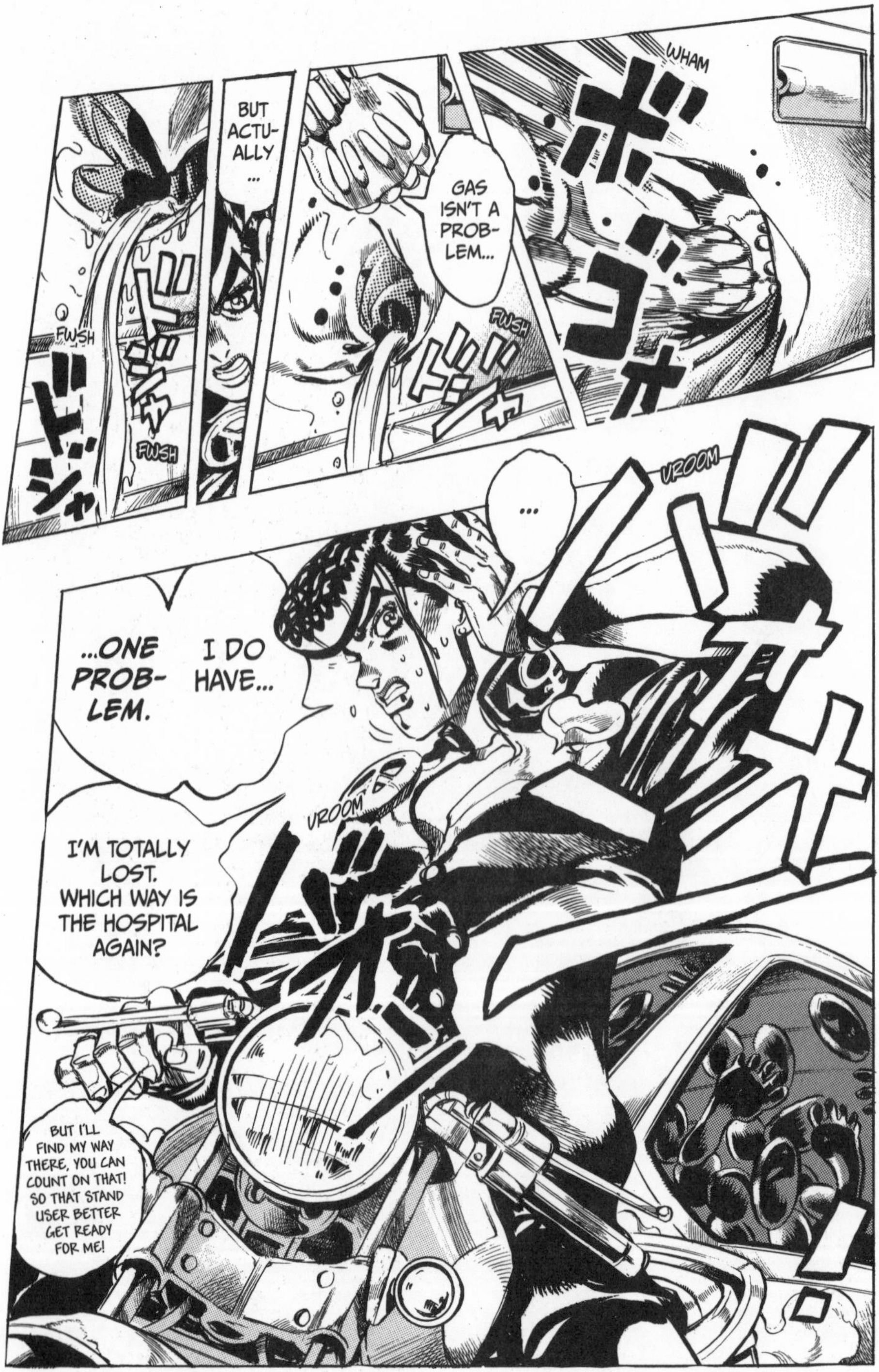
WHAM
GAS ISN'T A PROB-LEM...
FWSH
BUT ACTU-ALLY ...
FWSH
FWSH
UROOM
...
I DO HAVE...
...ONE PROB-LEM.
UROOM
I'M TOTALLY LOST. WHICH WAY IS THE HOSPITAL AGAIN?
BUT I'LL FIND MY WAY THERE, YOU CAN COUNT ON THAT! SO THAT STAND USER BETTER GET READY FOR ME!

CHAPTER 125

HIGHWAY GO GO, PART 7

JoJo's BIZARRE ADVENTURE

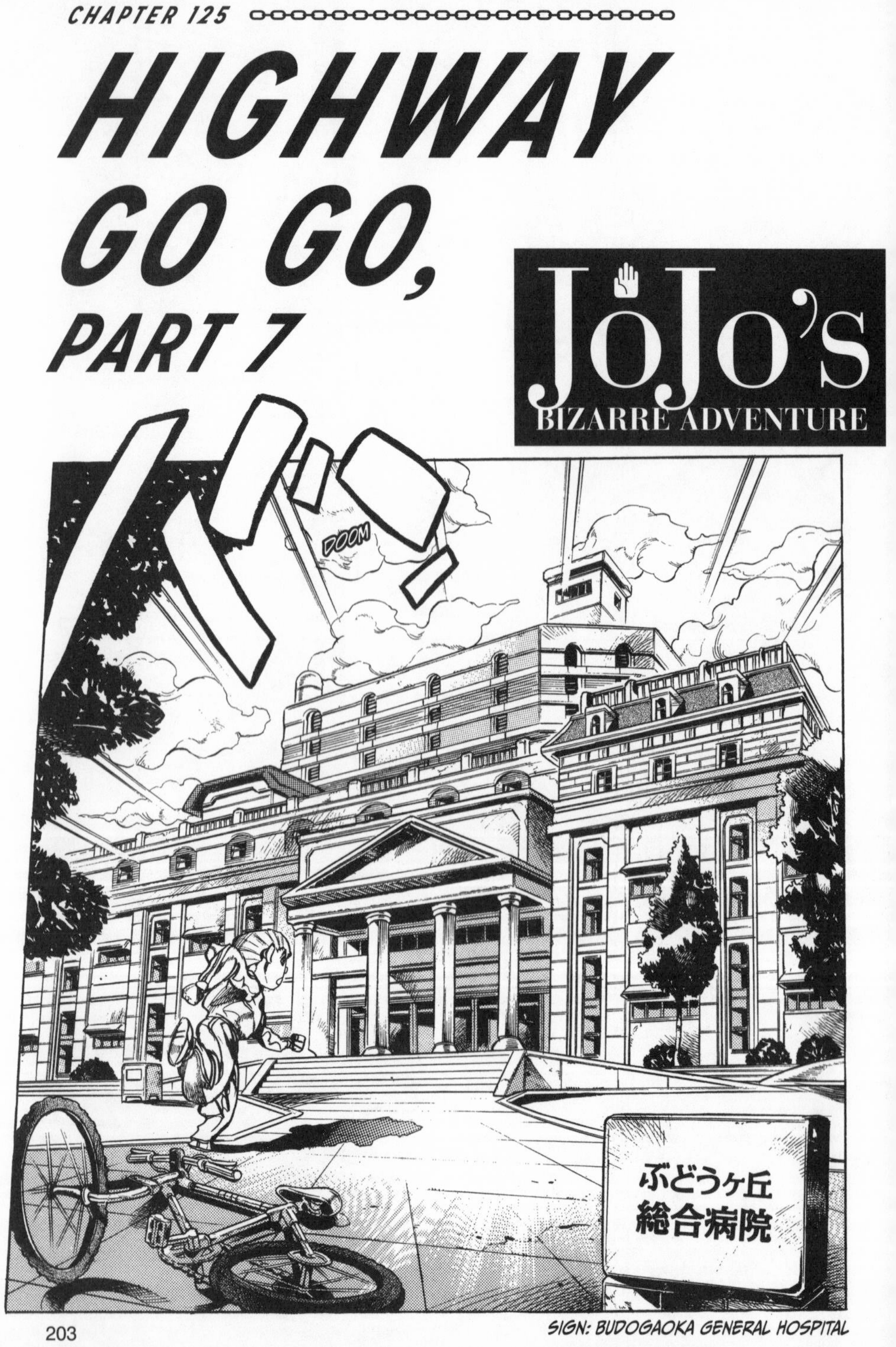
DOOM
ぶどうヶ丘
総合病院

SIGN: BUDOGAOKA GENERAL HOSPITAL

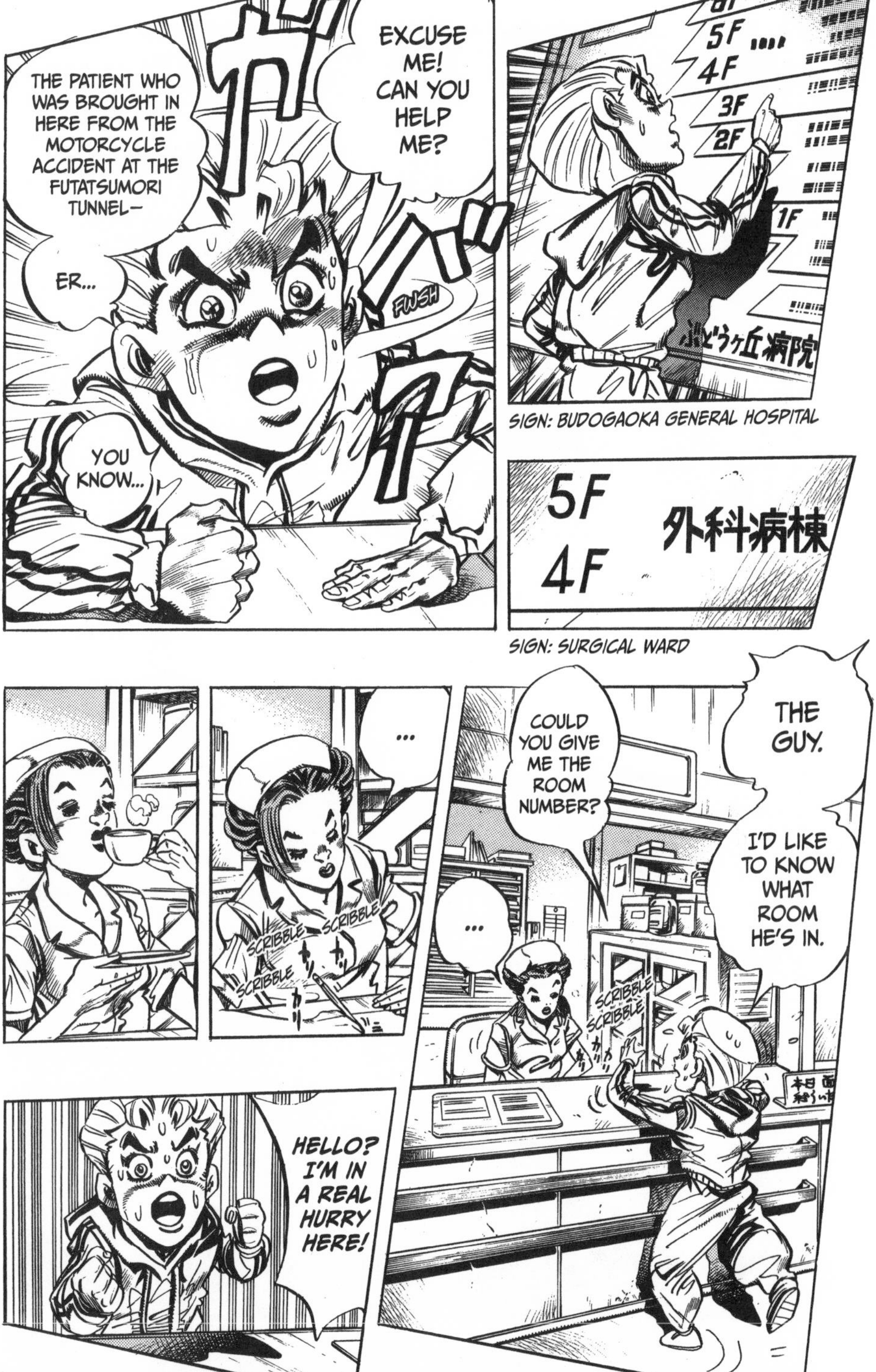
5F
4F
3F
2F
1F
ぶどうヶ丘病院
SIGN: BUDOGAOKA GENERAL HOSPITAL
5F
4F
外科病棟
SIGN: SURGICAL WARD
EXCUSE ME! CAN YOU HELP ME?
THE PATIENT WHO WAS BROUGHT IN HERE FROM THE MOTORCYCLE ACCIDENT AT THE FUTATSUMORI TUNNEL—
ER...
FWSH
YOU KNOW...
THE GUY.
I'D LIKE TO KNOW WHAT ROOM HE'S IN.
COULD YOU GIVE ME THE ROOM NUMBER?
...
SCRIBBLE SCRIBBLE
...
SCRIBBLE SCRIBBLE
SCRIBBLE
HELLO? I'M IN A REAL HURRY HERE!

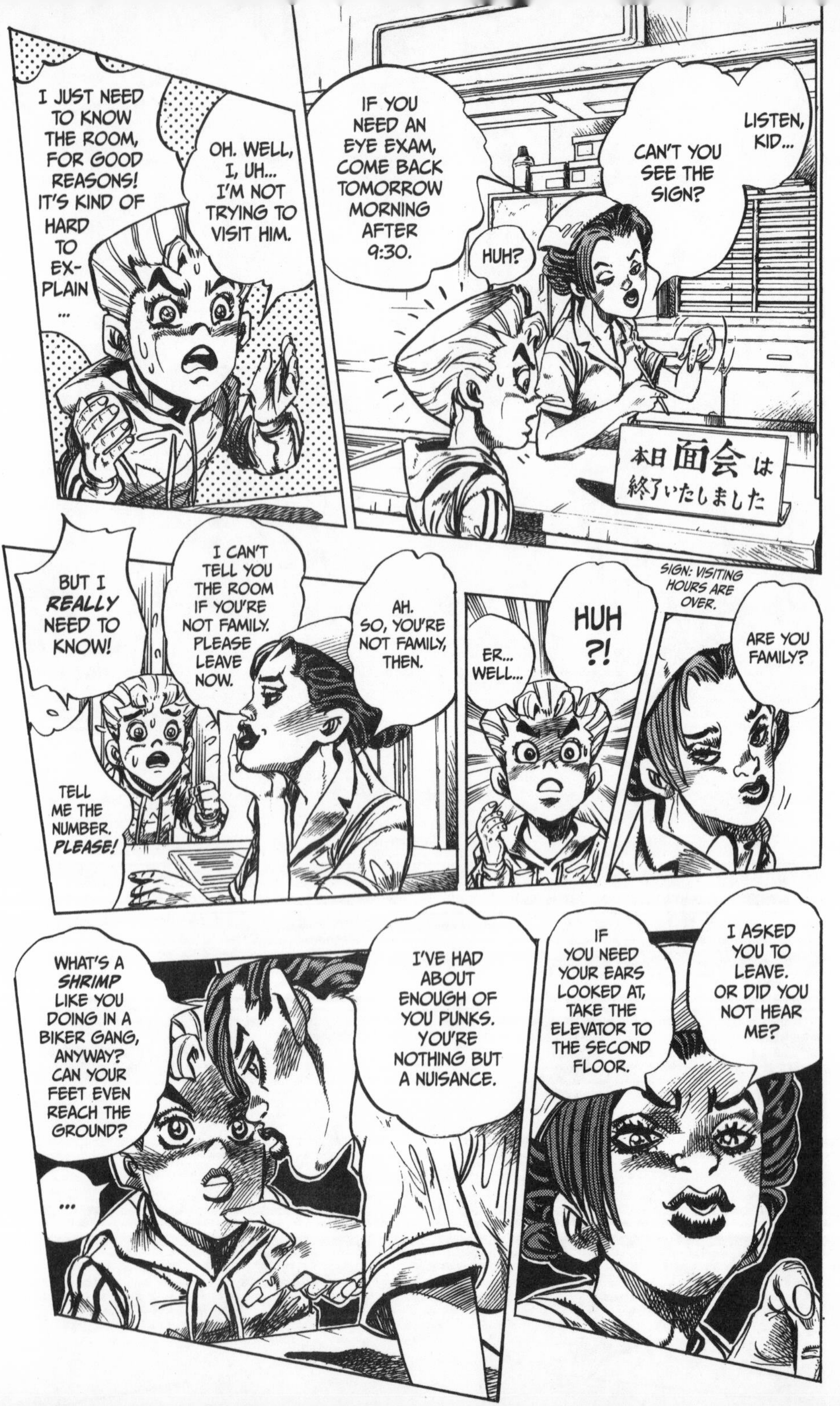
LISTEN, KID...
CAN'T YOU SEE THE SIGN?
IF YOU NEED AN EYE EXAM, COME BACK TOMORROW MORNING AFTER 9:30.
HUH?
本日面会は終了いたしました
SIGN: VISITING HOURS ARE OVER.
OH. WELL, I, UH... I'M NOT TRYING TO VISIT HIM.
I JUST NEED TO KNOW THE ROOM, FOR GOOD REASONS! IT'S KIND OF HARD TO EX-PLAIN...
ARE YOU FAMILY?
HUH ?!
ER... WELL...
AH. SO, YOU'RE NOT FAMILY, THEN.
I CAN'T TELL YOU THE ROOM IF YOU'RE NOT FAMILY. PLEASE LEAVE NOW.
BUT I *REALLY* NEED TO KNOW!
TELL ME THE NUMBER. *PLEASE!*
I ASKED YOU TO LEAVE. OR DID YOU NOT HEAR ME?
IF YOU NEED YOUR EARS LOOKED AT, TAKE THE ELEVATOR TO THE SECOND FLOOR.
I'VE HAD ABOUT ENOUGH OF YOU PUNKS. YOU'RE NOTHING BUT A NUISANCE.
WHAT'S A *SHRIMP* LIKE YOU DOING IN A BIKER GANG, ANYWAY? CAN YOUR FEET EVEN REACH THE GROUND?
...

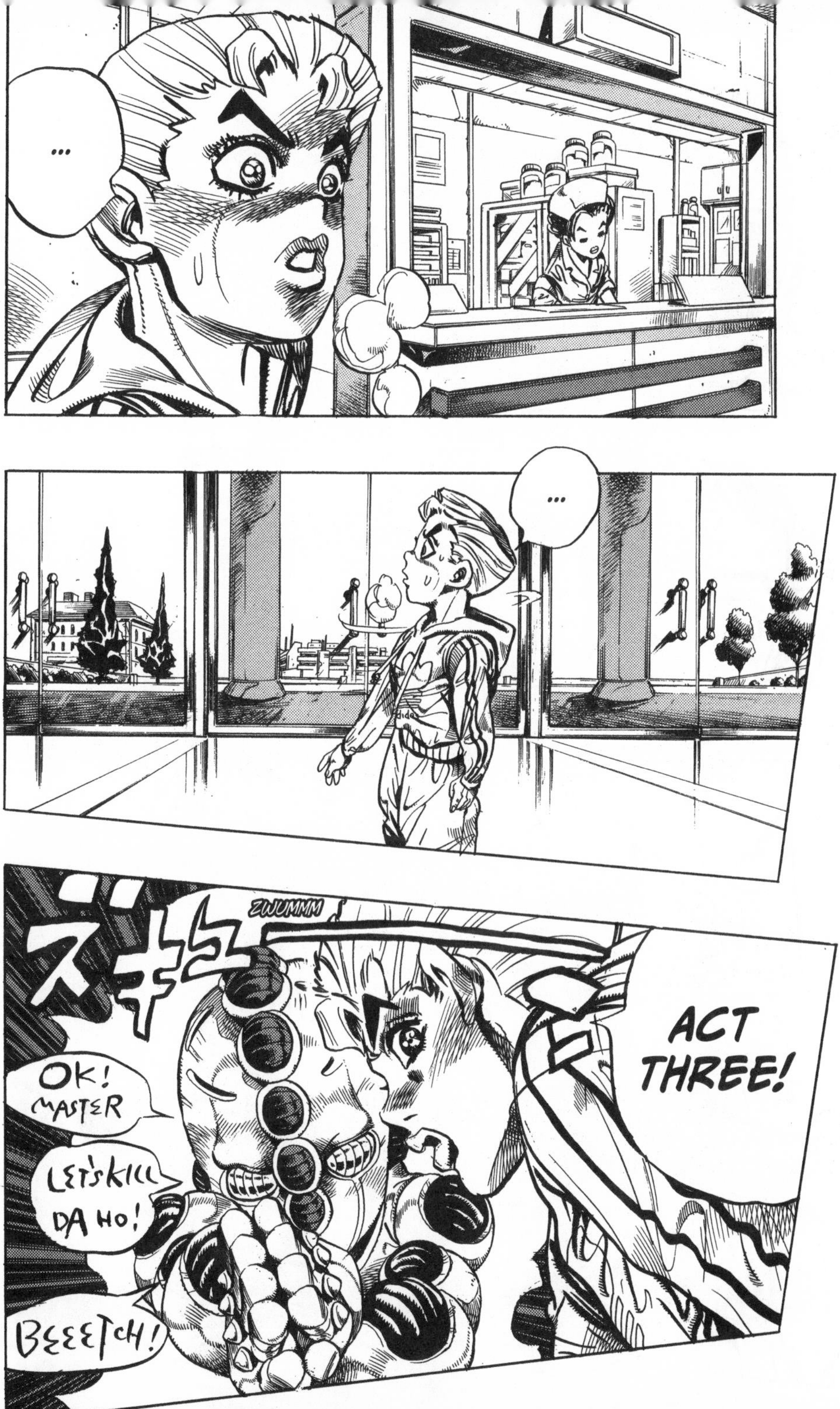
...
...
ZWUMMM
ACT THREE!
ズキュ
OK! MASTER
LET'S KILL DA HO!
BEEETCH!

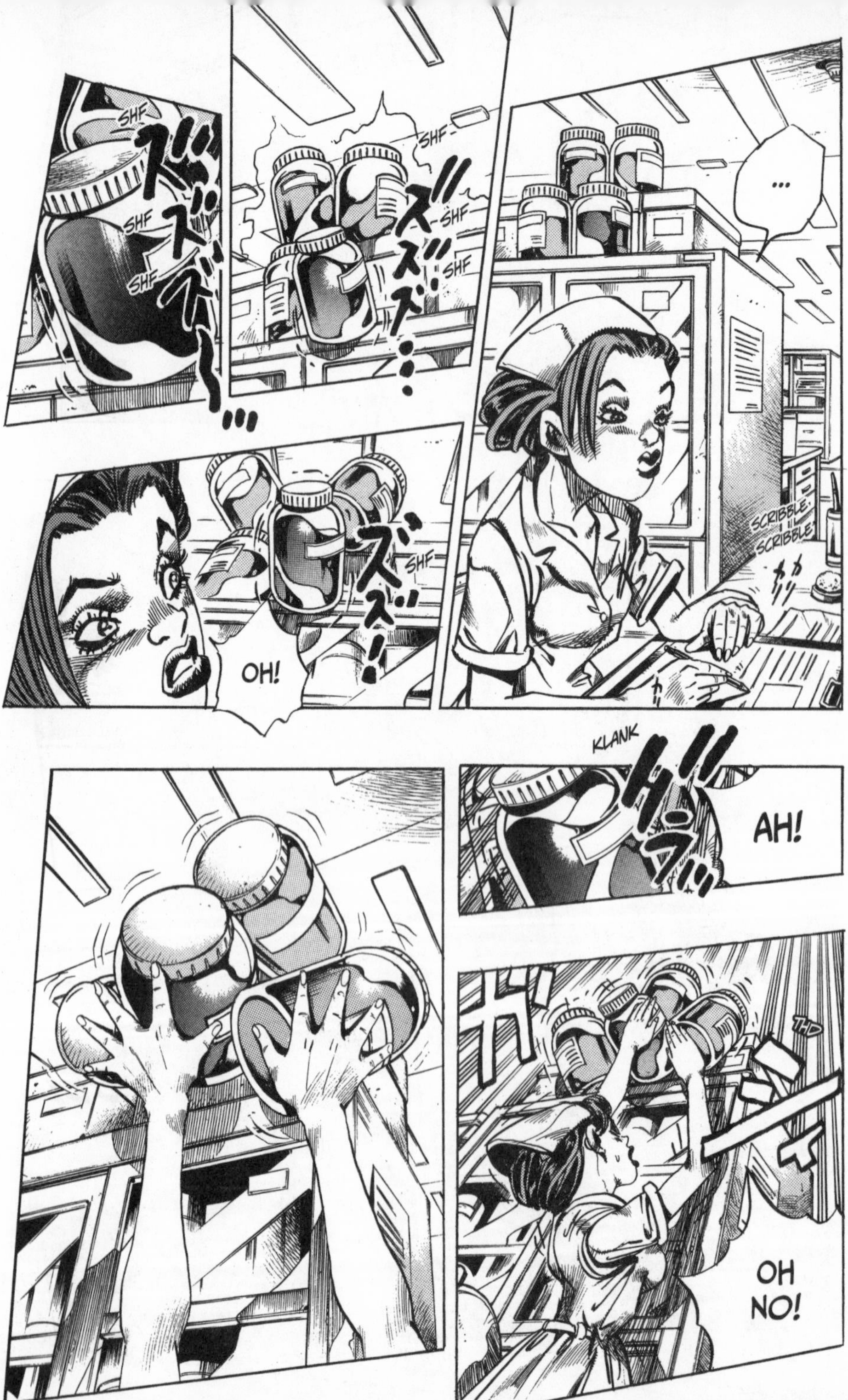
...
SCRIBBLE
SCRIBBLE
SHF
SHF
SHF
SHF
SHF
SHF
SHF
OH!
KLANK
AH!
THD
OH NO!

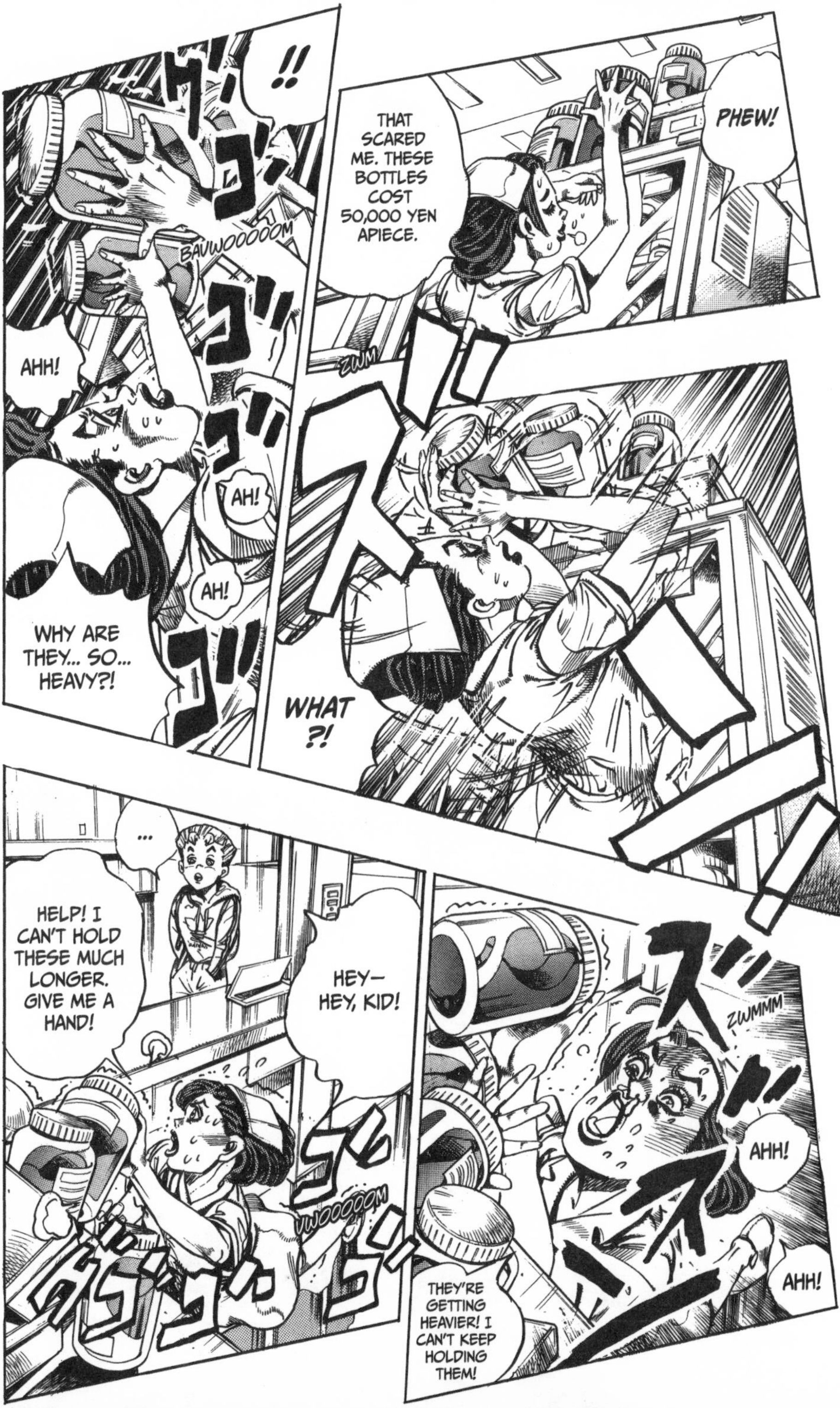
PHEW!
THAT SCARED ME. THESE BOTTLES COST 50,000 YEN APIECE.
ZWM
WHAT ?!
!!
BAWOOOOOOM
AHH!
AH!
AH!
WHY ARE THEY... SO... HEAVY?!
ZWMMM
AHH!
AHH!
THEY'RE GETTING HEAVIER! I CAN'T KEEP HOLDING THEM!
...
HEY— HEY, KID!
HELP! I CAN'T HOLD THESE MUCH LONGER. GIVE ME A HAND!
UWOOOOOM

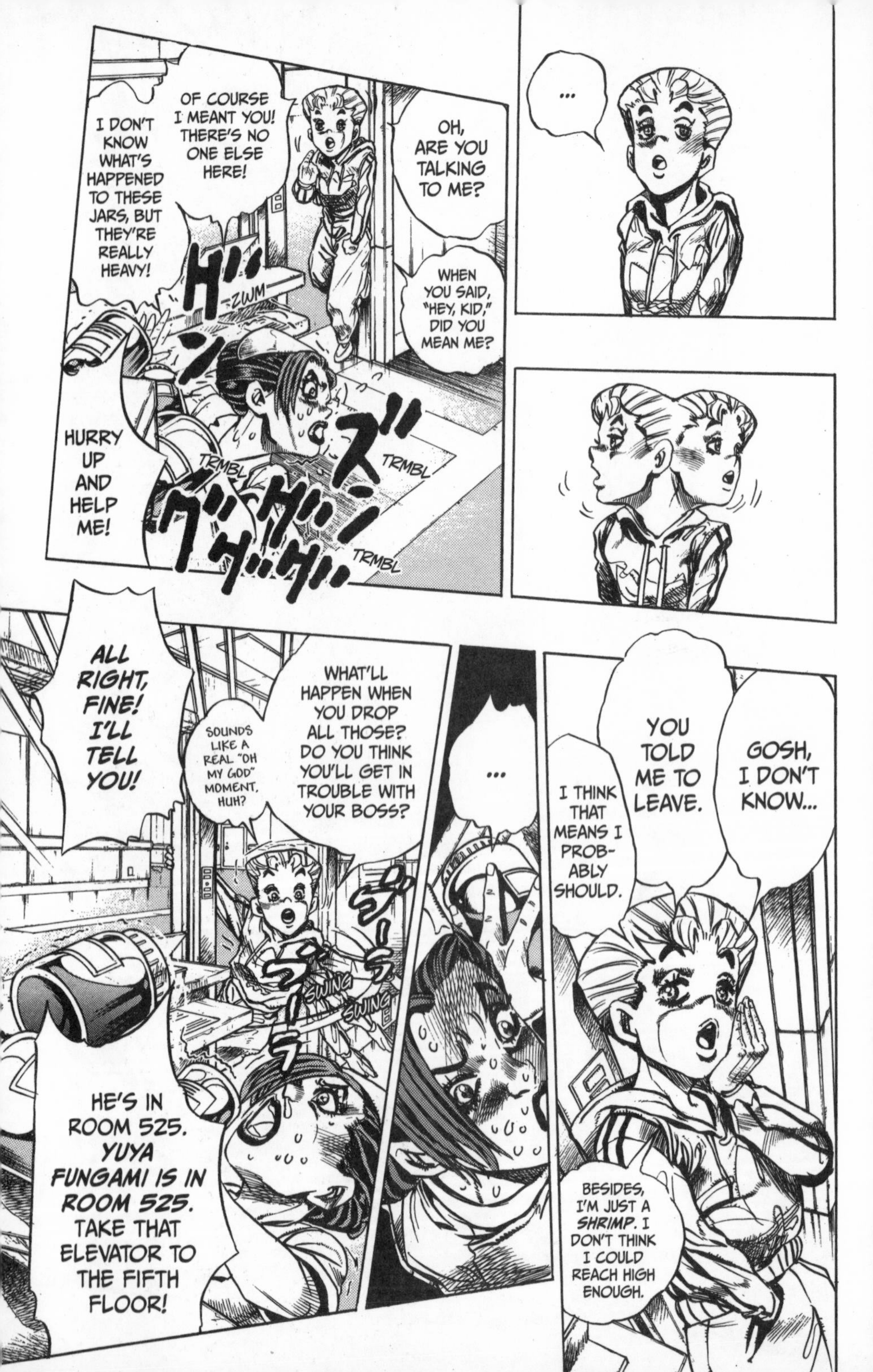
...
OH, ARE YOU TALKING TO ME?
WHEN YOU SAID, "HEY, KID," DID YOU MEAN ME?
OF COURSE I MEANT YOU! THERE'S NO ONE ELSE HERE!
I DON'T KNOW WHAT'S HAPPENED TO THESE JARS, BUT THEY'RE REALLY HEAVY!
ZWM
TRMBL
HURRY UP AND HELP ME!
TRMBL
TRMBL
GOSH, I DON'T KNOW...
YOU TOLD ME TO LEAVE.
I THINK THAT MEANS I PROB-ABLY SHOULD.
BESIDES, I'M JUST A *SHRIMP*. I DON'T THINK I COULD REACH HIGH ENOUGH.
...
WHAT'LL HAPPEN WHEN YOU DROP ALL THOSE? DO YOU THINK YOU'LL GET IN TROUBLE WITH YOUR BOSS?
SOUNDS LIKE A REAL "OH MY GOD" MOMENT, HUH?
ALL RIGHT, FINE! I'LL TELL YOU!
SWING
SWING
HE'S IN ROOM 525. *YUYA FUNGAMI IS IN ROOM 525.* TAKE THAT ELEVATOR TO THE FIFTH FLOOR!

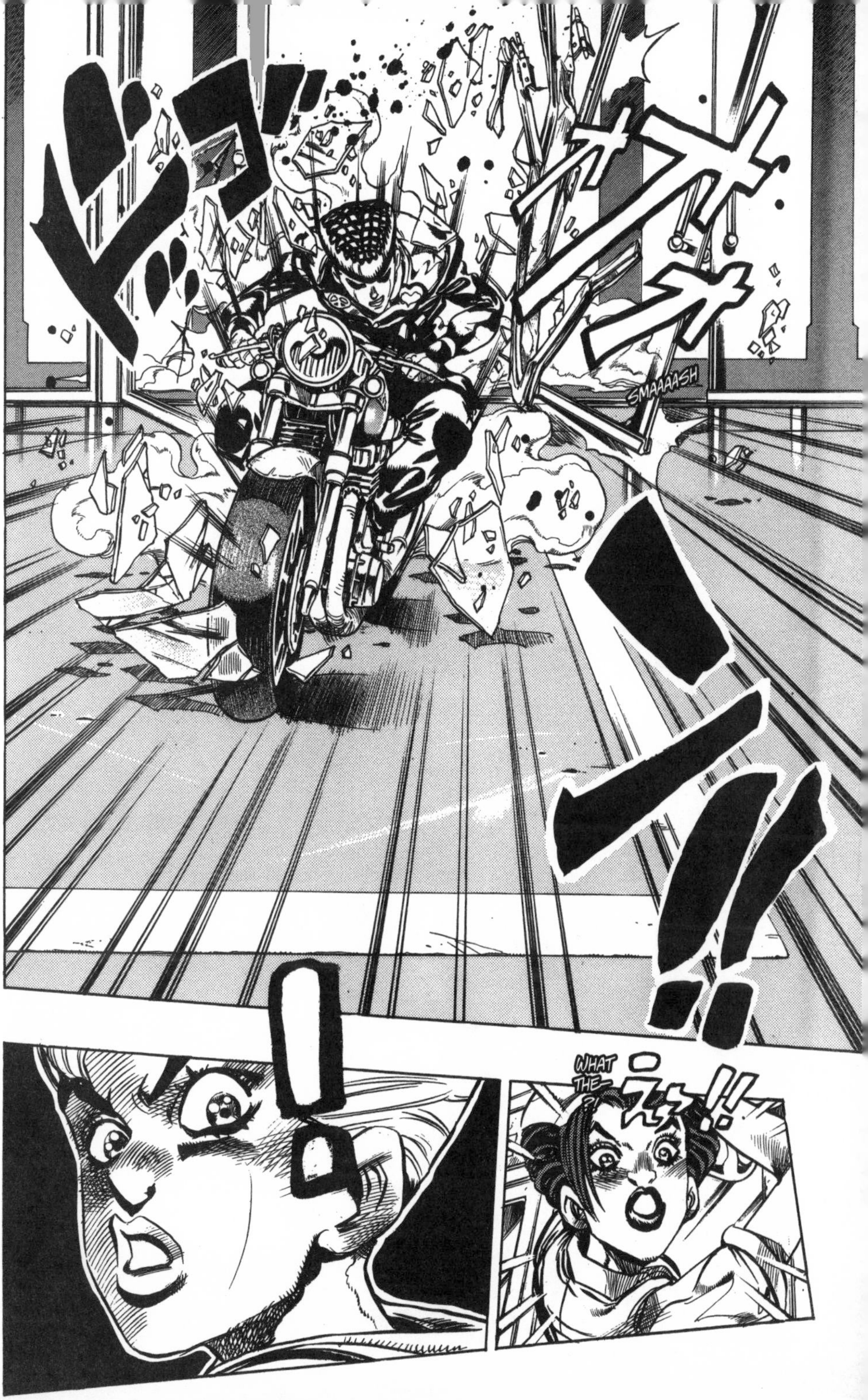
SMAAAASH
WHAT THE—?

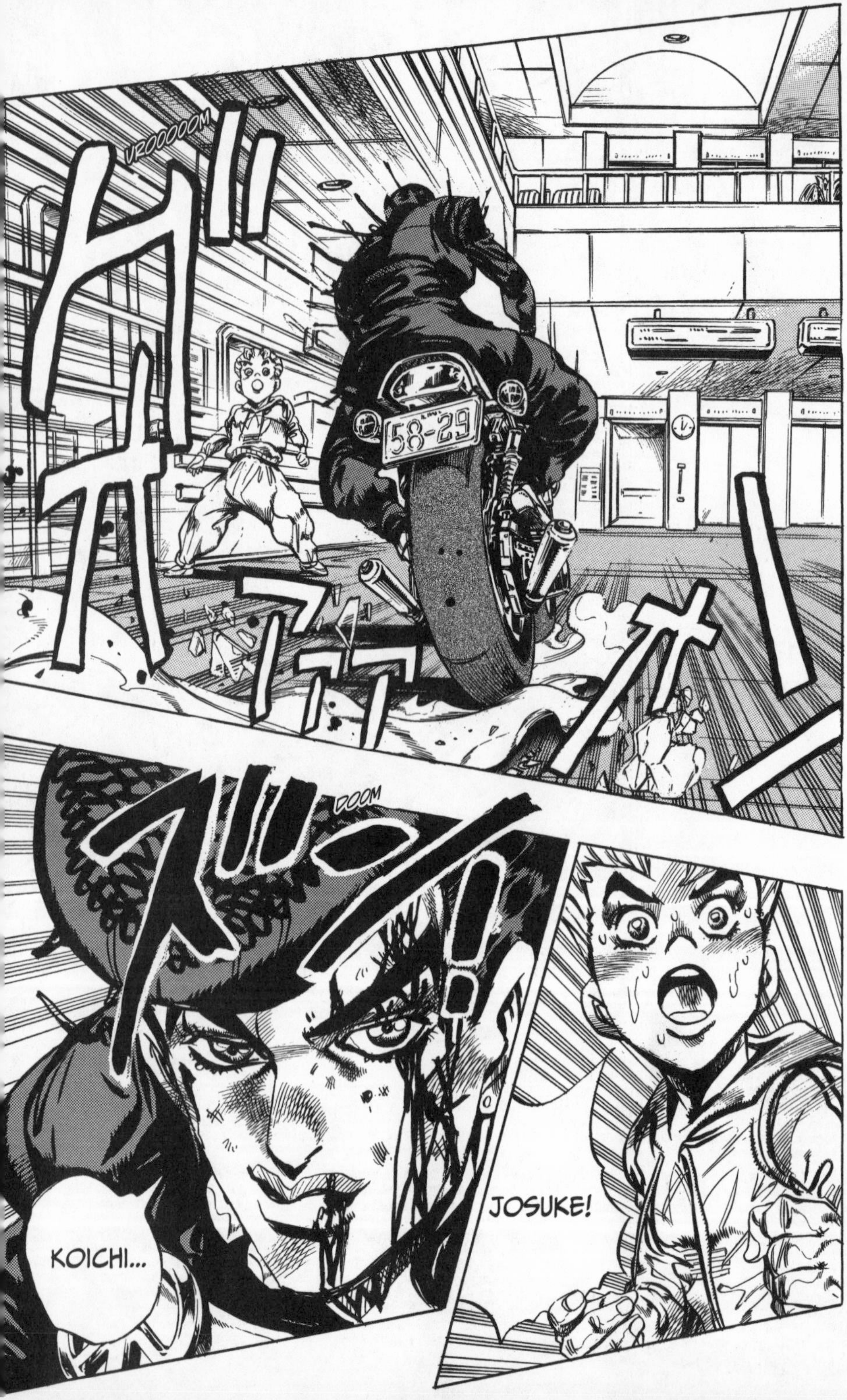
VROOOOOM
58-29
JOSUKE!
DOOM
KOICHI...

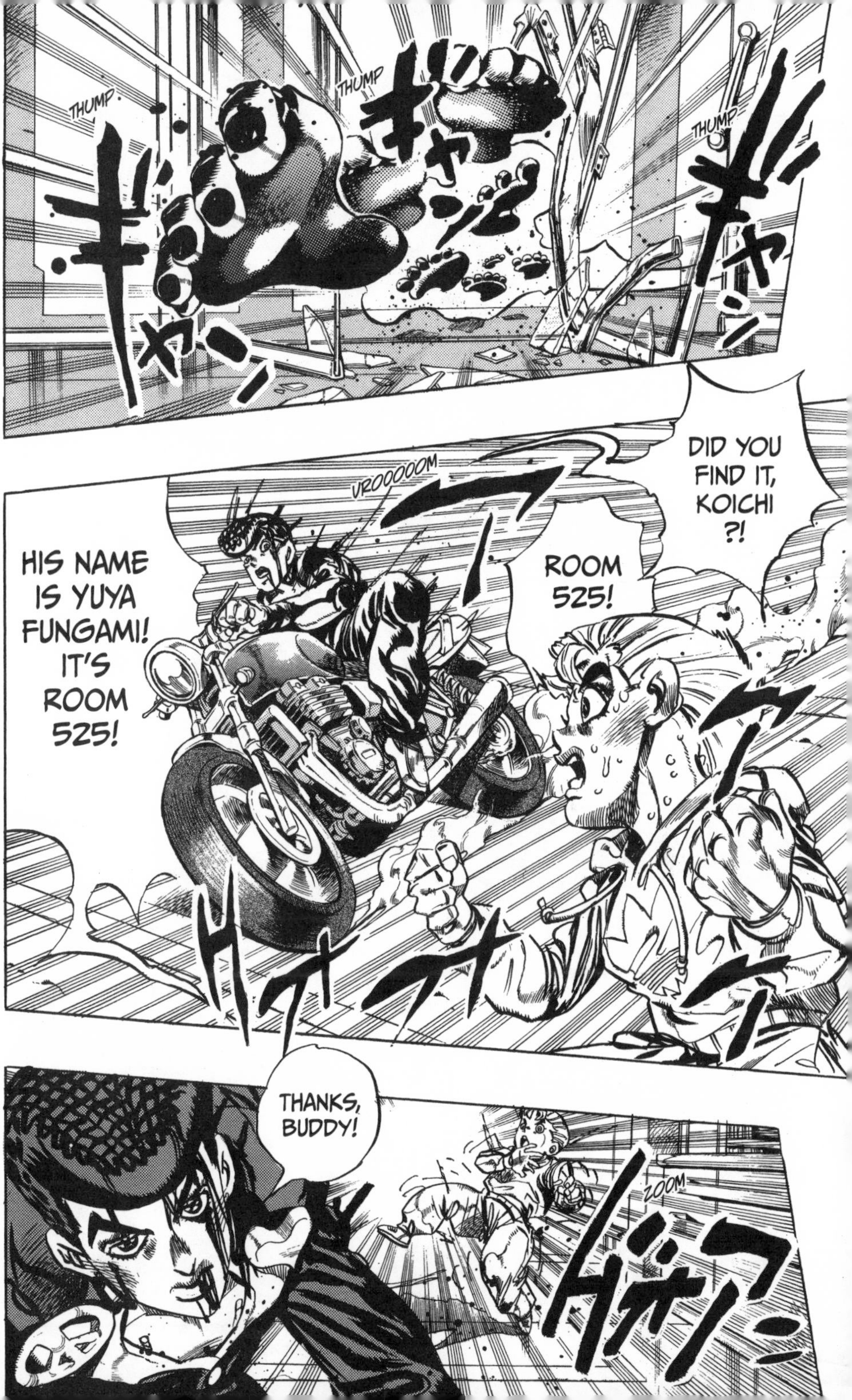
THUMP
THUMP
THUMP
DID YOU FIND IT, KOICHI ?!
ROOM 525!
VROOOOOM
HIS NAME IS YUYA FUNGAMI! IT'S ROOM 525!
THANKS, BUDDY!
ZOOM

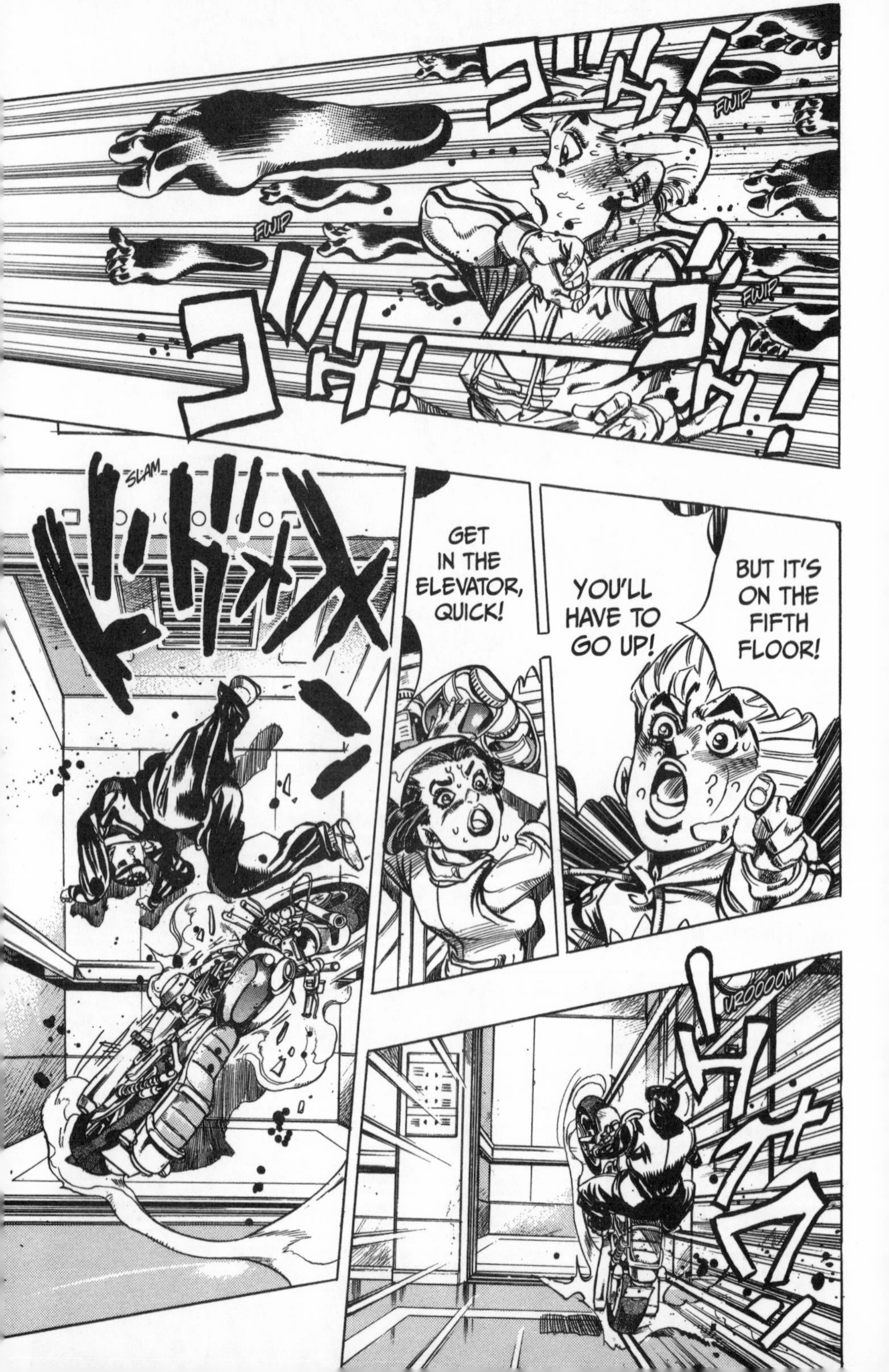
FWIP
FWIP
FWIP
FWIP
BUT IT'S ON THE FIFTH FLOOR!
YOU'LL HAVE TO GO UP!
GET IN THE ELEVATOR, QUICK!
VROOOOM
SLAM

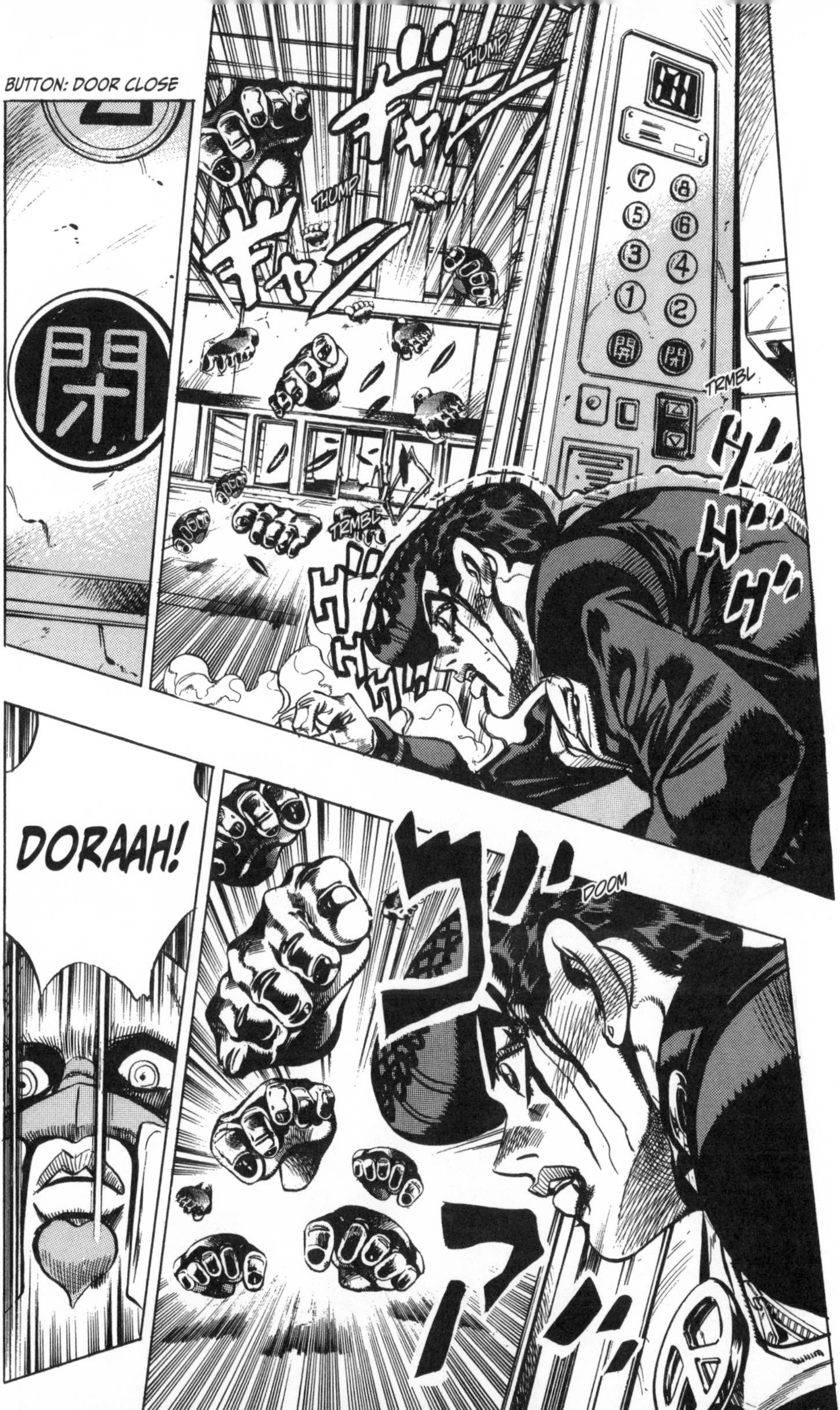
THUMP
THUMP
TRMBL
TRMBL
BUTTON: DOOR CLOSE
DOOM
DORAAH!

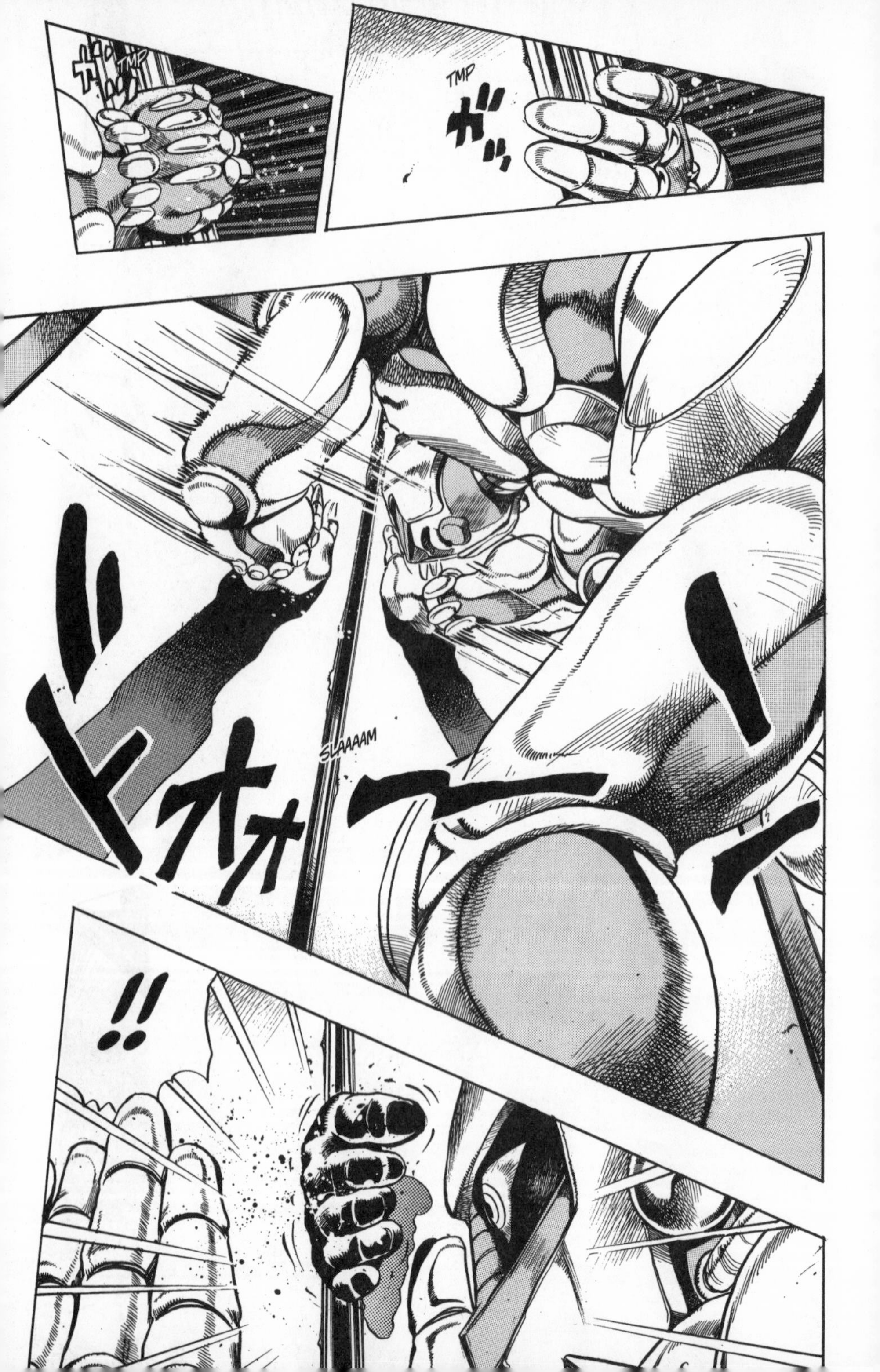
TMP
ガッ
TMP
ガッ
SLAAAAM
!!

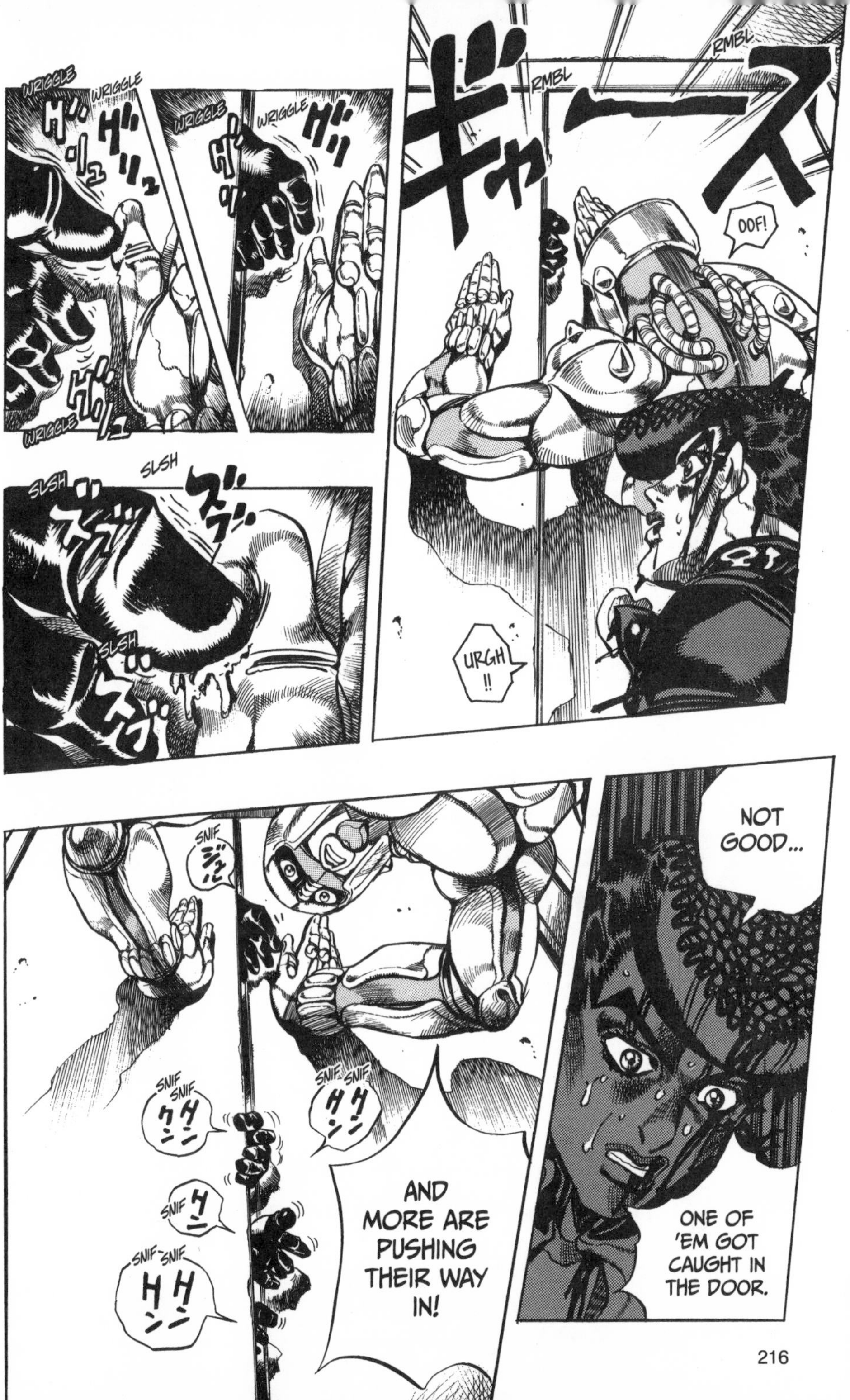

ギャース
RMBL
RMBL
OOF!
URGH!!
WRIGGLE
WRIGGLE
WRIGGLE
WRIGGLE
WRIGGLE
SLSH
SLSH
SLSH
NOT GOOD...
ONE OF 'EM GOT CAUGHT IN THE DOOR.
SNIF
SNIF SNIF
AND MORE ARE PUSHING THEIR WAY IN!
SNIF SNIF
SNIF
SNIF SNIF

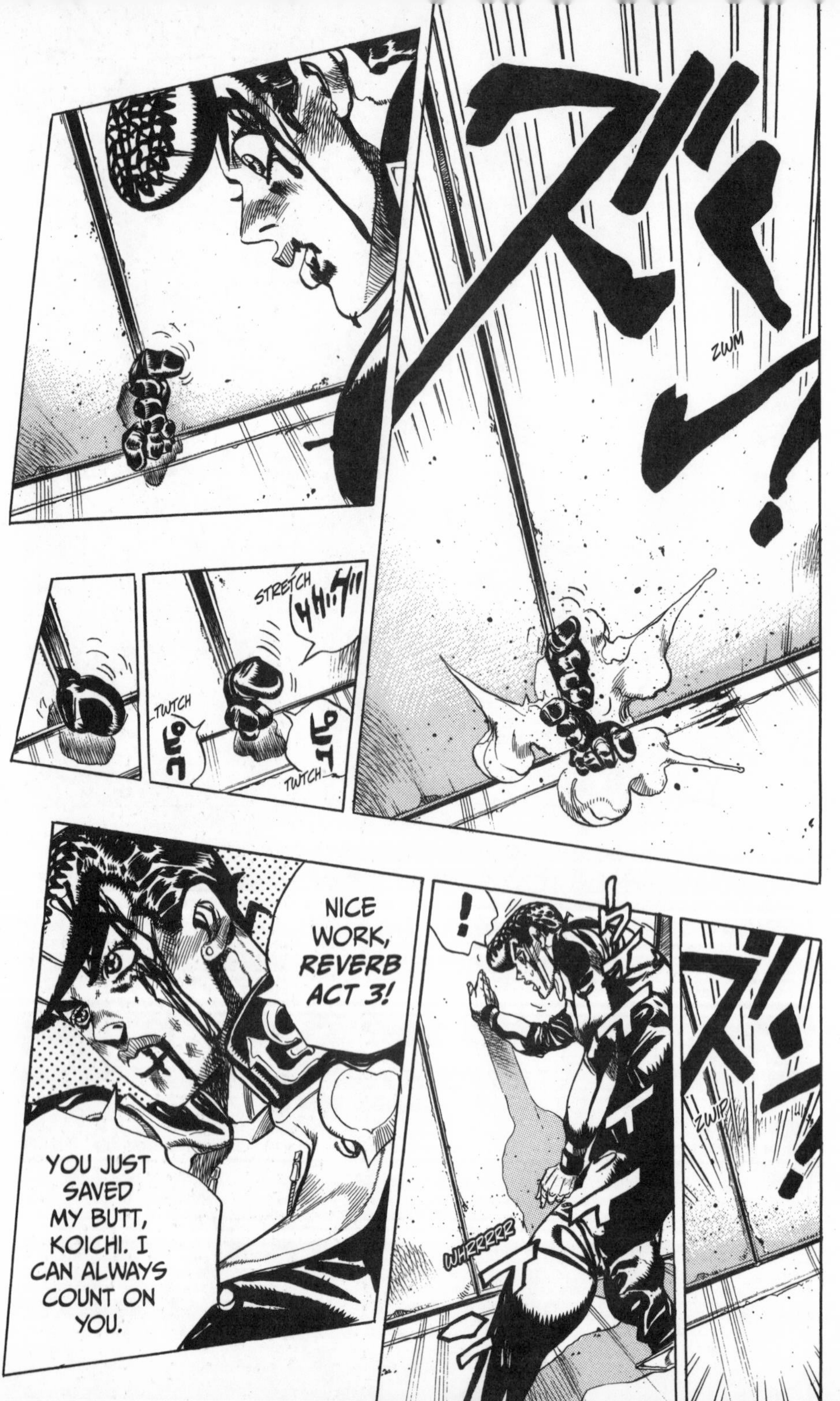
ZWM
STRETCH
TWTCH
TWTCH
ZWIP
!
WHRRRRR
NICE WORK, REVERB ACT 3!
YOU JUST SAVED MY BUTT, KOICHI. I CAN ALWAYS COUNT ON YOU.

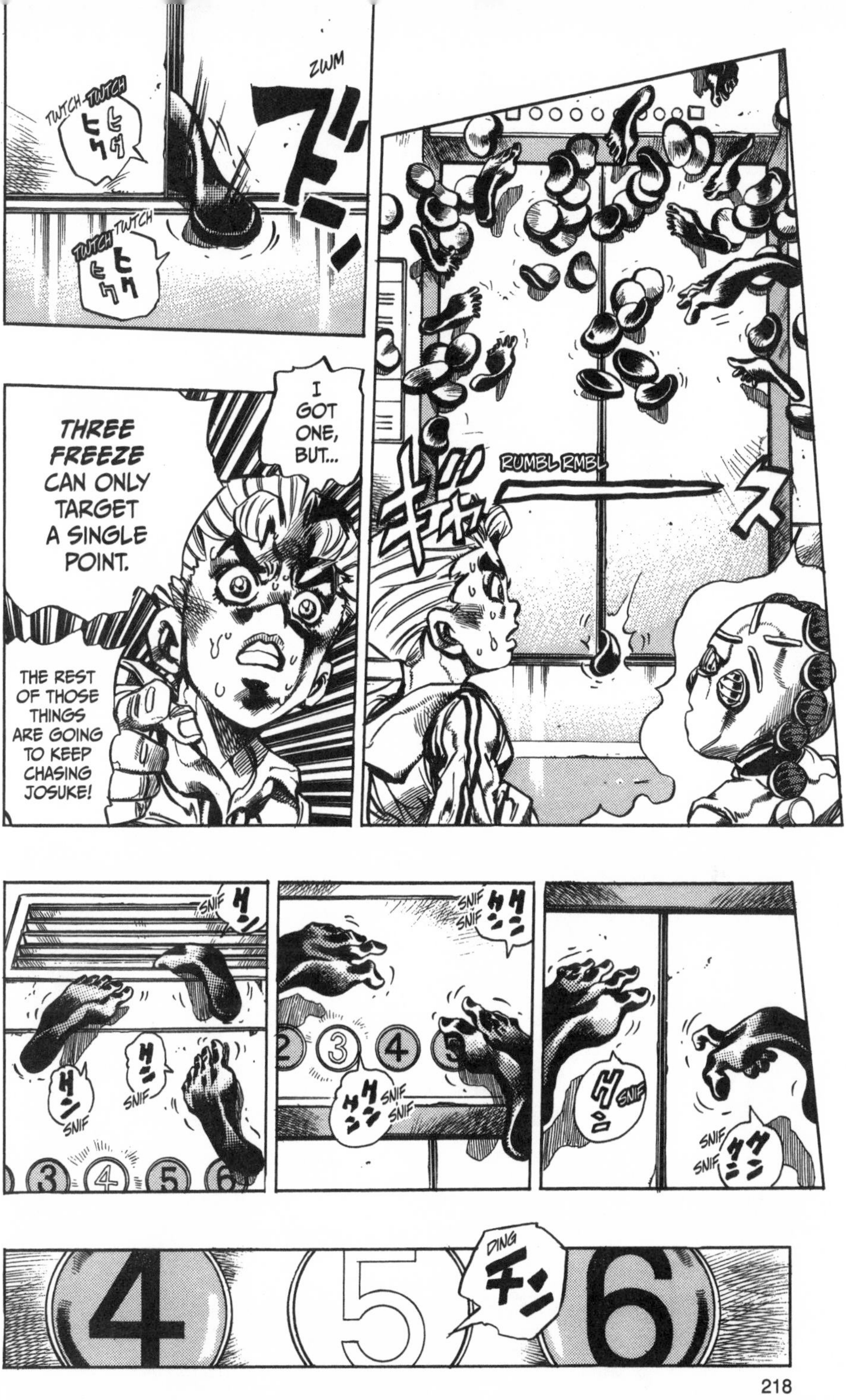
RUMBL RMBL
ZWUM
ズドン
TWITCH TWITCH
TWITCH TWITCH
I GOT ONE, BUT...
THREE FREEZE CAN ONLY TARGET A SINGLE POINT.
THE REST OF THOSE THINGS ARE GOING TO KEEP CHASING JOSUKE!
SNIF
SNIF SNIF
SNIF SNIF
SNIF SNIF
SNIF
SNIF
SNIF
DING
チン

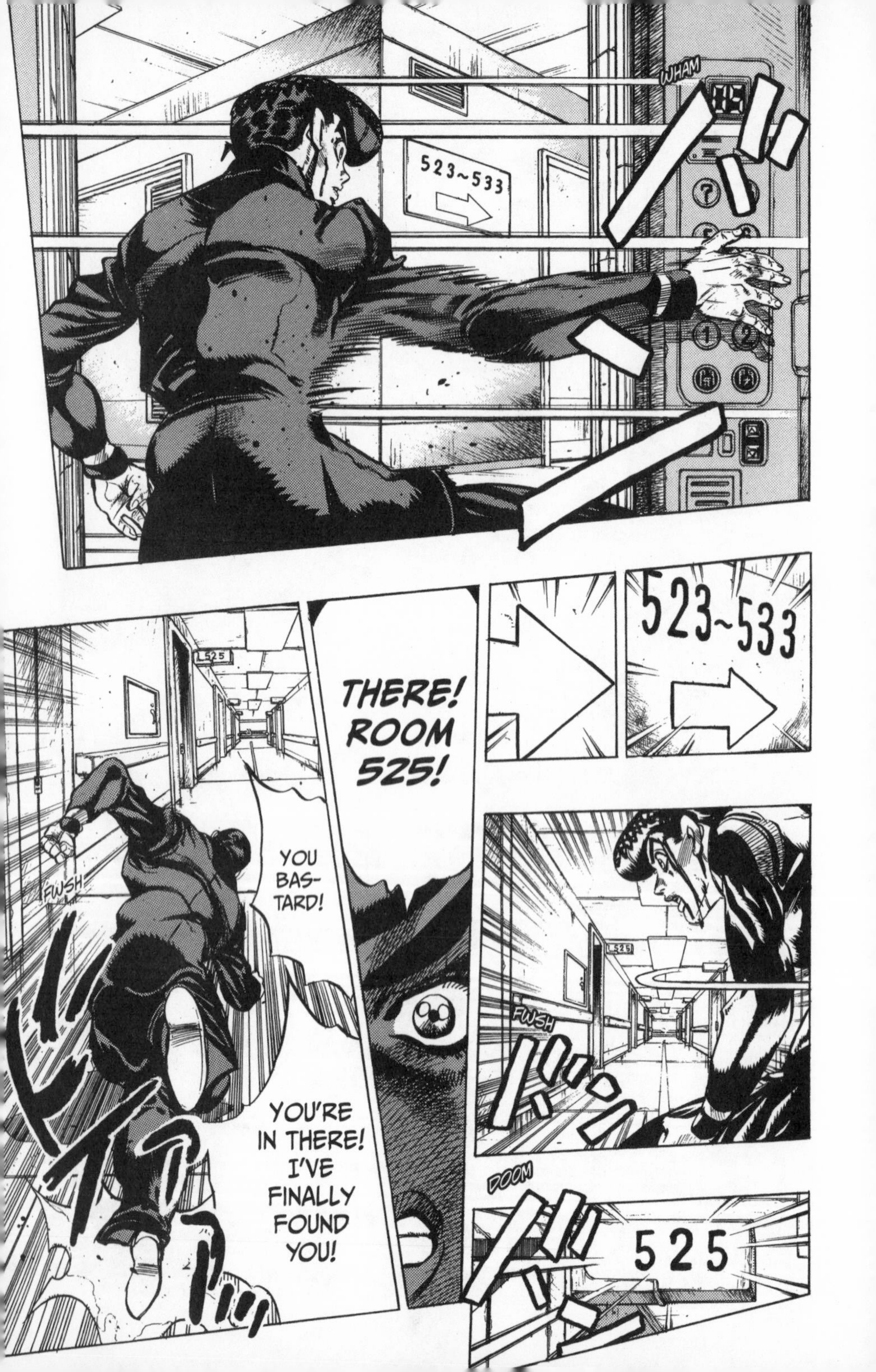
WHAM
523~533
523~533
FWSH
DOOM
525
THERE! ROOM 525!
YOU BAS-TARD!
YOU'RE IN THERE! I'VE FINALLY FOUND YOU!
FWSH

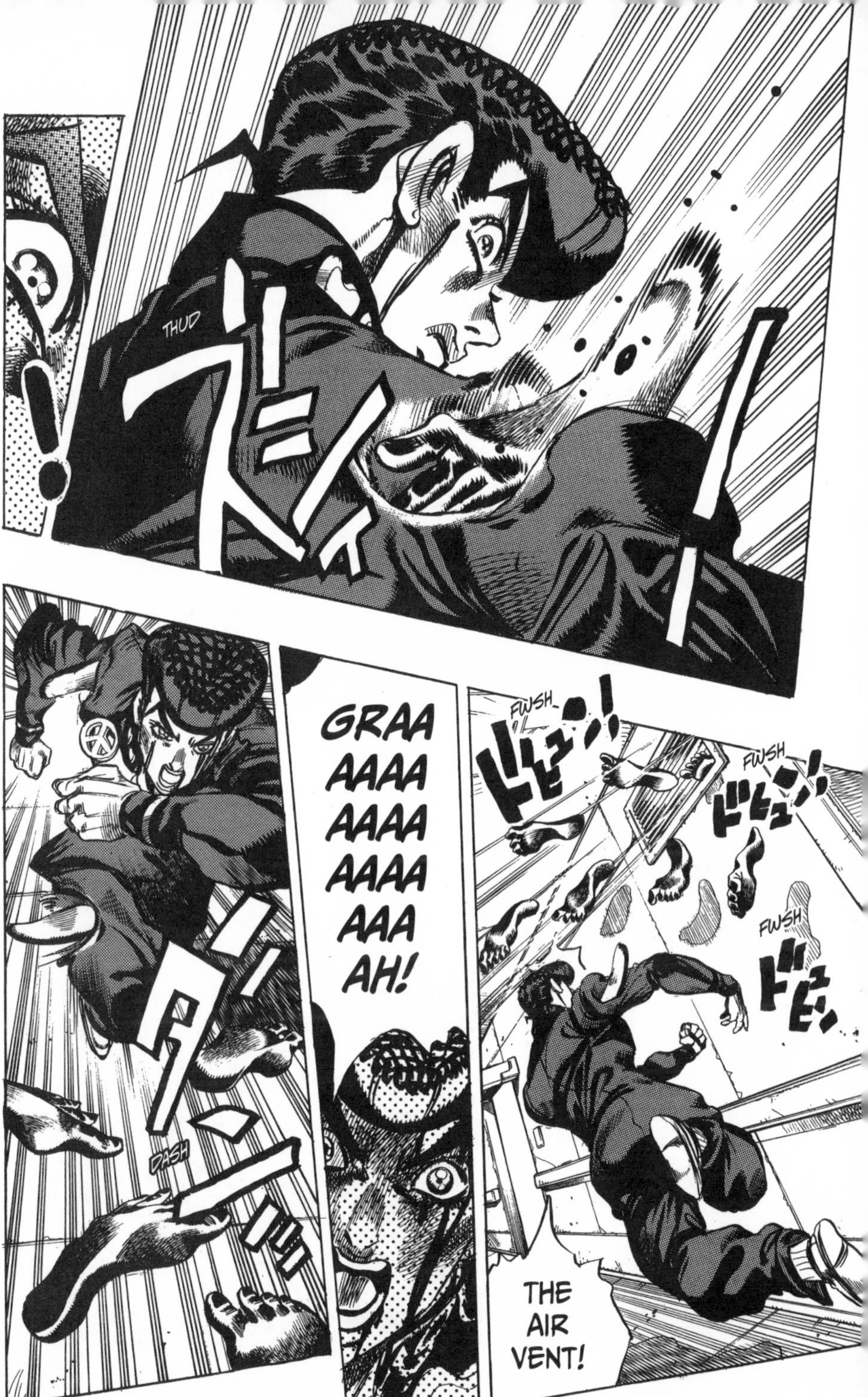
THUD
FWSH
FWSH
FWSH
THE AIR VENT!
GRAA AAAA AAAA AAAA AAA AH!
DASH

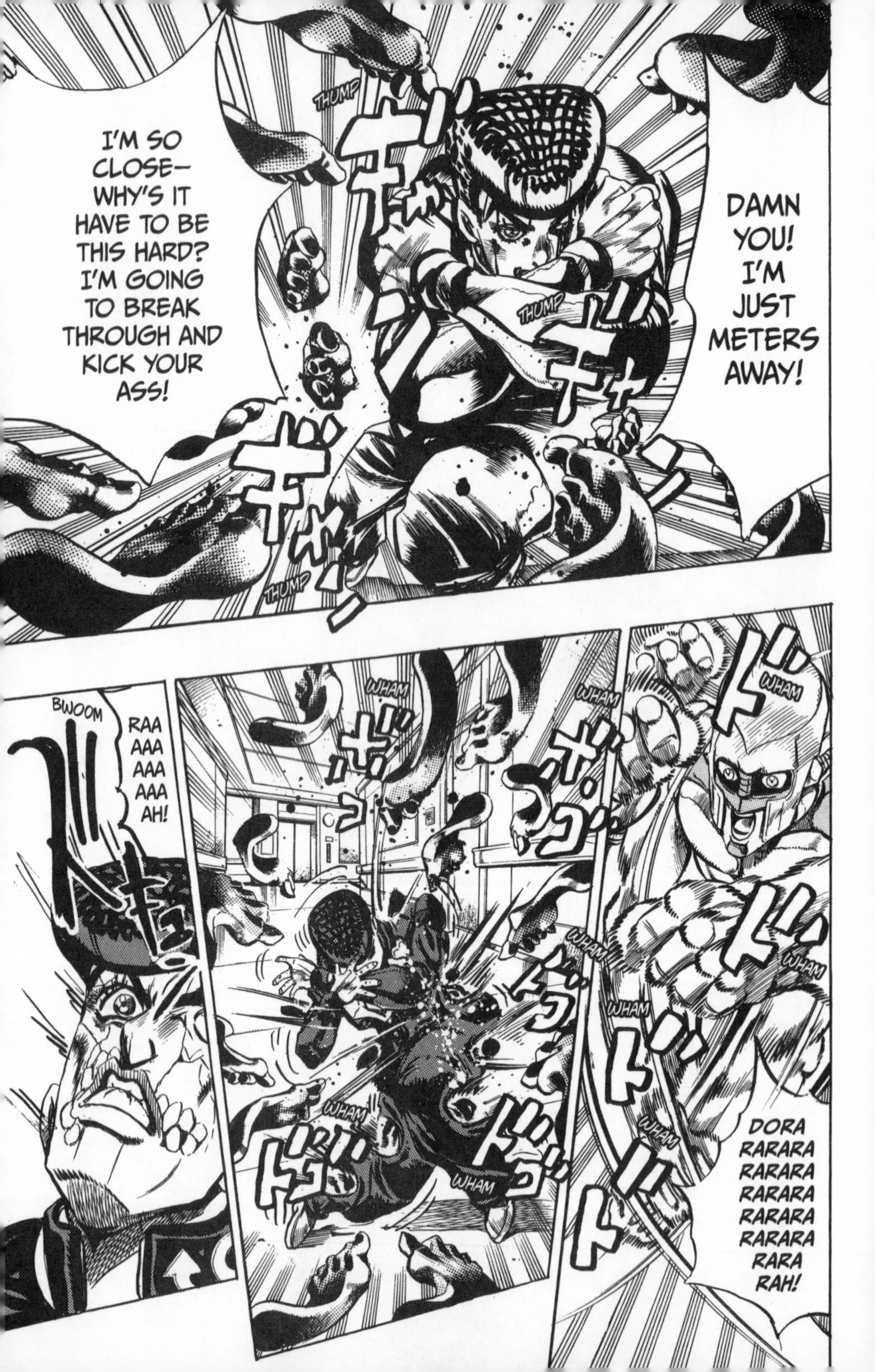
DAMN YOU! I'M JUST METERS AWAY!
THUMP
THUMP
I'M SO CLOSE—WHY'S IT HAVE TO BE THIS HARD? I'M GOING TO BREAK THROUGH AND KICK YOUR ASS!
THUMP
WHAM
WHAM
WHAM
WHAM
DORA RARARA RARARA RARARA RARARA RARARA RARA RAH!
WHAM
WHAM
WHAM
WHAM
BWOOM
RAA AAA AAA AAA AH!

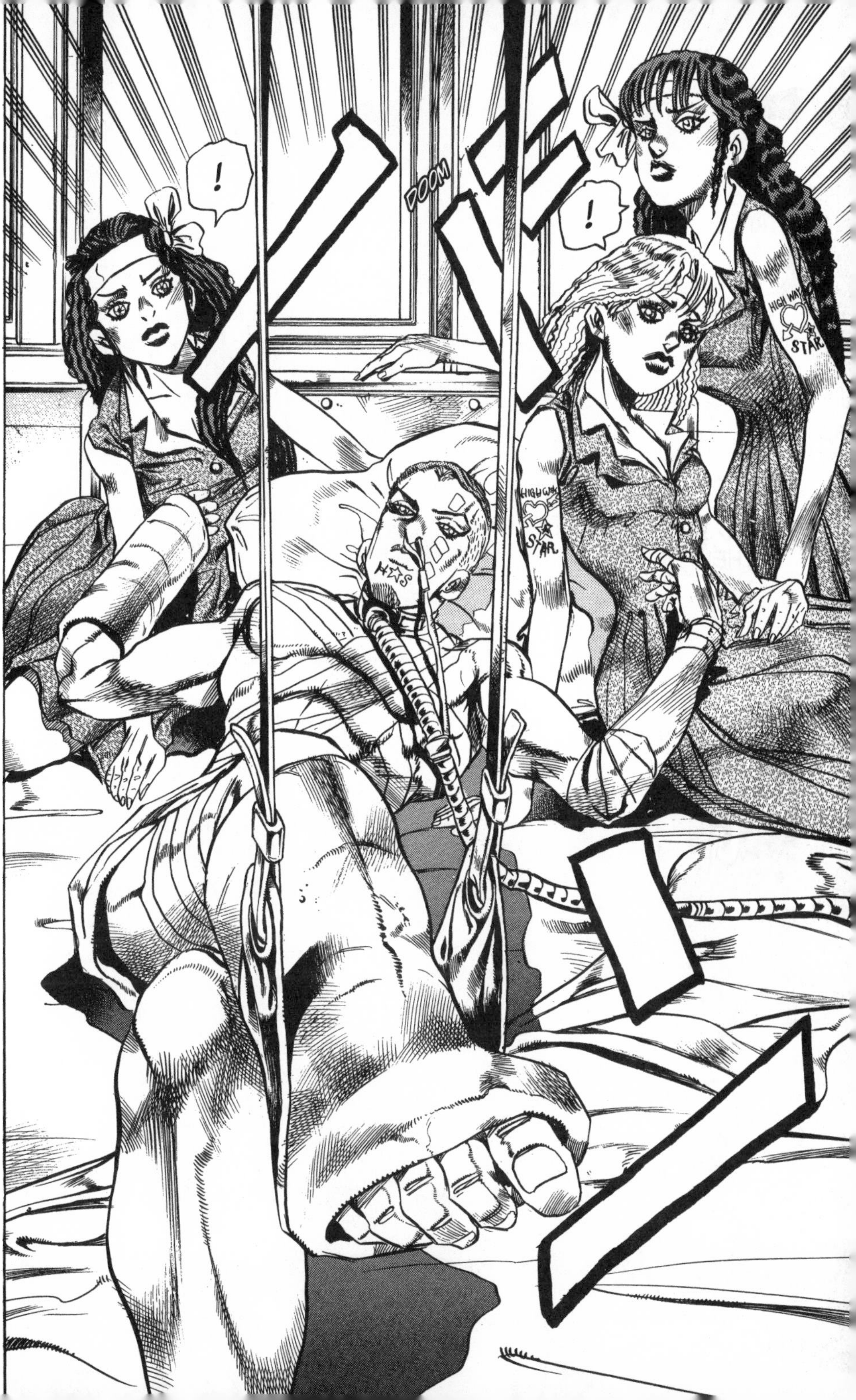

!
DOOM
!
HIGH WAY
STAR
HIGH WAY
STAR

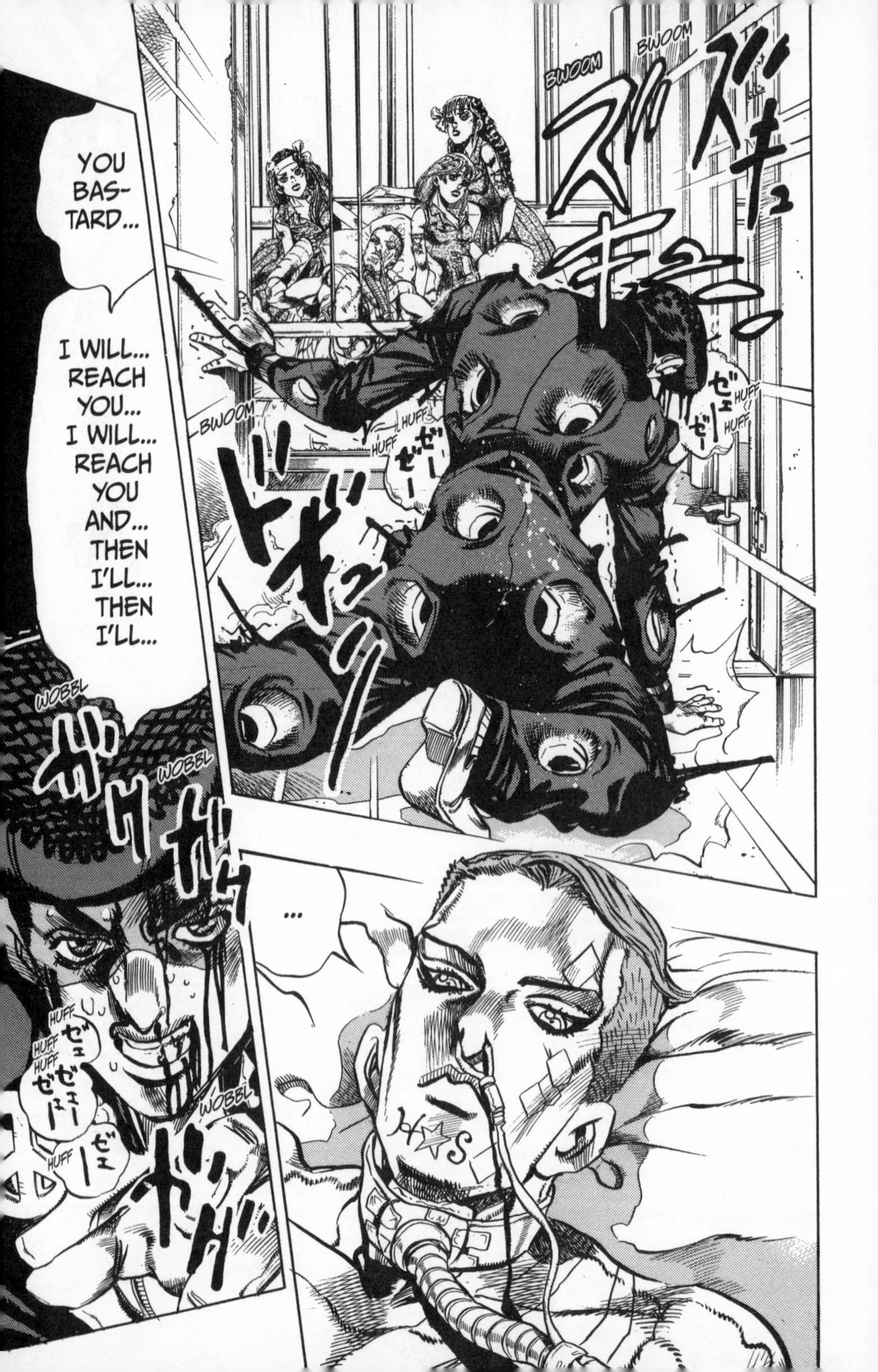
BWOOM
BWOOM
HUFF
HUFF
BWOOM
HUFF
...
YOU BASTARD...
I WILL... REACH YOU... I WILL... REACH YOU AND... THEN I'LL... THEN I'LL...
WOBBL
WOBBL
HUFF
HUFF
HUFF
WOBBL
HUFF

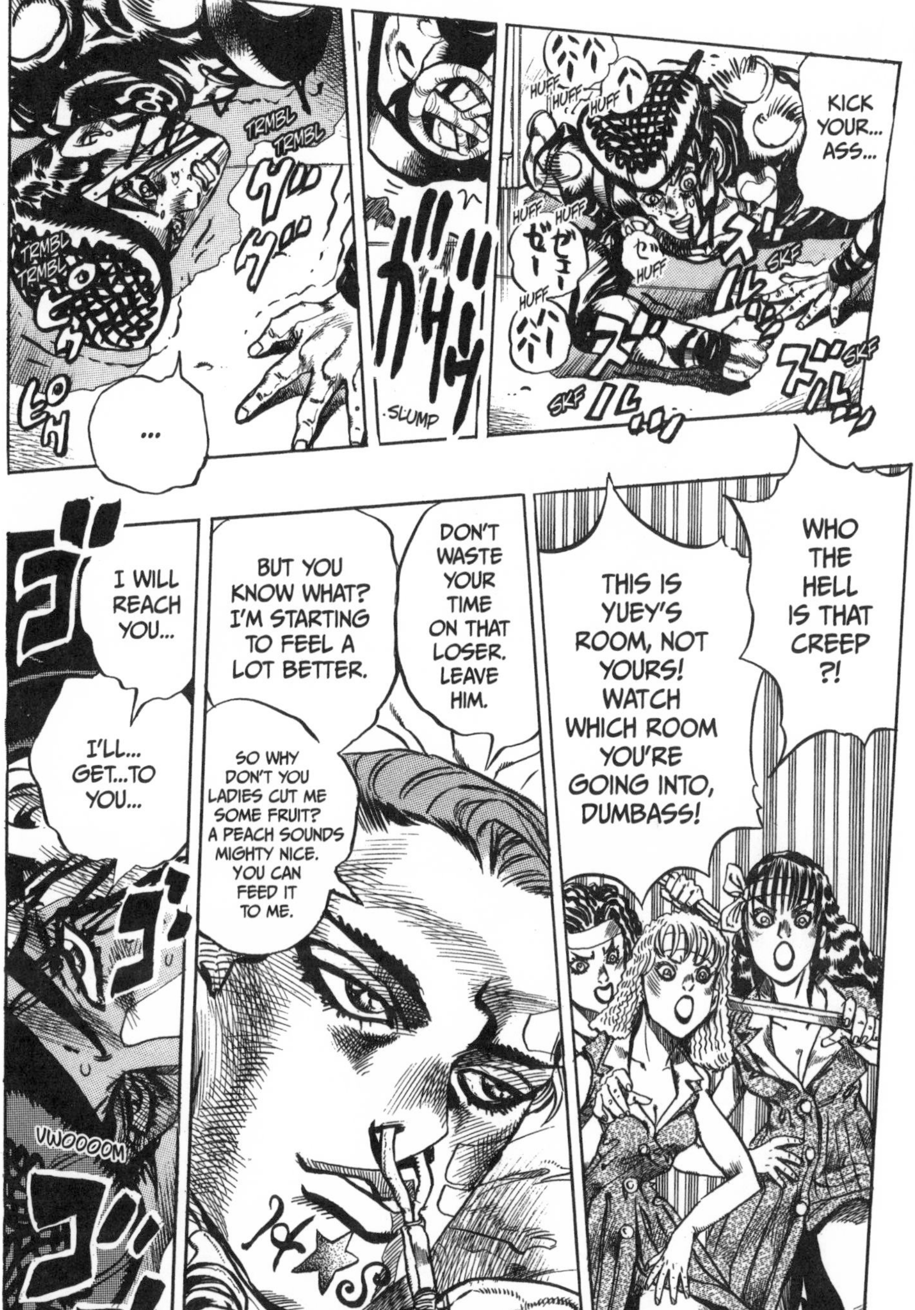
KICK YOUR... ASS...
HUFF HUFF HUFF
HUFF HUFF HUFF HUFF
SKF SKF SKF
SLUMP
TRMBL TRMBL
TRMBL TRMBL
...
WHO THE HELL IS THAT CREEP?!
THIS IS YUEY'S ROOM, NOT YOURS! WATCH WHICH ROOM YOU'RE GOING INTO, DUMBASS!
DON'T WASTE YOUR TIME ON THAT LOSER. LEAVE HIM.
BUT YOU KNOW WHAT? I'M STARTING TO FEEL A LOT BETTER.
SO WHY DON'T YOU LADIES CUT ME SOME FRUIT? A PEACH SOUNDS MIGHTY NICE. YOU CAN FEED IT TO ME.
I WILL REACH YOU...
I'LL... GET...TO YOU...
VWOOOOM

CHAPTER 126

HIGHWAY GO GO, PART 8

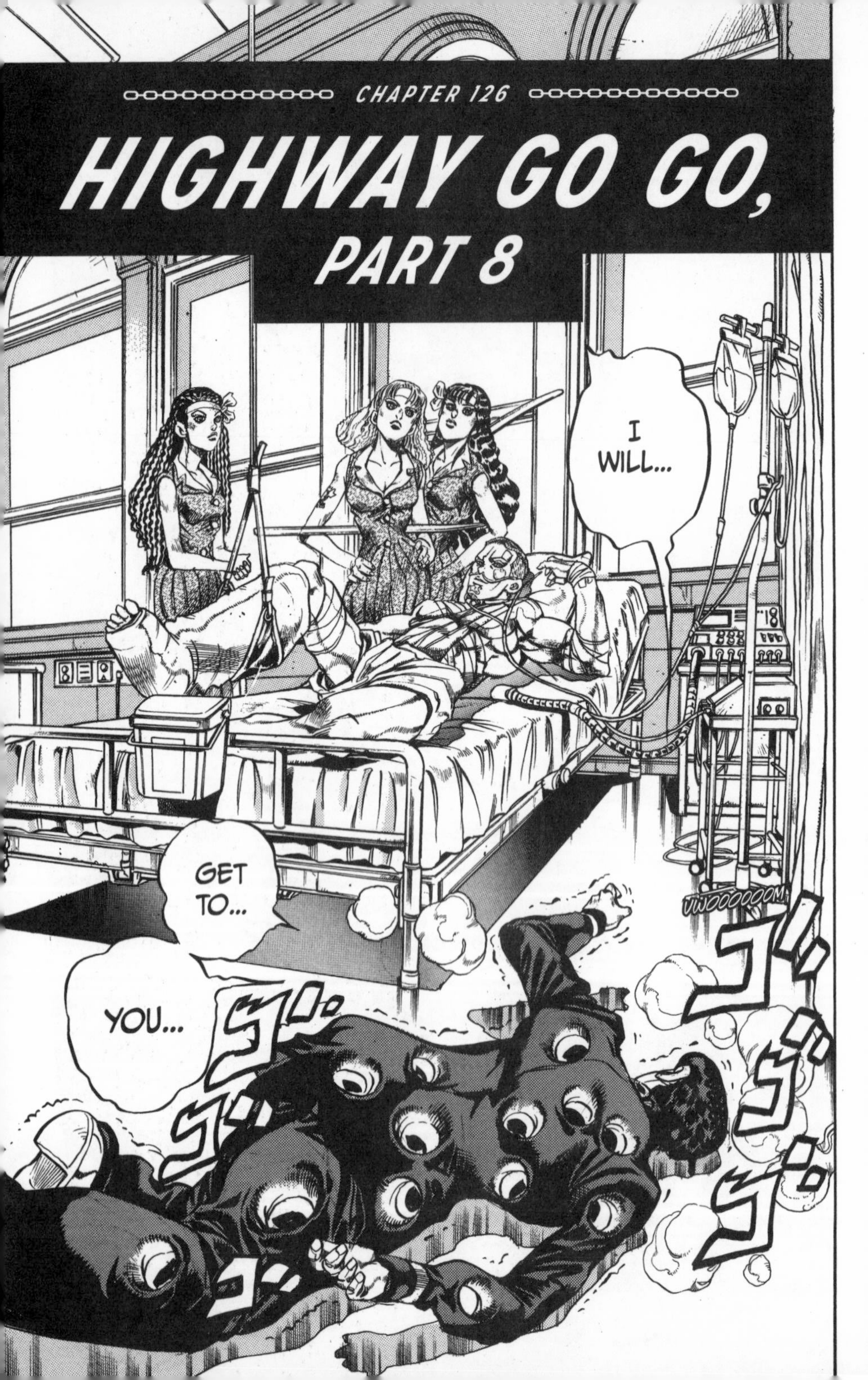
I WILL...
GET TO...
YOU...
VWOOOOOOM

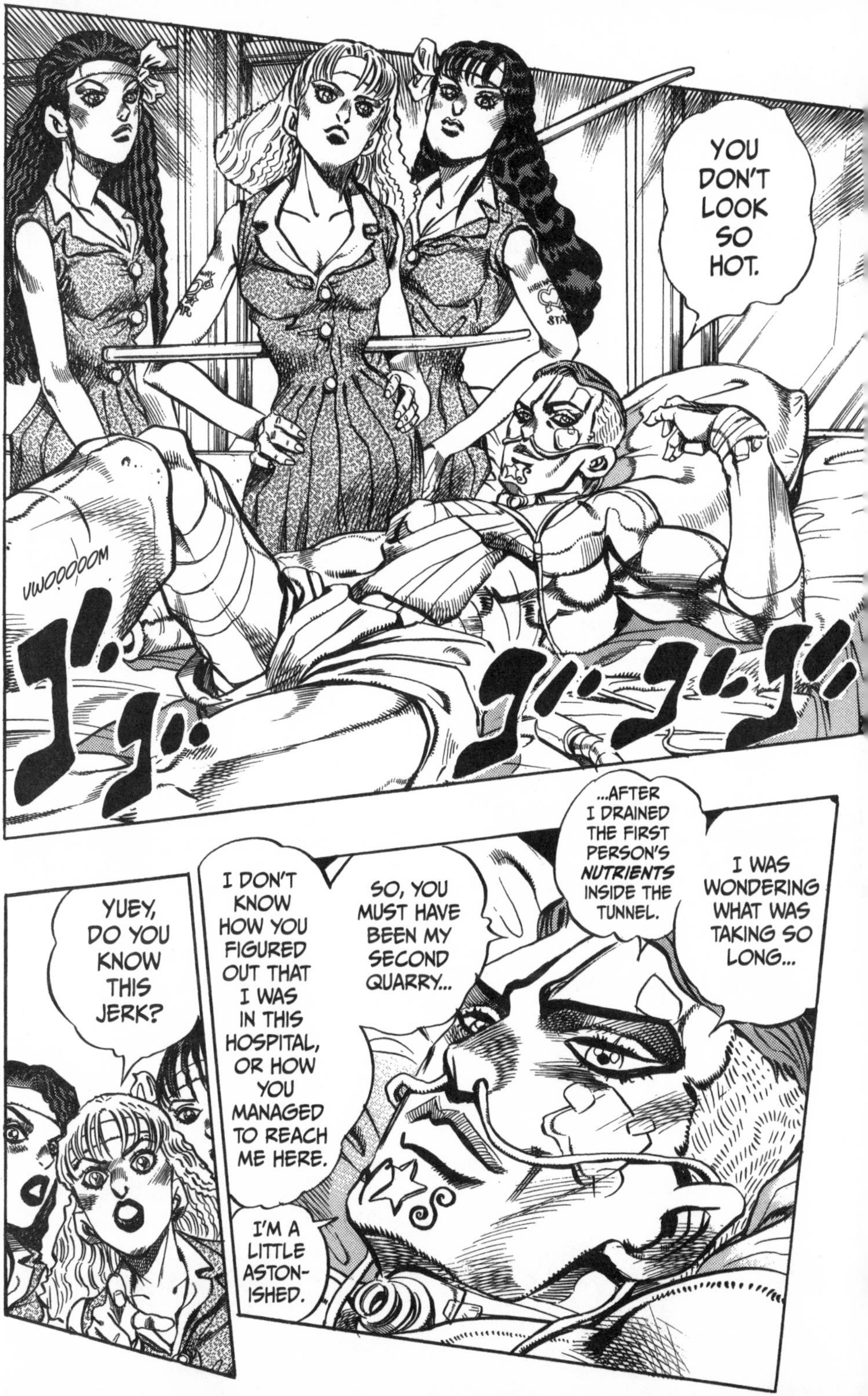
YOU DON'T LOOK SO HOT.
VWOOOOOM
I WAS WONDERING WHAT WAS TAKING SO LONG...
...AFTER I DRAINED THE FIRST PERSON'S ***NUTRIENTS*** INSIDE THE TUNNEL.
SO, YOU MUST HAVE BEEN MY SECOND QUARRY...
I DON'T KNOW HOW YOU FIGURED OUT THAT I WAS IN THIS HOSPITAL, OR HOW YOU MANAGED TO REACH ME HERE.
I'M A LITTLE ASTON-ISHED.
YUEY, DO YOU KNOW THIS JERK?

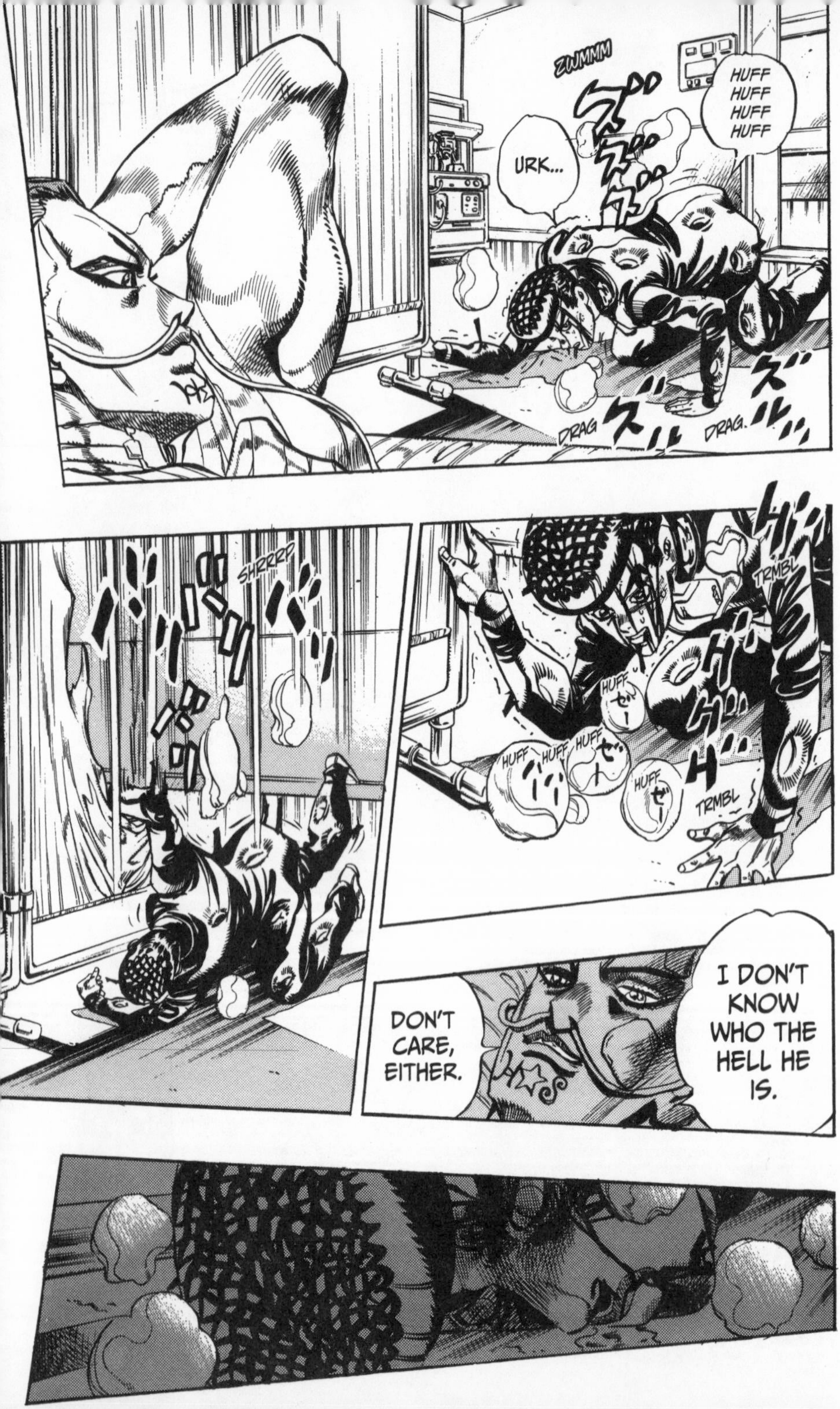
HUFF HUFF HUFF HUFF
ZWUMMM
URK...
DRAG.
DRAG
TRMBL
HUFF
HUFF
HUFF
HUFF
HUFF
TRMBL
SHRRRP
I DON'T KNOW WHO THE HELL HE IS.
DON'T CARE, EITHER.

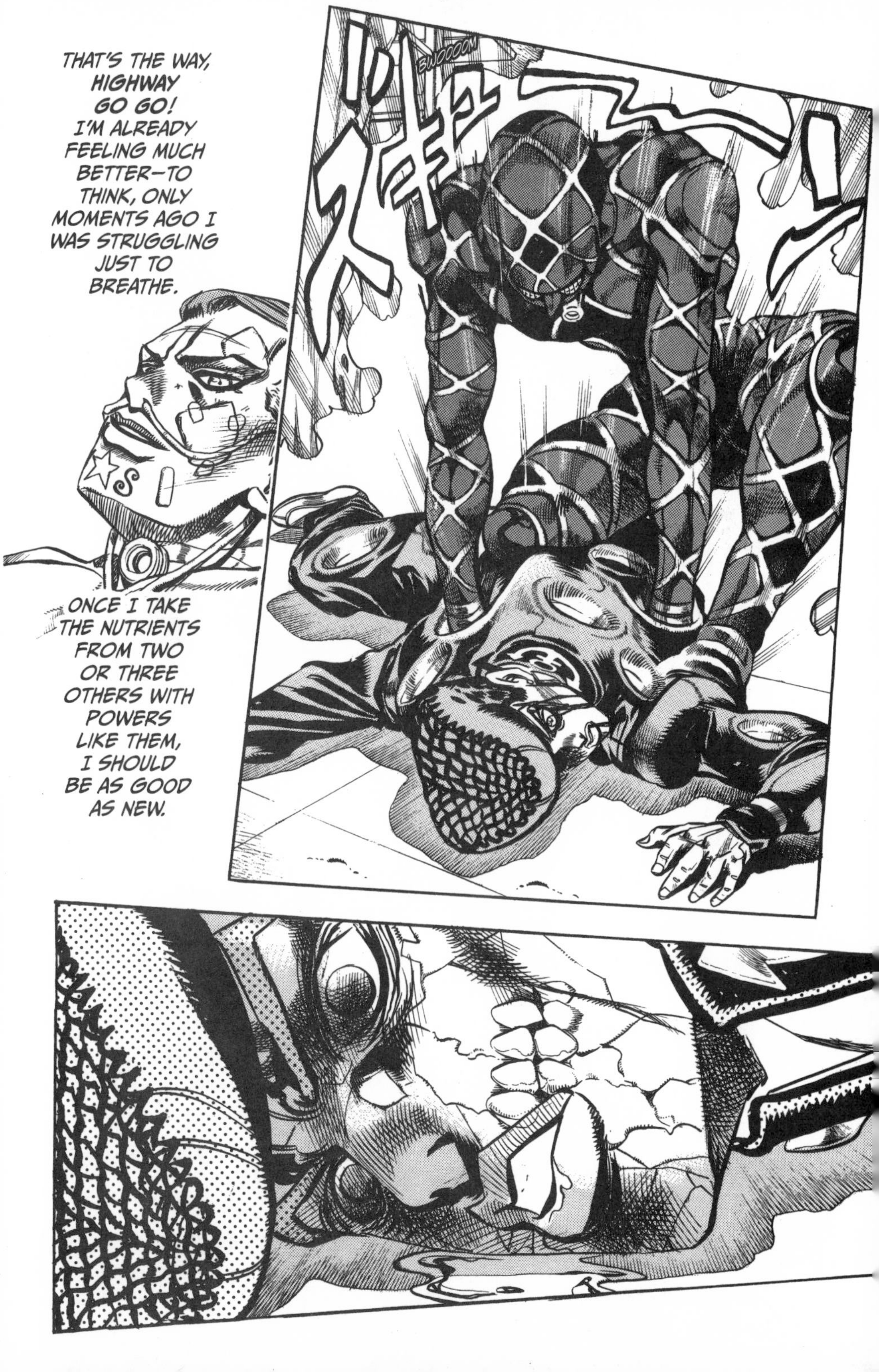
BWOOOOM
THAT'S THE WAY, HIGHWAY GO GO! I'M ALREADY FEELING MUCH BETTER—TO THINK, ONLY MOMENTS AGO I WAS STRUGGLING JUST TO BREATHE.
ONCE I TAKE THE NUTRIENTS FROM TWO OR THREE OTHERS WITH POWERS LIKE THEM, I SHOULD BE AS GOOD AS NEW.

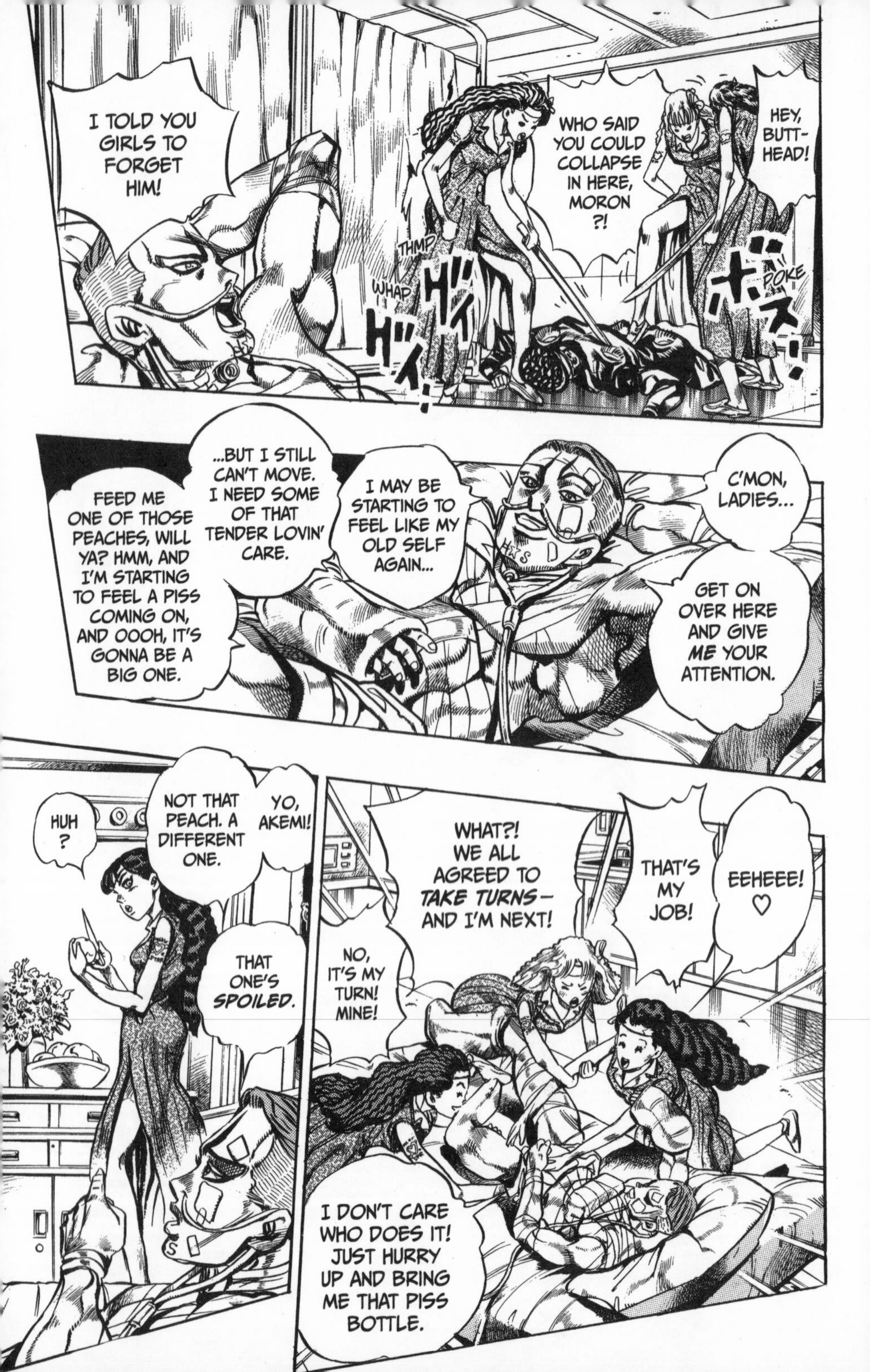
HEY, BUTT-HEAD!
POKE
WHO SAID YOU COULD COLLAPSE IN HERE, MORON?!
THMP
WHAP
I TOLD YOU GIRLS TO FORGET HIM!
C'MON, LADIES...
GET ON OVER HERE AND GIVE *ME* YOUR ATTENTION.
I MAY BE STARTING TO FEEL LIKE MY OLD SELF AGAIN...
...BUT I STILL CAN'T MOVE. I NEED SOME OF THAT TENDER LOVIN' CARE.
FEED ME ONE OF THOSE PEACHES, WILL YA? HMM, AND I'M STARTING TO FEEL A PISS COMING ON, AND OOOH, IT'S GONNA BE A BIG ONE.
EEHEEE! ♡
THAT'S MY JOB!
WHAT?! WE ALL AGREED TO *TAKE TURNS*— AND I'M NEXT!
NO, IT'S MY TURN! MINE!
I DON'T CARE WHO DOES IT! JUST HURRY UP AND BRING ME THAT PISS BOTTLE.
YO, AKEMI!
NOT THAT PEACH. A DIFFERENT ONE.
HUH?
THAT ONE'S *SPOILED*.

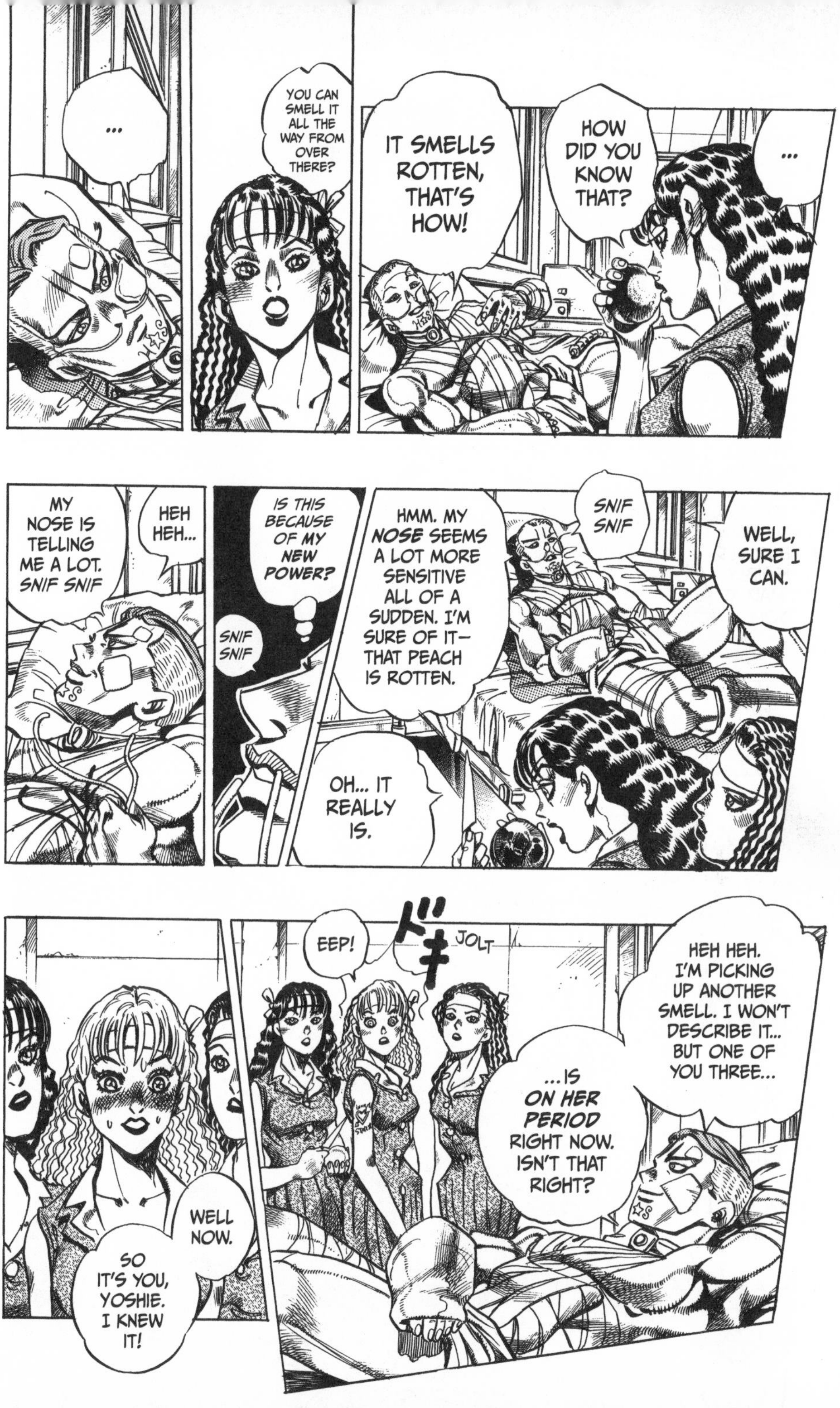
...
HOW DID YOU KNOW THAT?
IT SMELLS ROTTEN, THAT'S HOW!
YOU CAN SMELL IT ALL THE WAY FROM OVER THERE?
...
WELL, SURE I CAN.
SNIF SNIF
HMM. MY *NOSE* SEEMS A LOT MORE SENSITIVE ALL OF A SUDDEN. I'M SURE OF IT— THAT PEACH IS ROTTEN.
OH... IT REALLY IS.
IS THIS BECAUSE OF MY NEW POWER?
SNIF SNIF
HEH HEH...
MY NOSE IS TELLING ME A LOT. *SNIF SNIF*
HEH HEH. I'M PICKING UP ANOTHER SMELL. I WON'T DESCRIBE IT... BUT ONE OF YOU THREE...
...IS ***ON HER PERIOD*** RIGHT NOW. ISN'T THAT RIGHT?
ドキ
JOLT
EEP!
WELL NOW.
SO IT'S YOU, YOSHIE. I KNEW IT!

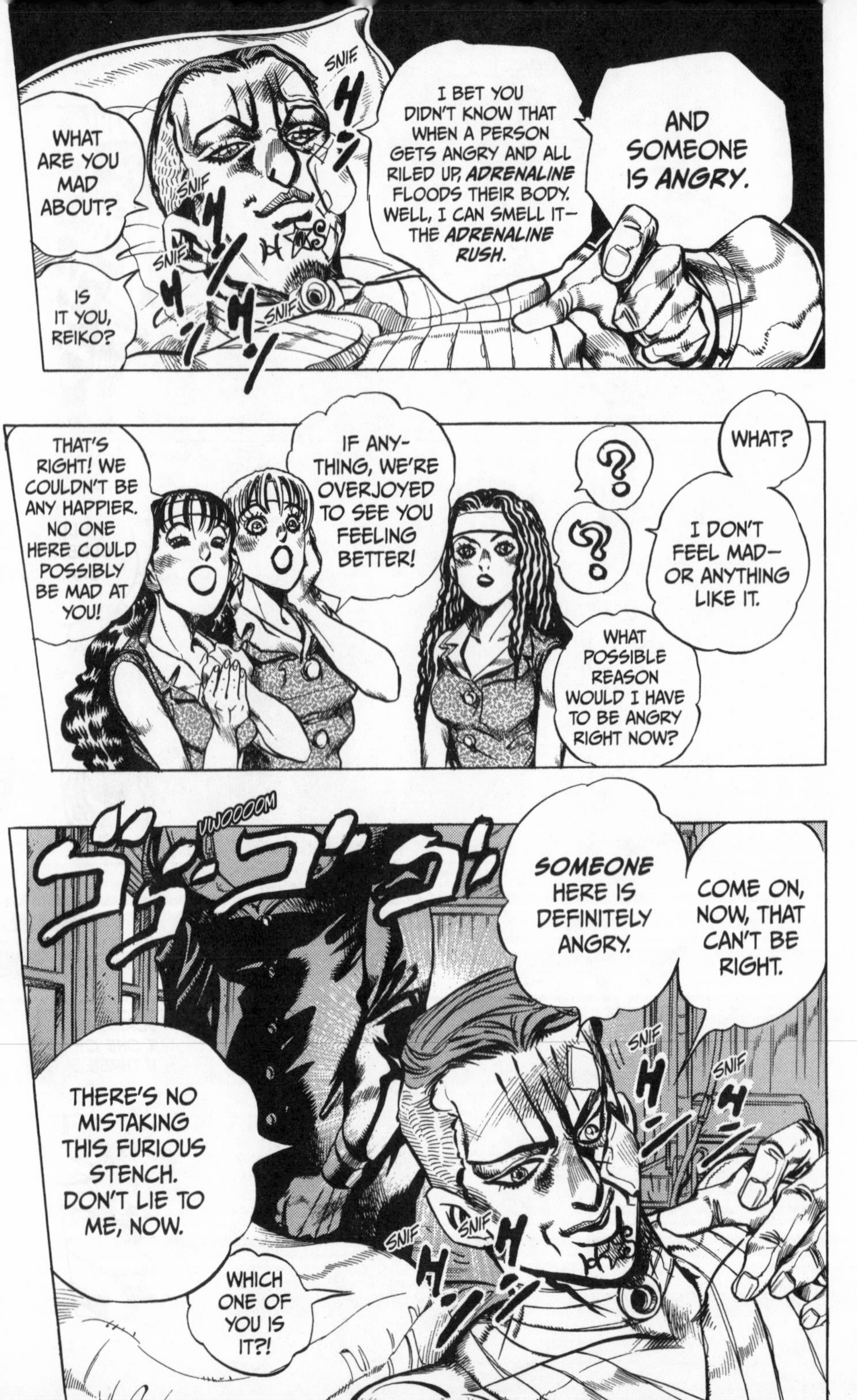
AND SOMEONE IS ANGRY.
I BET YOU DIDN'T KNOW THAT WHEN A PERSON GETS ANGRY AND ALL RILED UP, ADRENALINE FLOODS THEIR BODY. WELL, I CAN SMELL IT— THE ADRENALINE RUSH.
SNIF
SNIF
SNIF
SNIF
WHAT ARE YOU MAD ABOUT?
IS IT YOU, REIKO?
WHAT?
I DON'T FEEL MAD— OR ANYTHING LIKE IT.
WHAT POSSIBLE REASON WOULD I HAVE TO BE ANGRY RIGHT NOW?
?
?
IF ANY-THING, WE'RE OVERJOYED TO SEE YOU FEELING BETTER!
THAT'S RIGHT! WE COULDN'T BE ANY HAPPIER. NO ONE HERE COULD POSSIBLY BE MAD AT YOU!
COME ON, NOW, THAT CAN'T BE RIGHT.
SOMEONE HERE IS DEFINITELY ANGRY.
UWOOOOM
SNIF
SNIF
THERE'S NO MISTAKING THIS FURIOUS STENCH. DON'T LIE TO ME, NOW.
SNIF
SNIF
WHICH ONE OF YOU IS IT?!

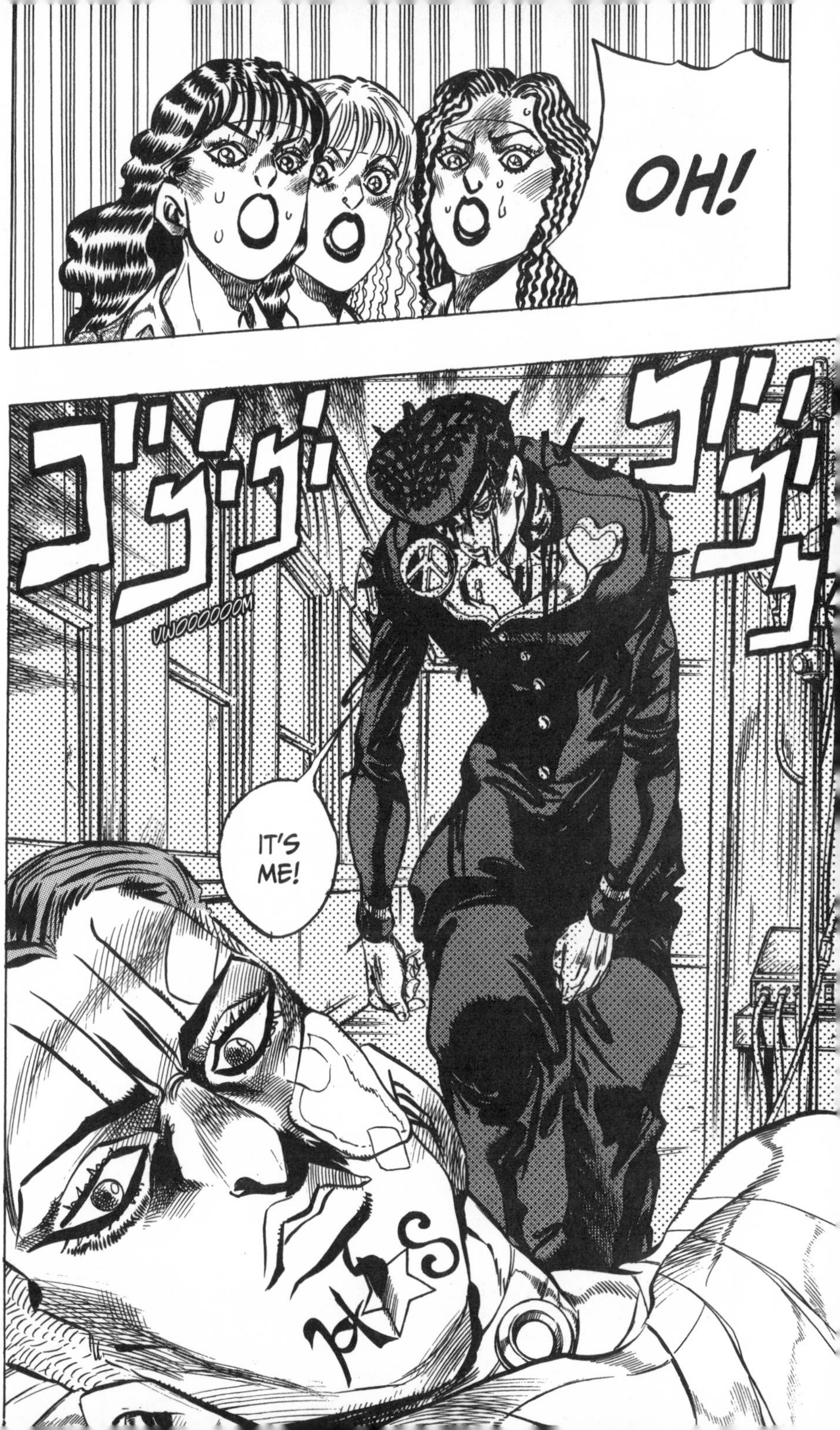
OH!
ゴゴゴ
ゴゴゴ
VWOOOOOOOM
IT'S ME!

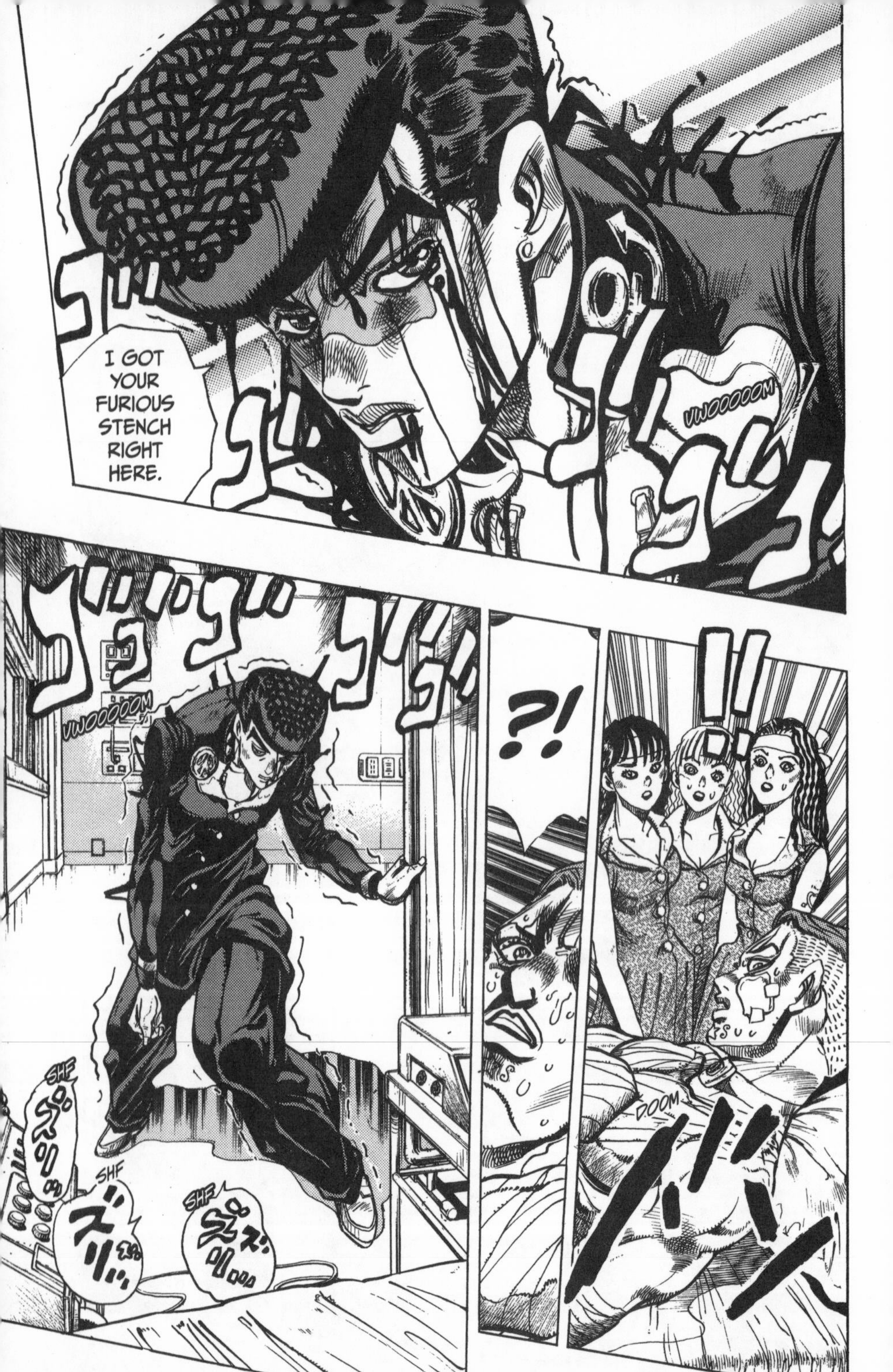
I GOT YOUR FURIOUS STENCH RIGHT HERE.
UWOOOOOM
!!
DOOM
?!
UWOOOOOM
SHF
SHF
SHF

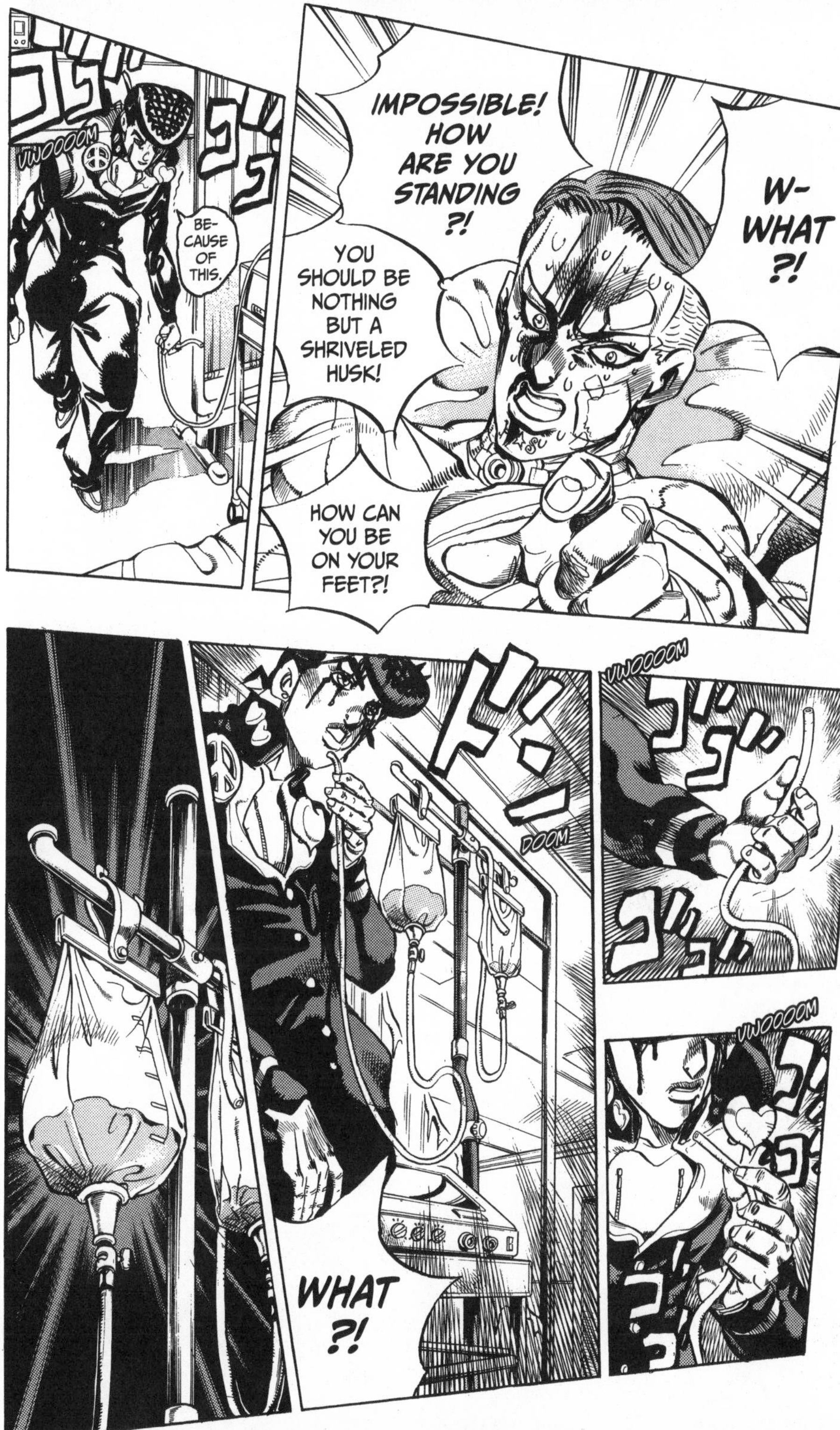
W-WHAT ?!
IMPOSSIBLE! HOW ARE YOU STANDING ?!
YOU SHOULD BE NOTHING BUT A SHRIVELED HUSK!
HOW CAN YOU BE ON YOUR FEET?!
VWOOOOM
BE-CAUSE OF THIS.
VWOOOOM
VWOOOOM
DOOM
WHAT ?!

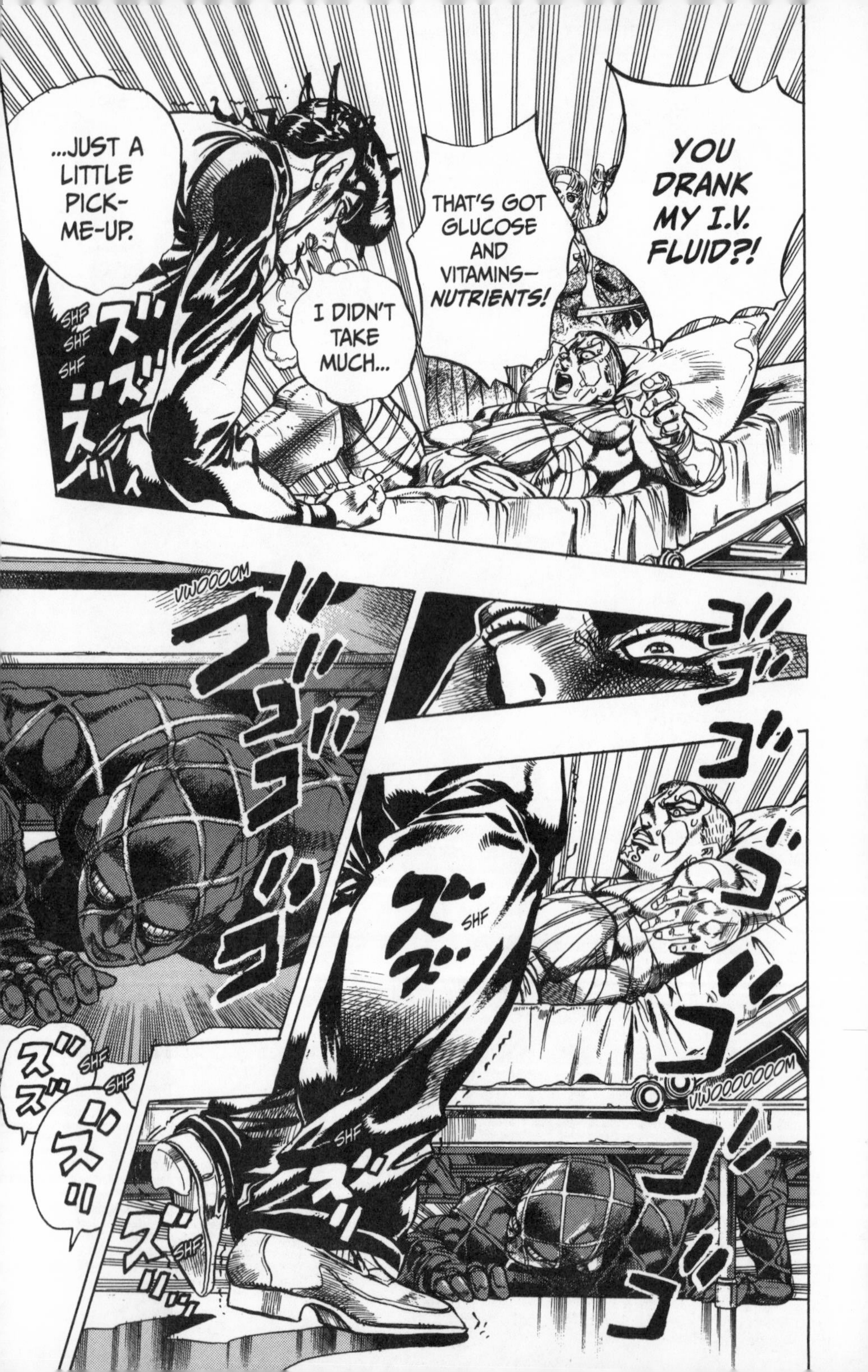
YOU DRANK MY I.V. FLUID?!
THAT'S GOT GLUCOSE AND VITAMINS— NUTRIENTS!
I DIDN'T TAKE MUCH...
...JUST A LITTLE PICK-ME-UP.
SHF SHF SHF
VWOOOOOOOOM
SHF
SHF
VWOOOOM
SHF
SHF
SHF

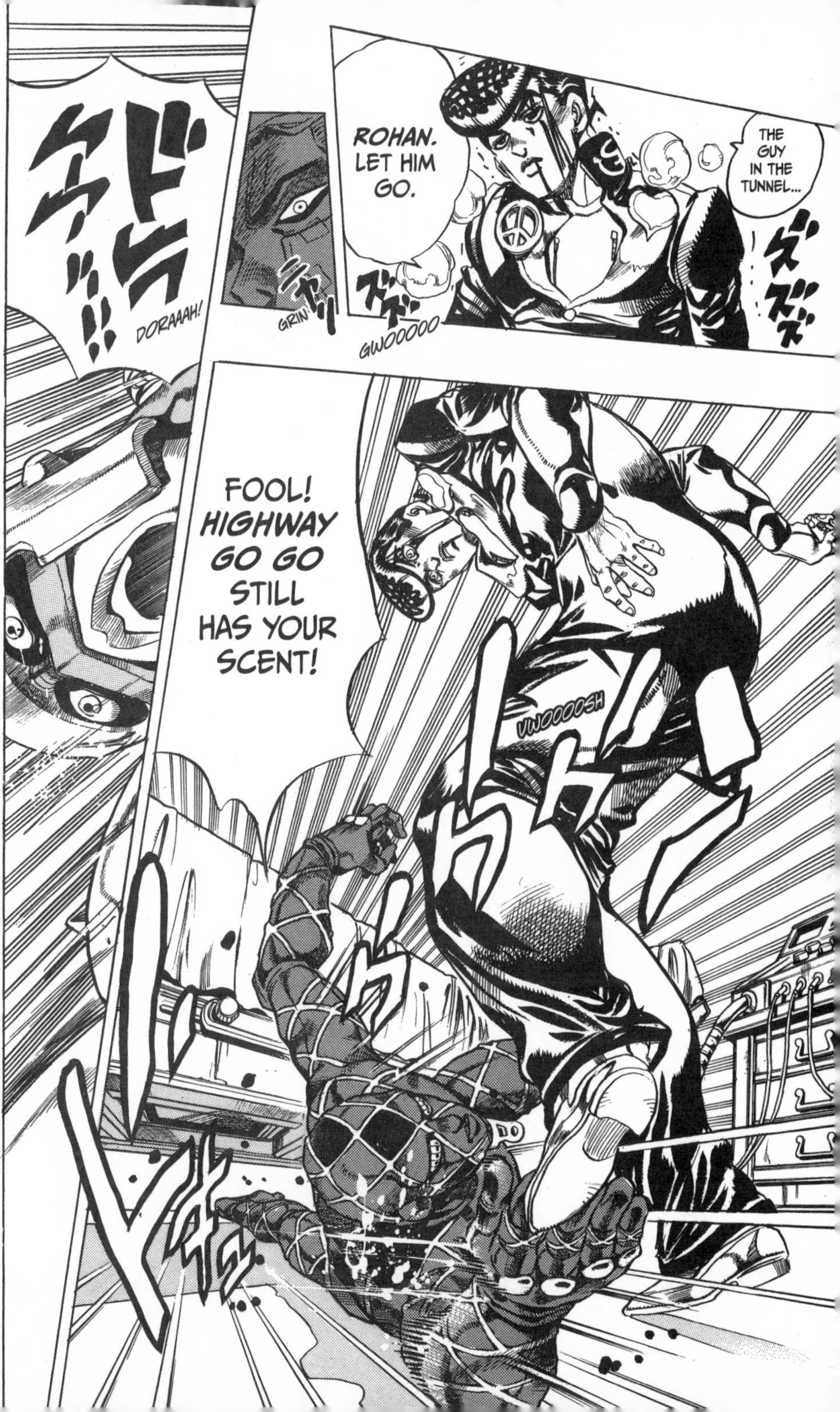
THE GUY IN THE TUNNEL...
ROHAN. LET HIM GO.
GWOOOOO
GRIN
FOOL! HIGHWAY GO GO STILL HAS YOUR SCENT!
VWOOOOSH
DO
DORAAAH!

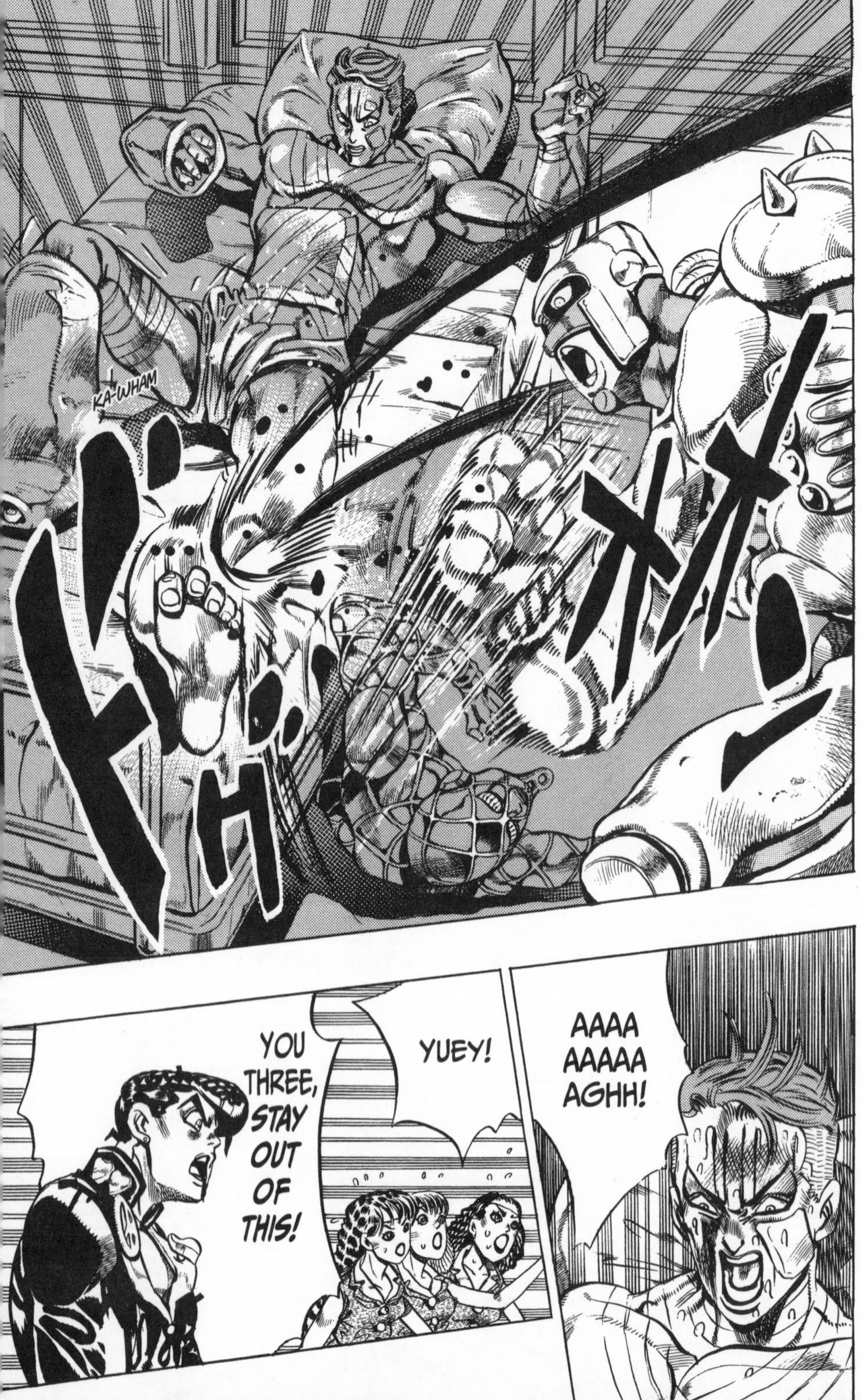
KA-WHAM
AAAA AAAAA AGHH!
YUEY!
YOU THREE, STAY OUT OF THIS!

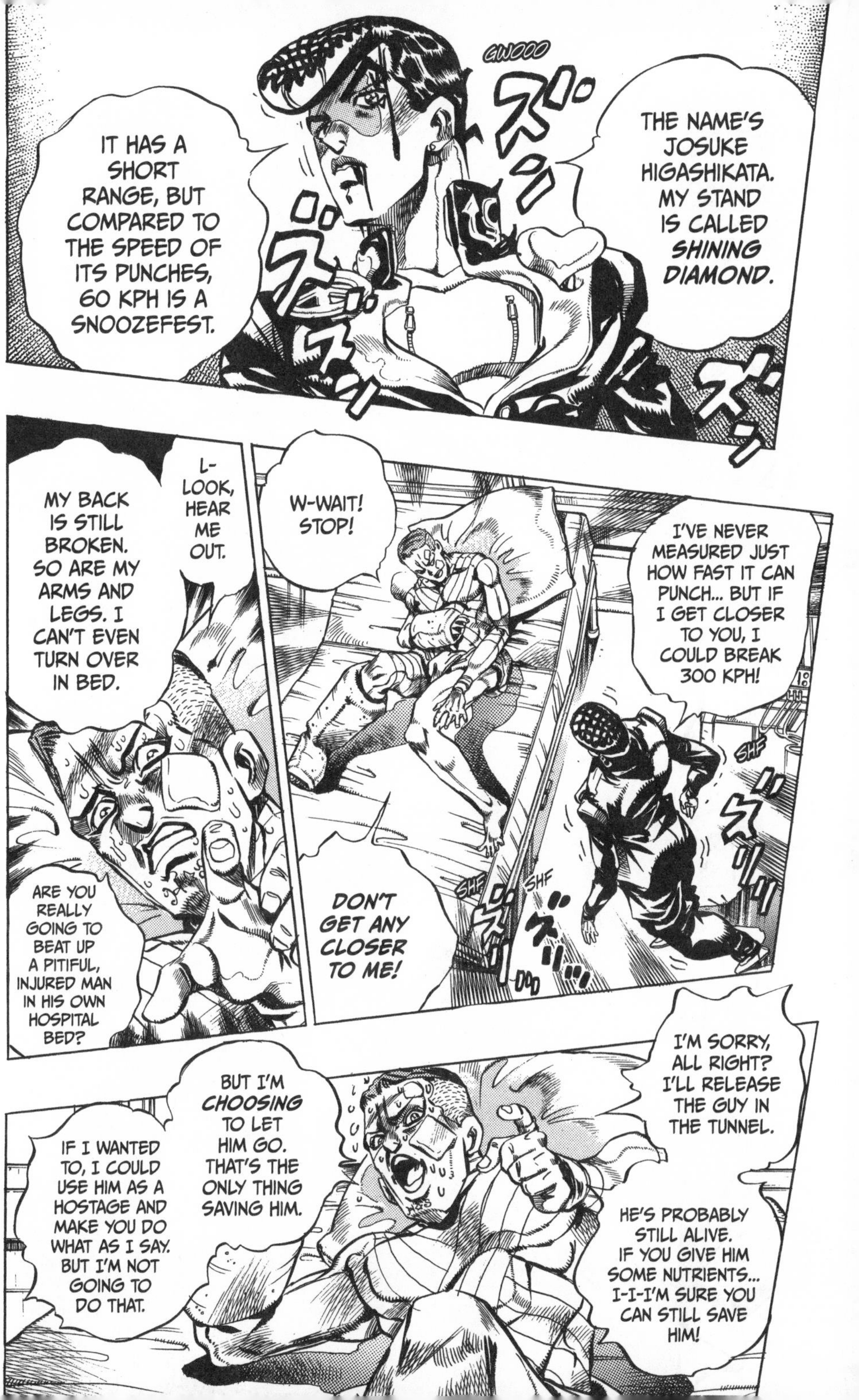
GWOOO
THE NAME'S JOSUKE HIGASHIKATA. MY STAND IS CALLED *SHINING DIAMOND*.
IT HAS A SHORT RANGE, BUT COMPARED TO THE SPEED OF ITS PUNCHES, 60 KPH IS A SNOOZEFEST.
I'VE NEVER MEASURED JUST HOW FAST IT CAN PUNCH... BUT IF I GET CLOSER TO YOU, I COULD BREAK 300 KPH!
W-WAIT! STOP!
SHF
SHF
SHF
DON'T GET ANY CLOSER TO ME!
L-LOOK, HEAR ME OUT.
MY BACK IS STILL BROKEN. SO ARE MY ARMS AND LEGS. I CAN'T EVEN TURN OVER IN BED.
ARE YOU REALLY GOING TO BEAT UP A PITIFUL, INJURED MAN IN HIS OWN HOSPITAL BED?
I'M SORRY, ALL RIGHT? I'LL RELEASE THE GUY IN THE TUNNEL.
HE'S PROBABLY STILL ALIVE. IF YOU GIVE HIM SOME NUTRIENTS... I-I-I'M SURE YOU CAN STILL SAVE HIM!
BUT I'M *CHOOSING* TO LET HIM GO. THAT'S THE ONLY THING SAVING HIM.
IF I WANTED TO, I COULD USE HIM AS A HOSTAGE AND MAKE YOU DO WHAT AS I SAY. BUT I'M NOT GOING TO DO THAT.

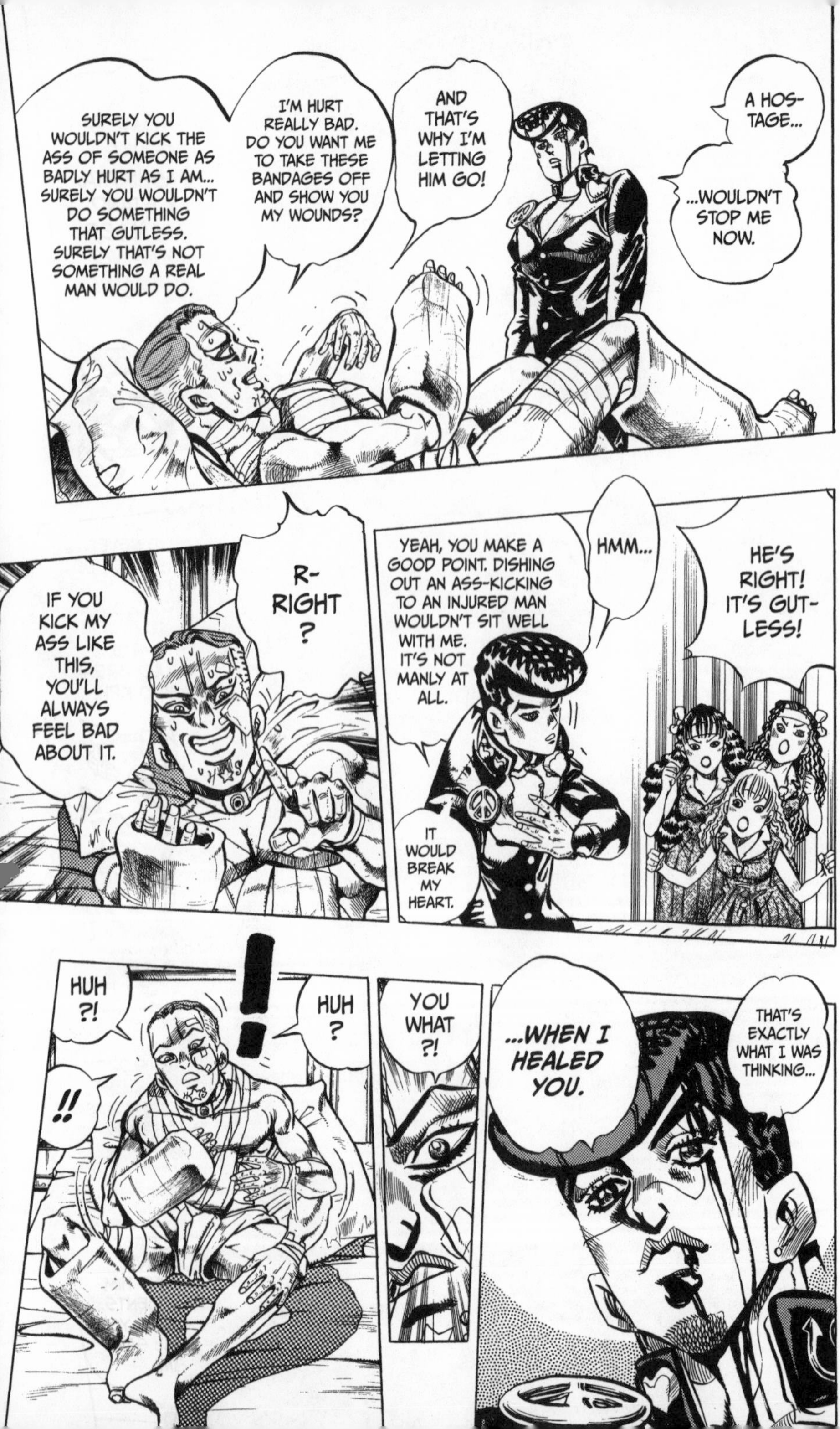
A HOS-TAGE...
...WOULDN'T STOP ME NOW.
AND THAT'S WHY I'M LETTING HIM GO!
I'M HURT REALLY BAD. DO YOU WANT ME TO TAKE THESE BANDAGES OFF AND SHOW YOU MY WOUNDS?
SURELY YOU WOULDN'T KICK THE ASS OF SOMEONE AS BADLY HURT AS I AM... SURELY YOU WOULDN'T DO SOMETHING THAT GUTLESS. SURELY THAT'S NOT SOMETHING A REAL MAN WOULD DO.
HE'S RIGHT! IT'S GUT-LESS!
HMM...
YEAH, YOU MAKE A GOOD POINT. DISHING OUT AN ASS-KICKING TO AN INJURED MAN WOULDN'T SIT WELL WITH ME. IT'S NOT MANLY AT ALL.
IT WOULD BREAK MY HEART.
R-RIGHT?
IF YOU KICK MY ASS LIKE THIS, YOU'LL ALWAYS FEEL BAD ABOUT IT.
THAT'S EXACTLY WHAT I WAS THINKING...
...WHEN I HEALED YOU.
YOU WHAT?!
HUH?
HUH?!
!!

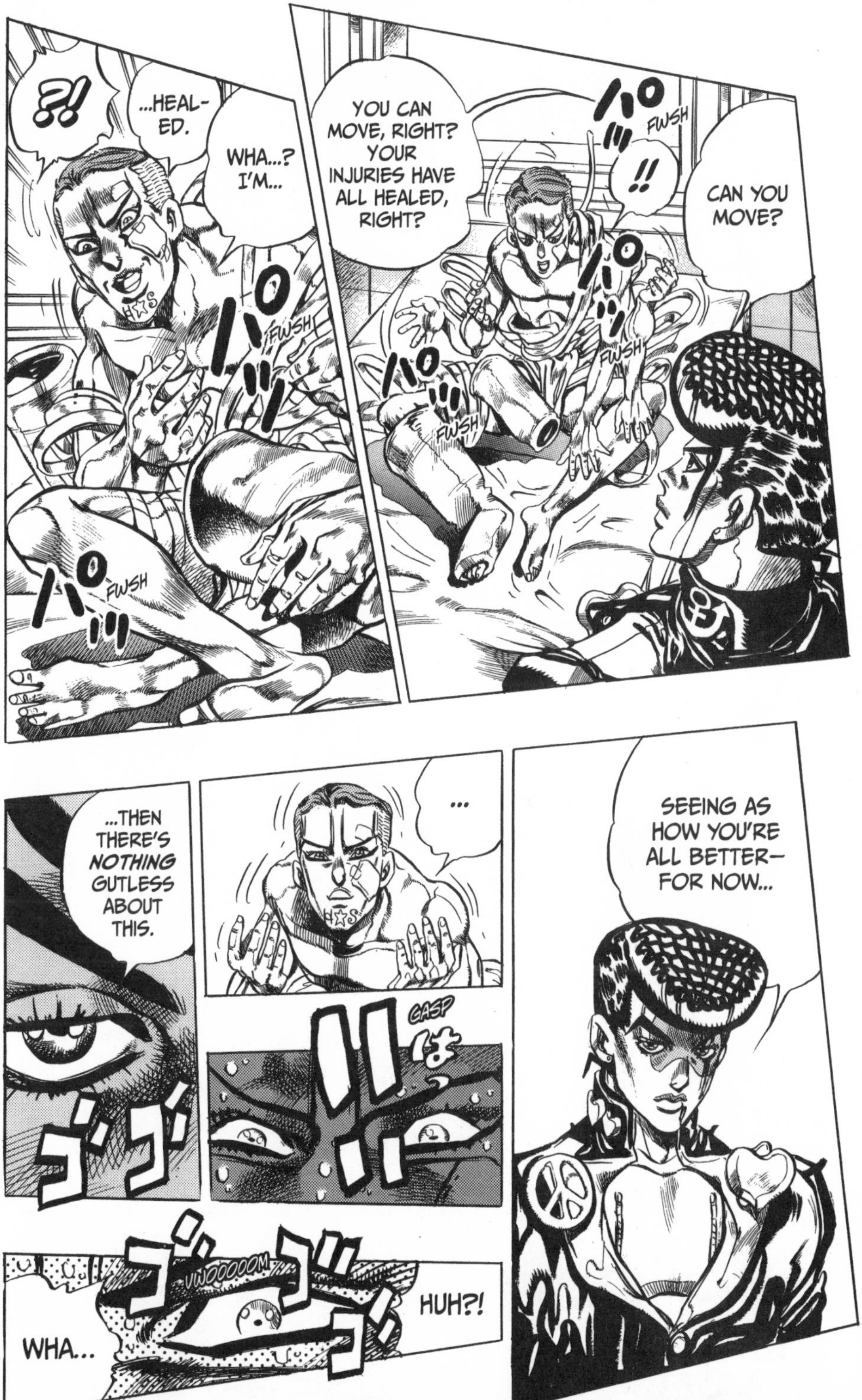
CAN YOU MOVE?
!!
FWSH
YOU CAN MOVE, RIGHT? YOUR INJURIES HAVE ALL HEALED, RIGHT?
FWSH
FWSH
FWSH
WHA...? I'M...
...HEAL-ED.
?!
FWSH
FWSH
SEEING AS HOW YOU'RE ALL BETTER— FOR NOW...
...
...THEN THERE'S *NOTHING* GUTLESS ABOUT THIS.
GASP
HUH?!
VWOOOOOM
WHA...

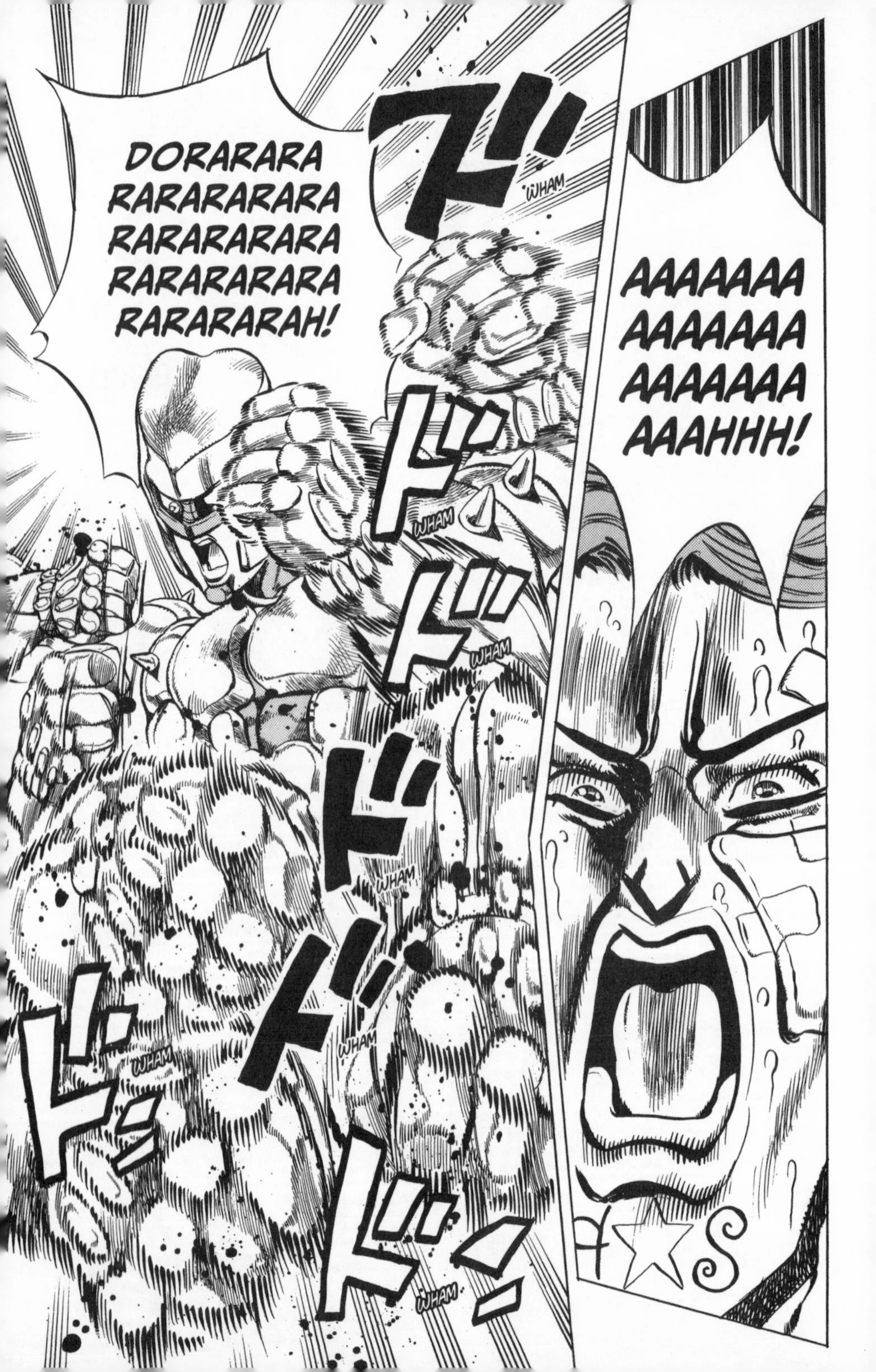
AAAAAAA
AAAAAAA
AAAAAAA
AAAHHH!
WHAM
DORARARA
RARARARARA
RARARARARA
RARARARARA
RARARARAH!
WHAM
WHAM
WHAM
WHAM
WHAM
WHAM

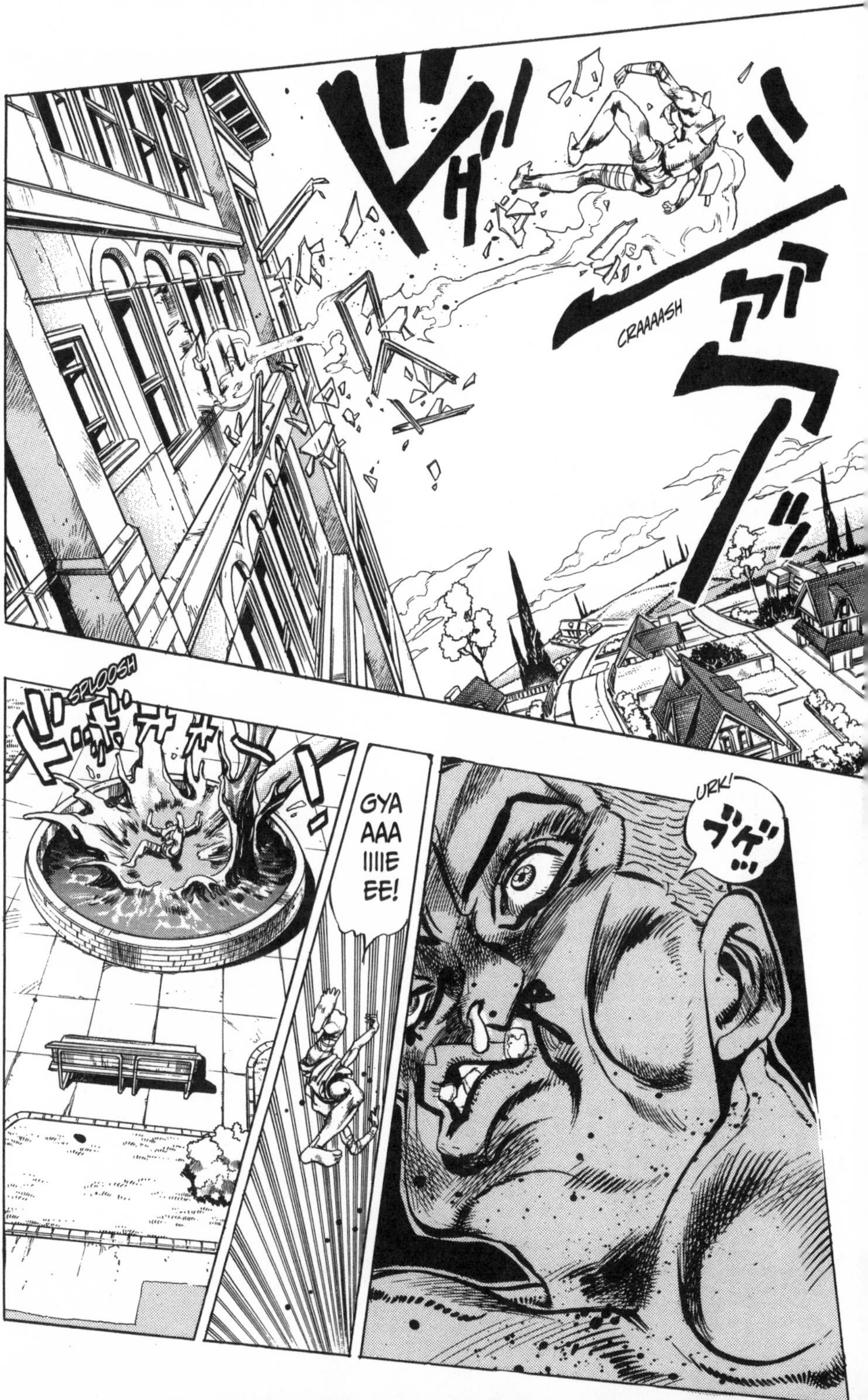
CRAAAASH
URK!
ブゲッ
GYA AAA IIIIE EE!
SPLOOSH

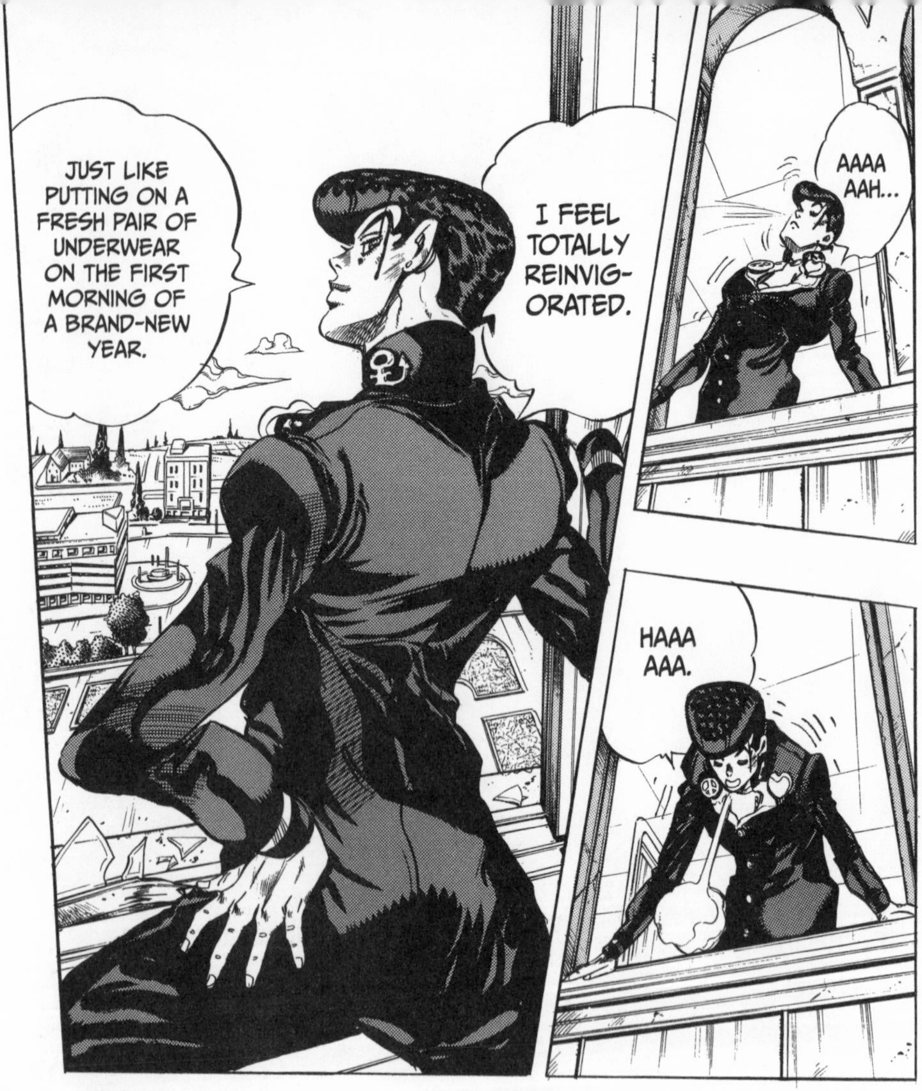
AAAA AAH...
HAAA AAA.
I FEEL TOTALLY REINVIG-ORATED.
JUST LIKE PUTTING ON A FRESH PAIR OF UNDERWEAR ON THE FIRST MORNING OF A BRAND-NEW YEAR.

YUYA FUNGAMI: HIS STAY IN BUDOGAOKA HOSPITAL WAS EXTENDED. JOSUKE WARNED HIM THAT IF HE EVER TRIED TO USE HIGHWAY GO GO TO HEAL HIMSELF AGAIN, HE'D KICK HIS ASS HOWEVER MANY TIMES IT TOOK. EVEN SO, JOSUKE WAS STILL JEALOUS THE BIKER HAD GROUPIES TO NURSE HIM BACK TO HEALTH.

ROHAN KISHIBE: JOSUKE RESCUED HIM FROM THE TUNNEL AND EXPECTED THE DEED WOULD FINALLY KINDLE A STRONG FRIENDSHIP, BUT THE MANGA ARTIST WAS STILL ANGRY AT JOSUKE FOR REFUSING TO RUN AWAY IN THE FIRST PLACE. ROHAN CONSIDERED THEM EVEN, AND THE PAIR'S SOUR RELATIONSHIP CONTINUED.

KOICHI HIROSE: HE TOOK HIS DOG FOR A WALK.

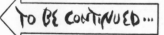

TO BE CONTINUED...

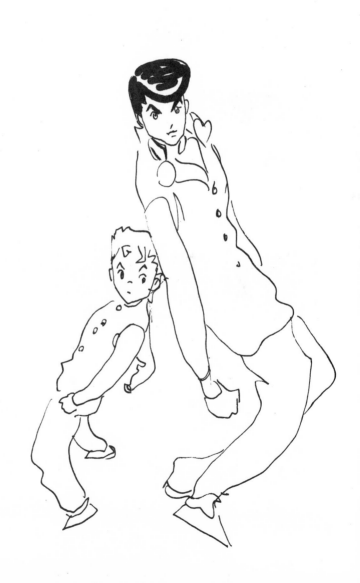

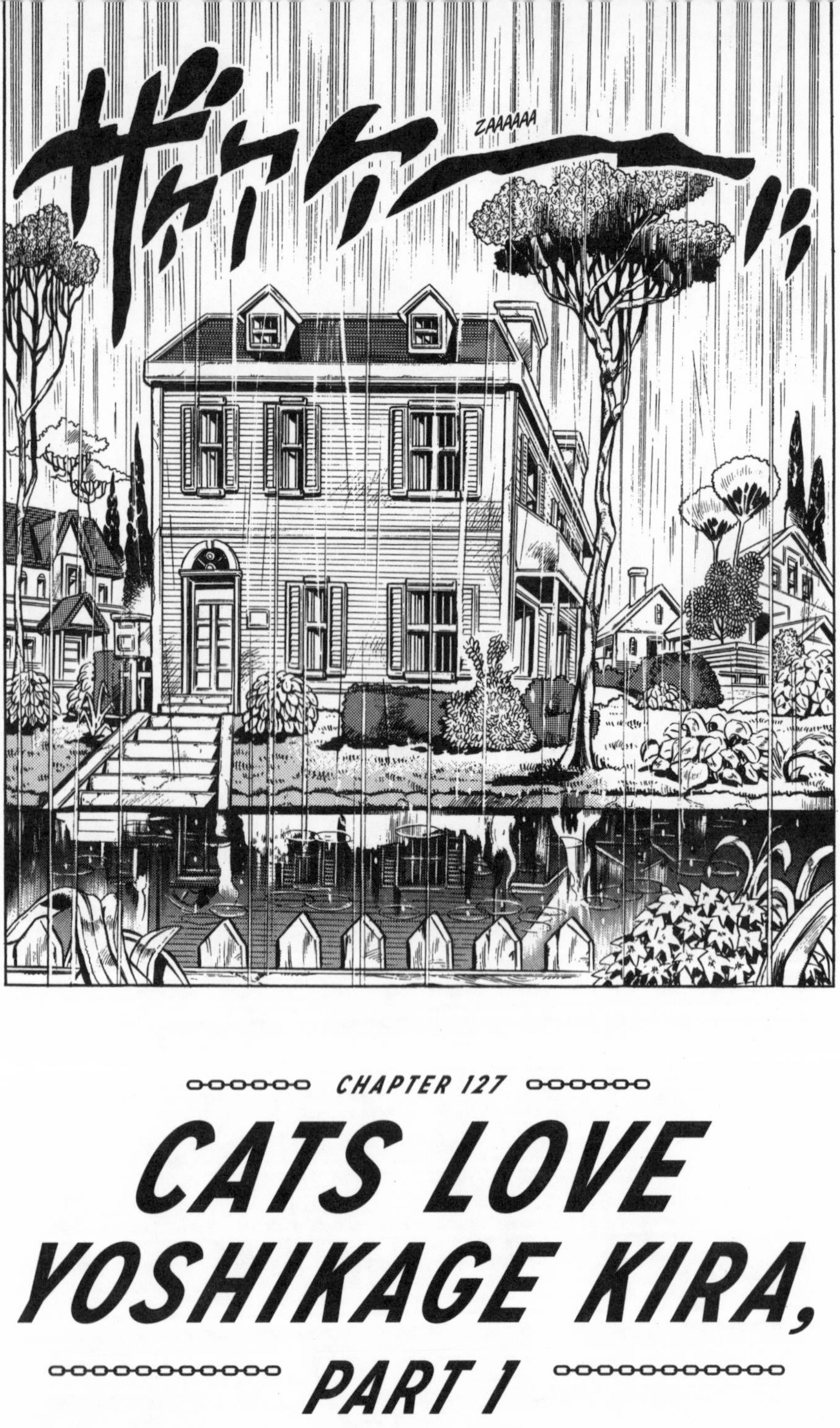
ZAAAAAA

CHAPTER 127

CATS LOVE YOSHIKAGE KIRA, PART 1

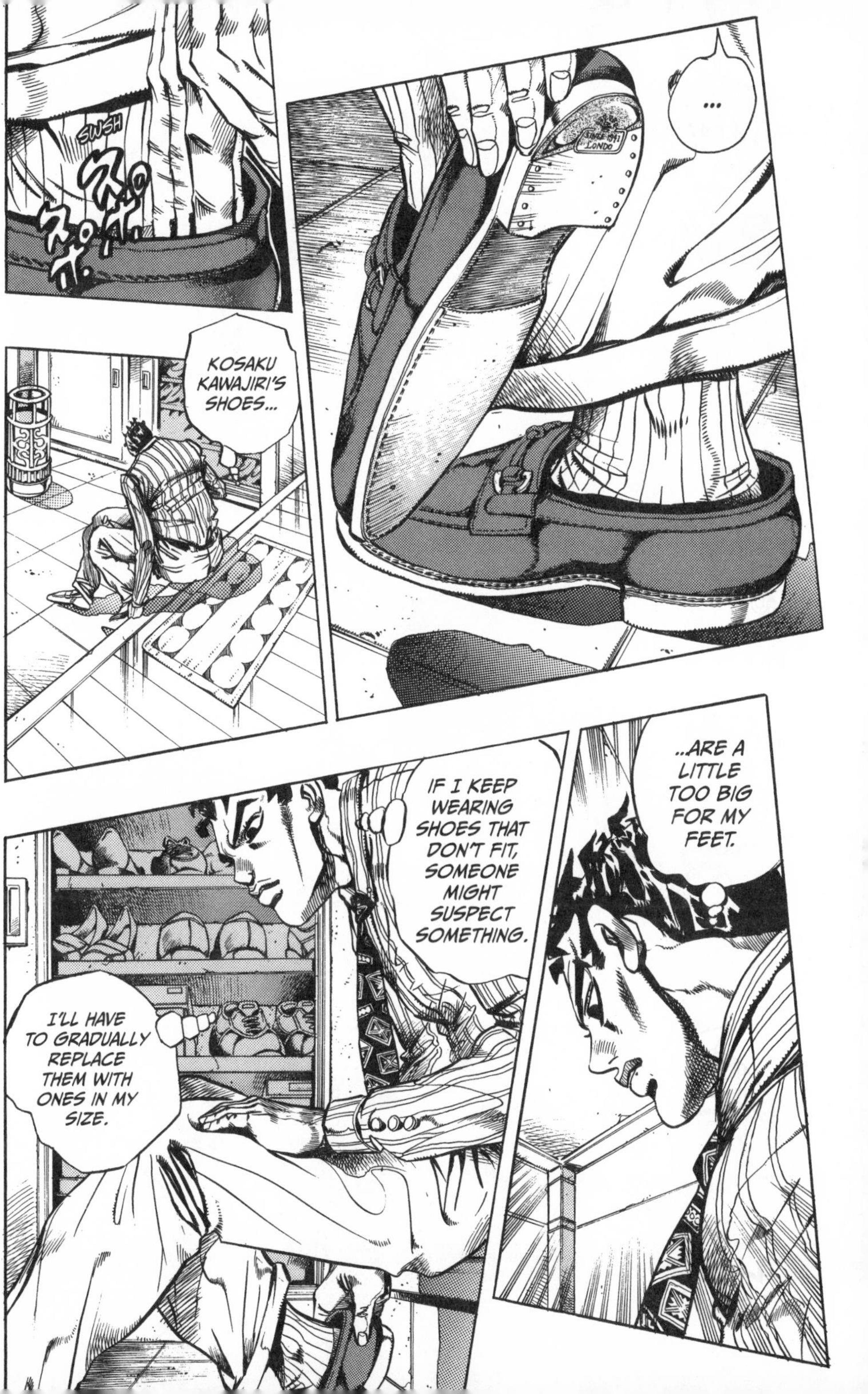
...
SINCE 1941 LONDO
SWSH
KOSAKU KAWAJIRI'S SHOES...
...ARE A LITTLE TOO BIG FOR MY FEET.
IF I KEEP WEARING SHOES THAT DON'T FIT, SOMEONE MIGHT SUSPECT SOMETHING.
I'LL HAVE TO GRADUALLY REPLACE THEM WITH ONES IN MY SIZE.

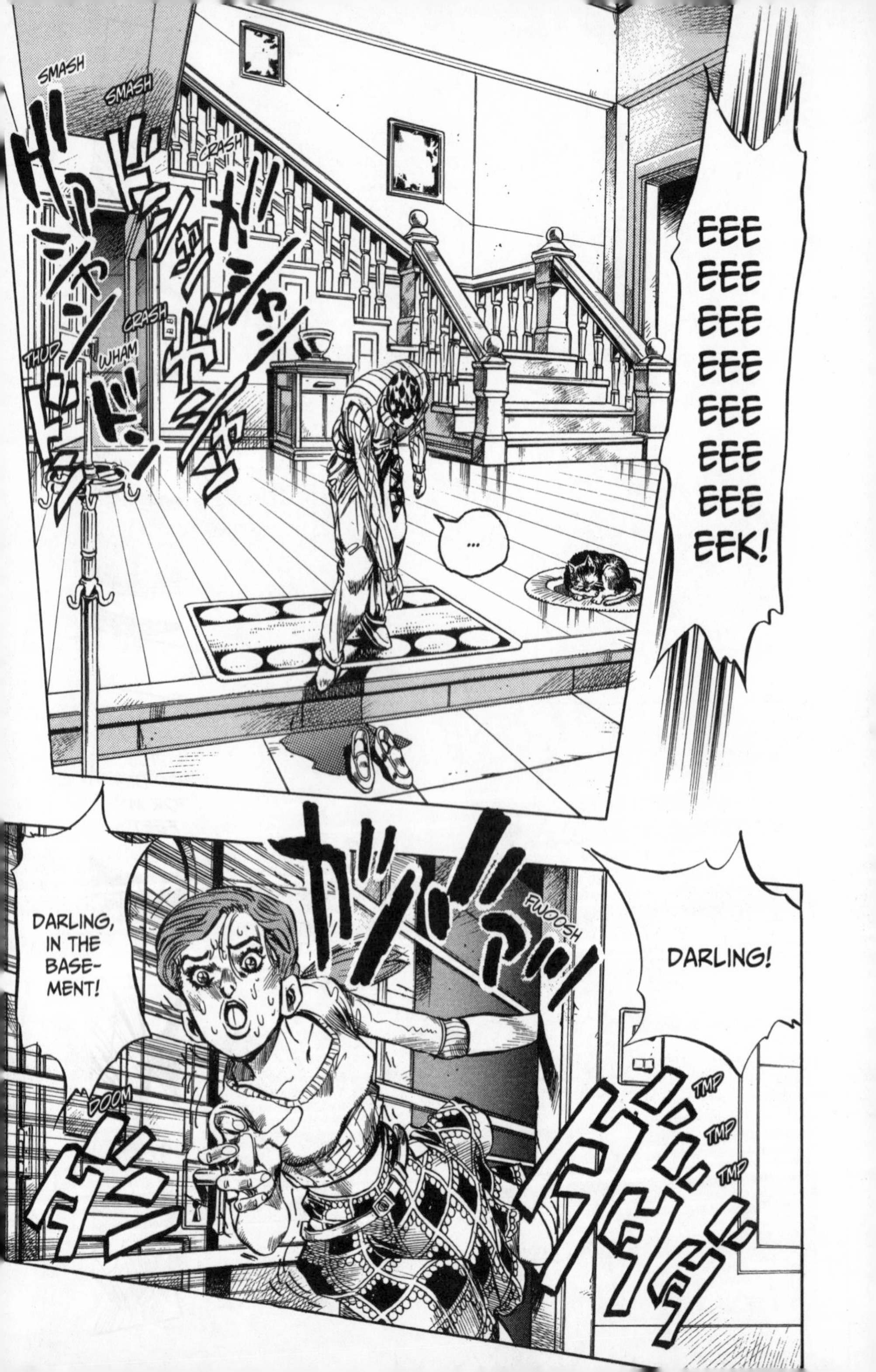
EEE
EEE
EEE
EEE
EEE
EEE
EEE
EEK!
SMASH
SMASH
CRASH
CRASH
THUD
WHAM
...
DARLING!
FWOOSH
DARLING, IN THE BASE- MENT!
TMP
TMP
TMP
DOOM

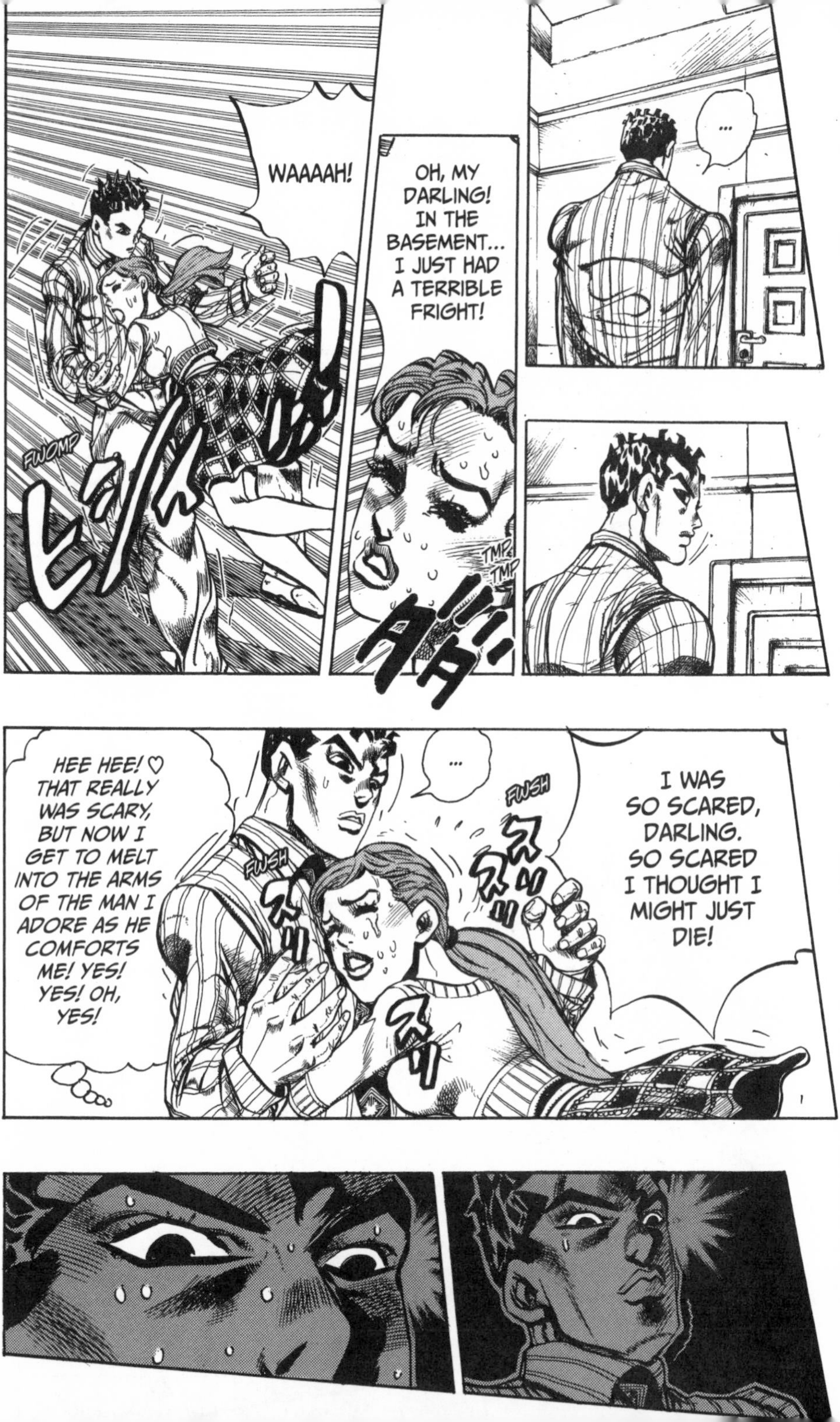

...
OH, MY DARLING! IN THE BASEMENT... I JUST HAD A TERRIBLE FRIGHT!
TMP TMP
WAAAAH!
FWOMP
I WAS SO SCARED, DARLING. SO SCARED I THOUGHT I MIGHT JUST DIE!
FWSH
...
FWSH
HEE HEE! ♡ THAT REALLY WAS SCARY, BUT NOW I GET TO MELT INTO THE ARMS OF THE MAN I ADORE AS HE COMFORTS ME! YES! YES! OH, YES!

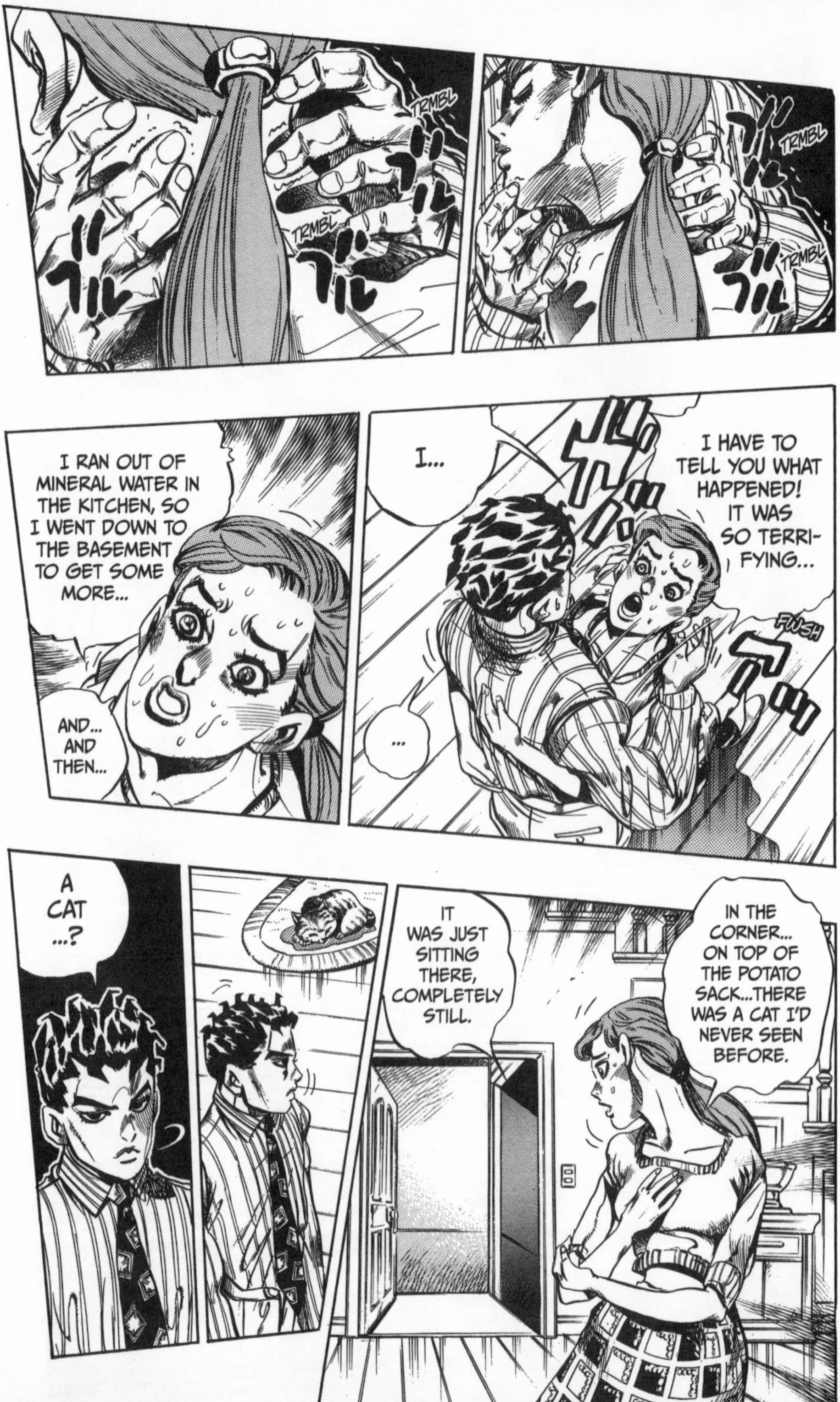
TRMBL
TRMBL
TRMBL
TRMBL
I HAVE TO TELL YOU WHAT HAPPENED! IT WAS SO TERRIFYING...
I...
FWSH
...
I RAN OUT OF MINERAL WATER IN THE KITCHEN, SO I WENT DOWN TO THE BASEMENT TO GET SOME MORE...
AND... AND THEN...
IN THE CORNER... ON TOP OF THE POTATO SACK...THERE WAS A CAT I'D NEVER SEEN BEFORE.
IT WAS JUST SITTING THERE, COMPLETELY STILL.
A CAT ...?

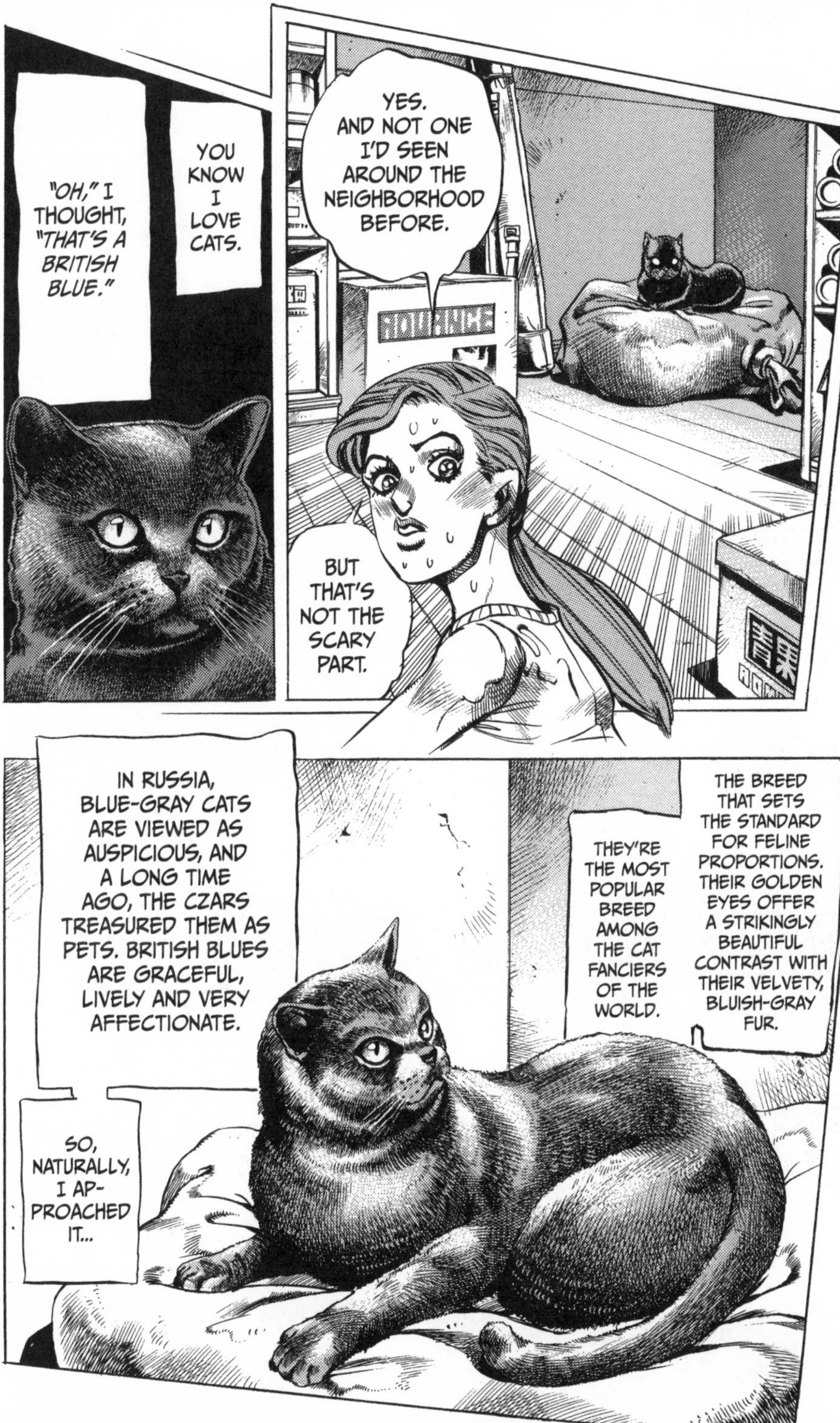
YES. AND NOT ONE I'D SEEN AROUND THE NEIGHBORHOOD BEFORE.
BUT THAT'S NOT THE SCARY PART.
YOU KNOW I LOVE CATS.
"OH," I THOUGHT, "THAT'S A BRITISH BLUE."
THE BREED THAT SETS THE STANDARD FOR FELINE PROPORTIONS. THEIR GOLDEN EYES OFFER A STRIKINGLY BEAUTIFUL CONTRAST WITH THEIR VELVETY, BLUISH-GRAY FUR.
THEY'RE THE MOST POPULAR BREED AMONG THE CAT FANCIERS OF THE WORLD.
IN RUSSIA, BLUE-GRAY CATS ARE VIEWED AS AUSPICIOUS, AND A LONG TIME AGO, THE CZARS TREASURED THEM AS PETS. BRITISH BLUES ARE GRACEFUL, LIVELY AND VERY AFFECTIONATE.
SO, NATURALLY, I AP-PROACHED IT...

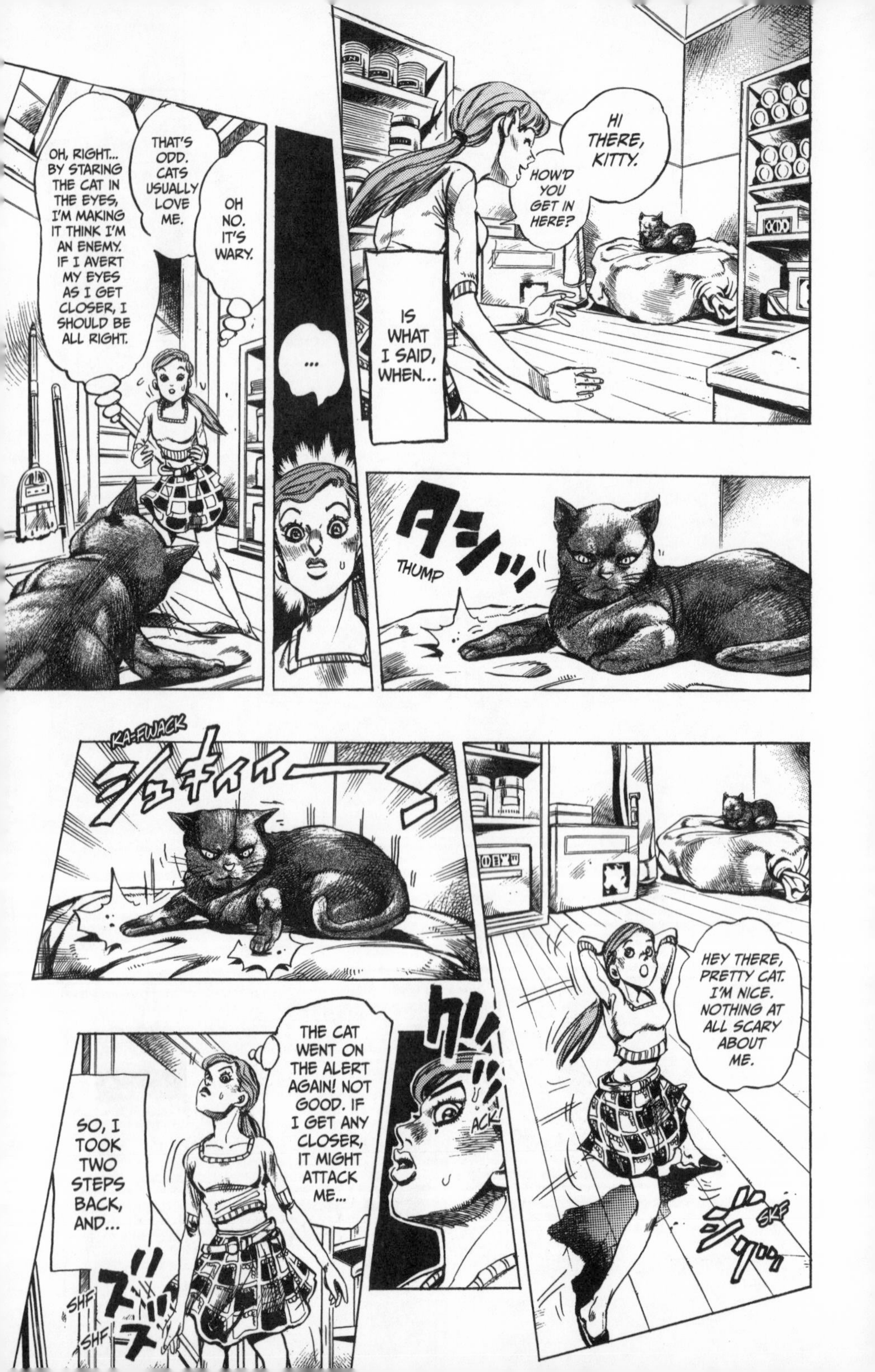
HI THERE, KITTY.
HOW'D YOU GET IN HERE?
IS WHAT I SAID, WHEN...
THUMP
...
OH NO. IT'S WARY.
THAT'S ODD. CATS USUALLY LOVE ME.
OH, RIGHT... BY STARING THE CAT IN THE EYES, I'M MAKING IT THINK I'M AN ENEMY. IF I AVERT MY EYES AS I GET CLOSER, I SHOULD BE ALL RIGHT.
HEY THERE, PRETTY CAT. I'M NICE. NOTHING AT ALL SCARY ABOUT ME.
SKF
KA-FWACK
ACK!
THE CAT WENT ON THE ALERT AGAIN! NOT GOOD. IF I GET ANY CLOSER, IT MIGHT ATTACK ME...
SO, I TOOK TWO STEPS BACK, AND...
SHF
SHF

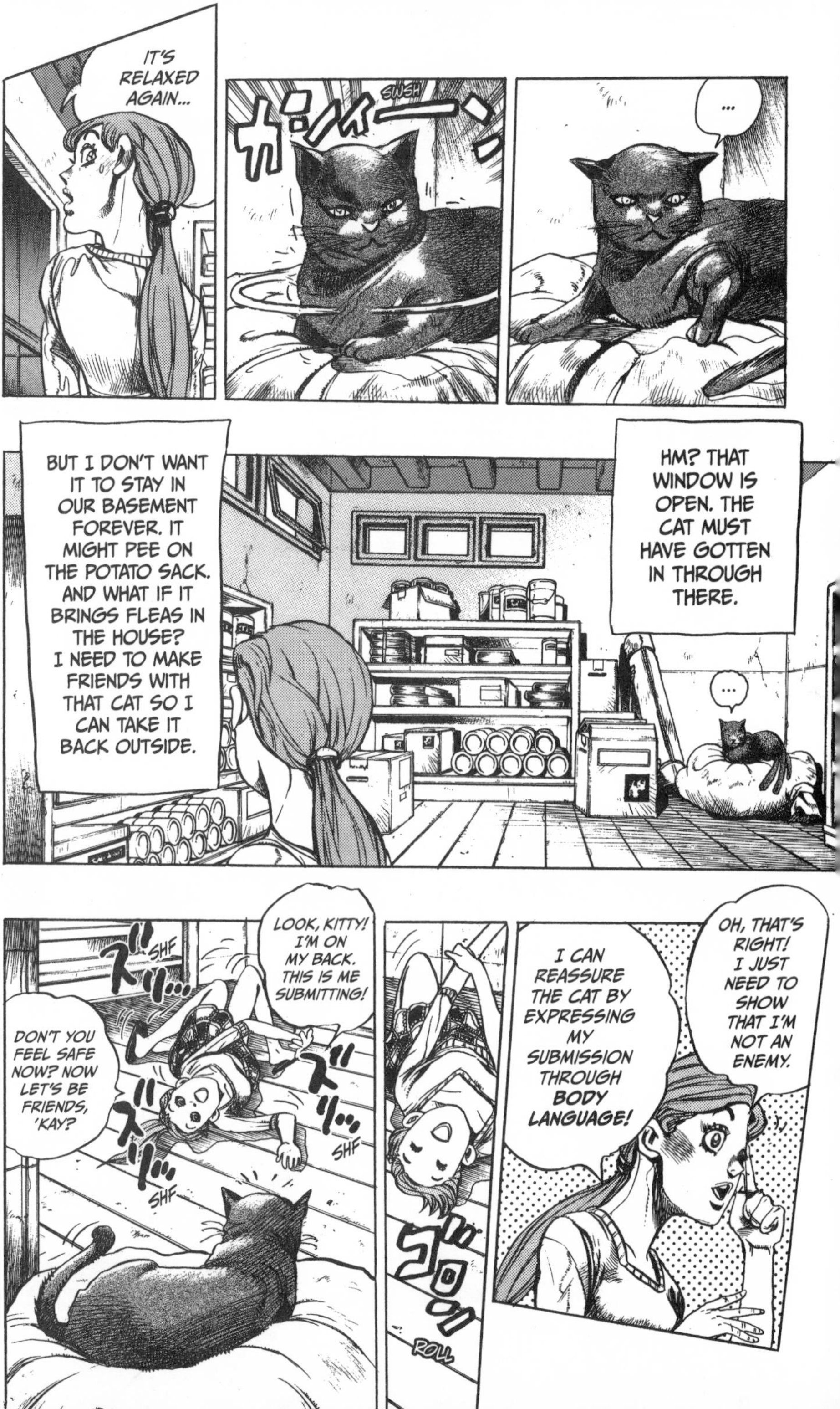
...
SWSH
IT'S RELAXED AGAIN...
HM? THAT WINDOW IS OPEN. THE CAT MUST HAVE GOTTEN IN THROUGH THERE.
BUT I DON'T WANT IT TO STAY IN OUR BASEMENT FOREVER. IT MIGHT PEE ON THE POTATO SACK. AND WHAT IF IT BRINGS FLEAS IN THE HOUSE? I NEED TO MAKE FRIENDS WITH THAT CAT SO I CAN TAKE IT BACK OUTSIDE.
...
OH, THAT'S RIGHT! I JUST NEED TO SHOW THAT I'M NOT AN ENEMY.
I CAN REASSURE THE CAT BY EXPRESSING MY SUBMISSION THROUGH BODY LANGUAGE!
ROLL
LOOK, KITTY! I'M ON MY BACK. THIS IS ME SUBMITTING!
SHF
SHF
DON'T YOU FEEL SAFE NOW? NOW LET'S BE FRIENDS, 'KAY?
SHF

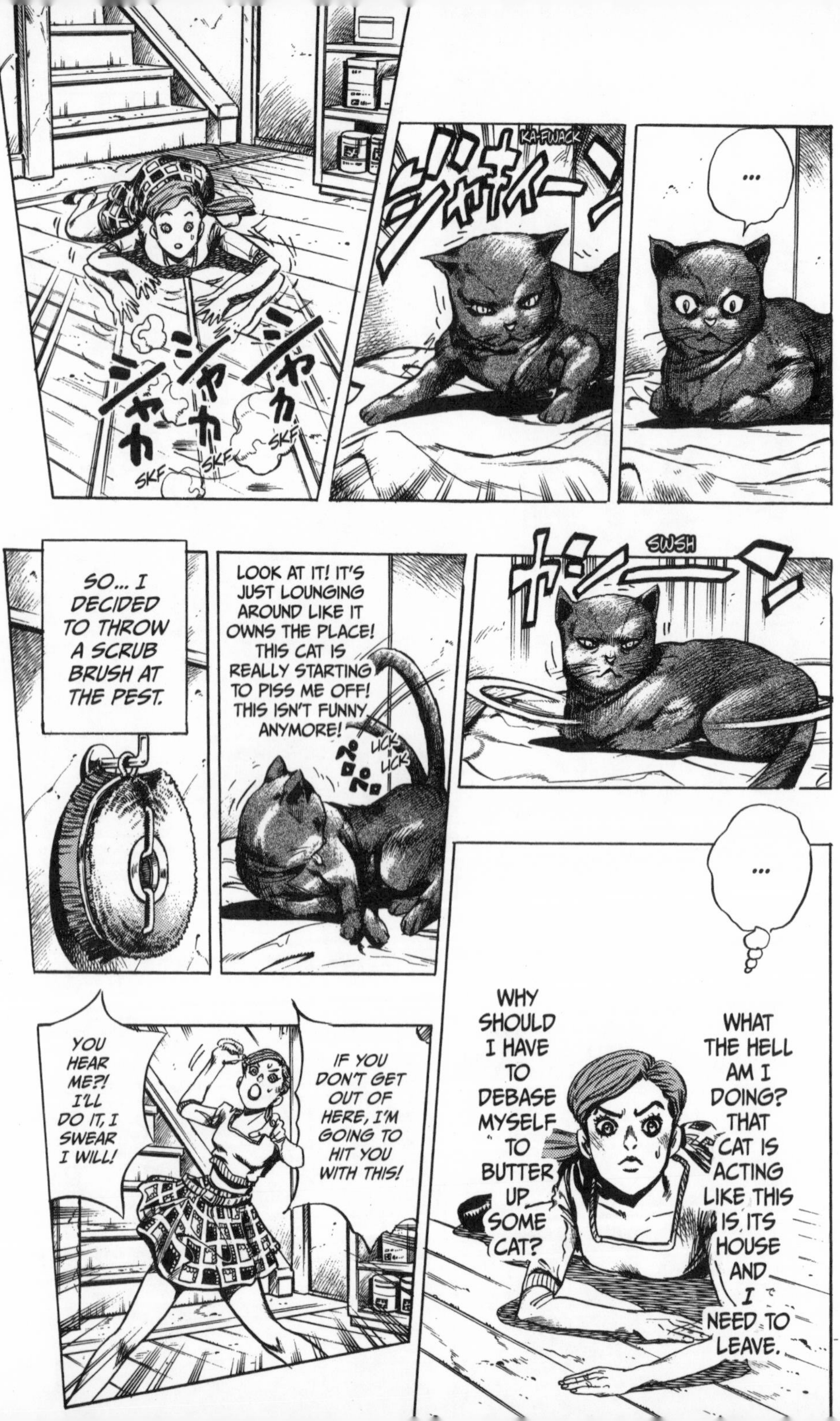

...
KA-FWACK
SKF
SKF
SKF
SWSH
LOOK AT IT! IT'S JUST LOUNGING AROUND LIKE IT OWNS THE PLACE! THIS CAT IS REALLY STARTING TO PISS ME OFF! THIS ISN'T FUNNY ANYMORE!
LICK LICK
SO... I DECIDED TO THROW A SCRUB BRUSH AT THE PEST.
...
WHAT THE HELL AM I DOING? THAT CAT IS ACTING LIKE THIS IS ITS HOUSE AND I NEED TO LEAVE.
WHY SHOULD I HAVE TO DEBASE MYSELF TO BUTTER UP SOME CAT?
IF YOU DON'T GET OUT OF HERE, I'M GOING TO HIT YOU WITH THIS!
YOU HEAR ME?! I'LL DO IT, I SWEAR I WILL!

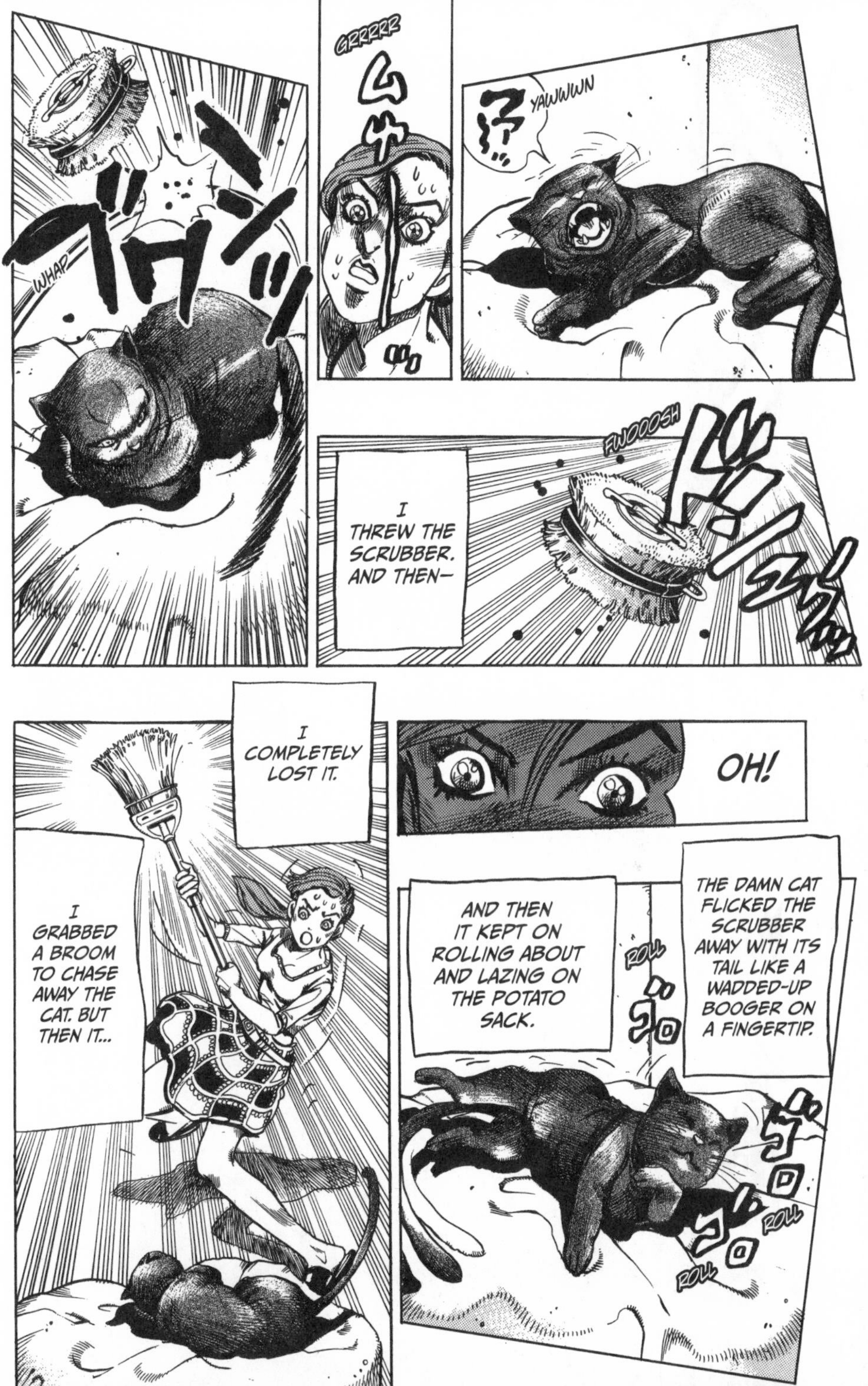
YAWWWN
GRRRRR
I THREW THE SCRUBBER. AND THEN—
FWOOOSH
WHAP
OH!
THE DAMN CAT FLICKED THE SCRUBBER AWAY WITH ITS TAIL LIKE A WADDED-UP BOOGER ON A FINGERTIP.
AND THEN IT KEPT ON ROLLING ABOUT AND LAZING ON THE POTATO SACK.
ROLL
ROLL
ROLL
I COMPLETELY LOST IT.
I GRABBED A BROOM TO CHASE AWAY THE CAT. BUT THEN IT...

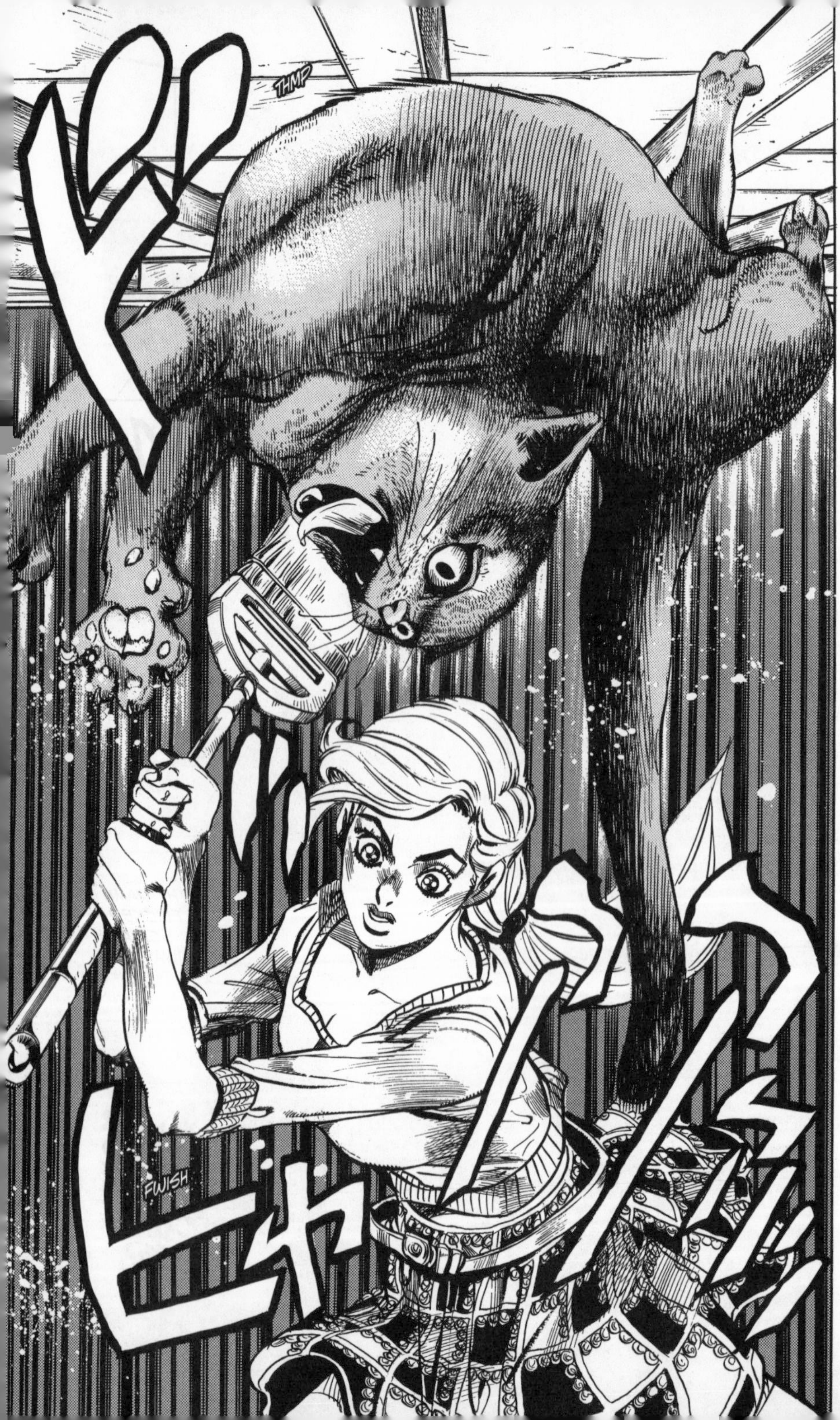
THMP
FWISH

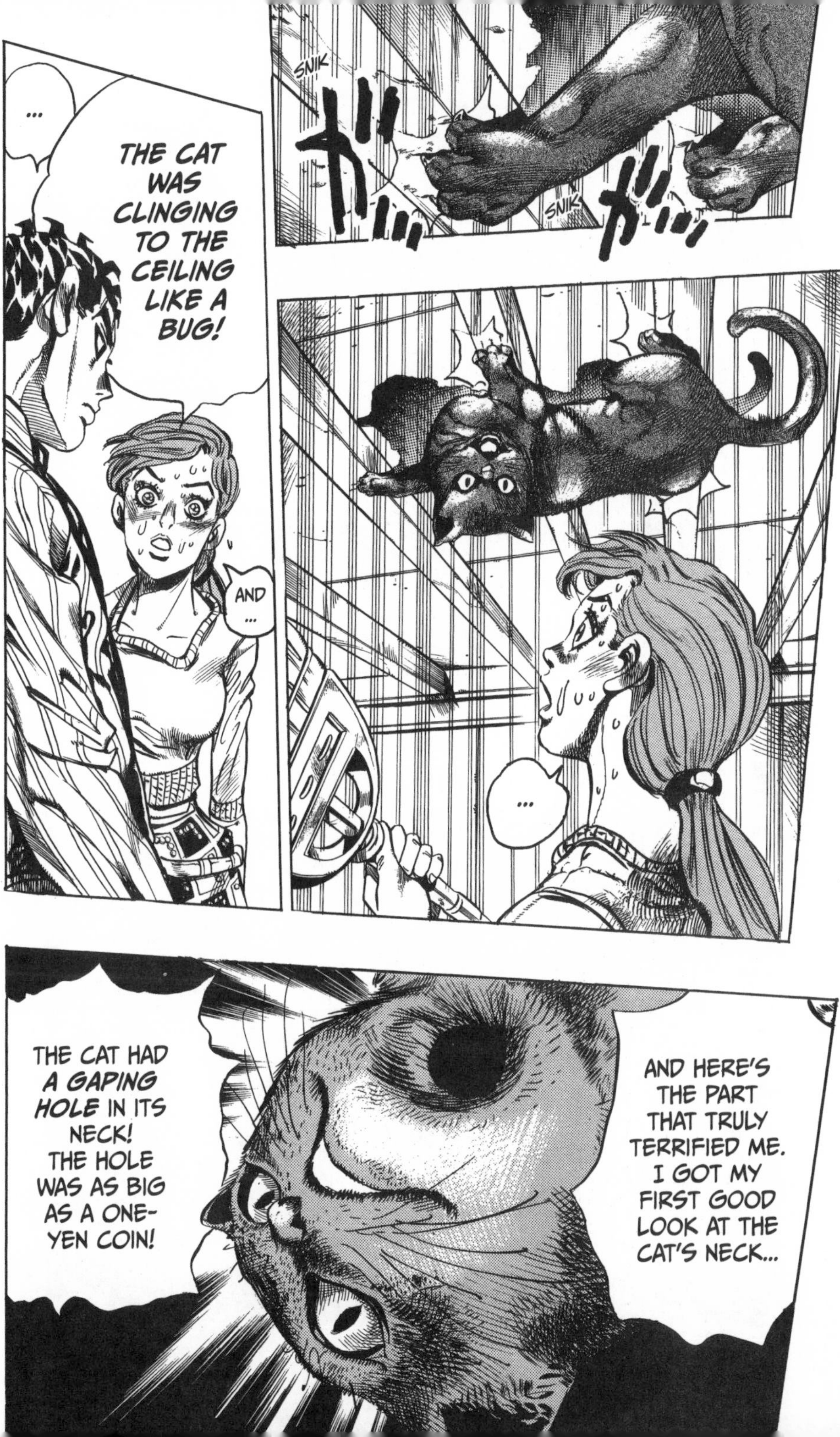
SNIK
SNIK
...
...
THE CAT WAS CLINGING TO THE CEILING LIKE A BUG!
AND ...
AND HERE'S THE PART THAT TRULY TERRIFIED ME. I GOT MY FIRST GOOD LOOK AT THE CAT'S NECK...
THE CAT HAD *A GAPING HOLE* IN ITS NECK! THE HOLE WAS AS BIG AS A ONE-YEN COIN!

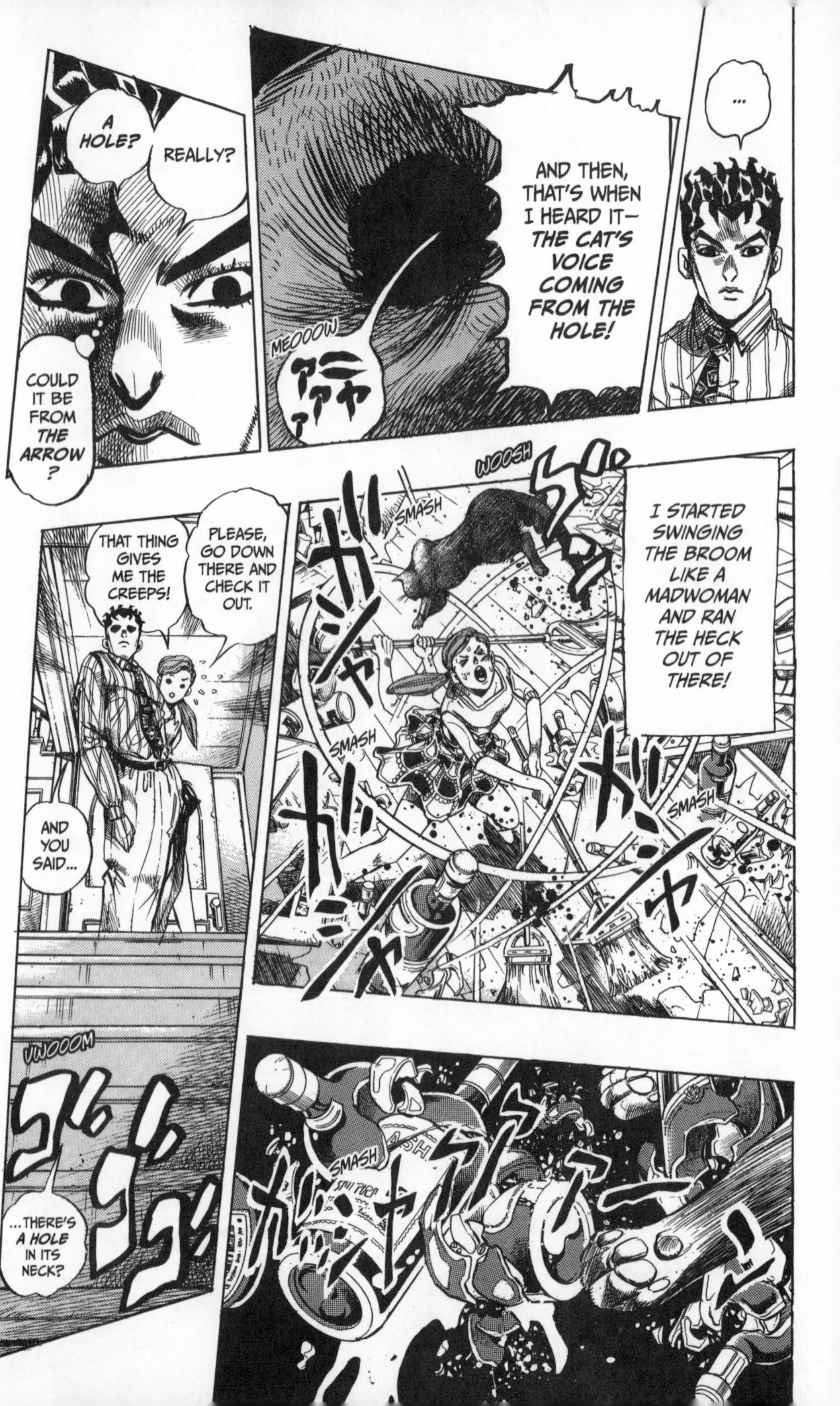
...
AND THEN, THAT'S WHEN I HEARD IT— THE CAT'S VOICE COMING FROM THE HOLE!
MEOOOW
A HOLE?
REALLY?
COULD IT BE FROM THE ARROW?
I STARTED SWINGING THE BROOM LIKE A MADWOMAN AND RAN THE HECK OUT OF THERE!
WOOSH
SMASH
SMASH
SMASH
PLEASE, GO DOWN THERE AND CHECK IT OUT.
THAT THING GIVES ME THE CREEPS!
AND YOU SAID...
SMASH
UWOOOM
...THERE'S A HOLE IN ITS NECK?

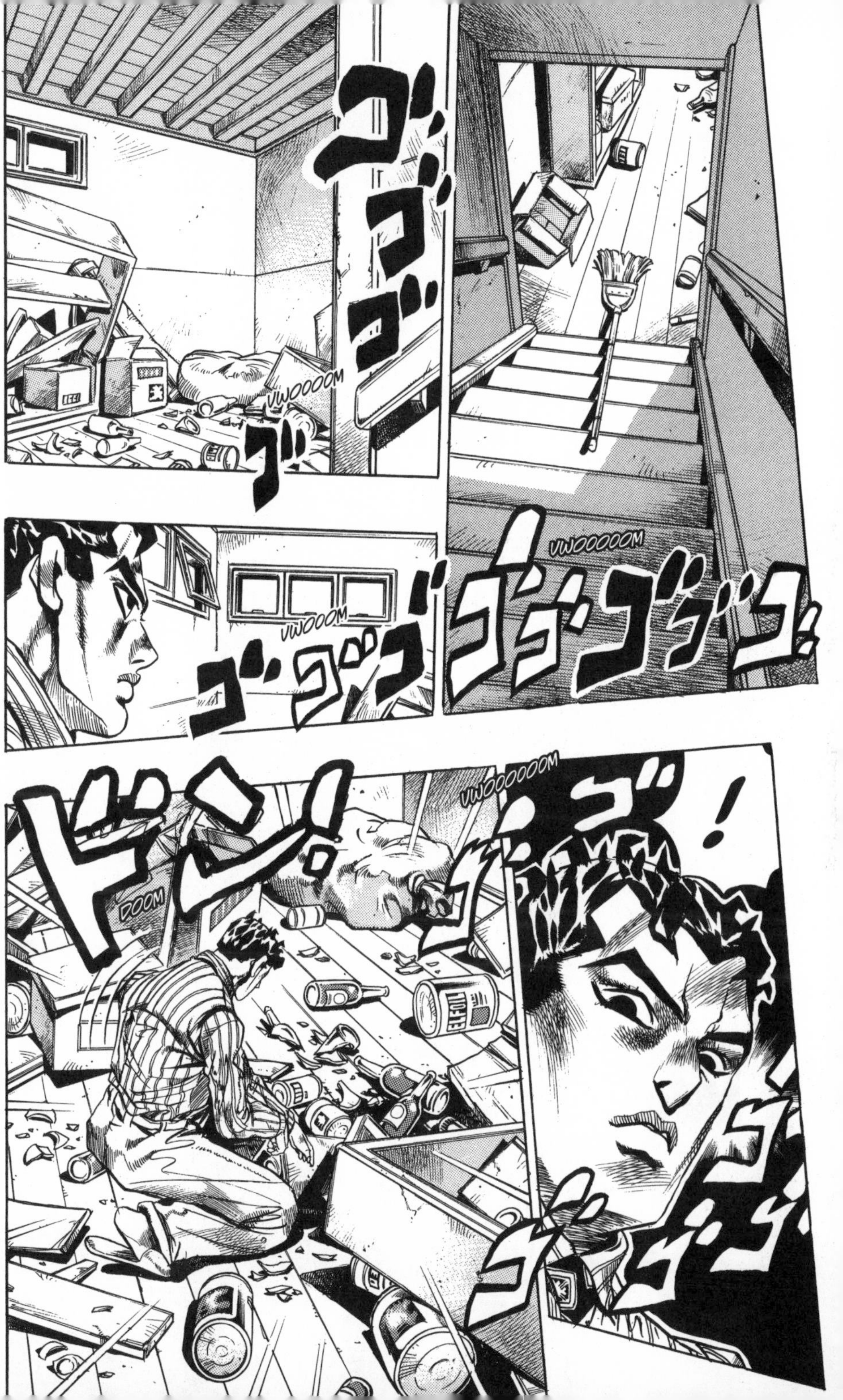
VWOOOOOM
ゴゴゴゴゴゴン!
ゴゴゴゴ
VWOOOOM
VWOOOM
ゴゴゴゴ
VWOOOOOOOM
ゴ!
ゴゴゴゴ
ドン!
DOOM

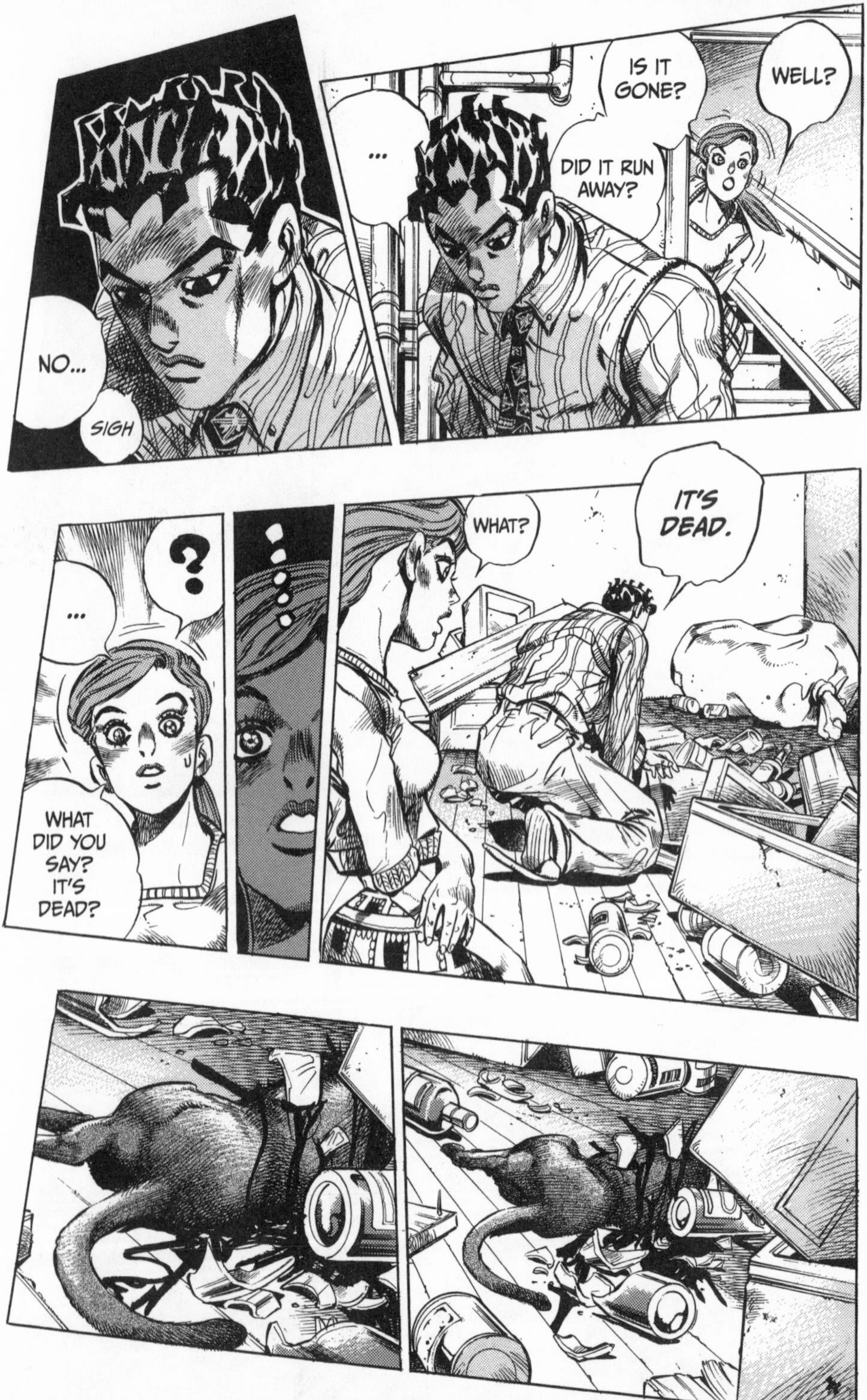
WELL?
IS IT GONE?
DID IT RUN AWAY?
...
NO...
SIGH
IT'S DEAD.
WHAT?
?
...
WHAT DID YOU SAY? IT'S DEAD?

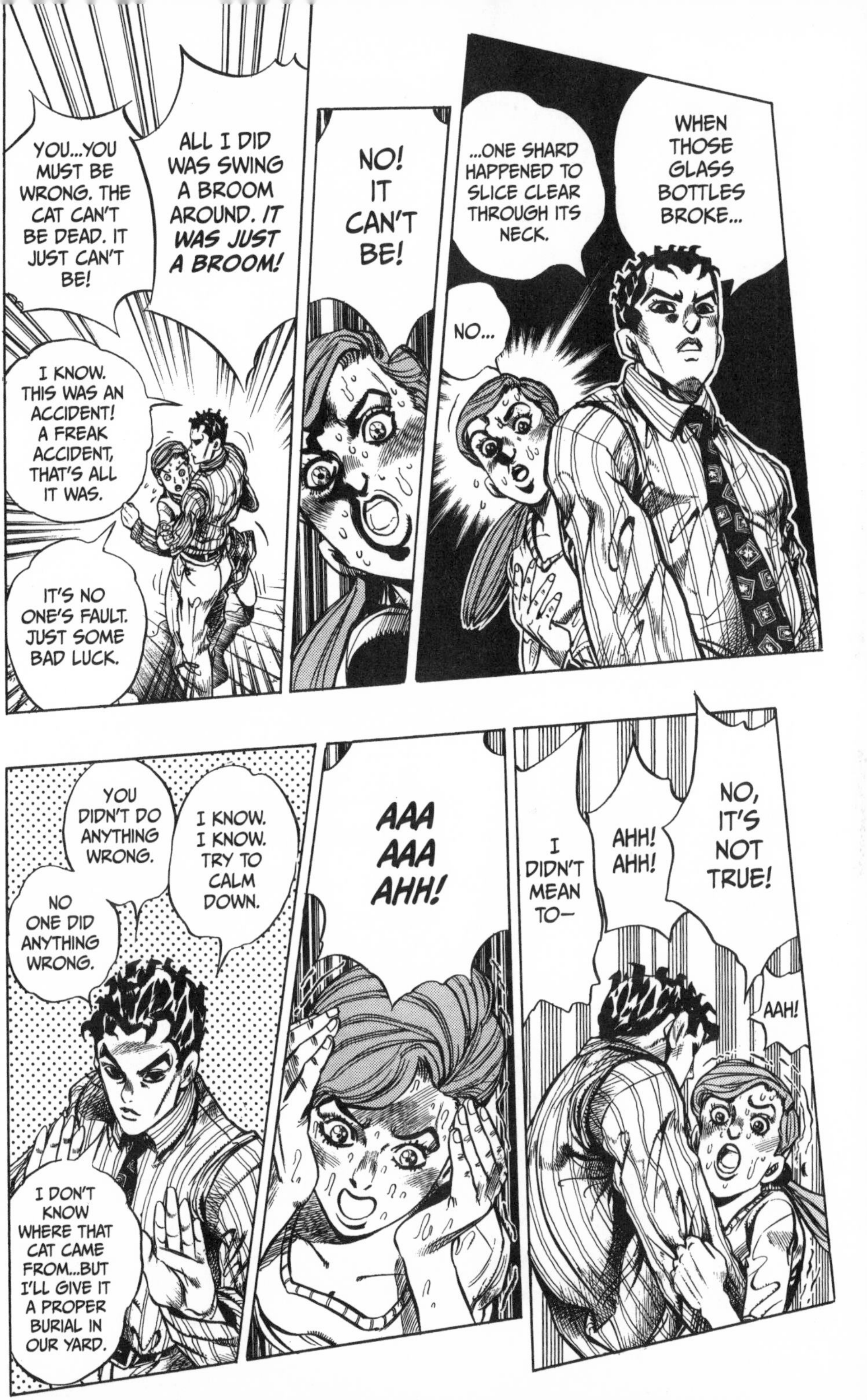
WHEN THOSE GLASS BOTTLES BROKE...
...ONE SHARD HAPPENED TO SLICE CLEAR THROUGH ITS NECK.
NO...
NO! IT CAN'T BE!
ALL I DID WAS SWING A BROOM AROUND. *IT WAS JUST A BROOM!*
YOU...YOU MUST BE WRONG. THE CAT CAN'T BE DEAD. IT JUST CAN'T BE!
I KNOW. THIS WAS AN ACCIDENT! A FREAK ACCIDENT, THAT'S ALL IT WAS.
IT'S NO ONE'S FAULT. JUST SOME BAD LUCK.
NO, IT'S NOT TRUE!
AHH! AHH!
I DIDN'T MEAN TO—
AAH!
AAA AAA AHH!
I KNOW. I KNOW. TRY TO CALM DOWN.
YOU DIDN'T DO ANYTHING WRONG.
NO ONE DID ANYTHING WRONG.
I DON'T KNOW WHERE THAT CAT CAME FROM...BUT I'LL GIVE IT A PROPER BURIAL IN OUR YARD.

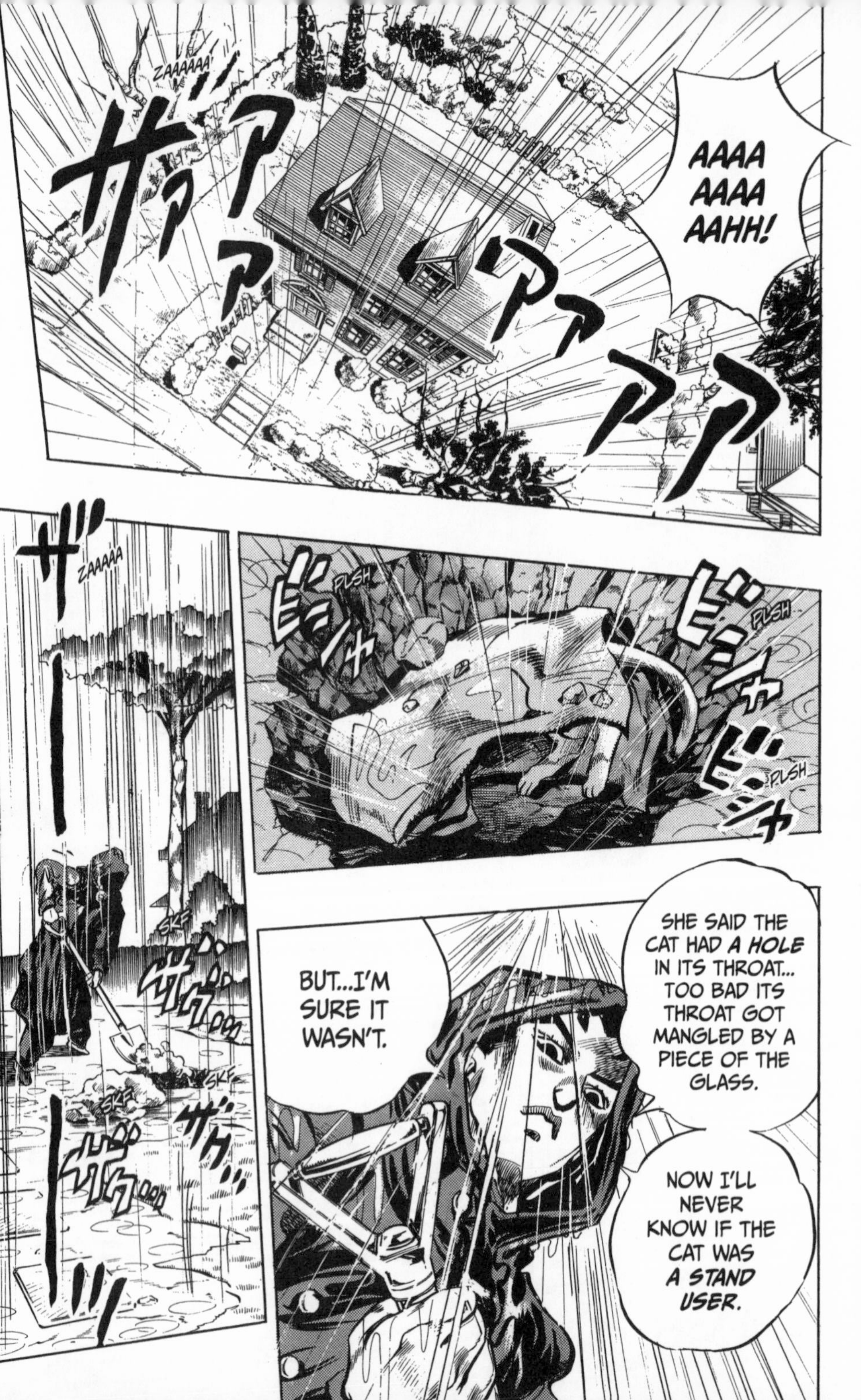
AAAA AAAA AAHH!
ZAAAAAA
PUSH
PUSH
PUSH
SHE SAID THE CAT HAD A ***HOLE*** IN ITS THROAT... TOO BAD ITS THROAT GOT MANGLED BY A PIECE OF THE GLASS.
BUT...I'M SURE IT WASN'T.
NOW I'LL NEVER KNOW IF THE CAT WAS ***A STAND USER.***
ZAAAAA
SKF
SKF
SKF

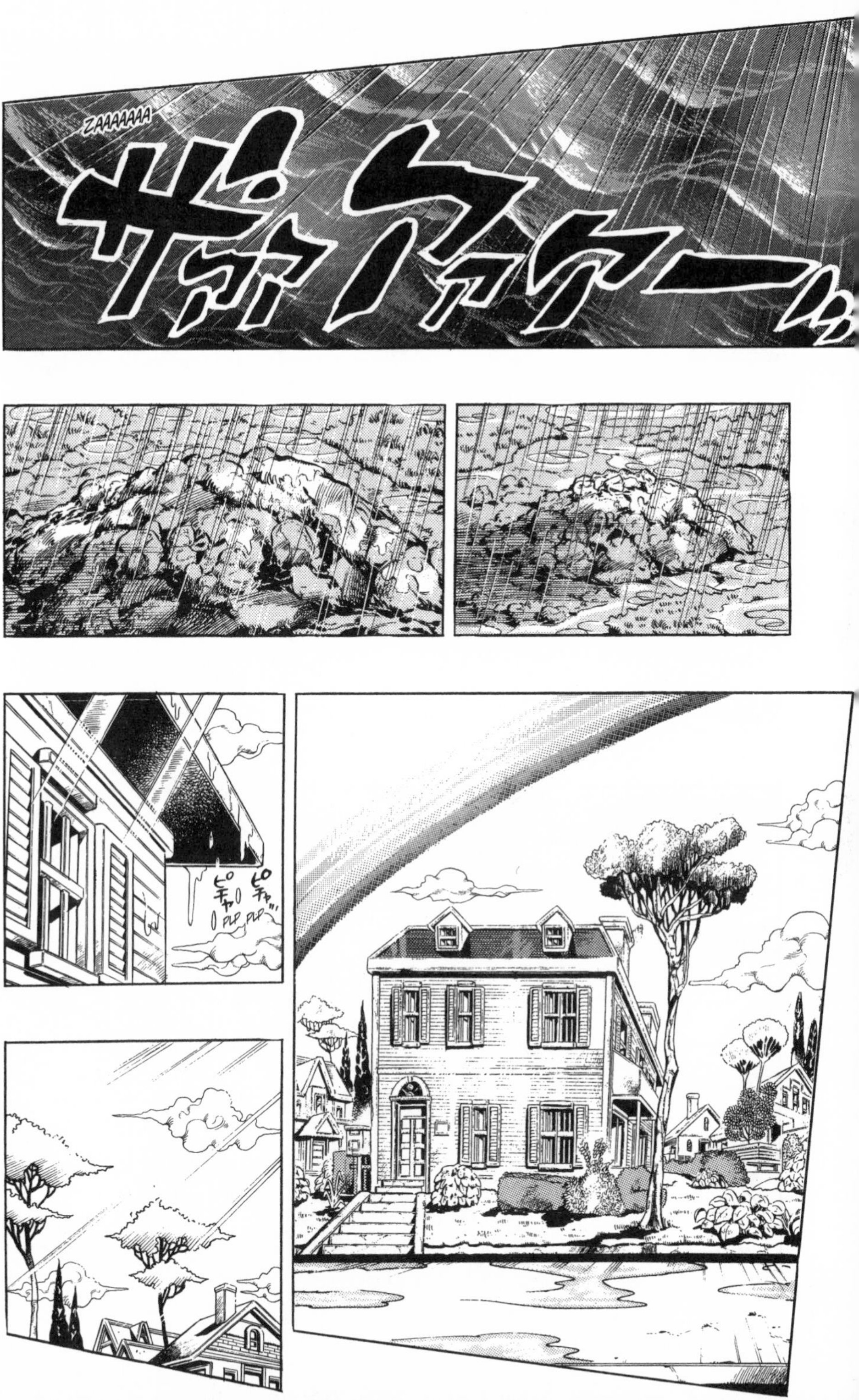
ZAAAAAAA
ザァァァァァーーーッ
ピチャ
ピチャ…
PLP PLP

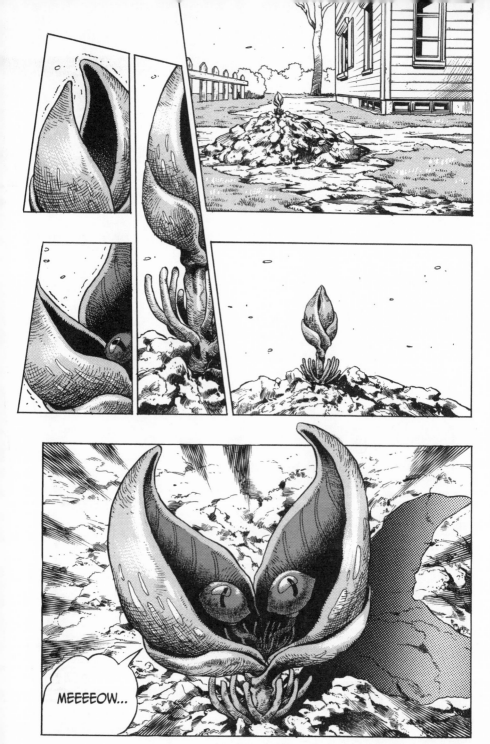

MEEEEOW...

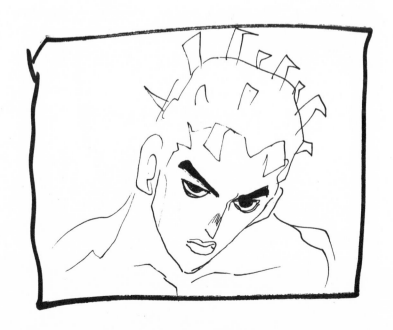

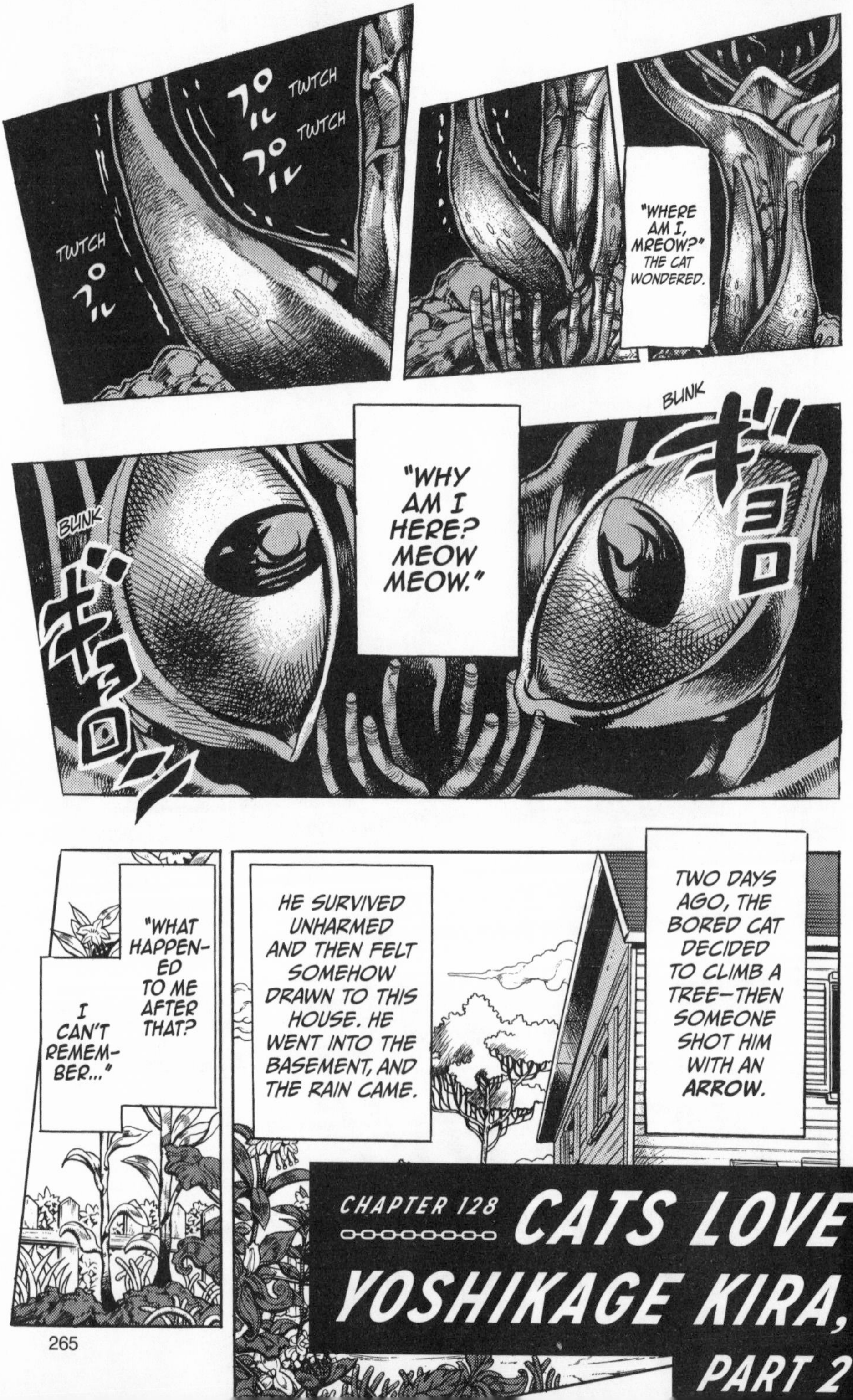
"WHERE AM I, MREOW?" THE CAT WONDERED.
TWTCH
TWTCH
TWTCH
BLINK
"WHY AM I HERE? MEOW MEOW."
BLINK
TWO DAYS AGO, THE BORED CAT DECIDED TO CLIMB A TREE—THEN SOMEONE SHOT HIM WITH AN ARROW.
HE SURVIVED UNHARMED AND THEN FELT SOMEHOW DRAWN TO THIS HOUSE. HE WENT INTO THE BASEMENT, AND THE RAIN CAME.
"WHAT HAPPENED TO ME AFTER THAT?
I CAN'T REMEMBER..."
CHAPTER 128
CATS LOVE YOSHIKAGE KIRA, PART 2

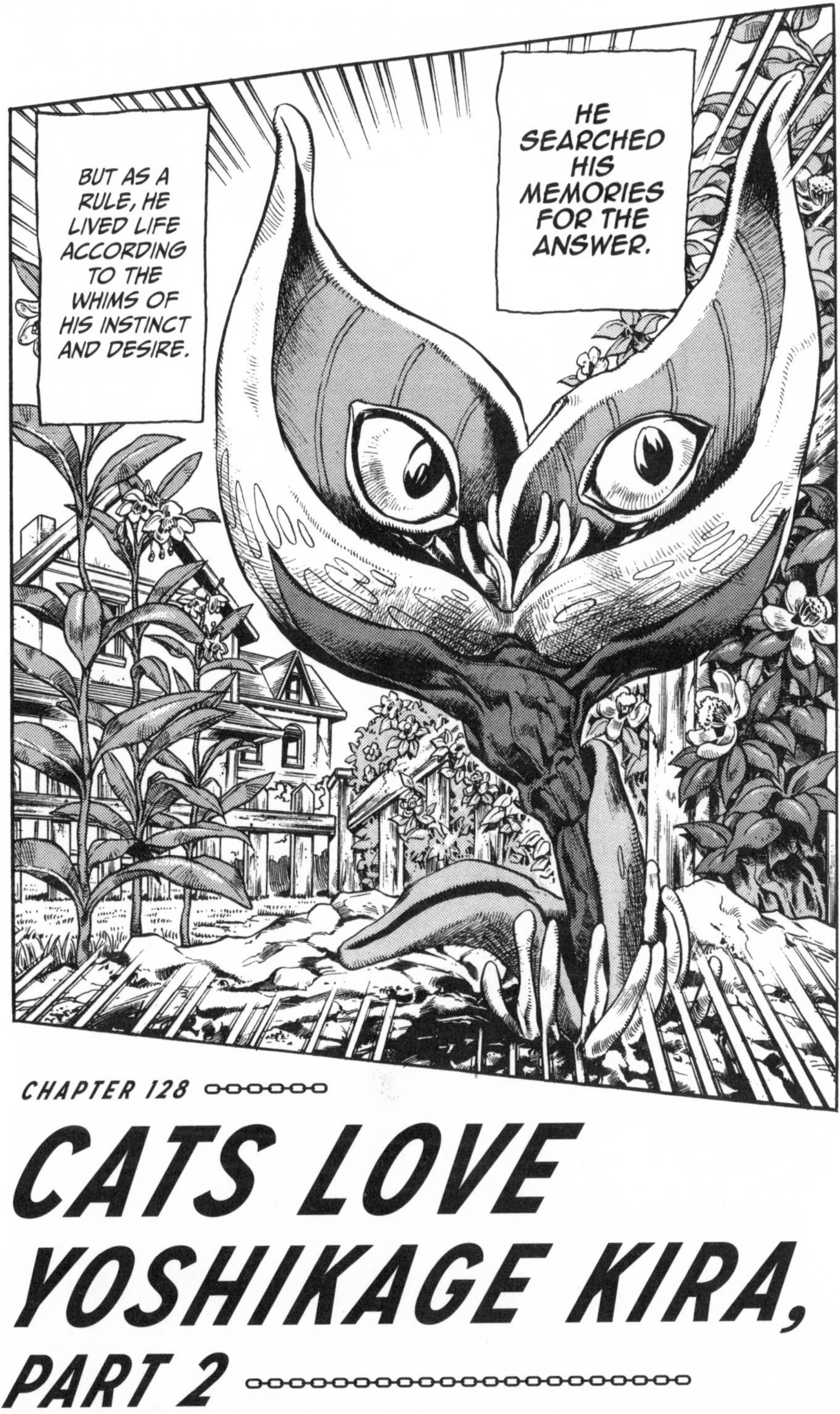
HE SEARCHED HIS MEMORIES FOR THE ANSWER.
BUT AS A RULE, HE LIVED LIFE ACCORDING TO THE WHIMS OF HIS INSTINCT AND DESIRE.

CHAPTER 128

CATS LOVE YOSHIKAGE KIRA, PART 2

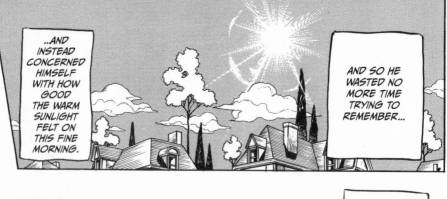

AND SO HE WASTED NO MORE TIME TRYING TO REMEMBER...
...AND INSTEAD CONCERNED HIMSELF WITH HOW GOOD THE WARM SUNLIGHT FELT ON THIS FINE MORNING.
"FIRST UP— GROOMING! DOESN'T MY FUR DESERVE TO BE BRUSHED?"
MEOW MEOW
ミャン ミャン
MEOW
LICK
LICK
LICK
MEOW
HM?
SNIF SNIF
...?
SNIF SNIF
WHAT'S THAT GRASSY SMELL?
MY FORELEGS SMELL LIKE GRASS. I WONDER WHERE THAT SMELL GOT ON ME...
?
OH WELL. NEXT UP— MY TAIL!
FWSH

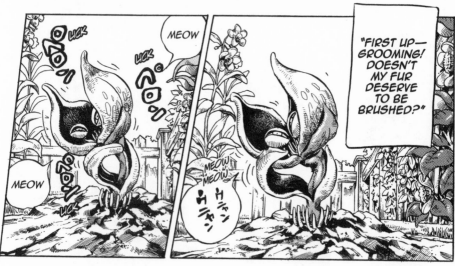

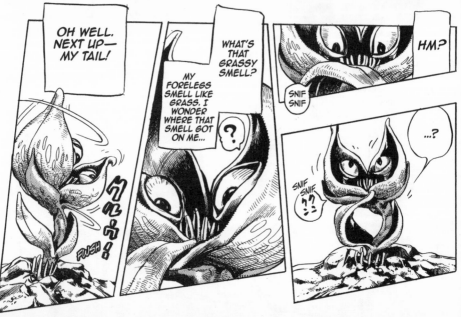

MEOW ?!
MYA-MEOW ?
!
キョロ
キョロ
GLANCE GLANCE
WHAT'S GOING ON? WHERE'S MY TAIL?
WHERE'S MY PRECIOUS TAIL?!
AFTER I GROOM MY FACE, MY TAIL COMES NEXT. I SO LOVE TO BITE AT THE FUR TO SOFTEN IT, THEN COMB IT BACK INTO PROPER PLACE WITH MY TONGUE.
BUT MY TAIL IS GONE! WHERE DID IT GO?!
HM?
HM ??
BZZZZZ
...
BZZZZ
BZZZZ
...
MEOW
ニャッ
PWSH
BZZZZ
GRR!

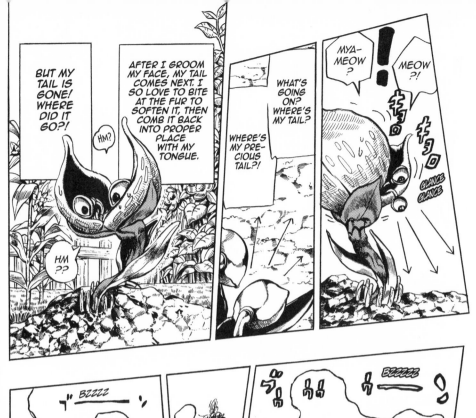

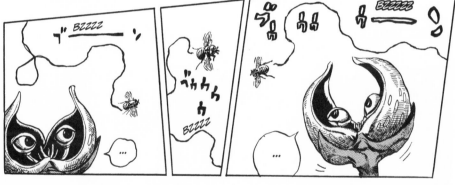

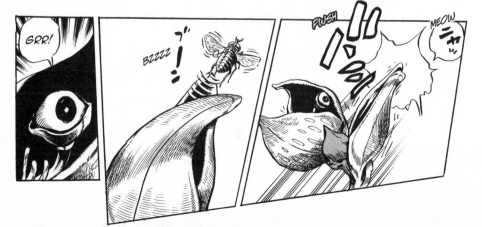

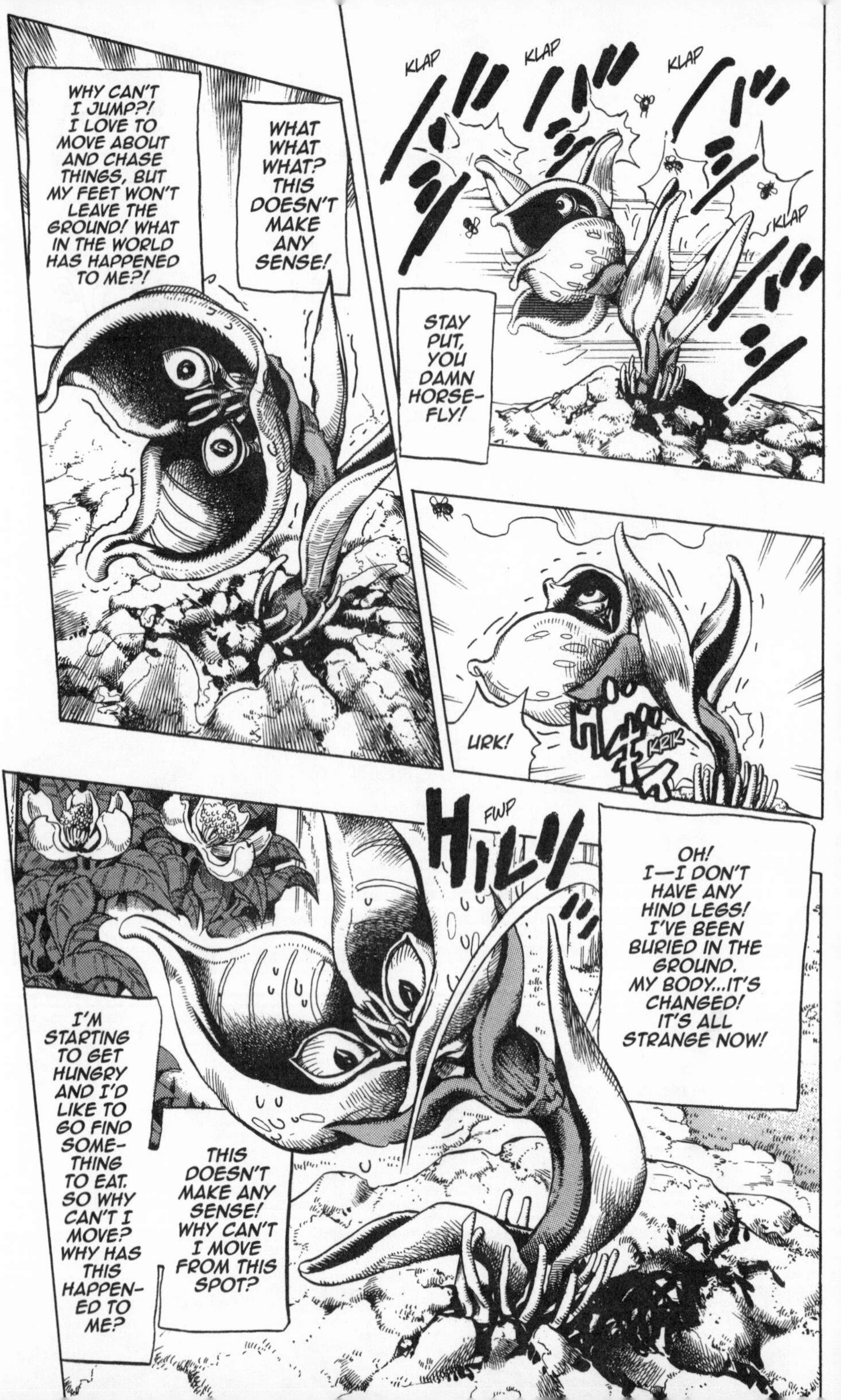

KLAP
KLAP
KLAP
KLAP
STAY PUT, YOU DAMN HORSE-FLY!
URK!
KRIK
WHY CAN'T I JUMP?! I LOVE TO MOVE ABOUT AND CHASE THINGS, BUT MY FEET WON'T LEAVE THE GROUND! WHAT IN THE WORLD HAS HAPPENED TO ME?!
WHAT WHAT WHAT? THIS DOESN'T MAKE ANY SENSE!
FWP
OH! I—I DON'T HAVE ANY HIND LEGS! I'VE BEEN BURIED IN THE GROUND. MY BODY...IT'S CHANGED! IT'S ALL STRANGE NOW!
I'M STARTING TO GET HUNGRY AND I'D LIKE TO GO FIND SOME-THING TO EAT. SO WHY CAN'T I MOVE? WHY HAS THIS HAPPEN-ED TO ME?
THIS DOESN'T MAKE ANY SENSE! WHY CAN'T I MOVE FROM THIS SPOT?

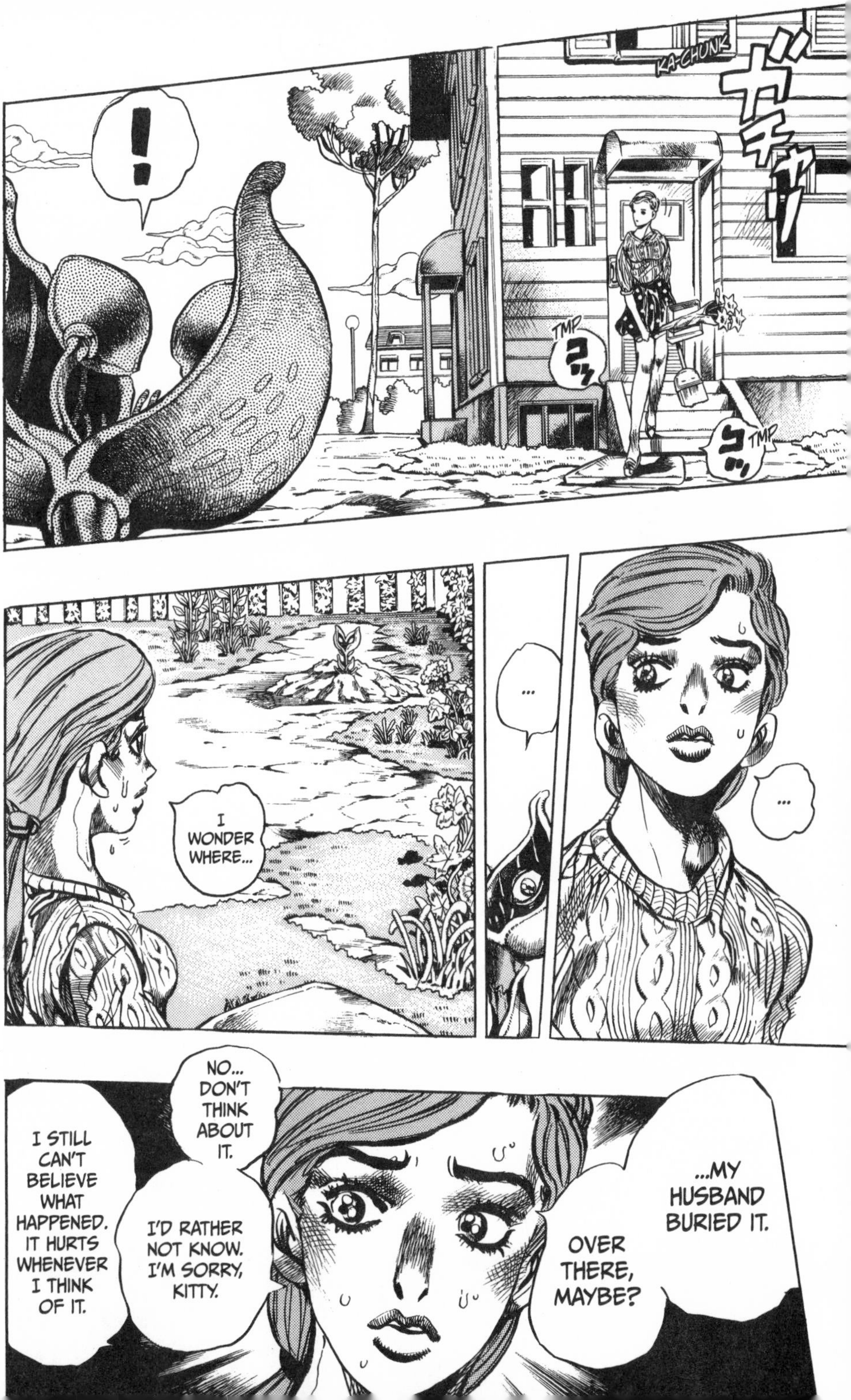
KA-CHUNK
TMP
TMP
!
...
...
I WONDER WHERE...
...MY HUSBAND BURIED IT.
OVER THERE, MAYBE?
NO... DON'T THINK ABOUT IT.
I'D RATHER NOT KNOW. I'M SORRY, KITTY.
I STILL CAN'T BELIEVE WHAT HAPPENED. IT HURTS WHENEVER I THINK OF IT.

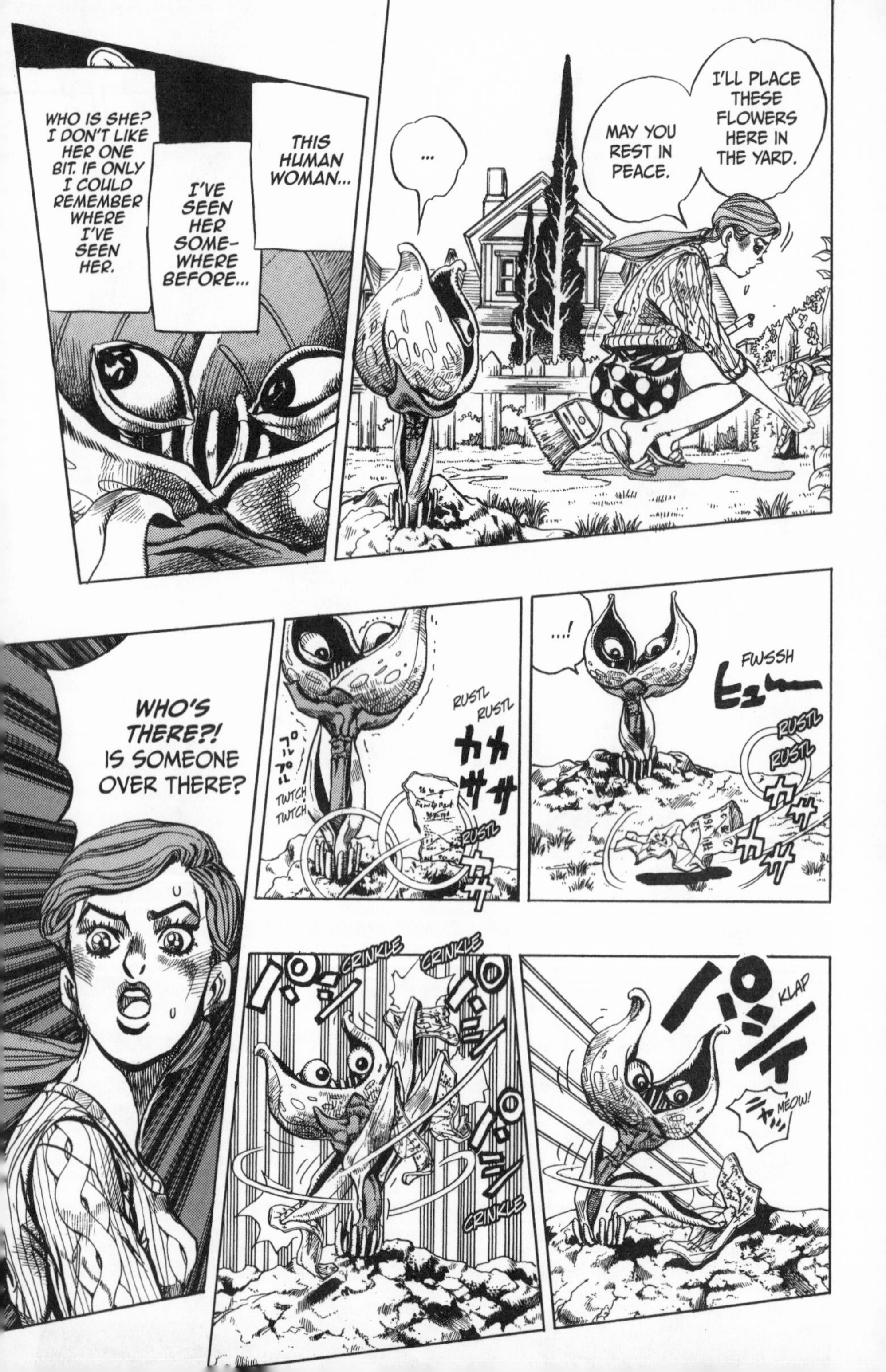
I'LL PLACE THESE FLOWERS HERE IN THE YARD.
MAY YOU REST IN PEACE.
...
THIS HUMAN WOMAN...
I'VE SEEN HER SOMEWHERE BEFORE...
WHO IS SHE? I DON'T LIKE HER ONE BIT. IF ONLY I COULD REMEMBER WHERE I'VE SEEN HER.
...!
FWSSH
ヒュー
RUSTL
RUSTL
カサ
カサ
RUSTL RUSTL
カカ
ササ
プルプル
TWTCH TWTCH
RUSTL
カサ
KLAP
パシィ
ニャ
MEOW!
CRINKLE
CRINKLE
パシ
パシ
CRINKLE
WHO'S THERE?! IS SOMEONE OVER THERE?

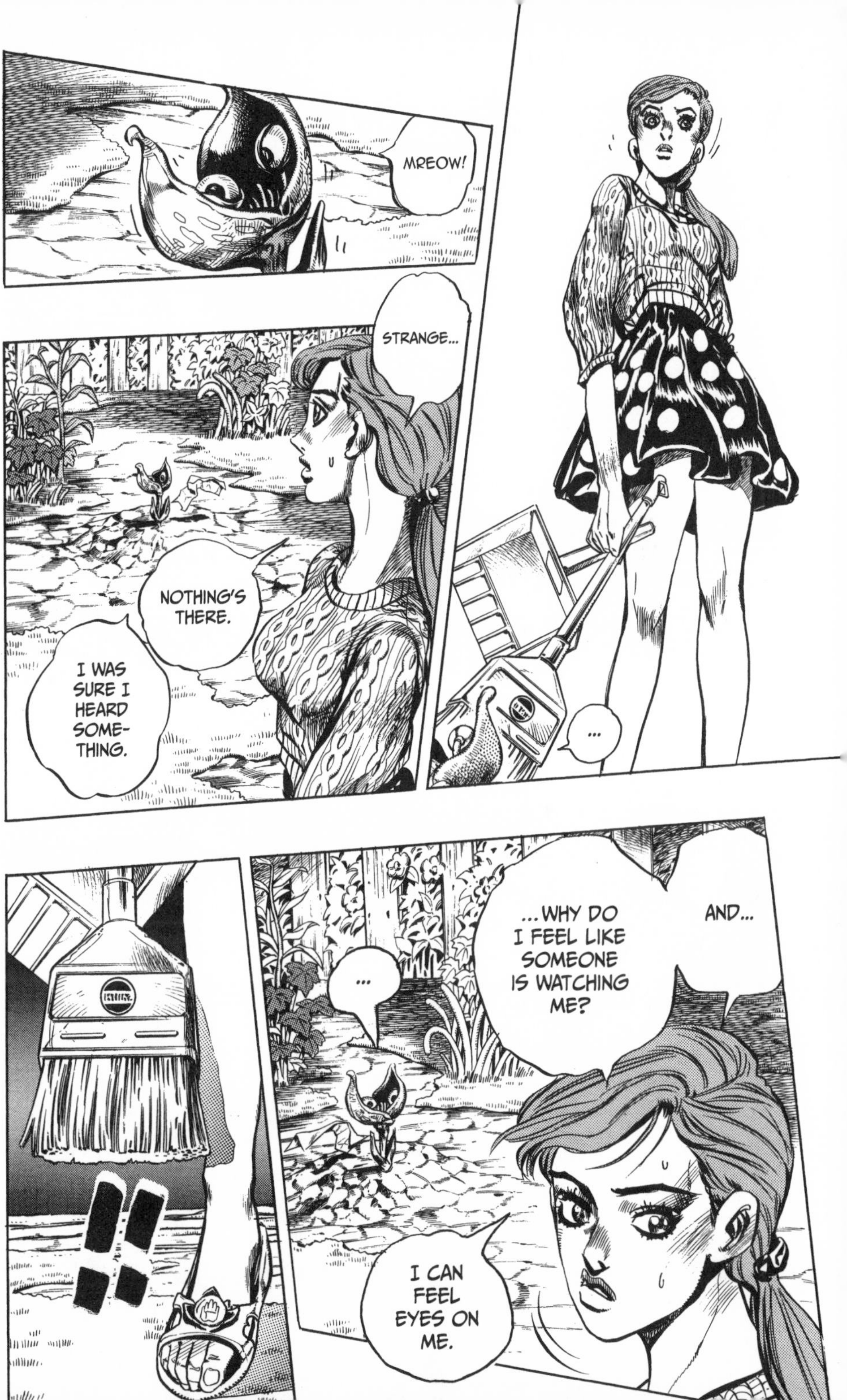
...
MREOW!
STRANGE...
NOTHING'S THERE.
I WAS SURE I HEARD SOME-THING.
AND...
...WHY DO I FEEL LIKE SOMEONE IS WATCHING ME?
...
I CAN FEEL EYES ON ME.

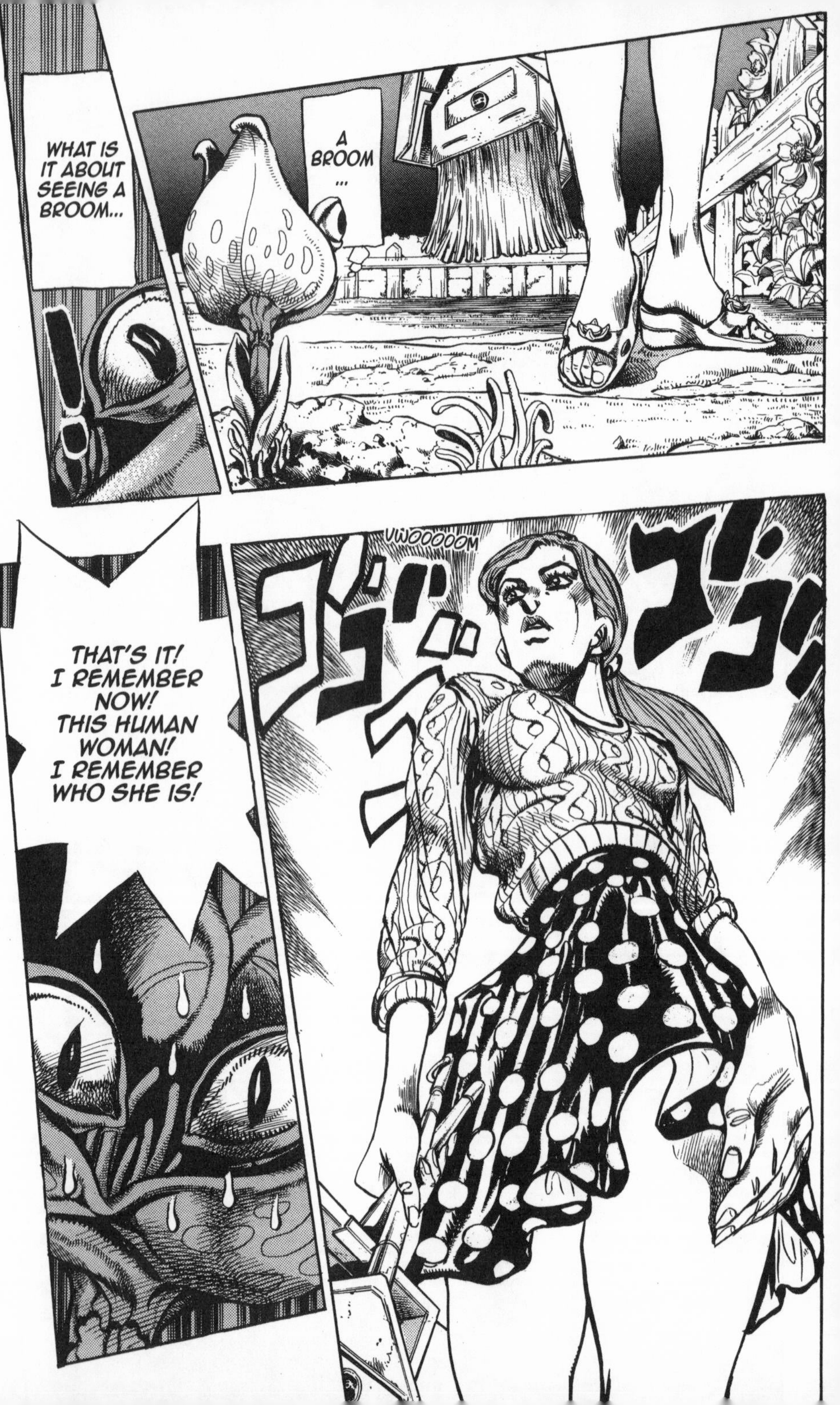
A BROOM ...
WHAT IS IT ABOUT SEEING A BROOM...
VWOOOOOM
THAT'S IT! I REMEMBER NOW! THIS HUMAN WOMAN! I REMEMBER WHO SHE IS!

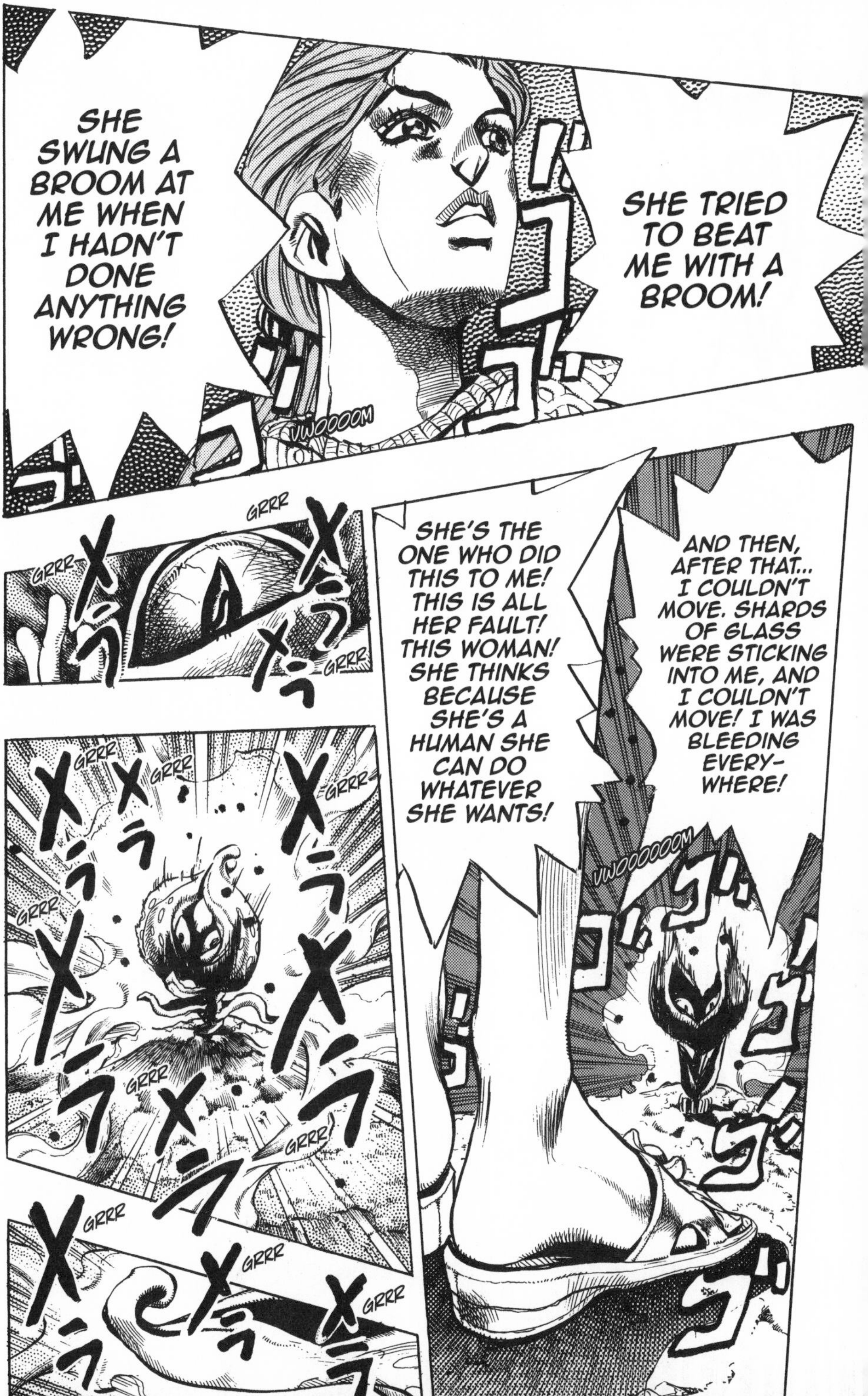
SHE TRIED TO BEAT ME WITH A BROOM!
SHE SWUNG A BROOM AT ME WHEN I HADN'T DONE ANYTHING WRONG!
VWOOOOM
AND THEN, AFTER THAT... I COULDN'T MOVE. SHARDS OF GLASS WERE STICKING INTO ME, AND I COULDN'T MOVE! I WAS BLEEDING EVERY-WHERE!
SHE'S THE ONE WHO DID THIS TO ME! THIS IS ALL HER FAULT! THIS WOMAN! SHE THINKS BECAUSE SHE'S A HUMAN SHE CAN DO WHATEVER SHE WANTS!
VWOOOOOOM
GRRR
GRRR
GRRR
GRRR
GRRR
GRRR
GRRR
GRRR
GRRR
GRRR
GRRR
GRRR

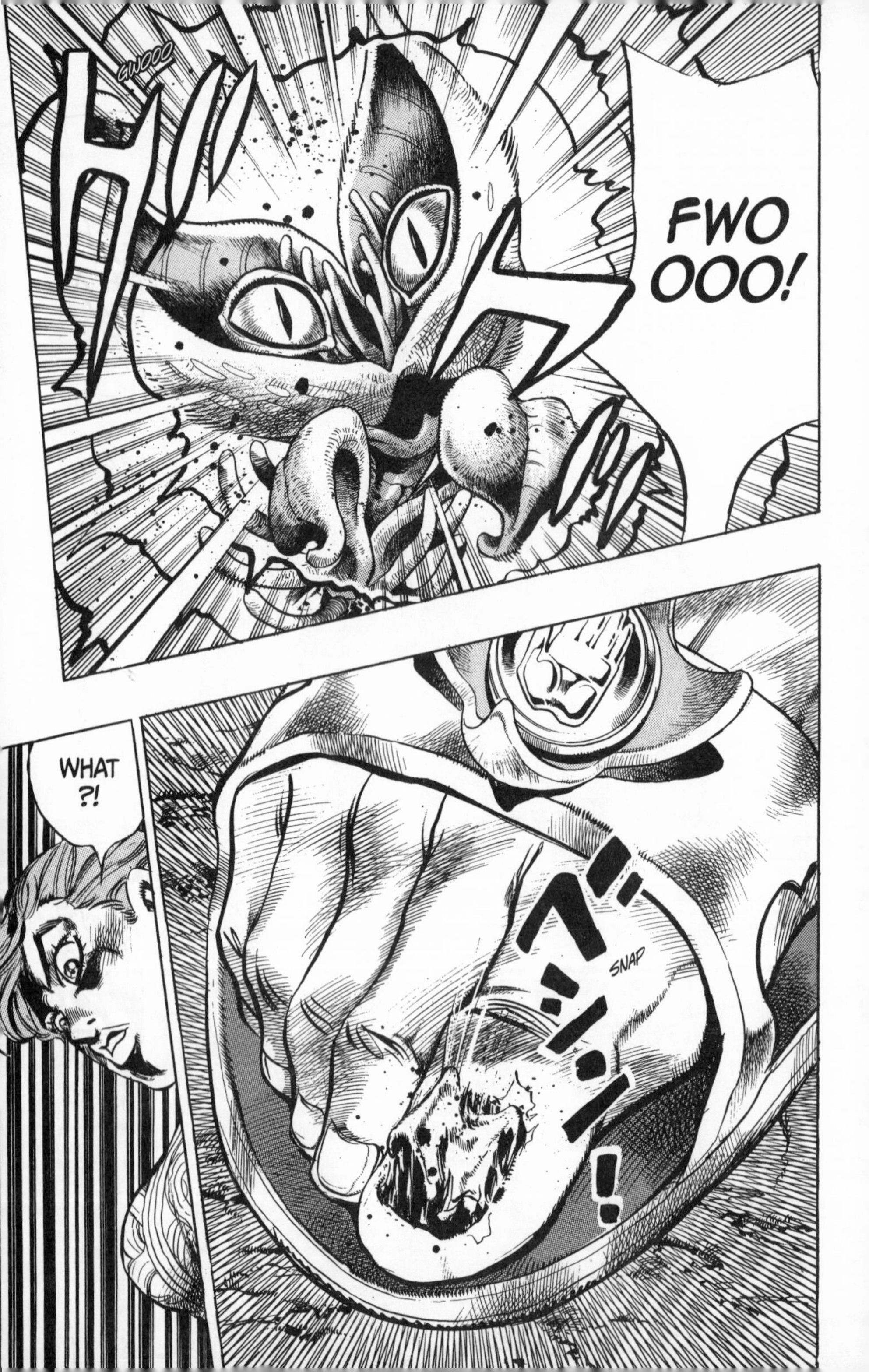
FWO
OOO!
GWOOO
SNAP
WHAT
?!

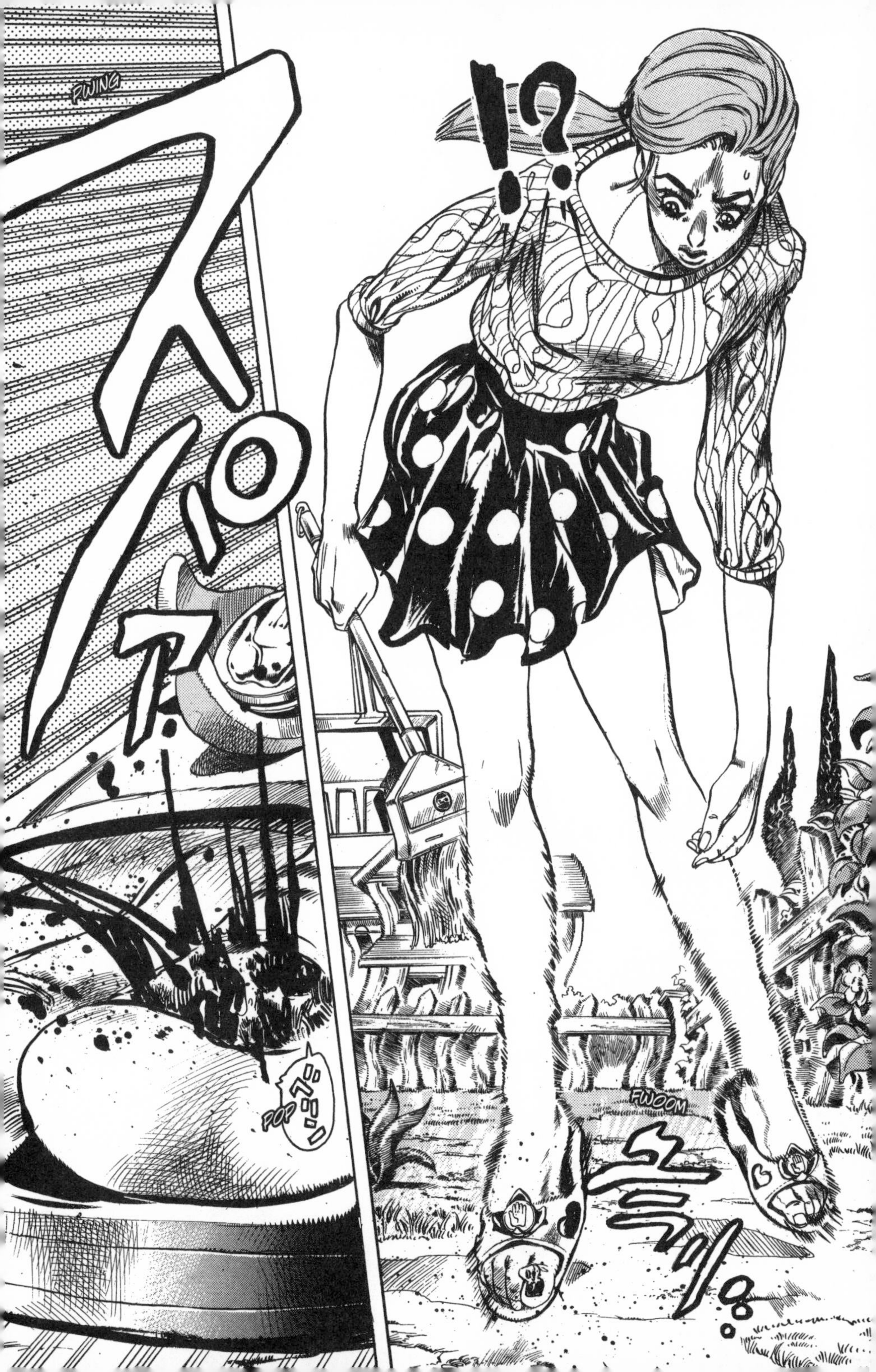
FWOOM
PWING
POP

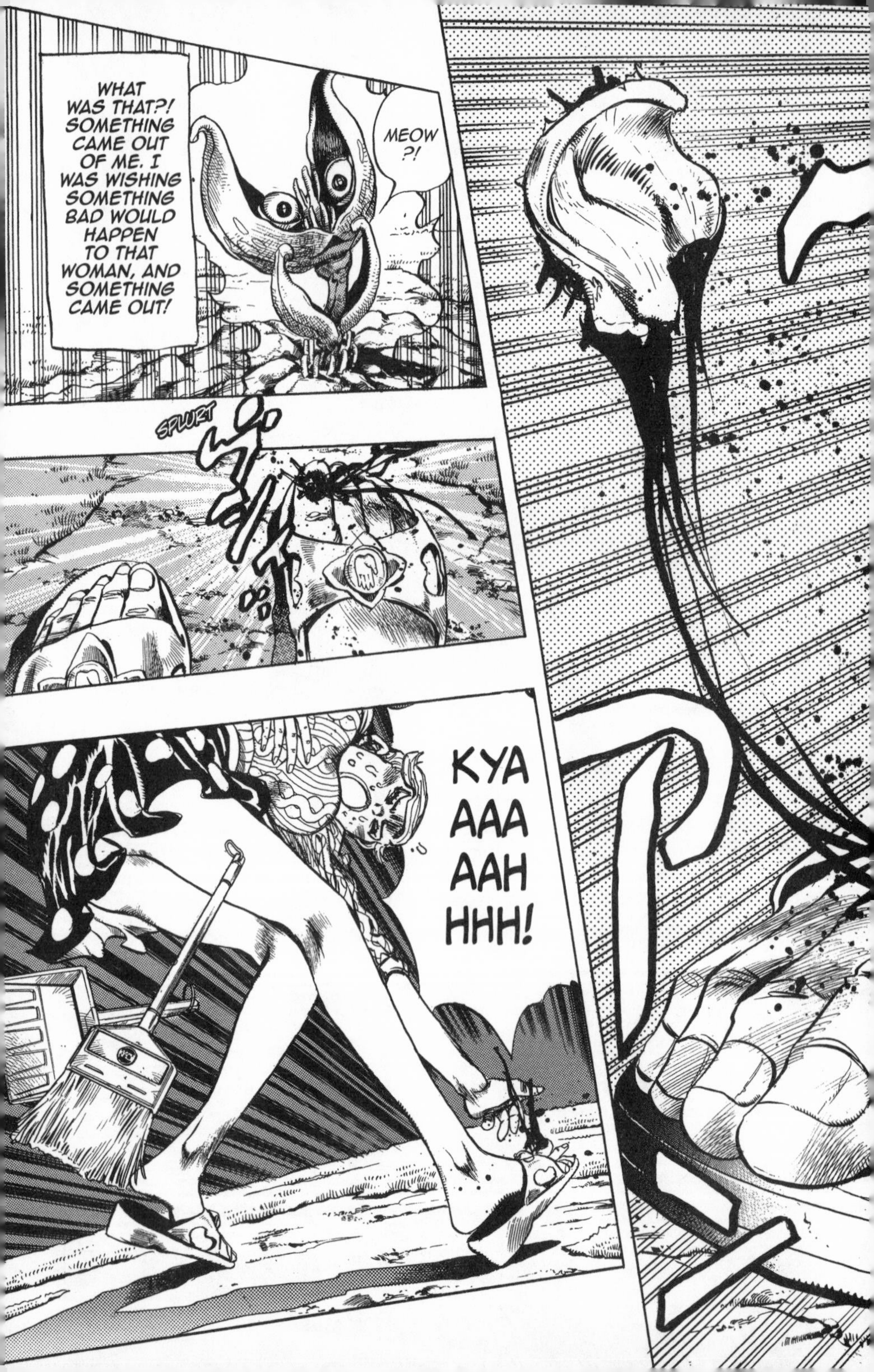
MEOW ?!
WHAT WAS THAT?! SOMETHING CAME OUT OF ME. I WAS WISHING SOMETHING BAD WOULD HAPPEN TO THAT WOMAN, AND SOMETHING CAME OUT!
SPLURT
KYAAAAAHHHH!

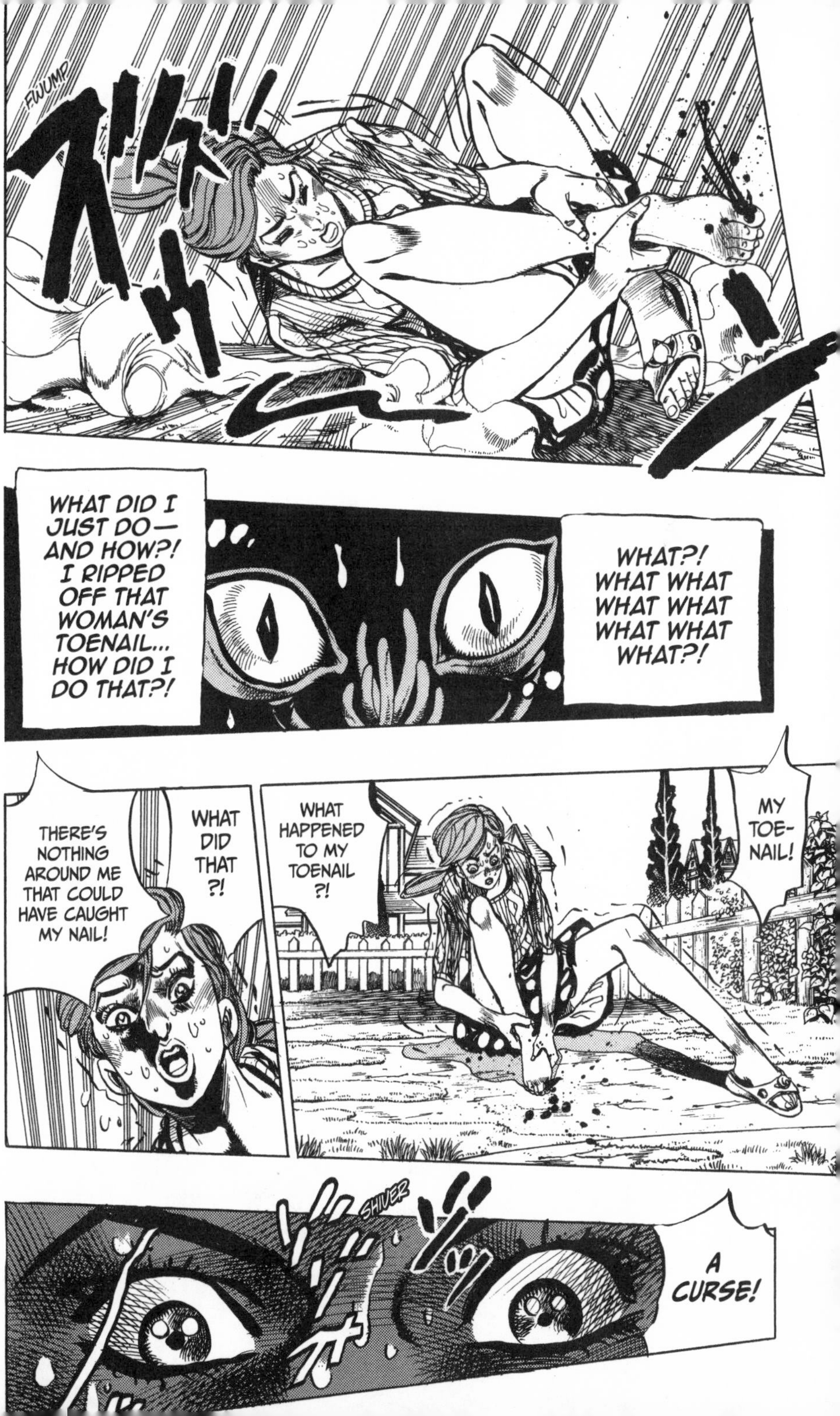
FWUMP
WHAT?! WHAT WHAT WHAT WHAT WHAT WHAT WHAT?!
WHAT DID I JUST DO—AND HOW?! I RIPPED OFF THAT WOMAN'S TOENAIL... HOW DID I DO THAT?!
MY TOE-NAIL!
WHAT HAPPENED TO MY TOENAIL ?!
WHAT DID THAT ?!
THERE'S NOTHING AROUND ME THAT COULD HAVE CAUGHT MY NAIL!
SHIVER
A CURSE!

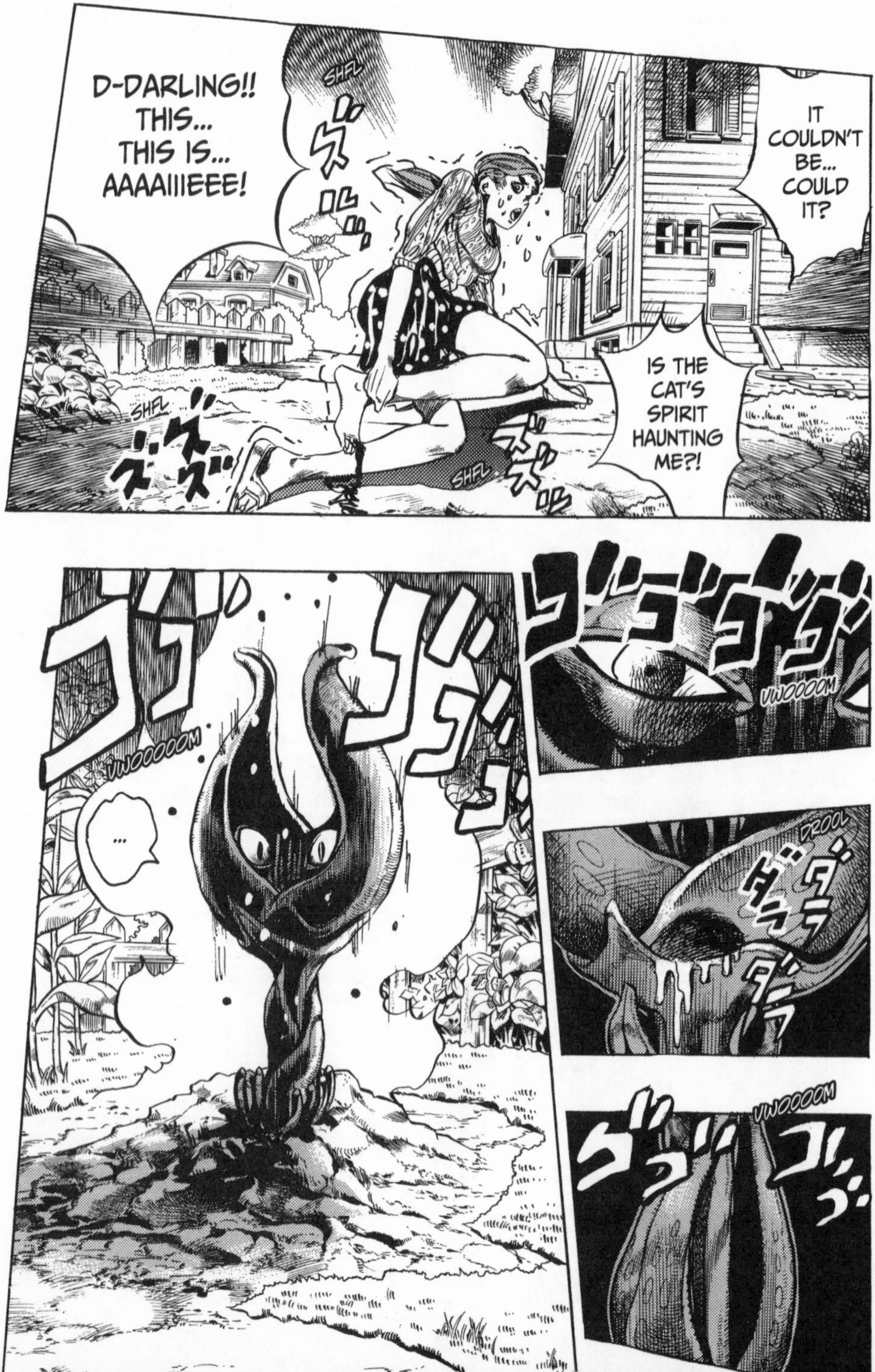
IT COULDN'T BE... COULD IT?
SHFL
D-DARLING!! THIS... THIS IS... AAAAIIIEEE!
IS THE CAT'S SPIRIT HAUNTING ME?!
SHFL
SHFL
UWOOOOM
DROOL
UWOOOOM
UWOOOOOM
...

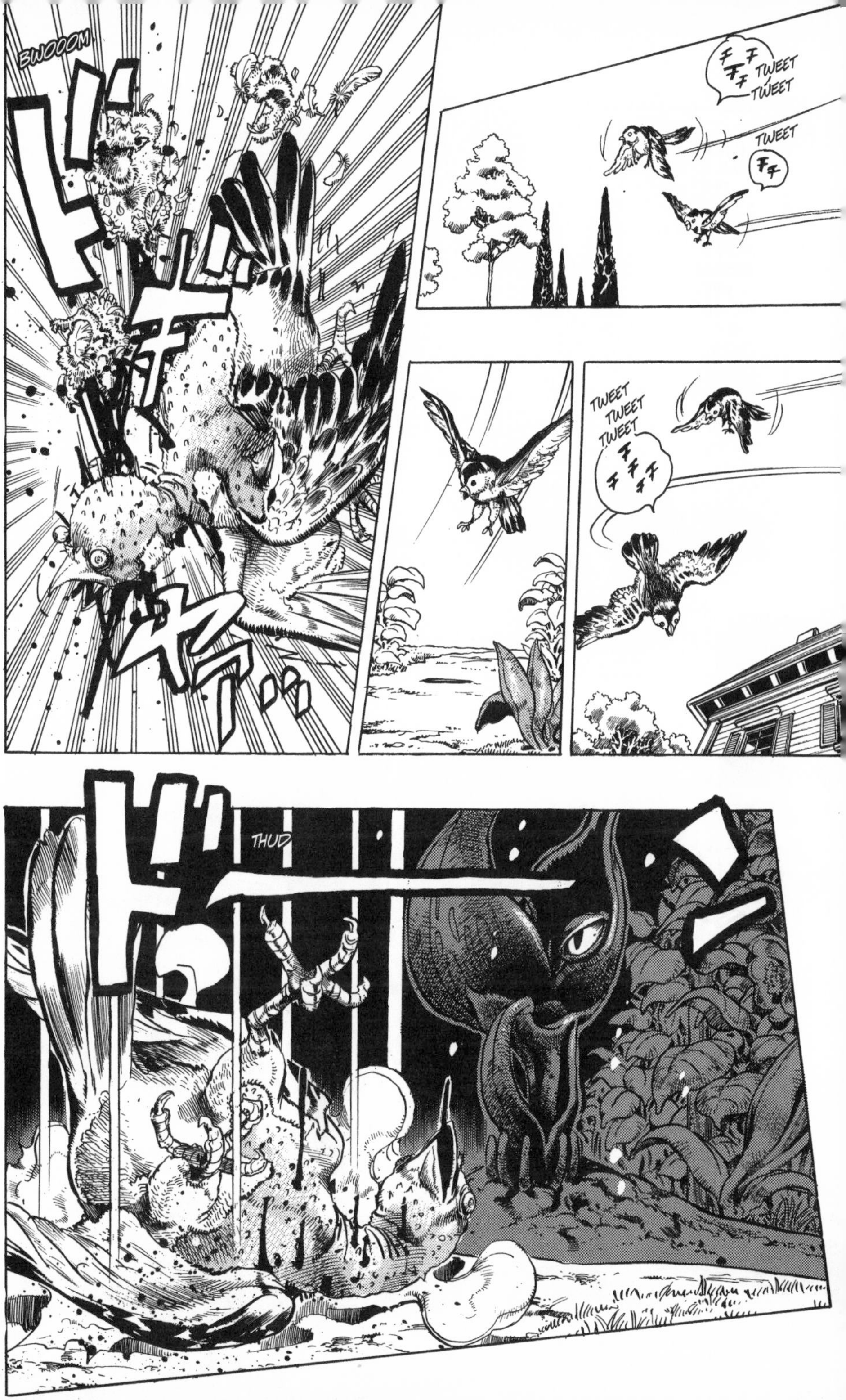
チチチ
TWEET TWEET
TWEET
チチ
TWEET TWEET TWEET
チチチチ
BWOOOM
THUD

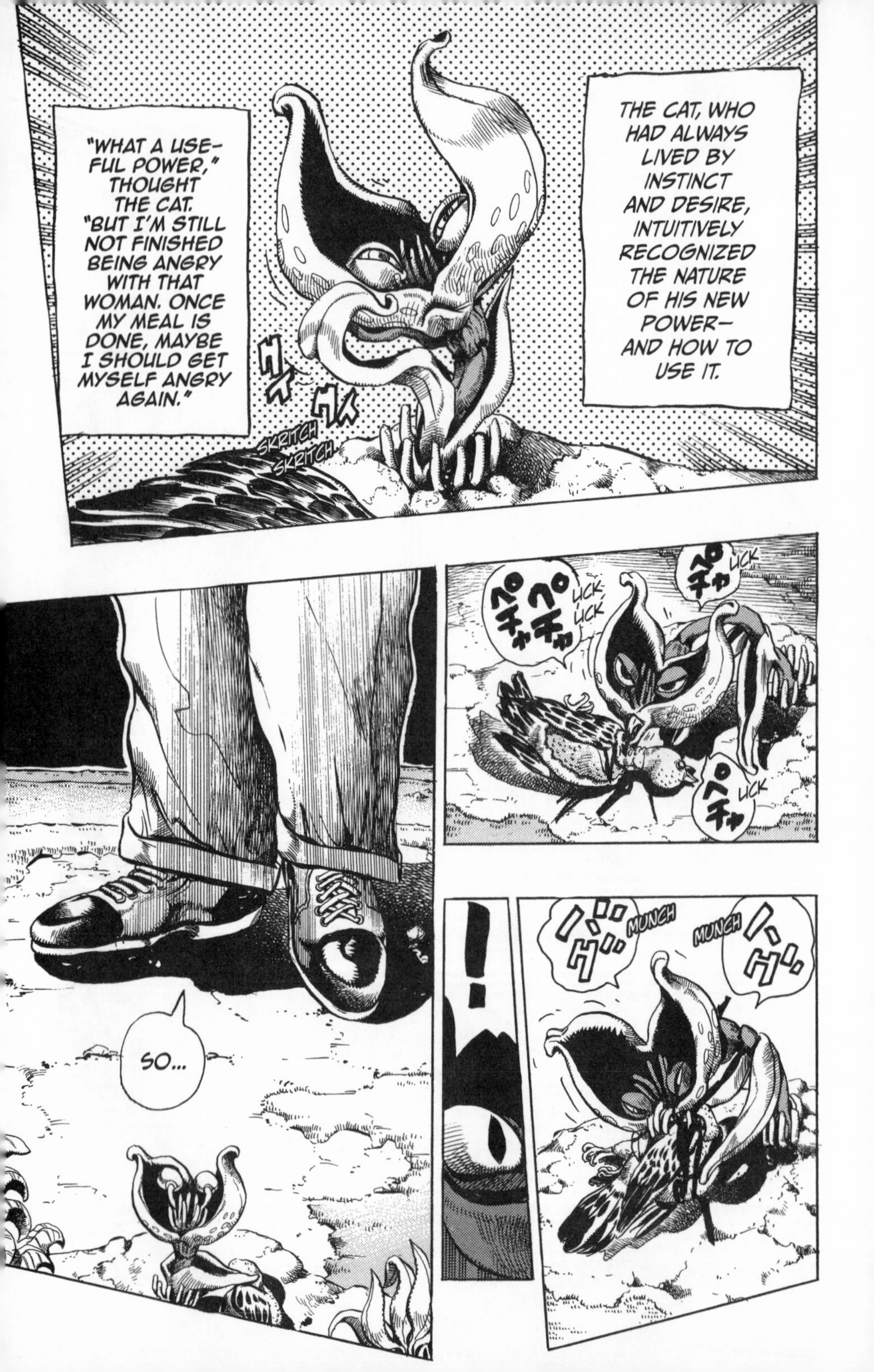

THE CAT, WHO HAD ALWAYS LIVED BY INSTINCT AND DESIRE, INTUITIVELY RECOGNIZED THE NATURE OF HIS NEW POWER—AND HOW TO USE IT.
"WHAT A USEFUL POWER," THOUGHT THE CAT. "BUT I'M STILL NOT FINISHED BEING ANGRY WITH THAT WOMAN. ONCE MY MEAL IS DONE, MAYBE I SHOULD GET MYSELF ANGRY AGAIN."
SKRITCH SKRITCH
LICK
LICK LICK
LICK
MUNCH
MUNCH
!
SO...

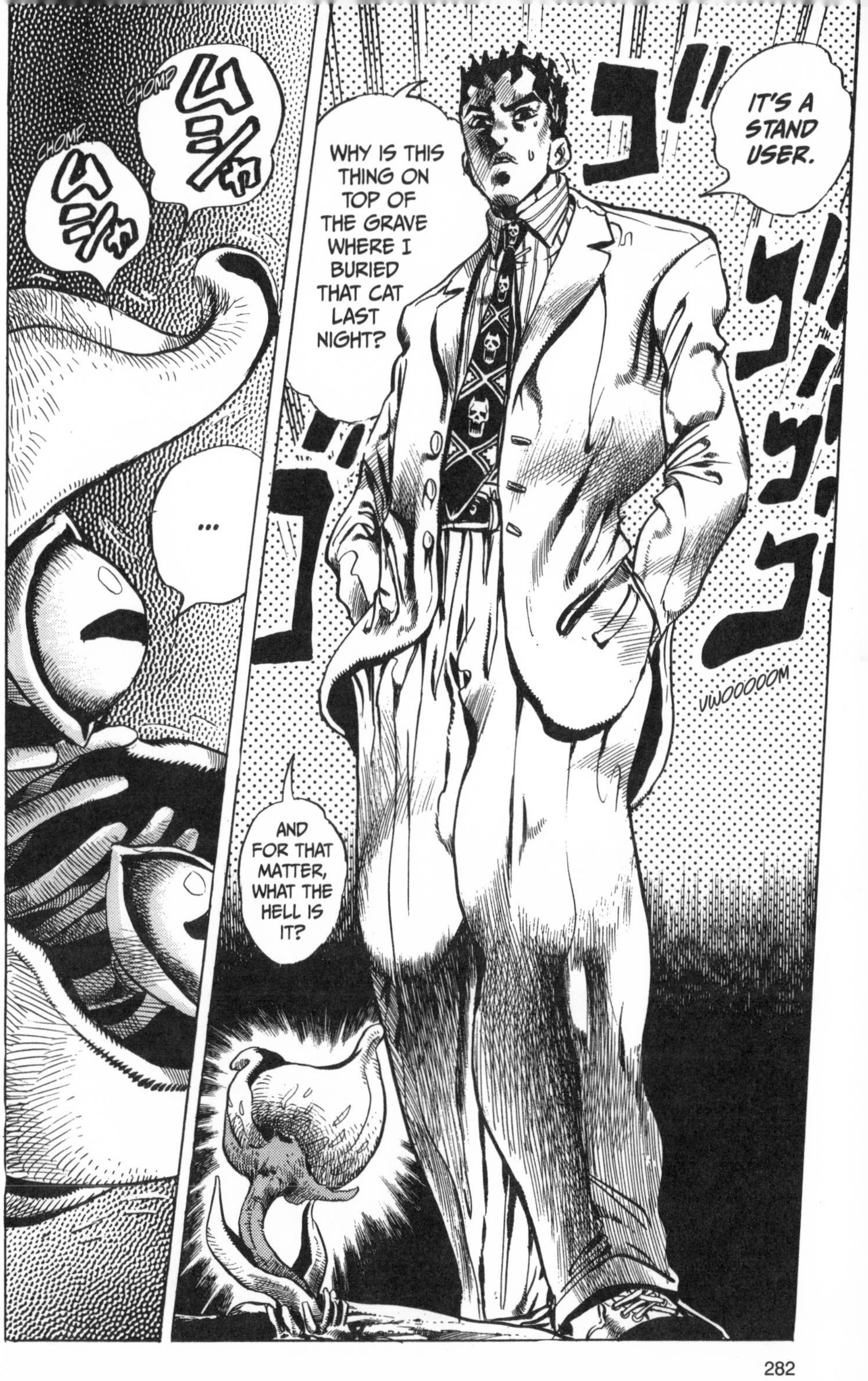
IT'S A STAND USER.
WHY IS THIS THING ON TOP OF THE GRAVE WHERE I BURIED THAT CAT LAST NIGHT?
VWOOOOOM
AND FOR THAT MATTER, WHAT THE HELL IS IT?
CHOMP
CHOMP
...

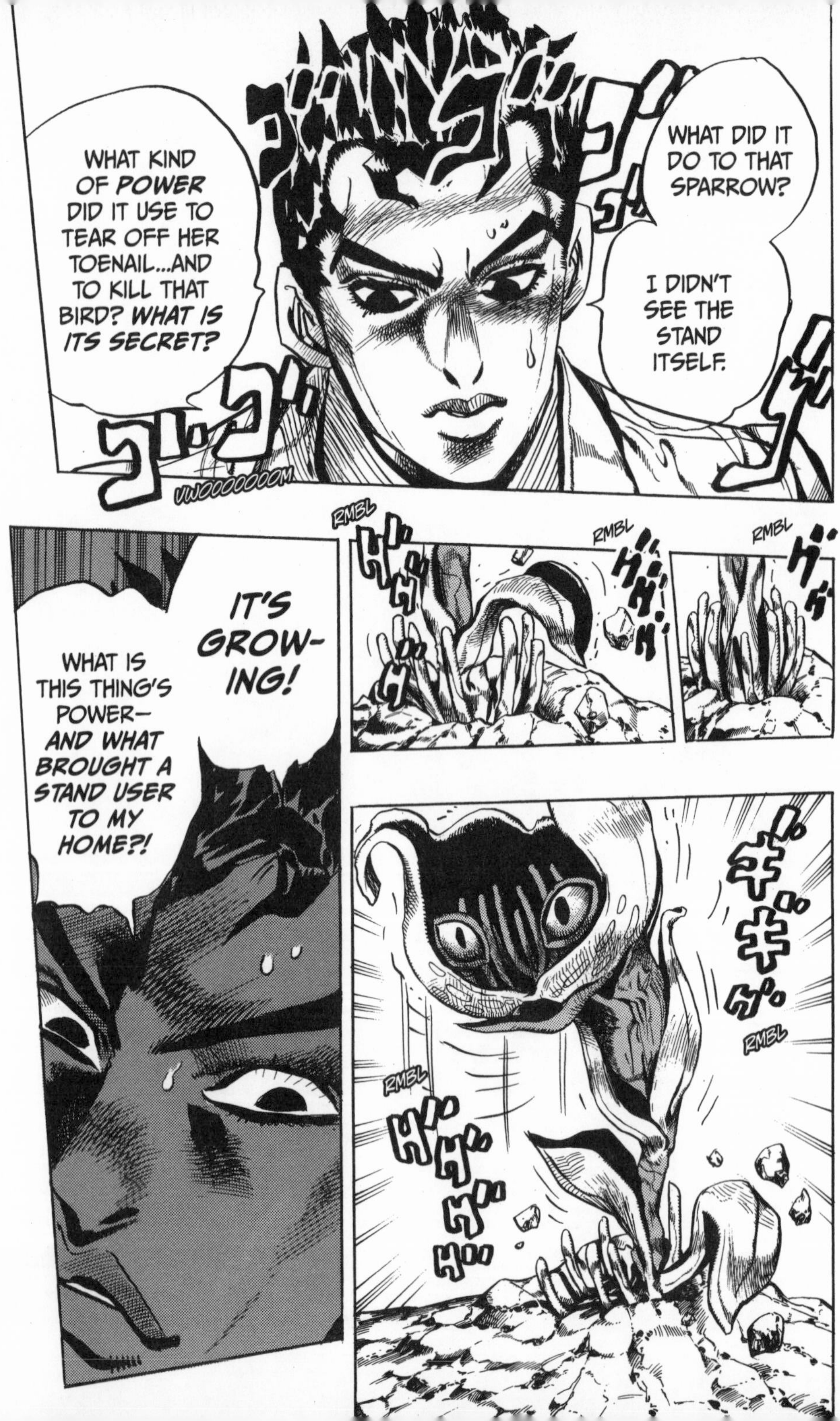
WHAT DID IT DO TO THAT SPARROW?
I DIDN'T SEE THE STAND ITSELF.
WHAT KIND OF *POWER* DID IT USE TO TEAR OFF HER TOENAIL...AND TO KILL THAT BIRD? *WHAT IS ITS SECRET?*
UWOOOOOOOOM
RMBL
RMBL
RMBL
RMBL
RMBL
IT'S GROWING!
WHAT IS THIS THING'S POWER—*AND WHAT BROUGHT A STAND USER TO MY HOME?!*

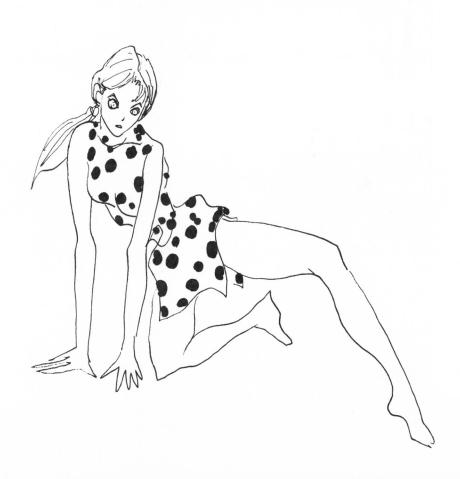

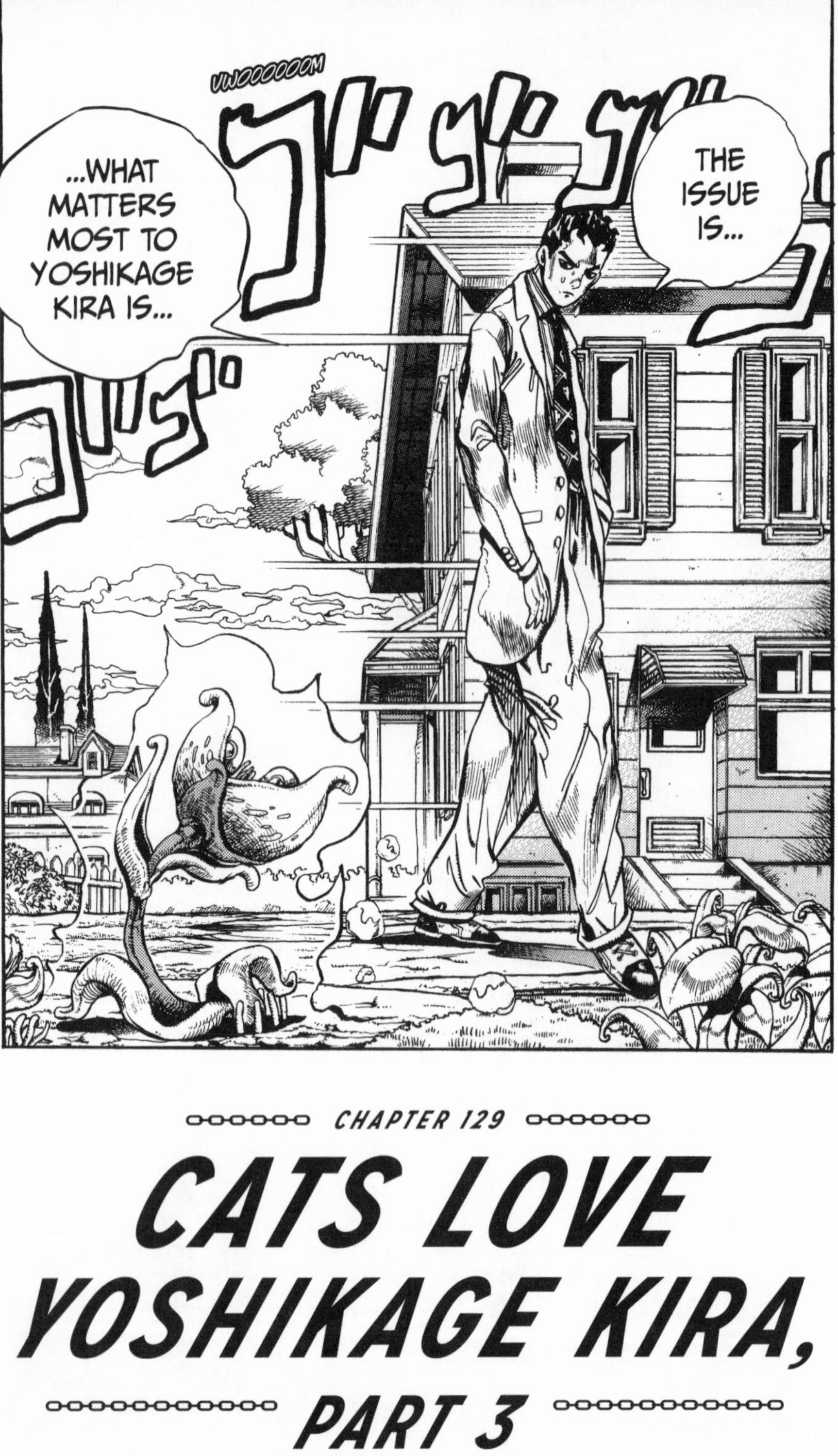
VWOOOOOOOM
THE ISSUE IS...
...WHAT MATTERS MOST TO YOSHIKAGE KIRA IS...

CHAPTER 129

CATS LOVE YOSHIKAGE KIRA, PART 3

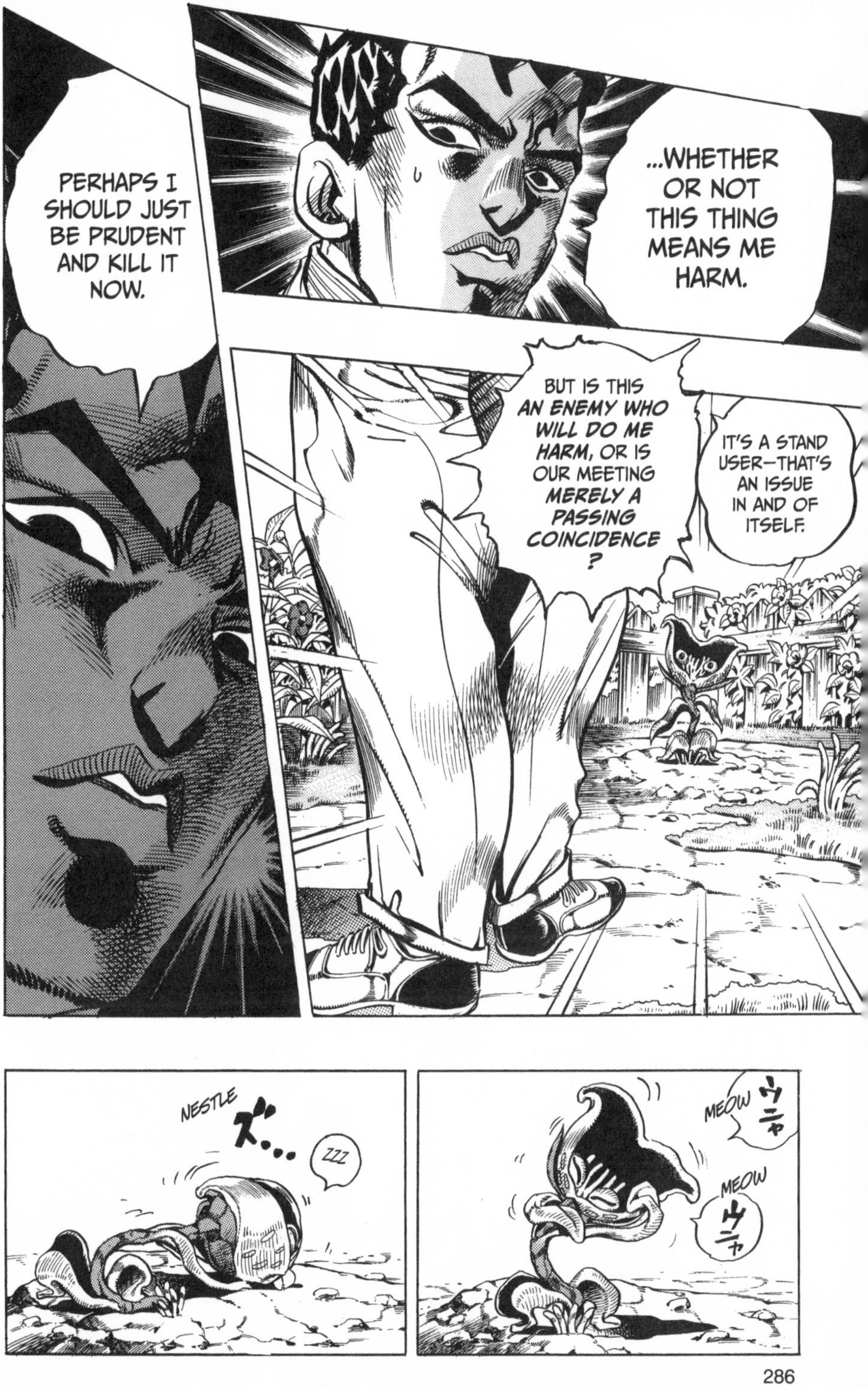
...WHETHER OR NOT THIS THING MEANS ME HARM.
IT'S A STAND USER—THAT'S AN ISSUE IN AND OF ITSELF.
BUT IS THIS *AN ENEMY WHO WILL DO ME HARM,* OR IS OUR MEETING *MERELY A PASSING COINCIDENCE* ?
PERHAPS I SHOULD JUST BE PRUDENT AND KILL IT NOW.
ウニャ MEOW
ウニャ MEOW
ズ... NESTLE
ZZZ

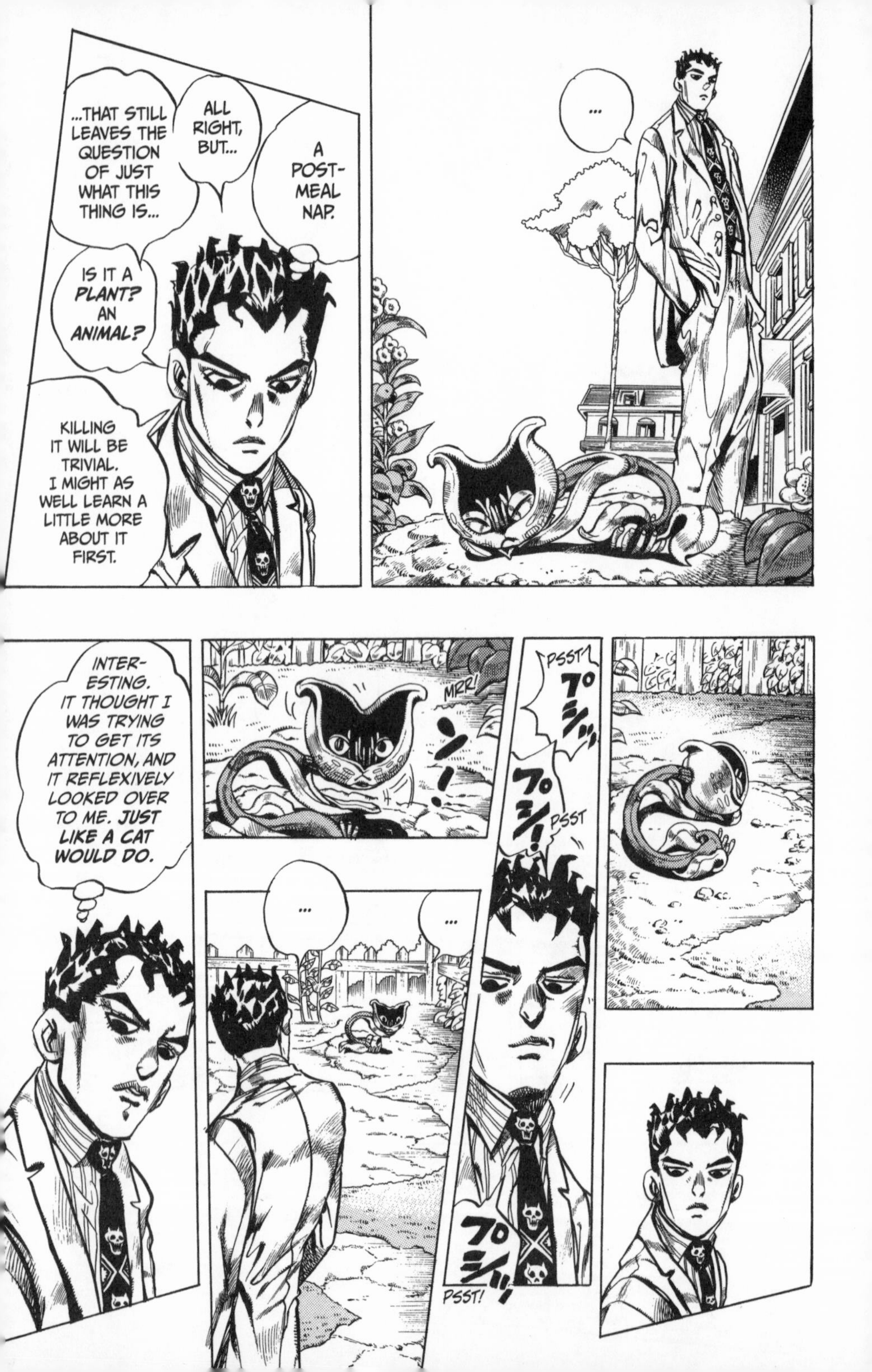
...
A POST-MEAL NAP.
ALL RIGHT, BUT...
...THAT STILL LEAVES THE QUESTION OF JUST WHAT THIS THING IS...
IS IT A PLANT? AN ANIMAL?
KILLING IT WILL BE TRIVIAL. I MIGHT AS WELL LEARN A LITTLE MORE ABOUT IT FIRST.
PSST!
プシッ
プシッ!
PSST
プシッ
PSST!
MRR!
ン!
...
...
INTERESTING. IT THOUGHT I WAS TRYING TO GET ITS ATTENTION, AND IT REFLEXIVELY LOOKED OVER TO ME. JUST LIKE A CAT WOULD DO.

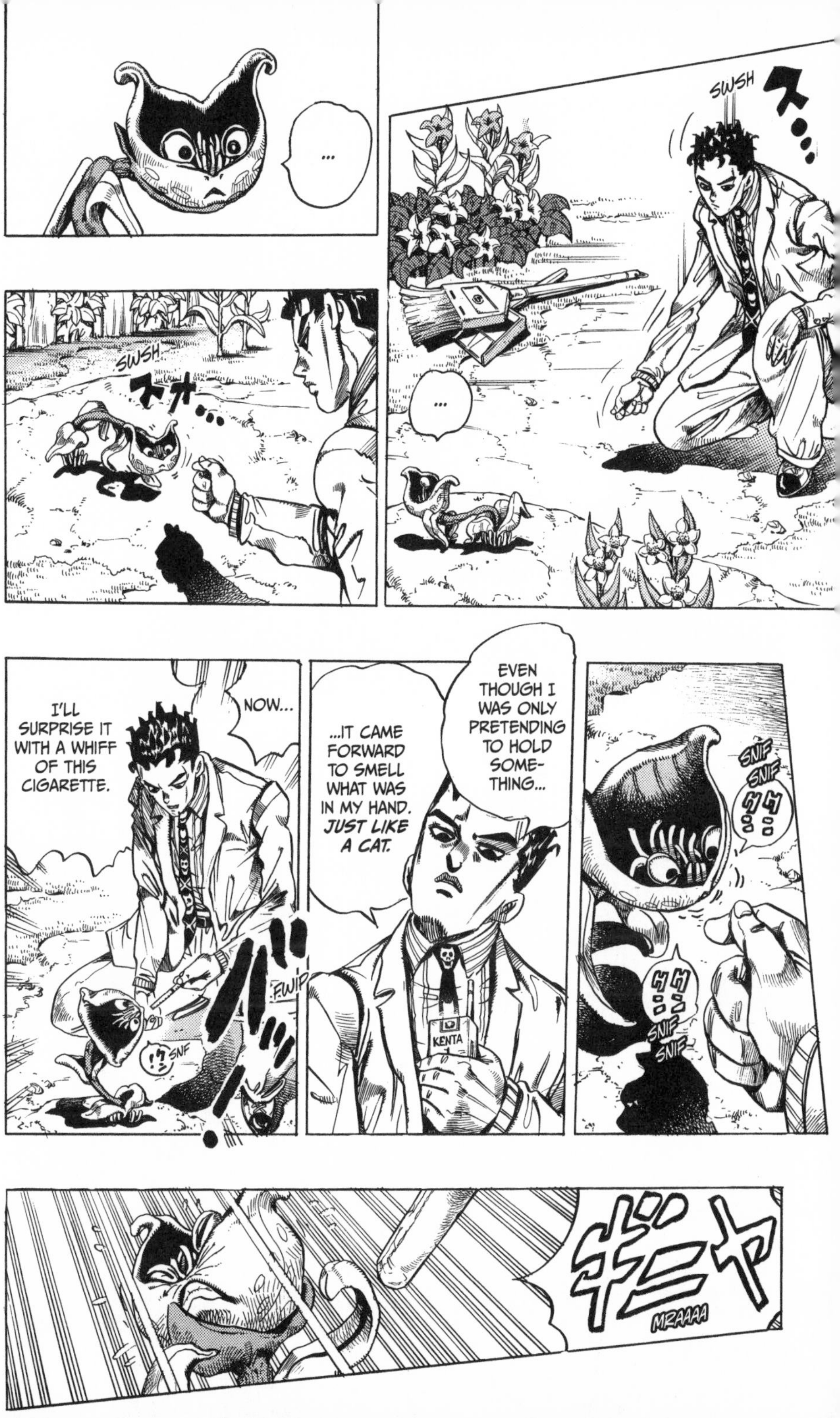
SWSH
ス…
...
...
SWSH
スォ…
SNIF
SNIF
SNIF
SNIF
EVEN THOUGH I WAS ONLY PRETENDING TO HOLD SOME-THING...
...IT CAME FORWARD TO SMELL WHAT WAS IN MY HAND. *JUST LIKE A CAT.*
KENTA
NOW...
I'LL SURPRISE IT WITH A WHIFF OF THIS CIGARETTE.
FWIP
!?
SNF
ギニャ
MRAAAA

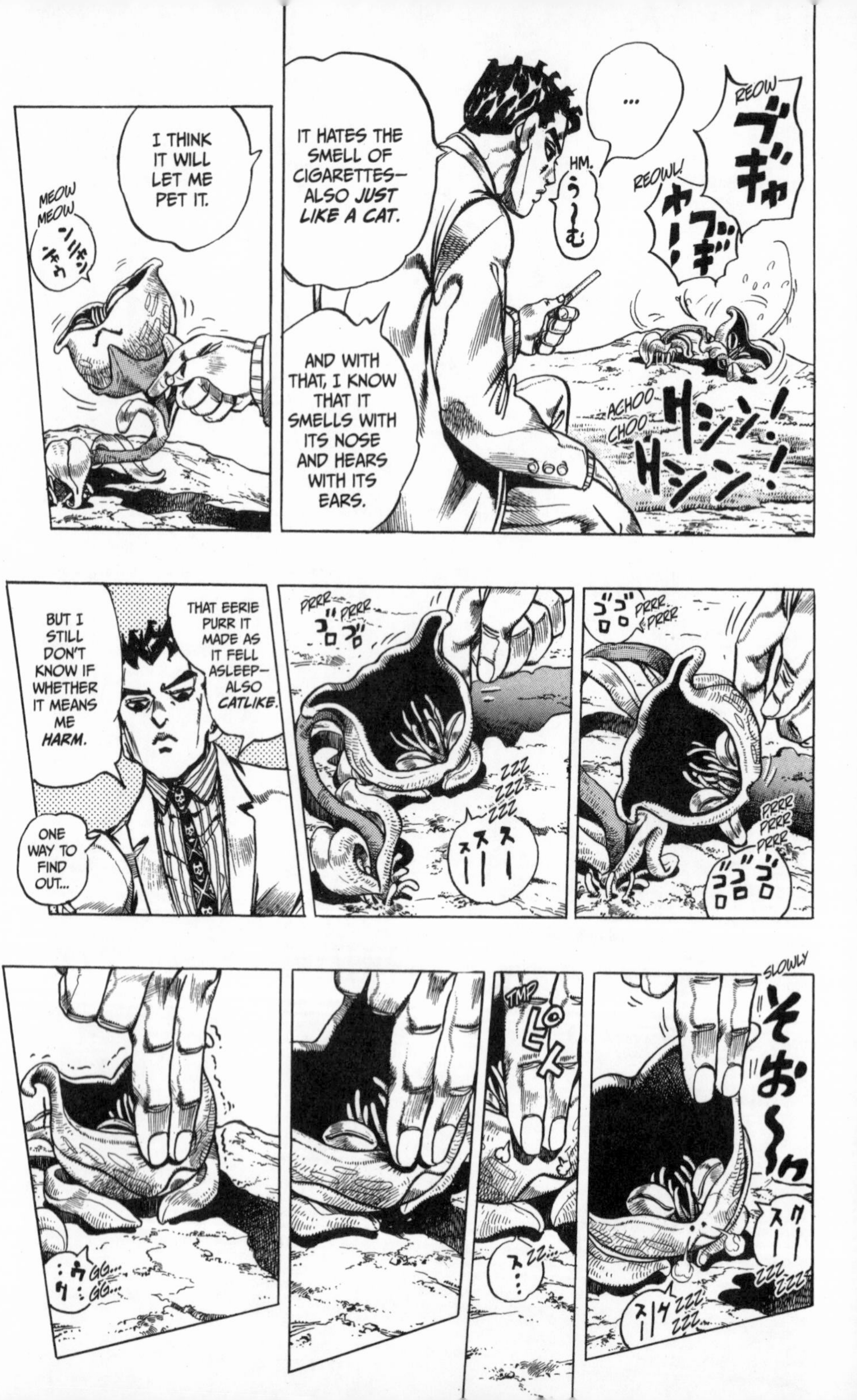
...
HM.
うーむ
REOW
REOWL!
ACHOO
CHOO
IT HATES THE SMELL OF CIGARETTES— ALSO JUST LIKE A CAT.
AND WITH THAT, I KNOW THAT IT SMELLS WITH ITS NOSE AND HEARS WITH ITS EARS.
I THINK IT WILL LET ME PET IT.
MEOW MEOW
PRRR PRRR
PRRR PRRR PRRR
PRRR PRRR
ZZZ ZZZ ZZZ
THAT EERIE PURR IT MADE AS IT FELL ASLEEP— ALSO CATLIKE.
BUT I STILL DON'T KNOW IF WHETHER IT MEANS ME HARM.
ONE WAY TO FIND OUT...
SLOWLY
そお～っ
ZZZ ZZZ
ZZZ ZZZ
TMP
ZZZ...
GG... GG...

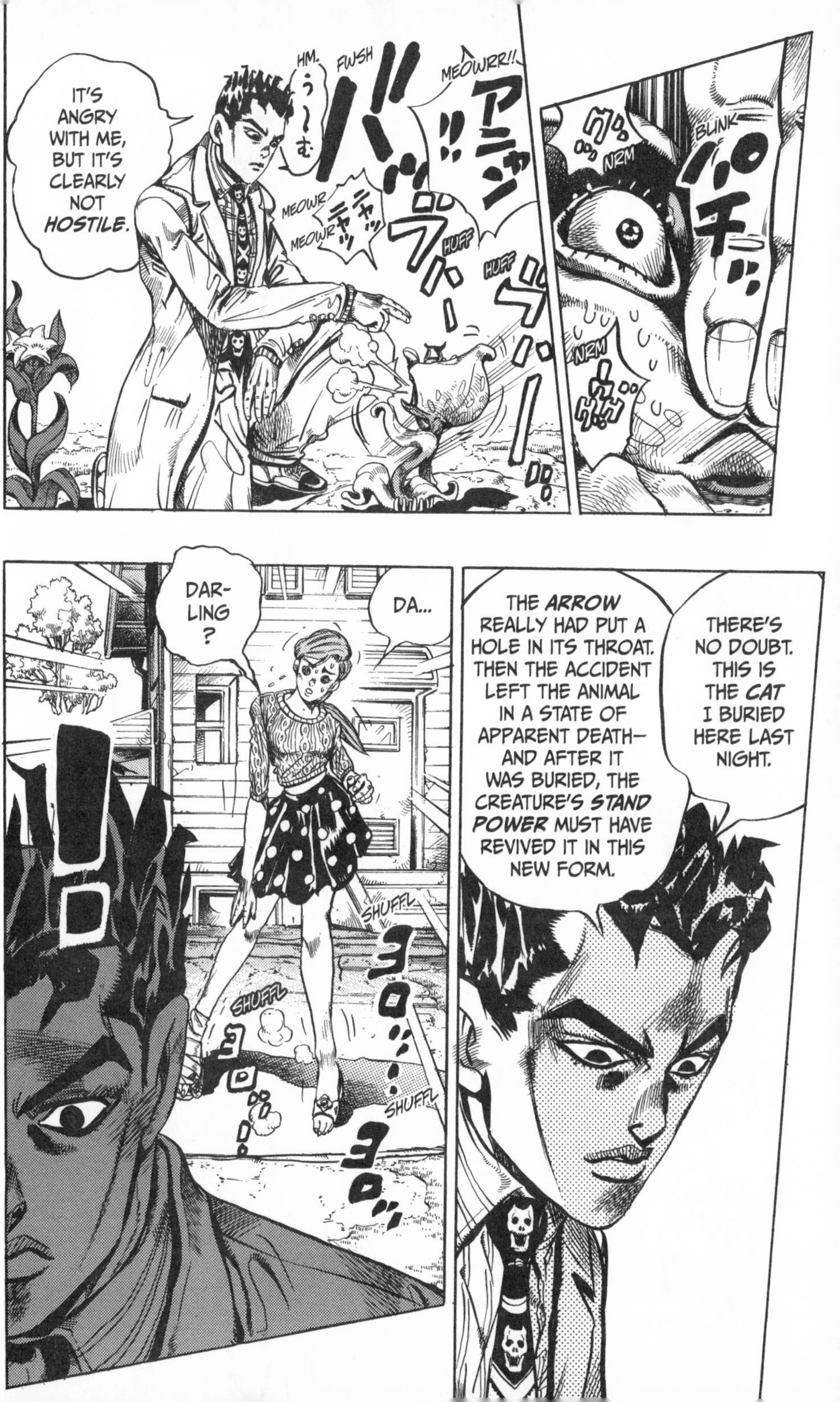
NRM
BLINK
NRM
MEOWRR!!
FWSH
HM.
IT'S ANGRY WITH ME, BUT IT'S CLEARLY NOT *HOSTILE*.
MEOWR
MEOWR
HUFF
HUFF
THERE'S NO DOUBT. THIS IS THE *CAT* I BURIED HERE LAST NIGHT.
THE *ARROW* REALLY HAD PUT A HOLE IN ITS THROAT. THEN THE ACCIDENT LEFT THE ANIMAL IN A STATE OF APPARENT DEATH— AND AFTER IT WAS BURIED, THE CREATURE'S *STAND POWER* MUST HAVE REVIVED IT IN THIS NEW FORM.
DA...
DAR- LING ?
SHUFFL
SHUFFL
SHUFFL

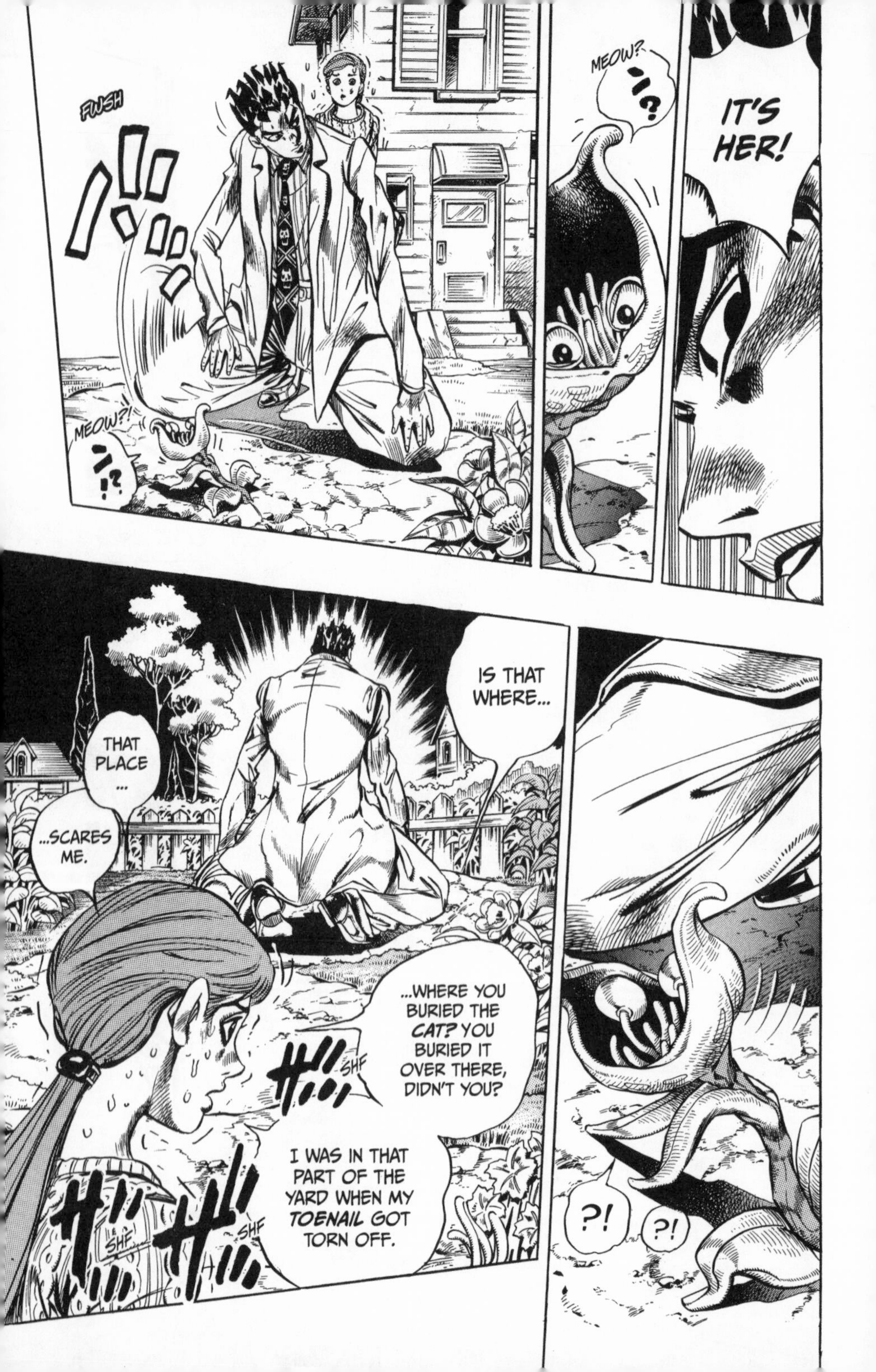
IT'S HER!
MEOW?
?
FWSH
MEOW?!
?
?!
?!
IS THAT WHERE...
THAT PLACE ...
...SCARES ME.
...WHERE YOU BURIED THE CAT? YOU BURIED IT OVER THERE, DIDN'T YOU?
SHF
I WAS IN THAT PART OF THE YARD WHEN MY TOENAIL GOT TORN OFF.
SHF
SHF

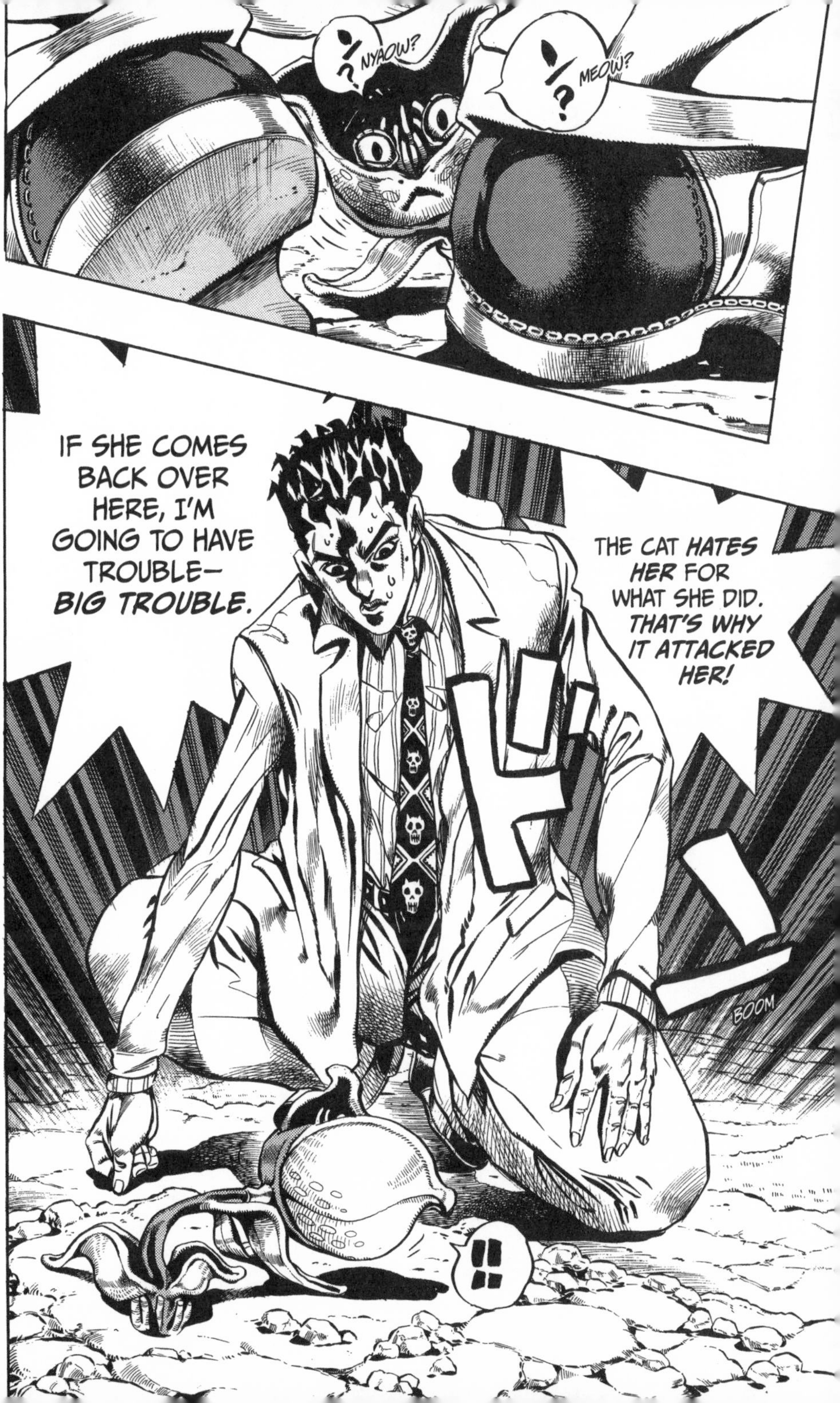

!? MEOW?
!? NYAOW?
THE CAT *HATES HER* FOR WHAT SHE DID. *THAT'S WHY IT ATTACKED HER!*
IF SHE COMES BACK OVER HERE, I'M GOING TO HAVE TROUBLE— *BIG TROUBLE.*
BOOM
!!

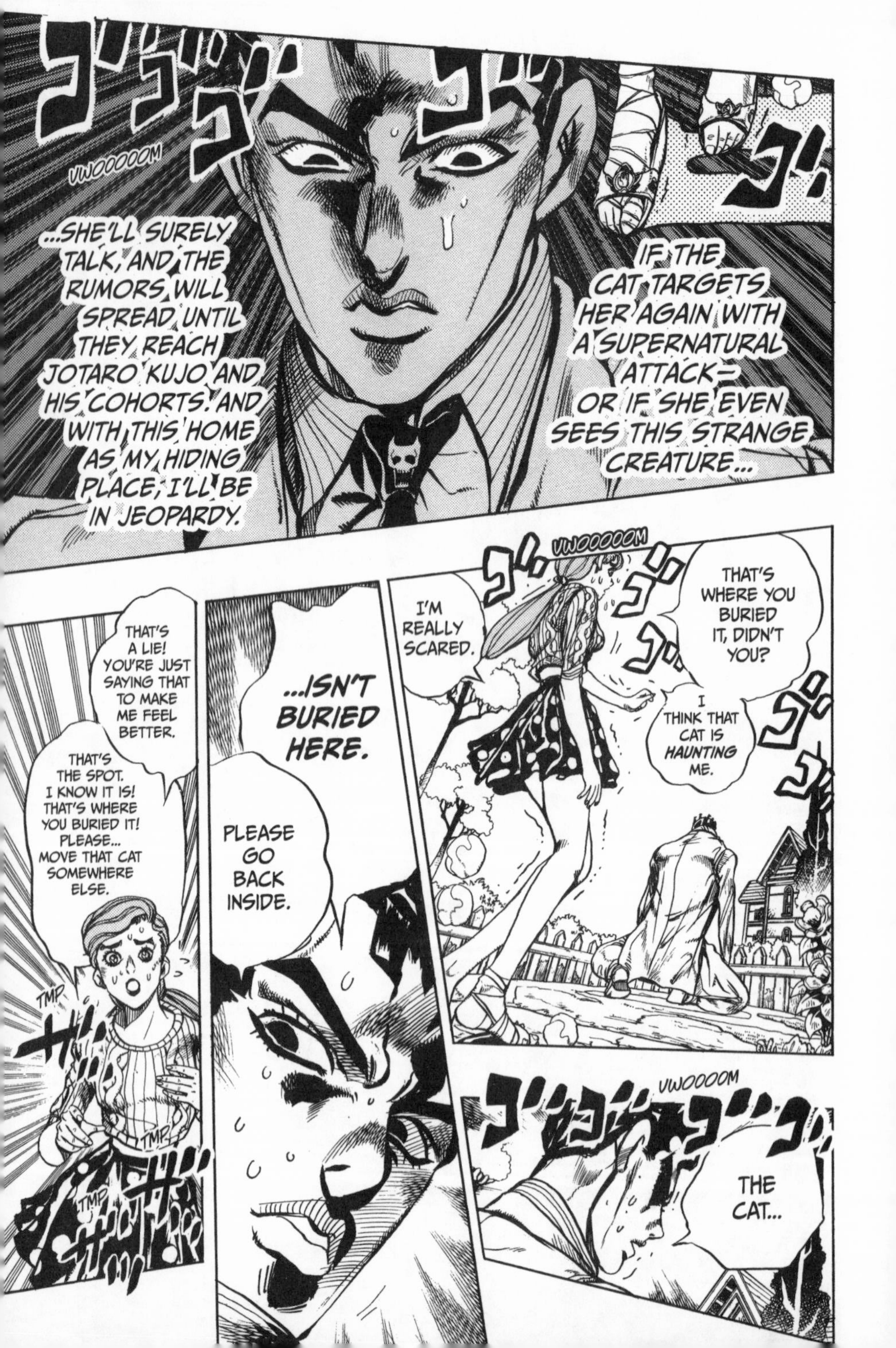
VWOOOOOM
IF THE CAT TARGETS HER AGAIN WITH A SUPERNATURAL ATTACK— OR IF SHE EVEN SEES THIS STRANGE CREATURE...
...SHE'LL SURELY TALK, AND THE RUMORS WILL SPREAD UNTIL THEY REACH JOTARO KUJO AND HIS COHORTS. AND WITH THIS HOME AS MY HIDING PLACE, I'LL BE IN JEOPARDY.
VWOOOOOM
THAT'S WHERE YOU BURIED IT, DIDN'T YOU?
I THINK THAT CAT IS HAUNTING ME.
I'M REALLY SCARED.
VWOOOOM
THE CAT...
...ISN'T BURIED HERE.
PLEASE GO BACK INSIDE.
THAT'S A LIE! YOU'RE JUST SAYING THAT TO MAKE ME FEEL BETTER.
THAT'S THE SPOT. I KNOW IT IS! THAT'S WHERE YOU BURIED IT! PLEASE... MOVE THAT CAT SOMEWHERE ELSE.
TMP
TMP
TMP

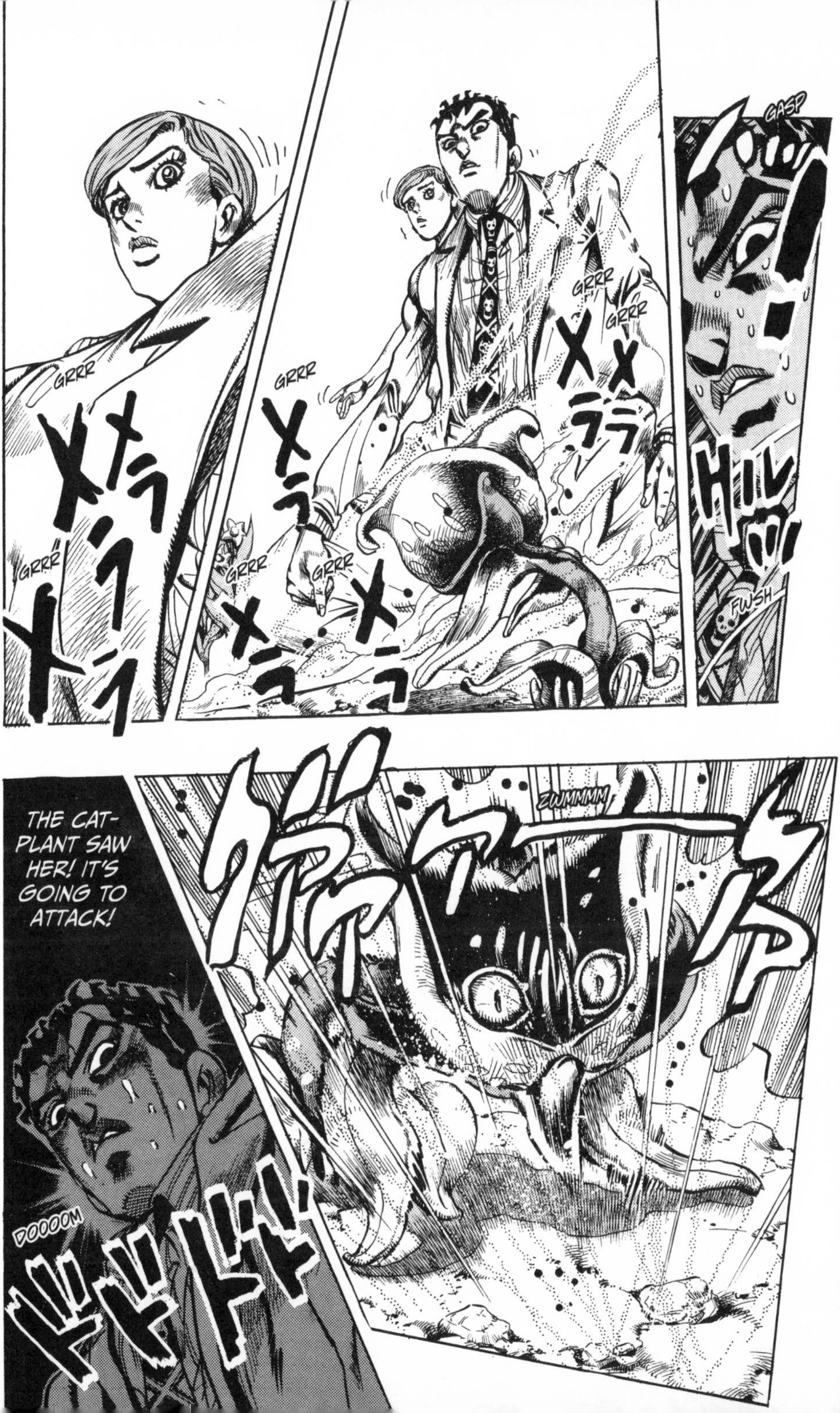
GASP
FWSH
GRRR
GRRR
GRRR
GRRR
GRRR
GRRR
GRRR
ZWMMMM
THE CAT-PLANT SAW HER! IT'S GOING TO ATTACK!
DOOOOM

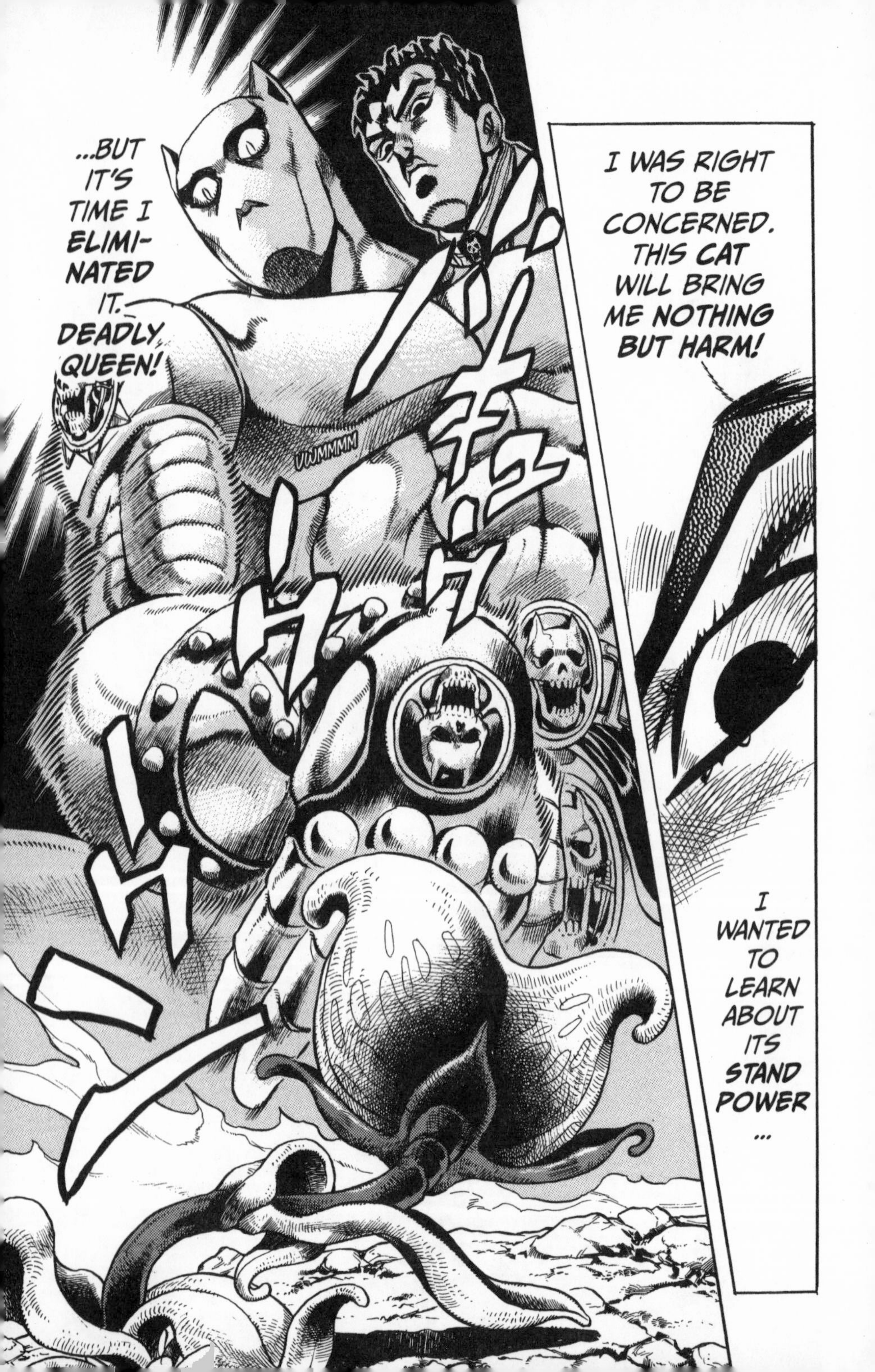
I WAS RIGHT TO BE CONCERNED. THIS CAT WILL BRING ME NOTHING BUT HARM!
I WANTED TO LEARN ABOUT ITS STAND POWER ...
...BUT IT'S TIME I ELIMINATED IT. DEADLY QUEEN!
UWMMMM

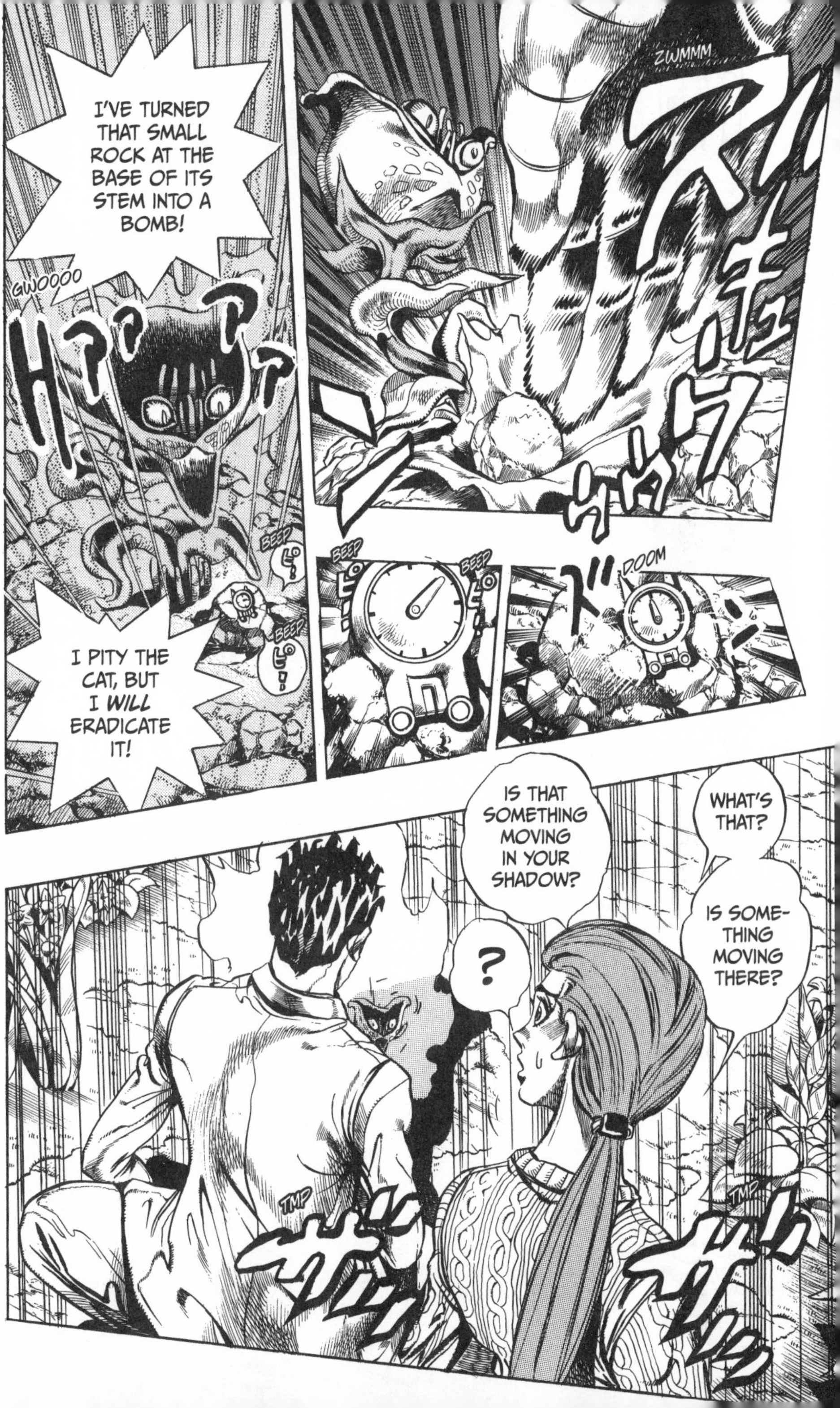
ZWMMM
DOOM
BEEP
BEEP
I'VE TURNED THAT SMALL ROCK AT THE BASE OF ITS STEM INTO A BOMB!
GWOOOO
H?? ??
BEEP
BEEP
I PITY THE CAT, BUT I *WILL* ERADICATE IT!
WHAT'S THAT?
IS SOMETHING MOVING THERE?
IS THAT SOMETHING MOVING IN YOUR SHADOW?
?
TMP
TMP

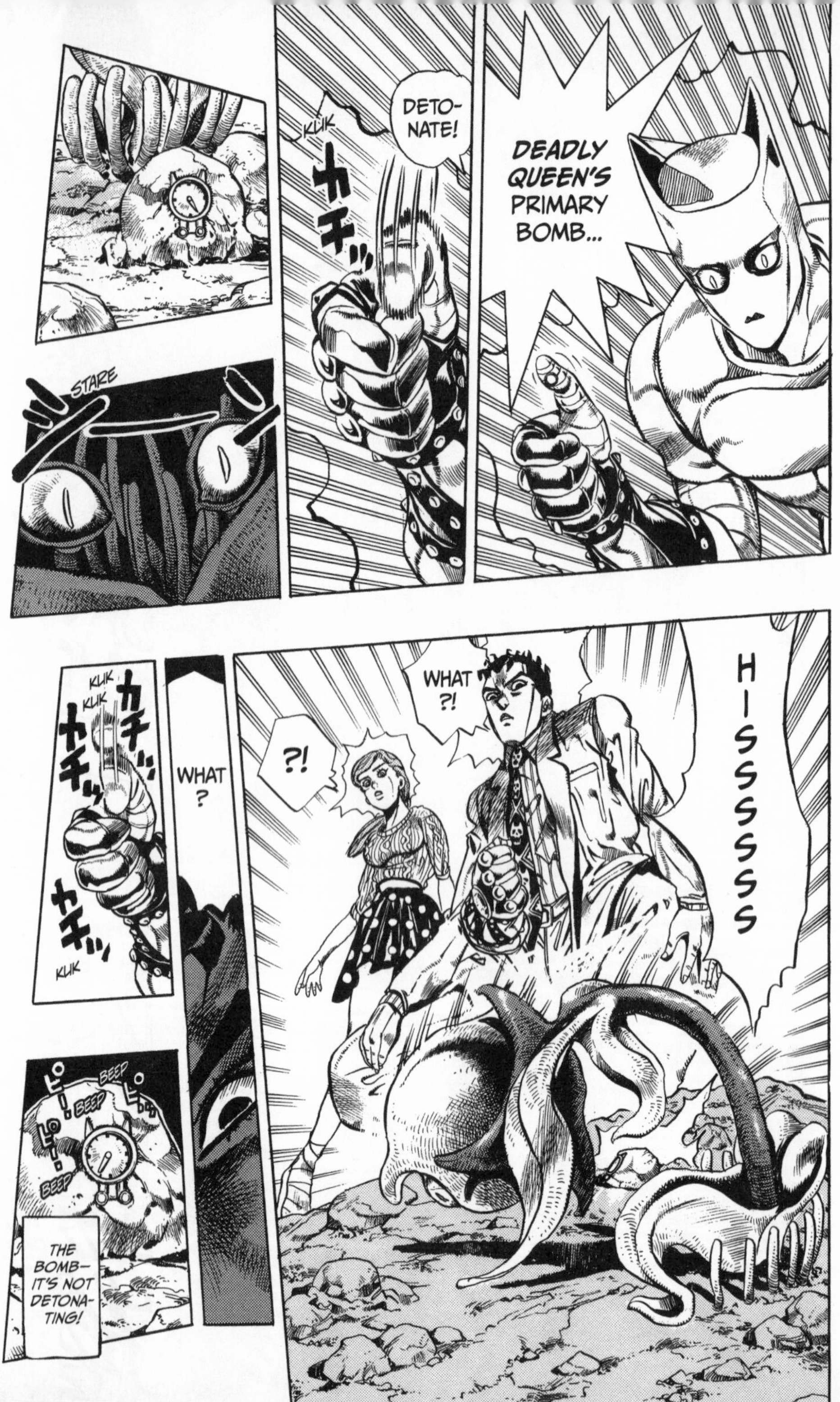
DEADLY QUEEN'S PRIMARY BOMB...
DETO-NATE!
KUK
カチッ
STARE
HISSSSSS
WHAT ?!
?!
WHAT ?
KUK KUK
カチッ カチッ
カチッ
KUK
BEEP BEEP BEEP
THE BOMB— IT'S NOT DETONATING!

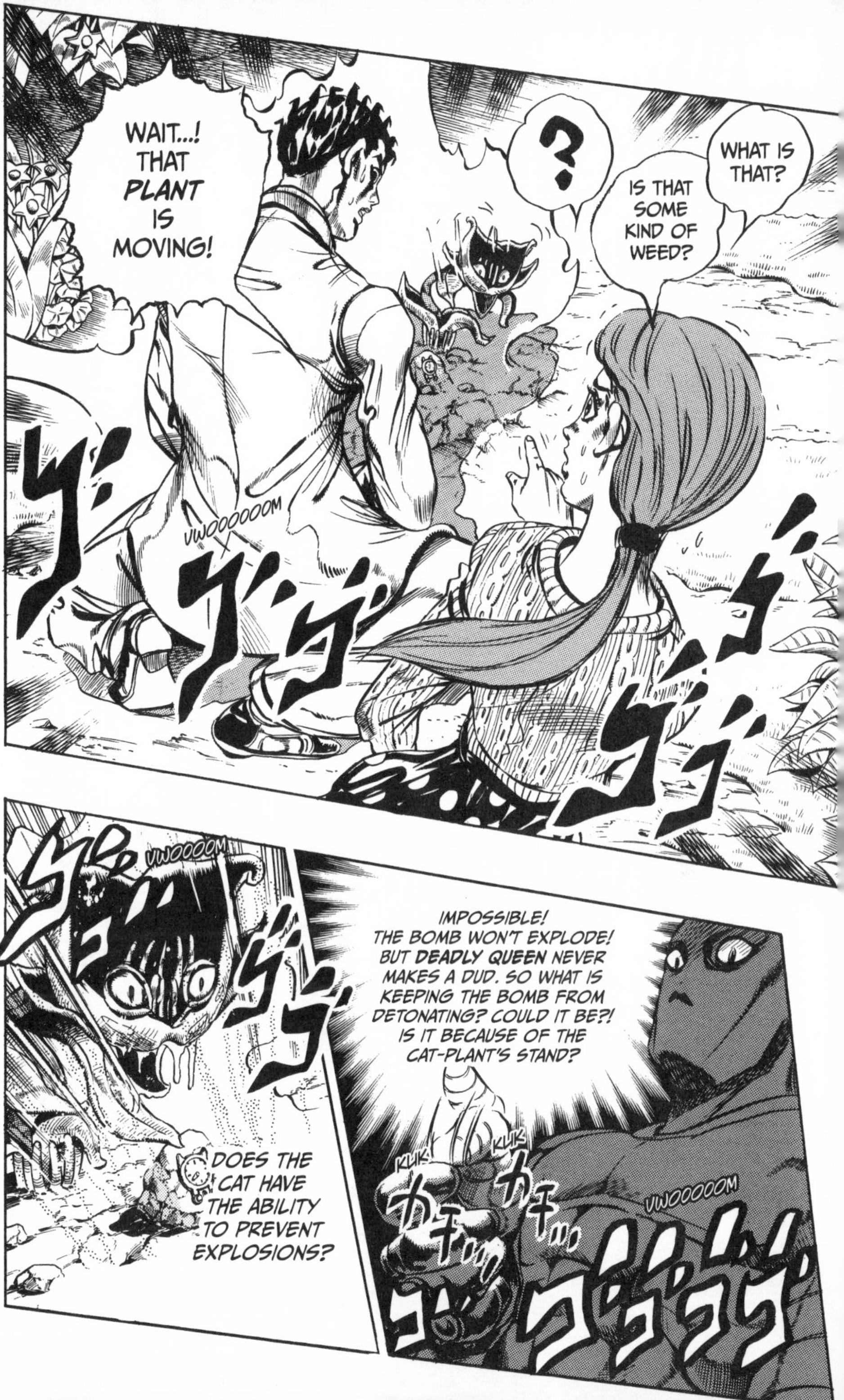
WHAT IS THAT?
IS THAT SOME KIND OF WEED?
?
WAIT...! THAT PLANT IS MOVING!
VWOOOOOOM
IMPOSSIBLE! THE BOMB WON'T EXPLODE! BUT DEADLY QUEEN NEVER MAKES A DUD. SO WHAT IS KEEPING THE BOMB FROM DETONATING? COULD IT BE?! IS IT BECAUSE OF THE CAT-PLANT'S STAND?
KUK
KUK
VWOOOOOM
VWOOOOM
DOES THE CAT HAVE THE ABILITY TO PREVENT EXPLOSIONS?

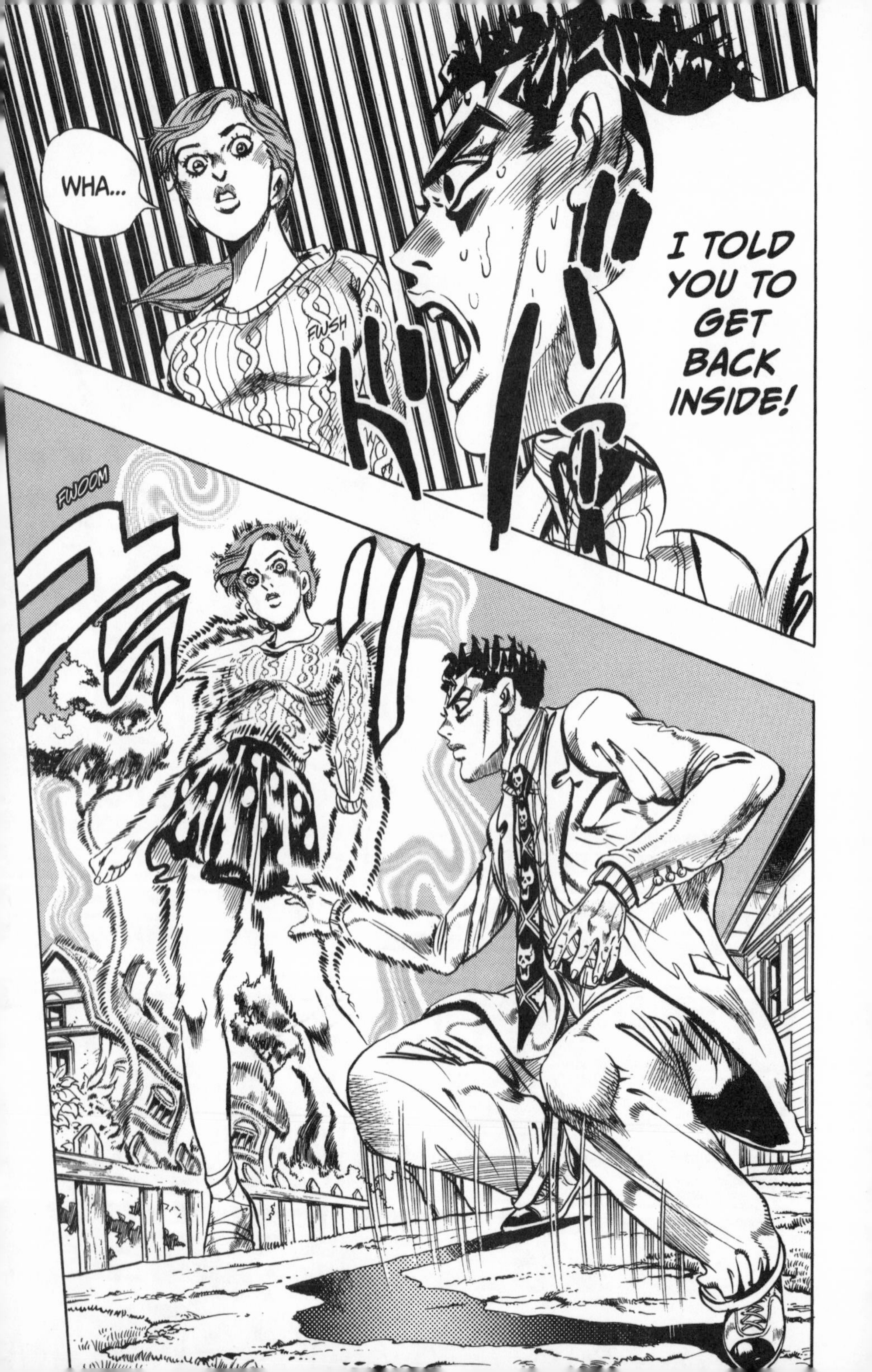
I TOLD YOU TO GET BACK INSIDE!
FWSH
WHA...
FWOOM

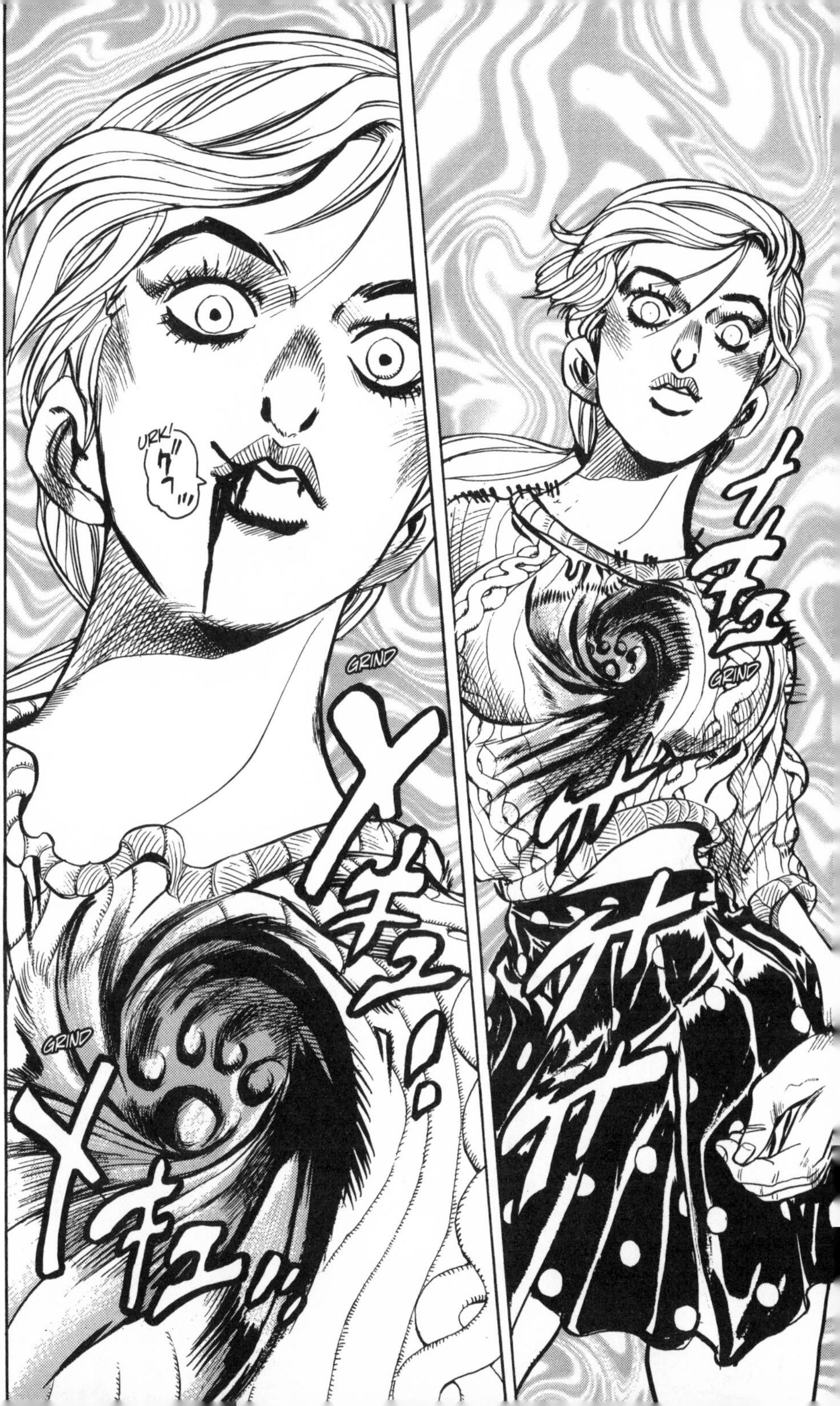
GRIND
URK!
GRIND
GRIND

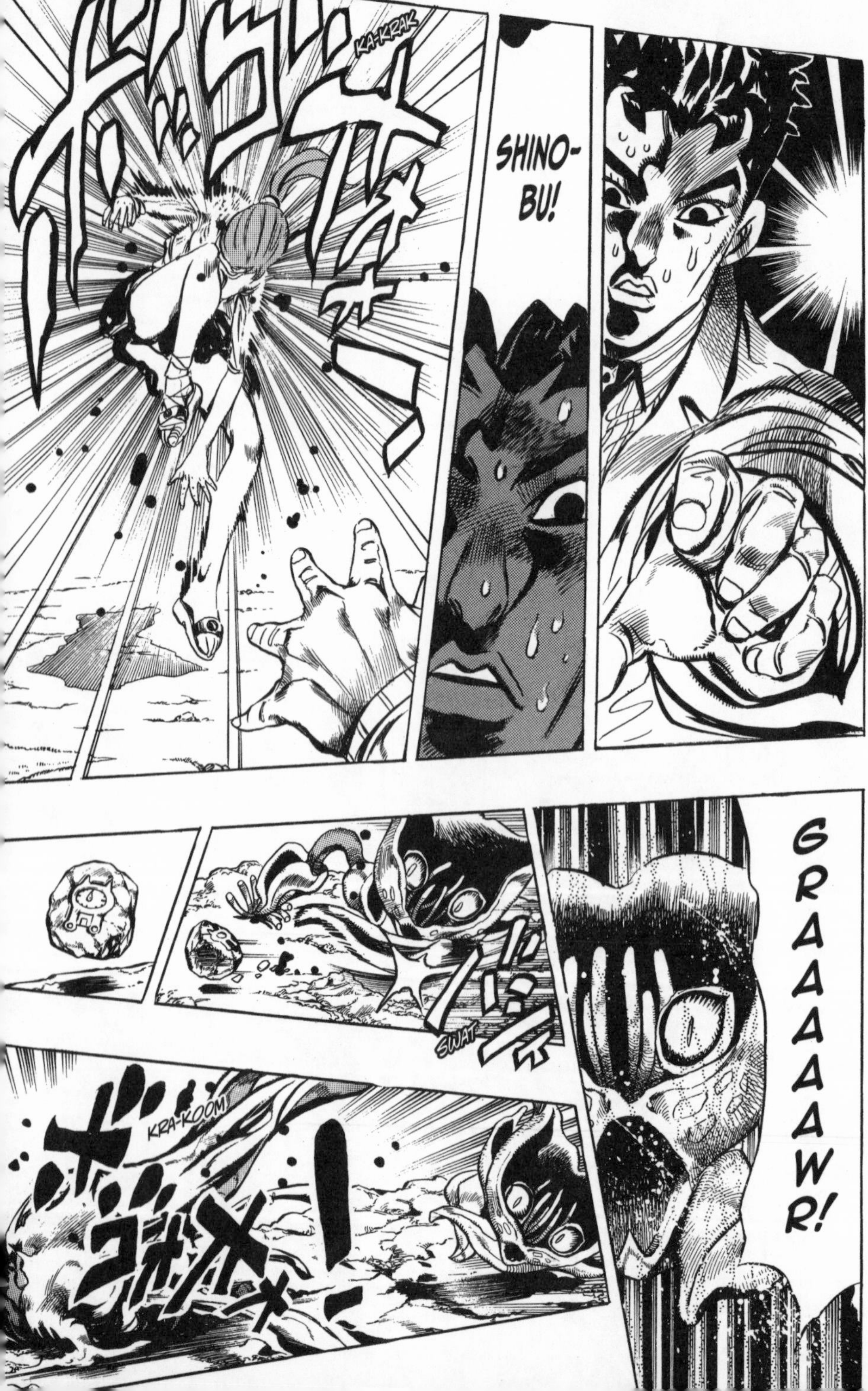

SHINO-BU!
KA-KRAK
GRAAAAAAWR!
SWAT
KRA-KOOM

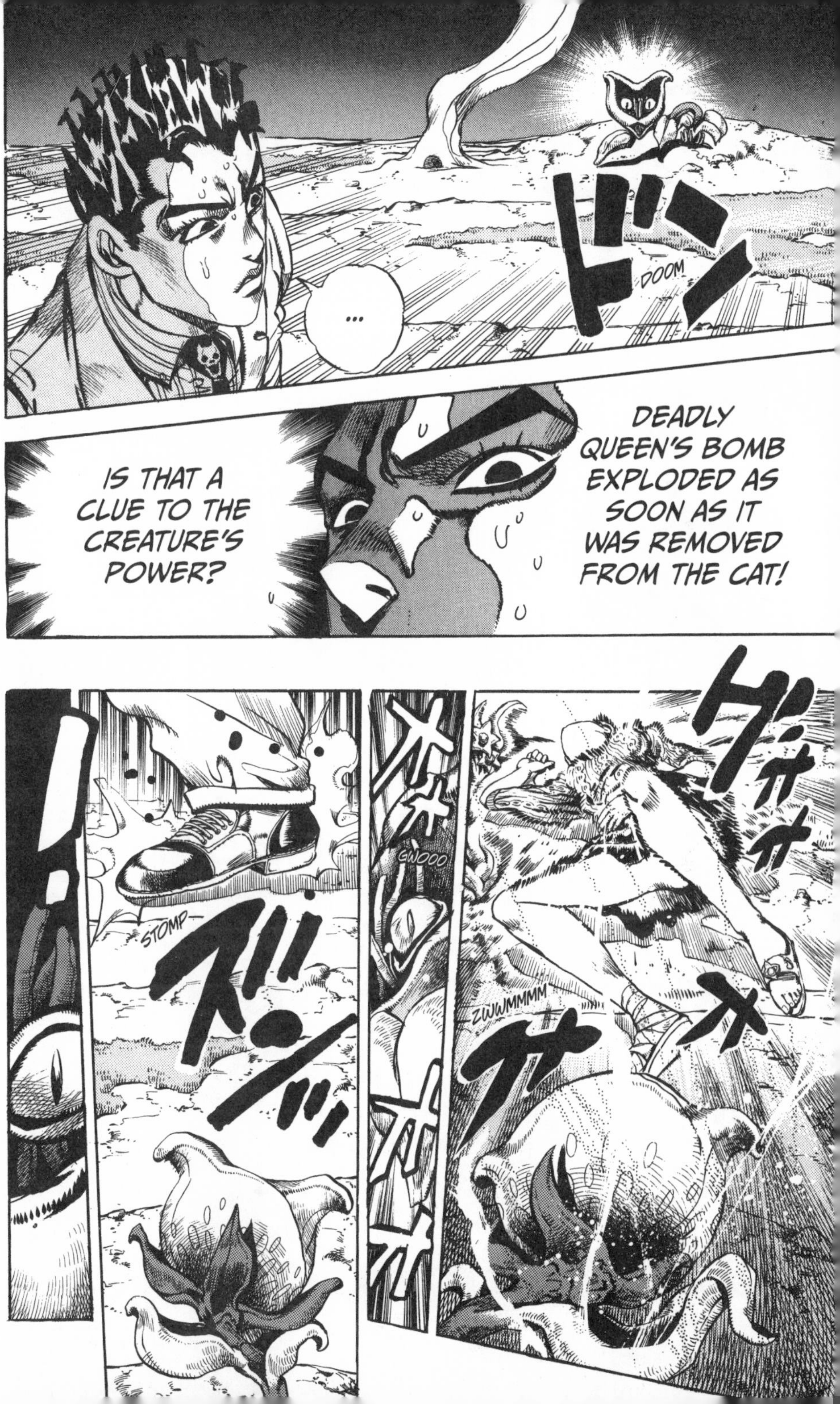
DOOM
...
DEADLY QUEEN'S BOMB EXPLODED AS SOON AS IT WAS REMOVED FROM THE CAT!
IS THAT A CLUE TO THE CREATURE'S POWER?
ZWWMMMM
GWOOO
STOMP

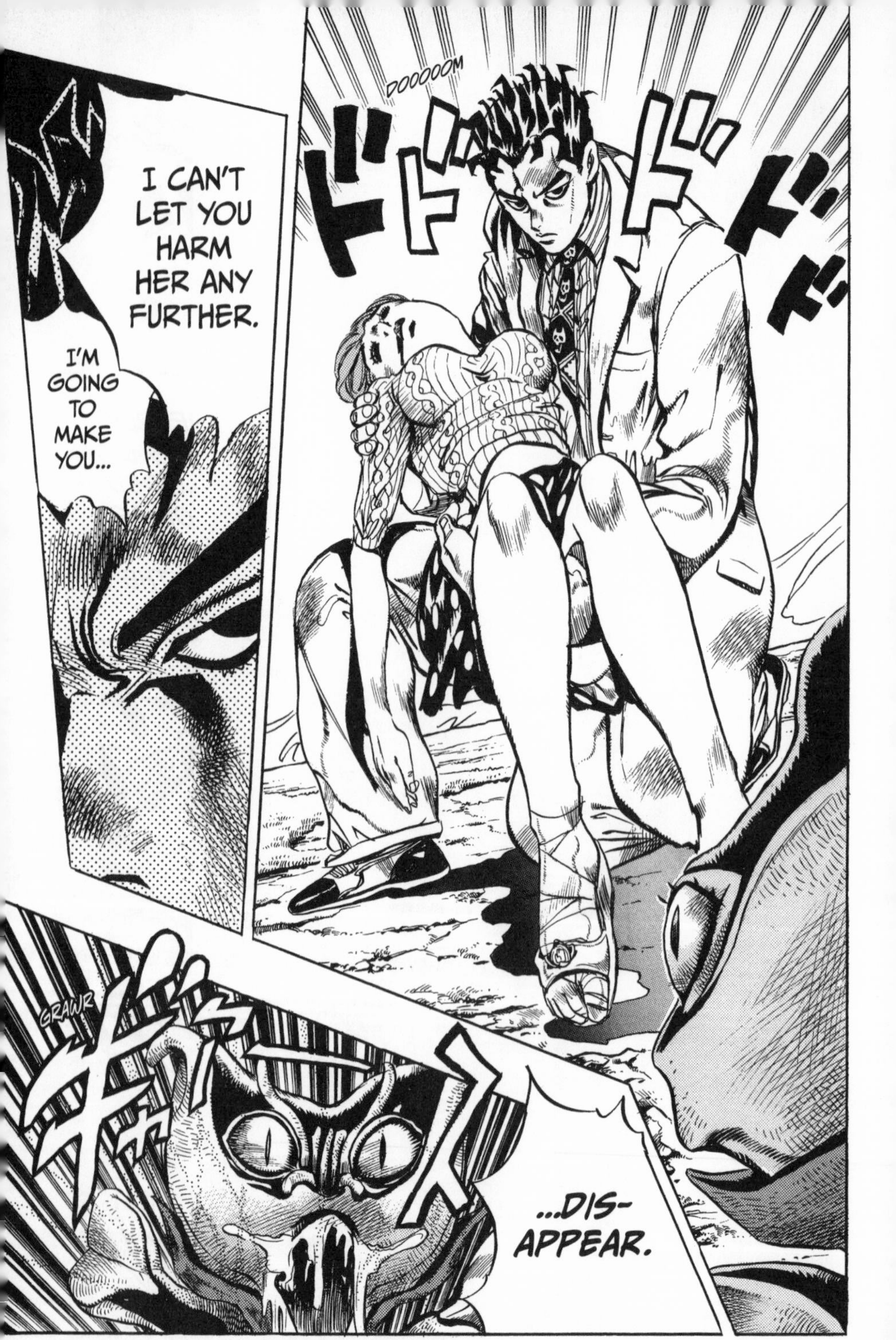
DOOOOOM
I CAN'T LET YOU HARM HER ANY FURTHER.
I'M GOING TO MAKE YOU...
...DIS-APPEAR.
GRAWR

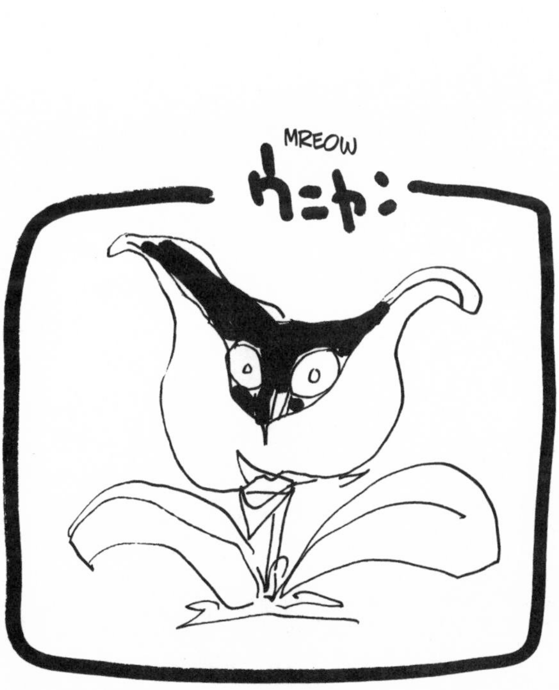
MREOW

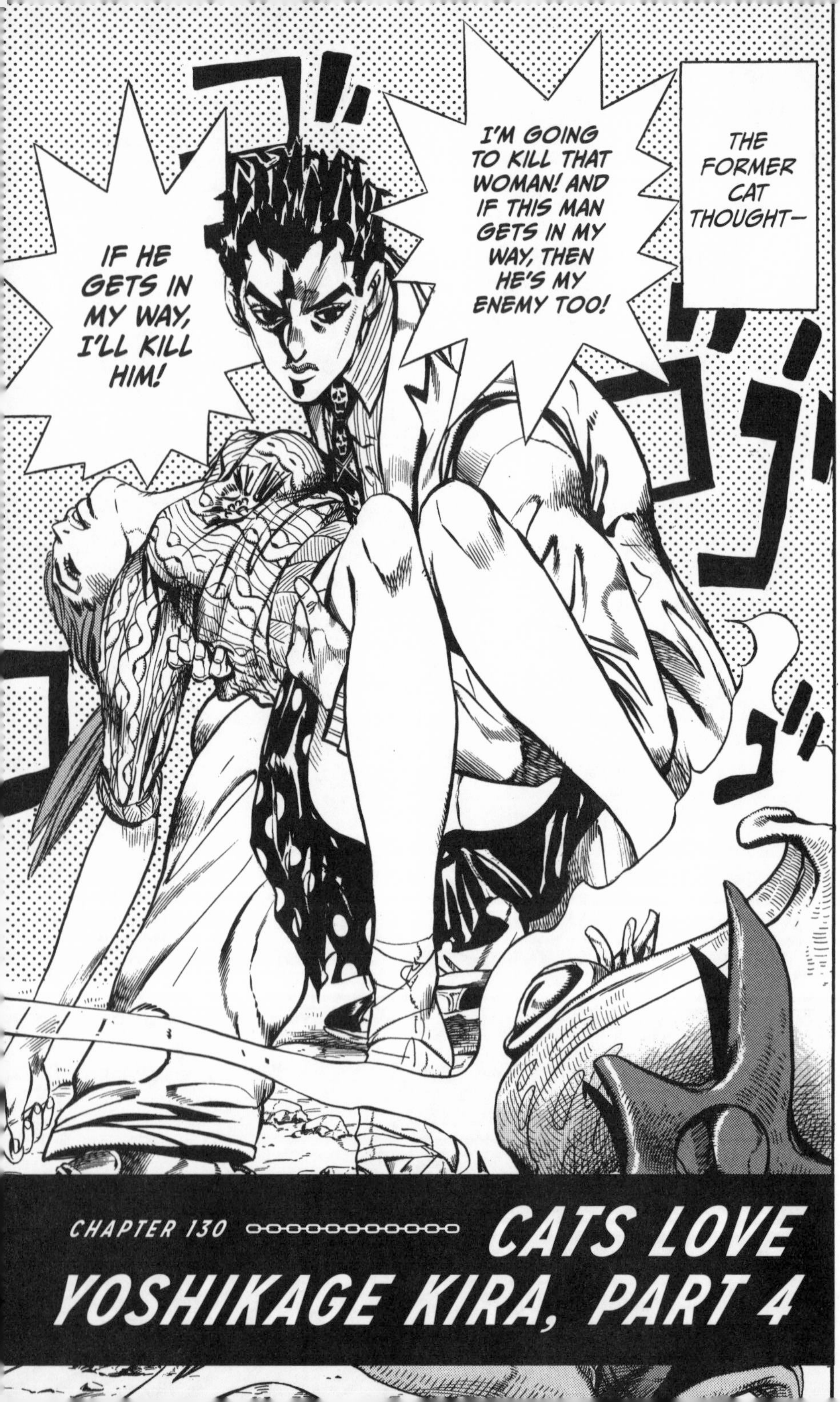
THE FORMER CAT THOUGHT—
I'M GOING TO KILL THAT WOMAN! AND IF THIS MAN GETS IN MY WAY, THEN HE'S MY ENEMY TOO!
IF HE GETS IN MY WAY, I'LL KILL HIM!

CHAPTER 130

CATS LOVE YOSHIKAGE KIRA, PART 4

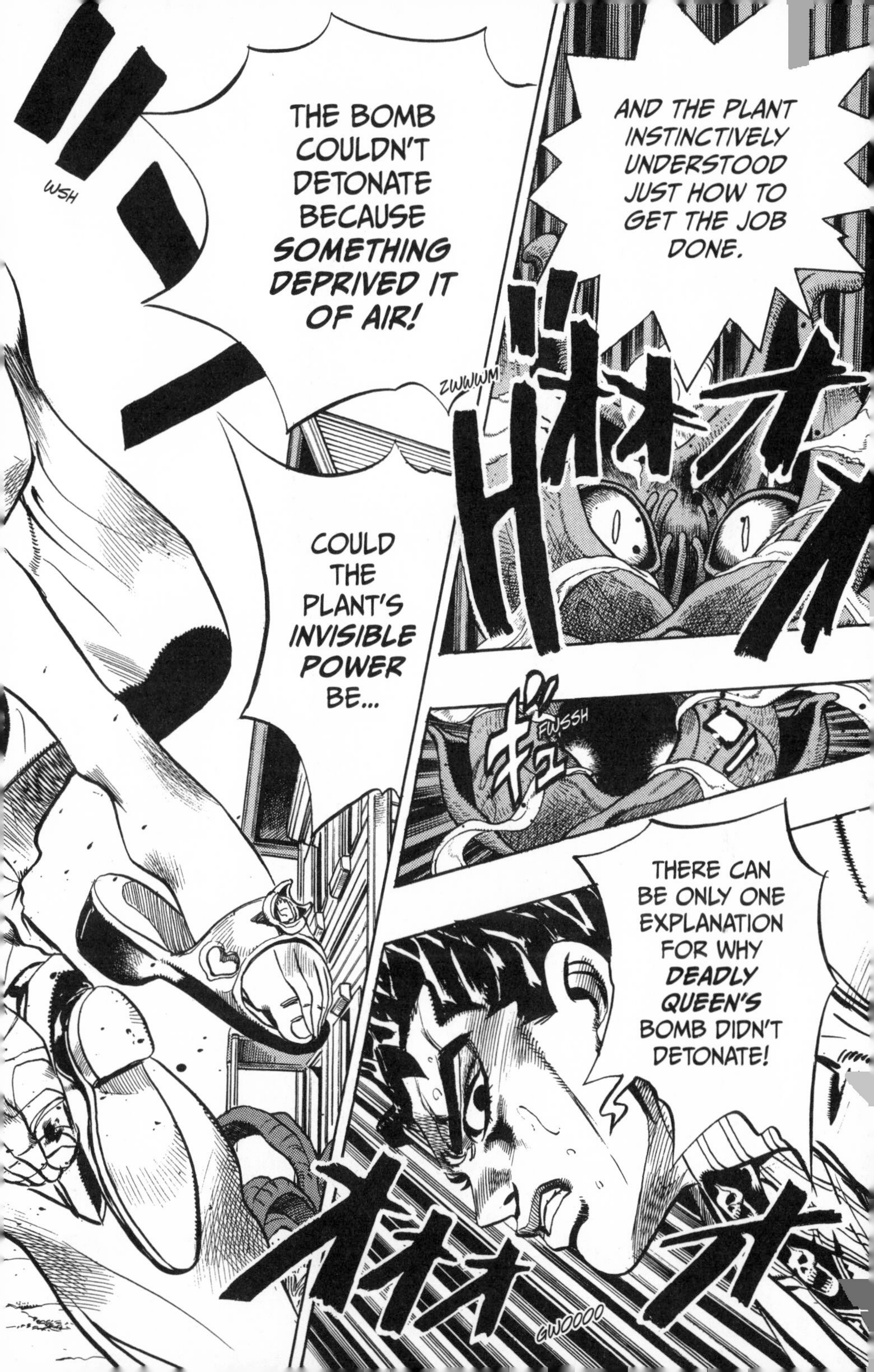
AND THE PLANT INSTINCTIVELY UNDERSTOOD JUST HOW TO GET THE JOB DONE.
ZWWWM
FWSSH
THERE CAN BE ONLY ONE EXPLANATION FOR WHY DEADLY QUEEN'S BOMB DIDN'T DETONATE!
GWOOOO
WSH
THE BOMB COULDN'T DETONATE BECAUSE SOMETHING DEPRIVED IT OF AIR!
COULD THE PLANT'S INVISIBLE POWER BE...

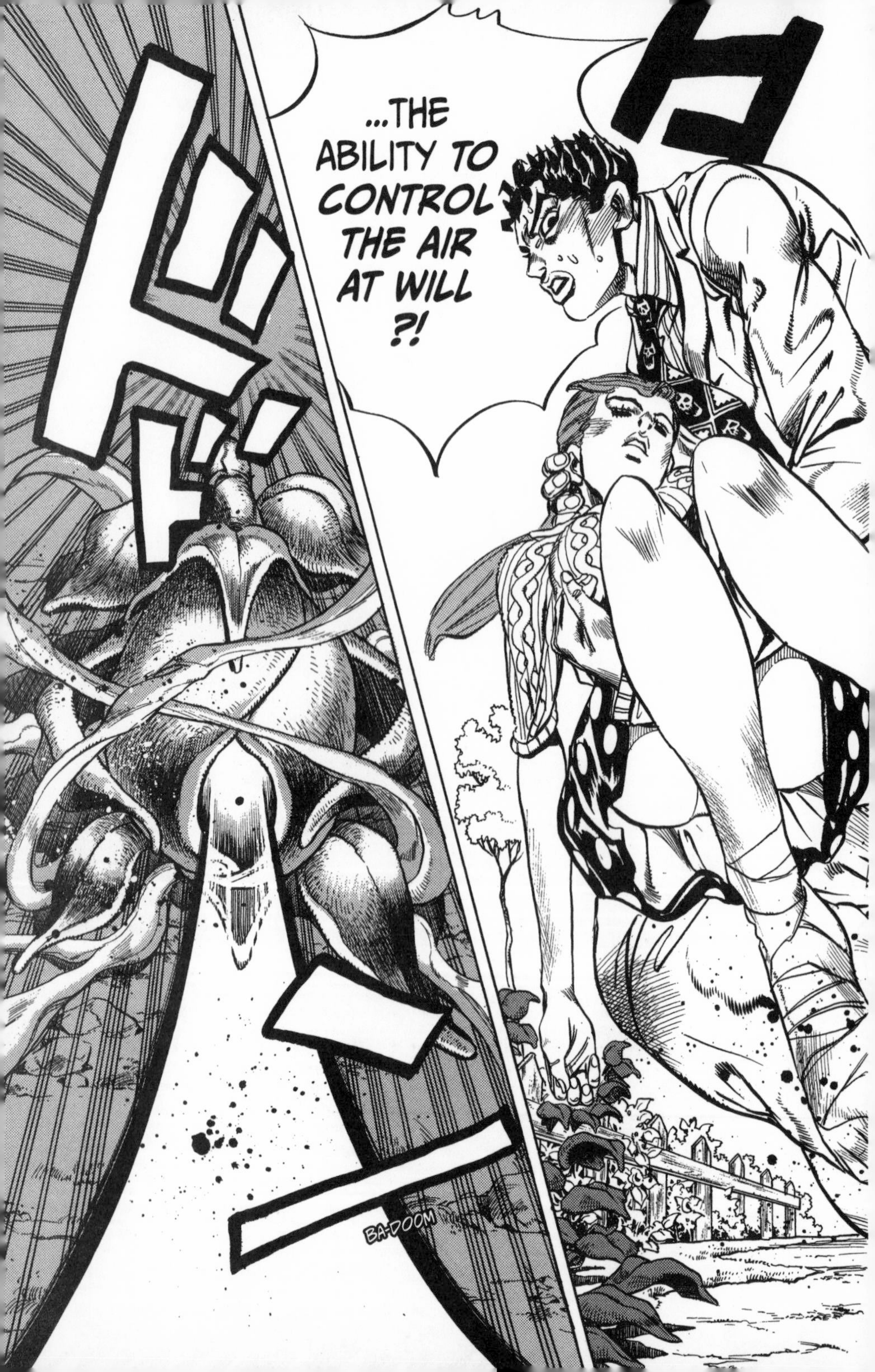
...THE ABILITY TO CONTROL THE AIR AT WILL ?!
BA-DOOM

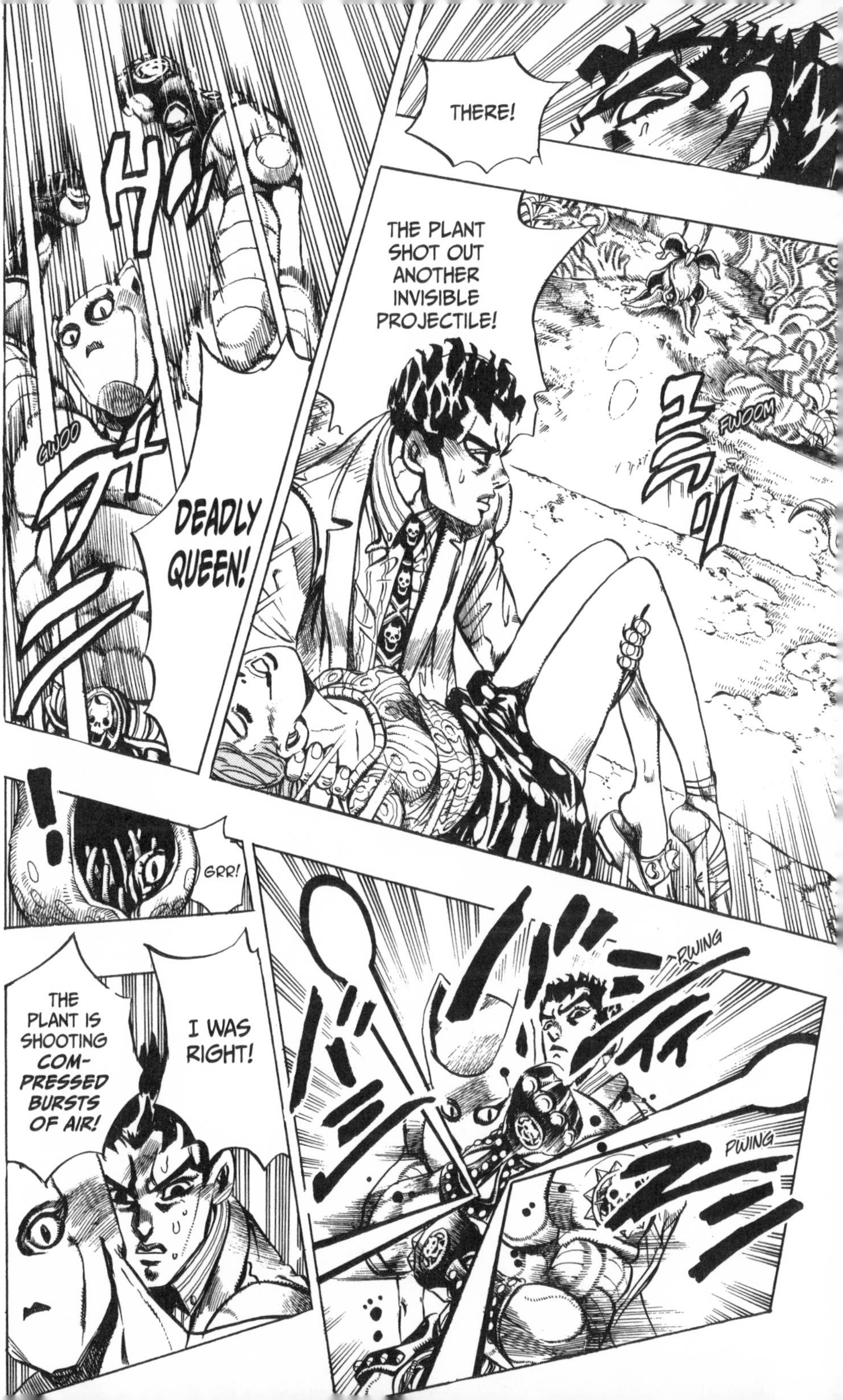
THERE!
THE PLANT SHOT OUT ANOTHER INVISIBLE PROJECTILE!
FWOOM
DEADLY QUEEN!
GWOO
GRR!
PWING
PWING
I WAS RIGHT!
THE PLANT IS SHOOTING COM-PRESSED BURSTS OF AIR!

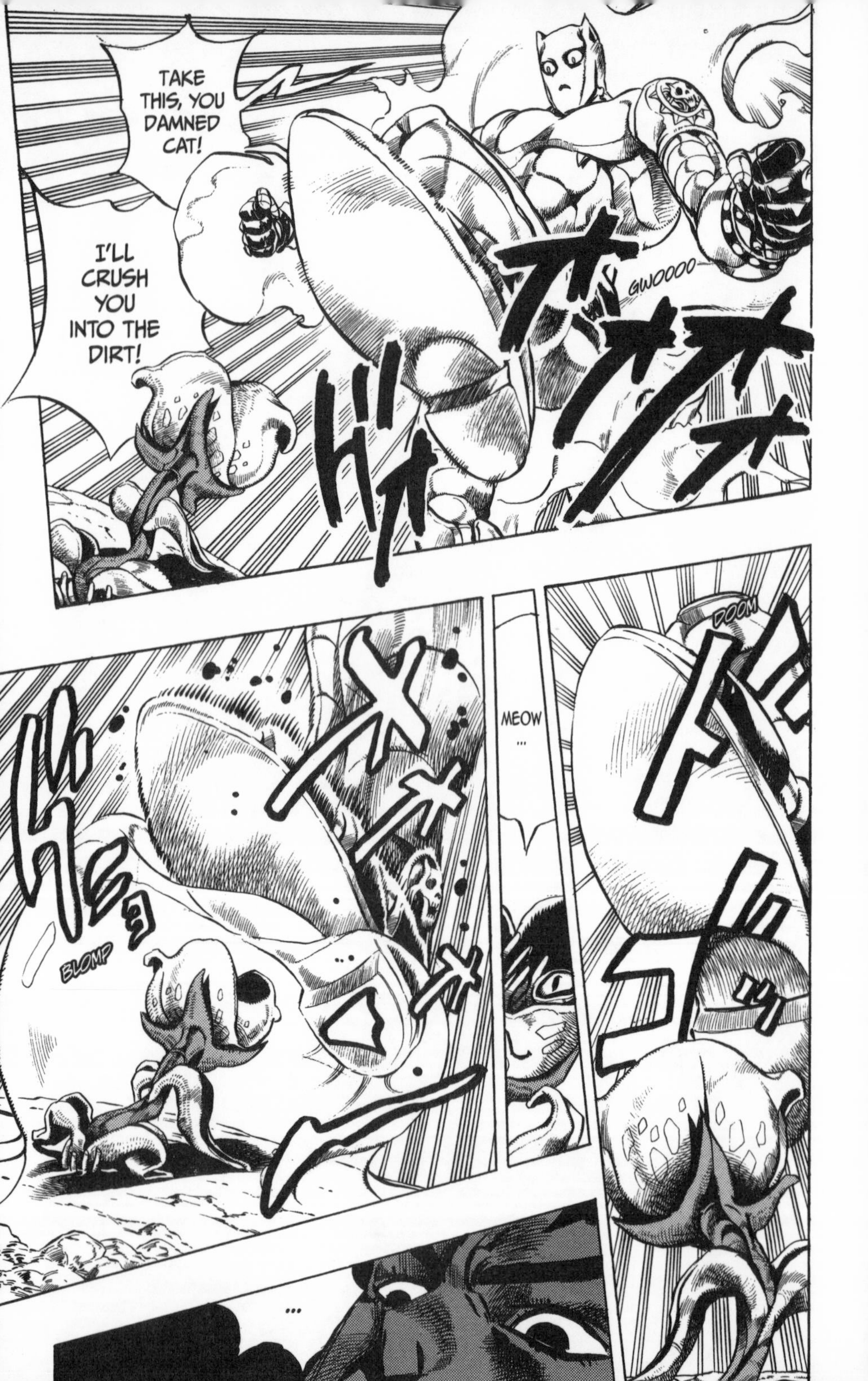
TAKE THIS, YOU DAMNED CAT!
I'LL CRUSH YOU INTO THE DIRT!
GWOOOO
DOOM
MEOW ...
BLOMP
...

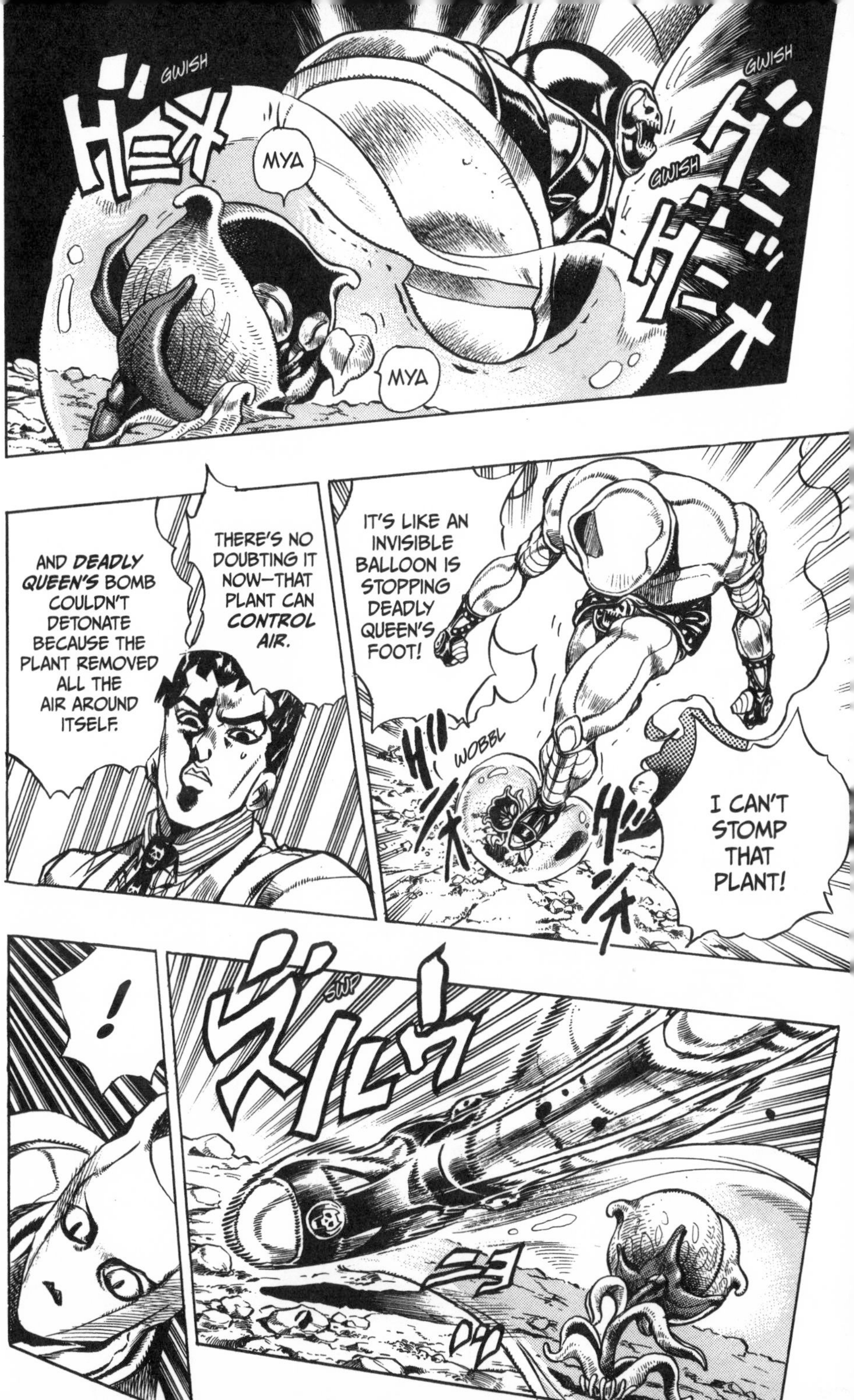
GWISH
GWISH
MYA
GWISH
MYA
I CAN'T STOMP THAT PLANT!
IT'S LIKE AN INVISIBLE BALLOON IS STOPPING DEADLY QUEEN'S FOOT!
WOBBL
THERE'S NO DOUBTING IT NOW—THAT PLANT CAN *CONTROL AIR.*
AND *DEADLY QUEEN'S* BOMB COULDN'T DETONATE BECAUSE THE PLANT REMOVED ALL THE AIR AROUND ITSELF.
SWP
!

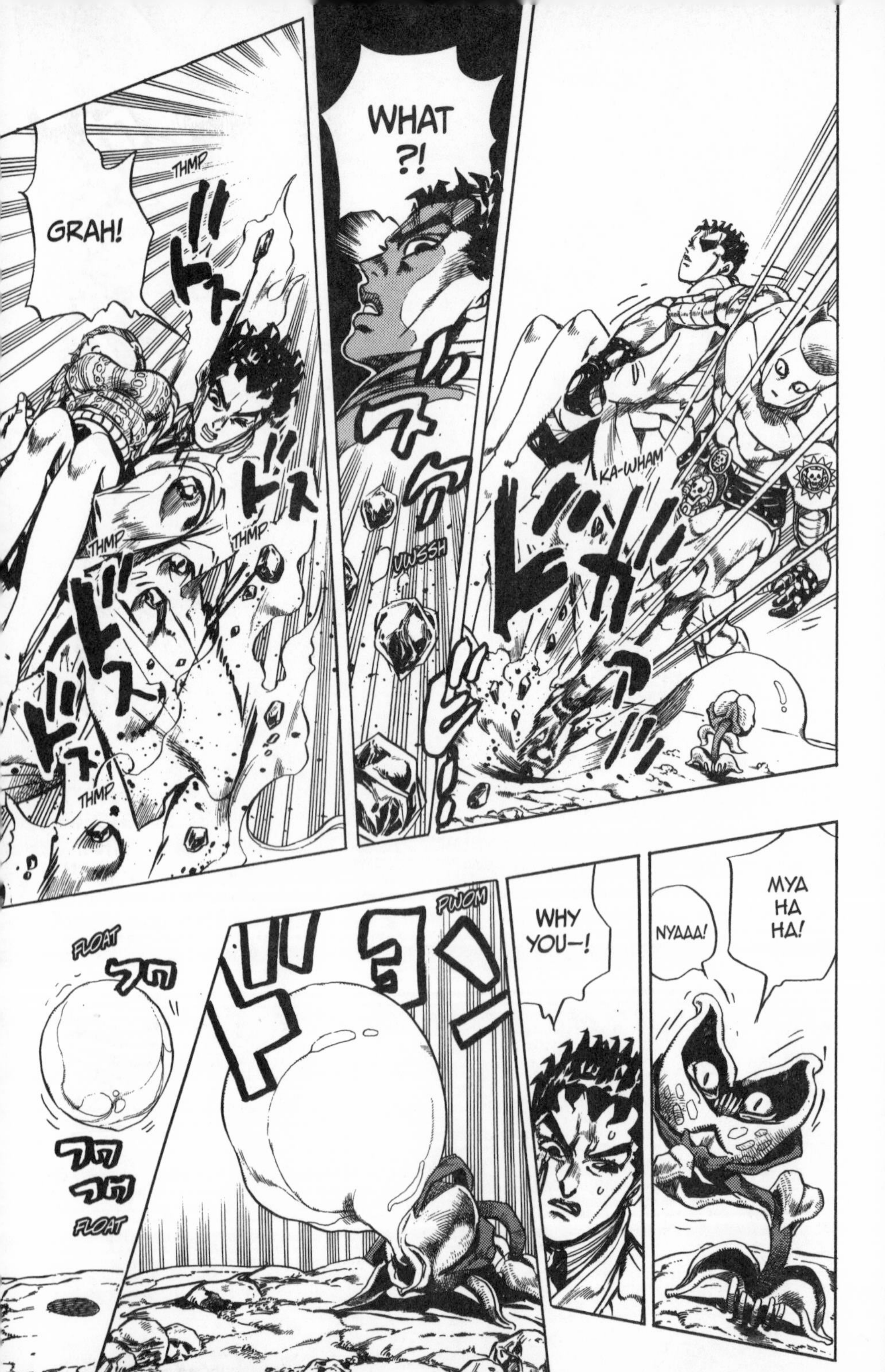
KA-WHAM
WHAT ?!
UWSSH
GRAH!
THMP
THMP
THMP
THMP
MYA HA HA!
NYAAA!
WHY YOU—!
PWOM
FLOAT
FLOAT

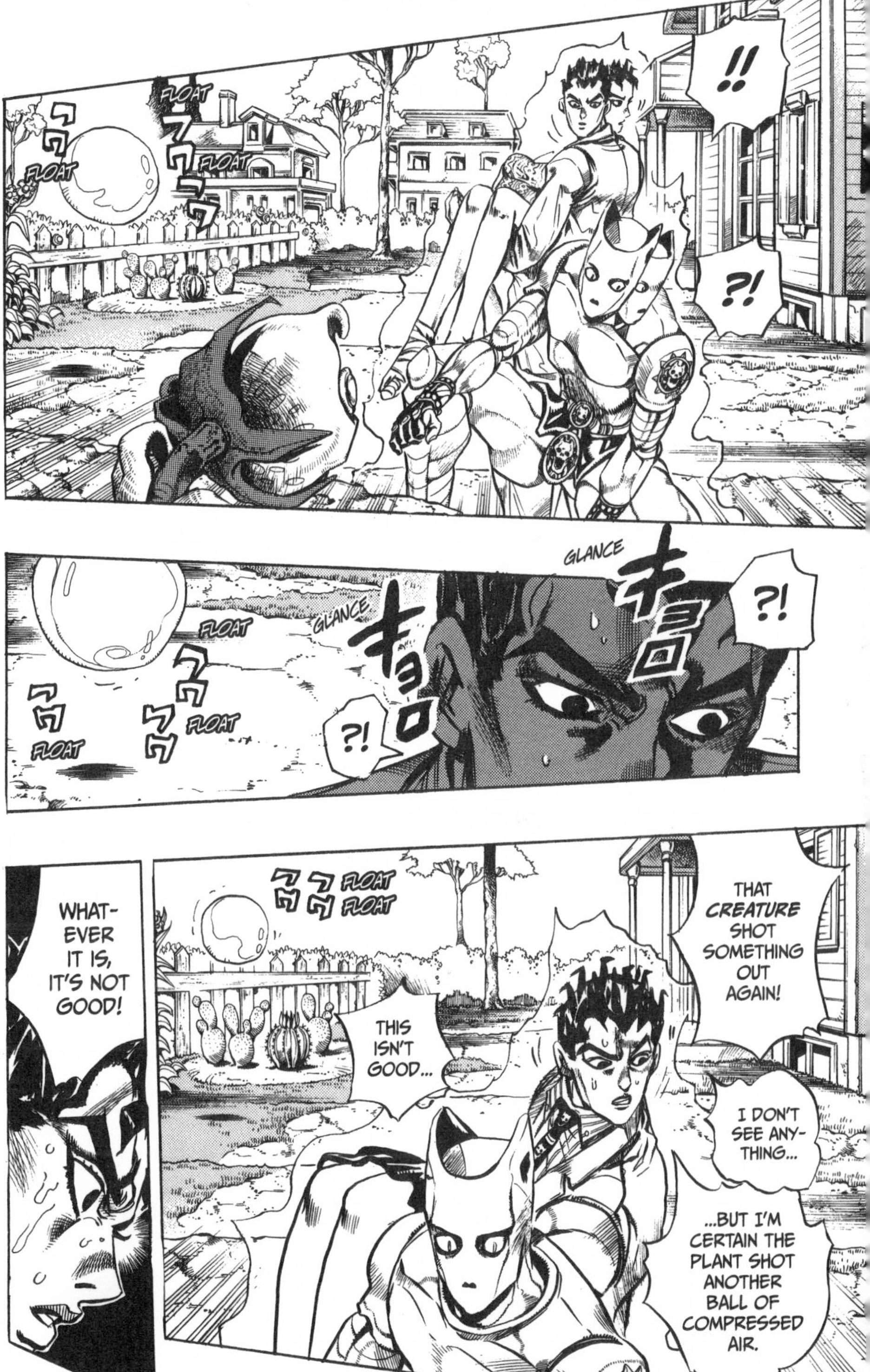
!!
?!
FLOAT
FLOAT
FLOAT
GLANCE
?!
GLANCE
?!
FLOAT
FLOAT
FLOAT
THAT CREATURE SHOT SOMETHING OUT AGAIN!
FLOAT
FLOAT
THIS ISN'T GOOD...
I DON'T SEE ANYTHING...
...BUT I'M CERTAIN THE PLANT SHOT ANOTHER BALL OF COMPRESSED AIR.
WHATEVER IT IS, IT'S NOT GOOD!

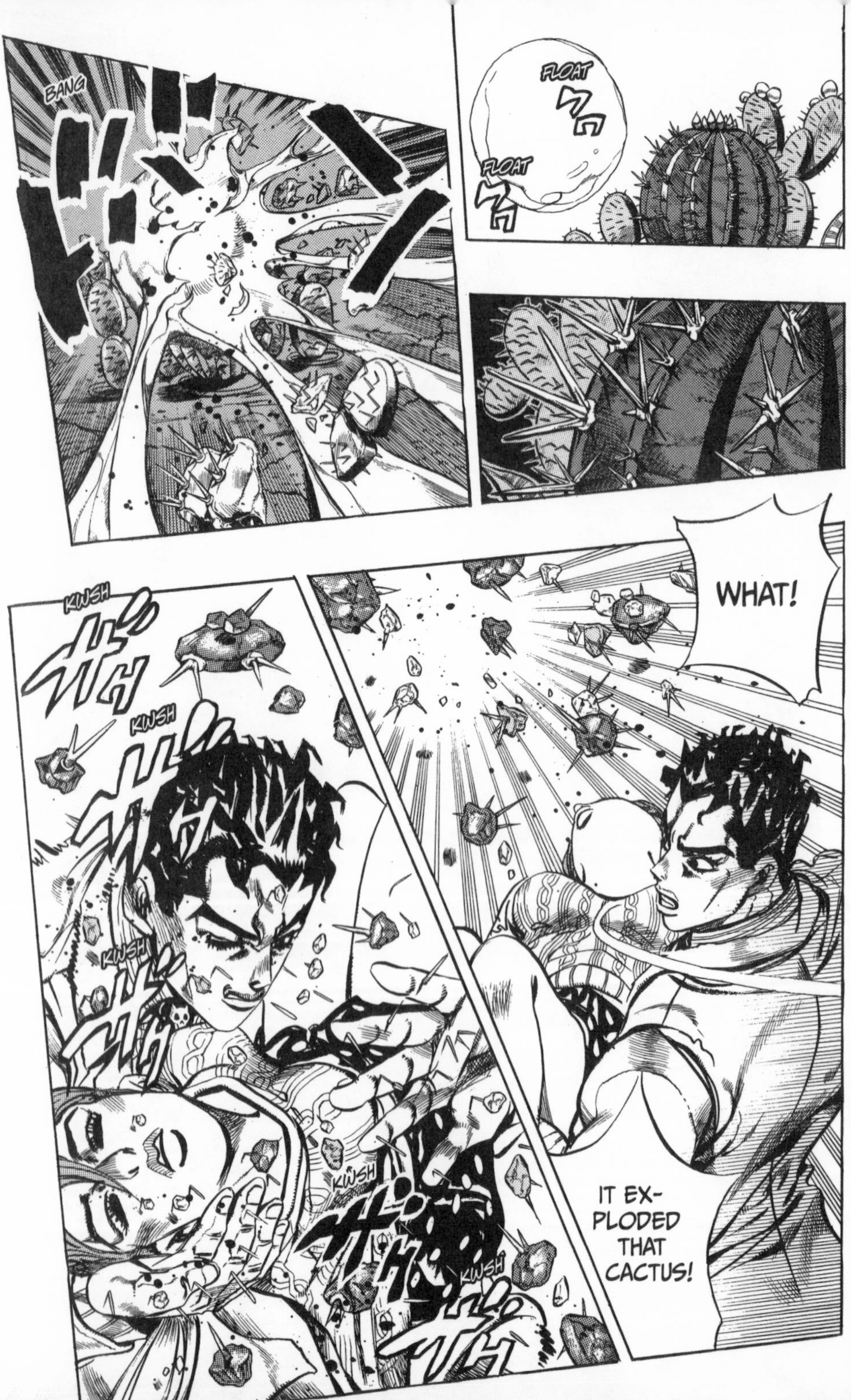
FLOAT
FLOAT
BANG
WHAT!
IT EX-
PLODED
THAT
CACTUS!
KWSH
KWSH
KWSH
KWSH
KWSH

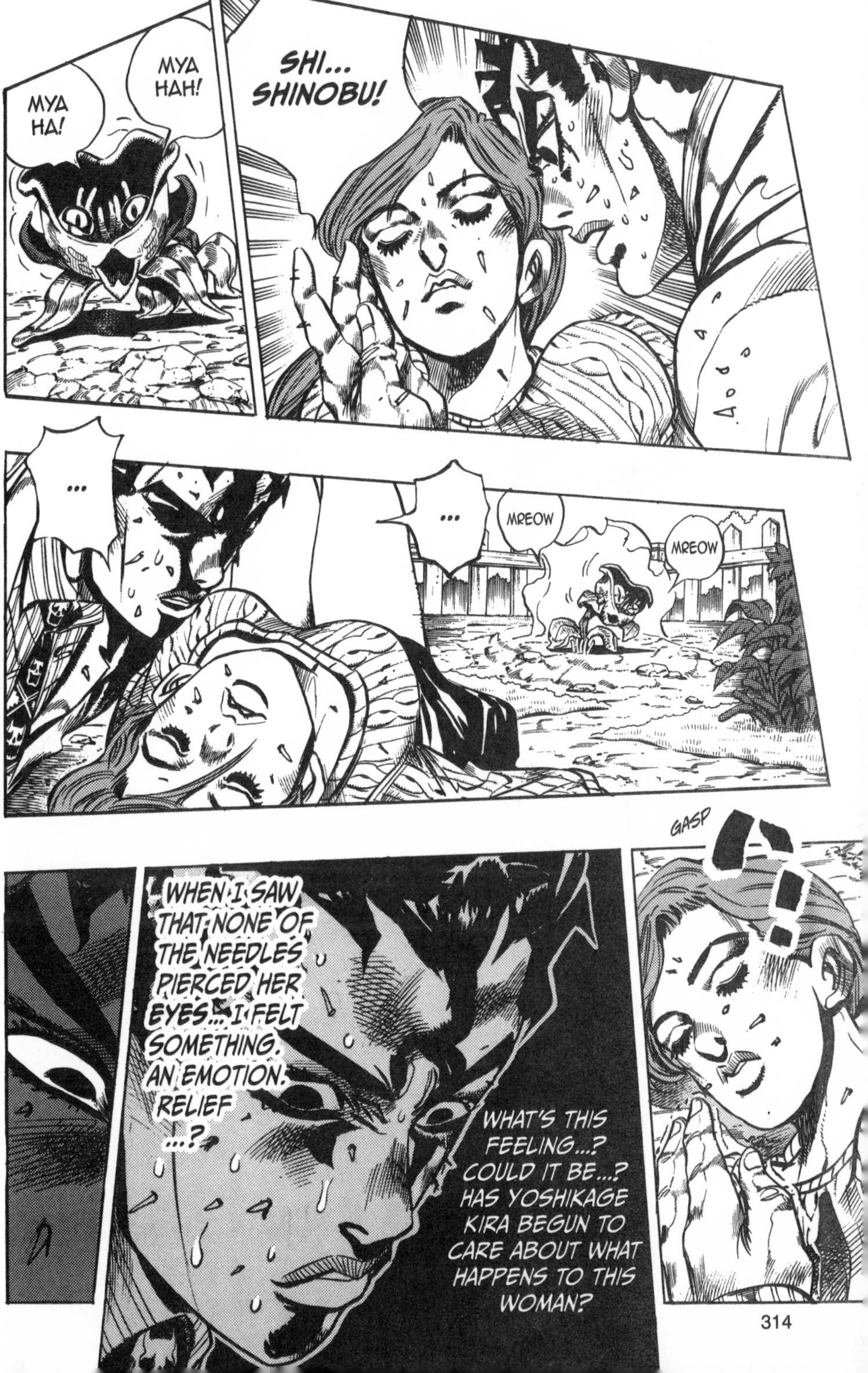
SHI... SHINOBU!
MYA HAH!
MYA HA!
MREOW
MREOW
...
...
GASP
WHEN I SAW THAT NONE OF THE NEEDLES PIERCED HER EYES... I FELT SOMETHING. AN EMOTION. RELIEF ...?
WHAT'S THIS FEELING...? COULD IT BE...? HAS YOSHIKAGE KIRA BEGUN TO CARE ABOUT WHAT HAPPENS TO THIS WOMAN?

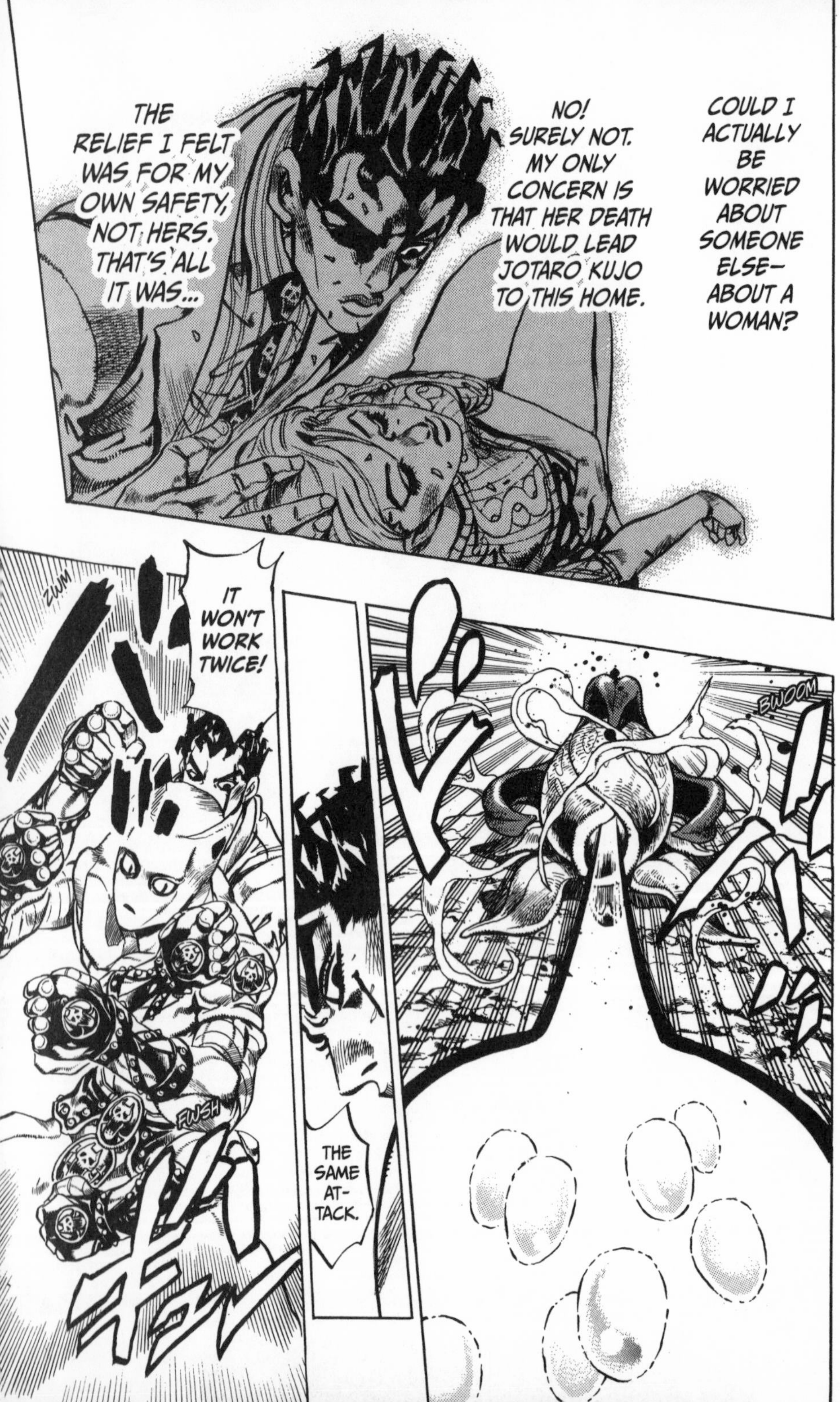
COULD I ACTUALLY BE WORRIED ABOUT SOMEONE ELSE— ABOUT A WOMAN?
NO! SURELY NOT. MY ONLY CONCERN IS THAT HER DEATH WOULD LEAD JOTARO KUJO TO THIS HOME.
THE RELIEF I FELT WAS FOR MY OWN SAFETY, NOT HERS. THAT'S ALL IT WAS...
BWOOM
THE SAME AT-TACK.
IT WON'T WORK TWICE!
ZWM
FWSH

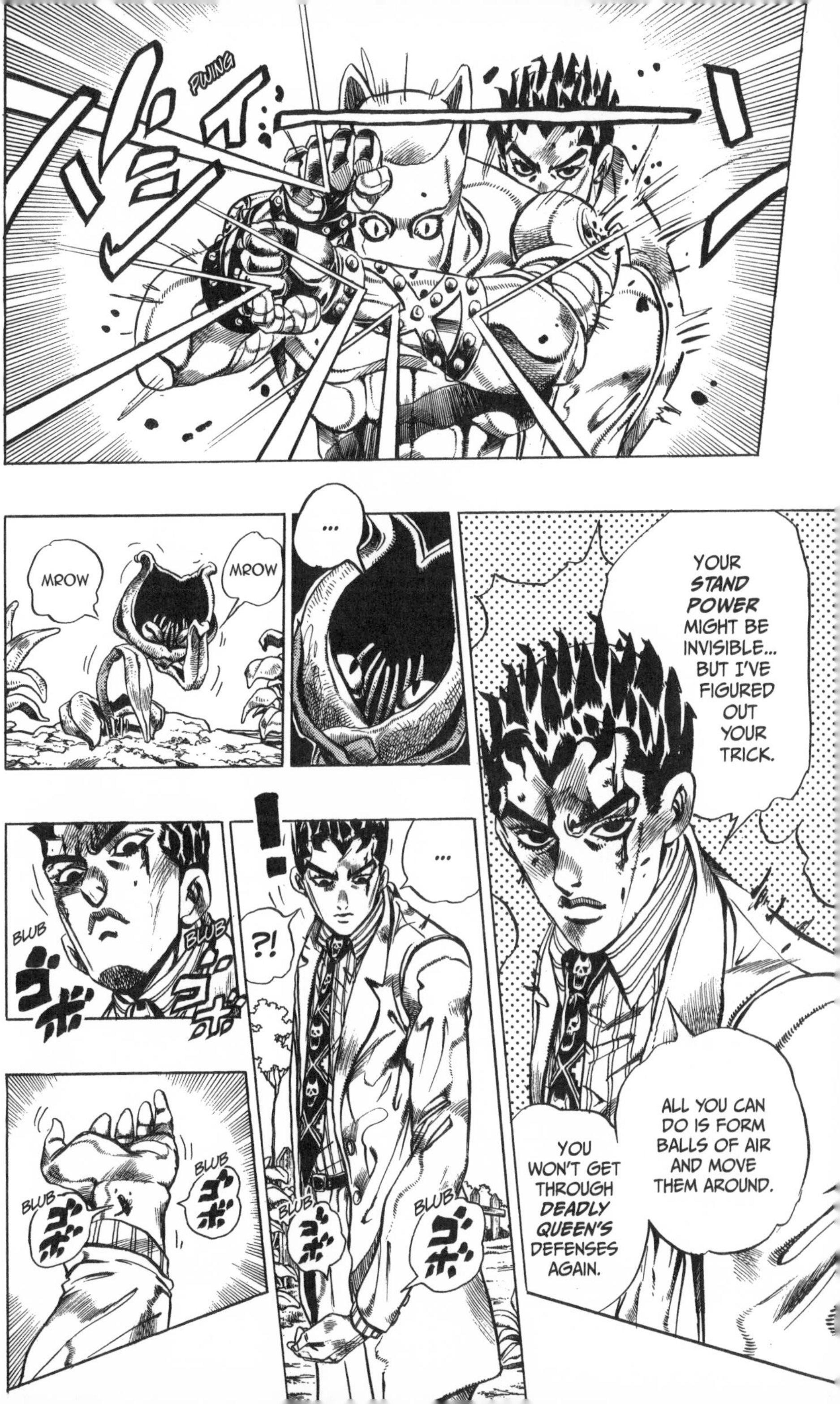
PWING
YOUR STAND POWER MIGHT BE INVISIBLE... BUT I'VE FIGURED OUT YOUR TRICK.
ALL YOU CAN DO IS FORM BALLS OF AIR AND MOVE THEM AROUND.
YOU WON'T GET THROUGH DEADLY QUEEN'S DEFENSES AGAIN.
...
MROW
MROW
!
...
?!
BLUB
ゴボ
BLUB
ゴボ
BLUB
ゴボ
BLUB
ゴボ
BLUB
ゴボ
BLUB
ゴボ

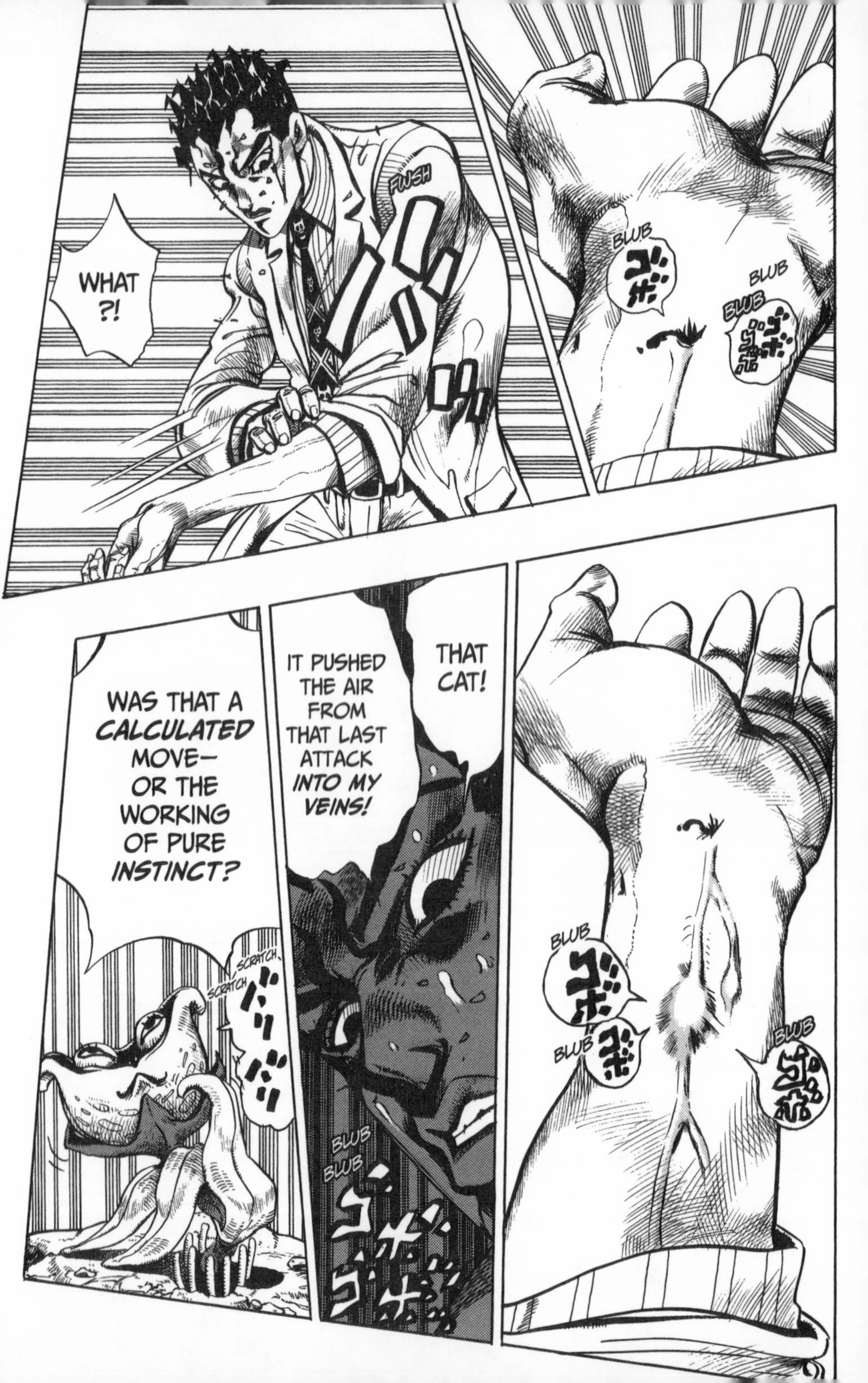
BLUB
BLUB
BLUB
FWSH
WHAT ?!
BLUB
BLUB
BLUB
THAT CAT!
IT PUSHED THE AIR FROM THAT LAST ATTACK *INTO MY VEINS!*
BLUB BLUB
WAS THAT A *CALCULATED* MOVE— OR THE WORKING OF PURE *INSTINCT?*
SCRATCH SCRATCH

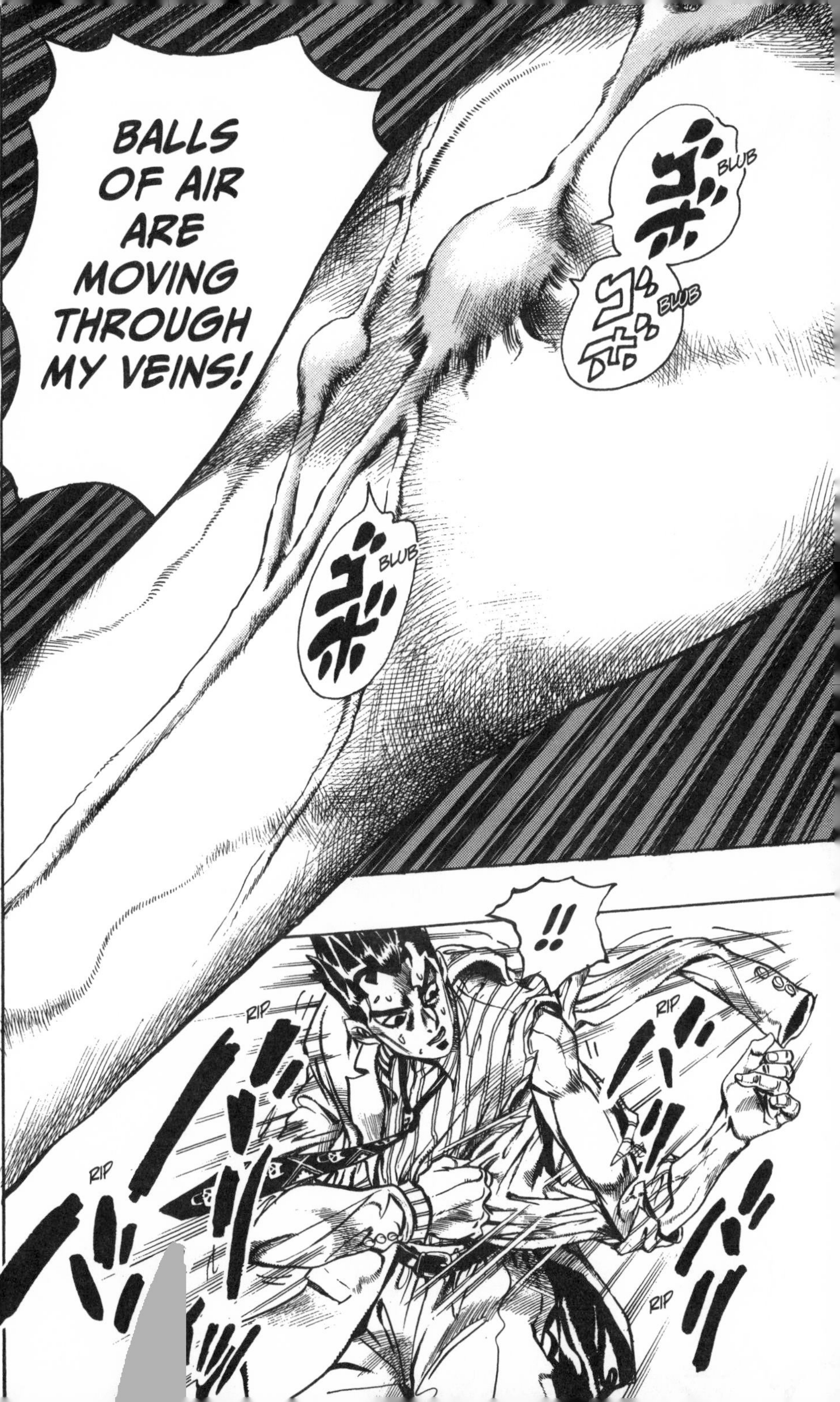
BALLS OF AIR ARE MOVING THROUGH MY VEINS!
ゴボ BLUB
ゴボゴボ BLUB
ゴボ BLUB
!!
RIP
RIP
RIP
RIP

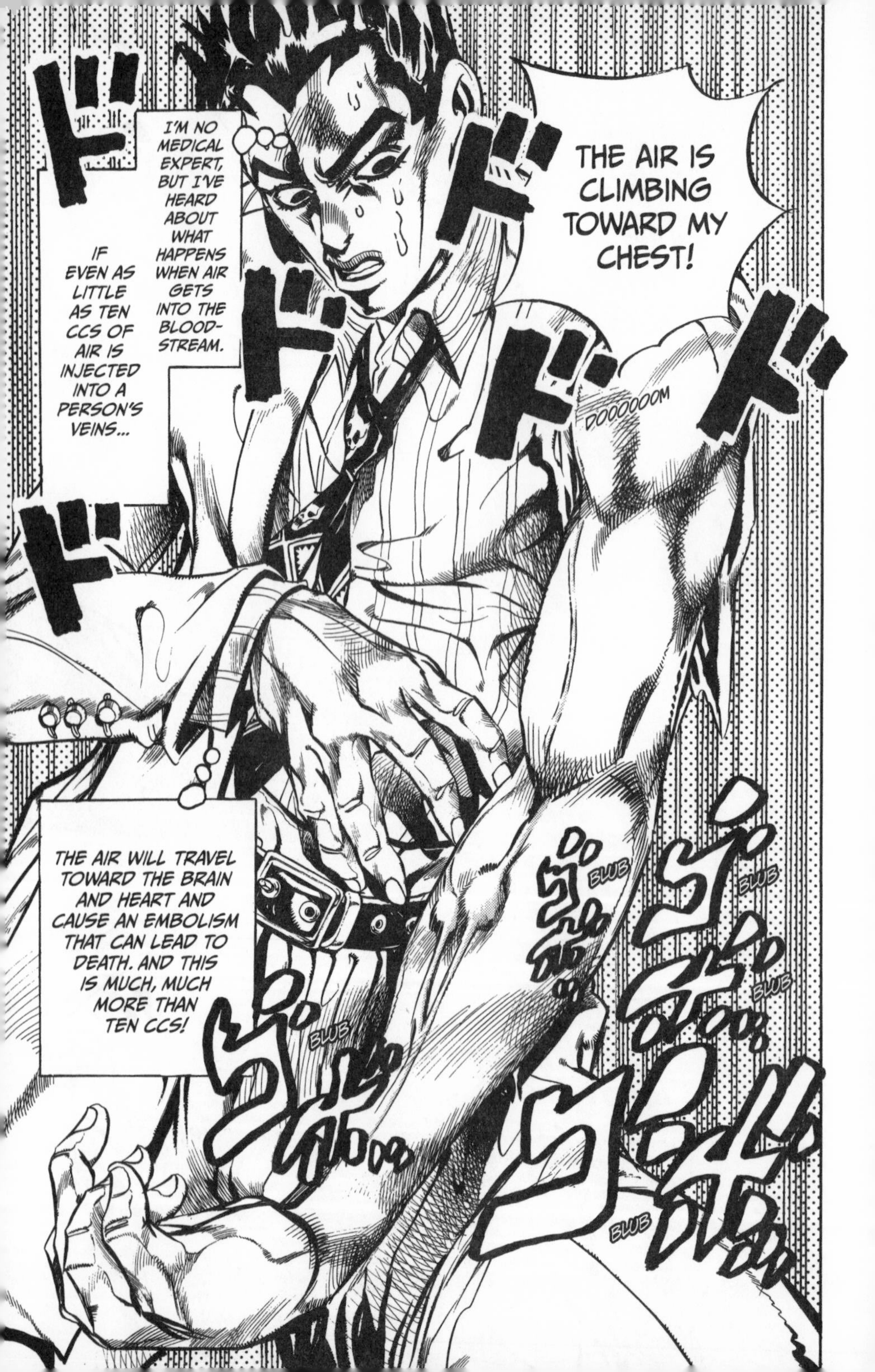
THE AIR IS CLIMBING TOWARD MY CHEST!
I'M NO MEDICAL EXPERT, BUT I'VE HEARD ABOUT WHAT HAPPENS WHEN AIR GETS INTO THE BLOOD-STREAM.
IF EVEN AS LITTLE AS TEN CCS OF AIR IS INJECTED INTO A PERSON'S VEINS...
DOOOOOOOM
THE AIR WILL TRAVEL TOWARD THE BRAIN AND HEART AND CAUSE AN EMBOLISM THAT CAN LEAD TO DEATH. AND THIS IS MUCH, MUCH MORE THAN TEN CCS!
BLUB
BLUB
BLUB
BLUB
BLUB

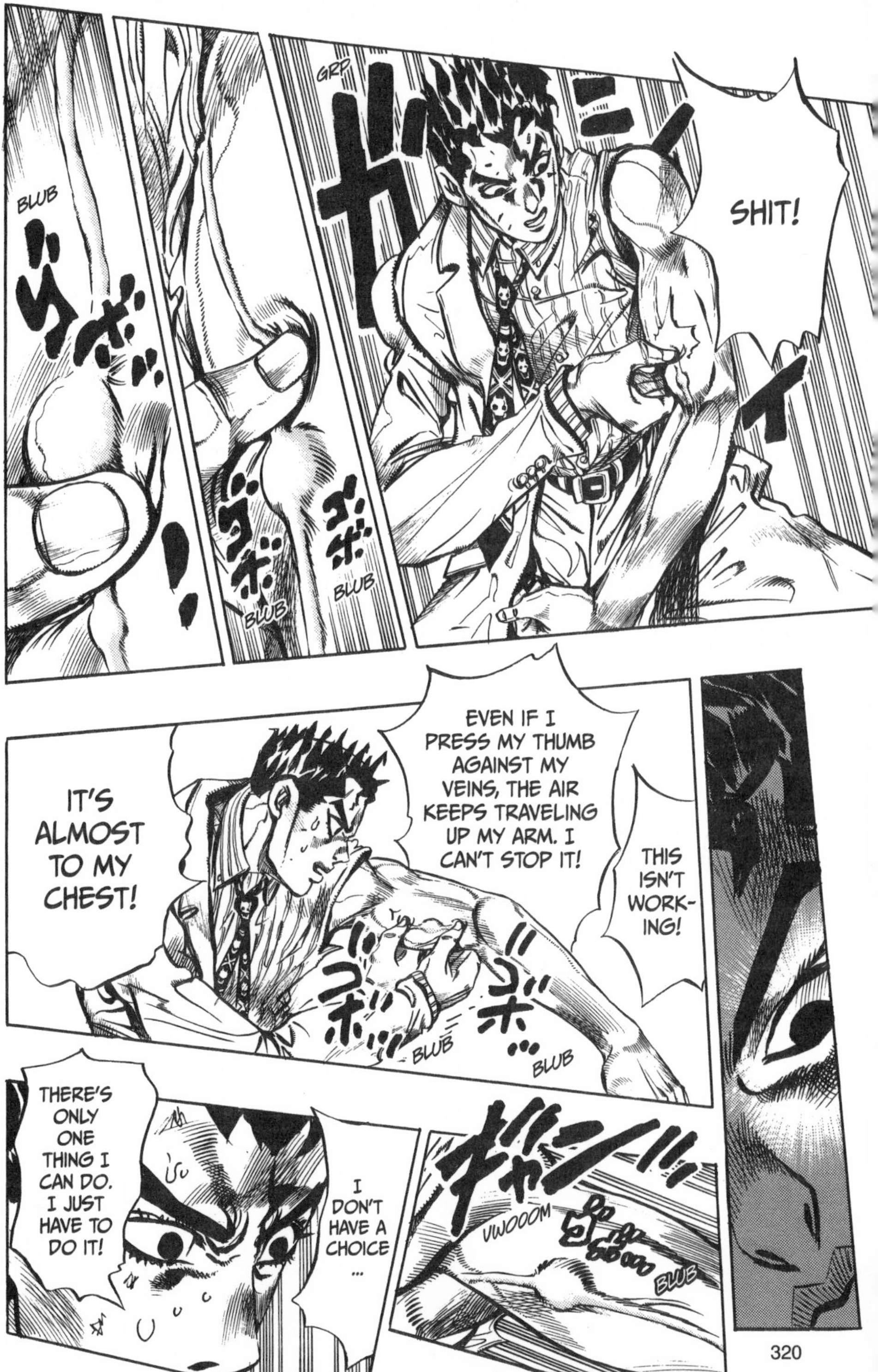
GRP
SHIT!
BLUB
BLUB
BLUB
EVEN IF I PRESS MY THUMB AGAINST MY VEINS, THE AIR KEEPS TRAVELING UP MY ARM. I CAN'T STOP IT!
THIS ISN'T WORKING!
IT'S ALMOST TO MY CHEST!
BLUB
BLUB
VWOOOM
BLUB
I DON'T HAVE A CHOICE...
THERE'S ONLY ONE THING I CAN DO. I JUST HAVE TO DO IT!

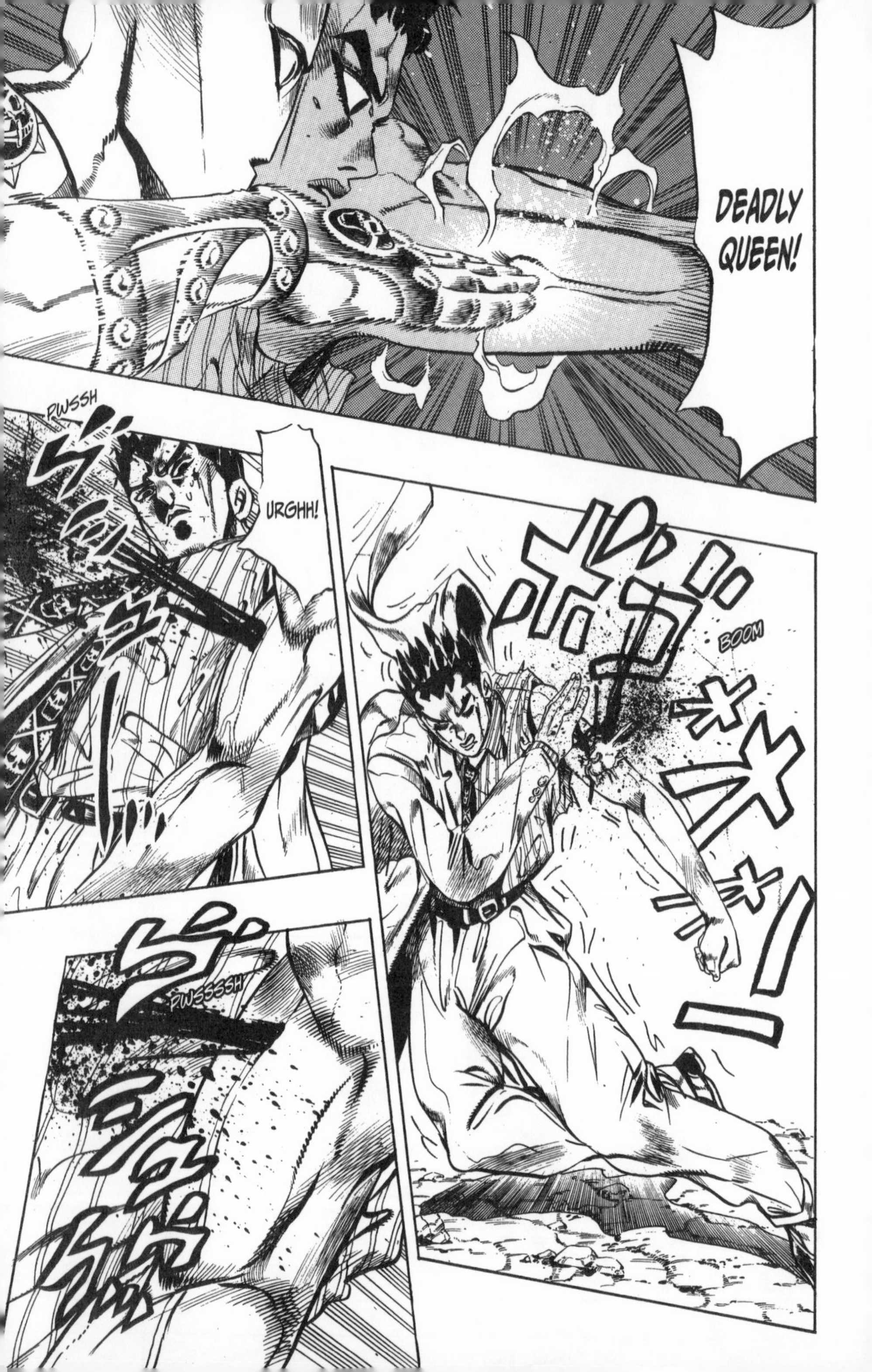
DEADLY QUEEN!
PWSSH
URGHH!
BOOM
PWSSSSH

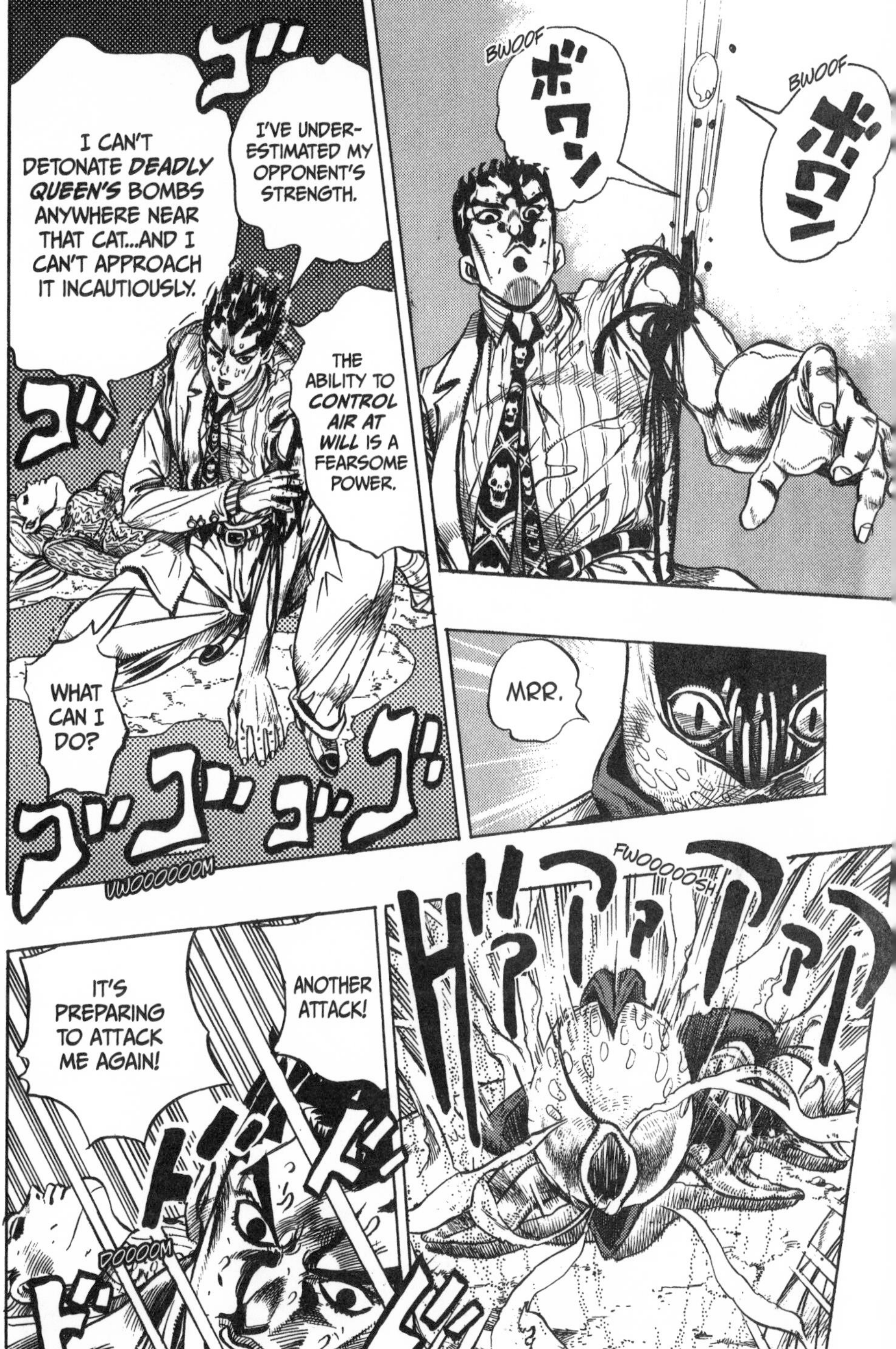
BWOOF
ボワン
BWOOF
ボワン
MRR.
I'VE UNDER-ESTIMATED MY OPPONENT'S STRENGTH.
I CAN'T DETONATE ***DEADLY QUEEN'S*** BOMBS ANYWHERE NEAR THAT CAT...AND I CAN'T APPROACH IT INCAUTIOUSLY.
THE ABILITY TO ***CONTROL AIR AT WILL*** IS A FEARSOME POWER.
WHAT CAN I DO?
UWOOOOOOOM
FWOOOOOSH
ANOTHER ATTACK!
IT'S PREPARING TO ATTACK ME AGAIN!
DOOOOM

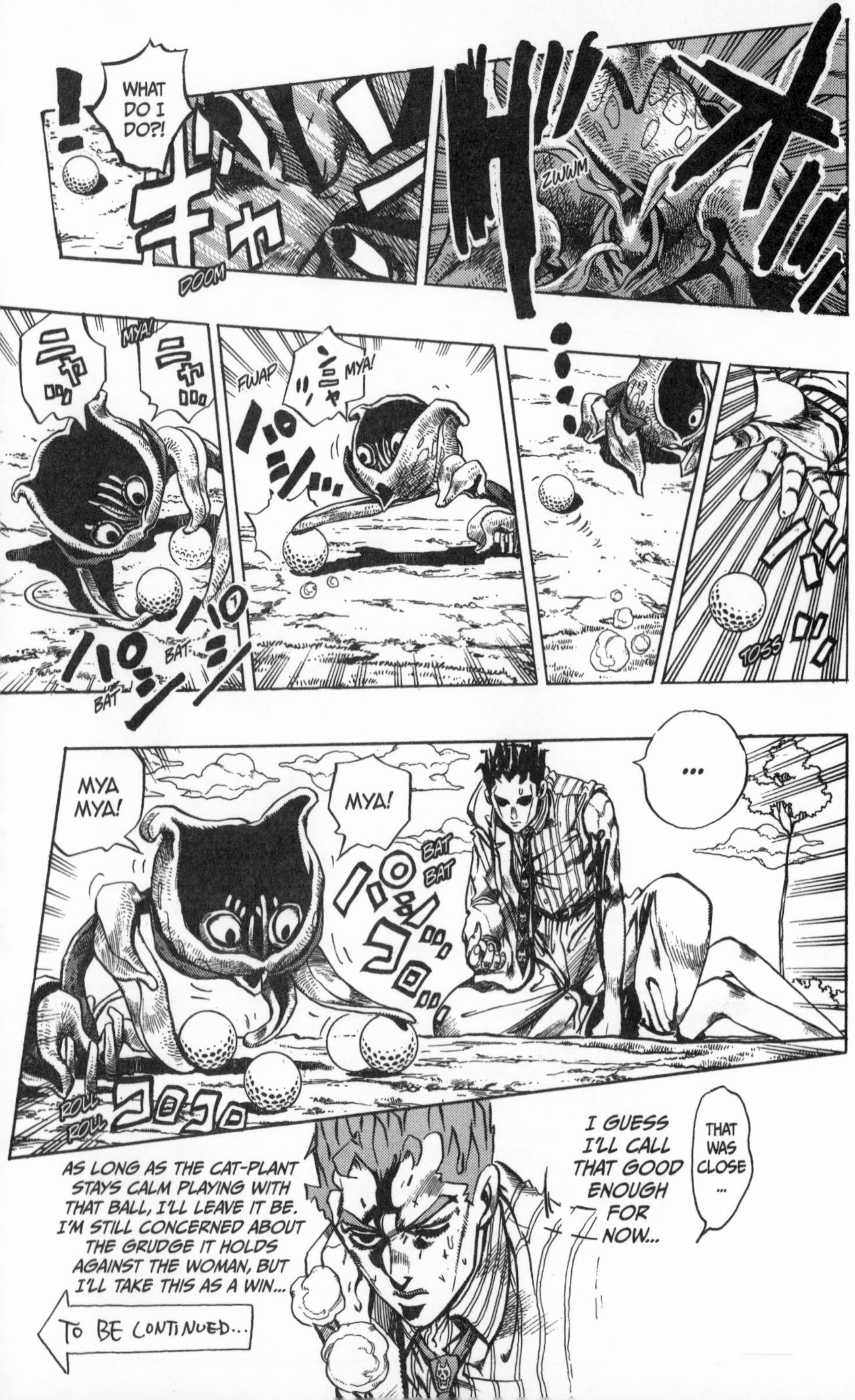
ZWWM
WHAT DO I DO?!
DOOM
TOSS
FWAP
MYA!
MYA!
BAT
BAT
...
BAT BAT
MYA!
MYA MYA!
ROLL ROLL
THAT WAS CLOSE...
I GUESS I'LL CALL THAT GOOD ENOUGH FOR NOW...
AS LONG AS THE CAT-PLANT STAYS CALM PLAYING WITH THAT BALL, I'LL LEAVE IT BE. I'M STILL CONCERNED ABOUT THE GRUDGE IT HOLDS AGAINST THE WOMAN, BUT I'LL TAKE THIS AS A WIN...
TO BE CONTINUED...

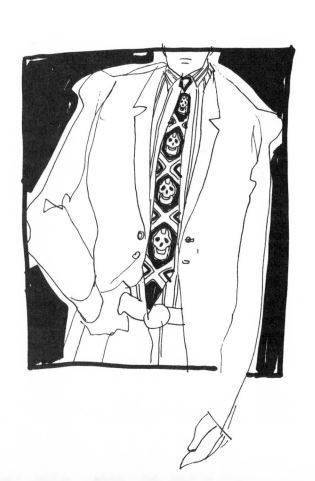

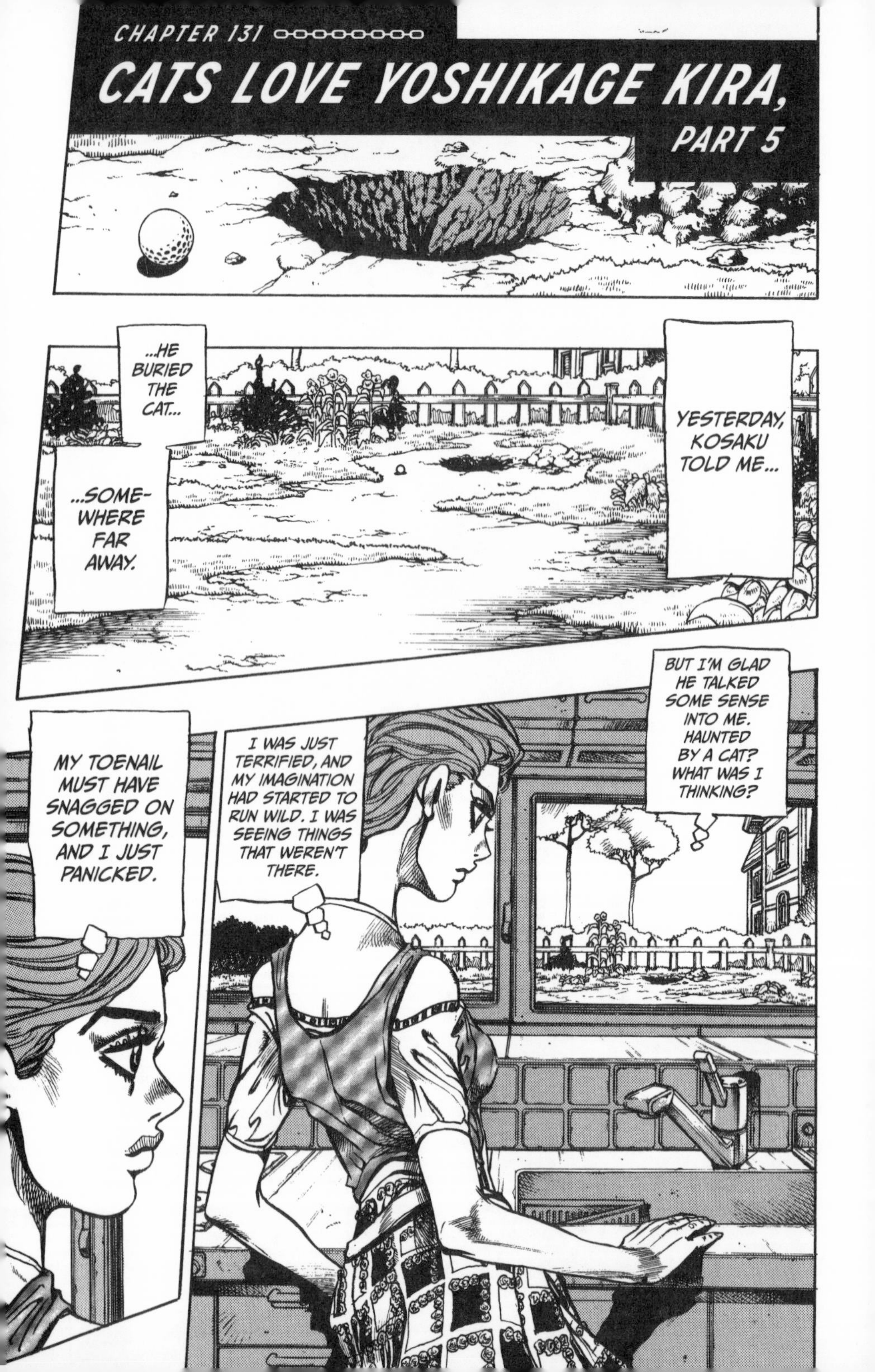
CHAPTER 131
CATS LOVE YOSHIKAGE KIRA, PART 5
YESTERDAY, KOSAKU TOLD ME...
...HE BURIED THE CAT...
...SOME-WHERE FAR AWAY.
BUT I'M GLAD HE TALKED SOME SENSE INTO ME. HAUNTED BY A CAT? WHAT WAS I THINKING?
I WAS JUST TERRIFIED, AND MY IMAGINATION HAD STARTED TO RUN WILD. I WAS SEEING THINGS THAT WEREN'T THERE.
MY TOENAIL MUST HAVE SNAGGED ON SOMETHING, AND I JUST PANICKED.

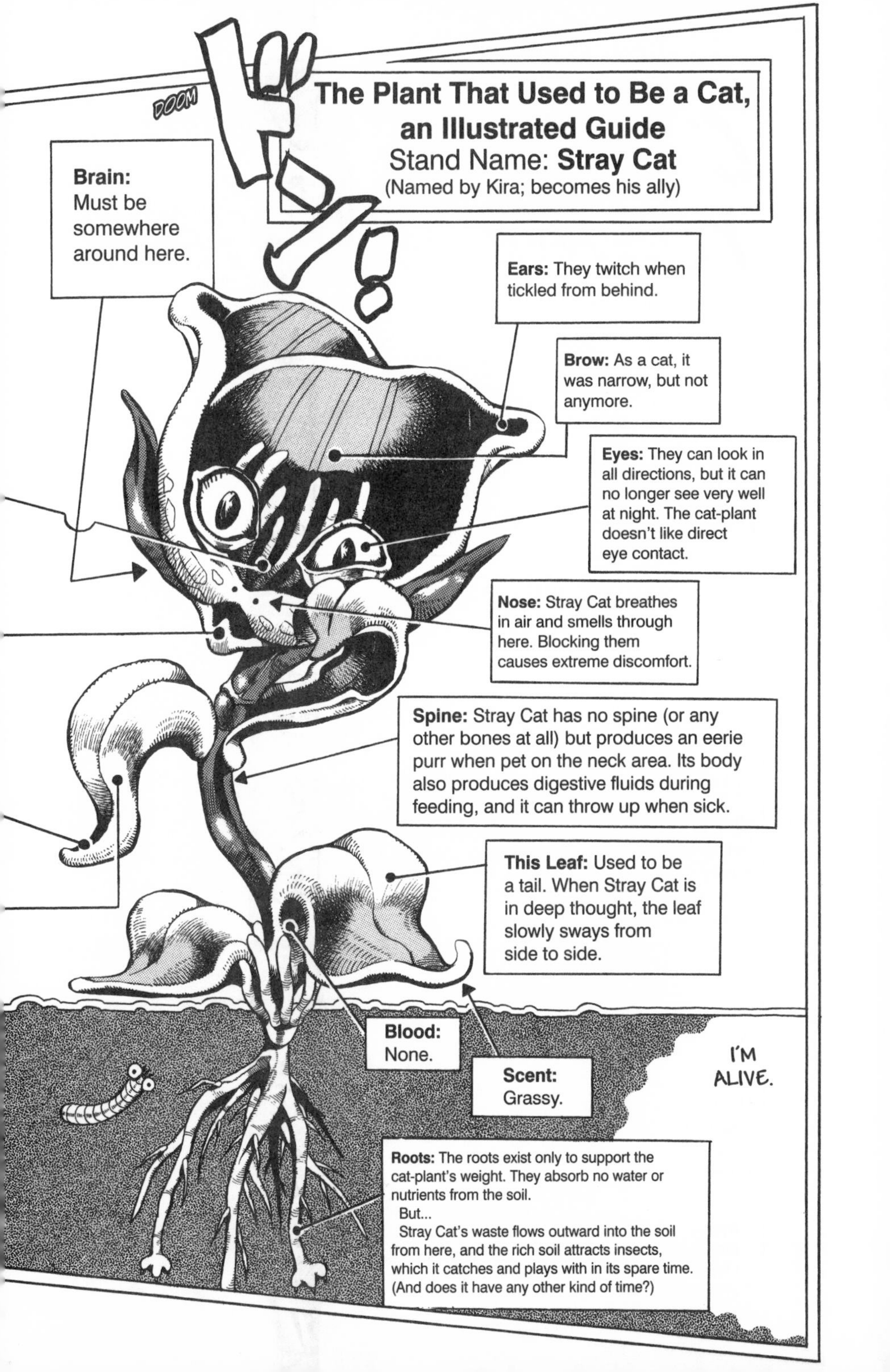

The Plant That Used to Be a Cat, an Illustrated Guide
Stand Name: Stray Cat
(Named by Kira; becomes his ally)
DOOM
Brain: Must be somewhere around here.
Ears: They twitch when tickled from behind.
Brow: As a cat, it was narrow, but not anymore.
Eyes: They can look in all directions, but it can no longer see very well at night. The cat-plant doesn't like direct eye contact.
Nose: Stray Cat breathes in air and smells through here. Blocking them causes extreme discomfort.
Spine: Stray Cat has no spine (or any other bones at all) but produces an eerie purr when pet on the neck area. Its body also produces digestive fluids during feeding, and it can throw up when sick.
This Leaf: Used to be a tail. When Stray Cat is in deep thought, the leaf slowly sways from side to side.
Blood: None.
Scent: Grassy.
I'M ALIVE.
Roots: The roots exist only to support the cat-plant's weight. They absorb no water or nutrients from the soil.
But...
Stray Cat's waste flows outward into the soil from here, and the rich soil attracts insects, which it catches and plays with in its spare time. (And does it have any other kind of time?)

CHAPTER 131

CATS LOVE YOSHIKAGE KIRA, PART 5

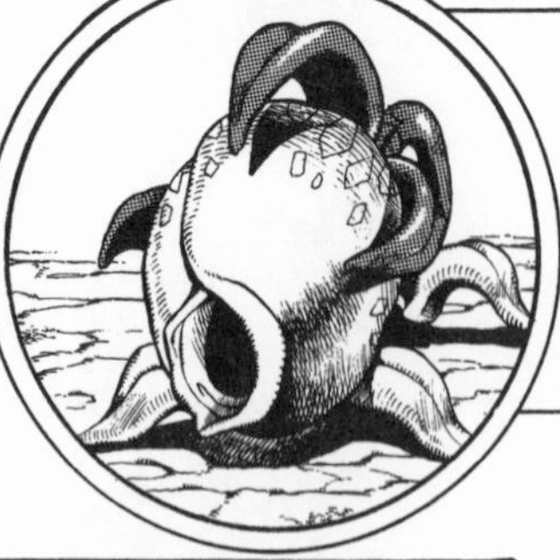

Whiskers: Stray Cat uses them to manipulate air. When it is about to fire a compressed burst of air, the cat-plant curls up as shown on the left.

Mouth: Where Stray Cat produces its meowing sounds. It also ingests water and food. Also, the cat-plant sometimes drools.

Claws: None.

Leaves: They are capable of grabbing objects. Stray Cat instinctively pounces on anything that moves with its leaves.

Stray Cat's air manipulation relies on heliotropism

Stray Cat's body can exhibit heliotropism (a movement response to sunlight) when exposed to brightness over 20,000 lux, the typical brightness of a rainy day.

Its chlorophyll allows it to breathe in and manipulate air.

Its ability to control air strengthens corresponding to the intensity of the sunlight. At night, however, its ability weakens.

Yoshikage Kira has Discovered that when kept in the dark, the cat plant remains docile.

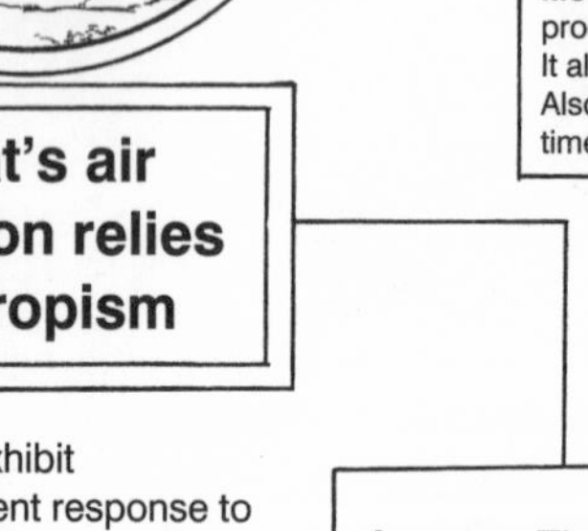
Chloroplasts
Xylem
Phloem
Stomata

Range of Air Manipulation Ability: Limited only by line of sight.

Likes:
- Fatty tuna
- Shrimp
- Sticking its head into paper bags
- Watching TV
- Receiving praise

Dislikes:
- Tobacco
- Wasabi
- Citrus fruit
- Cold places
- Shinobu Kawajiri

Method of Reproduction: Unknown
Sex: Unknown
Life Span: Unknown
Method of Wintering: Sleeps through most of the winter, except when underneath a kotatsu, in which case it becomes active again.

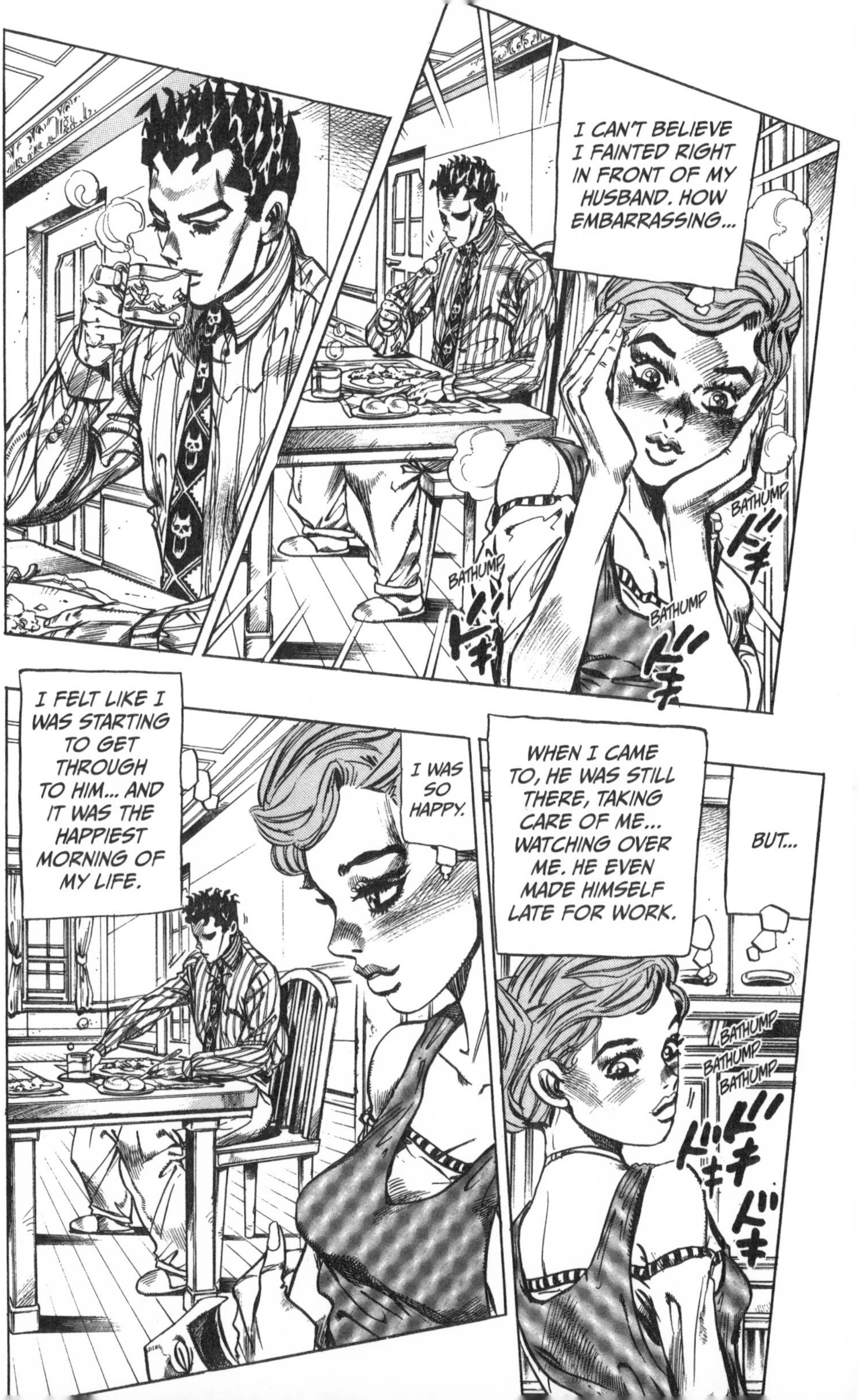
I CAN'T BELIEVE I FAINTED RIGHT IN FRONT OF MY HUSBAND. HOW EMBARRASSING...
BATHUMP
ドキ
BATHUMP
ドキ
BATHUMP
ドキ
WHEN I CAME TO, HE WAS STILL THERE, TAKING CARE OF ME... WATCHING OVER ME. HE EVEN MADE HIMSELF LATE FOR WORK.
BUT...
BATHUMP
BATHUMP
BATHUMP
ドキドキドキ
I WAS SO HAPPY.
I FELT LIKE I WAS STARTING TO GET THROUGH TO HIM... AND IT WAS THE HAPPIEST MORNING OF MY LIFE.

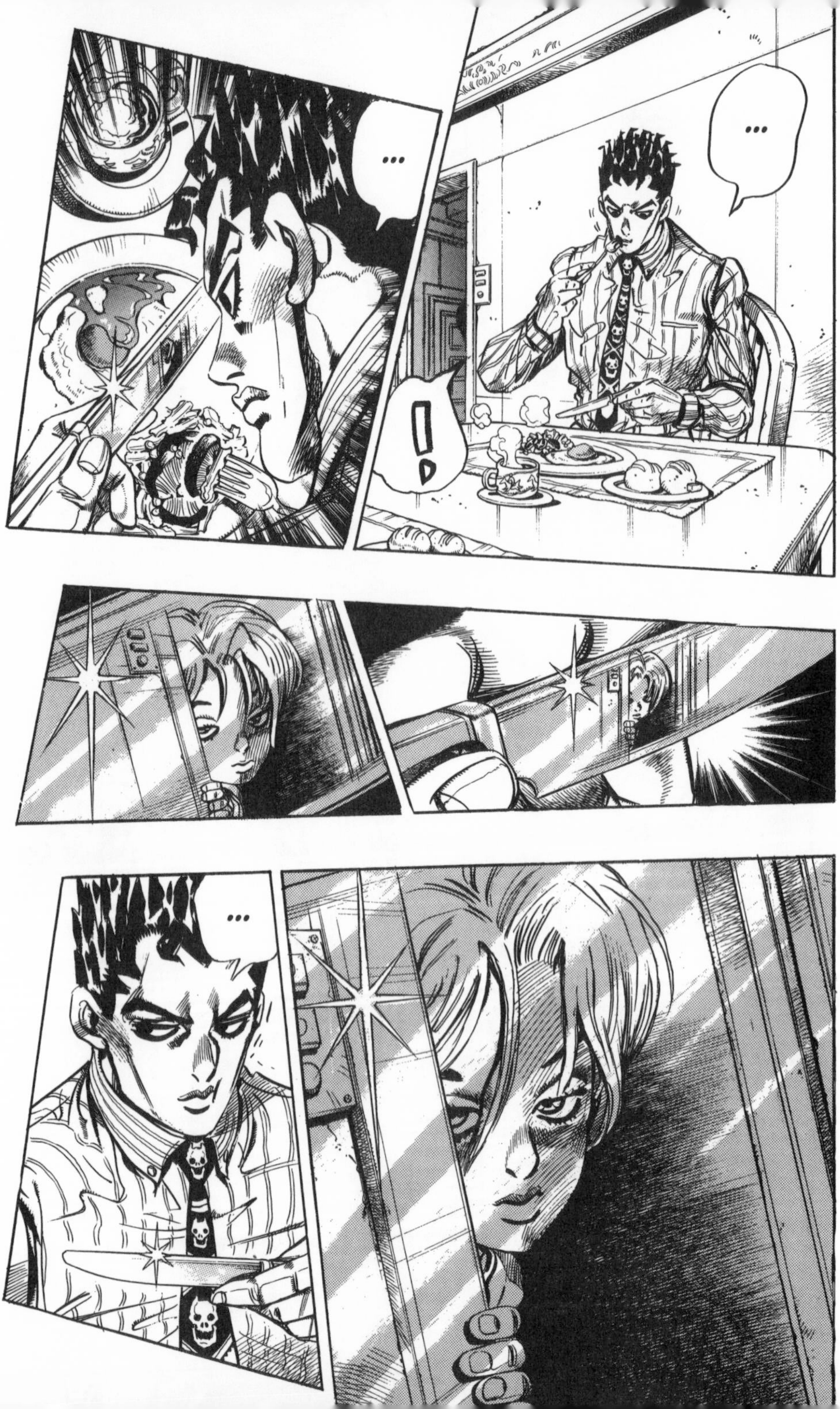
...
!?
...
...

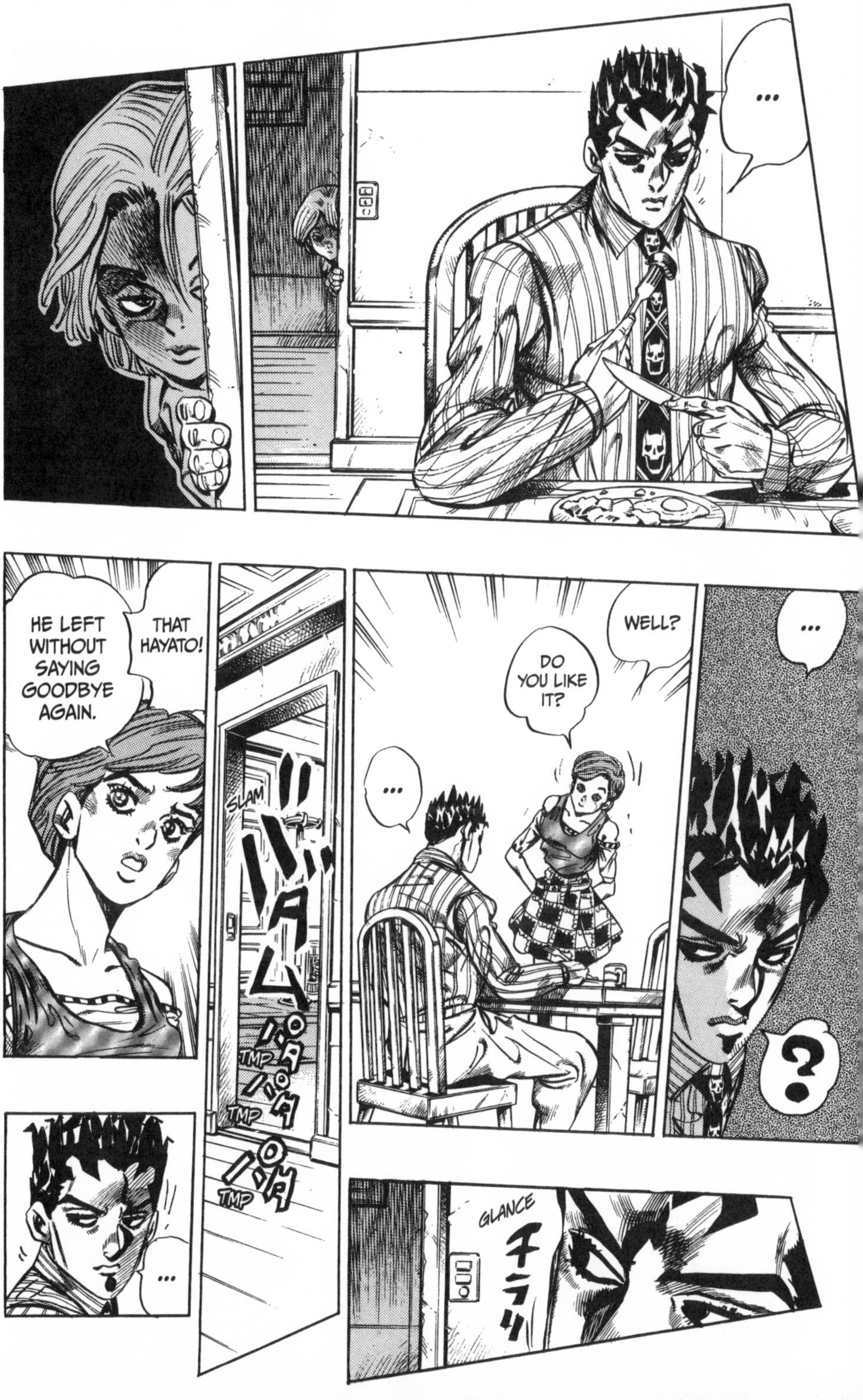
...
...
?
WELL?
DO YOU LIKE IT?
...
SLAM
TMP
TMP
TMP
THAT HAYATO!
HE LEFT WITHOUT SAYING GOODBYE AGAIN.
GLANCE
...

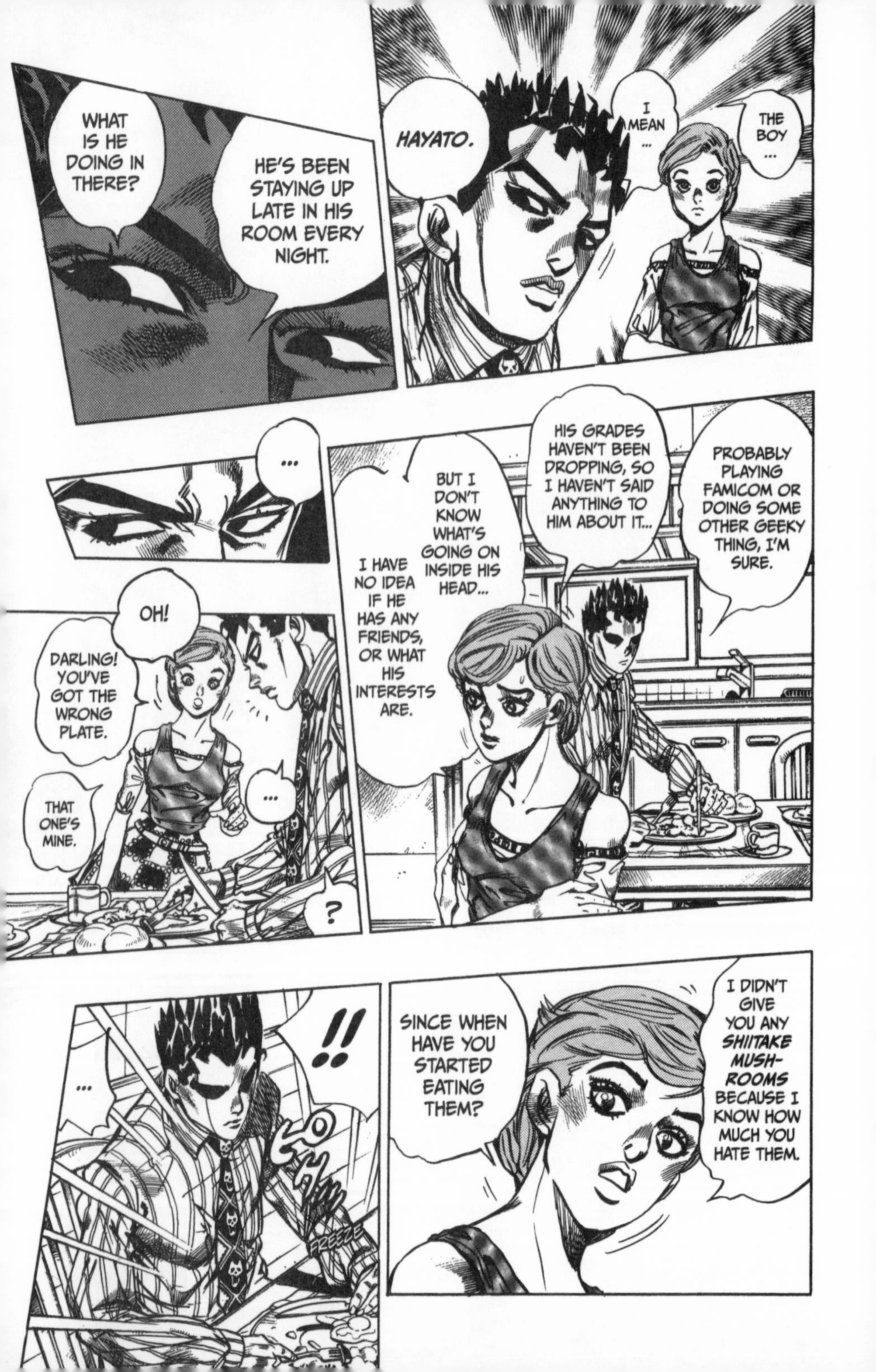
THE BOY ...
I MEAN ...
HAYATO.
HE'S BEEN STAYING UP LATE IN HIS ROOM EVERY NIGHT.
WHAT IS HE DOING IN THERE?
PROBABLY PLAYING FAMICOM OR DOING SOME OTHER GEEKY THING, I'M SURE.
HIS GRADES HAVEN'T BEEN DROPPING, SO I HAVEN'T SAID ANYTHING TO HIM ABOUT IT...
BUT I DON'T KNOW WHAT'S GOING ON INSIDE HIS HEAD...
I HAVE NO IDEA IF HE HAS ANY FRIENDS, OR WHAT HIS INTERESTS ARE.
...
OH!
DARLING! YOU'VE GOT THE WRONG PLATE.
...
THAT ONE'S MINE.
?
I DIDN'T GIVE YOU ANY *SHIITAKE MUSHROOMS* BECAUSE I KNOW HOW MUCH YOU HATE THEM.
SINCE WHEN HAVE YOU STARTED EATING THEM?
!!
...
FREEZE

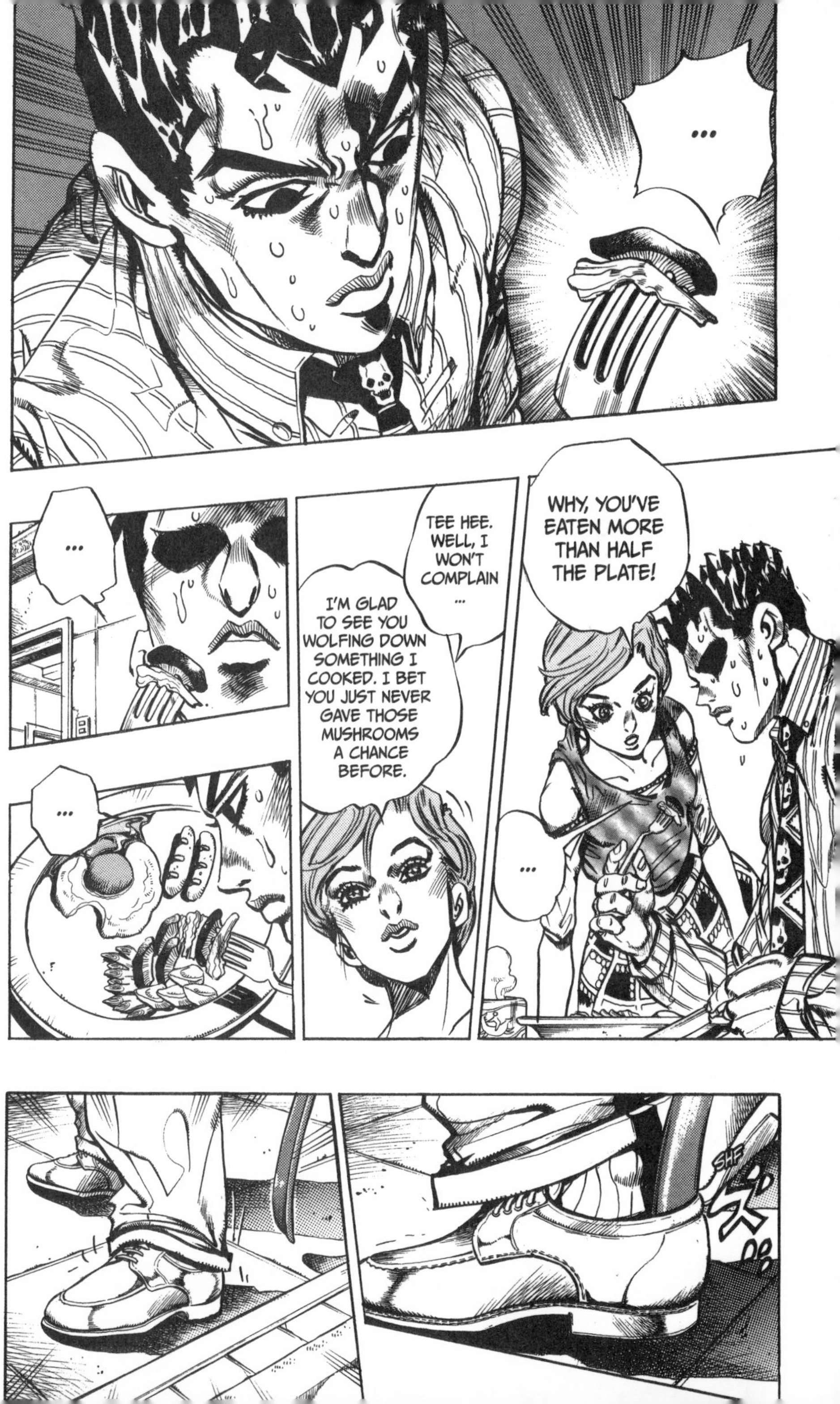
...
WHY, YOU'VE EATEN MORE THAN HALF THE PLATE!
...
TEE HEE. WELL, I WON'T COMPLAIN ...
I'M GLAD TO SEE YOU WOLFING DOWN SOMETHING I COOKED. I BET YOU JUST NEVER GAVE THOSE MUSHROOMS A CHANCE BEFORE.
...
...

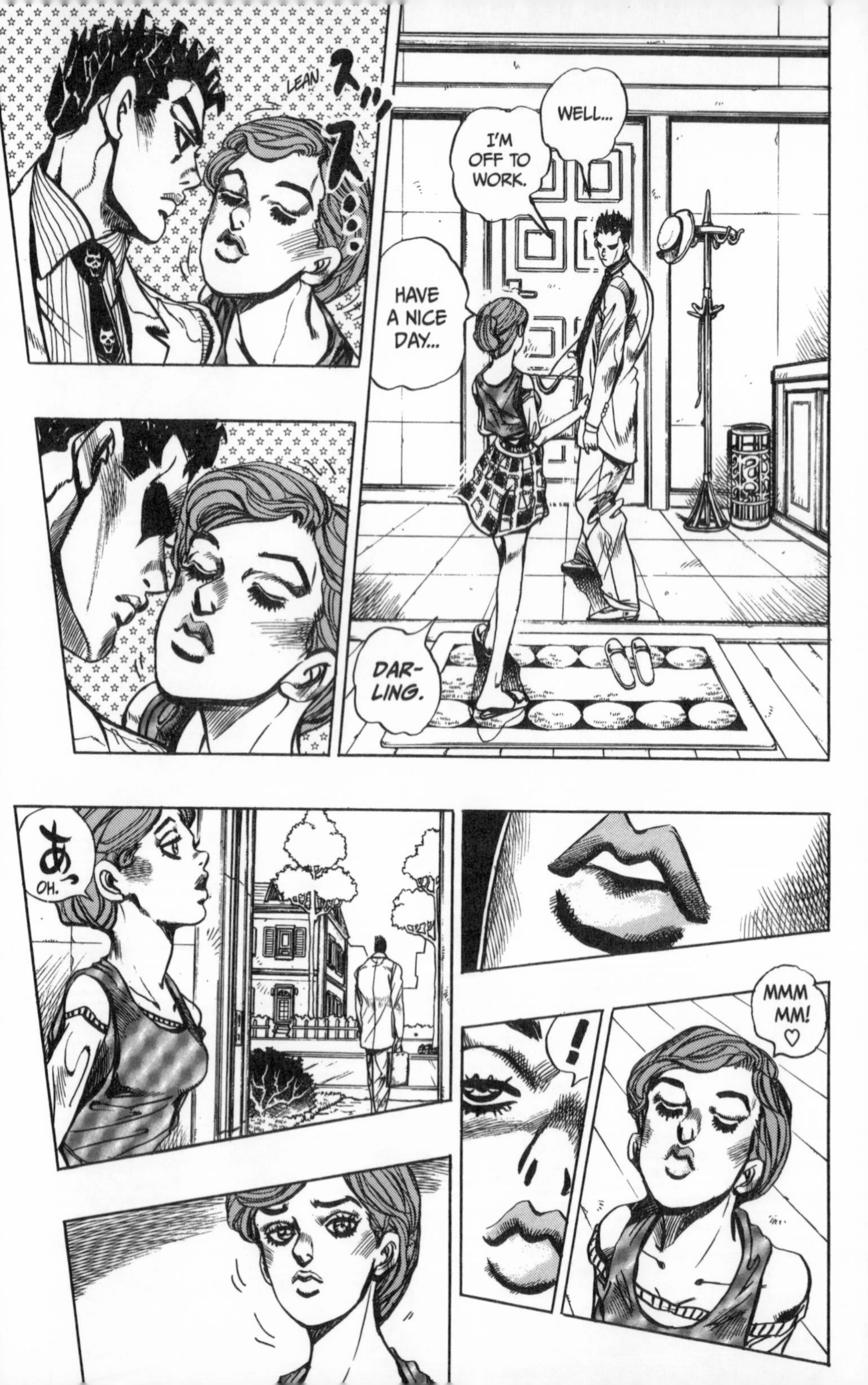
WELL...
I'M OFF TO WORK.
HAVE A NICE DAY...
DAR-LING.
LEAN
スッ
MMM MM! ♡
!
あっ
OH.

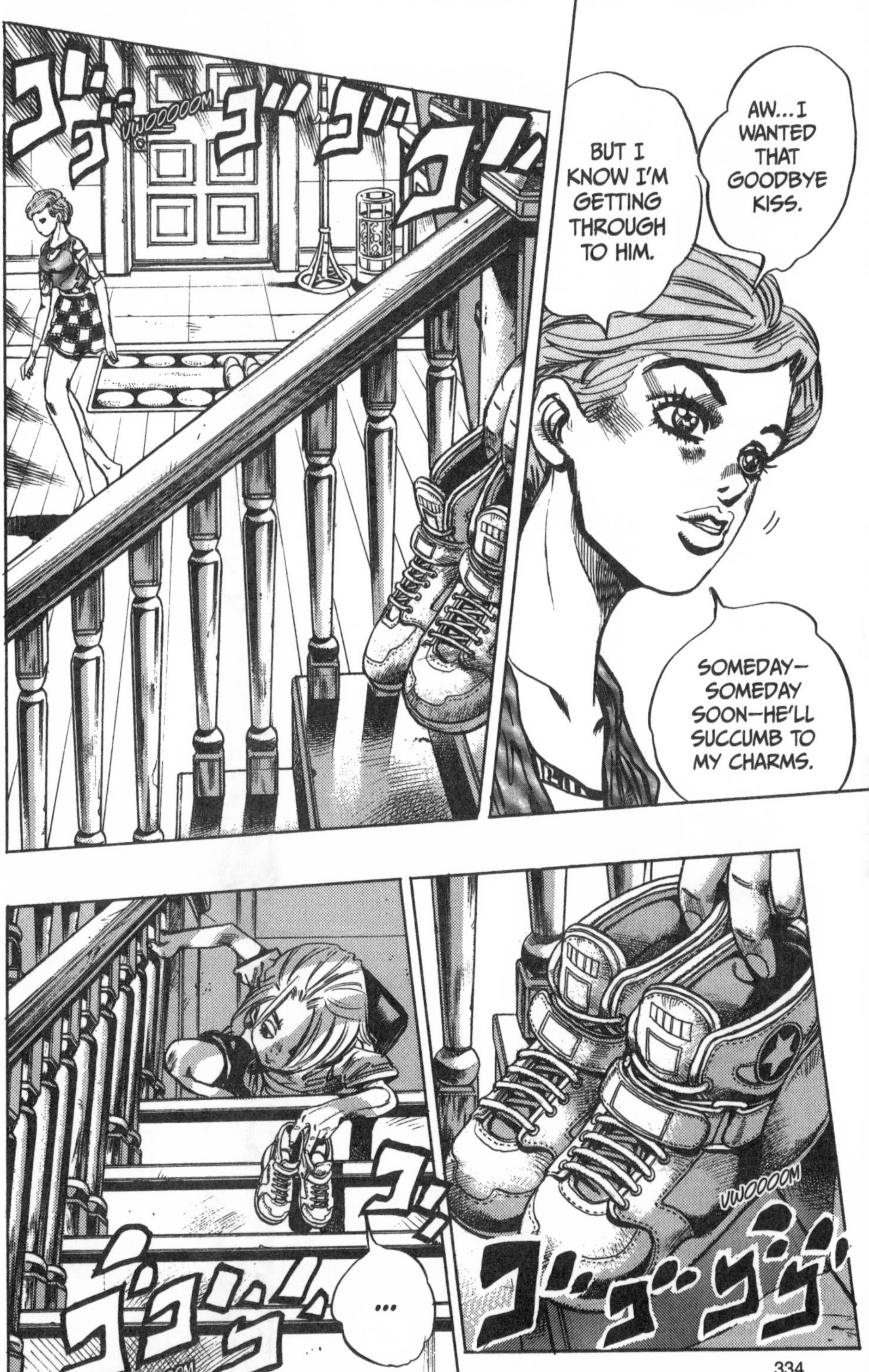
AW...I WANTED THAT GOODBYE KISS.
BUT I KNOW I'M GETTING THROUGH TO HIM.
SOMEDAY—SOMEDAY SOON—HE'LL SUCCUMB TO MY CHARMS.
UWOOOOOM
UWOOOOM
...
UWOOOOM

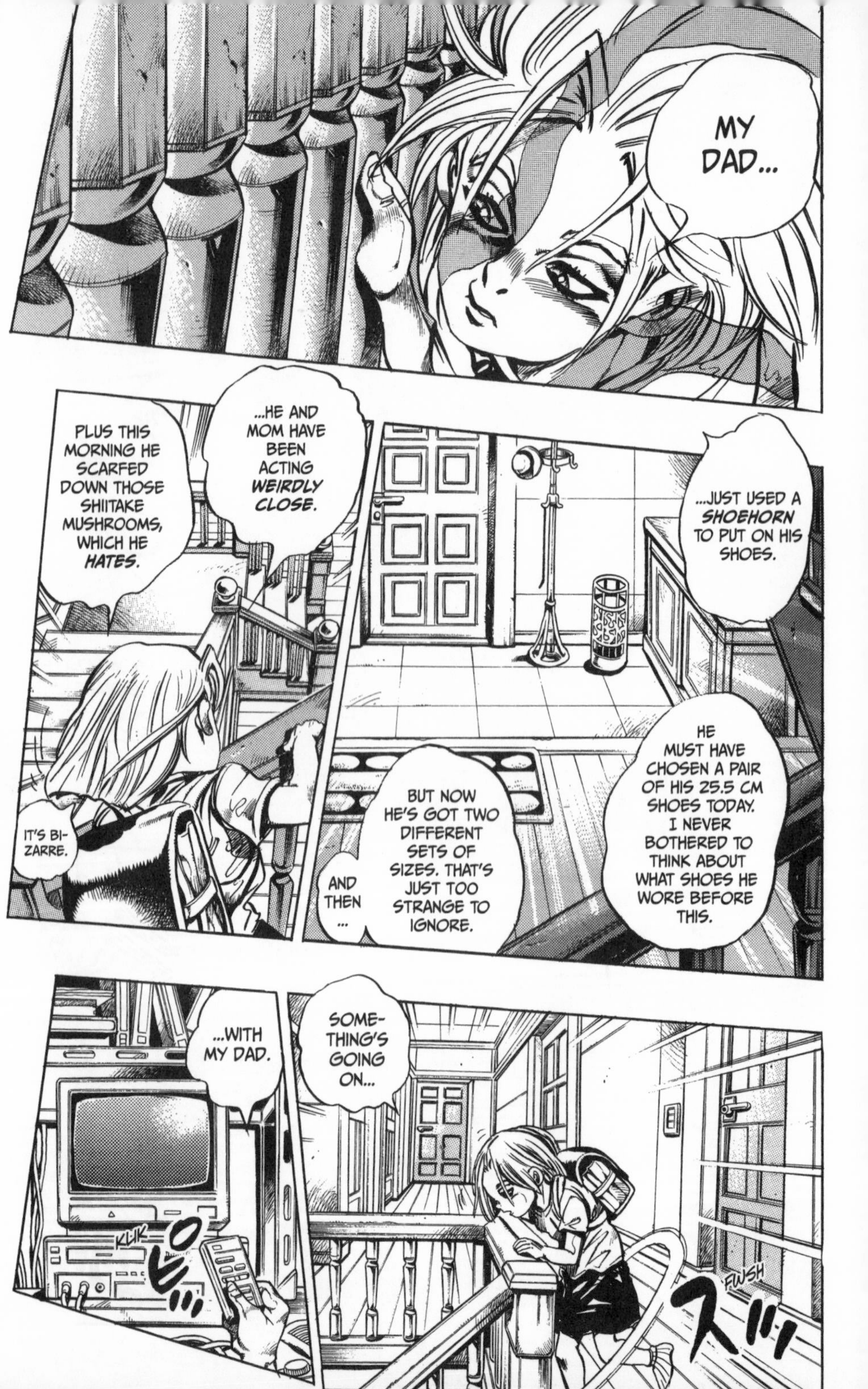
MY DAD...
...JUST USED A *SHOEHORN* TO PUT ON HIS SHOES.
HE MUST HAVE CHOSEN A PAIR OF HIS 25.5 CM SHOES TODAY. I NEVER BOTHERED TO THINK ABOUT WHAT SHOES HE WORE BEFORE THIS.
BUT NOW HE'S GOT TWO DIFFERENT SETS OF SIZES. THAT'S JUST TOO STRANGE TO IGNORE.
AND THEN ...
...HE AND MOM HAVE BEEN ACTING *WEIRDLY CLOSE*.
PLUS THIS MORNING HE SCARFED DOWN THOSE SHIITAKE MUSHROOMS, WHICH HE *HATES*.
IT'S BI-ZARRE.
SOME-THING'S GOING ON...
FWSH
...WITH MY DAD.
KLIK

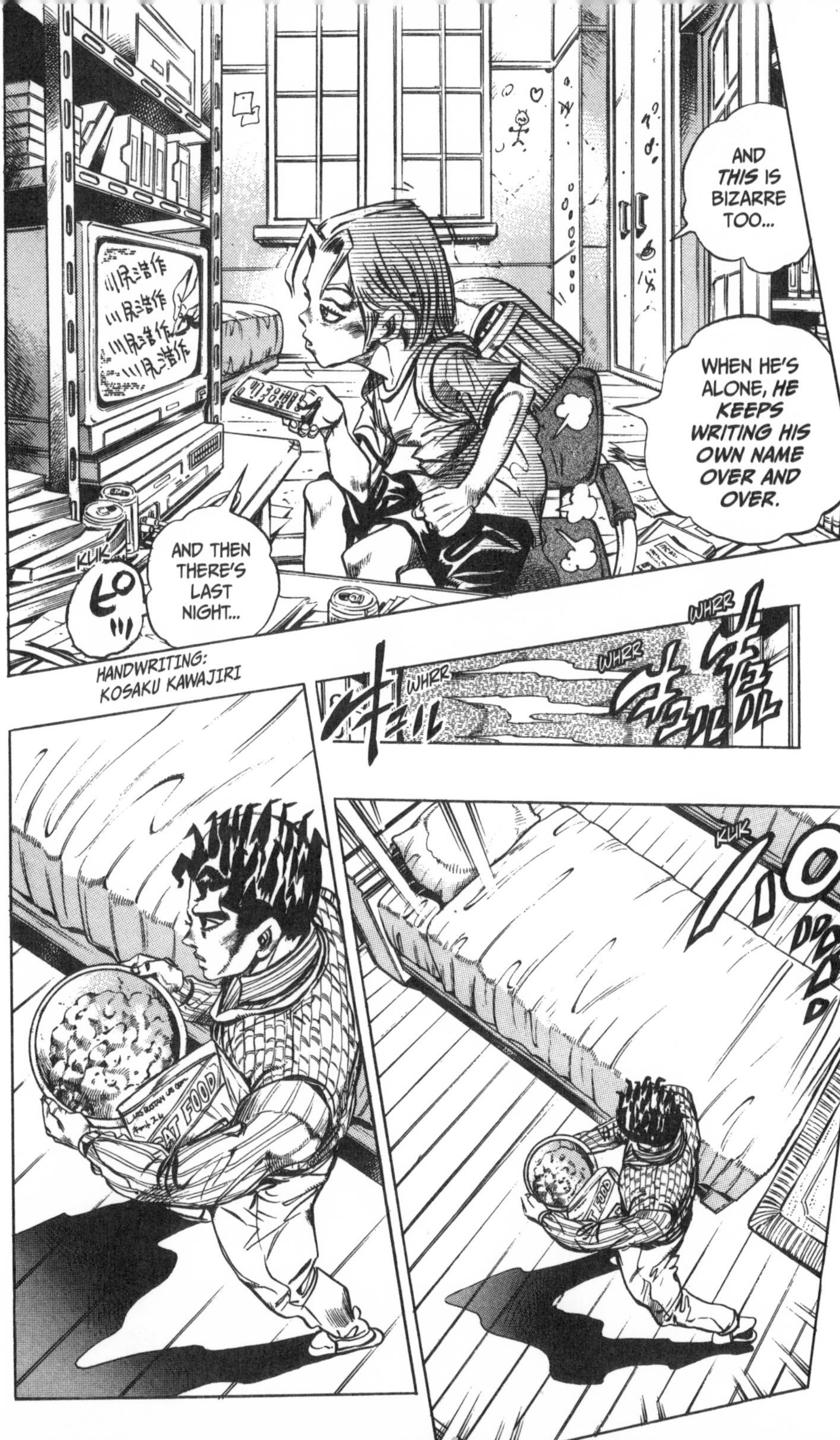
AND THIS IS BIZARRE TOO...
WHEN HE'S ALONE, HE KEEPS WRITING HIS OWN NAME OVER AND OVER.
AND THEN THERE'S LAST NIGHT...
KUK
HANDWRITING: KOSAKU KAWAJIRI
WHRR
WHRR
WHRR
KUK

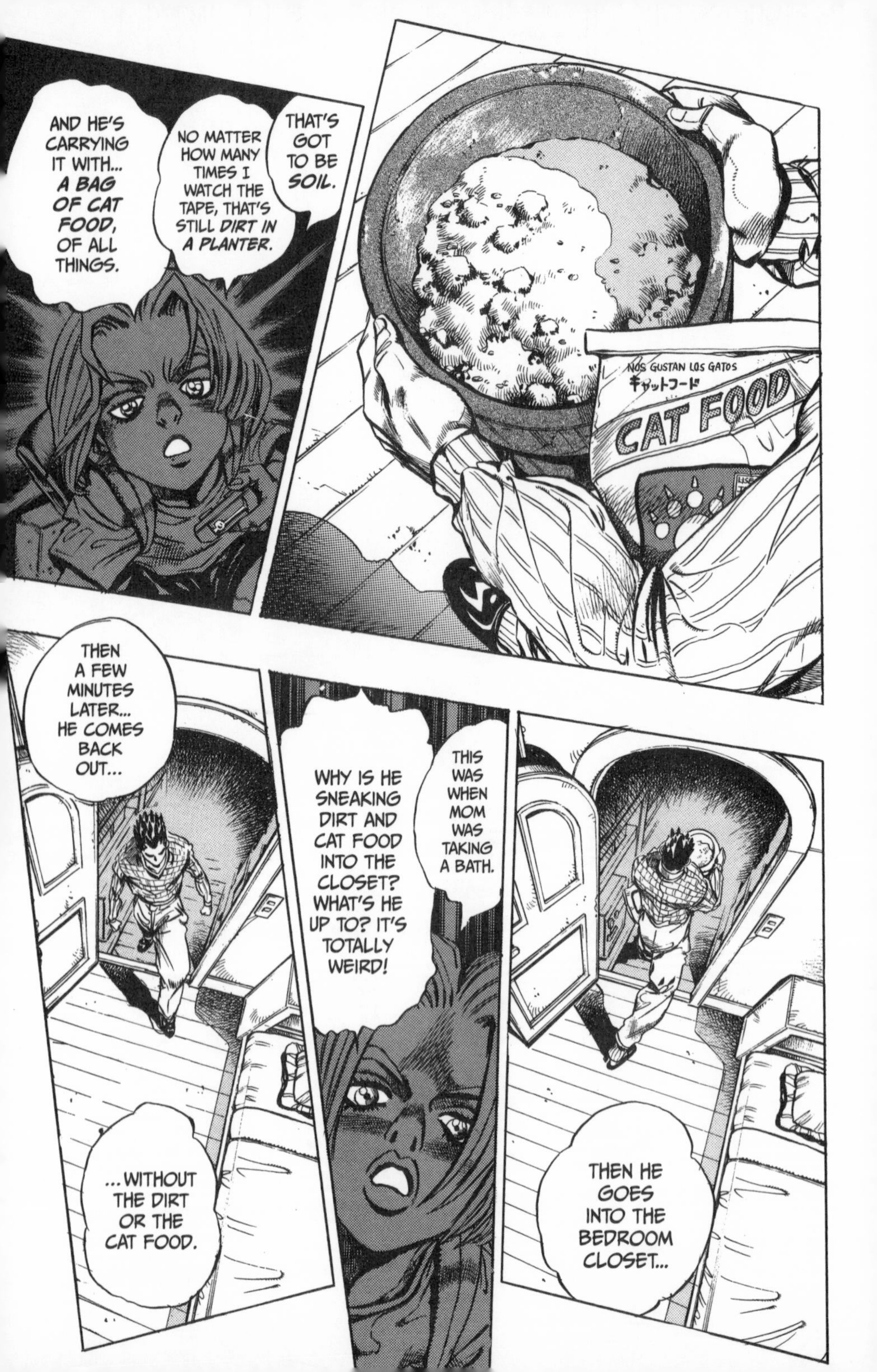
NOS GUSTAN LOS GATOS
キャットフード
CAT FOOD
THAT'S GOT TO BE *SOIL*.
NO MATTER HOW MANY TIMES I WATCH THE TAPE, THAT'S STILL *DIRT IN A PLANTER*.
AND HE'S CARRYING IT WITH... *A BAG OF CAT FOOD*, OF ALL THINGS.
THEN HE GOES INTO THE BEDROOM CLOSET...
THIS WAS WHEN MOM WAS TAKING A BATH.
WHY IS HE SNEAKING DIRT AND CAT FOOD INTO THE CLOSET? WHAT'S HE UP TO? IT'S TOTALLY WEIRD!
THEN A FEW MINUTES LATER... HE COMES BACK OUT...
...WITHOUT THE DIRT OR THE CAT FOOD.

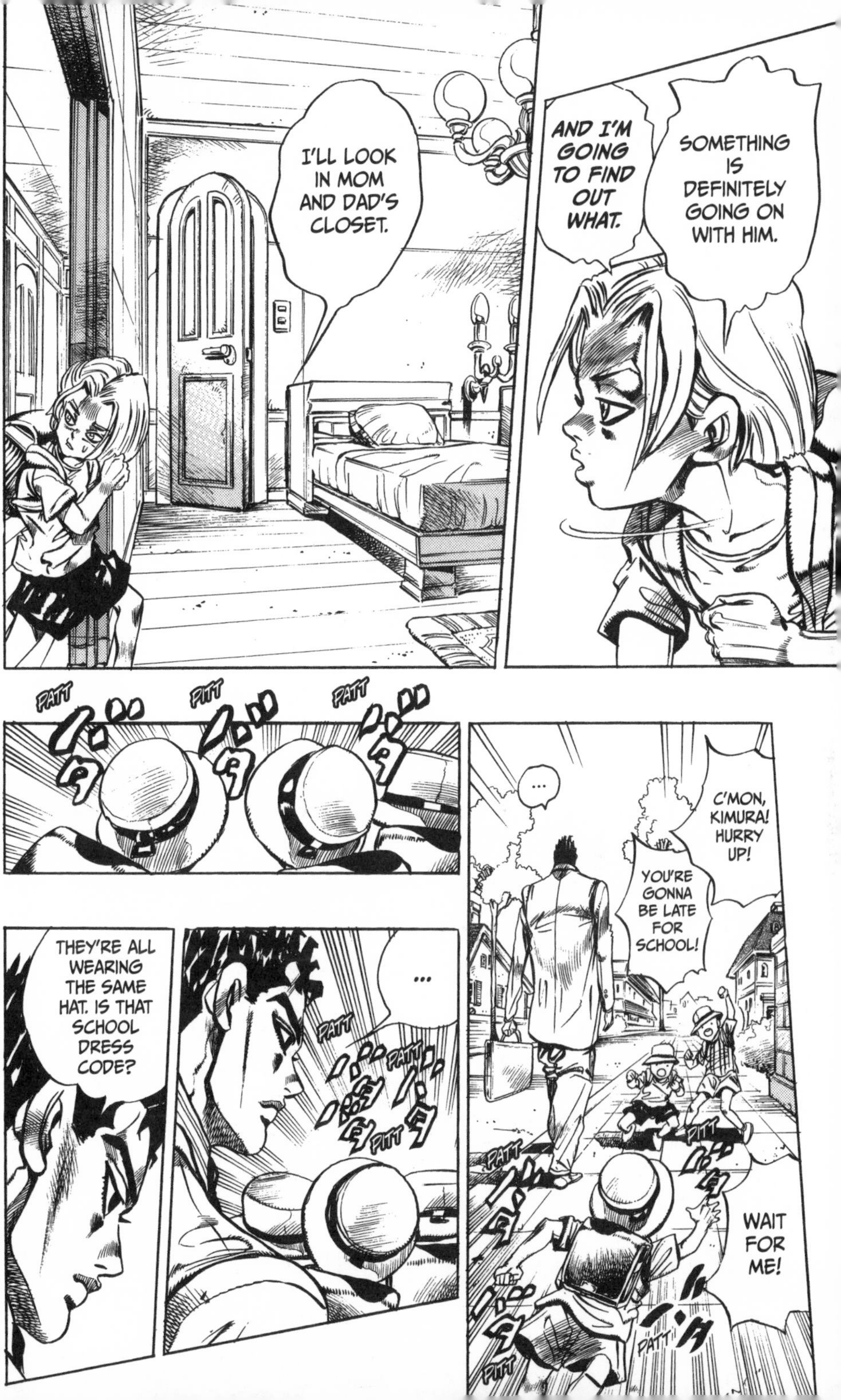
SOMETHING IS DEFINITELY GOING ON WITH HIM.
AND I'M GOING TO FIND OUT WHAT.
I'LL LOOK IN MOM AND DAD'S CLOSET.
C'MON, KIMURA! HURRY UP!
...
YOU'RE GONNA BE LATE FOR SCHOOL!
PITT
PATT
WAIT FOR ME!
PATT
PITT
PATT
PITT
PATT
...
PATT
PATT
PITT
THEY'RE ALL WEARING THE SAME HAT. IS THAT SCHOOL DRESS CODE?

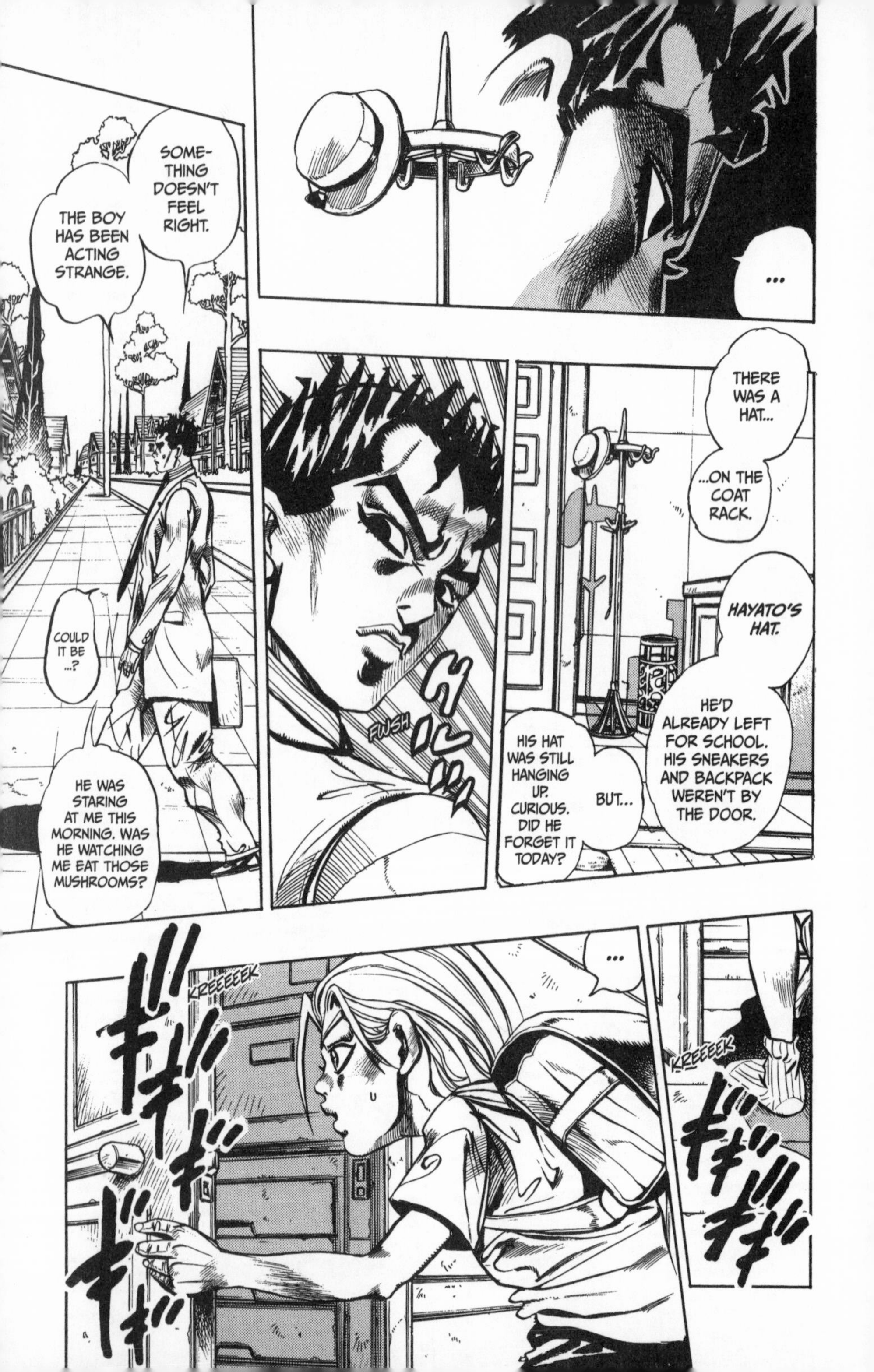
...
THERE WAS A HAT...
...ON THE COAT RACK.
HAYATO'S HAT.
HE'D ALREADY LEFT FOR SCHOOL. HIS SNEAKERS AND BACKPACK WEREN'T BY THE DOOR.
BUT...
HIS HAT WAS STILL HANGING UP. CURIOUS. DID HE FORGET IT TODAY?
FWSH
SOMETHING DOESN'T FEEL RIGHT.
THE BOY HAS BEEN ACTING STRANGE.
COULD IT BE ...?
HE WAS STARING AT ME THIS MORNING. WAS HE WATCHING ME EAT THOSE MUSHROOMS?
KREEEEK
...
KREEEEEK

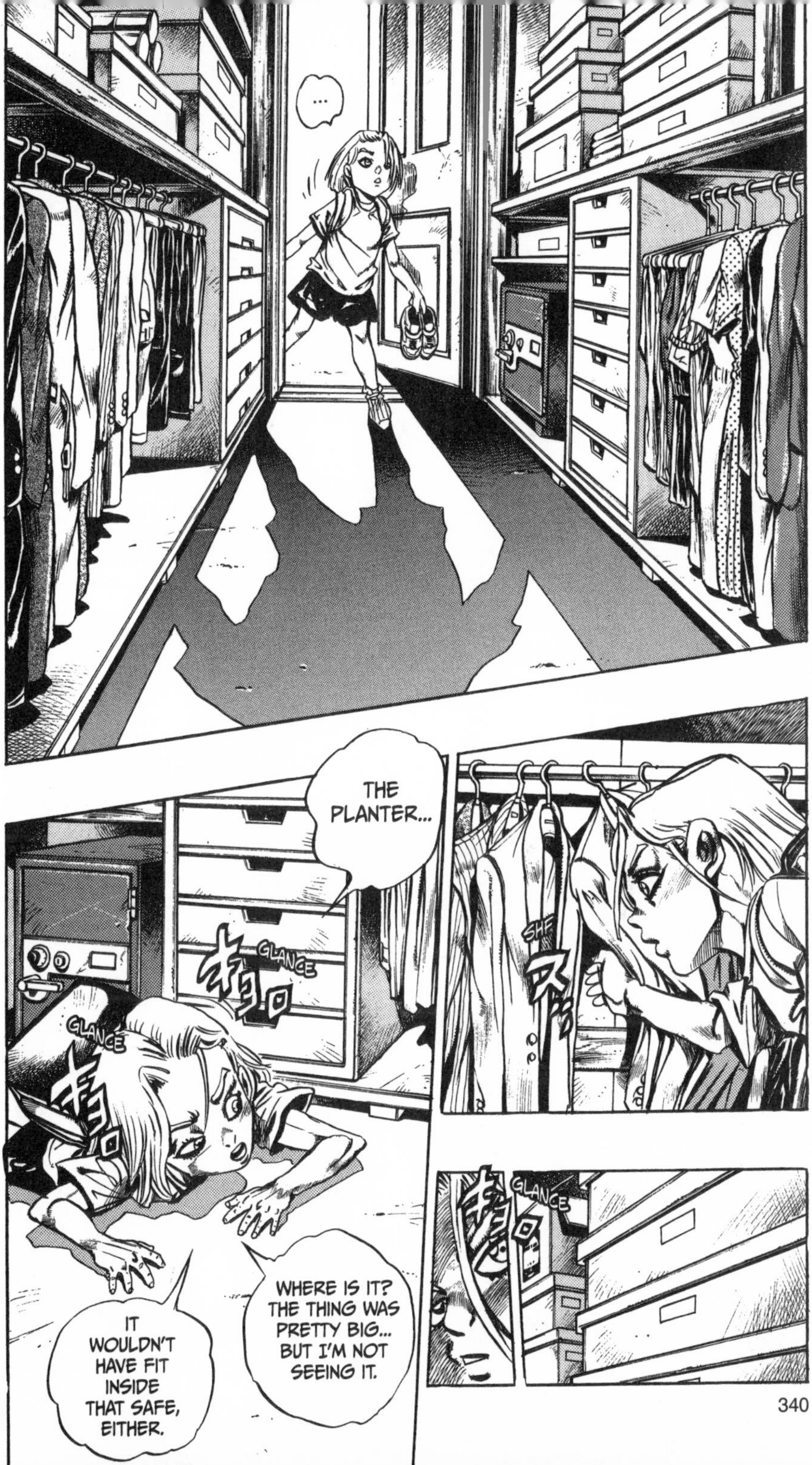
...
SHF
GLANCE
THE PLANTER...
GLANCE
GLANCE
WHERE IS IT? THE THING WAS PRETTY BIG... BUT I'M NOT SEEING IT.
IT WOULDN'T HAVE FIT INSIDE THAT SAFE, EITHER.

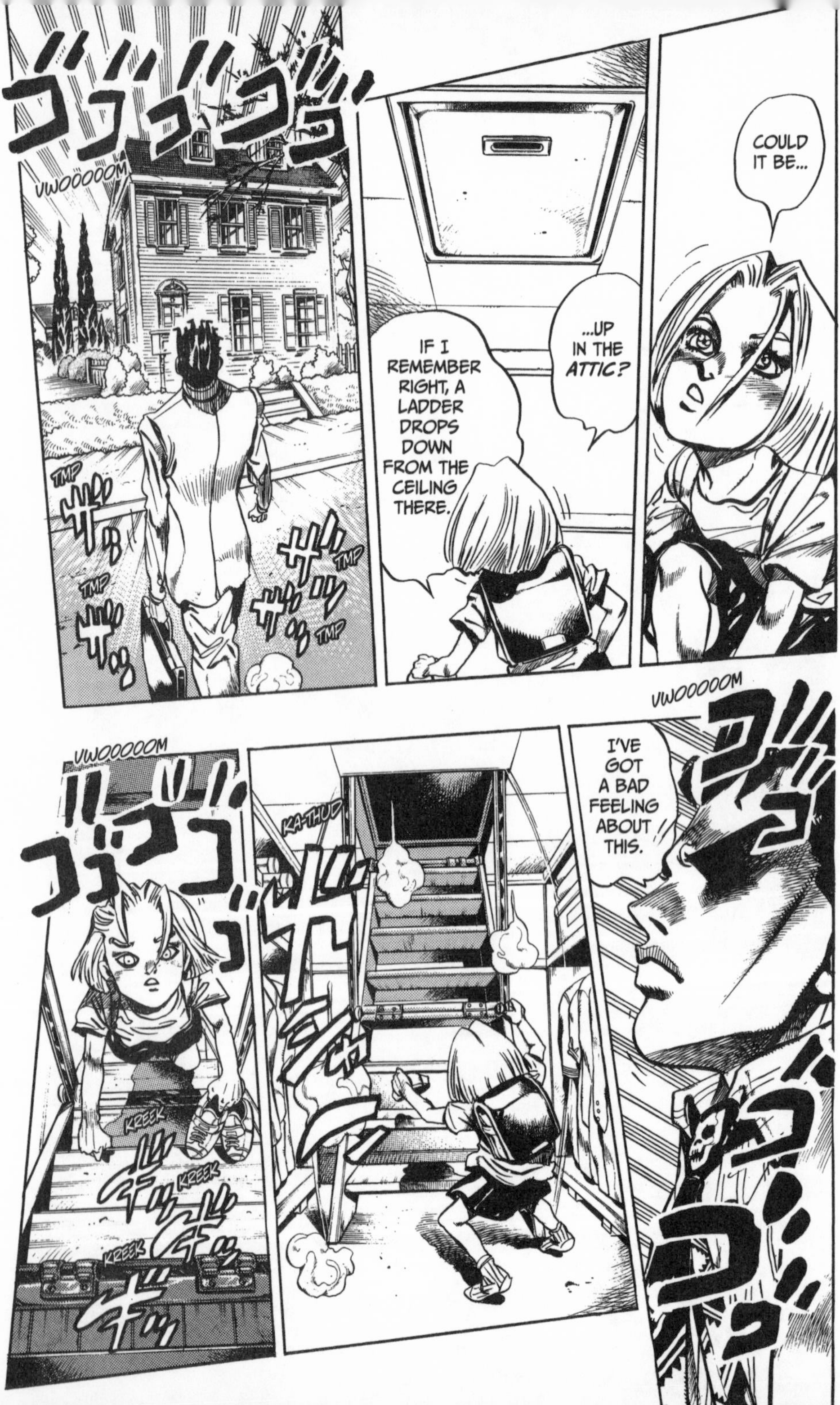
COULD IT BE...
...UP IN THE ATTIC?
IF I REMEMBER RIGHT, A LADDER DROPS DOWN FROM THE CEILING THERE.
VWOOOOOM
TMP
TMP
TMP
TMP
VWOOOOOM
I'VE GOT A BAD FEELING ABOUT THIS.
KA-THUD
VWOOOOOM
KREEK
KREEK
KREEK

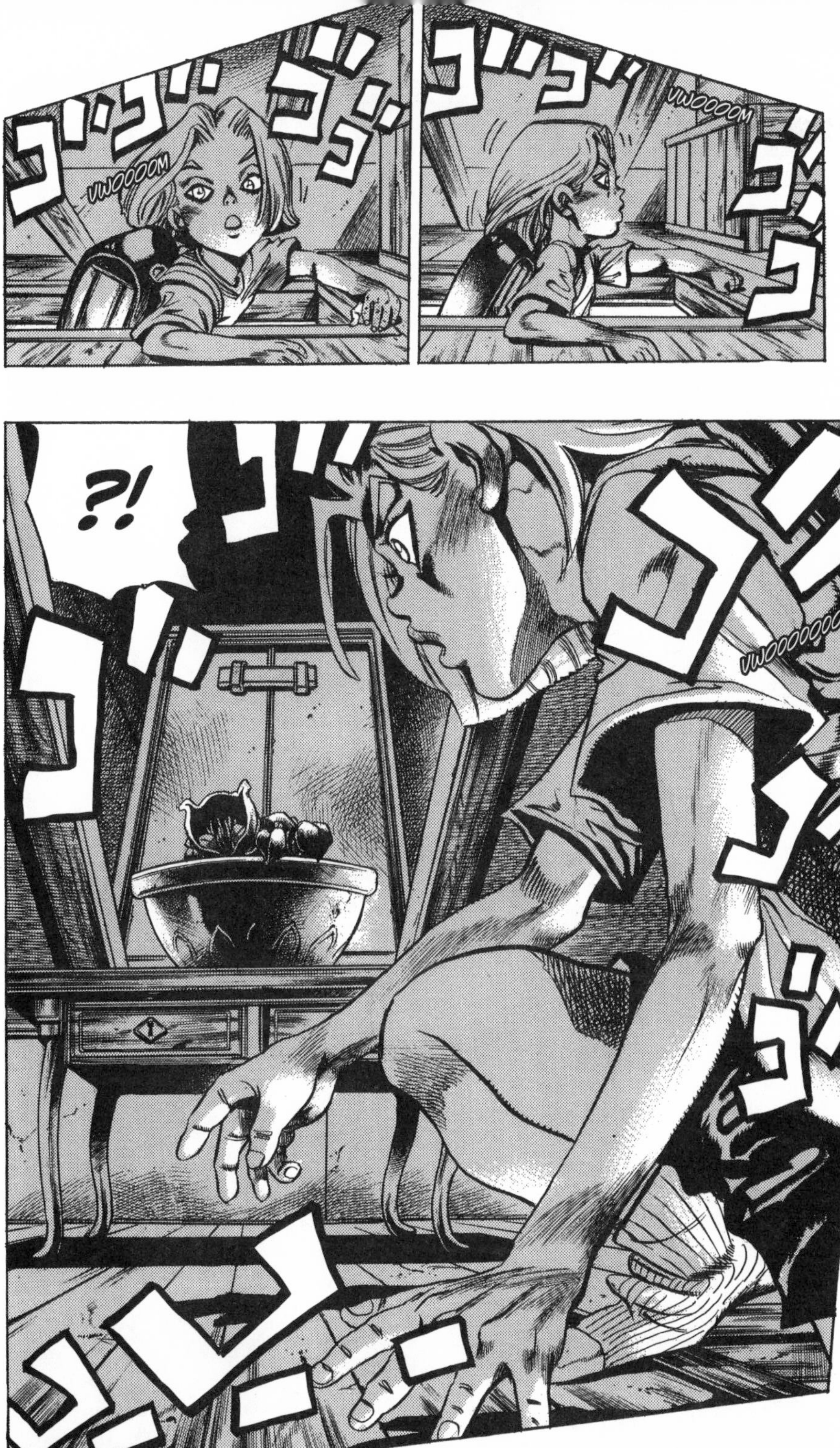
VWOOOOM
VWOOOOM
?!
VWOOOOOOOM

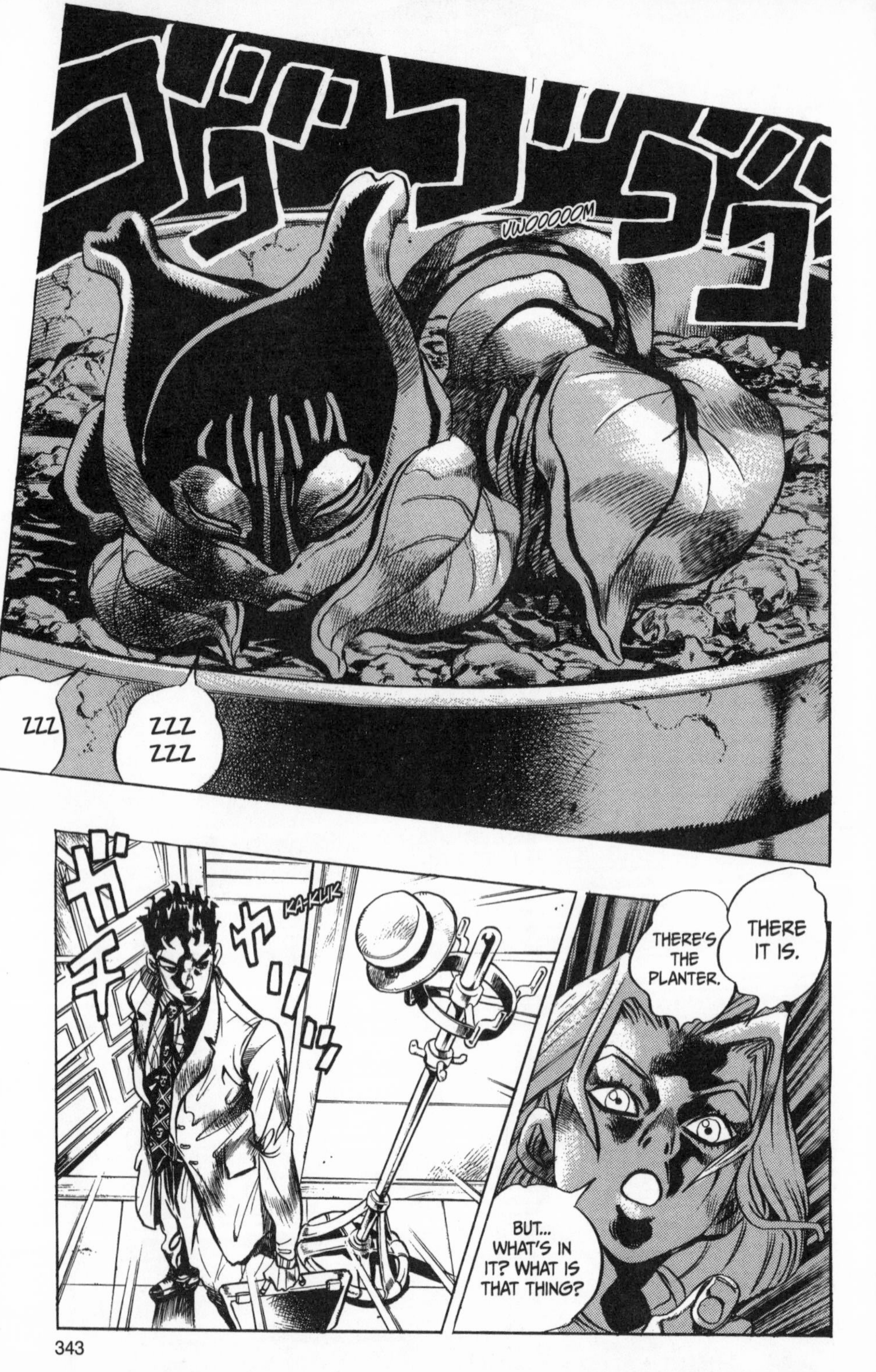
VWOOOOOM
ZZZ
ZZZ
ZZZ
THERE IT IS.
THERE'S THE PLANTER.
BUT... WHAT'S IN IT? WHAT IS THAT THING?
KA-KLIK

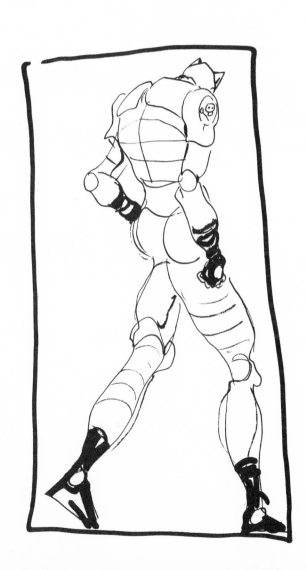

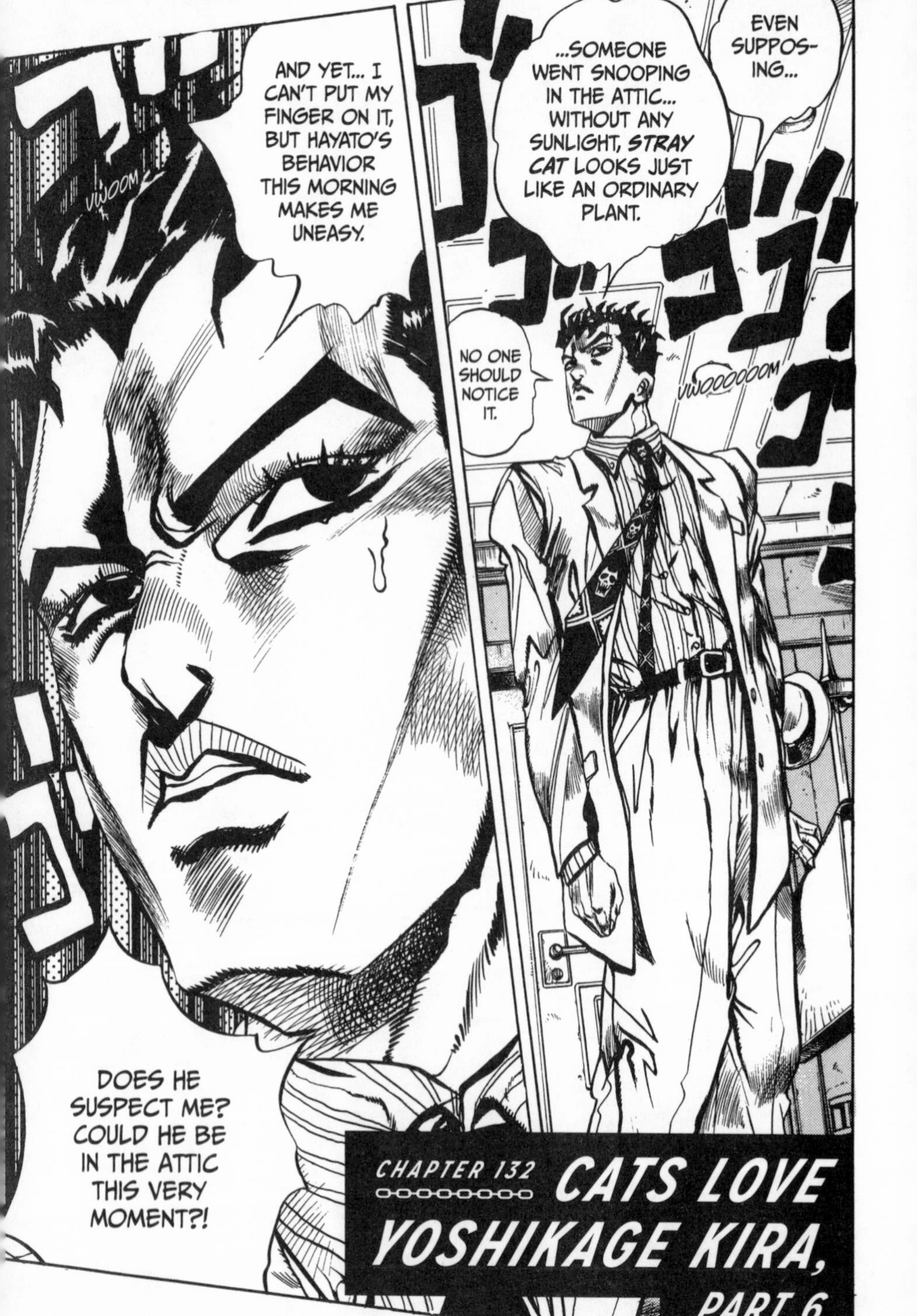
EVEN SUPPOSING...
...SOMEONE WENT SNOOPING IN THE ATTIC... WITHOUT ANY SUNLIGHT, STRAY CAT LOOKS JUST LIKE AN ORDINARY PLANT.
VWOOOOOOM
NO ONE SHOULD NOTICE IT.
AND YET... I CAN'T PUT MY FINGER ON IT, BUT HAYATO'S BEHAVIOR THIS MORNING MAKES ME UNEASY.
VWOOM
DOES HE SUSPECT ME? COULD HE BE IN THE ATTIC THIS VERY MOMENT?!

CHAPTER 132

CATS LOVE YOSHIKAGE KIRA, PART 6

CHAPTER 132

CATS LOVE YOSHIKAGE KIRA, PART 6

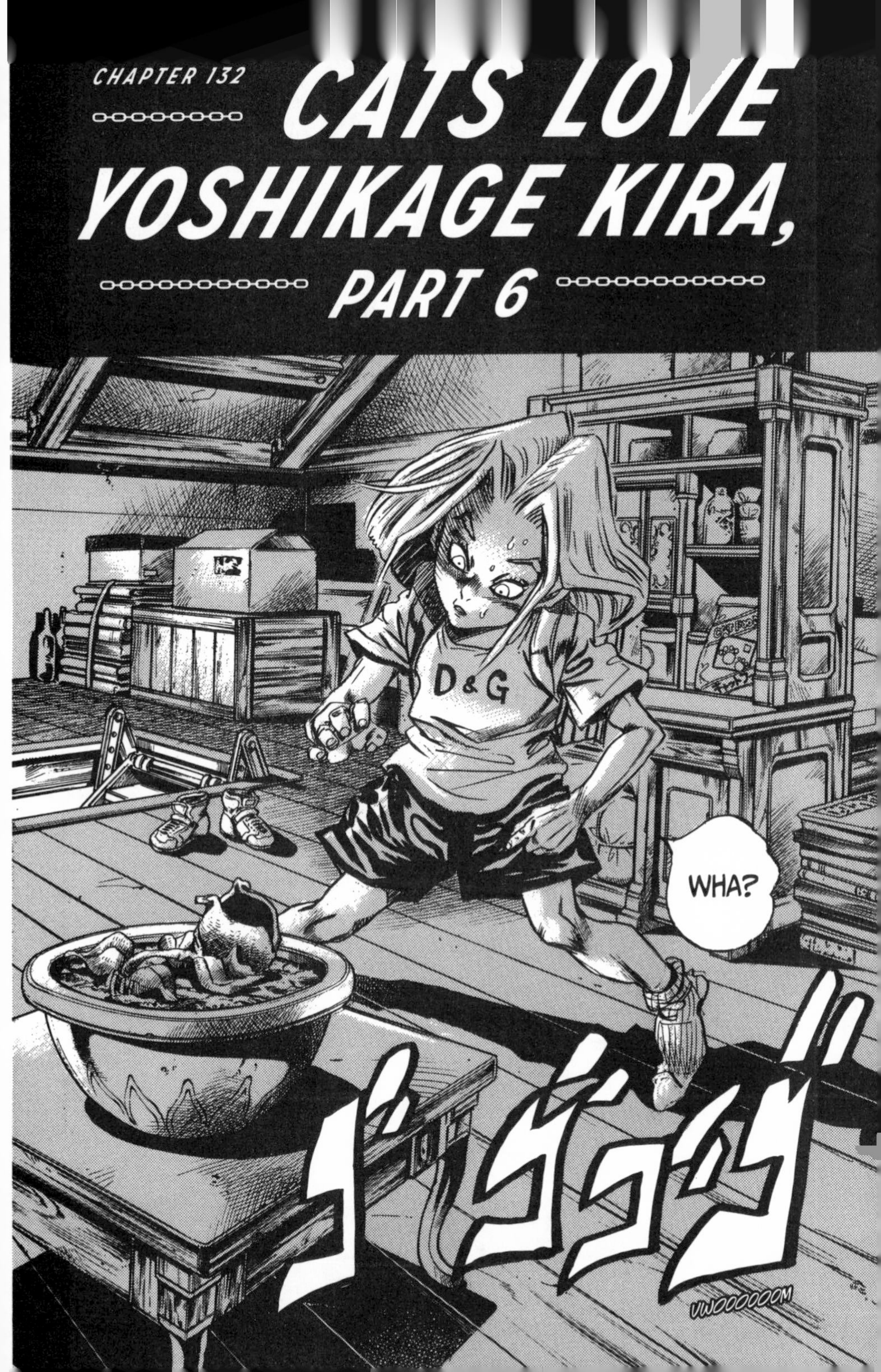
WHA?
ゴゴゴゴ
VWOOOOOOOM

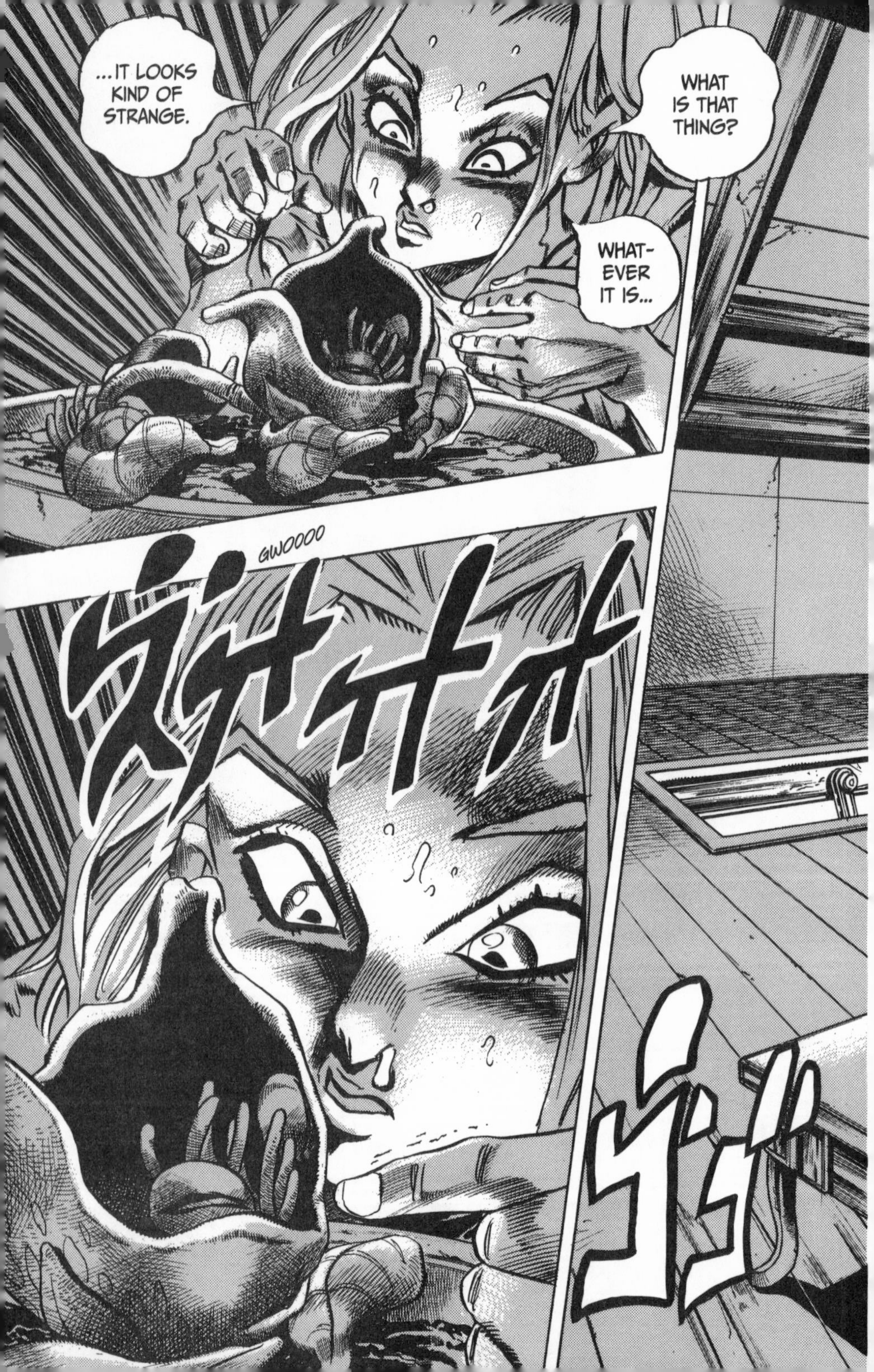
WHAT IS THAT THING?
...IT LOOKS KIND OF STRANGE.
WHAT-EVER IT IS...
GWOOOO

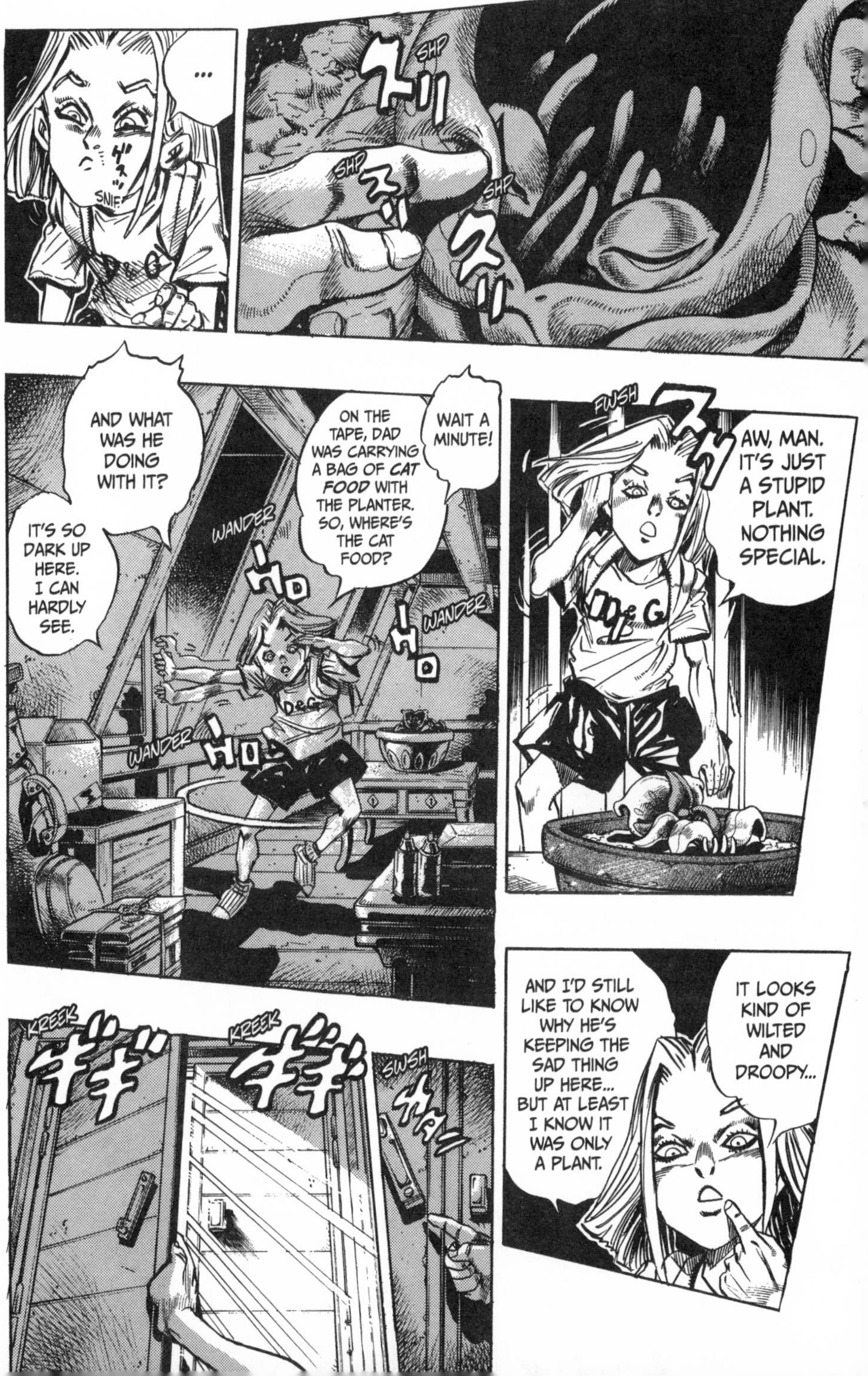
SHP
SHP
SHP
...
SNIF
FWSH
AW, MAN. IT'S JUST A STUPID PLANT. NOTHING SPECIAL.
WAIT A MINUTE!
ON THE TAPE, DAD WAS CARRYING A BAG OF *CAT FOOD* WITH THE PLANTER. SO, WHERE'S THE CAT FOOD?
AND WHAT WAS HE DOING WITH IT?
IT'S SO DARK UP HERE. I CAN HARDLY SEE.
WANDER
WANDER
WANDER
IT LOOKS KIND OF WILTED AND DROOPY...
AND I'D STILL LIKE TO KNOW WHY HE'S KEEPING THE SAD THING UP HERE... BUT AT LEAST I KNOW IT WAS ONLY A PLANT.
SWSH
KREEK
KREEK

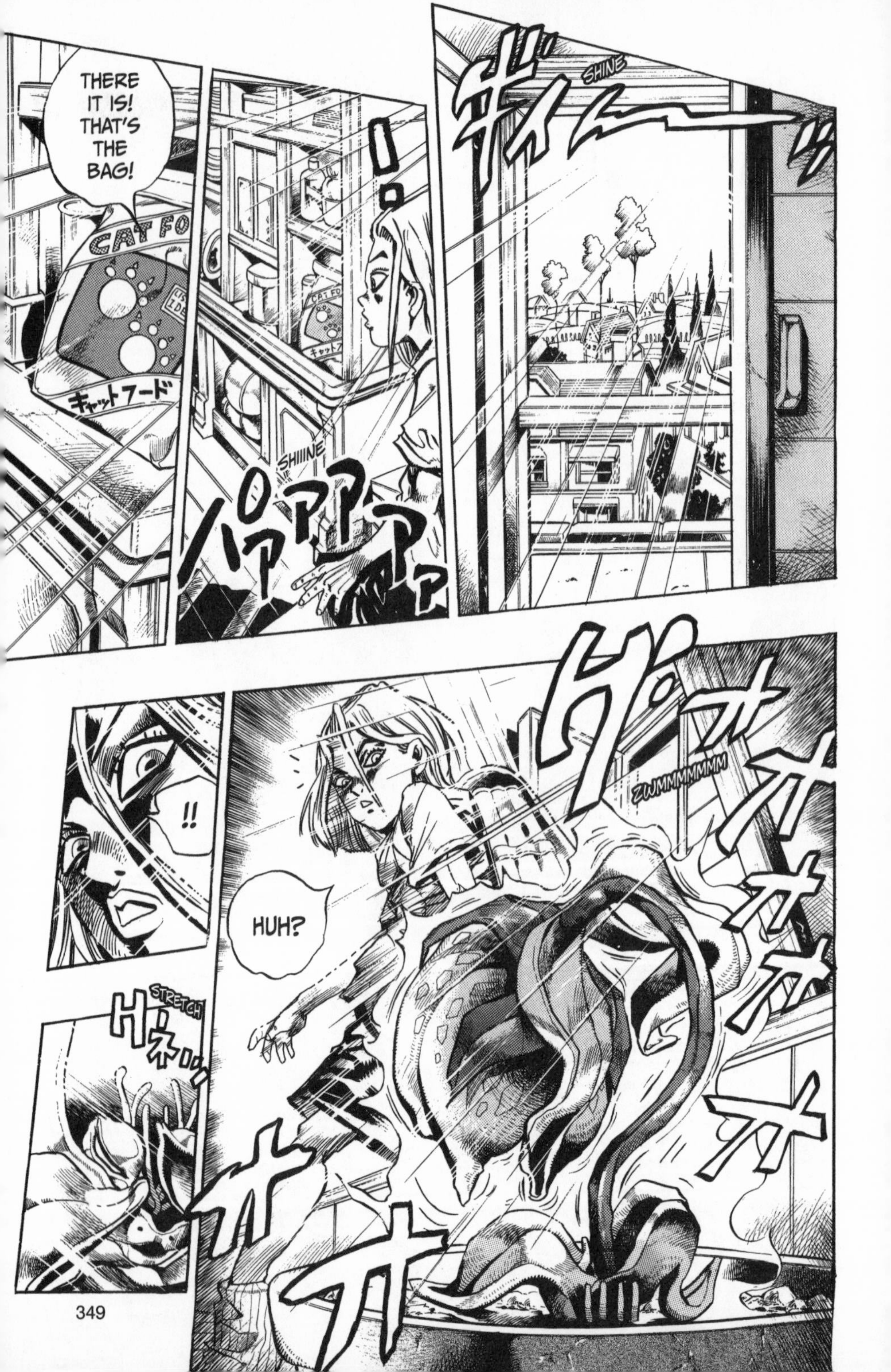
SHINE
!
SHIIINE
THERE IT IS! THAT'S THE BAG!
CAT FO
キャットフード
ZWMMMMMMM
HUH?
!!
STRETCH

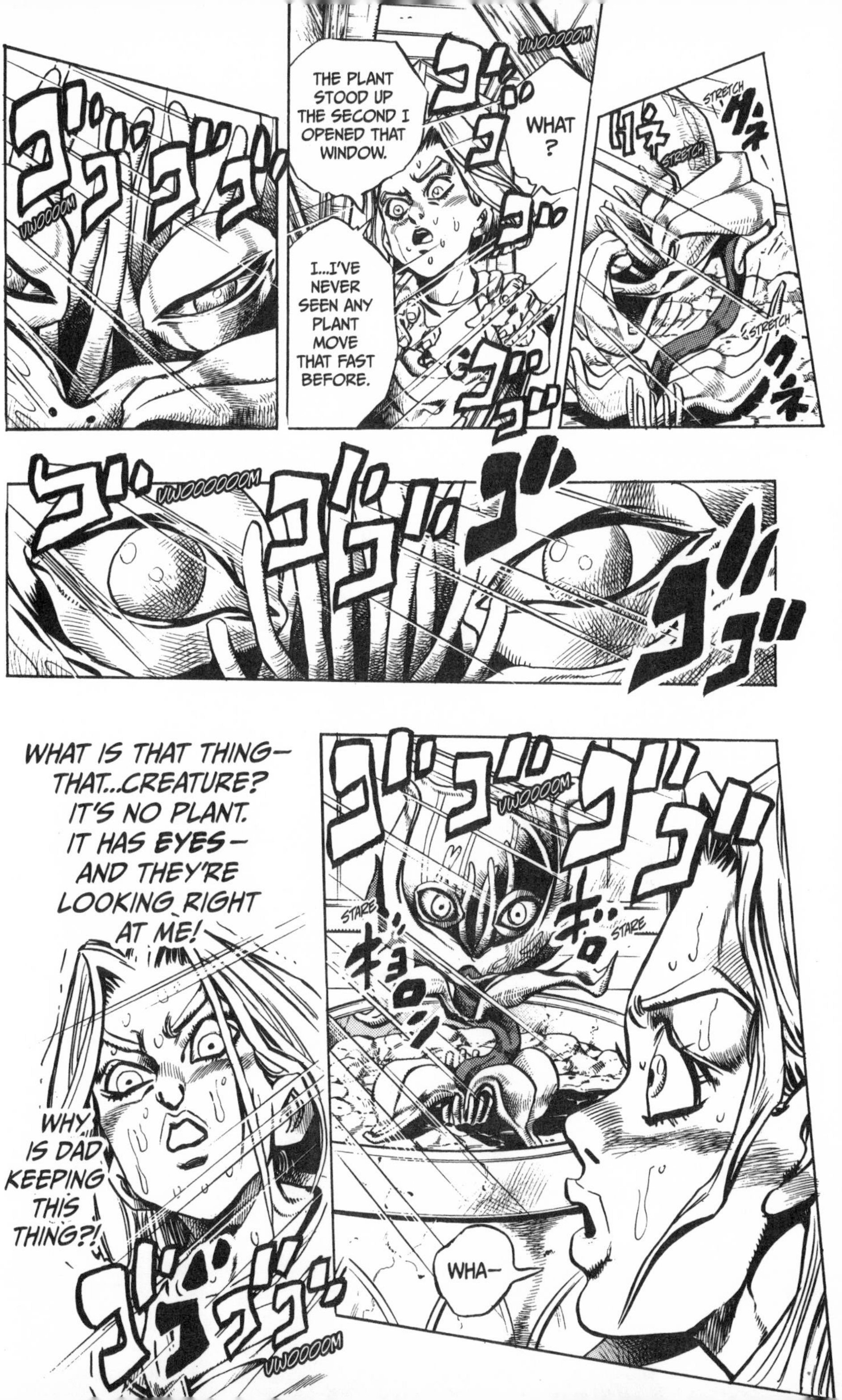
STRETCH
STRETCH
STRETCH
UWOOOOOM
THE PLANT STOOD UP THE SECOND I OPENED THAT WINDOW.
WHAT?
I...I'VE NEVER SEEN ANY PLANT MOVE THAT FAST BEFORE.
UWOOOOM
UWOOOOOOOM
UWOOOOM
STARE
STARE
WHA-
WHAT IS THAT THING— THAT...CREATURE? IT'S NO PLANT. IT HAS EYES— AND THEY'RE LOOKING RIGHT AT ME!
WHY IS DAD KEEPING THIS THING?!
UWOOOOM

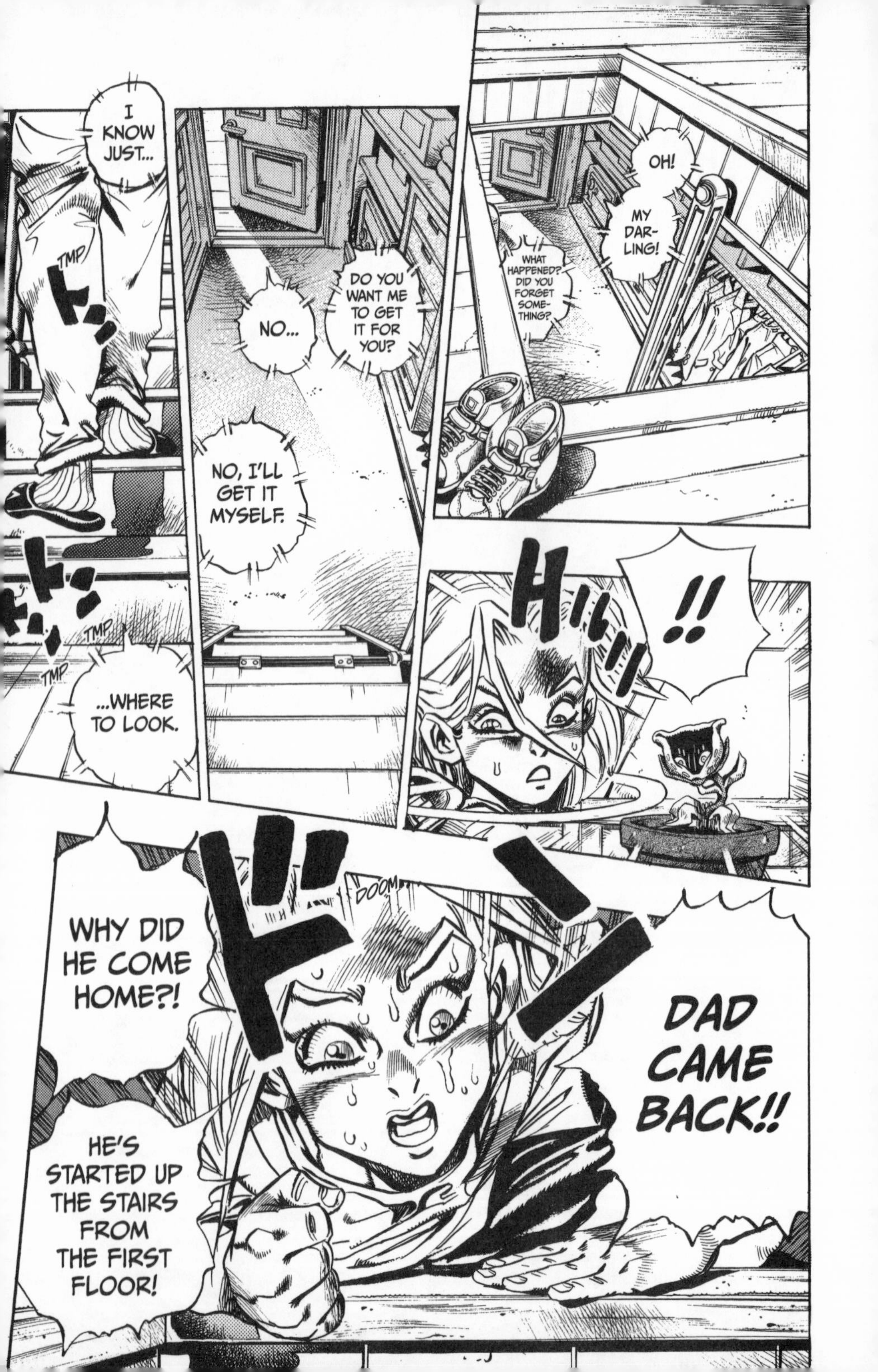
OH!
MY DARLING!
WHAT HAPPENED? DID YOU FORGET SOMETHING?
!!
DO YOU WANT ME TO GET IT FOR YOU?
NO...
NO, I'LL GET IT MYSELF.
I KNOW JUST...
TMP
TMP
TMP
...WHERE TO LOOK.
DOOM
DAD CAME BACK!!
WHY DID HE COME HOME?!
HE'S STARTED UP THE STAIRS FROM THE FIRST FLOOR!

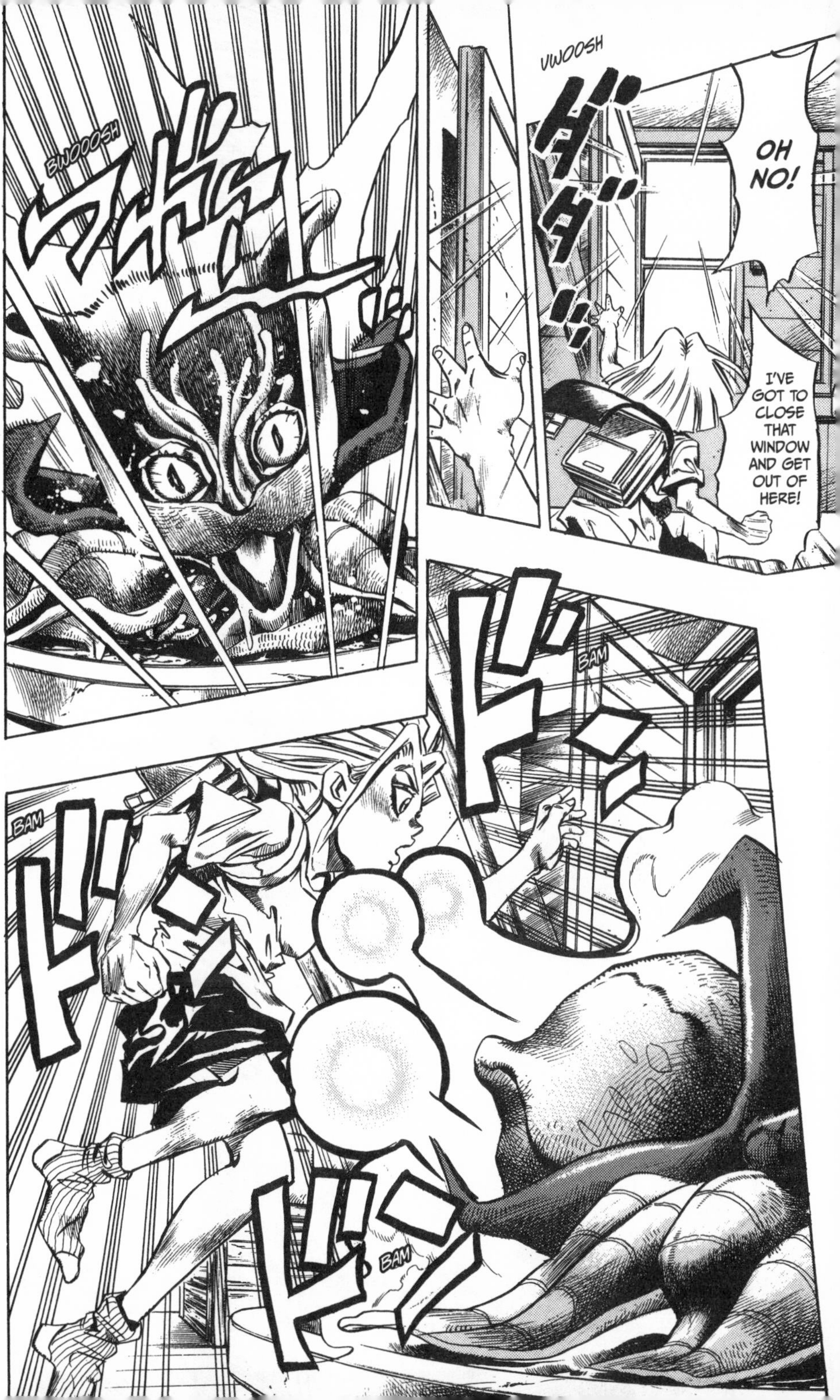
VWOOSH
OH NO!
I'VE GOT TO CLOSE THAT WINDOW AND GET OUT OF HERE!
BWOOOSH
BAM
BAM
BAM

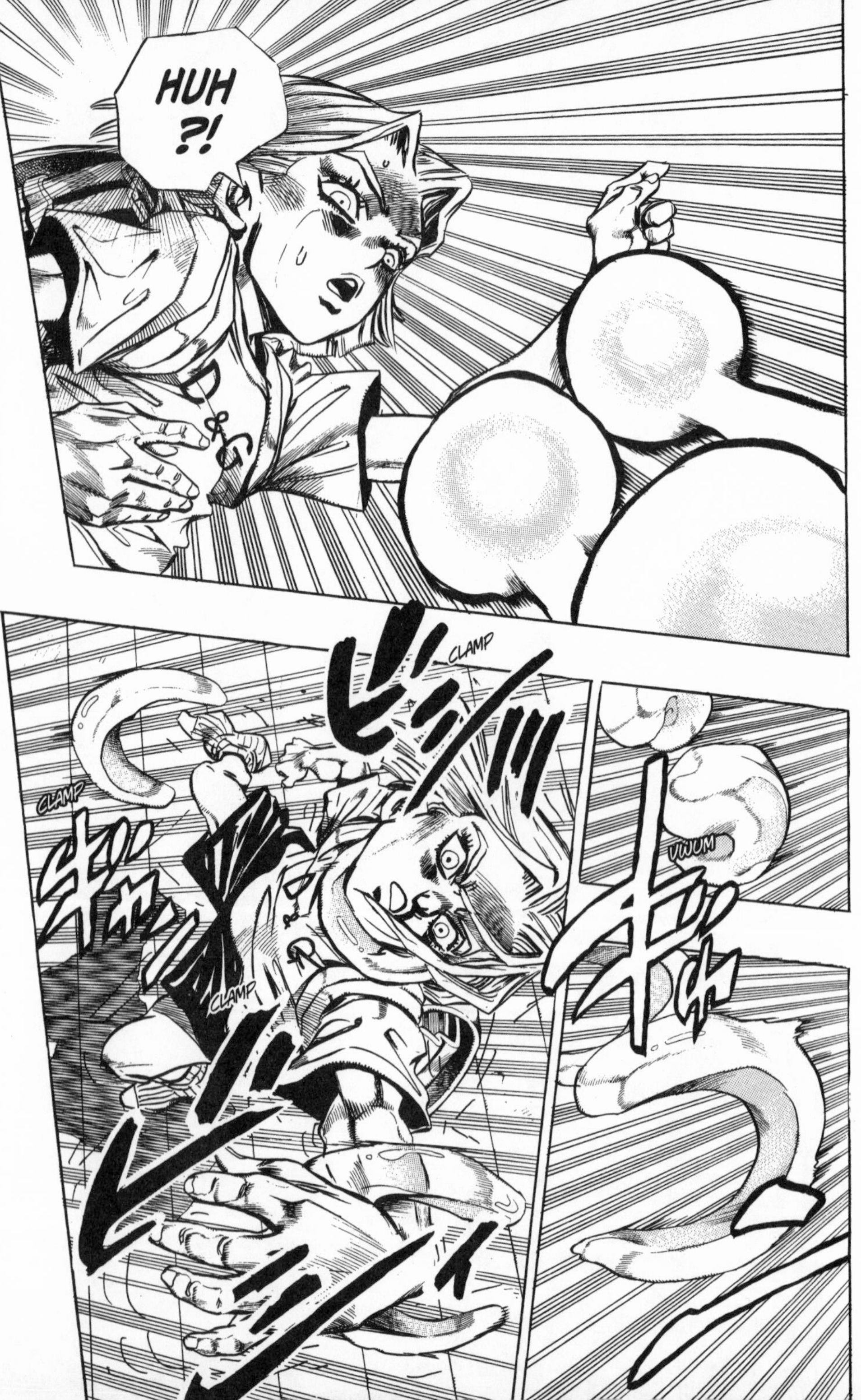
HUH ?!
UWUM
CLAMP
CLAMP
CLAMP

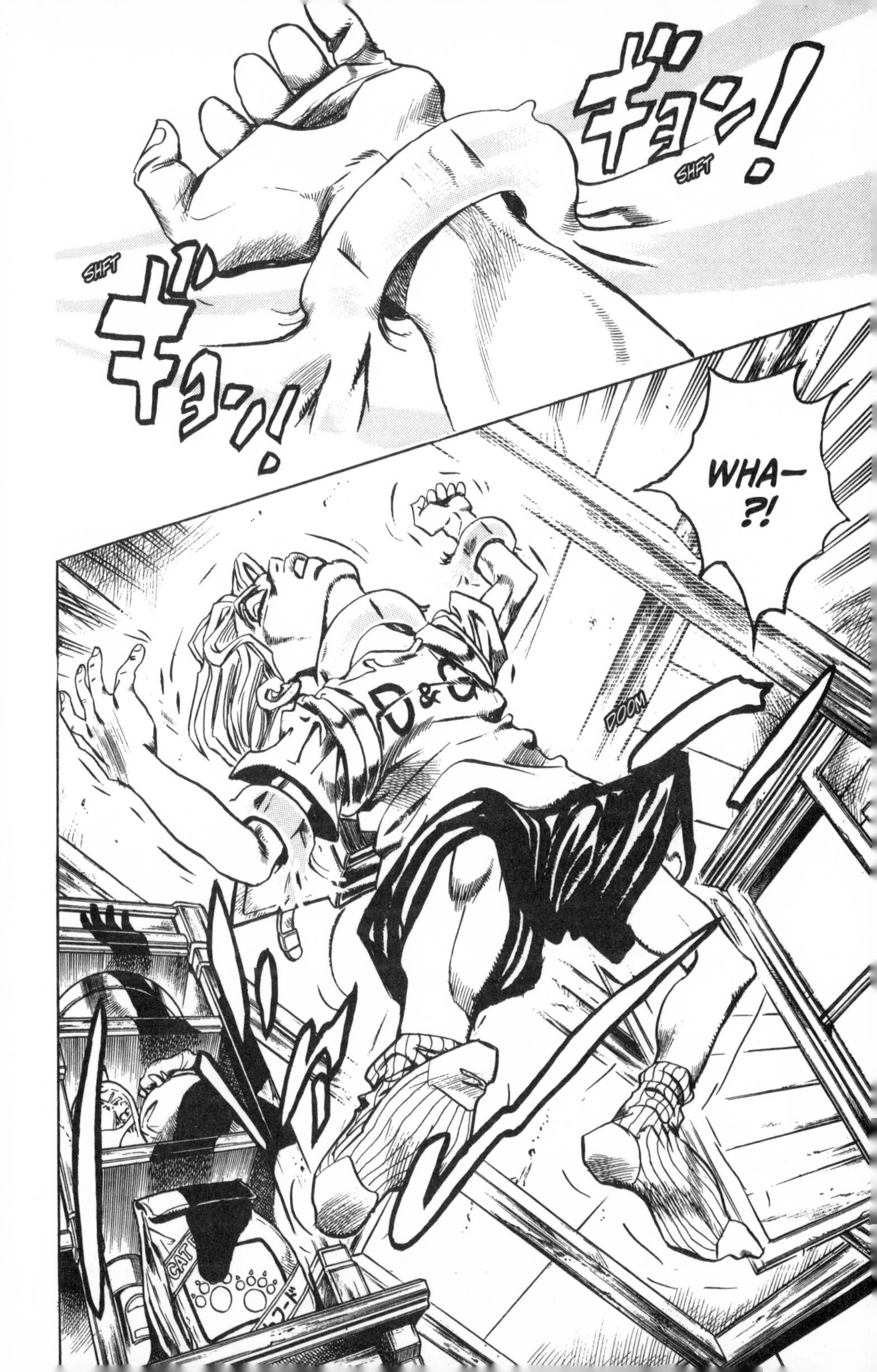
ギョン!
SHFT
ギョン!
SHFT
WHA—?!
DOOM
CAT

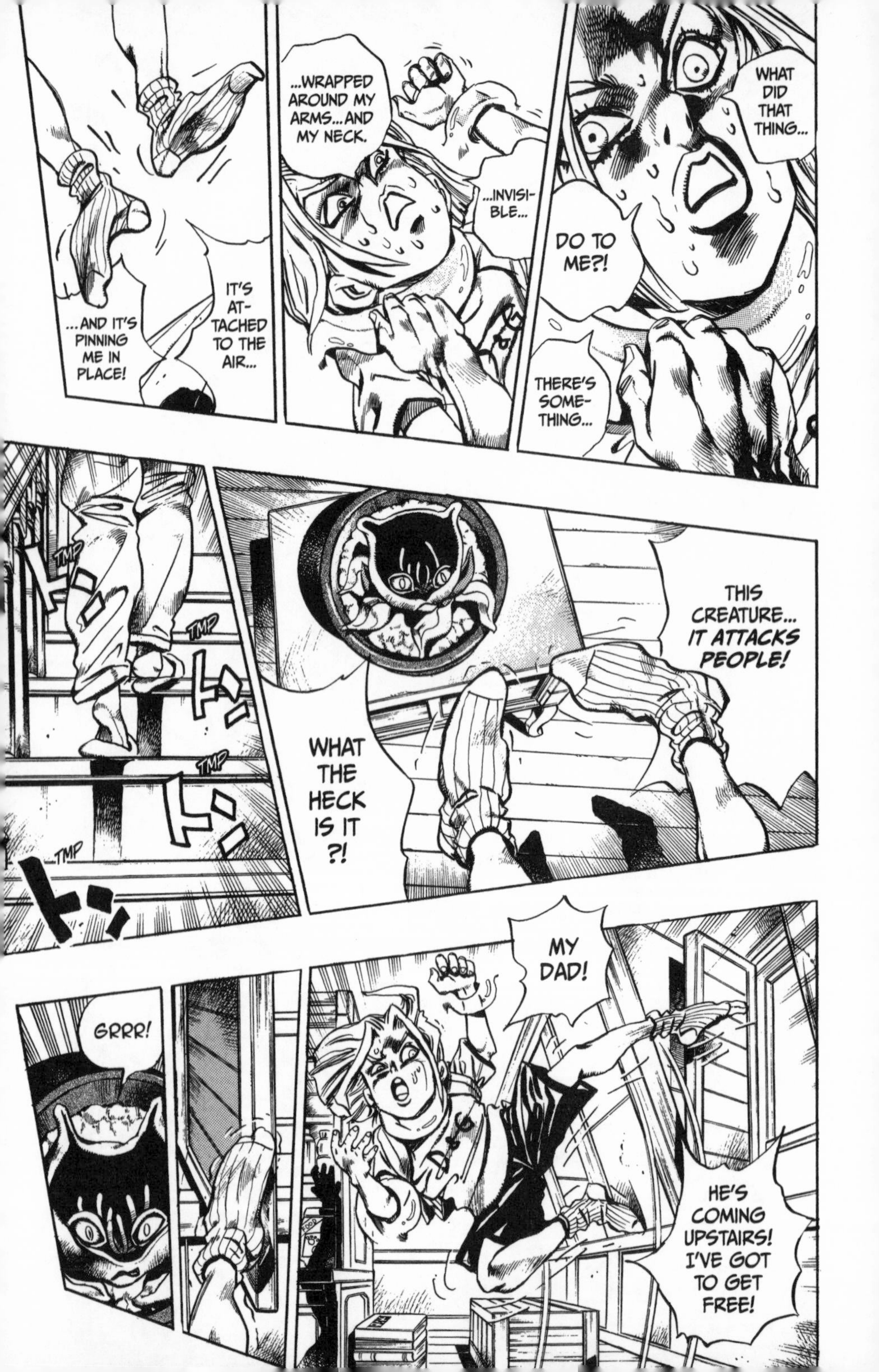
WHAT DID THAT THING...
DO TO ME?!
THERE'S SOME-THING...
...INVISI-BLE...
...WRAPPED AROUND MY ARMS...AND MY NECK.
IT'S AT-TACHED TO THE AIR...
...AND IT'S PINNING ME IN PLACE!
THIS CREATURE... *IT ATTACKS PEOPLE!*
WHAT THE HECK IS IT ?!
TMP
TMP
TMP
TMP
MY DAD!
HE'S COMING UPSTAIRS! I'VE GOT TO GET FREE!
GRRR!

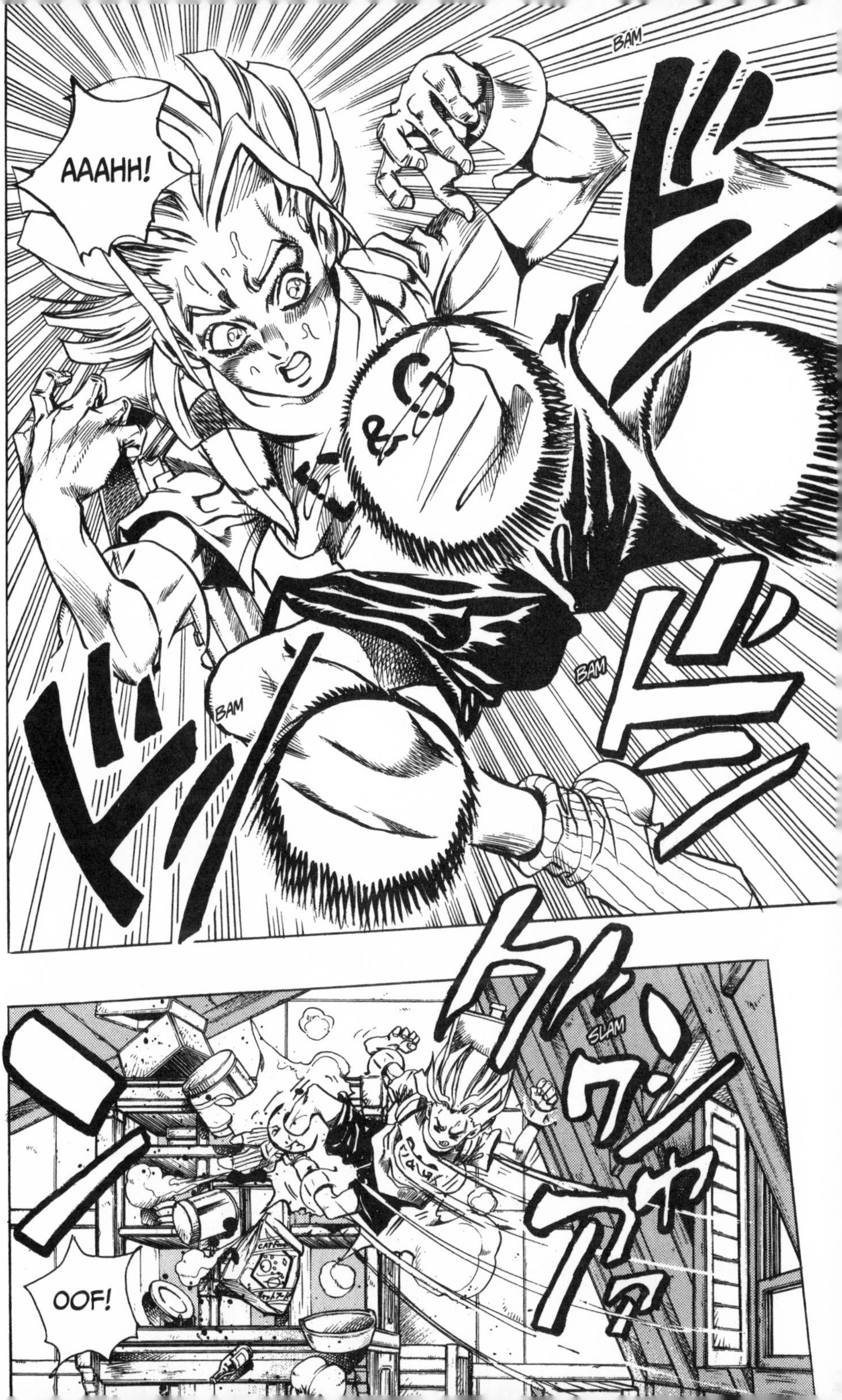
BAM
AAAHH!
BAM
BAM
SLAM
OOF!

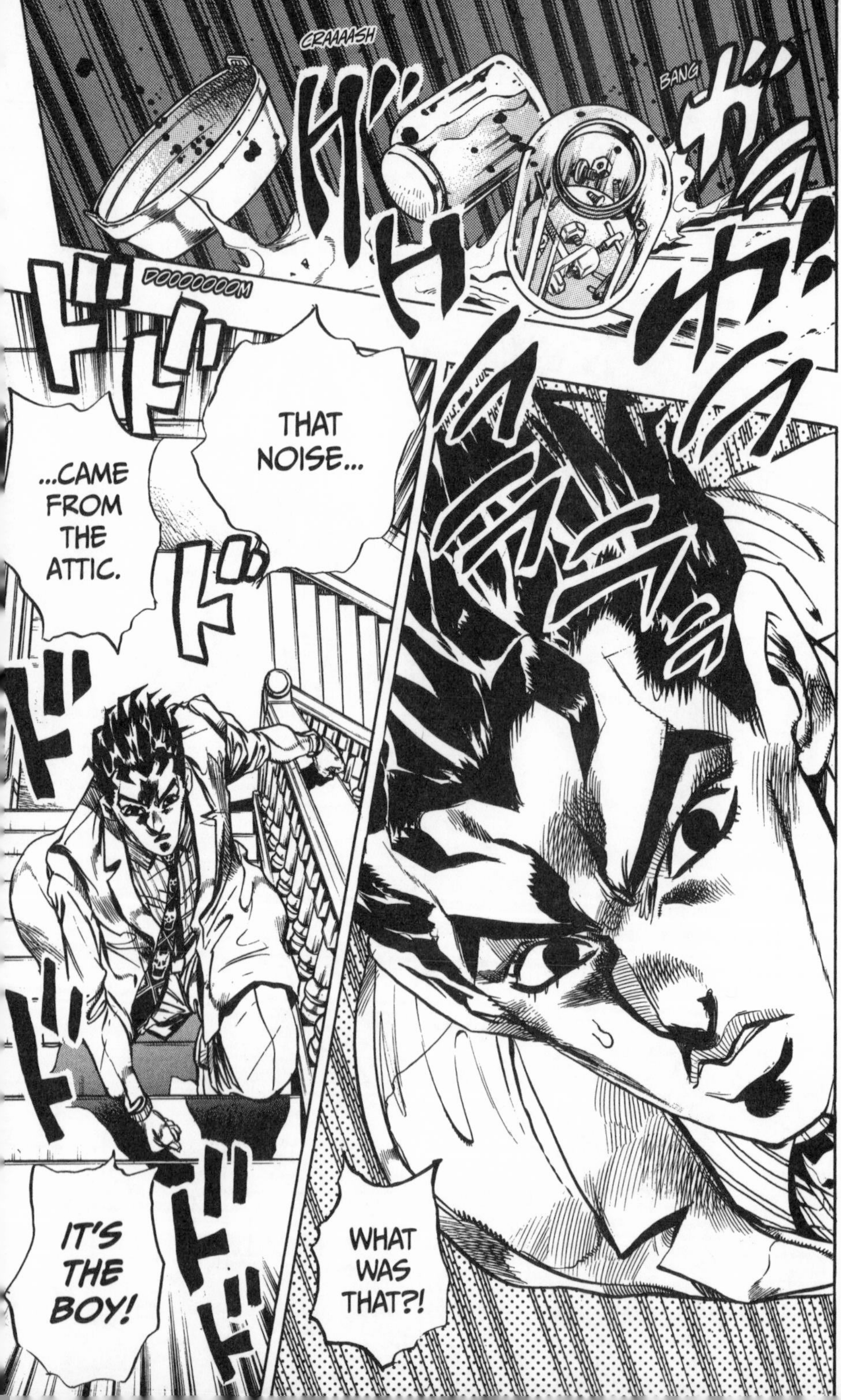
BANG
CRAAASH
DOOOOOOOOM
WHAT WAS THAT?!
THAT NOISE...
...CAME FROM THE ATTIC.
IT'S THE BOY!

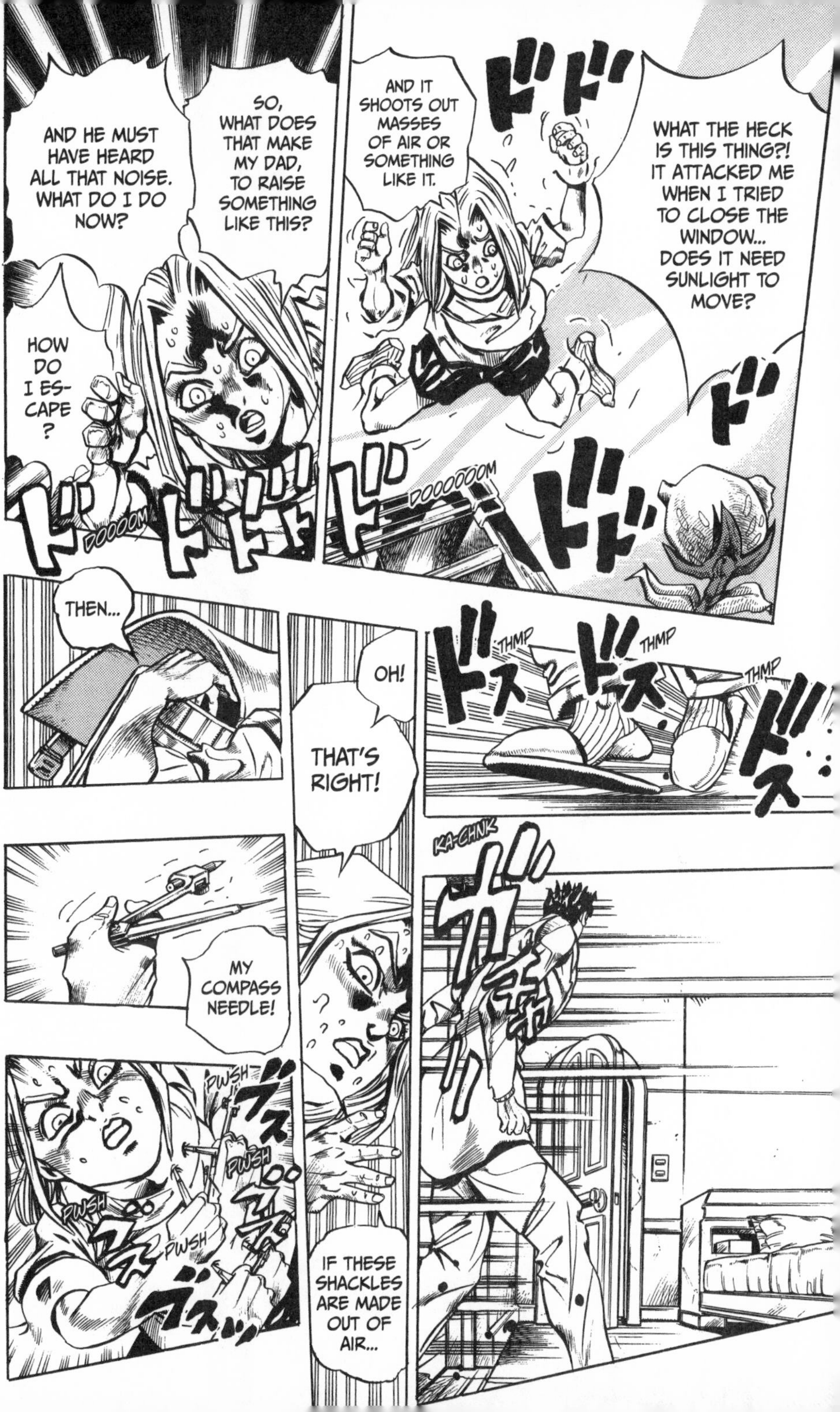
WHAT THE HECK IS THIS THING?! IT ATTACKED ME WHEN I TRIED TO CLOSE THE WINDOW... DOES IT NEED SUNLIGHT TO MOVE?
AND IT SHOOTS OUT MASSES OF AIR OR SOMETHING LIKE IT.
DOOOOOOM
SO, WHAT DOES THAT MAKE MY DAD, TO RAISE SOMETHING LIKE THIS?
AND HE MUST HAVE HEARD ALL THAT NOISE. WHAT DO I DO NOW?
HOW DO I ES-CAPE?
DOOOOOM
THMP
THMP
THMP
OH!
THAT'S RIGHT!
THEN...
KA-CHNK
IF THESE SHACKLES ARE MADE OUT OF AIR...
MY COMPASS NEEDLE!
PWSH
PWSH
PWSH
PWSH

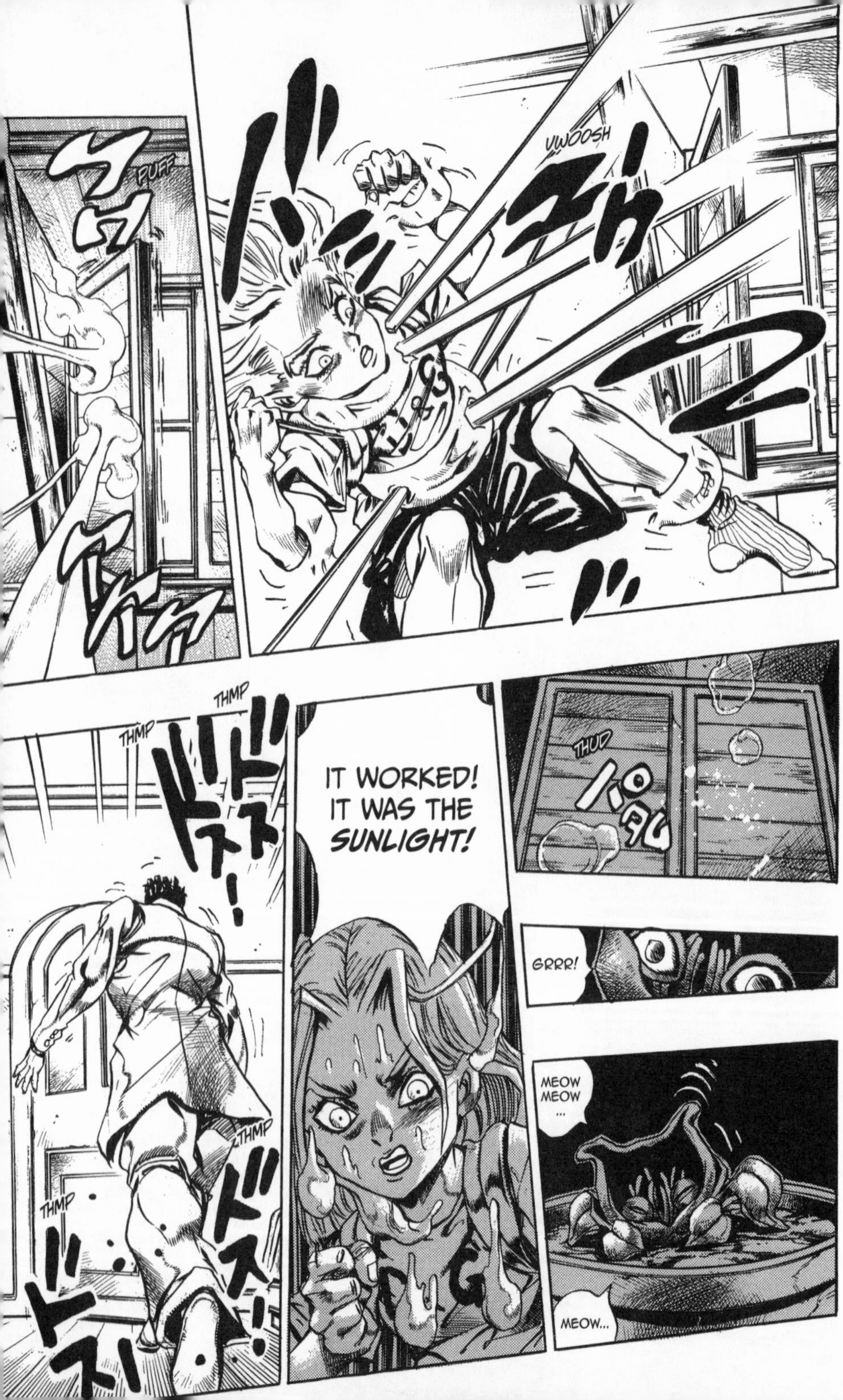
VWOOSH
PUFF
THUD
GRRR!
MEOW
MEOW
...
MEOW...
IT WORKED!
IT WAS THE
SUNLIGHT!
THMP
THMP
THMP
THMP

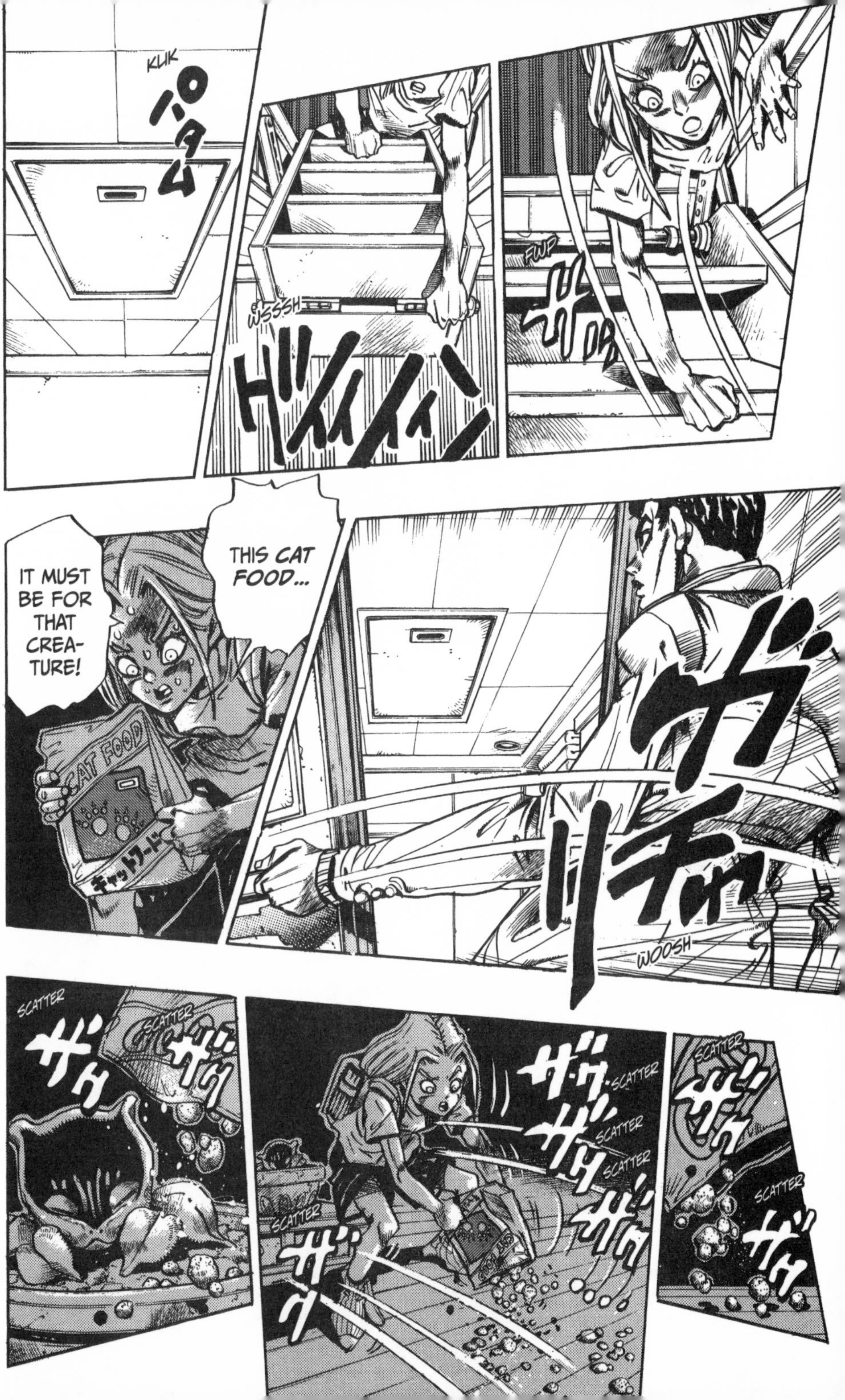
FWUP
DR
WSSSH
KLIK
パタム
WOOSH
THIS CAT FOOD...
IT MUST BE FOR THAT CREATURE!
CAT FOOD
SCATTER
SCATTER
SCATTER
SCATTER
SCATTER
SCATTER
SCATTER
SCATTER

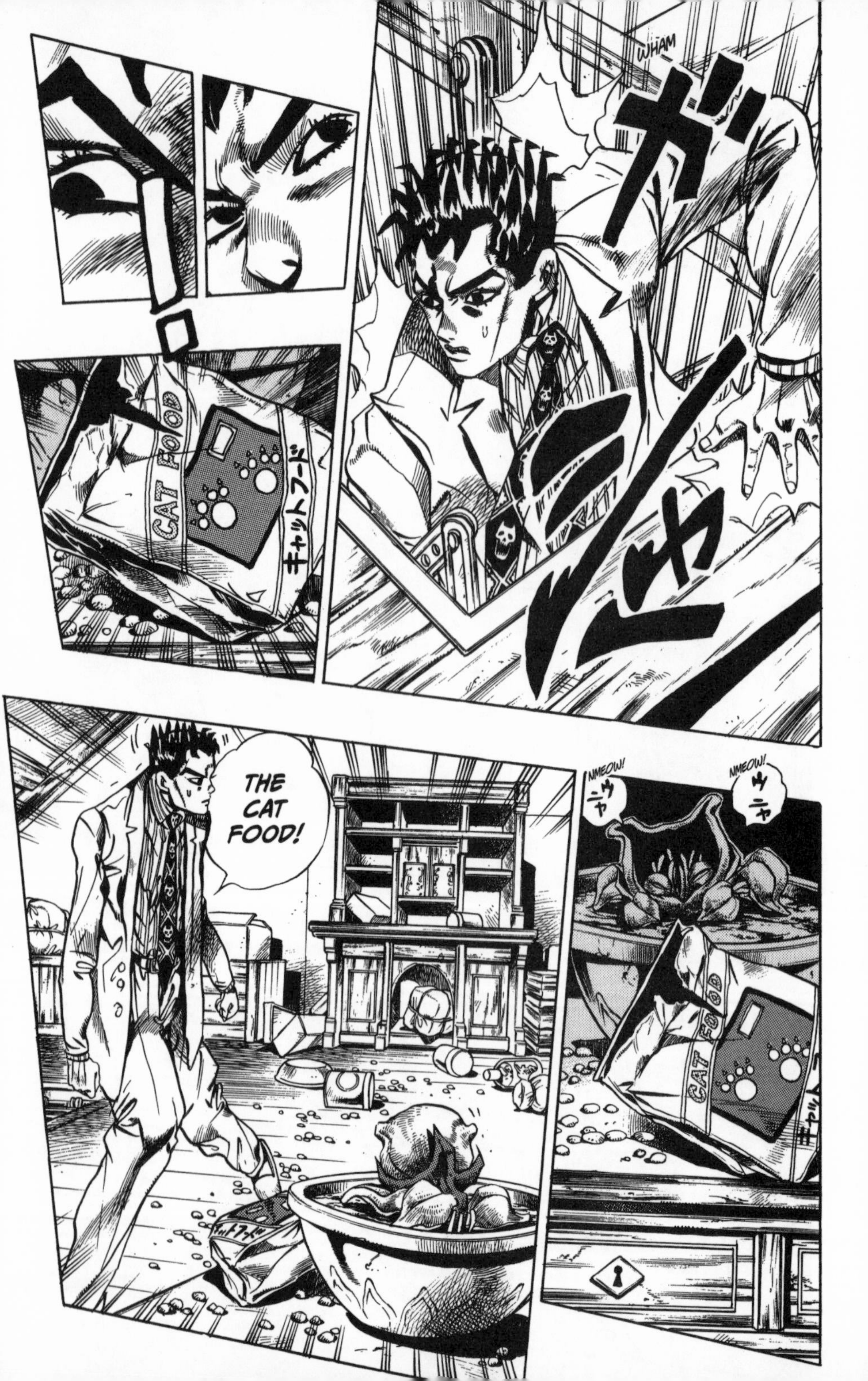
WHAM
CAT FOOD
キャットフード
NMEOW!
NMEOW!
CAT FOOD
THE CAT FOOD!

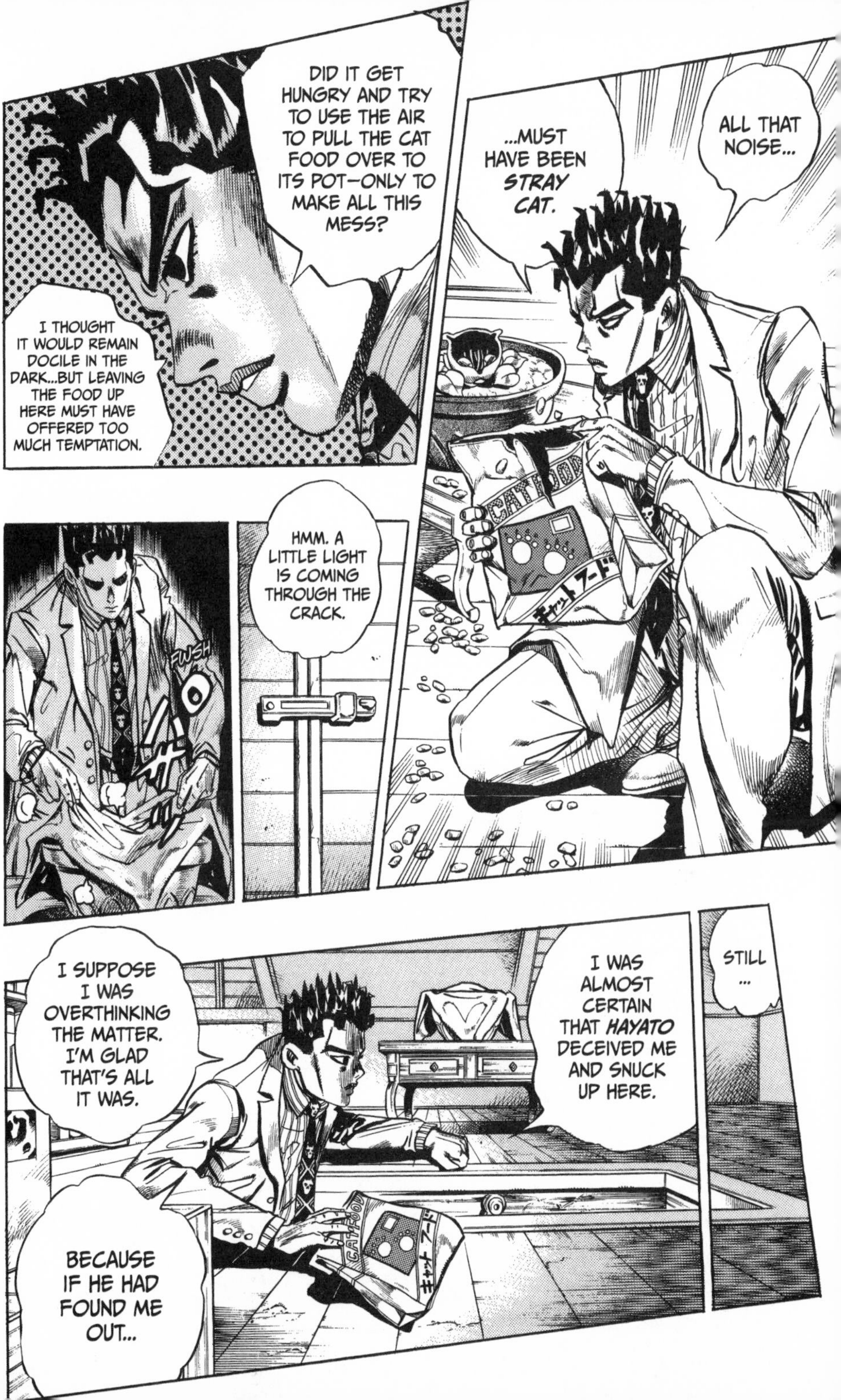
ALL THAT NOISE...
...MUST HAVE BEEN *STRAY CAT.*
CATFOOD
キャットフード
DID IT GET HUNGRY AND TRY TO USE THE AIR TO PULL THE CAT FOOD OVER TO ITS POT—ONLY TO MAKE ALL THIS MESS?
I THOUGHT IT WOULD REMAIN DOCILE IN THE DARK...BUT LEAVING THE FOOD UP HERE MUST HAVE OFFERED TOO MUCH TEMPTATION.
HMM. A LITTLE LIGHT IS COMING THROUGH THE CRACK.
FWSH
STILL ...
I WAS ALMOST CERTAIN THAT *HAYATO* DECEIVED ME AND SNUCK UP HERE.
I SUPPOSE I WAS OVERTHINKING THE MATTER. I'M GLAD THAT'S ALL IT WAS.
CATFOOD
BECAUSE IF HE HAD FOUND ME OUT...

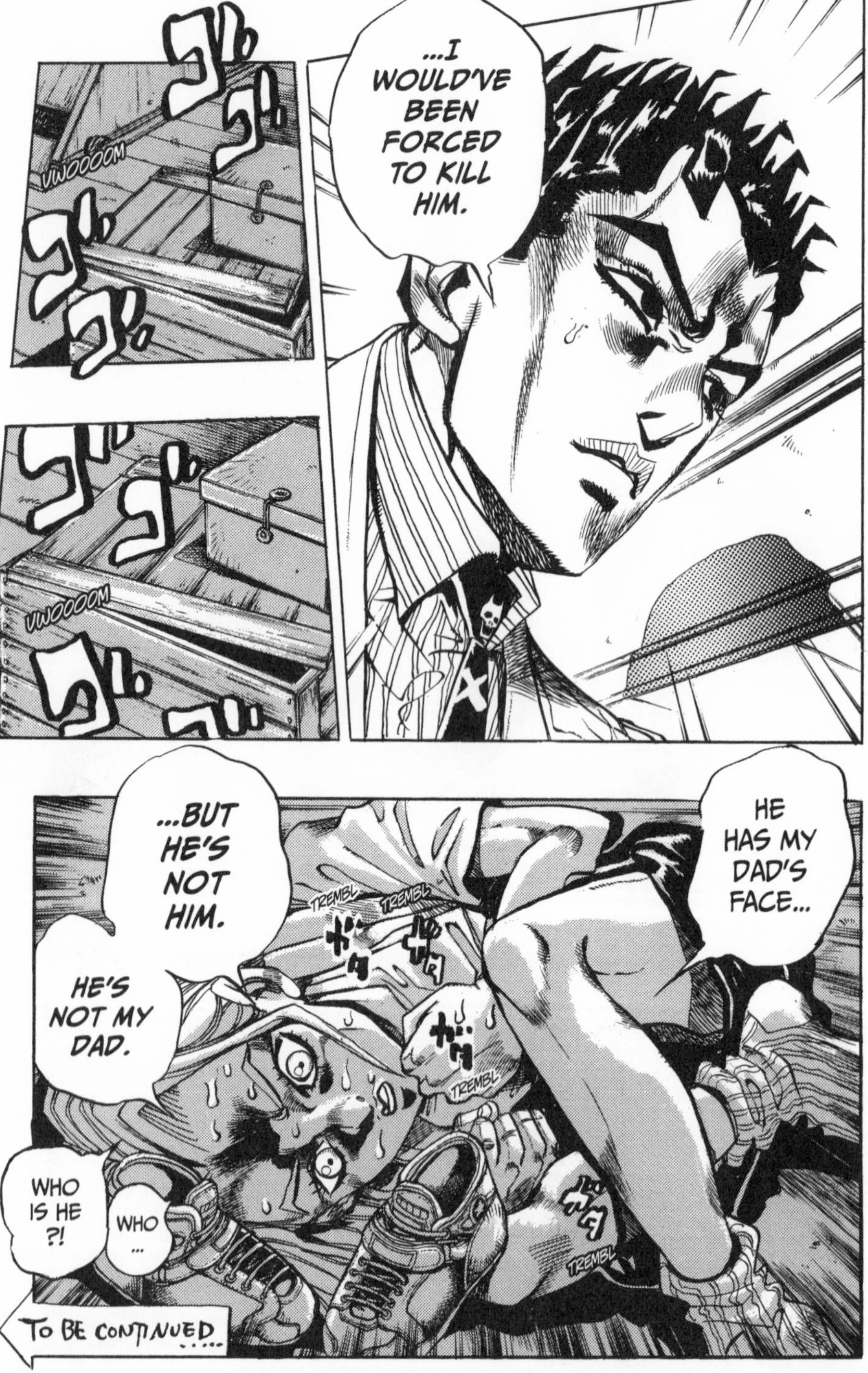
...I WOULD'VE BEEN FORCED TO KILL HIM.
UWOOOOM
UWOOOOM
HE HAS MY DAD'S FACE...
...BUT HE'S NOT HIM.
TREMBL
TREMBL
HE'S NOT MY DAD.
TREMBL
TREMBL
WHO ...
WHO IS HE ?!
TO BE CONTINUED...

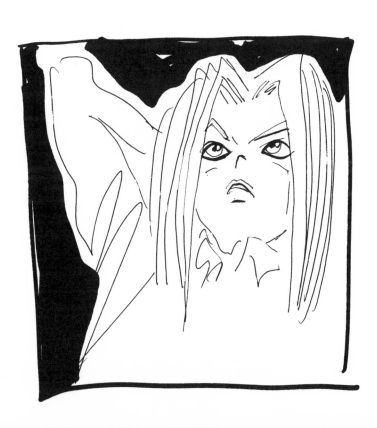

CHAPTER 133 ★ LET'S LIVE ON A TRANSMISSION TOWER, PART 1

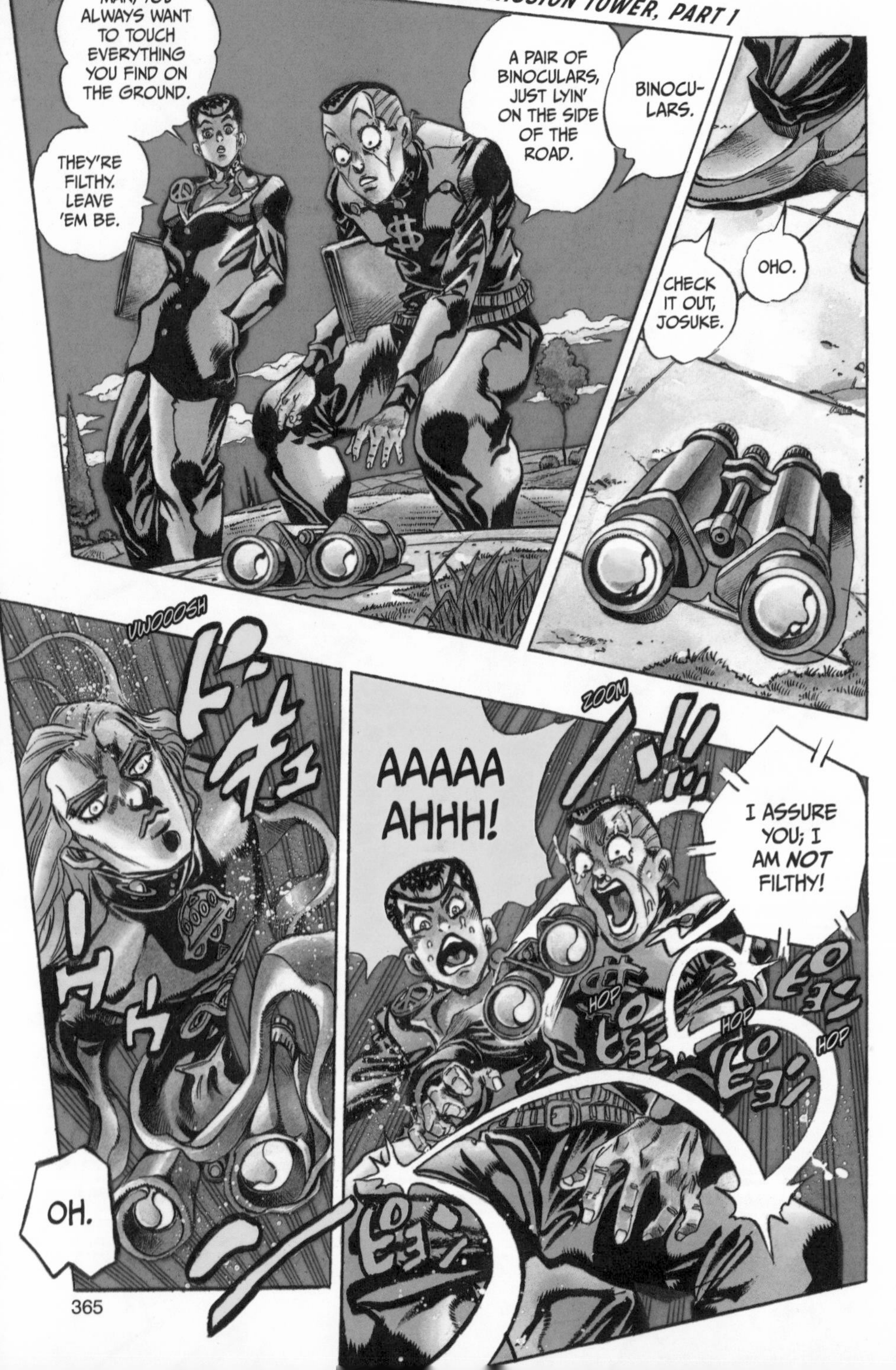
OHO.
CHECK IT OUT, JOSUKE.
BINOCU-LARS.
A PAIR OF BINOCULARS, JUST LYIN' ON THE SIDE OF THE ROAD.
MAN, YOU ALWAYS WANT TO TOUCH EVERYTHING YOU FIND ON THE GROUND.
THEY'RE FILTHY. LEAVE 'EM BE.
ZOOM
AAAAA AHHH!
I ASSURE YOU; I AM *NOT* FILTHY!
HOP
HOP
HOP
UWOOOSH
OH.

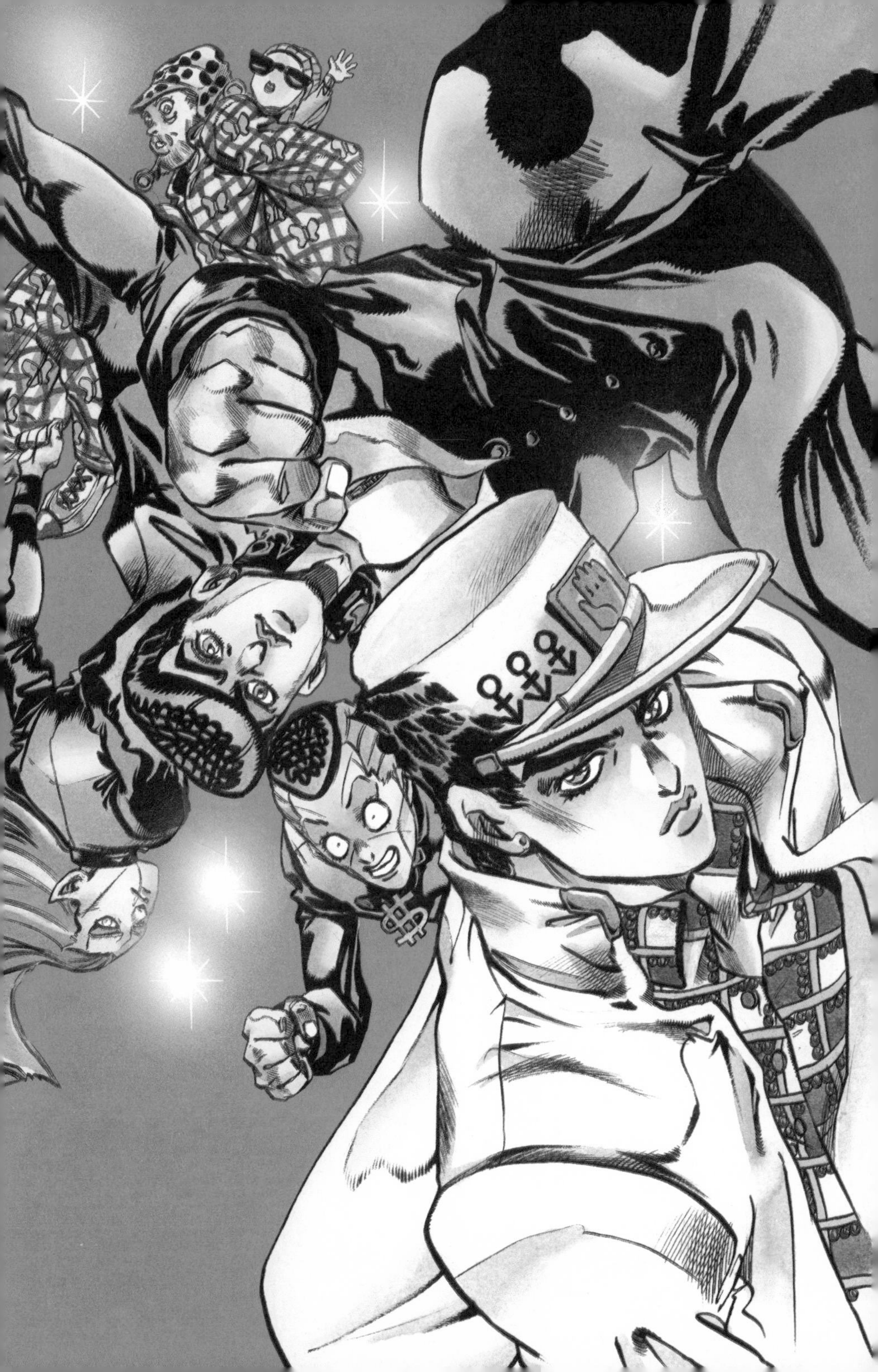

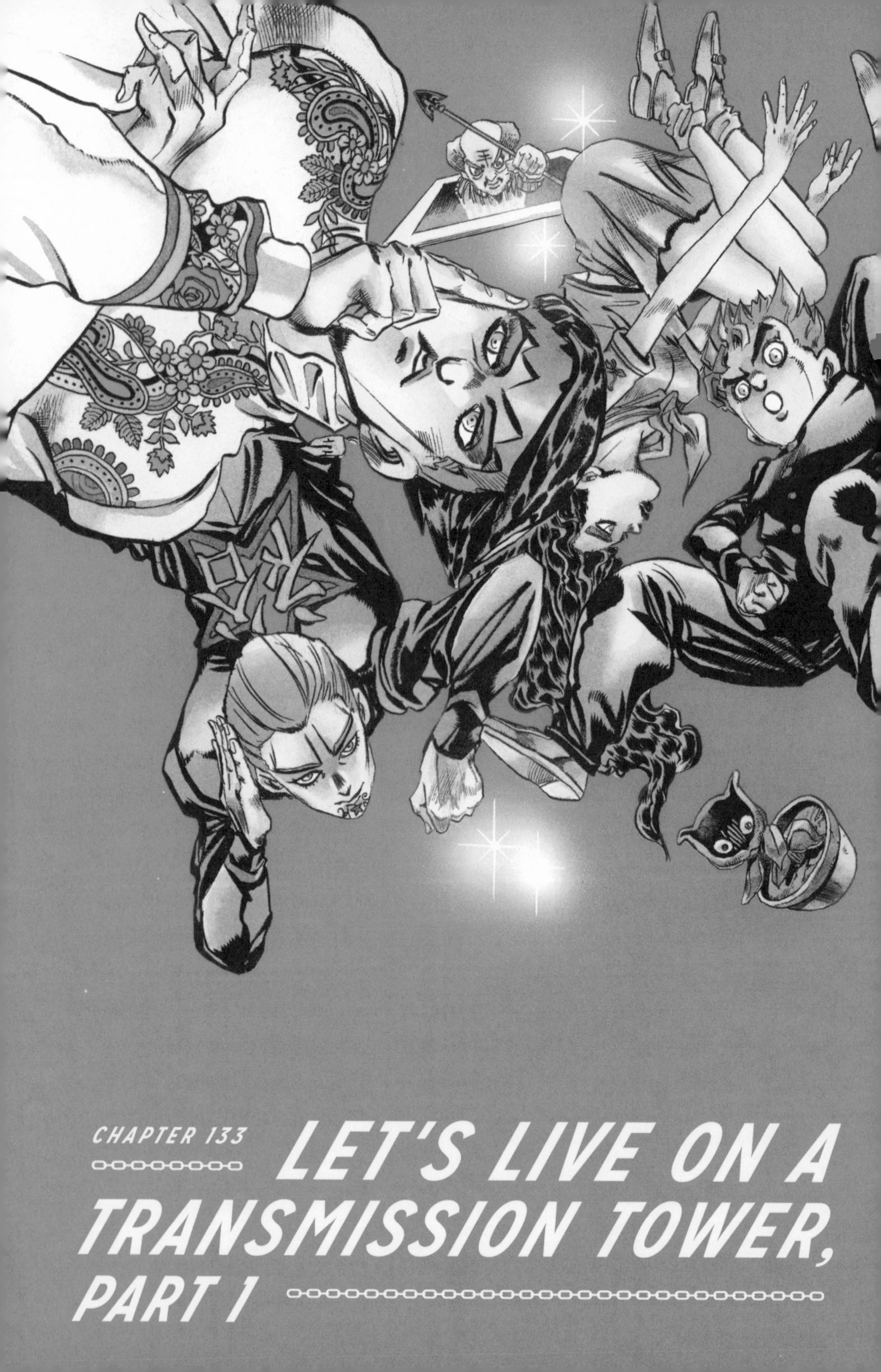

CHAPTER 133

LET'S LIVE ON A TRANSMISSION TOWER, PART 1

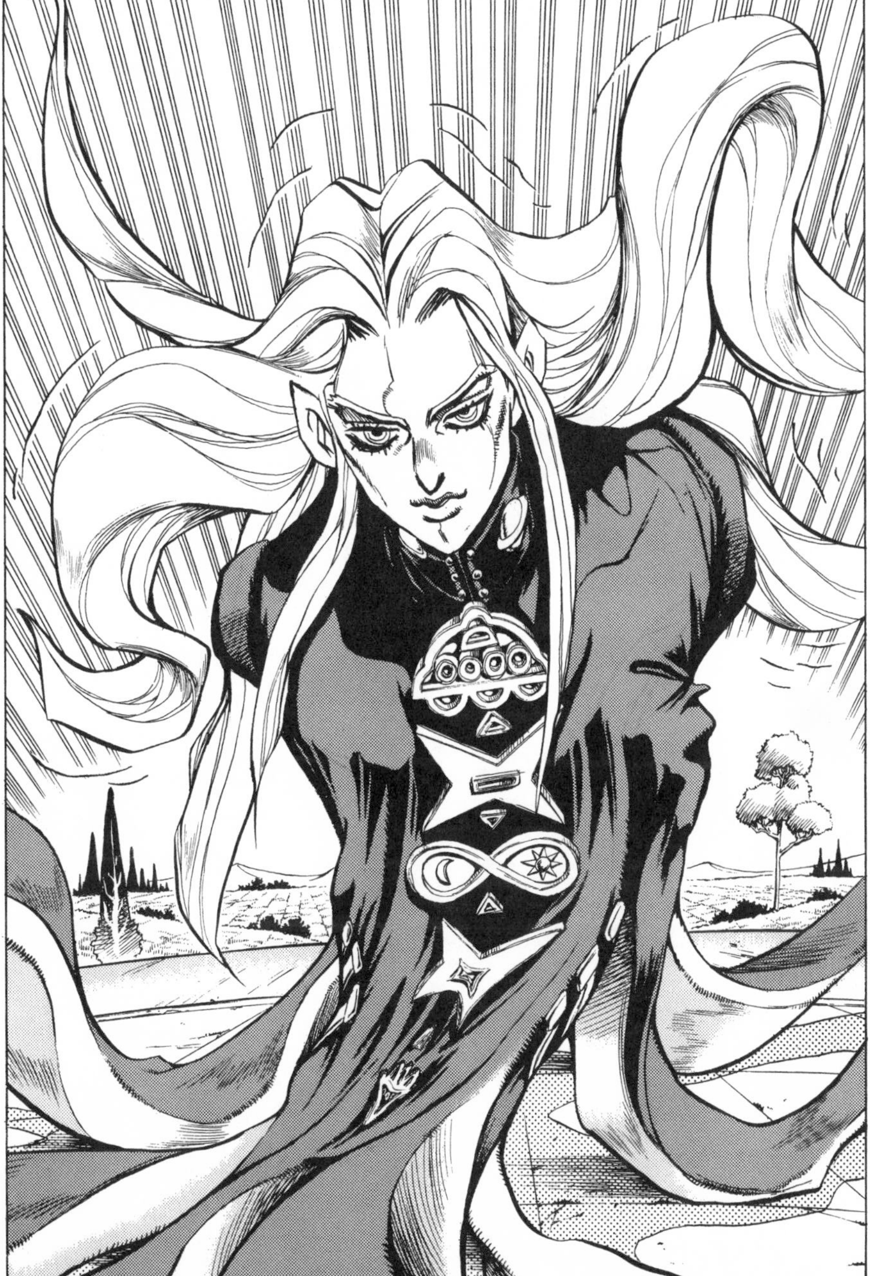

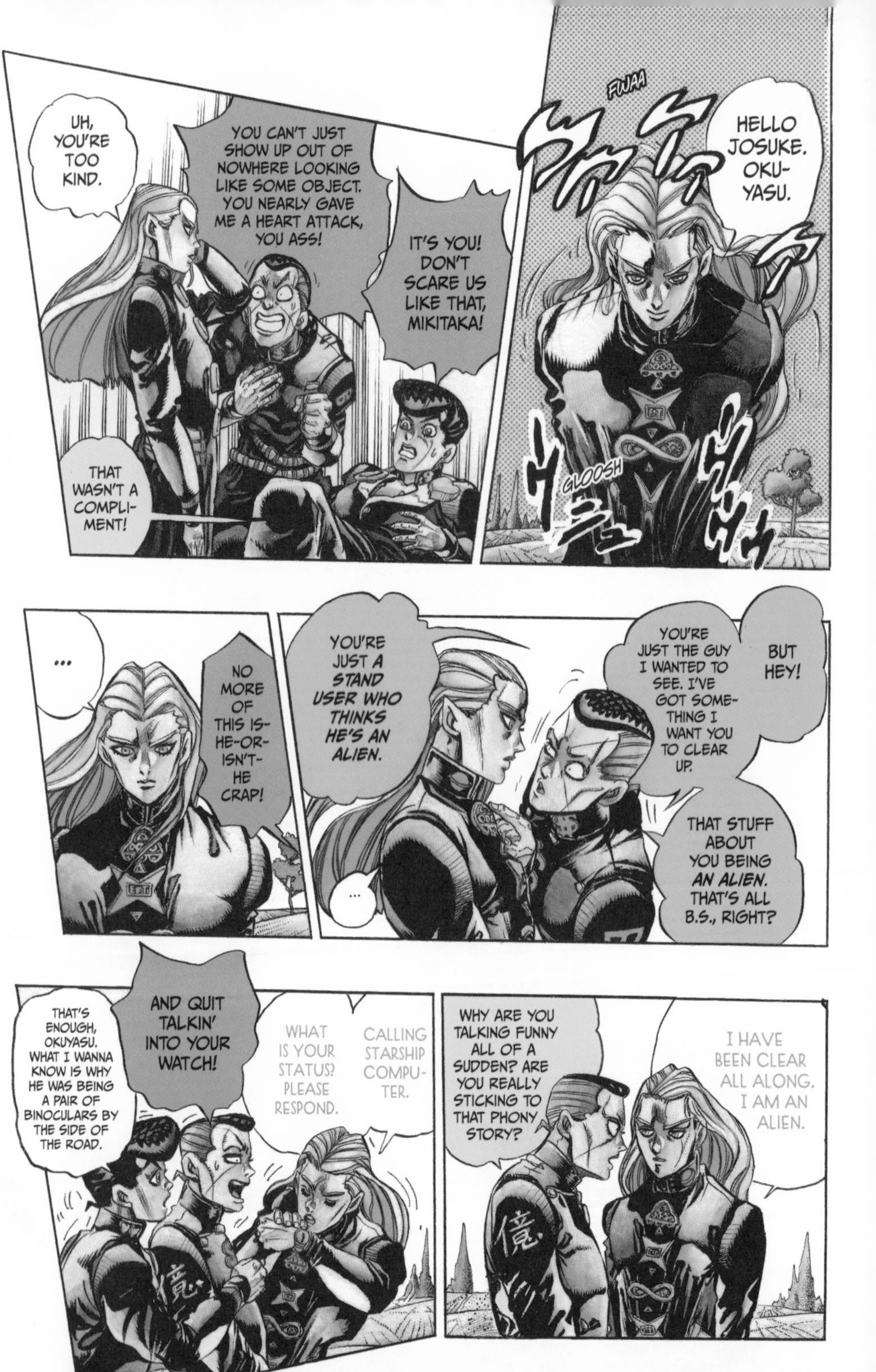
FUJAA
HELLO JOSUKE. OKU-YASU.
GLOOSH
IT'S YOU! DON'T SCARE US LIKE THAT, MIKITAKA!
YOU CAN'T JUST SHOW UP OUT OF NOWHERE LOOKING LIKE SOME OBJECT. YOU NEARLY GAVE ME A HEART ATTACK, YOU ASS!
UH, YOU'RE TOO KIND.
THAT WASN'T A COMPLI-MENT!
BUT HEY!
YOU'RE JUST THE GUY I WANTED TO SEE. I'VE GOT SOME-THING I WANT YOU TO CLEAR UP.
THAT STUFF ABOUT YOU BEING AN ALIEN. THAT'S ALL B.S., RIGHT?
YOU'RE JUST A STAND USER WHO THINKS HE'S AN ALIEN.
...
NO MORE OF THIS IS-HE-OR-ISN'T-HE CRAP!
...
I HAVE BEEN CLEAR ALL ALONG. I AM AN ALIEN.
WHY ARE YOU TALKING FUNNY ALL OF A SUDDEN? ARE YOU REALLY STICKING TO THAT PHONY STORY?
CALLING STARSHIP COMPU-TER.
WHAT IS YOUR STATUS? PLEASE RESPOND.
AND QUIT TALKIN' INTO YOUR WATCH!
THAT'S ENOUGH, OKUYASU. WHAT I WANNA KNOW IS WHY HE WAS BEING A PAIR OF BINOCULARS BY THE SIDE OF THE ROAD.

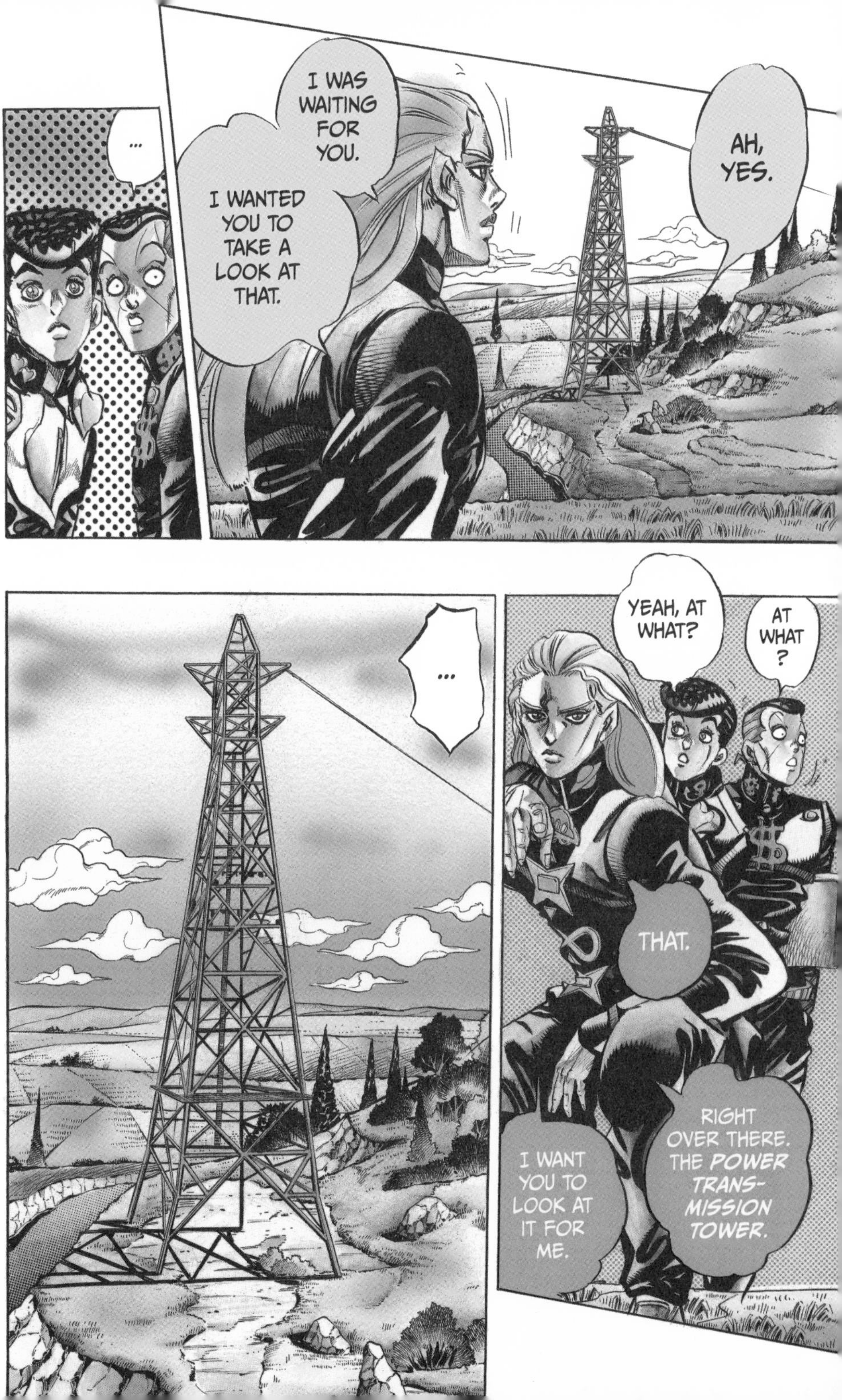
AH, YES.
I WAS WAITING FOR YOU.
I WANTED YOU TO TAKE A LOOK AT THAT.
...
AT WHAT?
YEAH, AT WHAT?
THAT.
RIGHT OVER THERE. THE *POWER TRANS-MISSION TOWER.*
I WANT YOU TO LOOK AT IT FOR ME.
...

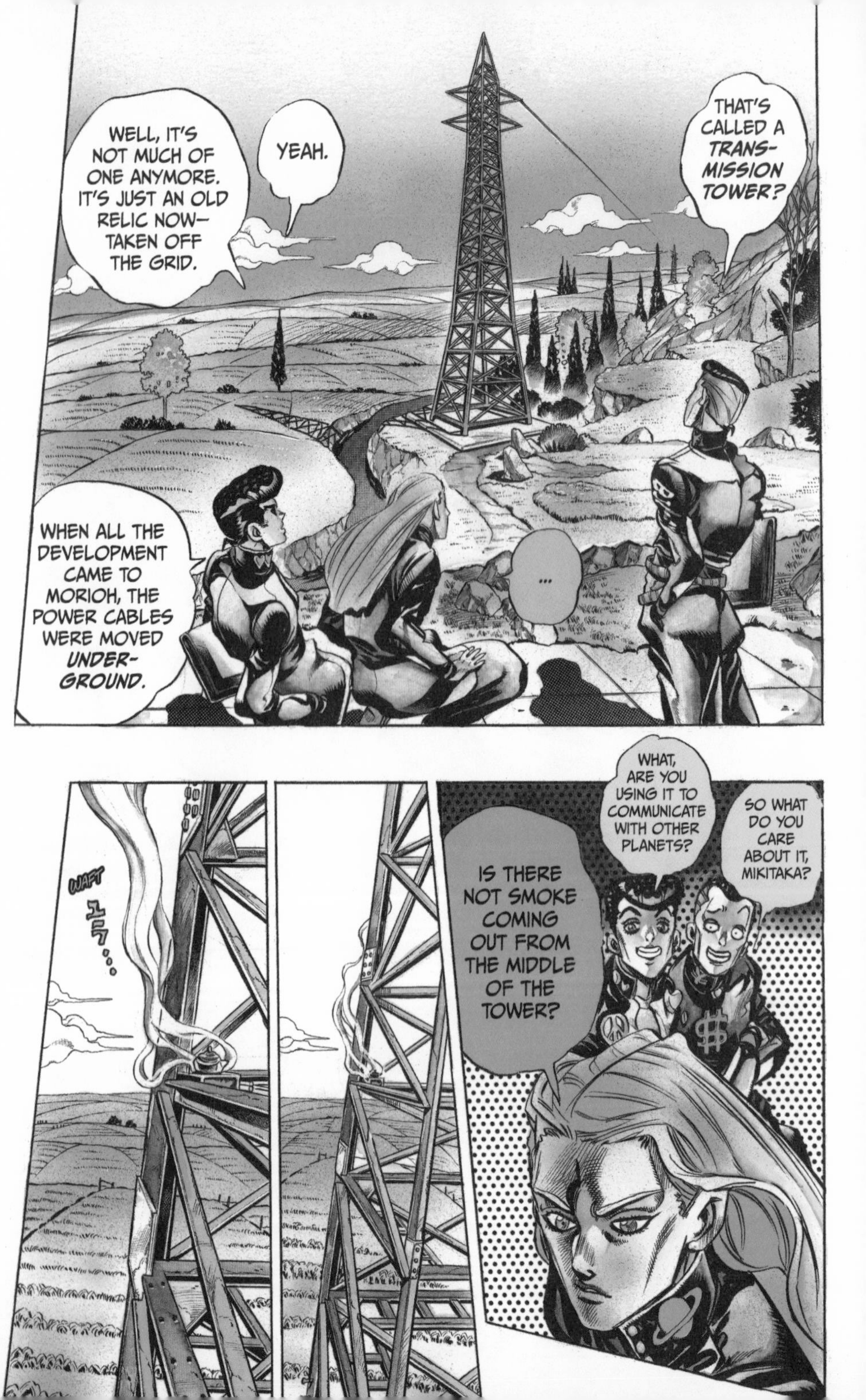
THAT'S CALLED A TRANSMISSION TOWER?
YEAH.
WELL, IT'S NOT MUCH OF ONE ANYMORE. IT'S JUST AN OLD RELIC NOW—TAKEN OFF THE GRID.
...
WHEN ALL THE DEVELOPMENT CAME TO MORIOH, THE POWER CABLES WERE MOVED UNDERGROUND.
IS THERE NOT SMOKE COMING OUT FROM THE MIDDLE OF THE TOWER?
WHAT, ARE YOU USING IT TO COMMUNICATE WITH OTHER PLANETS?
SO WHAT DO YOU CARE ABOUT IT, MIKITAKA?
WAFT
ユラ...

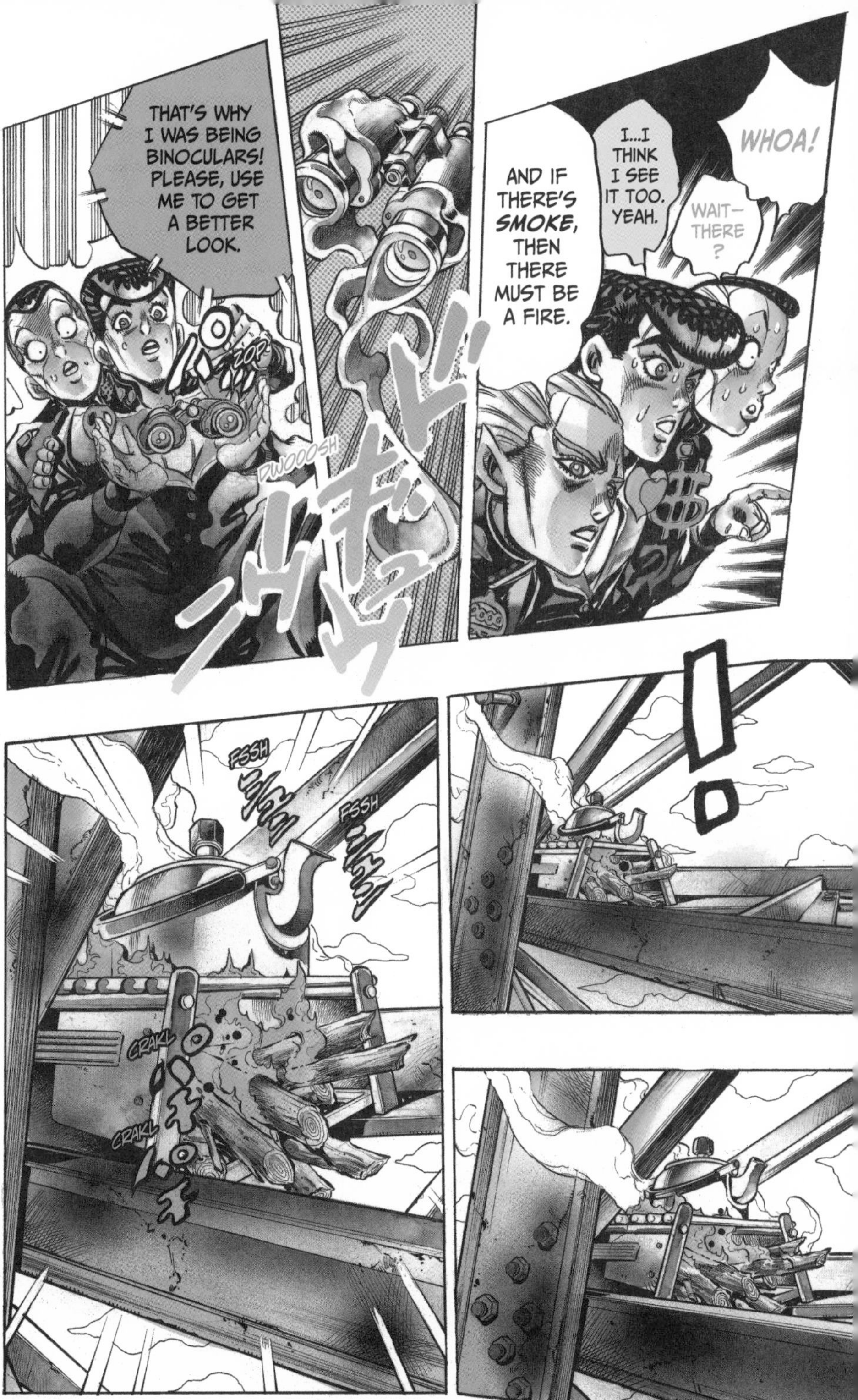
WHOA!
WAIT—THERE?
I...I THINK I SEE IT TOO. YEAH.
AND IF THERE'S *SMOKE*, THEN THERE MUST BE A FIRE.
DWOOOSH
ZOP
THAT'S WHY I WAS BEING BINOCULARS! PLEASE, USE ME TO GET A BETTER LOOK.
FSSH
FSSH
CRAKL
CRAKL

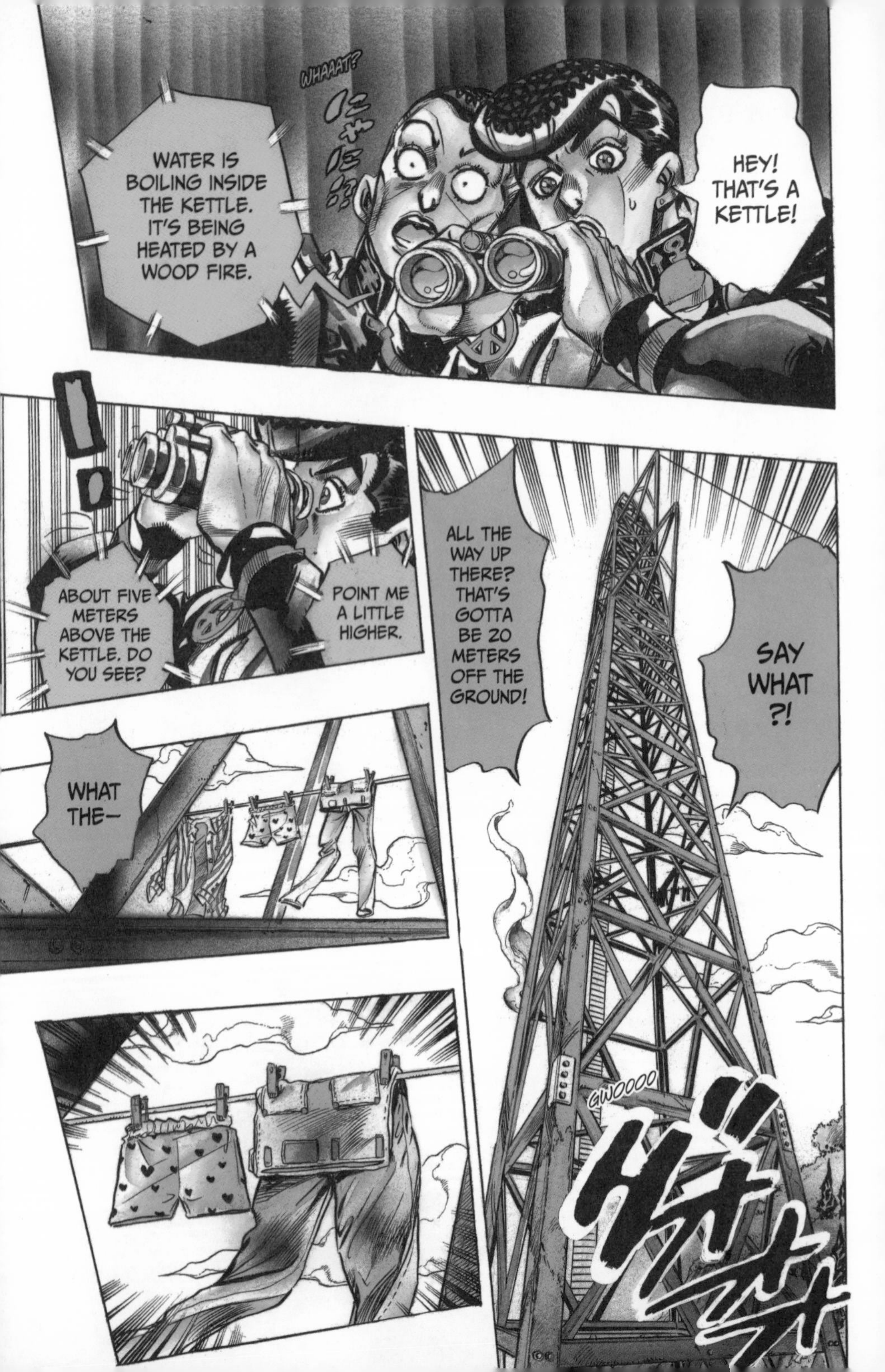
HEY! THAT'S A KETTLE!
WHAAAT?
WATER IS BOILING INSIDE THE KETTLE. IT'S BEING HEATED BY A WOOD FIRE.
SAY WHAT?!
ALL THE WAY UP THERE? THAT'S GOTTA BE 20 METERS OFF THE GROUND!
GWOOOO
POINT ME A LITTLE HIGHER.
ABOUT FIVE METERS ABOVE THE KETTLE. DO YOU SEE?
WHAT THE–

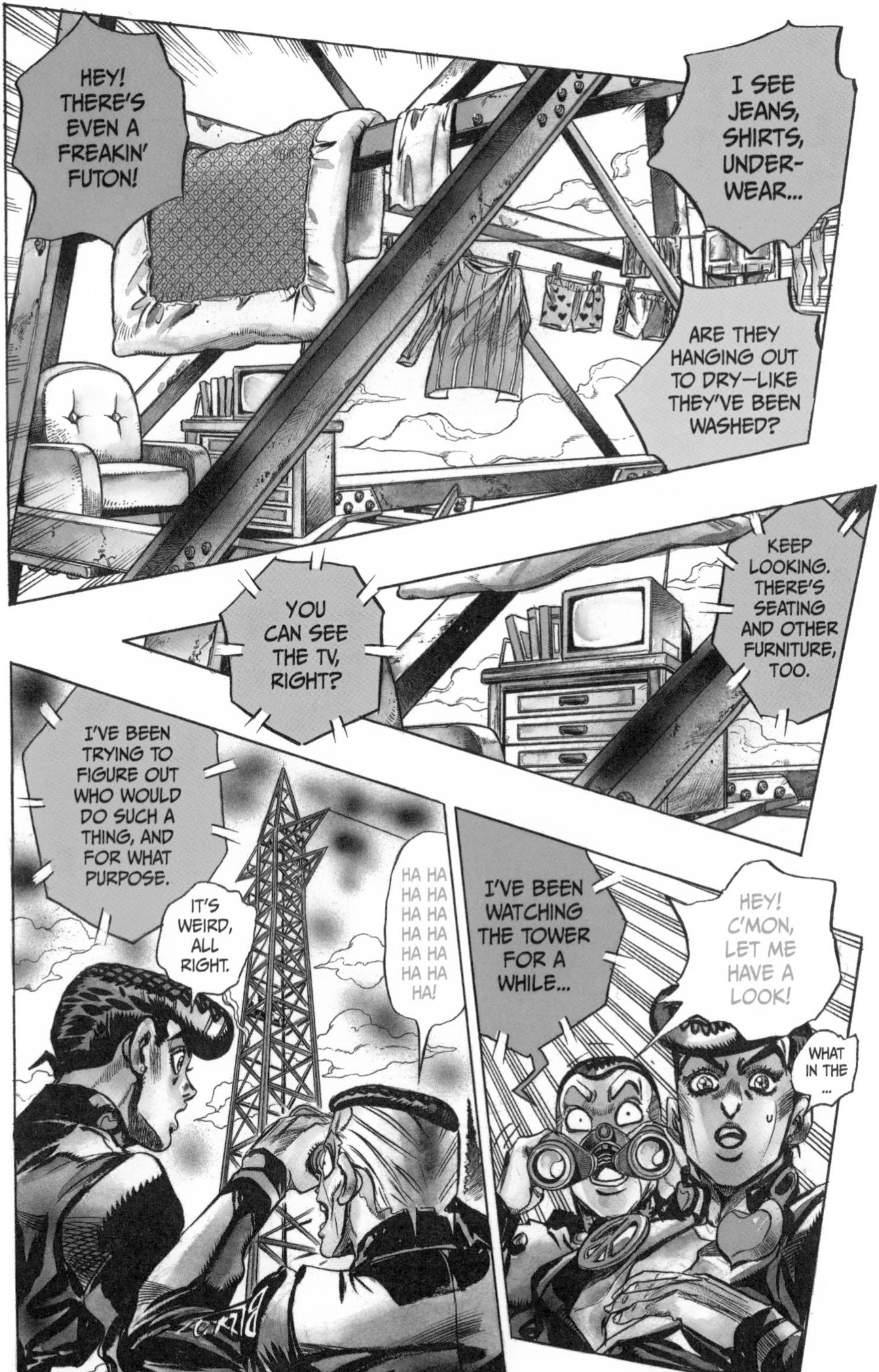
I SEE JEANS, SHIRTS, UNDER-WEAR...
HEY! THERE'S EVEN A FREAKIN' FUTON!
ARE THEY HANGING OUT TO DRY—LIKE THEY'VE BEEN WASHED?
KEEP LOOKING. THERE'S SEATING AND OTHER FURNITURE, TOO.
YOU CAN SEE THE TV, RIGHT?
HEY! C'MON, LET ME HAVE A LOOK!
I'VE BEEN WATCHING THE TOWER FOR A WHILE...
WHAT IN THE ...
HA HA HA HA HA HA HA HA HA HA HA HA HA!
I'VE BEEN TRYING TO FIGURE OUT WHO WOULD DO SUCH A THING, AND FOR WHAT PURPOSE.
IT'S WEIRD, ALL RIGHT.

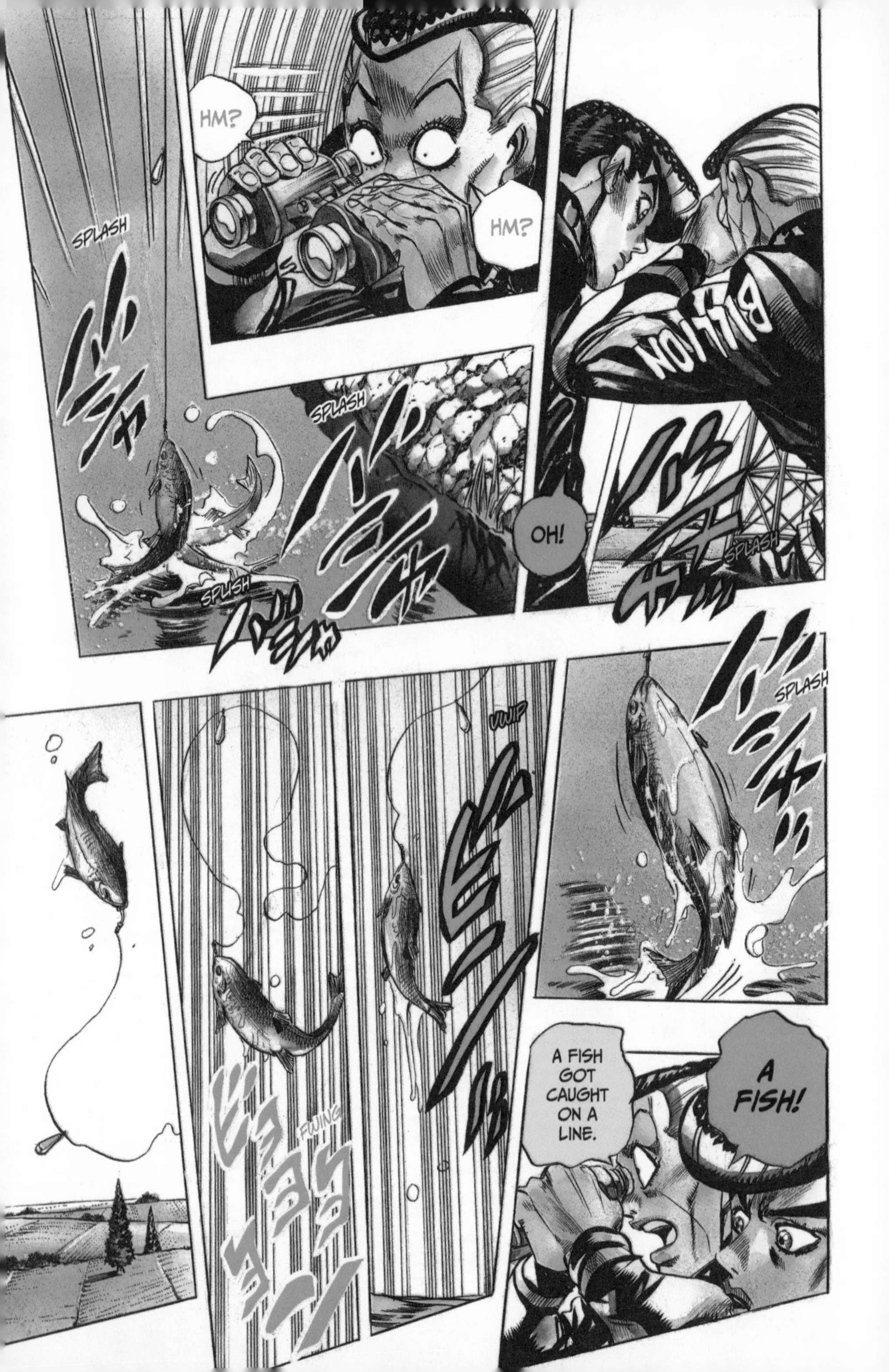

OH!
SPLASH
HM?
HM?
SPLASH
SPLISH
SPLASH
SPLASH
A FISH!
A FISH GOT CAUGHT ON A LINE.
UWIP
FWING

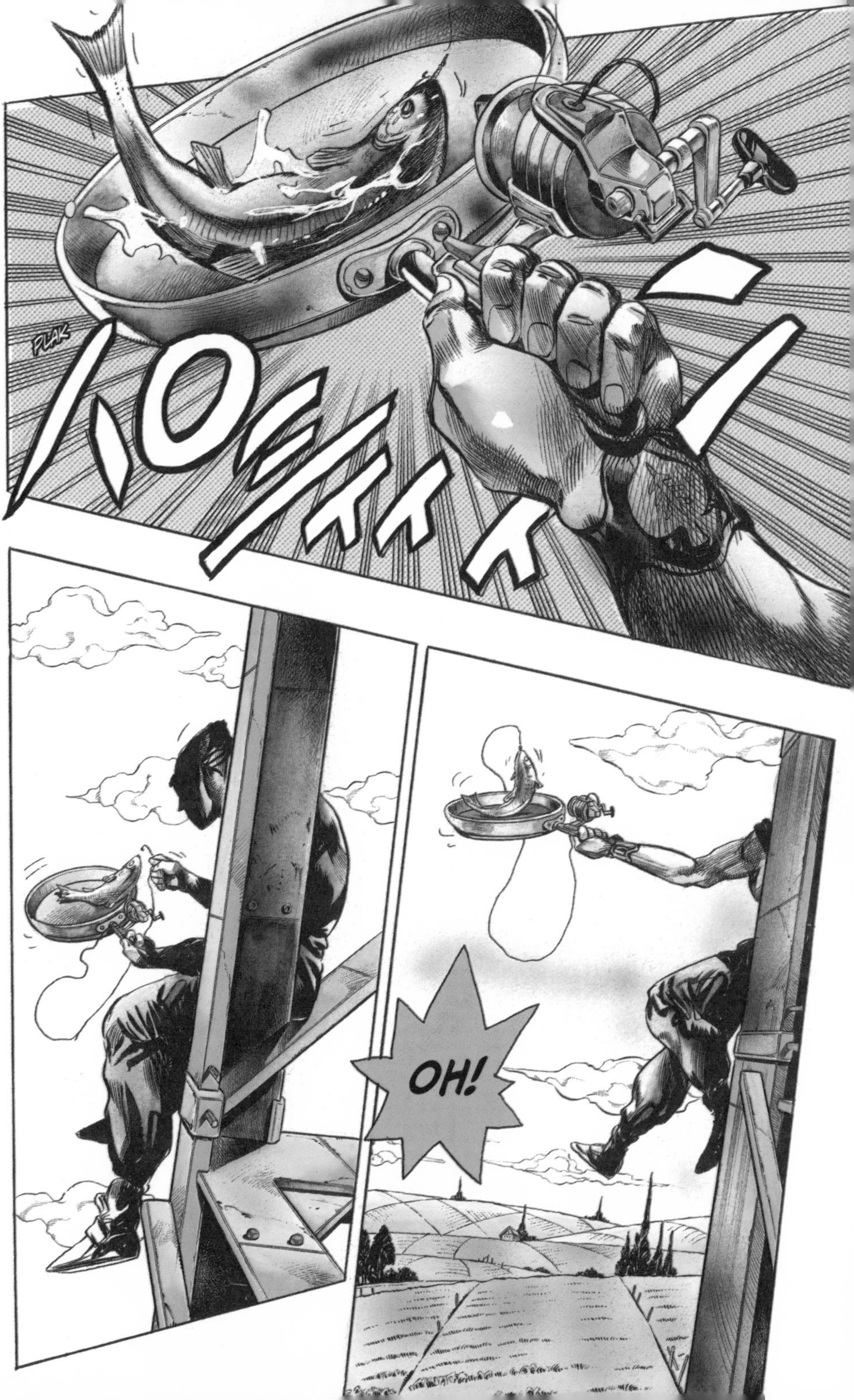
PLAK
パシィィィィ
OH!

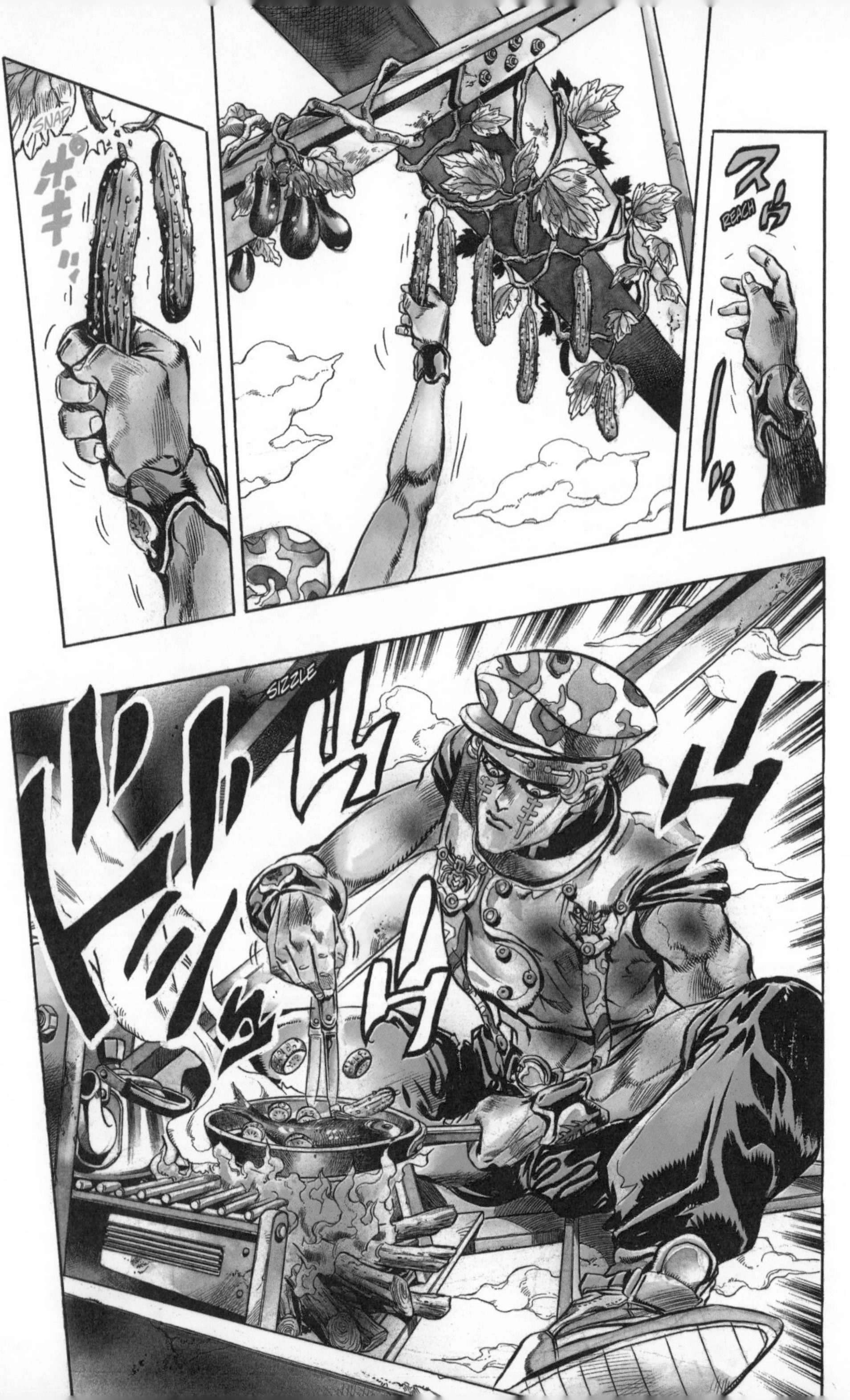
スッ
REACH
SNAP
ポキッ
SIZZLE

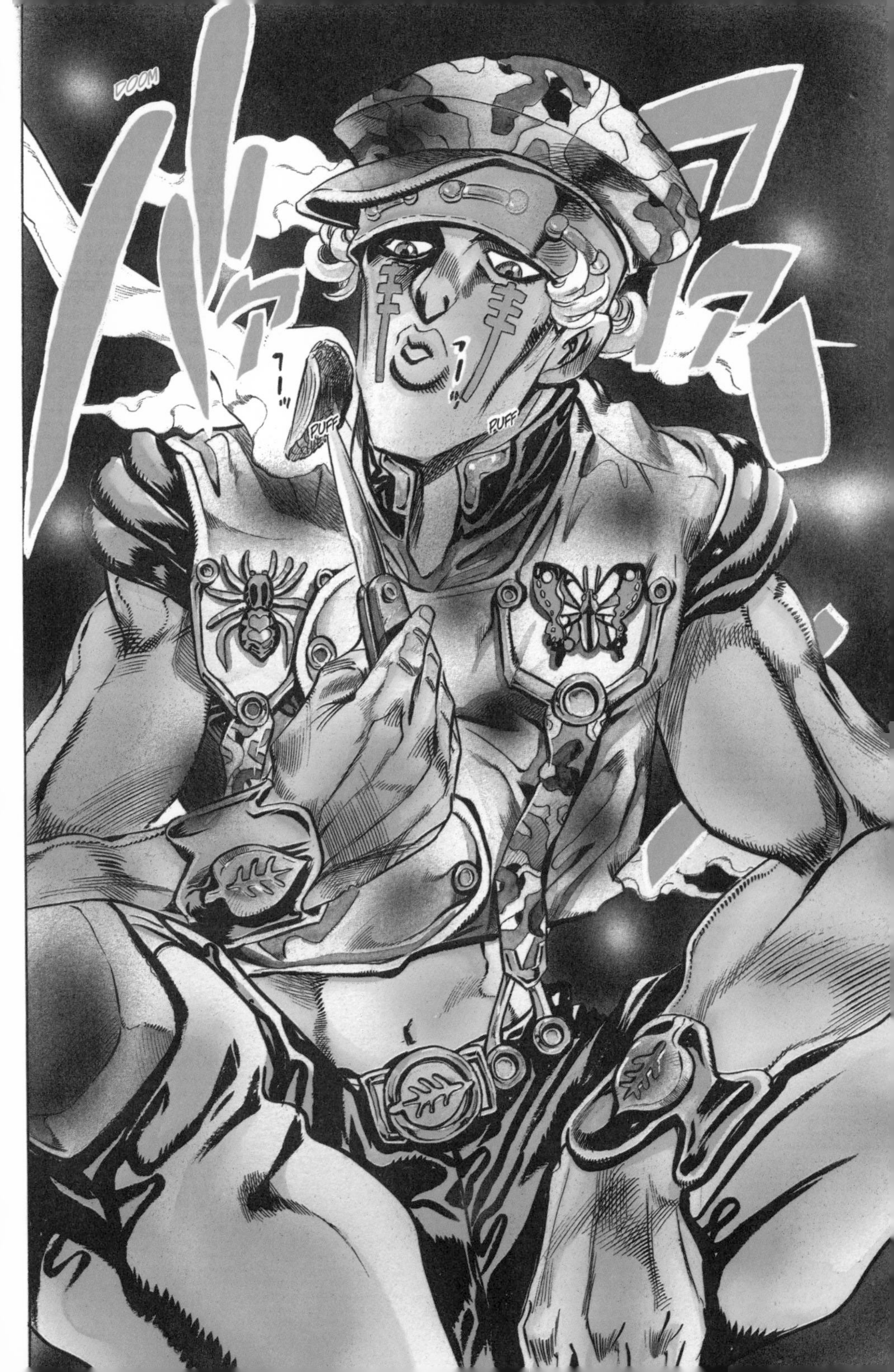
DOOM
PUFF
PUFF

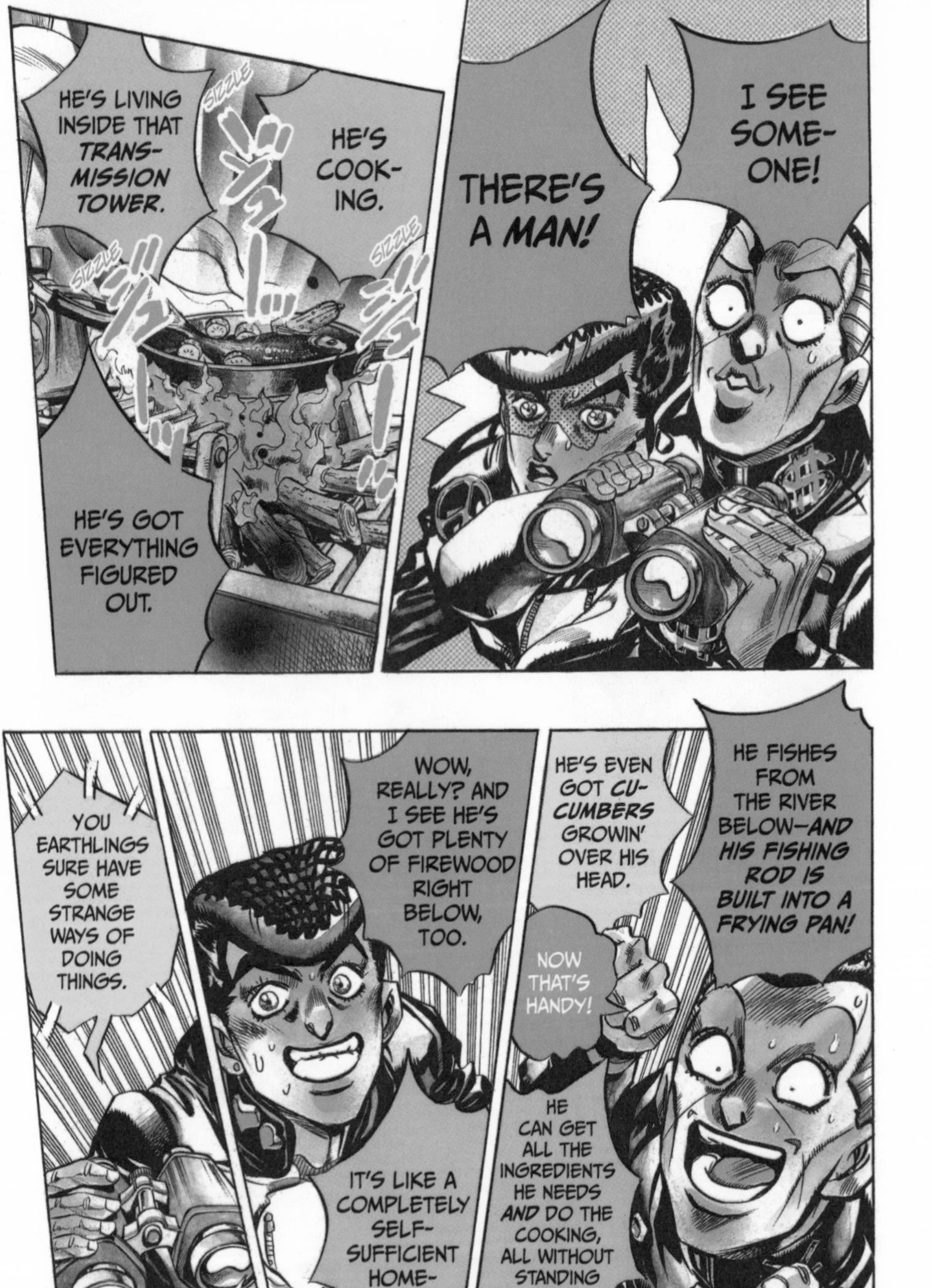

I SEE SOME-ONE!
THERE'S A MAN!
HE'S LIVING INSIDE THAT TRANS-MISSION TOWER.
SIZZLE
SIZZLE
SIZZLE
HE'S COOK-ING.
HE'S GOT EVERYTHING FIGURED OUT.
HE FISHES FROM THE RIVER BELOW—AND HIS FISHING ROD IS BUILT INTO A FRYING PAN!
HE'S EVEN GOT CU-CUMBERS GROWIN' OVER HIS HEAD.
NOW THAT'S HANDY!
HE CAN GET ALL THE INGREDIENTS HE NEEDS AND DO THE COOKING, ALL WITHOUT STANDING UP!
WOW, REALLY? AND I SEE HE'S GOT PLENTY OF FIREWOOD RIGHT BELOW, TOO.
IT'S LIKE A COMPLETELY SELF-SUFFICIENT HOME-STEAD!
YOU'RE ONE TO TALK.
YOU EARTHLINGS SURE HAVE SOME STRANGE WAYS OF DOING THINGS.

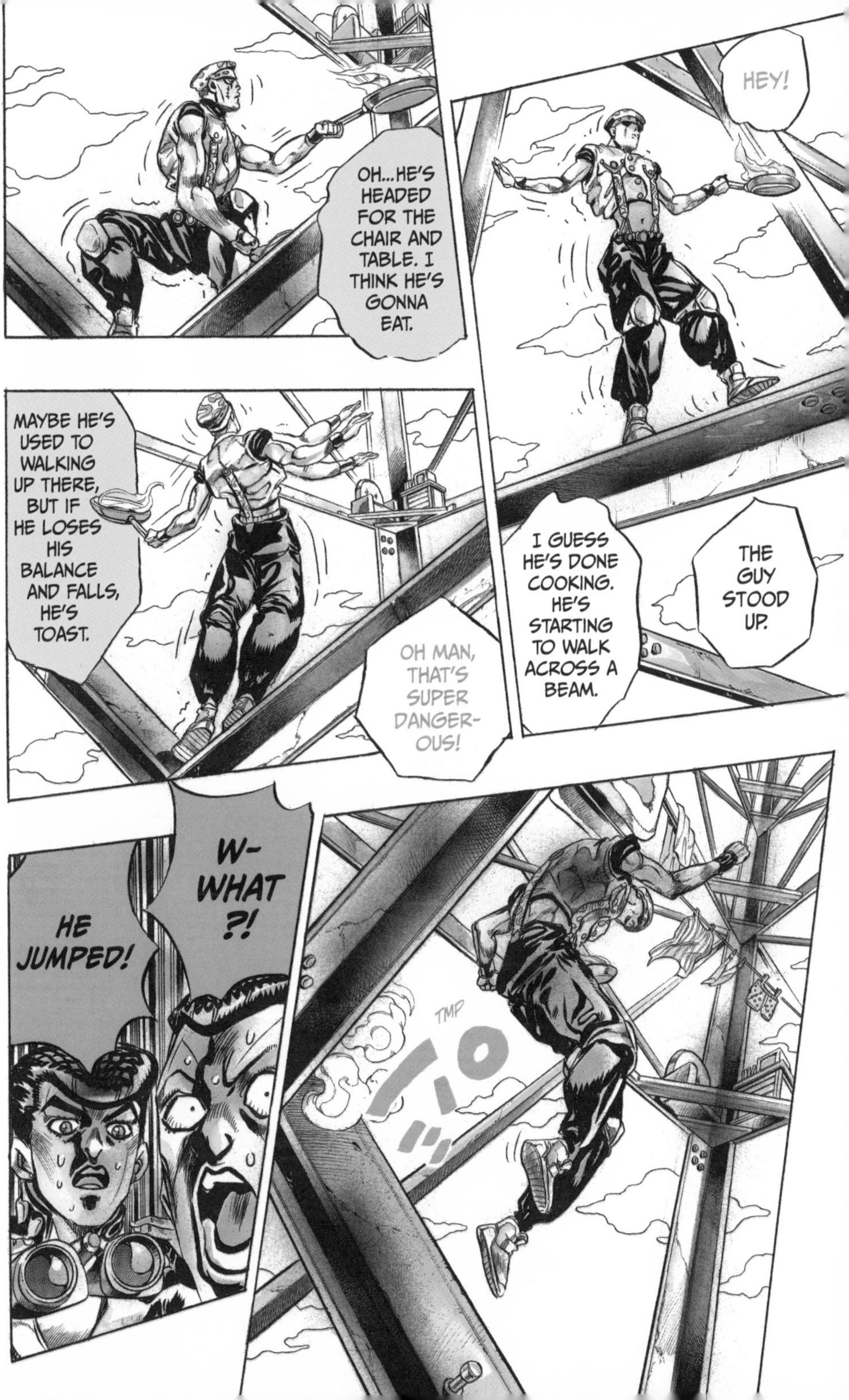
HEY!
THE GUY STOOD UP.
I GUESS HE'S DONE COOKING. HE'S STARTING TO WALK ACROSS A BEAM.
OH...HE'S HEADED FOR THE CHAIR AND TABLE. I THINK HE'S GONNA EAT.
OH MAN, THAT'S SUPER DANGER-OUS!
MAYBE HE'S USED TO WALKING UP THERE, BUT IF HE LOSES HIS BALANCE AND FALLS, HE'S TOAST.
TMP
W-WHAT?!
HE JUMPED!

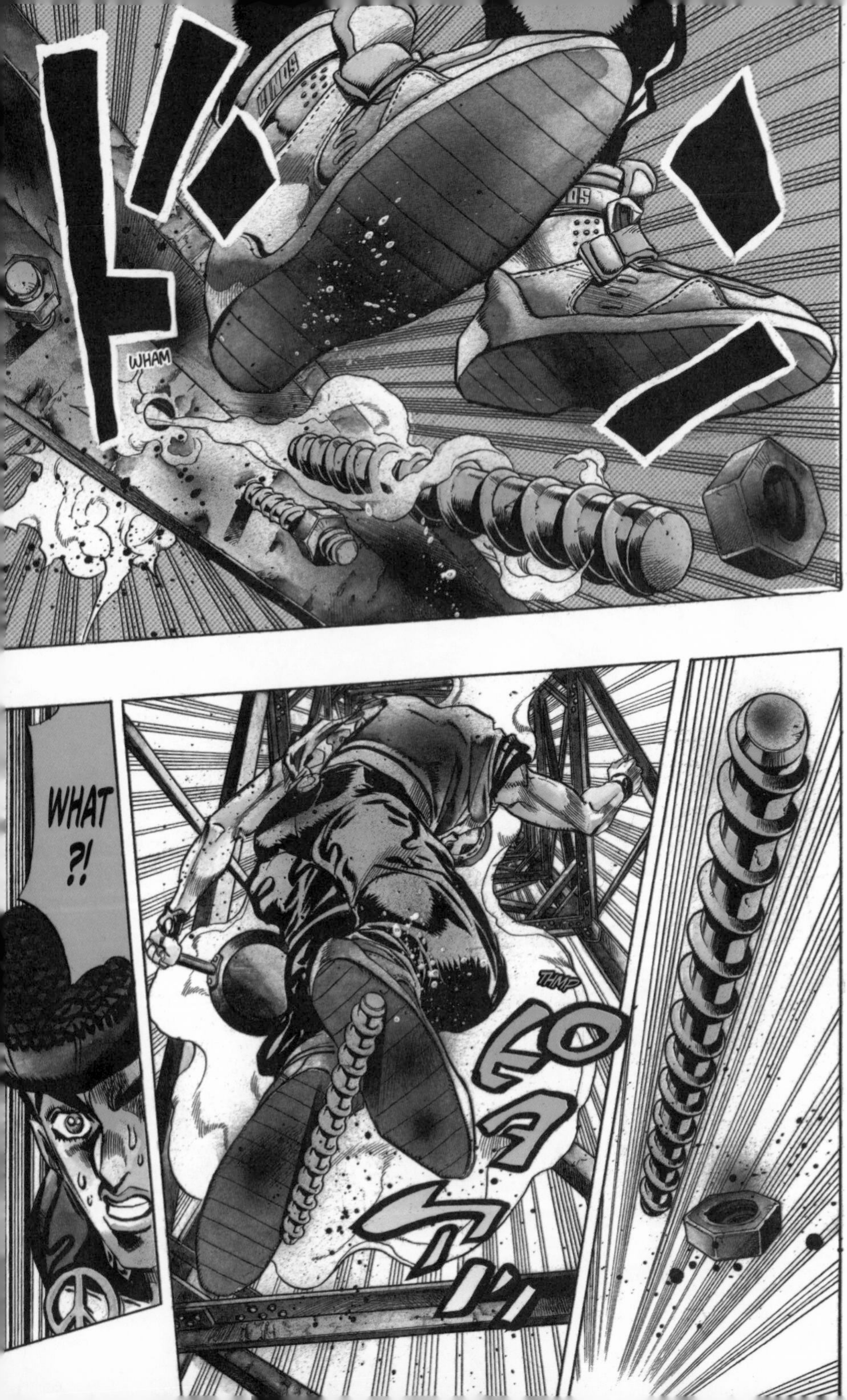
WHAM
THMP
WHAT ?!

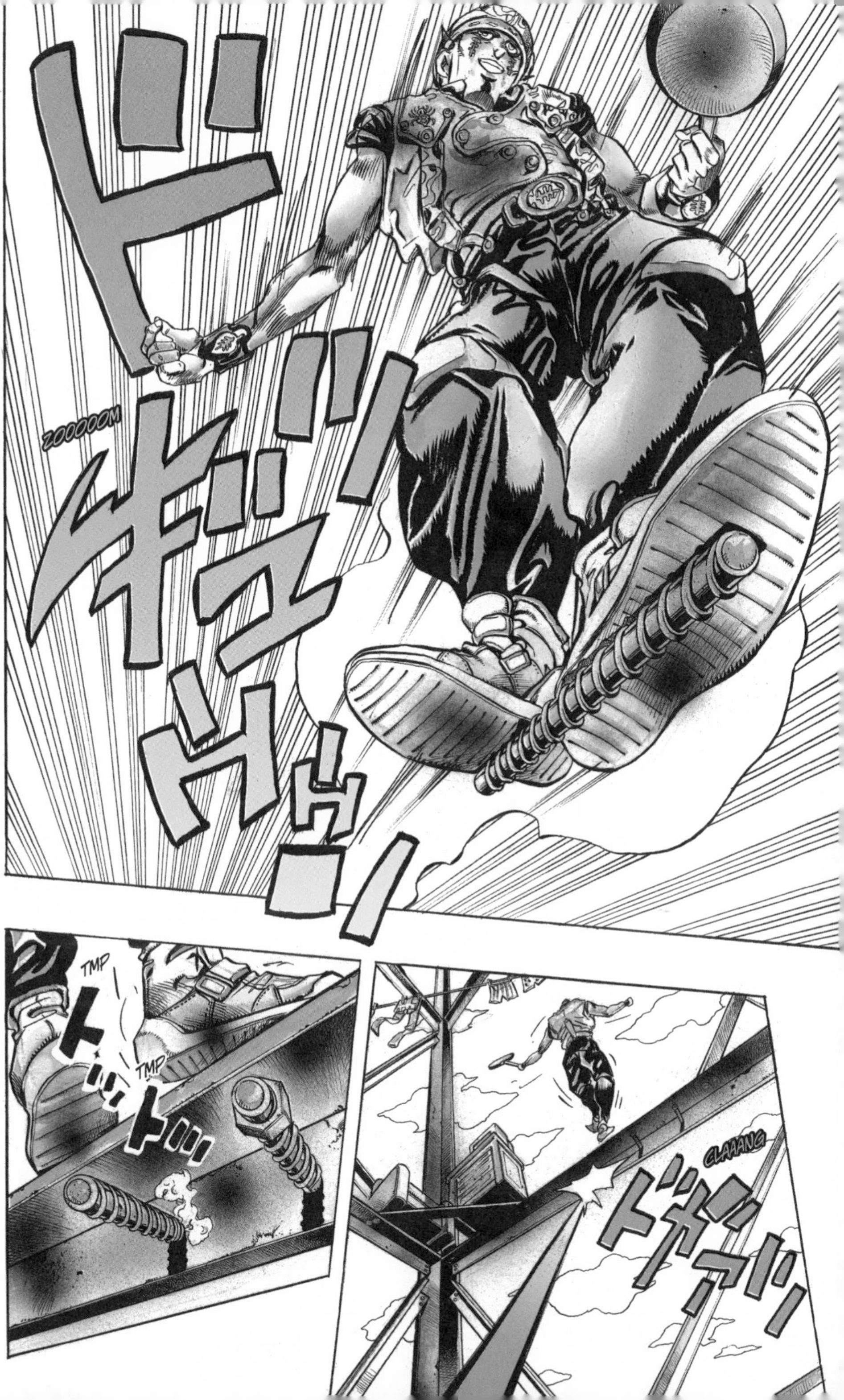
ZOOOOOM
CLAAANG
TMP
TMP

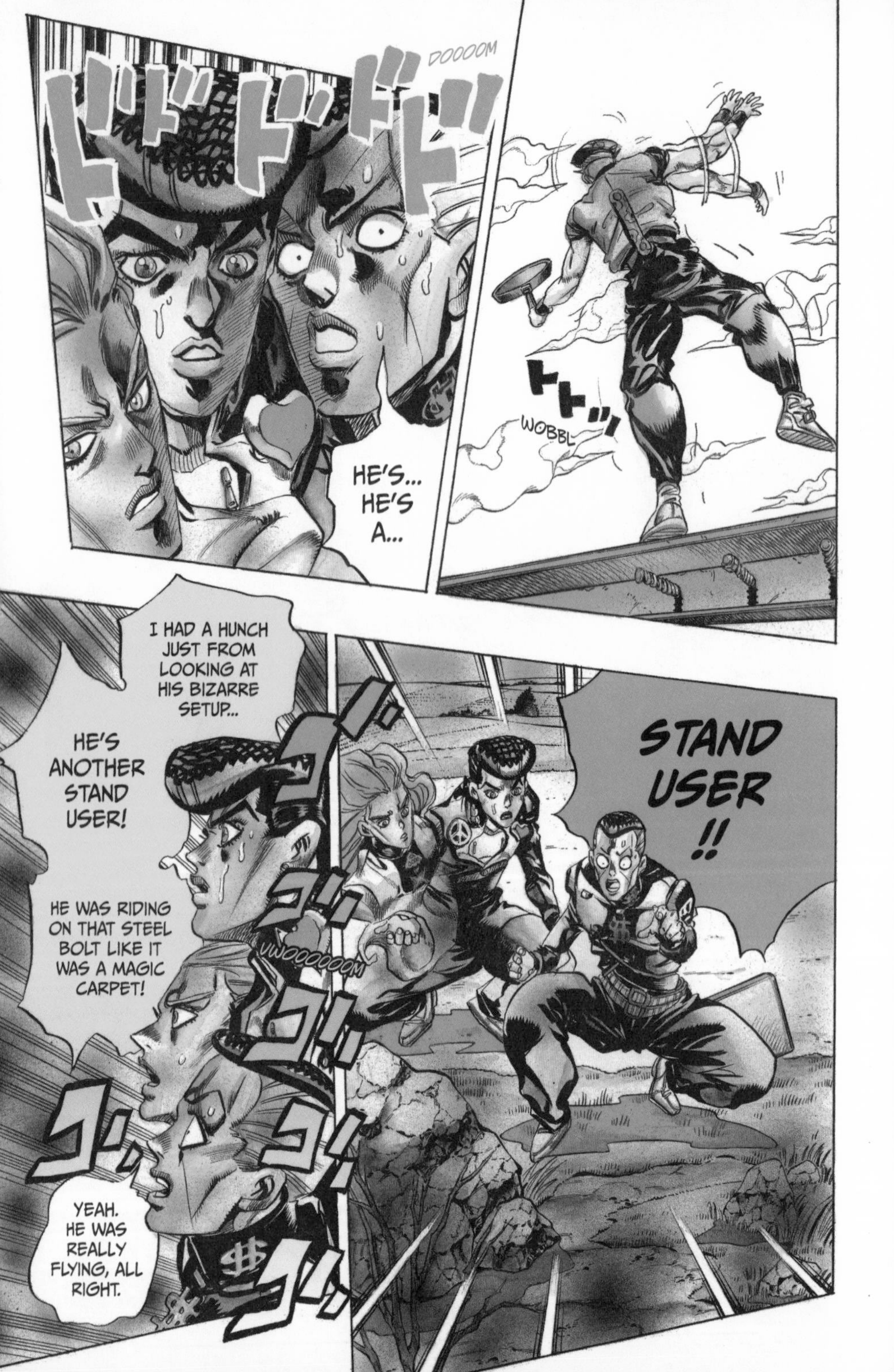
WOBBL
DOOOOM
HE'S... HE'S A...
STAND USER!!
I HAD A HUNCH JUST FROM LOOKING AT HIS BIZARRE SETUP...
HE'S ANOTHER STAND USER!
HE WAS RIDING ON THAT STEEL BOLT LIKE IT WAS A MAGIC CARPET!
VWOOOOOOM
YEAH. HE WAS REALLY FLYING, ALL RIGHT.

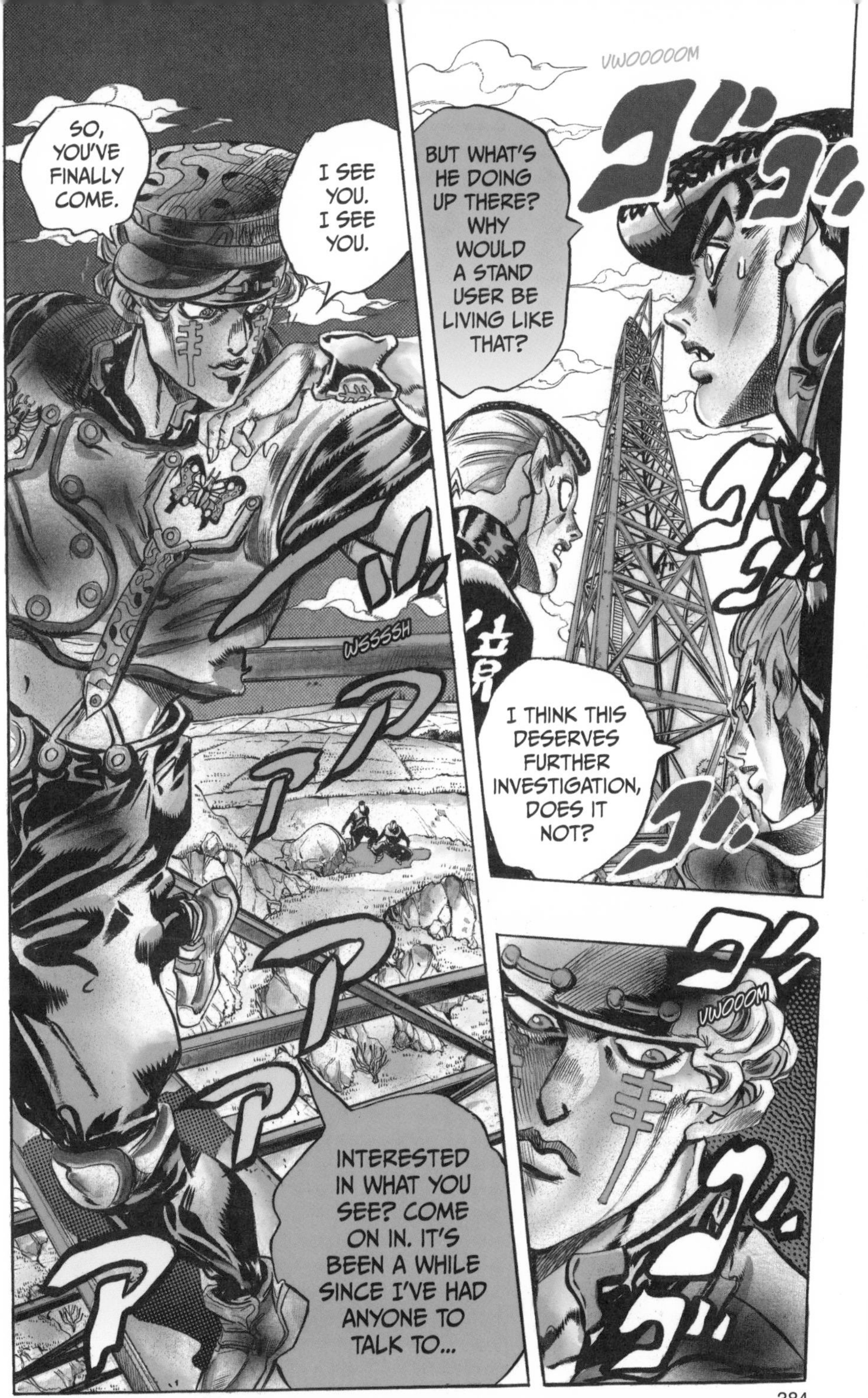
VWOOOOOM
BUT WHAT'S HE DOING UP THERE? WHY WOULD A STAND USER BE LIVING LIKE THAT?
I THINK THIS DESERVES FURTHER INVESTIGATION, DOES IT NOT?
VWOOOM
I SEE YOU. I SEE YOU.
SO, YOU'VE FINALLY COME.
WSSSSH
INTERESTED IN WHAT YOU SEE? COME ON IN. IT'S BEEN A WHILE SINCE I'VE HAD ANYONE TO TALK TO...

AUTHOR'S COMMENTS

Whenever I have to draw a location in my manga, such as the interior of a hospital or pharmacy, or the grounds of a shrine, I take photographs of a real-world example to use as references. But that kind of photography can be rather nerve-racking.

If I ask an employee for permission to take pictures, they'll ask me all sorts of prying questions back, like "What are you using them for?" and "Do you work for a magazine?" and "Who are you?" And then, after all that, they'll usually say something like, "The manager isn't here right now, so come back tomorrow." I'm only using the photos for reference. Just let me take them, all right? (I'll even give you candy.)

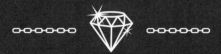

ALBUMS TO MAKE YOU CRY

These are my top 10 from the 1970s (in no particular order). Everyone's tastes are different, but no matter how many times I listen to these, they never fail to bring tears to my eyes.

#1 Led Zeppelin, *Physical Graffiti*
#2 Chicago, *Chicago VII*
#3 *Saturday Night Fever* soundtrack
#4 Curtis Mayfield, *Super Fly*
#5 Marvin Gaye, *What's Going On*
#6 Jackson Browne, *Late for the Sky*
#7 Pink Floyd, *The Dark Side of the Moon*
#8 Sex Pistols, *Never Mind the Bollocks, Here's the Sex Pistols*
#9 George Benson, *Breezin'*
#10 The Carpenters, *Now & Then*

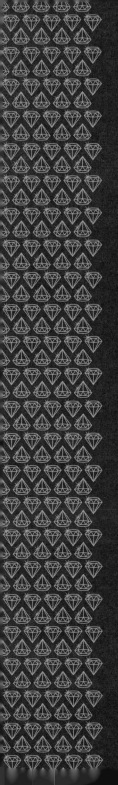

JoJo's
BIZARRE ADVENTURE

PART 4: DIAMOND IS UNBREAKABLE
VOLUME 7
BY HIROHIKO ARAKI

DELUXE HARDCOVER EDITION
Translation: Nathan A Collins
Touch-Up Art & Lettering: Mark McMurray
Design: Adam Grano
Editor: David Brothers

Printed in the U.S.A.

Published by VIZ Media, LLC
P.O. Box 77010
San Francisco, CA 94107

10 9 8 7 6 5 4 3 2 1
First printing, November 2020

VIZ MEDIA
viz.com

SHONEN JUMP
shonenjump.com

THIS IS THE LAST PAGE

JoJo's BIZARRE ADVENTURE

has been printed in the original
Japanese format in order to preserve
the orientation of the original artwork.

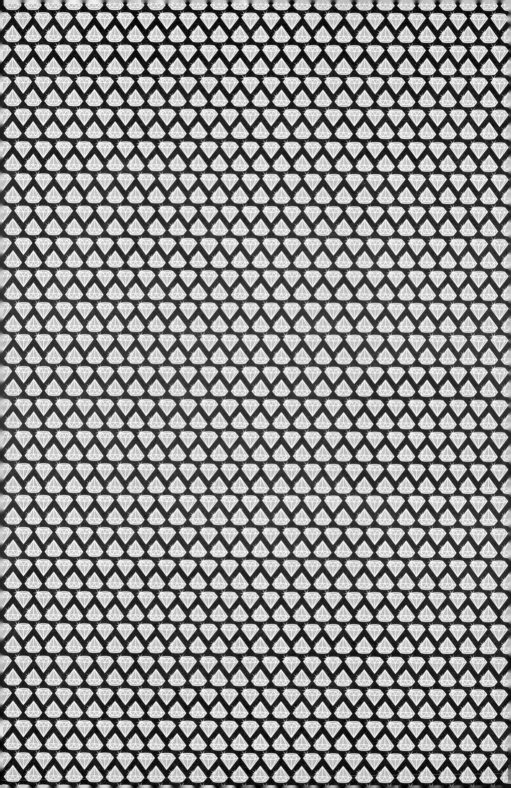